Islamic Architecture
of the Indian Subcontinent

Bianca Maria Alfieri
Photographs by Federico Borromeo

te Neues Publishing Company
New York

Published in 2000 by Laurence King Publishing
an imprint of Calmann & King Ltd
71 Great Russell Street
London WC1B 3BN
Telephone: +44 20 7831 6351
Fax: +44 20 7831 8356
e-mail: enquiries@calmann-king.co.uk
www.laurence-king.com

Distributed in the United States by
te Neues Publishing Company
16 West 22nd Street
New York, NY 10010
Telephone: 212 627 9090
Fax: 212 627 9511
www.teneues.com

Text and photographs copyright
© Arte e Moneta SA, Savosa (Switzerland)

Copyright © 2000 Calmann & King Ltd
This book was designed and produced by
Calmann & King Ltd, London

All rights reserved. No part of this publication
may be reproduced or transmitted in any
form or by any means, electronic or
mechanical, including photocopy, recording
or any information storage and retrieval
system, without permission in writing
from the publisher.

Library of Congress Cataloging-in-Publication
Data is available.

USA ISBN 3-8238-5443-7
UK ISBN 1 85669 189 6

Designed by hdr design
(Hans Dieter Reichert and Peter Black)

Map by Advanced Illustration,
Andrea Fairbrass and Ailsa Heritage

Frontispiece: The Shah Najaf Mausoleum
at Lucknow, India
photograph by Federico Borromeo

Printed in China

Contents

	Historical Introduction	7
Part 1: The Origins		
	1 The Origins	14
	2 The Mamluks of Delhi (1206–1290)	20
	3 The Khaljis (1290–1320)	30
	4 The Tughluqs (1320–1413)	36
	5 The Sayyid and Lodi (1414–1451 and 1451–1526)	50
Part 2: Provincial Styles		
	6 The Punjab and Sind (1150–*c.*1550 and 1053–*c.*1592)	62
	7 Bengal (*c.*1300–*c.*1550)	80
	8 Jaunpur (1394–1483)	94
	9 Gujarat (*c.*1300–*c.*1500)	104
	10 Malwa (*c.*1400–*c.*1550)	130
	11 Deccan (1347–1687)	144
	12 Kashmir (1346–1586)	174
Part 3: The Mughals		
	13 The arrival of the Mughals	182
	14 The classic Mughal period I: Akbar (1556–1605)	202
	15 The classic Mughal period II: Jahangir (1605–1627)	226
	16 The classic Mughal period III: Shah Jahan (1628–1657)	240
	17 The classic Mughal period IV: Aurangzeb (1658–1707)	264
	18 The final phase of Mughal architecture	274
	19 The Mughal provincial style	284
	Glossary	296
	Table of Dynasties	300
	Bibliography	302
	Index	315

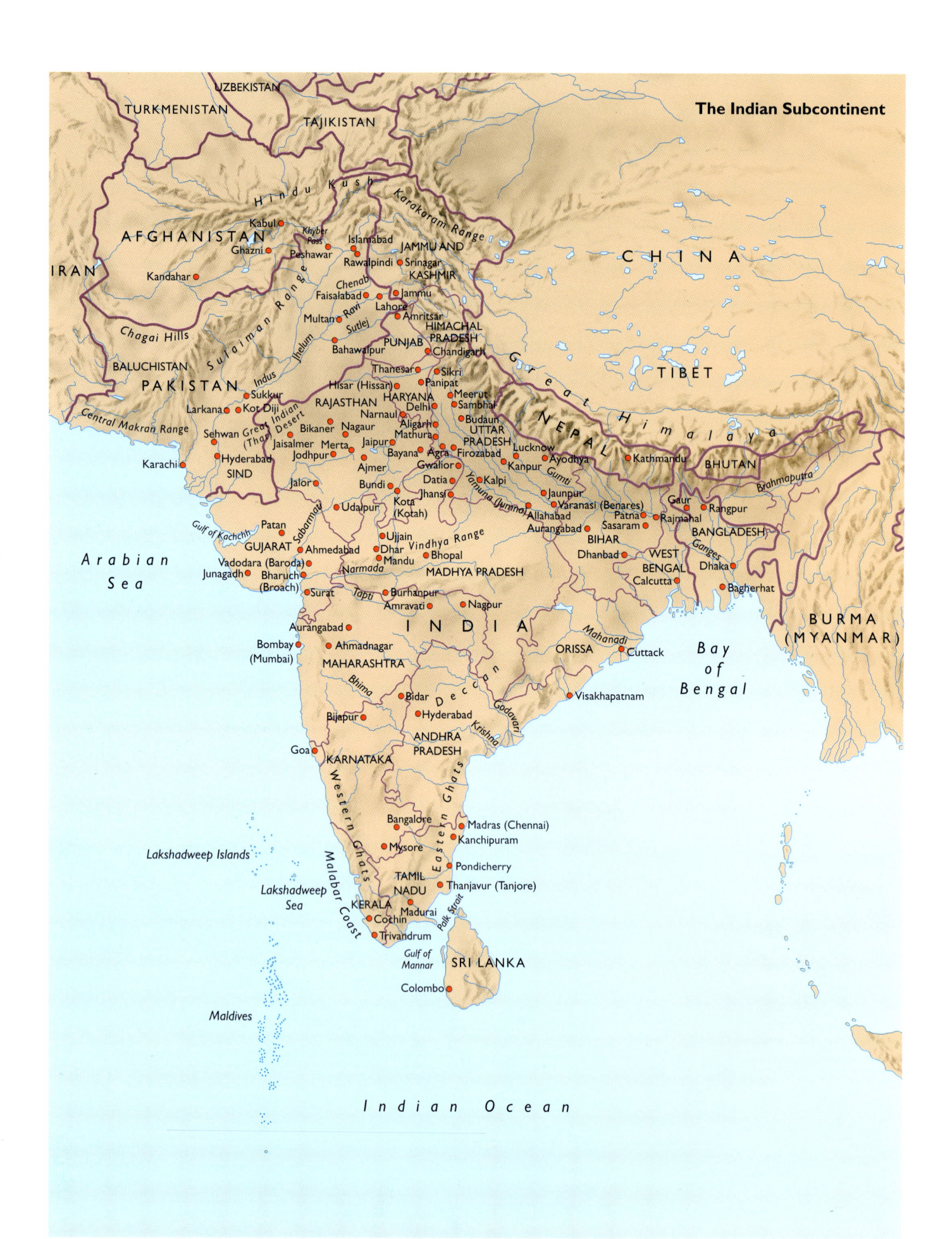

The Indian Subcontinent

Historical Introduction

A modern political map of the Indian subcontinent.

The encounter between Muslim civilization and the Hindu world, despite its initial dramatic contrasts, proved to be fertile in every field of the visual arts. But its greatest achievements were attained in the domain of building, worthy of the evaluation provided by Wheeler that 'in the whole history of architecture there is no more fascinating episode'.[1] It would be difficult to imagine anything more different from the sober, elegant, airy simplicity of Islamic architecture than the rich, entangled 'swarming, monstrous, sinister, fantastically beautiful'[2] Hindu architecture. Born of two entirely opposite worlds, and with different aims – one tied to the desert and the wide, bare horizons of the tableland, the other to the mysterious, luxurious intrigue of the 'vast and trackless forests'[3] – they seemed totally irreconcilable. And yet, after a first inevitable clash, the two traditions ended by meeting and influencing each other in different and ingenious ways, animating one of the highest and most balanced moments on Islam's artistic parabola.

There is no doubt that some visible aspects of India's complex religiosity – expressed iconographically in a mass of divine simulacra of often scabrous symbolism – must have been incomprehensible, indeed intolerable, to the Turkish conquerors who, with overriding force, spread across the fertile lands of northern India in the name of Islam at the beginning of the twelfth century. It is possible that beyond the instinctive disgust for the anthropomorphic images that populated the Hindu religious buildings, the Muslims also experienced an unconfessed terror for the world of demons and saints, with its sinister magic. This would explain the Muslims' first, furious, almost thoughtless destruction of the Indian artistic heritage. It was only later that the receptiveness of the Islamic spirit was to absorb, even then slowly, the more enduring influences of traditional Hindu taste, thus giving rise under the greatest and the most glorious of the foreign dynasties – the Mughals – to the new face of India. In their harmonious lines, splendid use of colour, and simplicity of design, the works of this period carry the inimitable mark of Islam. They also carry, in a myriad of decorative elements, the sign of the inexhaustible Hindu imagination.

Islam's first contact with the Indian world came under the caliphate of Umar (634–44) with the occupation by the Arabs of some ports on the Malabar coast, where they quickly established a permanent commercial port. Indeed, according to local tradition, the first mosque in India was built at Cranganore in 629. Now, however, only a plaque records the event on the wall of a modern mosque built in 1984.[4]

The real campaign against India, however, began in 711–12, when the governor of Basra, al-Hajjaj, sent Muhammad bin Qasim on an expedition against Sind, which culminated in the conquest of the port of Debal, on the ruins of which was built the first mosque (now in Pakistani territory). Muhammad subsequently conquered Brahmanabad and Multan, thus creating a base in the Punjab. From the ruins of Brahmanabad rose Mansura, which, after 871 with the weakening of the caliphate, became the capital of a small Arab realm in Sind, just as Multan had been for the Punjab. The inhospitable Thar desert, home of the warlike Rajputs, slowed the eastern expansion of the Muslims, while at the same time creating a natural defence for the territory which they had already conquered. These first Muslim invasions did not bring dramatic consequences for the indigenous peoples; in fact, with subtle political calculation, the Arabs guaranteed, in return for conversion to the new faith, exemption for people and property from the payment of the *jizia*, just as the *dhimmi* enjoyed.[5]

With the end of the tenth century and the beginning of the eleventh, a much more substantial tide of Islamicized peoples replaced the original invaders. The Turkish Ghaznavids, under the orders of Mahmud, spread towards the Indus basin through the Khyber Pass, and under the ideological shield of a holy war they indulged in all types of pillaging, not confining themselves to religious motives. Indeed India, with her almost defenceless fertile plains and her rich attractive cities, must have appeared to the nomadic Turco-Afghan tribes, conditioned by a life of hunger and privation, as a fantastic mirage of easily attainable prosperity. The resigned tolerance of the indigenous population, combined with the absolute lack of a national consciousness among the various Buddhist and Hindu dynasties, favoured the success of the invaders who enjoyed a further advantage in the extraordinary mobility of their efficient cavalry compared with the slow local armies, still predominantly made up of infantry troops and elephants. The easy victories, contrasting only with the unstinted though ill-fated resistance offered by some Rajput princes, only reinforced the Muslims' conviction of their own absolute superiority and determination to change, through the fortunes of a bellicose adventure, an otherwise miserable and wretched life. Thus the 17 expeditions carried out in India by Mahmud of Ghazni between the years 1000 and 1026 were organized more in search of glory and loot than as part of a premeditated plan of conquest. These expeditions nevertheless upset the political equilibrium of the Hindu world, demonstrating the intrinsic weakness of the great states of the Ganges basin, which the nascent power of the Ghurids later overran at Tarain in 1192, thus imposing on northern Indian the Muslim hegemony that lasted over 600 years. Indeed, the Ghurids instigated the historic mission definitively to destroy Hindu India and begin the construction of that Indo-Islamic world to which later dynasties contributed and then brought to an end. Retiring to Ghazni in 1193, Muhammad Ghuri entrusted the government of the Indian provinces to his erstwhile slave, the Turk Qutb al-Din Aibak, who on the death of Ghuri became the founder of the first Indo-Islamic dynasty (1206–90), called Mamluks because of the servile origins (*mamluk* means 'slave') of its principal representatives. Established in Delhi, Aibak soon conquered Bihar, Gujarat, Vindhya Pradesh and Bengal, while his son-in-law and successor, Iltutmish (1211–36), saw to the reinforcement of the north-west frontier against the impending Mongol threat. This last prevented the Muslim sovereigns of India from extending their territorial expansion towards the south of the peninsula for almost a century.

Only at the end of the thirteenth century with the accession to the throne of Ala al-Din (1296–1316) of the new Khalji dynasty (1290–1320) were the last Chagatayid Mongols finally expelled from Indian territory. Then, the Rajput rebels in the heart of the empire having been tamed, Malwa, Hoysala and the Deccan were all occupied, right to the very tip of the country.

Ala al-Din was the most eminent Muslim monarch to precede the great Mughal sovereigns. The empire of Delhi thus reached its apogee, even if in reality its rapid expansion was due simply to force of arms and the power of the state was based on the centralizing power of the despotic sultan. On his death, the dynasty lasted but four years. It was characterized by violent power struggles which culminated in the occupation of Delhi by Ghiyas al-Din Tughluq, an old Turkish general, son of an Indian mother and already an energetic defender of the western frontier. He founded the homonymous dynasty (1320–1413), under which Islam spread widely through large sections of the population and the Muslim leaders became ever more Indianized. Ghiyas al-Din proposed a reorganization of the state, creating a more complex system of taxes, which nonetheless succeeded simply in further dividing the two categories of citizen: the privileged Muslims together with the newly converted; and those almost totally deprived of their rights, the Hindus. This discrimination became intolerable under Muhammad Tughluq, the talented but unlucky son and successor of Ghiyas al-Din, who eventually caused the ruin of the kingdom with a series of disastrous initiatives. Among these was the issuing of nominal value money into the market, with an obligatory circulation of the official copper coin with the value of silver. On Muhammad's death in 1351 the economic difficulties that arose, aggravated by shortages and cruelly repressed popular revolts, provoked the territorial break up of the empire which fragmented into numerous Muslim states. His unifying example was not lost on the Muslims of India who allowed no Hindu restorations (Gwalior being the only exception and, later, the far south), but divided Indian territory into independent sultanates.

At the moment of the Delhi dynasty's greatest weakness, Timur's invasion passed through like a whirlwind. The terrible Turk first approached India in the summer of 1398 and on 17 December of that year he put the capital to fire and the sword while the last Tughluq sought

Historical Introduction

The mausoleum of Ghiyas-al Din, founder of the Tughluq dynasty (1320–1413), at Tughluqabad (Delhi).

escape in Gujarat. After a fortnight of massacres and merciless pillaging, Timur returned to his Turkestani dominions, leaving Delhi in the hands of an Indian descendant of the Prophet – his only act of government. Timur's nominee then founded the weakest and most inept of Delhi's dynasties (the Sayyids, 1414–51), whose power was limited to little more than the territory of the city itself. It was soon supplanted by the more energetic Afghan dynasty of the Lodis (1451–1526), which nonetheless, due to a lack of internal cohesion, opened the doors to a new foreign invasion.

The Turco-Mongol lord of Kabul, Babur, descendant of Timur – and on his mother's side of Chingiz (also Genghis) Khan – entered the rivalry between the Afghan generals, occupying Delhi in 1526 and founding the glorious Mughal dynasty that became the most powerful and the most famous of Islamic India. With this dynasty began a most brilliant period in the Muslim history of India and ended definitively the series of states founded by invaders coming from the borders. The Mughals resumed the plan for political unification of the immense country and carried it to fruition. They succeeded in giving the country a new, homogeneous face that lasted well beyond the collapse of the dynasty's effective power (1526–1707). In Bussagli's words:

If in the course of the eighteenth century the Mughal empire exhausted its historic mission and shattered into its component states, it continued until 1833 to exist nominally and exercised its sovereignty, as the theoretical source of all political power on the peninsula. And if the British government, after the great mutiny, eliminated the family dynasty, this did not prevent the fact that in 1876 when Queen Victoria took the imperial title, even at so great a distance, she seemed to insert herself into the long list of sovereigns that had begun with Babur.[6]

Even if it was rapid, the Mughal conquest of India was not easy. Caught out by an attempted Rajput rebellion and then by the rebellion led by the Afghan Sher Shah Sur, the valiant but strategically inept Humayun, son of Babur, who had succeeded his father on the throne in 1530, was defeated in 1540 and forced to seek refuge at the Persian Safavid court for several years. The brief Suri interregnum (1540–55), and in particular that of Sher Shah (1540–45), was nevertheless very advantageous for the organization of the state. Akbar, succeeding his father Humayun – who had returned to his dominion in 1555 but died in 1556 – benefited greatly from the useful ideas it gave him, especially in the administrative field.

Akbar was the most eminent and representative of the Mughals, the true creator of Indo-Islamic unity. An enlightened sovereign, a great politician and tolerant in spiritual matters, Akbar knew that to govern India properly it was necessary, above all else, to bridge the economic and social gap that existed between Muslim and Hindu. He therefore abolished the *jizia* and sought, even through personal contact, the friendship of the Rajput princes by opening up the most important positions in the state to them and by marrying their women. Subsequently, he sought to learn about all the other religious creeds, including Christianity (it seems that at one time he even wanted to become a Christian). He was convinced that spiritual unity was necessary in order to achieve political unity for India, and so he abandoned Muslim orthodoxy and founded a new syncretic religion, the Din-Ilahi, which represented the confluence of diverse metaphysical needs and which, according to the sovereign's intentions, was supposed to reconcile the positions of all his subjects. The Din-Ilahi unfortunately failed to take hold, primarily because it was too cerebral, and did not get beyond the confines of the court; it ended with the death of the sovereign. The far-sighted political plan that underpinned this generous effort was not understood by his successors, above all by his great-grandson, Aurangzeb. Indeed, Aurangzeb revived the most rigid orthodoxy and in the process shattered those ideals of unity and equality of which Akbar had dreamed. With Akbar's death the empire he had made splendid began to lose the perfect and coherent character that had been lent it purely by his gigantic personality.

Above The Ibrahim Khan mausoleum at Narnaul (c.1540), built during the Suri interregnum by Sher Shah for his grandfather.

Opposite The Itimad al-Daula mausoleum at Agra was built in 1626 by the Mughal emperor Jahangir's influential Persian wife Nur Jahan, in honour of her father.

Akbar's son Jahangir (1605–27), even if more cultured and refined than his father, lacked his amiability and, above all, suffered from the harmful influence of his beautiful Persian wife, Nur Jahan, who practically governed by proxy while Jahangir was under the influence of opium and alcohol. The policy of internal conquest initiated by Akbar was held up by the undefeated Deccani resistance, and struggles for the dynastic succession began to weaken the empire which seemed only to reach its maximum splendour under Shah Jahan (1627–57). In reality, despite able government under the new emperor and his sincere desire for peace, the wars continued in the Deccan (where the end of the Bahmanid Sultanate allowed the reinstatement of the Hindu Marathas) and on the western frontier, with Persian and Uzbek incursions, while at court corruption was rife. Shah Jahan himself, devastated by the fratricidal struggles of his four sons, heirs to the throne, died their prisoner in his palace at Agra.

Victor over his brothers by fair means or foul, Aurangzeb (1658–1707) became the last great Mughal emperor. Rigid and inflexible, capable of incredible cruelty in the name of religion become fanaticism, Aurangzeb totally inverted the policy of Akbar, persecuting the majority of his Hindu subjects in the name of Islam with an intransigence that was to carry him to ruin. The reintroduction of the *jizia* caused desperate revolts even among the Jat peasants of the Delhi area, to which were added the bloody rebellions of the Marathas, the Rajputs and the Sikhs. These revolts caused the break up of the army and the collapse of the economy, while even the Portuguese were persecuted with grave repercussions for sea trade. Portuguese maritime dominion was replaced by the East India Company, the English, the Dutch and eventually even the French too, the prelude to the colonial occupation of the subcontinent.

The death of Aurangzeb signalled the end of the effective power of the Mughals, even if the prestige of the immense empire was a vehicle used in the following century to lend the credibility of legitimate power to the various puppet governments that contested the Mughal legacy.

The Mughal empire will long be considered a national glory, at least until the new India, opening its eyes on its far-off past, recognizes in other historical sovereigns and in other empires a more genuine expression of the Indianness that is still even today the country's indisputable essence. [7]

[1] R.M. Wheeler, *Five Thousand Years of Pakistan*, London, 1950, p. 64.

[2] *Ibid.*

[3] *Ibid.*

[4] H. Sarkar, who describes it in *Monuments of Kerala*, ASI, 2nd edn, New Delhi, 1978, p. 49, says that 'there were corridors along all four sides of the central hall, reserved for the orantes, with a *mihrab* in the western wall'. See also B. Scarcia Amoretti, 'Qualche osservazione in margine all'ingresso dell'Islam nel Kerala', *Indo-Sino Tibetica, Studies in Honour of L. Petech*, ed. P. Daffinà, Rome, 1990, pp. 341–8.

[5] The *jizia* was a personal tax which was levied on all able, free men; the *dhimmi* were those non-Muslims, Christians and Jews who were protected by the Islamic state.

[6] M. Bussagli, *Profili dell'India antica e moderna*, Turin, 1959, p. 199.

[7] *Ibid.*, p. 213.

Part 1: The Origins

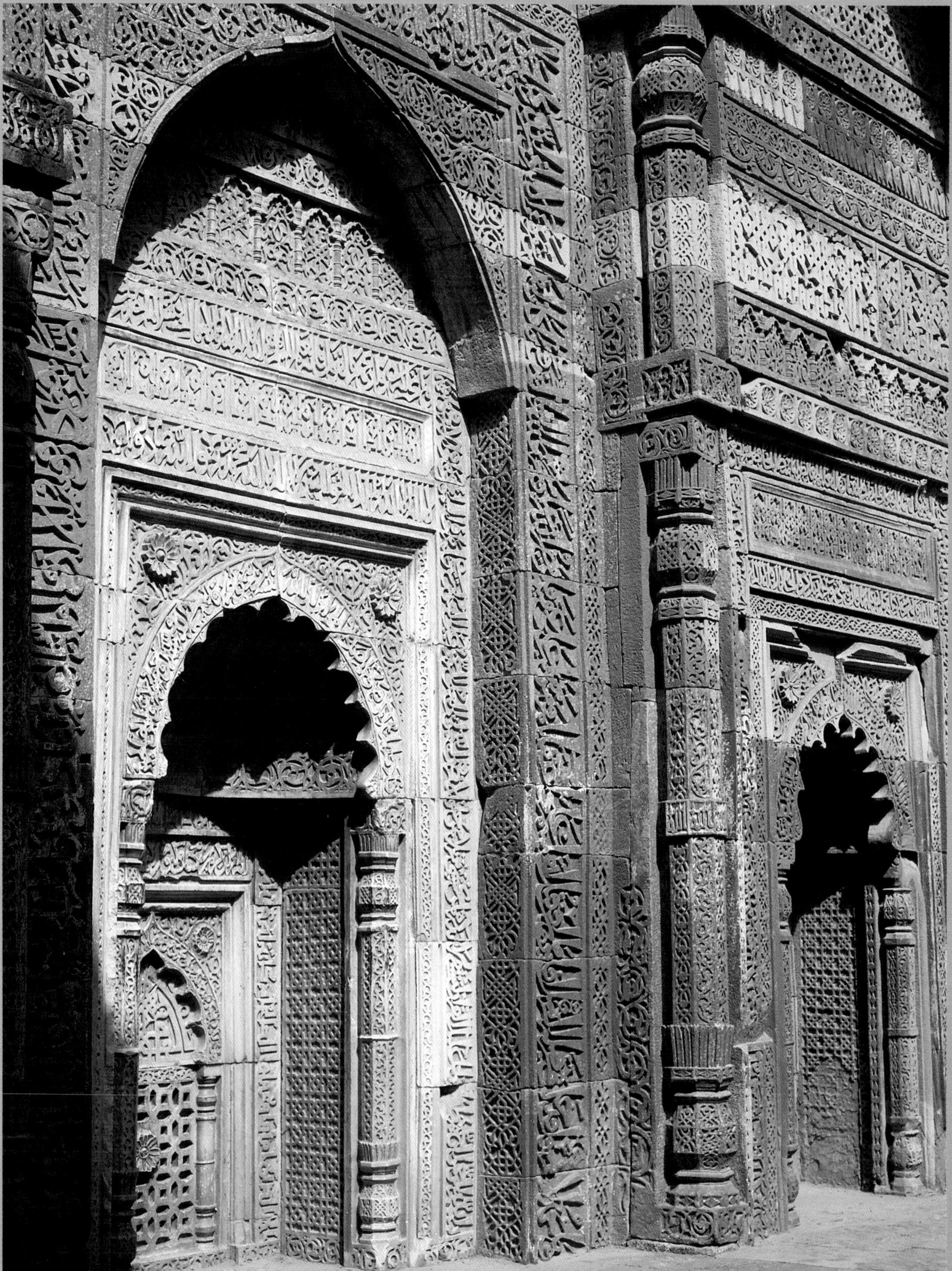

The Origins

1

The Mamluk-era mausoleum of Iltutmish at Delhi, built in 1235. The prototype for this tomb came from Bukhara in modern Uzbekistan, though the building incorporates Hindu elements introduced by local craftsmen (see p.27).

The Arab conquest of the Indian subcontinent began in southern Sind in AD 711–12, with three successive Arab expeditions against the port of Debal, whose Hindu sovereign, Dahir, had attacked and captured several Muslim merchantmen sailing from Ceylon. They were carrying women and gifts from the king of Ceylon for the caliph al-Walid. According to the historian Firishta, who relates the episode, some prisoners who managed to escape asked for justice from Hajjaj, the viceroy of the eastern provinces. It was he who mounted the punitive expeditions. The first two were repulsed by Dahir, but the third, better armed and equipped and led by Hajjaj's young son-in-law, Muhammad bin Qasim, defeated the Sind resistance. Debal was taken by force and on the ruins Muhammad built the first mosque of the entire Indian subcontinent on what is now Pakistani soil. After Muhammad, Sind was ruled by various Umayyad and Abbasid governors. But from 872–73 the Abbasids abandoned political control of Sind and the Arab leaders divided the country into many independent principalities, the most important being the emirates of Mansura and Multan. The first extended from Aror to the sea and took in the modern state of Sind and the former states of Lasbela and Makran in Baluchistan; it was governed by the Habbarg dynasty. The emirate of Multan extended from Aror to the borders of Kashmir and was held by another Qurayshiti family. The new cities that grew up in Sind under the Arabs included Nirun, Alor, Mansura and Malipura.

Banbhore

The location of Debal has not been identified with certainty. Some scholars place it at Thatta or in an area some 40 km to the south-west of the city. The confusion has arisen because of changes of place names and variations in the make up of the Indus delta. Nevertheless, it seems likely that the site of Debal is a low hill known as Bhambur (Banbhore; see p. 16), situated on a rocky plateau some 60 km east of Karachi on the north side of the Ghara estuary, once a main branch of the Indus delta. The hill is about 12m high and has substantial remains of sandstone walls, including fragments of a defensive wall more than 3 m wide with bastions. The interior was divided into two unequal parts by a transverse wall over 300 m long. Small, poorly preserved copper coins have been found on the site along with a large number of ceramics, many of them glazed, and some glass. Among the ceramics are also fragments of Chinese celadon of a kind that, from the ninth century onwards, is to be found widely distributed throughout Asia and has also been found at Brahmanabad. An ancient cistern runs along the northern edge of the hill and a little further north are walls and tombs. It seems that other mounds lie to the south of the inlet, but the entire area is still being excavated.

It would seem from finds already made that Banbhore existed from the first century BC to the twelfth century AD. Among the city's most important buildings is a mosque containing some beautifully designed Kufic inscriptions dated 727. The mosque was built in a very simple style, according to the pattern of the first Umayyad mosques of Kufa and Wasit, but is today reduced to a mere outline on the ground.[1] It was surrounded on three sides by ambulatories covered with flat roofs supported by double rows of wooden pillars. To the west was the prayer hall with three aisles parallel to the *qibla* wall, the wall indicating the direction of prayer. The *qibla* itself seems to have been without the *mihrab* niche, an innovation that in fact only appeared in the rebuilding of the Madina Mosque in 708–9.[2] In the oratory, the roof was supported by 33 wooden pillars, arranged in three rows and resting on stone bases as in the corridors. These bases are often storiated because they came from important pre-Islamic monuments. The apparatus for ritual ablutions was in the north-east corner of the mosque and at the two main entrances on the eastern and the northern sides. Another, smaller entrance was situated on the western side, with a small stairway leading to the outside.

The most important excavations at Banbhore began in 1958 and revealed three distinct periods: Scytho-Parthian, Hindu-Buddhist and Islamic, dating from the first to the thirteenth centuries. The excavation revealed a fortified citadel measuring some 670 x 335 m. Whether or not Banbhore was in fact Debal has yet to be decided, but the occupation of the site has been dated from the earliest period of Islamic government in Sind. The excavations suggest that during the Muslim period the city was well planned. The residential sectors were divided into blocks separated by well-orientated roads and thoroughfares. The homes of the elite were built in stone blocks and in some cases square-shaped fired bricks, with walls and floors dressed in stucco. The houses of the poor were made of unfired bricks and laid on a foundation of stone; the walls were dressed with smoothed mud. Remains of baths, thin tiles and wooden beams have also been found.

Although diminished in importance as a cultural and religious centre, Debal continued to be remembered in reports from the tenth century as a very active commercial port, even though, towards the end of the previous century, it had been badly damaged by an earthquake. In the thirteenth century, Khwarezmshah Jalal al-Din, who had temporarily occupied Sind, built the Great Mosque at Debal.[3] Immediately afterwards, for reasons that remain unclear, Debal disappeared from the historic and geographic record and its name passed on to other sites in the area; this has made identification very difficult.

After he conquered Debal, Muhammad bin Qasim continued his advance while Dahir retreated to the fortress of Brahmanabad, which fell in June 712 despite the bravery of the Hindus. The Arab forces advanced still further, gaining Aror, the Hindu capital of Sind, and causing the downfall of fortress after fortress. In 713 they took Multan, making it their bridgehead in the Punjab. A further advance was halted by the natural barrier of the Rajasthan desert and by Muhammad's return to his country; fallen from grace, he was executed.

Mansura

The Islamic capital, Mansura, of which there are few remains, was built on the site of the Hindu capital of Brahmanabad, situated some 70 km to the north-east of present-day Hyderabad.[4] The foundations of three small rectangular mosques have been found, with the *mihrab* projecting towards the exterior and an open entrance. In one mosque the roof was supported by four brick pillars, the square

Above The low hill known as Bhambur (Banbhore) is believed to be the site of the ancient port of Debal.

Right The remains of the foundations of the eighth-century mosque at Banbhore.

The archeological remains and fortifications of Banbhore suggest that the eighth-century Muslim part of the city was well planned.

bases of which remain; in another there were only two pillars. The perimeter walls of all three buildings were of brick. In front of the largest building there was a small court with a passage to the exterior. Circular clay wells of a type common in the Indo-Pakistani area have also been found together with numerous corroded copper coins that are difficult to identify. These last, nevertheless, seem to consist of two basic types: one, with beautiful Arab inscriptions on the edge, seems to have been minted in the caliphate itself; the other, rather small, flat and compressed, seems to have been minted in Sind, probably in Mansura where clay 'beehive' moulds were found just as at Banbhore. Fragments of carved brick, ivory pieces from chess sets turned on a lathe, glass beads and much run-of-the-mill pottery work mixed with Chinese celadon: all these have been found piled in chaotic disorder. A fourth mosque, somewhat larger than the others, has also been identified at Mansura. It seems to have had teak pillars in the Abbasid style and appears to date from about a century later than the other mosques.

Nothing remains of the monuments which were presumably built in the two capitals during the following centuries. After all, it was here that Muslim dominion in the subcontinent took shape. The authority of the caliphs was eroded almost completely with the slackening of the ties with the motherland, to the point where, from 871 onwards, the conquered region was divided into two independent principalities, governed respectively from Mansura in Sind and from Multan in the Punjab.

GHAZNAVIDS AND GHURIDS

At the beginning of the eleventh century, under the sword of Mahmud of Ghazni, Turkish conqueror of Afghanistan, the Muslim invasions began again.[5] This time, however, they were also directed against Islamic communities in the name of orthodoxy. Indeed, as a pretext for invading Multan, Mahmud, a Sunnite, declared his intention to punish the sovereign of the city who was an Ismailian and therefore a heretic. The attacks began in 1001, but only in 1011 did the Ghaznavid succeed in capturing the city and taking its riches to Ghazni. Gradually he extended his incursions to cover all the Punjab and Sind with some 17 successfully predatory expeditions, the sole aim of which was to enrich Ghazni and make it the most important city in eastern Islam. Mahmud's successors continued this policy of expansion, pushing on into other provinces and occupying Nagaur, in the heart of Rajasthan, until they, in their turn, were ensnared by the rising Ghurid dynasty which originated in a remote fortress in the mountains over 300 km to the north of Ghazni.[6] Twice Ala al-Din of Ghur attacked Ghazni and set fire to it (1149 and 1151), thus going down in the history as Jahansoz (the Scorcher of the World). His successor, Muizz al-Din Muhammad, took Ghazni definitively in 1173, forcing the last Ghaznavids to retreat to Lahore, which became their final refuge. Mahmud had already stayed in Lahore and, according to some sources, had built a mosque there known locally as Khisti Masjid, together with a minaret in the fortress.

Once his Afghan acquisitions had been consolidated, Muhammad dedicated himself to the conquest of the Punjab. He first occupied Multan, then the remainder of the region, followed by all of Sind. He went on to take Lahore from the great-grandson of Mahmud and turned towards Rajasthan and Gujarat, but his defeat was calamitous. After an equally unfortunate clash with the Chauhan Rajput sovereign Prithviraja III, Muhammad reorganized his armies and in 1192 succeeded in defeating a great alliance of Hindu sovereigns at Tarain, fully exhausting the resistance and initiating Muslim hegemony over India. He pushed on over the Ganges plain and set up a permanent occupation of Ajmer, which from then on became, almost without interruption, the fortress of the foreign ruler in Rajasthan. According to the historian Minhaj al-Din, on the capture of Ajmer victory trophies were sent to the Ghurid castle of Firozkoh: two large gold birds – perhaps *garudas*, vehicles of Vishnu, 'each about the size of a large camel' – together with five gold pinnacles. On returning home, Muhammad entrusted the government of the Indian provinces to his faithful lieutenant Qutb al-Din Aibak, who consolidated the conquest by first

Top The *jami masjid* (mid-fifteenth-century) at Bidar. Many of the structures built by the Deccani Bahmanid sultans, such as this mosque, show Persian influences.

Above The Diwan-i Khass at Fatehpur Sikri, one of the most famous structures built under the reign of the Mughal emperor Akbar (1556–1605).

occupying Delhi and then, with the help of the valiant general Muhammad ibn Bakhtiyar Khalji, Bihar (where many famous Buddhist monastic universities were destroyed), Bengal, Gujarat and Vindhya Pradesh. Some years later Muhammad Ghuri – murdered by two hired Ismailian assassins – died without heirs, leaving Aibak lord of his Indian territories. Aibak thus founded the Muizz dynasty, also called the Mamluks because, besides Qutb al-Din, many of his successors were also of servile origin. Indeed, in his youth, Aibak had been a Turkish slave who was freed and was started off on his army career with the aid of Muhammad.

Persian Influence

Aibak's dynasty lasted from 1206 to 1290, a period in which, for the first time, an Indo-Islamic art began to develop and take shape. From the beginning the dynasty itself, with much originality, was to be largely a tributary of the Iranian world (unsurprisingly if we consider the origin of the Ghurid sovereigns and their contact with Ghazni and the eastern Islamic regions). From here came many prototypes of monuments, the most conspicuous example of which is the minaret with a stellate plan. This plan provided the model for the Qutb Minar (see p. 23) which variously inspired local builders.[7] On the other hand, Indian influence on decorative techniques is apparent in some Afghan areas, especially in the Ghurid period. This is borne out by a certain number of funeral sculptures in marble from Ghazni and by a small stone mosque, the Masjid-i Sanji at Larvand (south-west Afghanistan). This last also provides evidence of the considerable influence of Rajasthan art.[8] The Iranian influence, although tempered by Turco-Afghan sources, was to remain a constant for some centuries in the area of Delhi; later, Timurid-Central Asiatic influences were felt, or even Ottoman in some of the regions that had become independent upon the fall of the Tughluqs; and with the Mughals, the Persian Timurid source of inspiration grew more direct. It was in this period that, after a number of experiments, Indo-Islamic architecture found a true unity of style.

With the first imperial dynasties, artistic production was concentrated above all at Delhi and Ajmer, but with the relaxing of central domination after the fall of the Tughluqs, architecture assumed different characteristics. These characteristics were often due to the prevalence of strong local traditions, such as in Gujarat, or were influenced by environmental conditions as in Bengal and Kashmir. Particular Persian influences, too, often arose, as in the Deccani Bahmanid sultanate and in the kingdoms that derived from it (Bidar, Bijapur, Golconda), even if in seventeenth-century Bijapur there were distinct Ottoman influences. The Iranian influence was exerted in all fields of culture such as literature, miniature painting and garden design. The official language of the empire was Persian, and numerous historical and poetic works were composed in it. The latter were of a most original style, called, appropriately enough, 'Indian', and later enjoyed extraordinary success from the sixteenth century onwards.

Characteristics of the Architecture

It has been stated more than once that during its Muslim period the Indian subcontinent saw the creation of a number of buildings remarkably superior to those of Islam's other regions. This is undoubtedly due to the fact that the material used most often, with the exception of Kashmir and Bengal, is stone. Usually this is a beautiful sandstone – red, grey or yellow – often complemented with white marble as decoration. It was only during the time of the Mughal Shah Jahan that marble became the preferred material and decoration was finished in hard or precious stones. The Muslim architecture of India, in contrast to the Hindu architecture that was almost exclusively religious, has produced a great variety of civic buildings designed for public use; private buildings such as palaces, fortresses, royal complexes, pavilions, bridges, houses, gardens and so on; and religious buildings, mosques, schools of theology (*madrasa*) and mausoleums. The structures are usually extremely simple in plan, even if the foreign influence often blends with elements of local tradition that are more obviously noticeable outside of Delhi. In the provinces, the design of the buildings – not simply the decoration – underwent considerable change, for example in Gujarat, Kashmir and Bengal. This close following of aesthetic canons was a conscious choice in the Mughal period, above all under Akbar, with the aim of achieving a reconciliation that was also aesthetic between the Hindu and Islamic worlds. Here we have the fundamental reason why Islam in India assumed an entirely original character compared with other Islamicized areas.

[1] *Pakistan Archaeology*, 1 (1964), pp. 49-55; 5, 1968, pp. 176-85.

[2] The house where the Prophet Muhammad had lived and died, at Medina, was immediately used as a mosque and, to commemorate the place where he used to stand up to lead the prayer or to preach, a niche called a *mihrab* was made. Being so full of symbolic meaning, it soon became the most sacred place in the mosque and was then fashioned and decorated in the most diverse and sumptuous ways throughout all the regions of Islam.

[3] Jalal al-Din Manguberti, last shah of Khwarezm, an oasis on the Oxus (Amu Darya) delta south of the Aral Sea, crossed the Indus in 1221 in an attempt to flee from his emirs' conspiracy and tried in vain to build up a new principality for himself. He was forced to retreat to Persia and died in 1231 at the hand of a Kurd while seeking refuge from the Mongols.

[4] H. Cousens, *Antiquities of Sind*, ASI, Calcutta, 1929.

[5] Mahmud (997-1050) was a descendant of Alptegin, the Turkish governor of Khorassan (north-western Iran). At the death of his father, Sebuktegin, who had managed to seize the throne of Ghazni, he extended his conquests from Afghanistan as far as Seistan (south-eastern Iran) and succeeded in persuading the Abbasid caliph al-Qadir to grant him the title of Yamin al-Daula (Right Hand of the State). Having come to terms with his powerful neighbours, the Ilek-khans, he vowed that he would make war every year on the pagans of India and began his raids, which the Indian princes, being at variance amongst themselves, found it difficult to resist, even as early as 1001. He went on to plunder Gwalior, Kanauj, Mathura and Anhilwara (the capital of Gujarat), where he is said to have broken into pieces with his own hands the idol of the famous temple of Somnath (1026) and to have had the pieces scattered before the entrance of the Great Mosque at Ghazni, so that the Muslims could tread all over them.

[6] The Ghurids (1148-1215), a people of Iranian origin, had settled in a mountainous region of Afghanistan between the Helmand valley and Herat and had been forced by Mahmud to embrace Islam. As their power increased, they ceased to be vassals of the Ghaznavids and established a kingdom that reached as far as Bamiyan and Balkh, giving themselves the title of sultan. Having come into conflict with the Ghaznavids because one of their princes had been killed by Bahram Shah (whom he had asked for protection), they destroyed the Ghaznavids' power and their capital city. In the fire that followed upon the general massacre of the inhabitants, Ala al-Din Ghuri even had the bodies of the deceased Ghaznavids dug up so that their remains could be burnt. Ala al-Din was subsequently defeated and taken prisoner by the Saljuq sultan Sanjar and died in 1162. He was succeeded by Ghiyas al-Din, who endowed his brother Muizz al-Din, commemorated on coins as Sultan al-Muazzam, with the possession of Ghazni, whence he set out on his conquest of India.

[7] N.A. Ahmad, 'Les monuments historiques et les mausolées de Ghazni', *Afghanistan*, 7/2 (1952), pp. 9-18; A. Bombaci, 'Ghazni', *East and West*, 8 (1957), pp. 247-59.

[8] G. Scarcia, M. Taddei, 'The Masjid-i Sangi of Larvand', *East and West*, 23 (1973), pp. 89-108.

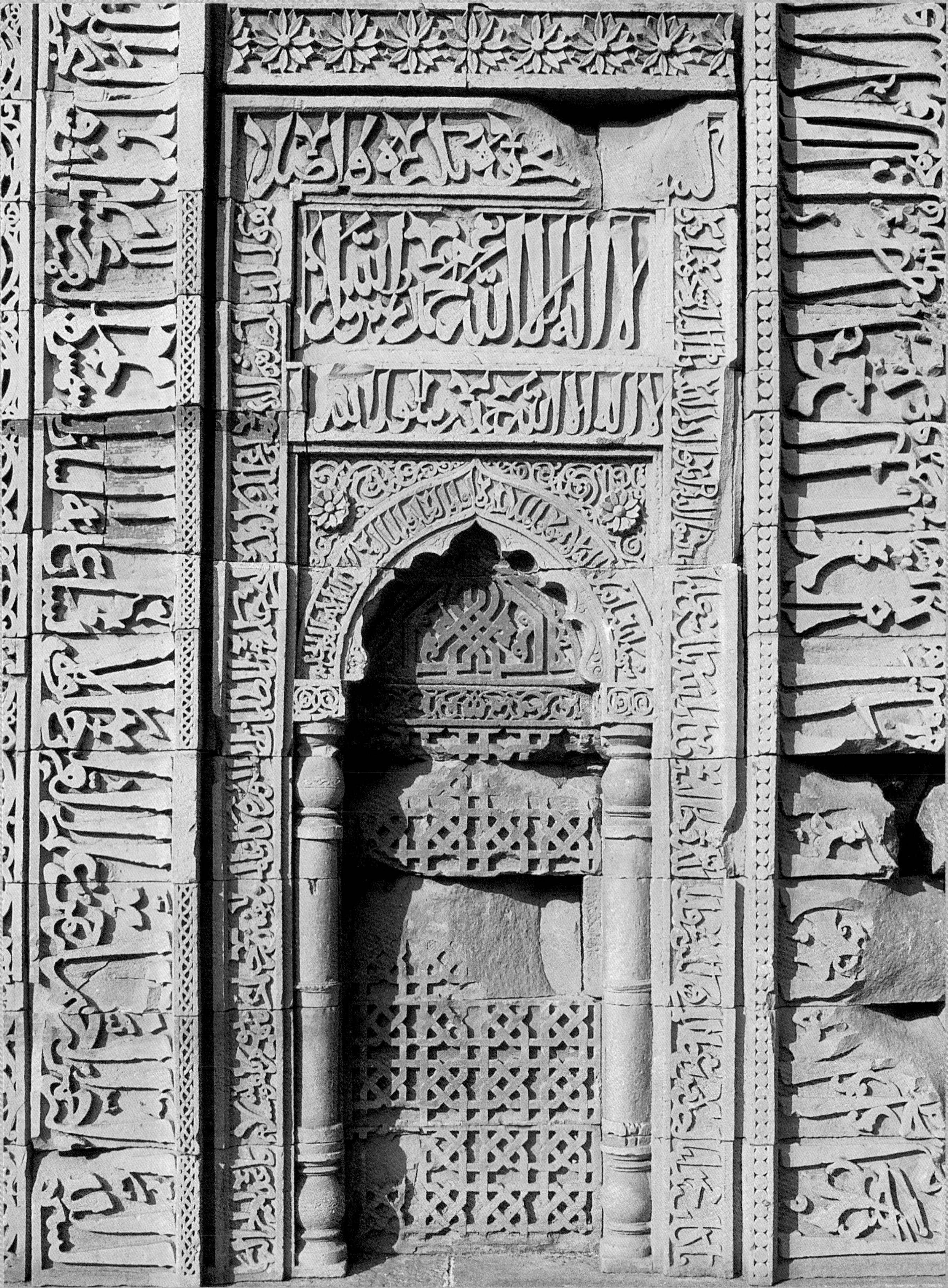

THE MAMLUKS OF DELHI (1206–1290)

2

The exterior of the Quwwat al-Islam mosque (1195) at Delhi is richly decorated in Kufic and naskhi inscriptions, although the materials, and many architectural elements, came from Hindu temples.

DELHI: QUWWAT AL-ISLAM

The oldest mosque in Delhi, the Quwwat al-Islam (Power of Islam), was built by Aibak in 1195 in the citadel of Rai Pithora, with materials from 27 Hindu and Jain temples demolished in the neighbourhood (according to an inscription on the interior architrave of the eastern portal). Its planimetry – somewhat complex owing to the successive alterations it underwent – was inspired by mosques with a wide hall preceded by a court, a type that was very common in this period throughout the eastern Muslim world. Hindu columns and pillars were superimposed to form the *riwaq* (covered galleries) that surround the *sahn* (courtyard of the mosque), at the corners of which were false domes built in the Hindu trabeated system. On the northern and southern sides, the *riwaq* were divided into two aisles: on the eastern side, where the entrance to the mosque was, there were three rows of pillars interrupted at the centre by a domed structure. The prayer hall to the west was four aisles deep: these aisles were formed by two rows of Hindu pillars placed one above the other and covered by Hindu roofs of the 'lantern' type. In 1199 a monumental façade was added to the hall. This had five arches, the central one being almost twice the height of the laterals. It was designed to recreate the imposing Iranian *iwan*, but because of the use of local craftsmen who were still inexpert in the art of Islamic construction, it remained out of harmony with the rest of the structure.[1] The pointed arches were built using the corbel technique of projecting stones, characteristic of Hindu architecture, which was well known from the *gavaksha* motif in the windows of the local *chaitya* sanctuary.[2] The pilasters that support the arches, created in various materials (red and grey sandstone, quartzite and black slate), are decorated with beautiful epigraphic friezes in Kufic and *naskhi* that reproduce for the most part Koranic verses.[3] These verses are placed among wave-like ornamental motifs that run vertically and rhythmically like Arab inscriptions. The Iron Pillar, a very tall iron column (see p. 22), was situated exactly in front of the main arch and in all probability dates from the Gupta period. It carries a dedication by

ISLAMIC ARCHITECTURE OF THE INDIAN SUBCONTINENT

a certain King Chandra, who may in fact correspond to Samudragupta (fourth century AD), who had the title of Chandra. Originally, the column must have been surmounted with a *garuda* (the mythical bird that was the vehicle of Vishnu) since the sovereign in the inscription claims to be a Vishnuite. The figure was of course removed by the Muslims when they set up the column in the mosque as a sign of the superiority of Islam over the defeated Hindu religion.

Delhi: Qutb Minar

Concurrent with the monumental façade, Aibak began the construction of the Qutb Minar, the well-known, beautiful minaret situated on the south-eastern outer corner of the mosque. Conceived as both a look-out and victory tower, 'to cast the shadow of God over the East and over the West', as one of its inscriptions states, it was directly inspired by the earlier Ghaznavid minarets of Masud III and Bahram Shah and the earlier Ghurid minarets of Jam and Khwaja Siah Posh.[4] Indeed, the stellate plan surmounted by a cylindrical shaft found its fullest expression in the Qutb Minar. Some 73 m tall, it has a base diameter of over 14 m and is currently made up of five superimposed tapering shafts, originally probably topped with a small domed pavilion (*chhatri*), as in the prototype at Jam. In the Mamluk period the shafts – polygonal, fluted and divided by protruding balconies on graceful *muqarnas* – must have been four in number. But in 1369 Firuz Shah Tughluq added a very ugly fifth storey after having restored, in dubious taste, the fourth floor which had been seriously damaged by a lightning bolt. This fifth storey was renovated by Sikandar Lodi in 1503 and again by the penultimate Mughal emperor, Akbar II, in 1828. Aibak only succeeded in completing the first storey and the others were finished by his successor, Iltutmish. The lower shaft has 24 ribs that are alternately angular and circular, the second shaft has only circular ribs, the third only angular, while the fourth and fifth are completely cylindrical. The entire minaret is in red sandstone and a particular local grey quartzite sandstone; the terminal parts are in white marble. The decoration – apart from the beautiful 'stalactite' balconies that separate the various storeys – consists of annular fasciae with *naskhi* inscriptions placed within vegetal and geometric borders.[5] Some stones have been taken from Hindu monuments and carry *chauhan* inscriptions or small epigraphs placed by local marble masons who worked there. This has led some Indian scholars to suggest that this was a Rajput building. However, quite apart from Aibak's inscriptions that allude to the Ghurid sovereigns Muizz al-Din and Ghiyas al-Din, the character of this tower is absolutely Islamic and differs totally from Hindu victory towers, *kirtisthambha*. According to Van Berchem, Qutb al-Din initially planned this tower as his own mausoleum. Successful imitations of the indigenous style are to be found instead in the lower decorative fasciae which are the work of local craftsmen. These do not clash with the arabesques and Kufic characters in best Persian taste that alternate on other parts of the minaret. On the northern side of the lowest shaft is a door, inside which is a spiral staircase that leads to each balcony and ends in a platform on the highest floor. Although one of the

Left The Iron Pillar, situated at the front of the main arch of the Quwwat al-Islam, was taken from an earlier Hindu site.

Opposite The Qutb Minar at the Quwwat al-Islam. Begun in 1199 by Aibak, the minaret was conceived as both a look out and a victory tower, and was inspired by earlier Ghaznavid and Ghurid examples.

most splendid and significant monuments of Indo-Islamic art, the Qutb Minar remained a practically unique phenomenon: in contrast with what happened in the Iranian and Turkish regions, in India the minaret did not develop greatly.

AJMER: ARHAI-DIN-KA JHOMPRA

In about 1200 at Ajmer, headquarters of the Muslim garrison of Rajasthan, Aibak began the building of the so-called Arhai-din-ka Jhompra mosque (literally the 'Two-and-a-Half-Days'-Refuge'; see p. 24). The name perhaps refers to the two-and-a-half-day market that was held regularly in the area, or perhaps to the time it took the Muslims to destroy the local Vishnuite temple; obviously it does not refer to the time taken to build the mosque. Like the Quwwat al-Islam, this was also built with spoil material from which the Hindu or Jain images had been stripped, sometimes perfunctorily. The greater experience of the local craftsmen in planning an Islamic building gave this monument a more harmonious and regular aspect. The Ajmer Mosque, which covers an area twice that of the Delhi Mosque, rises on a wide platform cut into a declivity in the centre of a valley surrounded on each side by hills; it is entirely of yellow sandstone. Access is from the eastern side by means of a high, wide stairway leading up to a pointed archway with a heavy horizontal architrave, flanked by two protruding balconies, in keeping with the typical style of Rajput and Gujarat cult buildings. Another entrance, consisting of a small pavilion, is to be found on the southern side. The planimetry of the mosque is based on the traditional layout, with a square court surrounded by arcades with corner towers. These last have a curved design with receding floors and are ornamented with beautiful carvings in Hindu style that are arranged on the shafts in horizontal fasciae. In both the arcades and the prayer hall on the western side, the ceilings are supported by three rows of Hindu pillars, one above the other. The colonnades therefore reach a considerable height, higher than those of the Delhi Mosque. The prayer hall is made up of five aisles parallel to the *qibla* wall, covered by elegantly patterned and varied lantern and corbel roofs that came from Hindu and Jain temples. The large number of pillars with their reliefs create a most evocative spiritual atmosphere which – although in contrast with the extreme simplicity of the niches of the *mihrab* – confers a sense of subtle mystery to the whole that is much more Hindu than it is Muslim.

Aibak's successor, Iltutmish, completed the mosque by adding, as in the Quwwat al-Islam, a monumental façade which, like the rest of the building and despite the fact that it is not perfectly matched to the pillared construction, is more harmonious and proportioned than the one at Delhi. It is made up of seven arches, of which the central one, larger than the others, has a bolder line and is surmounted by two stellate minarets, now for the most part in ruins. The main arch is pointed at the keystone, while the others are of the multifoil pointed variety and proved to be most important for the development of this form in Indo-Islamic architecture. The wall decoration is more refined than that at Delhi, with a bas-relief of geometric and floral motifs typical of the aniconic repertory of Islam. Extremely elegant Koranic inscriptions stand out from these motifs in high relief, creating a dynamic contrast. From this point onwards, such inscriptions were destined to play a leading role in the decoration of Muslim buildings.

KAMAN: CHAURASI KHAMBA

Maliq Baha al-Din Tughrul, another faithful general of Muhammad Ghuri (but a rival of Qutb al-Din Aibak), was responsible for several religious buildings in the Bayana area of south-eastern Rajasthan. Two mosques and an *idgah* (praying place for festivals) survive here.

The first mosque is in the village of Kaman and is known locally as Chaurasi Khamba (84 Columns; see p. 25). It is a built on an Arabic plan with a central courtyard surrounded by colonnades, and is entirely constructed from re-used material. The main entrance carries a somewhat damaged inscription on which the date of Ramadan AH 600 (May–June 1204) can be read. The columns, in some cases upside-down, still carry clear traces of the original Hindu decoration such as floral motifs, wreaths, rosettes, vases and figures, the faces of which have been chiselled away. The prayer hall, with three bays parallel to

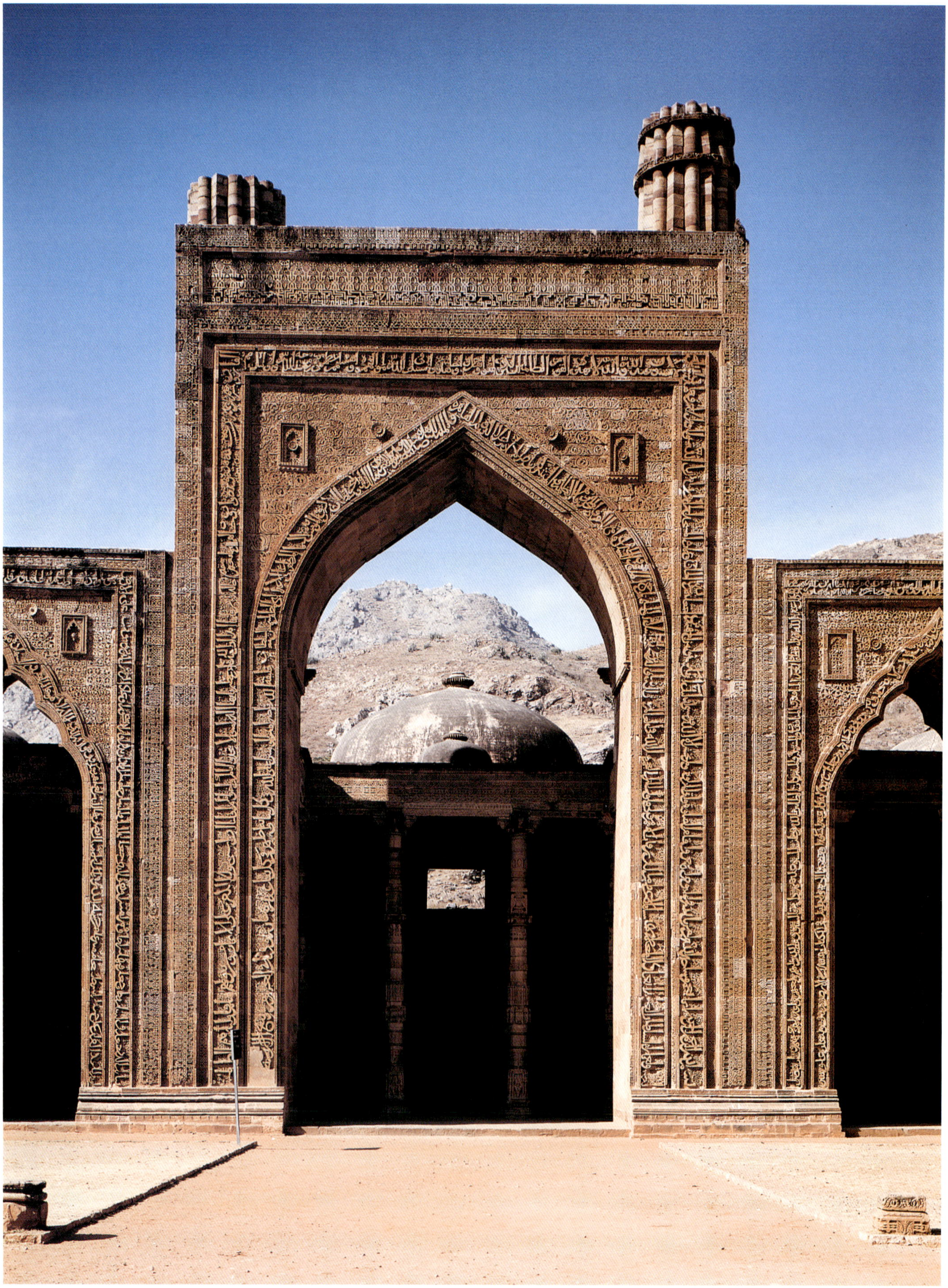

Left The mosque at Kaman, known as Chaurasi Khamba (84 Columns), was built on an Arabic plan – a central courtyard surrounded by collonnades – from entirely re-used materials.

Opposite The entrance of the Arhai-din-ka Jompra ('Two-and-a-Half-Days'-Refuge') mosque at Ajmer, begun around 1200 by Aibak and completed by Iltutmish.

the *qibla* wall, has seven bays, the central one being slightly wider than the others. As in the Quwwat al-Islam, the column shafts are placed one on top of the other so as to achieve the required height. The *mihrab* has a rectangular plan that projects strongly towards the exterior and a pointed arch decorated with floral volutes and a damaged Koranic inscription. The stone *minbar* (pulpit) is still in position and is exceptional for this period in India: it seems to have derived from Iranian wooden *minbars* such as the contemporary example at Nayin. It is made up of a series of steps and a platform covered by a dome. In the north-eastern corner of the *qibla* area there is the first example of a women's gallery, a feature that later spread throughout almost all pre-Mughal India; it is supported by four columns and was once screened by stone *jali* (screens), the jointing sockets of which can still be seen in the beams. The gallery was reached from the exterior through a door and a small stone staircase in the western corner of the northern wall. This last, like the eastern side of the courtyard, presents an unusual aspect because it rests on a high (1.76 m) platform, on top of which stand two rows of single-shafted columns. The mosque has been restored twice, but the lines of the original plan do not seem to have been altered. The eastern entrance juts out a long way on the outside so as to create a thick-walled space with heavy pilasters on the façade.

Bayana: Ukha Mandir

The mosque at Bayana – later transformed into a Hindu temple – known as Ukha Mandir, is also attributed to Baha al-Din Tughrul. This is a complex which includes a second mosque known as Ukha Mosque (see p. 33), adjacent to the first but built in 1320, during the Khalji period, and an unfinished minaret, the Ukha Minar from the Lodi period (1519–20). The Ukha Mandir, which unfortunately today is in a dilapidated state, has a plan similar to that of the Chaurasi Khamba, with a central courtyard surrounded by colonnades. These are deeper in the prayer hall and in the eastern area, while the courtyard has an impressive entrance way with a high pointed arch on the outside. Here, too, the columns have two superimposed shafts and come from Hindu temples: the spans are covered by corbelled arches, typical of indigenous construction. The *qibla* wall still has three rectangular *mihrab* of which only the central one projects towards the exterior. These are finely ornamented with spiral floral motifs, roses and epigraphic inscriptions. There is no *minbar* at all, but there is a raised ladies' gallery, screened by *jali* and furnished with a small supplementary *minbar*.

Qutb al-Din died in 1210 after a fall during a game of polo. His successor and son-in-law, Shams al-Din Iltutmish (1211–36), was an energetic warrior and an active builder. Although engaged in continuous wars designed to check the advance of the Mongols who were a constant threat to India, he dedicated himself with true commitment to the art of construction.

After completing the Qutb Minar, respecting the stylistic directions of his predecessor, he saw to the enlargement of the Quwwat al-Islam (1230; see p. 20), which by this time was not large enough to meet the needs of the capital's increased Muslim population. The original structures were left almost intact and were only slightly modified in order to duplicate the existing space. A new court was created incorporating the Qutb Minar; the northern and southern sides were bordered with cloisters two aisles deep, while the eastern side of the court had five rows of pillars. The façade was enlarged by three arches on each side, both to the north and to the south: the central arch was taller than the laterals, but all were pointed in the Persian style and were profusely ornamented with blind, shell-shaped niches and traceried windows. All the building material came, as always, from demolished Hindu and Jain temples.

Iltutmish was responsible for the introduction to India of a monument unknown in the local tradition, namely the mausoleum. The Hindu world had always cremated its dead, scattering the ashes in sacred rivers, so that it had never felt the need to build monumental tombs. Their models, therefore, were taken directly from Iranian countries. It is interesting to note, nevertheless, that even in this field the indigenous craftsmen succeeded in expressing their taste in some significant details of the decoration, so as to confer a truly Indian character to the monuments. This is apparent, for example, in the upside-down lotus flowers crowning the domes, the elaborate capitals, the false corbel supports with their complex forms, and above all, the small domes, supported by small pillars situated around the central dome (*chhatri*). These forms became more elaborate with time and were established variously in the Delhi sultanates and in the regional states; they later culminated in the splendid forms of the Mughal period.

Delhi: Sultan Ghari

The first of Iltutmish's funeral constructions is situated a short distance from Delhi and was built in 1231–2 for the son of the sovereign, Nasir al-Din Mahmud, who died very young in 1228 or 1229. The building is known by the name of Sultan Ghari (Sultan of the Cave) because the actual tomb is placed in an underground chamber. From the outside the building looks like a small fortress, built on a plinth 3 m high, with cylindrical, domed bastions at the corners. The walls are of grey sandstone with arched openings that are slightly pointed at the summit. Beyond the entrance there is a square court of roughly 21 m each side, at the centre of which is an octagonal platform which constitutes the roof of the burial chamber and which must have been surmounted by a small pillared pavilion with a pyramidal roof that has not survived. On the west side of the court is a small pillared mosque covered by an octagonal Hindu dome above the *mihrab*. This mosque also has a façade made up of columns of white marble which recall the Doric order. Another small pillared construction, again in white marble that contrasts strongly with the grey sandstone, rises at the centre of the eastern entrance side. The extreme simplicity of the forms and the complete lack of decoration confer a severe look to the monument, which is nonetheless not without a profound sense of peace and serenity. It was seriously damaged during the Chaghatai attacks at the beginning of the fourteenth century and was restored by Firuz Shah Tughluq, who had the six

Above Iltutmish's mausoleum (1235) at Delhi. The new approach to building the dome was structurally unsuccessful, and it has since fallen in.

Top The Sultan Ghari (1231–2) at Delhi was the first of Iltutmish's funeral constructions, built for his son, Nasir al-Din Mahmud. From the outside it looks like a small fortress.

Opposite The Shamsi *idgah* (1202–9) at Budaun. The *idgah* – virtually a wall with a *mihrab* – did not appear in other Islamic countries until the fourteenth century.

marble columns set up to form the protruding portico in front of the *mihrab*, with its vaguely classical air. According to Welch, it owed this classicism to the verbal descriptions of travellers from the west, perhaps Ibn Battuta, rather than any specific classic prototype.[6]

DELHI: ILTUTMISH MAUSOLEUM

The mausoleum that Iltutmish had built for himself in 1235 in the north-western corner of the Quwwat al-Islam is of a completely different character. Here, for the first time, the problem of the dome was tackled; and if the solution was aesthetically brilliant, it proved to be sadly lacking from a functional point of view: the dome has long since fallen in. The tomb is a cubic building with doors opening on three sides. The fourth side has no opening but is taken up by three *mihrab*, of which the central one, larger than the others, is protected by a multifoil arch. This is supported by small corner columns, and is framed by an architraved structure that in its turn is enclosed within a larger, ogival arch. In contrast with the exterior wall surfaces, which are without decoration, the interior walls of the mausoleum are covered with endless carving which elegantly mixes refined Koranic inscriptions in Kufic or *nastaliq*[7] with geometric elements, fine chain motifs, rosettes, crenellations, palmettes, triangular arches and Hindu pilasters that make the wall surfaces look like fine lace. The mediation between the square base of the building and the circle of the dome was provided by adding pendentives at the four corners, so as to obtain an octagonal base for the 16-sided structure on which the actual dome was to be erected. Evidently the Indian craftsmen who oversaw the construction had not yet physically mastered the new type of building even if they had understood the mechanical theory. At the centre of the mausoleum, on a double stone plinth, stands the sarcophagus of Iltutmish, but the real tomb is situated in an underground chamber reached by means of a narrow stair on the north side of the building. This tomb type was later altered over the course of centuries, but its prototype is to be found in the mausoleum of Ismail the Samanid, at Bukhara, which acted as model for countless Iranian funeral monuments.[8]

BUDAUN, SHAMSI *IDGAH*

As well as at Delhi and Ajmer, Iltutmish also commissioned some buildings at Budaun on the Ganges, including the Shamsi *idgah* (1202–9). The Shamsi *idgah* is a massive wall of bricks, which must have been more than 100 m long, with a *mihrab* at the centre whose inscription has been plastered over. On the upper part of the wall are traces of blue glazing, which was probably added to cover the original decoration. The *idgah* is thus little more than a wall with a *mihrab* where the entire community celebrated the major Islamic festivals: the Id al-Fitr (Festival at the End of Fasting) and the Id al-Kabir (Festival of the Sacrificed Lamb, held on the last day of the pilgrimage to Mecca). In Iranian territory and in the rest of Islam the *idgah* did not appear until the fourteenth century, while in India there are a certain number which date from Iltutmish's time. Perhaps the prototype of the *idgah* is to be found in the open-air mosque on the parade ground of Masud of Ghazni at Lashkari Bazar, apparently consisting of an archway with an *iwan* at the centre indicating the *qibla* and a huge space in front without perimeter walls. It seems that here the soldiers of the sultan would gather while the officers and the sovereign himself took their positions under the arch of the *iwan*. This model was probably adopted by the Ghurids and introduced by them into India so as to allow them to build in a short time large enough places of worship to accommodate the entire army.

BAYANA: *IDGAH*

The *idgah* of Bayana consists of a wall some 60 m long, built with blocks of re-used sandstone arranged in courses and terminating at the extremities with two circular towers which perhaps were once domed. At the centre is a square *mihrab* projecting towards the exterior with an arched niche and flanked on each side by four smaller niches; they are covered by false Hindu cupolas, which were probably added during restoration work. The original *minbar* is lost, but some traces can still be seen on the wall to the right of the central *mihrab*. This *idgah* is the oldest example of its kind still existing.

BUDAUN: *JAMI MASJID* AND OTHER BUILDINGS

Two structures worthy of mention at Budaun are a *musalla*, a type of open-air oratory, and a *jami masjid*, or Friday mosque (1222–4). This mosque had the same planimetry as the mosques of Delhi and Ajmer, including the arched façades, but it has been seriously modified by various renovations in the course of the centuries, the latest of which altered the monumental façade. The Great Mosque is of a remarkable size (some 84 x 65 m), with an internal courtyard of some 60 x 30 m, and is built with blocks of sandstone largely taken from the Manipal temple and other Hindu buildings nearby. It has faceted pillars with elegantly carved bases and capitals. The superstructure of the prayer hall was in brick, apart from the central dome which was in stone, a late restoration in Akbar's time. At the four corners of the perimeter rise four towers, decorated with geometric motifs. Both the *riwaq* of the courtyard and the prayer hall were formed by rows of pillars – two and four respectively – and the exterior façade must have been arcaded. According to Cunningham, the entire surface of the interior walls must have been faced in glazed tiles, but this theory is doubtful since no other contemporary example exists. If such decoration ever did exist, it must have been added at a later date.

HANSI: *IDGAH*

Another *idgah* from Iltutmish's time is at Hansi, a city to the north-west of Delhi on the old road to Khurasan. It was much ruined at the time of the Partition (1947) and has all but disappeared so that the traces of a *mihrab* and two towers at the extremities are only just recognizable. It carried an inscription in the name of Mahmud, Iltutmish's son, who had been governor of the city until his premature death. The inscription was perhaps carved on the slabs of stone that dressed two of the three original *mihrab*. Surprisingly, verse 144 from Sura five of the Koran is inscribed with the citation 'Jesus, son of Mary': at the very least an unusual choice for a building designed to celebrate Islamic festivals.

NAGAUR: ATARKIN-KA DARWAZA

At Nagaur, in Rajasthan, the gate of the city – called Atarkin-ka Darwaza – is still standing. This presents many decorative motifs similar to those found on the façade of the Arhai-din-ka Jhompra, to the point where they seem to have been executed by the same group of craftsmen. Its current appearance, however, would seem to indicate later additions; the date of its construction could be 1230, but it was restored in the course of the fourteenth and sixteenth centuries.

The secular works of Iltutmish and his successors, such as the citadel of Lalkot at Delhi and the palaces called Daulat Khana (Private Residence of the Ruler), Kushk-i Safid (White Palace) and Kushk-i Lal (Red Palace) have been completely lost because they were used in later times as quarries for building materials. Even the Kilokheri palace of Kai Qubad (1287–90), in which it seems there were grand murals that were removed by Firuz Shah Tughluq, suffered the same fate. The mausoleum of the sultan Balban (1266–87) at Delhi (Mehrauli) is also a ruin, and only a few fragments of its carved stucco

Above The *jami masjid* (1222–4) at Budaun. It has the same plan as the mosques of Delhi and Ajmer, though renovations have drastically altered it.

Opposite The mausoleum of the sultan Balban (1266–87) at Delhi (Mehrauli). Though ruined, it is important for having the first example in India of a true Islamic arch.

ornamentation have survived. This mausoleum is nonetheless very important because we find there the first example of a true Islamic arch, which was to be further developed in subsequent periods. On the road that leads from Delhi to Aligarh there are a few remains, including an inscription, of a small mosque at Jalali which was also built by Balban. He was also probably responsible for the mausoleum of the saint Baha al-Din Zakariya (1262) at Multan in Pakistan; this was, however, substantially modified in the sixteenth century.

[1] The *iwan* was an ancient Iranian structure going back to Parthian times, which continued to be used and was taken over throughout Islam. It is a quadrangular, vaulted structure and is closed on three sides only, with the front completely open. It originated perhaps in private houses in Khurasan (north-eastern Iran), where it stood at the centre of each side of an inner courtyard, and was introduced by the Saljuqs into the Iranian Great Mosques in the eleventh century. Its use spread rapidly in Central Asia, Iraq, Egypt and the Maghreb, where it became a characteristic feature of mosques and *madrasa*.

[2] The *gavaksha* motif consists of a double curved arch, slightly pointed at the apex, similar to the Gothic arch.

[3] Kufic and *naskhi* are different types of Arabian calligraphy: the first is a straight, monumental one, which probably gets its name from the city of Kufa (Iraq) where it was first used in the decoration of buildings; the second is a cursive style, used on various media.

[4] R. Nath, *History of Mughal Architecture*, vol. 1, New Delhi, 1982, p. 25 and pl. XXVII; U. Scerrato, *Islam*, Milan, 1972, p. 70.

[5] The western term 'stalactite' is used to denote the characteristic Islamic motif called *muqarnas*, which consists of rows of cells that extend vertically and horizontally, like honeycomb. It was first invented as a structure to conceal the joins in domes (the earliest examples are in Central Asia and Iran) and later became an ornamental motif that was widely used throughout Islam, in all different kinds of materials: stone, stucco, ceramic, wood and plaster. Examples can be found in *mihrab*, arches, capitals and in *iwan*, portals and minarets, where they support elements such as the *muezzin*'s balcony.

[6] A. Welch, H. Crane, 'The Tughluqs: Master Builders of the Delhi Sultanate', *Muqarnas*, 1 (1983), pp. 123–66 (154).

[7] *Nastaliq* (literally 'hanging') is a variety of the cursive style *naskhi*.

[8] Ismail, a descendant of Saman Khadat, was of Iranian stock. A Zoroastrian, he was converted to Islam in 874 and became governor of Bukhara in the name of his brother Nasr, the king of Transoxiana. When he himself had become king, he conquered Khurasan and Tabaristan, these being the first steps in the conquest of an empire that was to expand, within a short time, as far as the borders of India and Turkestan, almost as far as Baghdad. His tomb at Bukhara was built from about 907 to before 942. Square in plan, with a domed roof, it derived from the Iranian *char taq*, namely the tetrastyle structure that was the Zoroastrian fire temple in Sassanian times. The arcaded galleries concealing the transition between the central dome and the four small corner domes are also a Sassanian tradition and were to become very popular in Indian architecture.

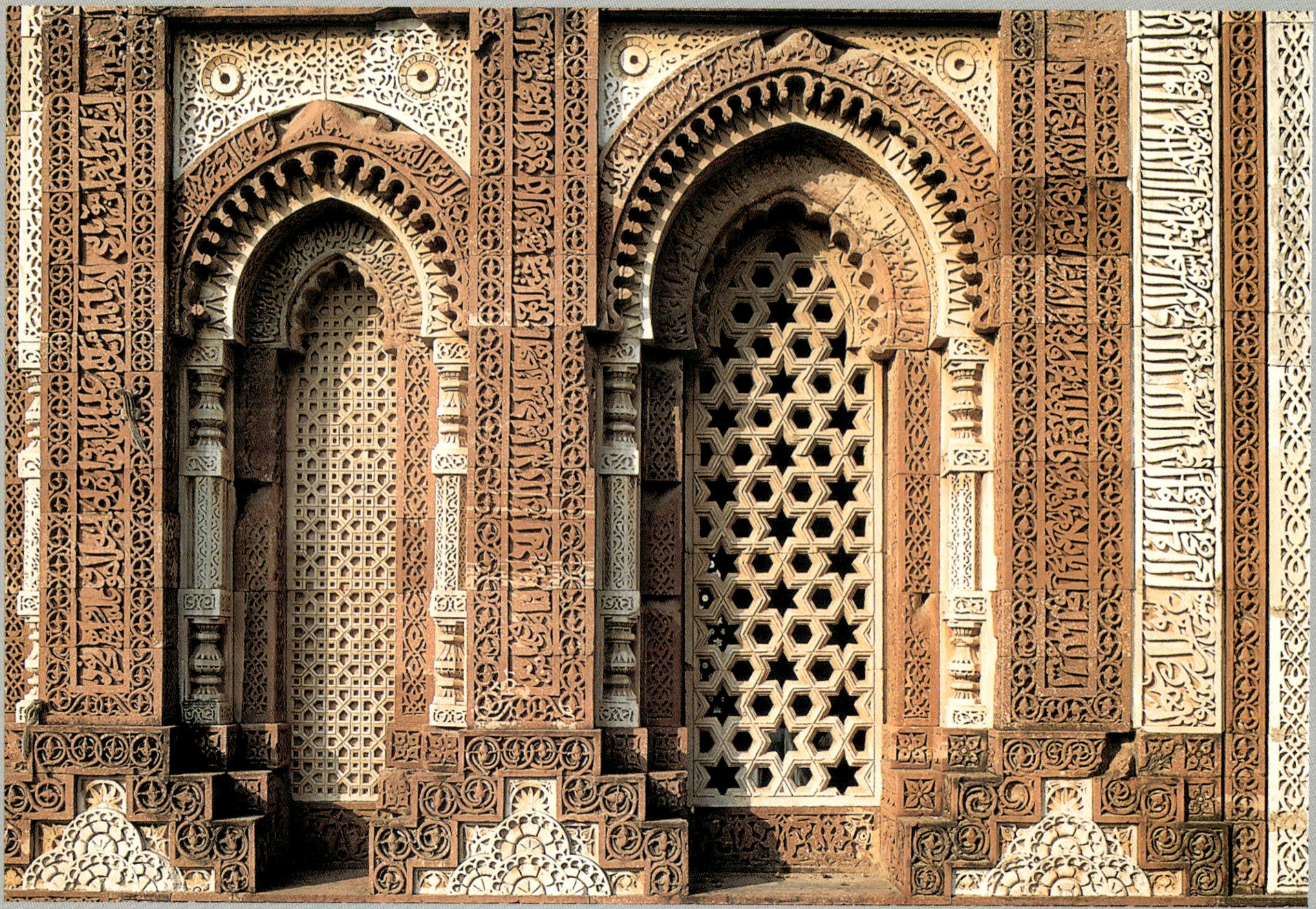

The Khaljis (1290-1320)

3

The façade of the Alai Darwaza (Gate of Ala al-Din; 1305), the entrance to the court of the Quwwat al-Islam at Delhi. Both architecturally and decoratively, this small building influenced later developments in Indian Islamic architecture.

Building activity declined after the death of Iltutmish, for the most part due to the growing Mongol threat on the north-west frontier. This decline ended, however, with the coming to power of the Khalji sovereigns, a Turco-Afghan dynasty from the village of Khalji near Ghazni. The first sovereign of the dynasty, Firuz Jalal al-Din (1290-96) soundly defeated a horde of Mongols that invaded India in 1292, but it was only with Ala al-Din (1296-1316), nephew and successor to Firuz, that the Mongols were chased out of India definitively after their siege of Delhi in 1303. Ala al-Din, who had not hesitated to assassinate his uncle in order to gain the throne, dedicated himself to the conquest of central and southern India and, in the space of a few years, secured Gujarat, Rajasthan, Malwa and Deccan, almost reaching the southernmost tip of the peninsula. In all India there was no Hindu state capable of measuring up to the Khalji empire. With Ala al-Din, the Islamic empire reached its apogee: he governed as an absolute despot and promulgated harsh laws, yet at the same time he was also a great patron of artists and religious men. At his court, Amir Khusrau, the greatest Indian poet in the Persian language, was greeted with honour, as was the historian al-Biruni and the great mystic Nizam al-Din Auliya. It is most probable that Ala al-Din also employed many craftsmen who were refugees from the area that was once part of the great Saljuq empire devastated by the Mongols. This would explain the great number of Iranian and Near Eastern influences to be found in many Khalji monuments.

Ala al-Din was convinced that the sovereign was the 'shadow of God' and declared himself Alexander II on his coins. He also embarked upon the reorganization of his immense state and began a series of great architectural projects which, however, were not carried to completion owing to their vast proportions and his own early death. This is the case with the enlargement of the Quwwat al-Islam which, according to the sultan's intentions, was to have combined the two earlier mosques of Qutb al-Din Aibak and Iltutmish, tripling the ground plan with the extension of the perimeter wall towards the north. There is now nothing left apart from the foundations of the prayer hall: Ala al-Din intended to build a colossal minaret at the centre of the new court with double the proportions – in both diameter and height – of the Qutb Minar. But his Alai Minar never rose beyond the first storey and today it is a huge mass of stones mixed with plaster. Inside, the first turn of the spiral staircase can be discerned.

Delhi: Alai Darwaza

Along the external perimeter of the walls an arrangement of four gates was planned, but only one was ever completed, or at least only one has survived to this day. The Alai Darwaza (Gate of Ala al-Din) is the southern entrance to the court from the mosque and was erected in 1305. Although small, it presents many new developments, both structural and decorative, which were later to have much influence in Indo-Islamic architecture. Built in red sandstone, it is endowed with luxurious decoration in white marble with inlay in black marble and blue schist. This ornamentation displays a direct influence from the art of Gujarat both in the treatment of

Above The Alai Darwaza at the Quwwat al-Islam, Delhi. The base of Aibak's Qutb Minar can be seen behind it.

Top The remains of the Tohfewala Gumbad mosque at Shahapur Jat (Delhi).

some designs and in the use of colour. It is a cubic structure resting on a plinth and covered by a low dome. It measures about 17 m in width and reaches over 20 m to the dome, which has a diameter of over 10 m. The façades are all opened by a high horseshoe arch, supported by pairs of slender columns of alternately red sandstone and white marble in an elegantly carved Persian style. The intrados of the arch is decorated with a series of lotus bud denticulations commonly called 'spear-head fringe'. Medallions once decorated the gables, which were filled with fine interlacing plant motifs. On the outside the walls are divided in two by a protruding cornice. In the lower storey are two arched windows framing the door, while in the upper storey there are panels containing superimposed niches. The decoration, carved both in bas-relief and high relief, is distributed liberally over the entire building and consists of elegant inscriptions, geometric arabesques and vegetal motifs of Hindu origin, all forming a delicate lacework on stone that is varied with the sober alternation of red sandstone and white marble. In later periods this last feature was to become a decorative technique which was used regularly. Nath maintains that the design of the Alai Darwaza was inspired by the Taq-i Kisra of Ctesiphon, the famous Sassanian palace of Khusrau I (531–79), with its enormous central *iwan* flanked by two wings and ornamented with small arches distributed over various false storeys.[1] The interior of the building, reached by means of a flight of steps, has walls that are carved with either floral or abstract arabesque motifs. The squinches of the dome are made up of angular niches, filled with receding horseshoe shaped arches that are highly decorative as well as functional. The light penetrates the interior from the windows of the lower storey, which are closed with gratings of white marble traceried with star motifs and hexagons, creating pleasing, intricate designs. This type of grating, derived from Hindu decoration, was later taken up by the Mughals and raised to the level of a fine art. Ala al-Din built a *madrasa* and his own tomb near the mosque. These were made up of simple halls and galleries covered with domes of moderate height.

SIRI: CITADEL

In 1303 Ala al-Din also planned a new citadel to the north-east of Lalkot which he called Siri; very little of it remains except a few sections of the fortifications. According to Amir Khusrau, writing in 1311, Ala al-Din re-established the practice of human sacrifice: he killed thousands of Mongols in this way and had them buried in the foundations of his city. According to Zia al-Din Bami, the great Hazar Sutun (Palace of the Thousand Columns) stood in Siri. It was the residence of the sovereign and his family and was probably where he received the dignitaries of the realm. There was also a Great Mosque there, which has not survived, and the tomb of Ala al-Din has also disappeared.

SHAHAPUR JAT (DELHI): TOHFEWALA GUMBAD

Although no remains of palaces have yet been found, in the village of Shahapur Jat some ruined buildings survive, among which various mosques and tombs have been identified. Among the former, the mosque known as Tohfewala Gumbad is worth noting; only the central part, covered by a dome, remains.

NIZAMU AL-DIN (DELHI): JAMAAT KHANA

Another building that is clearly Khalji is the mosque known as Jamaat Khana (meeting place), close to the tomb of Nizam al-Din Auliya. It was initially planned as a mausoleum for the saint – who in his humility preferred burial outdoors; his present tomb dates from 1808–9 – and was later changed into a prayer hall. The mosque is derived from the Alai Darwaza, but has a less definite character, perhaps because it was executed by different craftsmen. It has a rectangular plan and a façade with three large arches, decorated with spear-head fringe and Koranic inscriptions. Each arch corresponds to an internal space covered centrally by a low dome and laterally by two smaller domes. The central space more closely resembles the gate of Ala al-Din, especially in the type of squinch used for the dome, and seems to have been the only structure built by Ala al-Din. The two wings must have been added by Mubarak Khalji.

Though the fourteenth-century Ukha mosque at Bayana uses motifs from Delhi buildings, it exemplifies provincial style.

Bayana: Ukha Mosque

Outside Delhi at Bayana in the state of Bharatpur, Rajputana, the last Khalji sovereign built the Ukha Mosque (see p. 33). Although repeating some motifs from Delhi buildings such as the pointed arch with a spear-head fringe, it is a clear example of provincial style. Its plan is very similar to that of the adjacent mosque-temple, but it differs in some detail. One example is the main entrance, flanked by a colonnade, arranged on two levels and decorated, on the inside facing the courtyard, by two lateral turrets with stellate plans in imitation of the Qutb Minar (see p. 23). However, only the bases of these turrets remain. In the prayer hall there is no ladies' gallery; a raised section on the northern, southern and eastern colonnades perhaps served this purpose.

Bayana: other buildings

About 15 km from Bayana is a fort known locally as Banassar Qila. It is in a well-preserved state, probably because the place where it is situated is fairly inaccessible. Seen from the outside, it appears to be comparable with the Tughluq forts, but on the inside, among other remains, a minaret survives which is similar in style to the Lodi minaret at Bayana.

Daulatabad: Great Mosque

The Great Mosque of Daulatabad was built in 1318 by a successor of Ala al-Din, Qutb al-Din Mubarak Khalji. Within the interior perimeter this mosque was originally the Hindu fort of Devagiri (Home of the Gods). It has a very simple plan: a large square courtyard of some 78 m each side with a hypostyle prayer hall with 106 pillars (clearly stripped from local temples) which form 25 aisles, each 5 bays deep, and support a flat roof. In correspondence to the *mihrab*, which projects towards the outside as a square propylon, there is a dome erected on the four exterior pillars, while at the corners of the western wall are fluted bastions which recall the shape and design of the Qutb Minar.

At Hansi there still stands a gate of the ancient citadel which carries an inscription in the name of Ala al-Din Muhammad and the date 1302. It seems nevertheless that the fortifications of Hansi preceded the Khalji period and that therefore this gate, the Barsi Darwaza, was only reinforced by Ala al-Din as part of his general project to render the fortifications of the Multan–Delhi road more secure. The structure of the gate is extremely simple and presents a low pointed arch within a rectangular frame decorated by blind lateral niches and with heavy semi-circular keeps at the extremities. The roof is in fired brick. Some details of this gate are unusual: above all, the inscription which for the first time in India is written in Persian rather than Arabic. This practice did not become common until the end of the thirteenth century. The two decorative panels representing a man fighting with a lion are also uncommon; although they are frequently found in Iranian art, even during the Islamic period, in India only a few, certainly later, examples exist.

[1] R. Nath, *History of Sultanate Architecture*, New Delhi, 1978, p. 49.

Above The Great Mosque at Daulatabad, built in 1318 by
Qutb al-Din Mubarak Khalji inside the Hindu fort of Devagiri.

Opposite Banassar Qila, a fort outside Bayana. Its good state
of preservation is probably due to its difficult-to-reach site.

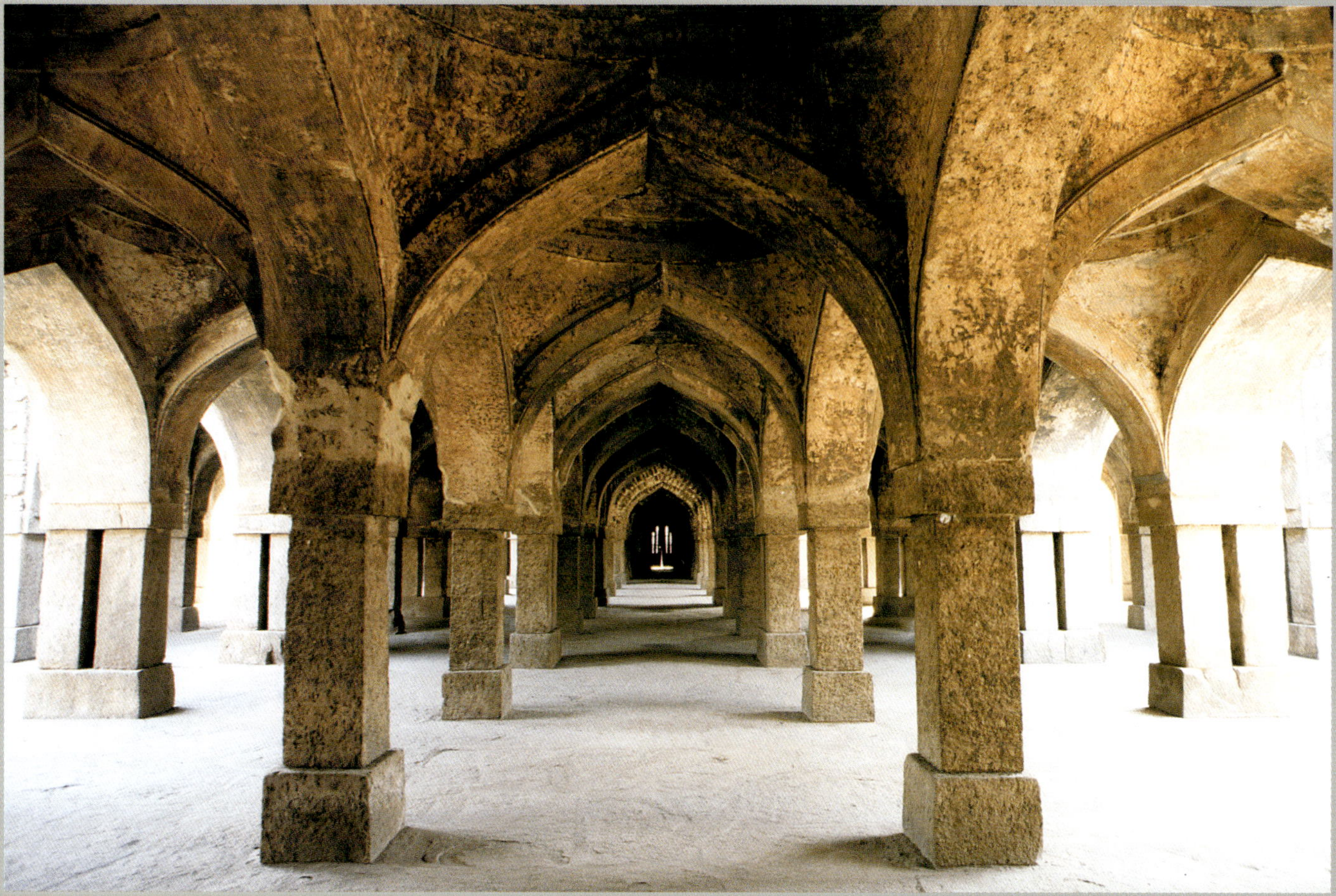

THE TUGHLUQS (1320–1413)

4

The interior of the fourteenth-century Khirki mosque at Jahan-Panah (Delhi). The building has a cruciform plan, making it rare in comparison to mosques with open-courtyard plans.

The energetic general Ghiyas al-Din Tughluq, son of a Qarauna Turk and an Indian woman, joined in the struggle for succession to the last inept Khaljis.[1] He claimed power and founded a new dynasty that ruled Delhi for almost a century. This period witnessed the increased Indianization of the ruling classes together with further consolidation of Islam and the conversion of large sections of the population.

The scope of Indo-Islamic art became wider, in terms of both geographic distribution and the development of a new style. The forced separation from the Iranian world – caused by the occupation of huge tracts of the Iranian regions by the pagan Mongols – diminished the force of the Persian Saljuq influence while allowing Indian influences to flourish. Constantly involved in the defence and enlargement of the realm, the Tughluq dynasty also gave the architecture a military character by fortifying almost all the buildings. Walls were steeply inclined, towers and bastions were tapered and cornices were surrounded by crenellated parapets. The sheer bulk of each monument and the speed with which it was built made the exuberant decoration used previously under earlier dynasties impossible. Ornament was achieved for the most part with polychrome techniques through alternating slabs in different colours of stone; later paint and colour-wash were used. Only the more important buildings were decorated with carved and moulded stucco. The most active builders of the dynasty were its founder, Ghiyas al-Din (1320–25), his son Muhammad Shah (1325–51) and Firuz Shah (1351–88), the most prolific of all.

TUGHLUQABAD (DELHI)

Ghiyas al-Din concentrated his efforts on the construction of his new capital, Tughluqabad, the third city of Delhi situated about 8 km to the east of Lalkot. Of his creation there now remain only some austere, imposing ruins of a cyclopean type on a rugged hill some 25 m high. The city, consisting of a high inner fort and a low outer fort, has an irregular rectangular outline that follows the side of the hill with a perimeter of over 6 km. At regular intervals there are immense circular bastions, often two storeys high, built on convex bases designed to impede the use of ladders during attacks. The bastion parapets are crenellated and the walls carry numerous lancet windows for the archers. Along the walls there were 13 gates, now for the most part ruined; those in best condition, on the southern side between the towers, have wide ramps for the passage of elephants. A moat surrounds the citadel that dominates all Tughluqabad. Evidently there was a fortress and a palace which were enclosed within two distinct walls: the first still carries the remains of casemates, galleries with embrasures and towers; the second wall enclosed the royal residence, the *zenana* (women's quarters) and halls for audiences. A long underground corridor with rooms opening on to the outer sides suggests that access to the citadel was possible by a rear entrance. The southern side of the citadel was protected by an artificial lake with water held by a fortified dam. On the other side there was a smaller hill on which Muhammad Shah Tughluq built the fort of Adilabad, now in ruins. The ancient stables and barracks are reasonably well preserved.

The great Maghrebian traveller Ibn Battuta, who stayed in Delhi from 1333 to 1342 and held the office of *qadi* under Muhammad Tughluq, has left a description of the site that is difficult to reconcile with the ruins, however imposing they may be: 'Here were the treasures and the palaces of the Tughluqs, and the great palace that he, Ghiyas al-Din, built in golden bricks so that when the sun rose it shone so brilliantly that no one succeeded in keeping his eye upon it.'

Tughluqabad (Delhi):
Ghiyas al-Din mausoleum

On the artificial lake, which is now dry, inside a very small fortress, stands the mausoleum of Ghiyas al-Din, which according to Ibn Battuta was built by Ghiyas himself. In contrast with the ruinous condition of Tughluqabad, the mausoleum is intact. It is connected to the city by means of a causeway some 220 m long and its circuit walls, in the form of an irregular pentagon, have huge circular bastions at the corners and are opened by an elegant gate which precedes a staggered entrance of obvious defensive intent. On the inside, the court, also asymmetric, is surrounded by arcades and conceals underground rooms with solid vaulted ceilings which, as they are not connected to the burial chamber, must have been for storing treasure. This theory would seem to be borne out by a reference from Ibn Battuta with regard to the construction of the city: 'He [the king] has gathered there a great treasure and they say that he has had a cistern built where he had molten gold poured, so that it became a solid mass.'

The tomb building is situated diagonally in the widest part of the court, the longest side of which is about 100 m. It is a severe building in red sandstone, with the dome and some decorative parts in white marble. Its outer walls are inclined to 75 degrees, the sides of the base are about 20 m long and the total height is over 28 m. At the centre of each side – apart from the west, which is closed to hold the *mihrab* – is a high, arched door, slightly pointed at the top with a spear-head fringe frieze as in the Alai Darwaza (see p. 30). In contrast to this last, however, here for the first time an architrave crosses the base of the arch, almost as if it were supporting it. This reappearance of an indigenous element in the construction of the Islamic arch is explained as an unconscious fusion on the part of the local workers of their trabeated method with the Muslim arcuated technique. This amalgam, technically irrational in as much as the beam, used this way, loses its functional character and becomes a purely ornamental feature, was later to have much success with the addition of a bracket under the terminal section of the beam. A border of white marble runs at the level of the arches, and above it there are arched niches framed by rectangles of white marble like the dome. These make a sober and elegant decorative feature which contrasts with the red sandstone of the base. Inside, the tomb is a simple square area with the dome supported by four pendentives akin to those of the Alai Darwaza. The dome is surmounted by the Hindu motif of *kalasha* and *amalaka* (vase and ribbed melon). Despite its solid and staid appearance, this monument has a convincing character which seems to embody the untamed and resolute spirit of the 'guardian of the frontier' that it was built to commemorate.

The Ghiyas al-Din mausoleum at Tughluqabad (Delhi) survives in perfect condition, unlike the ruined city to which it is connected.

In the northern corner of the small fortress is another small tomb some 8 m in diameter, octagonal in shape with a dome covered in white marble. It was built between 1323 and 1325 for the son of the sultan, Zafar Khan, but the burial chamber contains two cenotaphs surrounded by an ambulatory; it is said that one of them is the sepulchre of Muhammad Tughluq.

In Delhi there is the tomb of Shaikh Kabir al-Din Auliya, locally known as Lal Gumbad, which dates from a few years after that of Ghiyas al-Din and is a poor copy of considerably smaller proportions.

Delhi: Bijay Mandal

Muhammad bin Tughluq rid himself of his father by arranging the timely collapse of a heavy canopy erected in his honour. Before the disastrous transfer of the capital from Delhi to Daulatabad, of which only a few ruins remain, Muhammad built the city of Jahan-Panah (World's Refuge) connecting the city of Siri with the Qutb complex by means of an enormously thick fortified wall. At its centre he built a royal palace and a mosque. The palace is now almost in complete ruin, but it included the Bijay Mandal (Wonderful Mansion), which perhaps formed part of the Hazar Sutun (Palace of the Thousand Columns), a two-storey building with an exquisitely carved wooden ceiling supported by several rows of painted wooden columns, according to Ibn Battuta. It was so famous that when Timur occupied Delhi, the ladies of his harem wanted to visit it. The Bijay Mandal rises on a platform reached by means of an elaborate domed gate on its northern side; it perhaps made up only the north-western corner of the entire palace. The surviving ruins show a long hall with a ribbed vault and a low octagonal pavilion on the west side. Excavations carried out in this area in 1934 have revealed the bases of wooden pillars that were thought to be those of the Hazar Sutun. No other systematic exploration has subsequently been carried out, however, so that it remains difficult to give a reconstruction of the whole group of buildings.

Other buildings

Just as little remains of the Adilabad fort, built on a rocky outcrop to the south-east of Tughluqabad. It had heavy walls and

The Bijay Mandal at Delhi, built by Muhammad bin Tughluq. The building, now in ruins, may have formed part of the famous palace known as Hazar Sutun (now destroyed).

was accessible by means of two gates. Inside, a large rectangular courtyard and various grain silos have been identified.

Near Jahan-Panah, however, there remains an interesting work of hydraulic engineering: the Sath Pala bridge with seven spans (hence the name), two levels, and a supplementary arch and a tower at each extremity, which regulated the flow of water from a nearby artificial lake.

Other constructions from the reign of Muhammad are rare: for example the Gujarat mosques of Cambay (1325; see p. 109) and Dholka (1333) or the Deccani mosques of Qandahar and Bodhan (near Nizamabad, Hyderabad), all of little artistic interest. There are also a certain number of monumental tombs, among them one attributed to Kabir al-din Auliya at Delhi which, according to Husain and Welch, was initially planned by Muhammad as his own mausoleum in imitation of his father's. According to others (Percy Brown, Goetz, Sharma and Nath), however, the tomb is of a later period – 1388 or even 1397 – because it appears as a poor imitation of the earlier building. Whatever the truth, it seems that Muhammad Tughluq was buried at Tughluqabad in the small tomb of Zafar Khan, which has been identified by Nath as the 'Dar al-Aman' (Place of Peace) in which Firuz Shah buried his cousin, as he recounted in his memoirs.

Many of Muhammad Tughluq's projects, although brilliant, were destined to failure. This was the case with the forced transfer of the entire population of Delhi into the heart of the Deccan, 1,000 km to the south, of which one historian has given this account: 'His spirit was content and his mind rested only when, looking towards Delhi, he saw that there was neither smoke nor light, and that no cat or dog had been left among the buildings.' The new capital was too far from the Islamicized areas of the empire and before long proved to be inadequate for the needs of the government. Muhammad had the entire population return to Delhi with a disastrous march that caused hundreds of thousands of deaths. Delhi struggled to recover from the dramatic financial situation that followed and Muhammad tried to halt the disintegration that began to manifest itself in his reign. But he died suddenly during a military campaign in Sind.

Daulatabad

Some modern historians have revised this catastrophic view of Muhammad Tughluq's work. They maintain that Daulatabad (Mansion of Prosperity) was always considered by the sovereign only as a second capital, and that he did not transfer the entire population of Delhi there but only the court, the administration and various representatives of religious fraternities who, according to Muhammad's plan, would convert large sections of the local population. In the surrounding area, in fact, many *dargah* (tombs enclosed within perimeters) dedicated to Sufi saints are to be found.

The citadel of Daulatabad was built on an unattainable rocky hill over 200 m high and next to the ancient fort of Devagiri, which had been the home of the Yadava before the Islamic conquest at the hands of Ala al-Din Khalji. Muhammad Tughluq used the primitive Hindu nucleus, from which he took his building material, and added to it three sets of fortified walls which rendered his city one of the strongest fortifications in medieval India. In the outermost area, residential quarters were built; in the second strip, to the west of the first, which Ibn Battuta called Katak, rose the Great Mosque, not far from a smaller mosque built by Ala al-Din, and a bazaar. In the centre was the citadel itself, surrounded by a moat 15 m wide, whose water level could be varied, crossed by means of a bridge. Numerous fortified gates arranged on different axes and with varying batters to slow down enemy attacks were arranged along the walls. These gates were decorated with massive horizontal barbs to impede elephant attacks. From the lower city there was easy access to the bazaar by means of a massive stone gate with an arched entrance flanked by two semi-circular bastions. Today this gate is the main entrance to the citadel. In Katak, as well as two mosques and a bazaar there stands a beautiful three-storey minaret built in 1446 by Maliq Parviz in the Bahmanid period. There is also a large brickwork cistern which contained a supply of water. Not far from the bridge over the moat are the ruins of the small palace attributed to Nizam Shahi, called the Chini Mahall because of its covering in blue and white faience tiles (*chini*) of which there are still traces.

Daulatabad was begun in 1328–29 and was abandoned by Muhammad in 1335–6 when the incursions of the Chaghatai Turks threatened the security of Delhi and all of northern India. Nevertheless, it continued to function as an administrative centre until the end of the sultan's reign (1351).

Muhammad Tughluq's sudden return to Delhi caused many defections among his officers, who ended by claiming their own independence and founding an autonomous dynasty, the Bahmanids, who ruled the Deccan for over a century and a half. These events, together with the Chaghatai raids, undermined the political and economic structures of the state. Muhammad's sudden death prevented him from doing anything to reinforce them.

Muhammad was succeeded by the mild Firuz Shah who, in 38 years of his reign, dedicated himself to the development of the country, although he was hindered by the disorganized state of the empire and its upset finances. Firuz was dedicated to the art of building. In his own words:

Among the gifts that God bestowed upon me, His humble servant, was a desire to erect public buildings. I built many mosques and colleges and monasteries so that the learned and the elders, the devout and the Holy, might worship God in these edifices and aid the kind builder with their prayers.[2]

In fact, he built a great many important buildings – mosques, religious colleges, monasteries, palaces and hunting lodges – although all were constructed with inexpensive and not very durable materials put together in a style as simple as it was functional. According to contemporary historians, he also created 1,200 gardens around Delhi and at least '200 cities, 40 mosques, 30 villages, 100 public baths and 150 bridges'.[3] He also built a huge network of canals for the irrigation of the area around Delhi and in the Punjab and set about restoring buildings erected by his predecessors, such as the somewhat questionable repair and completion of the Qutb Minar. His buildings were constructed of crushed stone mixed with lime mortar and covered with plaster. Only the main structural elements, such as architraves, jambs and pillars, were of dressed stone, once painted in lively colours. Sometimes the decoration was made with modelled and painted stucco. Because of the poor quality of the materials used in the structures, they were often made extremely wide at the base and tapered towards the top, in order to ensure their stability and strength. The effect of inclination was often enhanced with the addition of corner bastions with turrets, or tower-like conical bastions that were crowned with low domes protruding from the four corners of the building. This similarity with the style of the slightly earlier brick tombs of Multan is not a pure coincidence, but rather a continuation of the vigorous Punjab style formerly used for the tomb of Ghiyas al-Din. Some buildings have an octagonal plan, others are cubic with a central body protruding vertically on each façade. The domes rest on octagonal drums, while less important buildings have pyramidal roofs. In the entrances, a Hindu architrave on columns separates the actual entrance from a window with a grating (*jali*) that closes the arch; smaller arches are arranged within wider ones while open galleries and balconies alternate with pavilions. In the interior there are complicated systems of vaults, with splays and decoration in carved stucco painted in bright colours which contrast with the deep blue of the ceiling.

Firuzabad (Delhi): Kotla Firuz Shah

The Kotla Firuz Shah at Firuzabad, on the river Jumna, was to become the prototype of the great Mughal city palace of the sixteenth century. As indicated by its name (Small Fortress) it was solidly fortified landwards with high walls from which bastions protruded at frequent intervals, while from the river it was adequately protected by the high bank. The Kotla Firuz Shah occupied an irregular rectangle of some 800 x 400 m, with the long side lying in a north–south direction. The eastern side runs parallel to the bank of the river. At the centre of the opposite side was the principal entrance, made up of a heavily fortified gate with a wide barbican protruding from the line of the wall, protected by a curtain wall and with the guards' quarters and the soldiers' barracks in the inner courtyard. Opposite the gate was a huge rectangular courtyard surrounded by a pillared verandah that

The entrance to the fort at Daulatabad, built by Muhammad Tughluq. The citadel's nearly unattainable position atop a 200 m high hill and fortified walls made it one of the strongest fortifications in medieval India.

formed the *diwan-i amm*, the hall for public audiences, where the king used to receive his subjects when in residence. Immediately behind this was the *diwan-i khass*, the hall for private audiences, where the sovereign received his counsellors and chiefs of administration. Along the banks of the river, relatively safe from military attack, were the private palaces, the mosques and the harems of the royal court. The areas to the north and south of the central axis were divided into various rectangular and square courts, in which there was a great variety of structures, 'such as pavilions of differing uses, tree-lined gardens with water, baths, fountains, barracks, armouries and the servants' quarters, all arranged so as to be connecting'.[4]

The historian Afif speaks of three palaces, each with different functions. The Mahall-i Sahan-i Gilin (Palace of the Clay Quadrangle), also called the Palace of Grapes, was reserved for receiving princes, governors, officers and men of letters. The Mahall-i Chhajja-i Chobin (Palace of the Wooden Gallery) was for staff close to the sovereign. The Mahall-i Bari Amm (Palace of the Public Court) was used for general receptions and was also called the Central Quadrangle.[5] All of these buildings have disappeared, except for the foundations of a square pillared hall that was probably a palace similar to the later *diwan-i khass* of the Mughals.

Documents speak of halls with mirrors, of sculptures in sandalwood and of murals with figures and landscapes, none of which has survived. They were destroyed in the civil wars that followed upon the death of Firuz Shah and the destruction wreaked by Timur in 1398. *The northern part of the Kotla still has a* baoli *(a deep well surrounded by underground rooms where the atmosphere was fresh even on the hottest days of the Indian summer), various pavilions and above all a* hawa mahall *('palace of the winds' or 'airy palace') in the form of a stepped pyramid with diminishing floors, which communicated with the private rooms via a secret passage in the western wall of the mosque, now for the most part in ruins*. The king's numerous concubines probably lived in this palace. On its top, Firuz Shah mounted one of the famous pillars (LAT) of Ashoka (third century bc),[6] which was moved with much difficulty from its original site at Thopra in the Ambala region (192 km to the north of Delhi). This was an imitation of the feat carried out 150 years earlier by Qutb al-Din Aibak with the pillar of Chandra in the court of the Quwwat al-Islam (see p. 22). For that reason the palace was also called the Lat Pyramid. Both this palace and the adjacent mosque stand on a high base and were probably connected.

FIRUZABAD (DELHI): *JAMI MASJID*

Although much ruined, the *jami masjid* must have presented a magnificent aspect. Since its eastern side was bordered by the Jumna, the main entrance was to the north and consisted of a square room situated on a series of wide steps and covered by a dome. The lower area was perhaps occupied by workshops, the income from which must have served to maintain the mosque. The central courtyard was surrounded by domed arcades, while behind the *qibla* wall ran a tall, narrow corridor reached by means of stairs in the north-west and south-west corners. This is the first time a corridor of this type has been found in a mosque and its precise function is unknown, but it became a

Above The Hawa Mahall (Palace of the Winds), part of the Kotla Firuz Shah complex on the Jumna river at Firuzabad (Delhi). The palace served as a prototype for sixteenth-century Mughal city-palaces.

Opposite The *jami masjid* in the Kotla Firuz Shah complex. Behind the *qibla* wall ran a tall, narrow corridor that became a common feature of mosques built later on in the sultanate.

common feature of mosques later in the sultanate. At the centre of the *sahn* (court) was a pool, perhaps covered by an octagonal dome supported by eight square pillars on which was carved the text of the emperor's memoirs. The Ashoka pillar fixed on the pyramidal palace immediately to the north of the mosque functioned as a symbolic minaret and was called Minar-i Zarin (Golden Minaret): it seems that it was richly decorated with gilt ornament and had a golden tip and crescent on top.

Despite the contemporary testimony to a great number of schools of theology built by Firuz Shah, the only one to have survived is that which extends along the two sides of the great cistern of the Hauz-i Khass, an artificial lake, today dried up, that had been dug by Ala al-Din Khalji in 1296 and had at its centre a small island with pleasure pavilions. On the eastern side (*c*.138 m) and the southern side (*c*.76 m) of the huge cistern, Firuz Shah began, in 1352, the construction of a *madrasa* and numerous connected buildings such as reading rooms, quarters for students, teachers and guests, a congregational mosque and cells for those wishing to devote themselves to meditation. The huge complex consisted of two wings of galleries with alternating domed pavilions. The lower galleries, on a level with the water, must have provided an oasis of freshness and included many cells, which were perhaps residential quarters. The upper floor, still more exposed to the breeze from the water, must have contained the teaching halls. At the junction of the two wings, a wide stairway led to the boats used on the islet. From the side facing landwards on the upper floor, the rooms opened over a long garden containing smaller quarters, pillared vestibules and open pavilions where, most probably, the women of the *zenana* passed the greater part of their time, being denied contact with the outside world by the solid walls. Indeed, it seems that walls surrounded the entire lake, which formed the sultan's private reserve. He himself was buried here, in the pleasant central pavilion, which is quite original. It is a building with a square plan, about 15 x 15 m, with slightly inclined exterior walls which are emphasized by projecting surfaces at their centre. It is covered by a fine dome slightly pointed at the summit and resting on an octagonal drum topped with ornamental merlons. To the front of the southern side is a low platform surrounded by a graceful stone railing. Inside, the dome rests on beautiful pendentives. The ornate epigraphs decorating the interior and exterior were added later in the Lodi period at the beginning of the sixteenth century.

In the garden, to the east, are various domed pavilions and tombs of the same shape. Further north, in the direction of the mosque, is an open, L-shaped building that was possibly the assembly hall, where the most important debates were held. There are also funeral buildings fairly similar to the previously mentioned ones in the area known as Chiragh-Delhi, around the mausoleum of Nasir al-Din Mahmud. One of them bears the name of Raushan Chiragh-i Dilhi (Illuminated Lamp of Delhi), who was a disciple of the saint Chishti Nizam al-Din and died in 1356.

Almost nothing remains of the other numerous structures built by Firuz Shah: only scanty ruins commemorate the famous Kushk-i Shikar (Hunting Palace), which contained another pillar of Ashoka, much admired by Timur.

JAHAN-PANAH (DELHI):
BEGAMPURI MOSQUE

The mosques surviving from this period are in reasonable condition.

At Jahan-Panah, near the Bijay Mandal, stands the Begampuri Mosque (*c.*1370), which according to local legend was built by the prime minister of the sovereign, Khan-i Jahan Tilangani (also known as Khan-i Jahan Maqbul Khan). This is a Friday or congregational mosque on a traditional model. Slightly rectangular (93.57 x 89.92 m), it has a courtyard surrounded on three sides by domed arcades supported by pillared arches with a protruding gate at the centre of each side, of which the eastern one is the largest. This last is the monumental entrance and is reached from the road by means of a wide stairway. The planimetric model is clearly Iranian, perhaps introduced into India by the architect of the sultan, Muhammad Zahir al-Din al-Jayush. The sanctuary is on the western side and has a central nave with two lateral aisles which are pillared and are also covered with domes. The entrance is made up of a high propylon in which there is an *iwan* flanked by tapering turrets. The mass of this propylon imposes on the dome of the central bay and spoils its lightness. This monumental set-up was used later on a much larger scale in the mosques of the Sharqis of Jaunpur, but in Delhi it became pure convention. Protruding at the northern extremity of the prayer hall, and perhaps connected via the outside to the royal palace, is a wide *maqsura* (screened or arched enclosure) with a fine stone *mihrab*. It seems that all the exterior surfaces were covered with glazed tiles of which there are some traces left. Because of the singularity of its construction – it is distinct from all the others built by Firuz Shah – and because it rises in the heart of Jahan-Panah, Nath has recently attributed the Begampuri

THE TUGHLUQS (1320–1413)

Above Staircase entrance to the Khirki Mosque at Jahan-Panah (Delhi). The mosque rests on a *tahkhana*, or low, arched structure, which not only gives it a more imposing appearance, but also provides a cool, dark retreat from hot summer weather.

Opposite The Begampuri Mosque at Jahan-Panah. The building is clearly modelled on an Iranian plan, which was perhaps introduced to India by Firuz Shah's architect, Muhammad Zahir al-Din al-Jayush.

Mosque to the reign of Muhammad Tughluq, taking back its construction by some decades (c.1345). He has also based this attribution on testimony from contemporary sources such as Ibn Battuta and Badr Chach.[7]

JAHAN-PANAH AND NIZAM AL-DIN (DELHI): KHIRKI AND KALAN MOSQUES

The Khirki and Kalan mosques, situated at Jahan-Panah and at Nizam al-Din respectively, apart from being very similar in their general plan, are both rendered more majestic by a *tah khana*, a low, arched structure on which they rest. The *tah khana* served to create a cool area during the hot days of summer and also provided space for the staff of the mosque, workshops and even dormitories for the pilgrims during festivals. This platform is 3 m above ground level and at the centre has a fine stairway that leads up to a protruding entrance flanked by sharply tapering turrets. Imposing round bastions ornament each corner of the boundary wall, giving the mosque the look of a fortress and resembling the tomb of Sultan Ghari (see p. 26) rather than a place of prayer.

Inside, the mosques have cloisters formed from a series of square bays, at each corner of which are heavy pillars carring ogival arches. Each of these bays is covered by a slightly pointed dome. Both mosques have a cruciform plan formed by two central naves that cross each other at a right angle. The Khirki Mosque, however, is more harmonious, being made up of 25 equal units, each measuring approximately 9 x 9 m, four of which are open, forming four small *sahn*. The entire building is covered alternately in flat roofs and pointed cupolas.

In the Kalan Mosque this pattern is less symmetrical and the building certainly loses in elegance. This is probably due to the fact that it was built by the vizier Khan Jahan Junan Shah in 1370, as we are told by an inscription, while the Khirki was of imperial origin. Some maintain that the Khirki is of later origin than the Kalan, while others date it to 1352–4. This type of mosque remains rather rare compared with the large, open courtyard type such as at Begampuri.

Khan Jahan Junan Shah also built another Kalan (or Kali) Mosque near the Turkmenian Gate in 1387, a year before the death of the sultan. Like its antecedents, the mosque rises on a plinth with vaulted cells and is reached by means of a long flight of steps on the eastern side, dominated by a domed entrance which leads to a rectangular courtyard. This is surrounded on three sides by arches resting on heavy square pillars which form bays surmounted by domes; it has five *mihrab*. The exterior corners carry the usual circular bastions.

OTHER MOSQUES

Certain Tughluq mosques consist of simple prayer halls, sometimes with one or two arcades and an open-air court. One such mosque was built near the tomb of Makhdum Shah Alam, a short distance from Firuzabad.

A much-revered sanctuary situated close to Delhi is the Qadam-i Sharif (1373), where a relic of the Prophet Muhammad is venerated in a small chapel built using Hindu spoils. The surrounding area, full of small mosques and houses for religious authorities and pilgrims, was enclosed by the sovereign with a solid protective wall.

DELHI: KHAN JAHAN TELANGANI MAUSOLEUM

Among the Tughluq buildings, worthy of note is the mausoleum of Khan Jahan Tilangani, which with its octagonal plan surmounted by a high dome seems to be modelled after the Qubba al-Sakhra (Dome of the Rock) in Jerusalem. The outer wall still carries fortifications with corner towers, although it seems to be the last example of this type. Inside the perimeter the tomb presents various innovations in both the plan and the elevation. Unlike the previous square mausoleums, this one has an octagonal form which, in spite of its rather squat and imperfect proportions, recalls the structure of the seventh-century building in Jerusalem that was very familiar to Muslims. Here, too, a verandah surrounds the building and each side has three low, pointed arches above which a wide *chhajja* (overhang) projects in the Hindu tradition. This particular architectural element was to enjoy much success later.

There were other examples of octagonal tombs in the Muslim world. The Qubba al-Sulaybiya, for example, was the most ancient funeral monument in Islam, built around 862 on the left bank of the Tigris for the Abbasid caliph al-Muntasir.[8] The tomb of the daughter of Hulagu at Maragha was also octagonal, but the mausoleum of the Ilkhanid Oljeytu, built at Sultaniya (c.1316), is the most complete and most successful of the type.[9] The Indian architect must only have had a sketch or an idea of the typical Islamic octagonal tomb to go by and had to use his own intuition to put it into practice. It is possible, however, that this tomb was inspired by the octagonal plan of the Rukn-i Alam mausoleum at Multan (see p. 67), in as much as this city had been Telangani's fief before he was appointed *wazir*. The mausoleum of Khan Jahan, perhaps begun in 1368 immediately following his death, was probably completed by his son. According to A. Welch, it could be considered as a development on the tomb of Zafar Khan, but in any case it was certainly the prototype of the large, octagonal funeral buildings that were to become so characteristic of Indo-Islamic architecture, and not only in northern India.

Outside Delhi, to protect the Punjab from possible attack from the north-west, Firuz Shah built the city of Hisar-i Firuza (modern Hissar) and equipped it with a water supply system which also served the surrounding areas. Its plan seems to have been based on the layout of the cities of Khurasan in north-eastern Iran, which in their turn had inherited it from pre-Islamic times. In the plan, the fort or citadel (*arg*) stands to one side of the city and not at its centre. Introduced into India by the Ghurids, this plan was used first at Tughluqabad then in a number of Firuz Shah's cities such as Fatehabad and Jaunpur, until it became very common in India. Later it was to be found at Bidar, Ahmedabad and Chanderi, and even in the Mughal period at Fatehpur Sikri and Delhi (Shahjahanabad).

Hisar: palace and other buildings

The ancient city of Hisar has now been swallowed up by modern buildings, but some notable ruins have survived as part of the fortified walls of the citadel: various canals and cisterns; the palace complex with the Lat-ki Mosque; the Talaqi Gate; the Gujara Mahall with its large garden; the Jahaz Kothi (a building, as its name suggests, in the shape of a ship); as well as many tombs of saints. The palace, partly in ruins and partly unexplored, stood on the north-western side of the citadel and seems to have been connected with a large garden. So far the north-western part of the complex has been excavated and consists of a gate, a mosque and four courtyards. The palace consisted originally of at least three levels, the lowest of which had arcades with massive pillars of rough stone, while the middle level had a brickwork arcade supported by columns with monolithic shafts; the upper level was colonnaded with beams and corbels in stone. On this last level there were probably a number of domed rooms and pavilions, but they have disappeared, as have many of the columns and the beams. It is

Above The Lat-ki Mosque at Hisar is one of the notable ruins of this ancient city. It is named for the ancient column (*lat*) that was set up in the courtyard.

Opposite The *idgah* at Fatehabad, with the *lat* of Firuz Shah in the foreground.

not impossible that there was a fourth level, though no visible traces of it remain. On the lower floors, many halls, rooms, guardrooms and narrow corridors, all without light, have been identified. As indicated by the position of the gates (apart from the Talaqi Gate there was another, the Nagauri Gate, which has not survived), the royal complex was accessible from the southern side while the administrative area and the public buildings must have been situated to the north. The Talaqi Gate, which leads into the southern courtyard, has a vaulted entrance with a pointed arch and is flanked by guardrooms. Its rubble-masonry walls have a strong batter, as in all Tughluq buildings.

HISAR: LAT-KI MOSQUE AND FATEHABAD *IDGAH*

On the opposite side of the courtyard, in front of the gate, stands the main mosque of the complex, the Lat-ki Mosque. Its name comes from an ancient column (*lat*) that was set up in the north-eastern corner of its courtyard. The cylindrical shaft, tapered towards the top, is in four registers divided by red sandstone drums and terminates with an iron pinnacle. According to Cunningham, the lower part, in yellow stone, carried pilgrims' inscriptions of the first century AD, and must have formed part of a shaft of which the upper section has been placed in front of the *idgah* at Fatehabad. This latter column has a shaft in two registers, of which the lower one is much older.

The Lat-ki Mosque stands on a platform and has massive walls, tapering towards the top. All that is left of the courtyard is part of the northern wing, while the prayer hall to the west is still standing, with a square room covered by a dome to the east which has not been identified precisely. This could have been a gate (but it is not exactly aligned), or perhaps a tomb. The mosque is built in spoil material and has two aisles parallel to the *qibla* wall covered by cross-vaults, apart from the north-east and north-west corners over which there are two small domes. At the northern extremity of the sanctuary is a small gallery in the form of a mezzanine supported by eight columns and eight rectangular pillars. This could have been the area reserved for the women, with a double *mihrab*, but it could also have been the *muluq khana* (the private room of the king) of which the historian Shams Siraj speaks when he says that Firuz Shah used to retire to pray in a space reserved for him during community prayers. The entire far wall of the mosque is patterned with rectangular-section *mihrab* of which the central one is larger, projects towards the exterior and is formed of multifoiled receding arches.

HISAR: GUJARA MAHALL

The Gujara Mahall stands on a massive rectangular platform just outside the citadel and must have been surrounded by other buildings, of which only ruins exist. The platform has two square towers to the east and is crossed by a water channel with a tank. It is reached by means of a series of steps situated in the north-western corner which have been much restored. At the centre of its eastern side rises a pavilion with inclined walls covered by nine small domes on pendentives, supported by four central columns in marble and a series of pilasters against the circuit walls. These walls each have three pointed-arch openings. To the north of the main pavilion is a small rectangular building with two rooms, one of which has a small *mihrab* and must have been the private mosque of the palace. The garden attached to the complex is largely in ruins, but the boundary walls, with two towers similar to those of the platform, are reasonably well preserved. The walls did not so much serve as a defense as provide protection from the desert winds and help retain humidity from the irrigation in order to render more fertile the orchards and the gardens that extended beyond the Gujara Mahall itself.

HISAR: JAHAZ KOTHI

To the east of the city, on another massive platform (perhaps once surrounded by water) stands the Jahaz Kothi, which seems to imitate the shape of a ship with a pointed bow. On the western side is a hall with pointed arches and cross-vaults resting on stone columns with monolithic shafts. This hall gives on to four connecting rooms, three of which stand on the same axis with the fourth a little further back, but still to the west. The central room in front is domed, but the dome seems to have been rebuilt or heavily restored at a later period. The westernmost room has three niches, one of which must have been a *mihrab* if, as some sources maintain, the entire building was originally a *madrasa*. The large hall was flanked by three vaulted rooms on each side, which at the extremities led in their turn to a domed room. To the north and south of the platform there must have been other rooms which have now fallen into ruin. The main entrance to the complex consists of a large square building covered by an almost hemispherical dome similar to that of Firuz Shah's tomb at Delhi. Not far from this building, on the north-western side of the platform, stands a small three-storey cylindrical tower, similar to the minaret of Chota Pandua in Bengal and dating from the fourteenth century. It is not improbable that this tower functioned as a minaret if the complex was a *madrasa*, but it must have been added later when the northern wing of the dome collapsed. The building has now been transformed into a Jain temple.

Other buildings by Firuz Shah

Firuz Shah built another palace complex, Kushk-i Shikar, this time for hunting expeditions. It was also known as Jahannuma Mahall, and in it he had erected another of the pillars of Ashoka. The chroniclers tell us that the palace was much admired by Timur who camped here while he prepared his attack on Delhi. Around the royal residence there were also many courtiers' buildings, but nothing has survived except for two badly ruined buildings. One, called Pir Ghalib, is thought to have formed part of a large mosque: there are various rooms on two levels and an extremely steep double stairway which crosses the whole southern façade from ground level to the roof. The other building, known as the Chauburji Mosque, must have been a tomb, but it underwent many alterations in Mughal times.

Another four buildings have been attributed to Firuz Shah's patronage, but without sure proof. These are mostly vaulted structures with a great many rooms, all with access to the roof, where it seems awnings could be used. Rather than residences, these appear to have been resting or amusement places for relaxation during hunting expeditions, which the sovereign greatly enjoyed. However, they are all badly ruined: the Kushk Mahall (see p. 140), the Malcha Mahall, the Bhuli Bhatiyari-ka Mahall at Delhi, as well as the Mahipalpur Mahall in the village of the same name a little to the south of the capital. Buildings for rest during hunting expeditions were later widely diffused during the Mughal period.

Firuz Shah also dedicated himself to the restoration of many monuments: apart from the Qutb Minar (see p. 23), he had restored the tomb of Nasir al-Din Mahmud (Sultan Ghari; see p. 26), with its 'Doric' columned portico in front of the *mihrab* and vaguely classical appearance. Perhaps it was inspired by the recollections of Ibn Battuta who knew Firuz Shah before he became a sultan.

Outside the capital, Firuz Shah's principal work was the foundation of Jaunpur, the new capital of Oudh which immediately afterwards became an independent kingdom. The mosque of the fortress (the latter was destroyed by the English) and part of the Atala Mosque (see p. 97) were built with spoil from Hindu buildings.

Irich: Jami Masjid

Towards the end of the Tughluq dominion (1402) the Friday mosque of Irich, a city approximately 60 km north of Jhansi, was constructed. This mosque seems to represent a transitional moment between the Tughluq style and the styles of subsequent dynasties in the contour arches which are emphasized and repeated in stepped floors. These arches became a constant feature in the buildings of the Sayyids and the Lodis, the last sultans of Delhi.

In the neighbourhood of Irich, the small three-domed mosque and the square-based domed tombs with unusual supports made out of Hindu pillars are perhaps from the Tughluq period. One building of considerable interest has a square ground-plan, bastions at the corners and a slightly pear-shaped dome. In both its structure and the decorative patterns formed by the brickwork it closely resembles the tomb of Ismail the Samanid at Bukhara, which dates to the first half of the tenth century.

Some echoes of the Tughluq style are to be seen much later in some fifteenth-century Bahmanid tombs at Gulbarga and in some buildings at Mandu (Hindola Mahall; see p. 130), Warangal (audience hall of Shitab Khan) and Ahmedabad (tombs of Azam and Muazam). But the Tughluq style quickly disappeared outside Delhi because the regional states chose to emphasize their distance from the centre of imperial power through their own art, with independent and original forms.

[1] Tughluq was the personal name of Ghiyas al-Din, which has been extended to his dynasty. Although this usage is not correct, it has been commonly accepted.

[2] H.M. Elliot, J. Dowson, *The History of India as told by its own historians: The Muhammadan Period. The posthumous Papers of the late Sir H.M. Elliot*, London 1867–77, vol. 3, pp. 382–3

[3] S. Grover, *The Architecture of India, Islamic (727–1707 A.D..)*, New Delhi 1981, p. 36.

[4] Ibid., p. 36.

[5] Nath, *op. cit.*, p. 63.

[6] Ashoka, the third king of the Maurya dynasty, reigned over a large part of India from about 268 to 232 BC. After being converted to Buddhism, he was one of its most enthusiastic propagators, by means of the edicts that he had carved on columns (*lat* or *stambha*) or on rock faces throughout his vast empire. Some of the columns have typical bell-shaped capitals surmounted by animal figures (lions, horses, humped oxen) that derive from Persepolitan examples.

[7] Nath, *op. cit.*, p. 56.

[8] The Abbasid caliph al-Muntasir died in 862, six months after he had murdered his father, al-Mutawwakil. The tomb that his Christian mother had built for him consisted of a square, domed room inside an octagonal ambulatory with a barrel-vaulted ceiling. This type of layout is reminiscent of the Dome of the Rock in Jerusalem and, in a way, clashes with Muslim doctrine which requires tombs to be at ground level, without superstructures, so as to emphasize the equality of all men in the face of death.

[9] Hulagu, the nephew of Chingiz Khan, was sent by his brother Mongke, great khan of the Mongols, to capture Baghdad and to defeat the Ismailite Assassins of Persia (1256). After he had devastated the city (1258) and killed Rukn al-Din, the supreme shaikh of the Assassins (from *hashashin*, 'consumers of hashish'), he was stopped by the Egyptian Mamluks. He died in 1265. At Maragha he had a fine tomb built for his daughter, as well as an astronomical observatory that was under the direction of the famous astrologer Nasir al-Din Tusi.

Oljeytu, the brother of Ghazan, the Mongol who had been converted to Islam, ruled over Iran from 1304 to 1316. As a baby, he had been baptized by his mother but later he embraced the Islamic faith, first as a Shiite, then as a Sunnite, then as a Shiite again. He extended the city of Sultaniya, which had been built by his father Arghun, and made it his capital, drawn by its natural beauty and its pleasant climate. His imposing mausoleum, surrounded by other buildings which are now in ruins, was a grandiose construction on an octagonal ground plan, and the beautiful dome was faced with turquoise tiles (1309–13).

Interior of the *jami masjid* at Irich. The mosque represents a transition between the Tughluq style and the styles of subsequent dynasties.

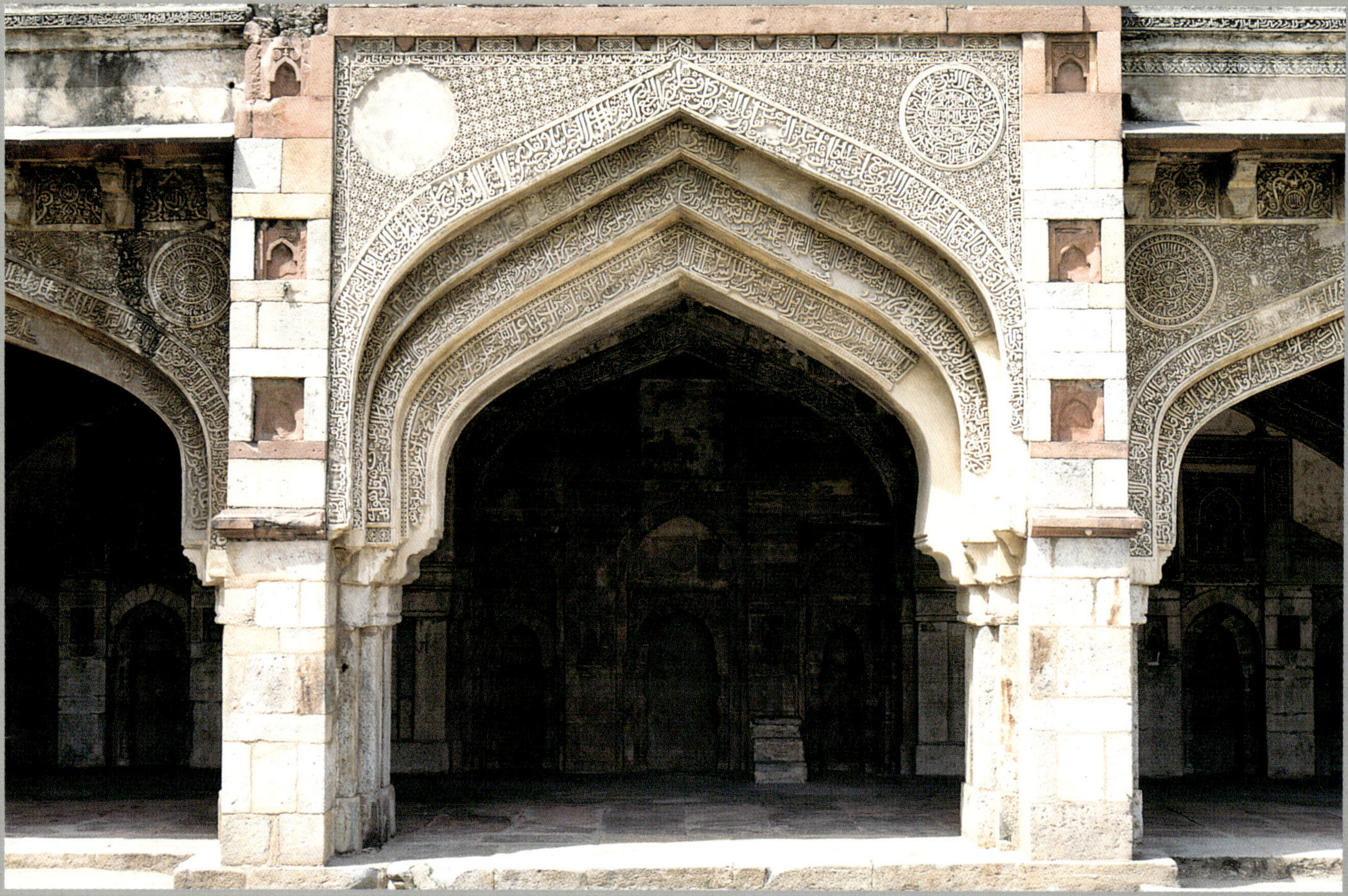

THE SAYYID AND LODI
(1414–1451 AND 1451–1526)

5

The main arch of the *jami masjid* of Sikandar Lodi (1494), in the Lodi Gardens at Delhi. The mosque is attached to the much larger domed building known as the Bara Gumbad.

Although a good politician and a shrewd administrator, Firuz Shah had been too rigid in his promulgation of Islamic orthodoxy. His anti-Hindu repression eventually left him without the possibility of achieving a working relationship between dominators and dominated, and on his death everything collapsed. His successors, weak and inept, followed one another on the throne but lacked true authority. Meanwhile, provincial governors repeatedly proclaimed independence and founded dynasties that were completely separate from Delhi. The last Tughluq sovereign, Nasir al-Din Mahmud (1394–1413), was a pale puppet in the hands of his ministers. Nasir governed a state that was by now restricted to eastern Punjab and parts of Uttar Pradesh. On this state the 'Scourge of God' – Tamerlane – fell like a thunderbolt.[1] He came down to India in the summer of 1398, quickly defeated the army of Mahmud (who found refuge in Gujarat) and entered Delhi, inflicting on it for two weeks the most terrible devastation. Thousands of citizens died by the sword and the Hindus, before being killed, were forced to set fire to their own homes with the women and children inside. Only the artists and the craftsmen were spared and transferred to Samarqand in order that they could contribute to the embellishment of the conqueror's capital. Delhi was left in desolation: many of its monuments were plundered and 90 elephants were used to transport the stones taken from the dismantled buildings to help the victor in his new building plans.

On 1 January 1399 Timur abandoned Delhi to its destiny and returned to Transoxiana, without troubling to consolidate his conquest. Timur was never to return to the Ganges valley and his only act of government was to appoint as his representative in the Punjab Khizr Khan, an Indian Sayyid (a descendant of the Prophet), while Mahmud Tughluq returned to Delhi (1401). With Mahmud's death in 1413 the Tughluq dynasty expired and Khizr Khan took the throne from the regent, Daulat Khan Lodi. The Sayyid dynasty founded by Khizr Khan (1414–51) – although he never took the title of sultan, continuing to consider himself a Timurid governor – was the weakest and most inefficient of all those that had come to govern India. It dominated only the capital and the surrounding area and was too limited to be able to support the burden of a court and an army. The only concern of the Sayyid sovereigns was the organization of semi-predatorial expeditions against the Hindu and Muslim feudatories of the Punjab and Doab, which were carried out in order to exact the tributes necessary for the survival of the capital.

In this climate of confusion and uncertainty, no monuments of any importance were constructed; no new cities, fortresses, mosques or schools of theology were built. The only buildings these sovereigns left were their mausoleums, a structure that displays dissolution and commemorates death, and is therefore a perfect expression of the spirit of the times.

In 1451 the sultans who ousted the Sayyids by force were the powerful Afghan Lodis who, under their founder, Bahlol, had already succeeded in extending their rule in the east as far as the borders of Bihar, in the west as far as Rajasthan and in the south as far as central India. However, the new Lodi reign (1451–1526) was troubled by struggles for domination and conquest so that building activity was rather limited. Although buildings of a certain elegance are not lacking, no great congregational mosque was built. Nevertheless, under the Lodis a new type of mosque developed that was also to become the more common type under the Mughals. Instead of the large hypostyle congregational mosques of the earlier sultanates, there was a preference for a type of prayer hall with a single nave parallel to the *qibla* wall and usually divided into three or five bays. We do not know how or why this type of mosque came into being, but the earliest example of it is the *jami masjid* of Sikandar Lodi, near the Bara Gumbad in the Lodi Gardens.

Mausoleums

Once again, however, many mausoleums were erected, which transformed the area surrounding Delhi into an enormous necropolis, to the point where this period is defined as the 'macabre' reign, a word that is perhaps derived from the Arab *maqbara* (cemetery). Some of these tombs are of large proportions and at least three belong to the sovereigns themselves, while many others were built by the nobility and other court personages. Some are simple, open pillared pavilions; others are built in a more imposing style and are surrounded by circuit walls that have high gates in them, with a small funeral mosque attached to the western side. The most important mausoleums can be classed in two principal types: the first has an octagonal plan, is on one level and is surrounded by an arched colonnade or a verandah with a wide overhang; the second has a square plan with two (sometimes three) storeys and is without a verandah. In both cases the structures are surmounted by a dome, often surrounded by a series of *chhatri* above each side of the octagon or at each corner of the square. Since the three great tombs attributed to the Sayyid and Lodi sovereigns are octagonal, it is probable that this form was reserved for royal personages, while the square tombs were for people of high rank.

The prototype of the octagonal mausoleum can be traced to the Tughluq tomb of Khan-i Jahan Tilangani erected at Delhi

THE SAYYID AND LODI
(1414–1451 AND 1451–1526)

Opposite The *jami masjid* of Sikandar Lodi in the Lodi Gardens at Delhi. It has a single nave prayer hall, and is the earliest example of this type of mosque.

Below The mausoleum of Adham Khan (1561) at Delhi is somewhat unusual in that it stands on a high platform and its dome rests on a hexagonal drum.

from 1368 to 1369. This type inspired several structures in subsequent periods, for example, the Suri tombs of Sasaram in Bihar, and those of Isa Khan and Adham Khan built at Delhi in 1547 and 1561 respectively after the fall of the dynasty. Isa Khan's tomb, which also includes a small mosque with three bays, a central dome and two lateral *chhatri*, has a well-balanced octagonal structure with an arched verandah whose corner pillars display the inclination characteristic of similar Sayyid and Lodi tombs inherited from the Tughluq period. The large central dome is not very high and is surrounded by domed *chhatri* and slender terminal turrets placed at the corners of the drum and the cornice below it. The tomb of Adham Khan differs from this plan in that it stands on a high platform and its dome is separated from the arched verandah that is its base by means of a high hexadecagonal drum decorated with deep blind niches that practically forms an intermediate storey for the building and lends it a vertical thrust. Nevertheless, the complex as a whole seems a little banal and prosaic, lacking in true inspiration.

The two Sayyid octagonal structures are dedicated to Muhammad and Mubarak, who died in 1444 and 1434 respectively, and both seem more or less contemporaneous with their deaths. Mubarak's, planned by himself, was probably finished by his son and successor, but the two tombs are so similar as to appear to have been built by the same person. The dome of Mubarak's mausoleum is slightly lower than the other and remains partially covered by the *chhatri* that surround it. The building stands on a low plinth, accessible by means of a few steps, and the octagonal pillared verandah that surrounds the sepulchral chamber has three archways on each side. The corners of each side are inclined, as in all mausoleums of this type. The overhang that covers the verandah is supported by simple stone corbels, while the terrace on which the *chhatri* rest is decorated with merlons. In Muhammad Sayyid's tomb, the defects of the earlier tomb have been eliminated, with a higher drum to support the dome which thus appears free and well proportioned. The width of each of the octagonal faces of the verandah is about 10 m, equivalent to the height including the base and the corner pinnacles (*guldasta*). This measurement is half the total height of the building including the terminal in the form of an upside-down lotus flower. The interior sepulchral chamber has an octagonal plan of about 8 m in diameter, with an architraved arch on each wall. The ceiling is decorated with carved stucco in the design of circles with arabesques and calligraphic motifs. On the peak of Mubarak's mausoleum there is still a small ornamental lantern.

Some square tombs have to be attributed to the Sayyid period even though their dates and their builders are unknown. For the most part these are isolated structures without perimeter walls, with vertical, not inclined, exterior walls and covered by domes on octagonal drums. It is probable that the mausoleums known locally as Dadi-ka Gumbad and Poli-ka Gumbad are of the Sayyid period. The façades are articulated with protruding entrances and false niches, which in the Dadi-ka Gumbad are arranged on three levels. In the Poli-ka Gumbad the dome is surmounted by a square *chhatri* that adds to the impression of height.

Some square tombs can be attributed to the Lodi period, among them the mausoleum of Bahlol, founder of the dynasty, situated at Chiragh-i Delhi. It has three arches on each façade and a central dome surrounded by four smaller domes. The other square tombs are higher than the octagonal ones and their façades are divided by arches so as to suggest two or three storeys. The central area, in the form of a projecting rectangle, contains a large archway with receding arches that occupies almost the entire height of the building. It encloses a gate framed by an architrave and a corbel, the upper space of which contains an arched window. The 'storeys' of the façade are ornamented with arched niches within rectangular panels, while there are window openings in the arches of the portals. Inside is a single square room with deep arches on each side: the *mihrab* is in the western side. The dome is supported by pendentives like those of the Alai Darwaza. These tombs can reach remarkable proportions: the Bare-Kan-ka Gumbad, for example, which is one of the largest, is almost 30 m high,

not including the terminal which has collapsed. This tomb is situated at Kotla Mubarakpur and can be dated to *c*.1510. Its façades are divided, externally, into three storeys with three arches on each side of the central *iwan*. At the corners there are turrets, also with three storeys, of which the middle one has alternately rounded and angular fluting, as in the Qutb Minar (see p. 23). Four fine octagonal *chhatri*, one of which is still in place, embellished the corners around the dome together with a series of pinnacles. The tomb must have belonged to a very powerful personage, perhaps a prime minister, who unfortunately remains unidentified.

Shish Gumbad is a tomb on a smaller scale, situated in the Lodi Gardens. Its exterior is divided into two storeys by a prominent cornice, the horizontal line of which contrasts rhythmically with the vertical lines of the central *iwan* and its lateral niches. Square panels with multi-coloured, predominantly turquoise, glazed tiles decorate the cornice that frames the *iwan* and have given the mausoleum its name (*shish* means 'mirror').

There are a number of other tombs with similar design: Kale-kan-ka Gumbad, Chote-Kan-ka Gumbad, Bagh-Alam-ka Gumbad and an unidentified mausoleum near the Bare-Kan-ka Gumbad.

Related to these mausoleums is the Bara Gumbad, which is attached to the Friday mosque of Sikandar Lodi in the Lodi Gardens (see p. 52). Some consider the Bara Gumbad to be a gate for this mosque which was built in 1494. In actual fact they are two completely different buildings – in scale, as well as in structure, style and spirit. The mosque is of rubble and plaster with a fine facing of stucco, while the mausoleum is built entirely in grey stone with architraves of red stone above the four entrances. These last are decorated with carved inscriptions. Furthermore, the dimensions of the mausoleum are considerably larger than those of the mosque over which it towers. Its style is in line with the square tombs, occupying a position midway between the Shish Gumbad and the Bagh-Alam-ka Gumbad, which are, without doubt, sepulchral buildings. This theory gains further credence from the fact that Sikandar Lodi was unlikely to have planned a gate of these imposing dimensions compared with the mosque, neither would he have built it using such completely different materials nor placed it on the southern side instead of the eastern side of the mosque according to tradition. Another decisive argument is that an examination of the structure shows that the mosque was built after the Gumbad which therefore had to be altered in order to connect it to the mosque. Nevertheless, it is also true that there are no tombs in the inner hall of the Bara Gumbad (although there are traces), nor are there *mihrab*. In fact, it is unusual that the building is open on all four sides, and it is this that gives rise to the idea that it could be a monumental

The Sayyid and Lodi
(1414–1451 and 1451–1526)

Above The mausoleum of Sikandar Lodi (died 1517) at Delhi is a fine example of an octagonal funerary building.

Opposite The Bara Gumbad, in the Lodi Gardens at Delhi, is believed to have been built in 1490 by a Lodi noble as a mausoleum, but the building was taken over by Sikandar Lodi four years later and used as an entrance to his mosque.

gate as opposed to a sepulchre. But the Koranic inscriptions that decorate the doors refer precisely to death, like the one on the eastern door, that ends: 'All that exists will perish, except for Him. He has the power and to Him all will be delivered'.[2] This quotation, like the others, is more appropriate to a mausoleum than to a gate and thus demonstrates, once again, that we have here an independent funeral building and not an adjunct to the mosque.[3] The Gumbad was erected in 1490, probably by some powerful Lodi noble, and was later modified to join it to the mosque, built four years later by Sikandar Lodi. According to Nath, the commissioning client of the mausoleum must have been a political adversary of Sikandar Lodi, who transformed the tomb into a magnificent entrance to his mosque as a punishment.

The mausoleum of Sikandar Lodi, who died in 1517, is a beautiful example of an octagonal tomb. It rises within a huge walled perimeter with octagonal turrets at the corners and is equipped with a monumental entrance on the southern side and a mosque on the western side. It resembles the Sayyid tombs of Mubarak and Muhammad Shah in terms of layout, the only change being in the lack of *chhatri*. It was once thought that the dome had a double shell, a lower one for the interior effect, another higher and slightly pear-

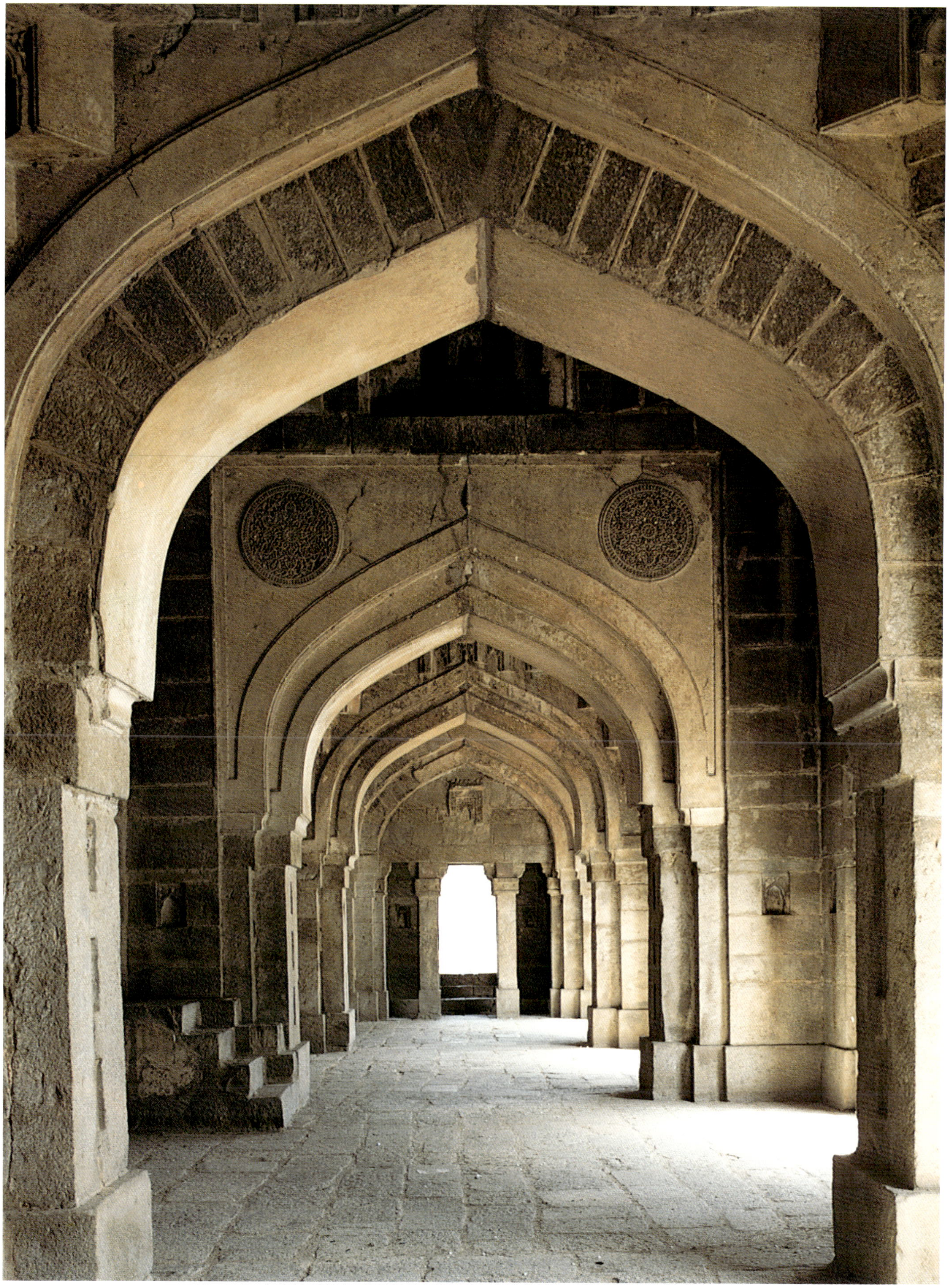

THE SAYYID AND LODI
(1414–1451 AND 1451–1526)

Right A small domed tomb attached to a mosque from the time of Sikandar Lodi, near the Rajon-ki Bain *baoli* at Mehrauli (Delhi).

Opposite The interior of the Moth Mosque at Delhi (c.1505). The building is unusually elegant and finely proportioned for a mosque of this period.

shaped one for the exterior effect. In reality, an accurate investigation has revealed that it is a single dome.

Delhi: Moth Mosque

Even though there is a lack of large congregational mosques in the period and the mosque attached to the Bara Gumbad is of rather modest proportions – almost a family chapel – around 1505 the prime minister of Sikandar Lodi built a remarkable structure. The Moth (or Moth-ki) Mosque combines ornamental grace with force of structure. Although its form resembles the Bara Gumbad mosque, its general proportions are more balanced – with its façade of five arches of which the central one is wider – and the lateral openings with three receding arches are better matched with the great middle arch which is framed by bastions decorated with arched niches. The extrados of the main archway is decorated above with a balconied window. The protruding *chhajja* on the wings are supported by rather ornate corbels. The three domes covering the prayer hall are better spaced and arranged with greater balance, as well as being of the right volume. The decoration, in the form of exquisite arabesques above the arches and medallions on the gables, is based on the alternation of colours and the use of stucco worked in bas-relief and painted in vivid colours. Inside there are *muqarnas* on the lateral domes and pendentives in the central nave, again like the Friday mosque of Sikandar Lodi. However, this last is more profusely decorated with epigraphic and floral motifs in stucco than is the Moth Mosque. The exterior aspect of the Moth Mosque is again Firuzian, with tapered turrets delimiting the rear of the central bay and large cylindrical corner towers, two floors high, with elegant pointed arches.

Delhi: other buildings

The mixture of Tughluq and Lodi elements, however, is one of the defects of this mosque and reveals the artistic uncertainty of the builders of the period. Despite this, mosques and mausoleums with these same characteristics continued to be built for about a further 50 years, although the techniques were gradually perfected and reached their culmination in the most complete example of the series, the Qila-i Kuhna Mosque, traditionally called the Royal Chapel of Sher Shah Sur, built in Delhi in about 1550. The conquest of the country by the Mughals (at the battle of Panipat, 1526) did not in fact prevent an acquired style from continuing in use for some years. Not until the arrival of Akbar, the third sovereign of the new dynasty, did a new, autonomous style take shape.

Among the civil buildings of the Lodi period that have reached us is a palace at Kharera, which is probably the only example of a private aristocratic residence of the fifteenth century. Known locally as Bara Khaumba (Twelve Pillars), it is rather damaged, but the reconstruction attempted by Percy Brown and others allows us to identify the principal elements.[4] The walls surrounded a courtyard, at the centre of which was a well or a type of pool and around which the stables and servants' quarters were situated. From the ground floor, an internal stair led to a large flat roof which was protected by a parapet and could be used as a terrace in the hot season. Connected to the courtyard is a pillared area, originally with a coffered ceiling, which perhaps gave the palace its name and must have been the private area of the house. Outside this area, surrounded by a high, protective wall, was a garden with a well and a *chaubutra*, a place to sit in the open air. The most interesting structure in the complex is a square tower which was originally three storeys high and was designed so as to be easily reached from all the ground-floor areas. It was probably the residence of the more important members of the family because the wide openings of the rooms allowed for a comfortable circulation of air and a fine view of the surrounding landscape. The strong batter of the tower walls and the possibly pyramidal nature of the roof continued the architectural style of the Tughluq period with its emphasis on defence and privacy.

Remains of other Lodi constructions are found at Mehrauli to the south of Lalkot: Jahaz Mahall, a pleasure palace or building

57

for pilgrims, perhaps with a private oratory as well, and Rajon-ki Bain. The latter is a splendid *baoli* with several arcaded floors; it is profusely decorated with stone and stucco reliefs with intricate baroque designs. Nearby is a small mosque carrying an inscription of AH 912 (1506), the time of Sikandar Lodi, and a domed tomb carried on pillars (see p. 57).

OTHER SITES

Other buildings of the Lodi period include the Kalan Mosque at Agra, where Sikandar Lodi transferred the centre of government; the congregational mosque at Lalitpur (in the Jhansi district); and at Sirhind the tomb of Sikandar Lodi's sister, similar to the Bare Khan tomb in Delhi. At Bayana is the Ukha Minar, built in Ibrahim Shah Lodi's time in 1519–20 by a governor of the city and just 10 m or so from the mosque of the same name. It has a circular shaft resting on an octagonal base but reaches no further than the first balcony because it was left unfinished, perhaps because of the pressure being exerted on the region in those years by Babur. A fairly similar but more complete minaret (including a balcony and a second cylindrical shaft) is situated in Banassar Qila.

Near Hisar, among the many tombs which for the most part are Mughal, there are some Lodi tombs, such as the tomb of Baba Pran Pir Padshah together with others without names. The nearby Hansi Rauza of Shah Nimatullah, a complex including two mosques, an ancient palace and portal, as well as the saint's tomb, also seems to belong to Lodi times, as do the mosque of Abu Bakr Jalwani, restored in Mughal times, the tomb of Ali Mir Tijara and the tomb known as Chahar Diwan (Baldachin Building). All of these buildings carry the characteristics of the buildings of the Delhi Lodis: domes on octagonal drums, façades opened by foiled arches framed by projecting portals and numerous decorative niches. Only the Chahar Diwan is set apart from this type because it consists of a platform surmounted by a building composed of two rows of columns covered by four domes, under which there were numerous tombs, now missing. Another example similar to this – the Bare Pir Sahib Dargah – is found at Nagaur and can be dated to the same period.

Above An imposing but incomplete Lodi minaret at Banassar Qila near Bayana. Only two shafts and one balcony remain.

Opposite Chaurasi Gumbad (1527–8) at Kalpi. The massive 45-dome building may be the tomb of the Lodi Shah Badshah.

THE SAYYID AND LODI
(1414–1451 AND 1451–1526)

In the Siri area there is another fine mosque, of smaller proportions, but very similar to the Moth Mosque, although in its decoration it does not fully exploit the two colours of the stone used. This is the Muhammadwali Mosque, still well preserved, surrounded by walls and entered by means of a graceful stone portal in red and white sandstone, with a pointed arch outlined with a double border in relief.

KALPI: CHAURASI GUMBAD

At Kalpi, the birthplace of Muhas-das, a poor Brahmin who later, at the time of Akbar, became famous as Raja Birbal, there is still a large funeral building called Chaurasi Gumbad (84 Domes) which is possibly the tomb of the Lodi Shah Badshah. This is an imposing and massive building, 42 m square and 27 m high, with domed corner towers reminiscent of the Tughluq style. Inside, the surface is divided into squares by eight rows of pillars alternating with seven rows of open bays, covered alternately by domes and flat roofs. At the centre is a large dome that rises from the terrace on a square drum. Another four smaller corner domes surround it, while at the centre of each façade there are four small kiosks with hipped roofs. There are 45 domes altogether, which makes it hard to account for the name given to the building. The decoration is in stucco.

The surrounding area has numerous square tombs covered by slightly pointed domes; these are plain in appearance but are not lacking in dignity.

[1] Tamerlane was born as Timur ('iron') in 1336 at Kesh (now Shahr-i Sabz, 'Green City') in Transoxiana, modern Uzbekistan. Later he was given the nickname *lang* ('lame') on account of an injury he had received, though the chroniclers are in disagreement as to its cause. He was the son of a local governor and belonged to the Turkized Balas tribe that had settled in Transoxiana, i.e. in the western part of the kingdom that had been allotted to Chaghatai, the turbulent son of Chingiz Khan. Although he thought of himself as a Mongol, Tamerlane must be considered as belonging to the Turkish race. His rise to power began in 1360 and ten years later he was already overlord of Transoxiana. He conquered a vast empire and wherever he went he left behind him pyramids of human heads and the memory of his cruelty. He died in 1405, while he was making preparations to attack China.

[2] Koran, 28.85–8.

[3] Nath, *op. cit.*, p. 80.

[4] P. Brown, *Indian Architecture (Islamic Period)*, 5th edn, Bombay, 1968, p. 22.

Part 2: Provincial Styles

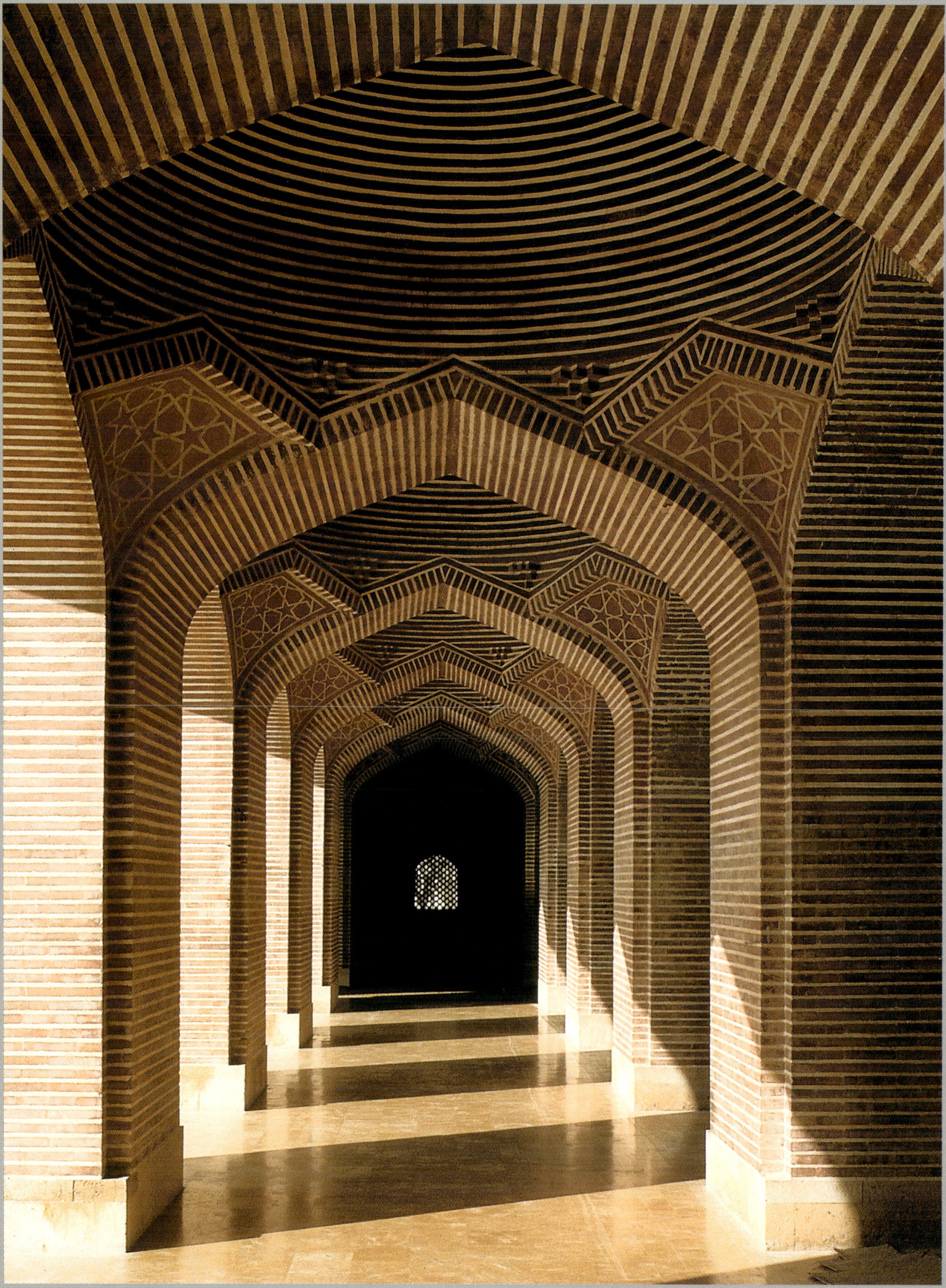

The Punjab and Sind
(1150–c.1550 and 1053–c.1592)

6

One of the courtyard arcades of the *jami masjid* at Thatta, built between 1644 and 1647 by Shah Jahan, when he was in exile from the court of his father, Jahangir.

While the Mughal dynasty established itself on the throne of Delhi, those parts of India that had not belonged to Firuz Shah Tughluq's empire developed their art in very different directions. Many remarkably beautiful buildings were created with characteristics that were completely original compared with the capital. This difference was due not just to the desire to express individual aesthetic ideals, but also to the degree of Islamic artistic influence exercised by Delhi on the various regions and the weight of indigenous traditions coupled with the skill of local craftsmen. Occasionally, climatic conditions had a hand in shaping provincial styles, as did the use of construction materials that were scarce in some regions and common in others. These materials often determined specific techniques that characterized different zones. There are eight principal provincial styles, but at the same time there were minor manifestations in various parts of the country that are not sufficiently important to warrant consideration as autonomous movements. The majority of these styles were absorbed into the Mughal style that dominated throughout India from the second half of the sixteenth century onwards. Only the Deccani states maintained their independence for about a further century.

The Punjab (1150–c.1550)

The Punjab, where the first contact with Islam was felt, has the oldest provincial style. Two main centres were developed here: Multan and Lahore. Multan was one of the first Muslim capitals after the Arab invasion of Sind and the seat of an independent Arab state. Its political life was extremely complicated. The first Arab emirate of the Banu Munabbah was gradually debilitated by the creeping power of the Ismailian missionaries who, towards the end of the tenth century, established themselves with a stable government in the city and introduced the socio-political atmosphere of Fatimid Egypt.[1] Mahmud of Ghazni took the opportunity to annihilate the heretics when he conquered Multan at the beginning of the eleventh century. But soon his dynasty was defeated by the

Ghurids, one of whose governors, Nasir al-Din Qubacha, proclaimed himself independent sovereign of Multan, Uchchh and Lahore. Nasir added lustre to the region by welcoming to his court deposed princes from the cities of Khurasan, Ghur and Ghazni, as well as poets, historians, calligraphers and famous men of letters.

Multan became one of the most important cities on the frontier, in the front line for the defence of the subcontinent from the Mongol peril. Here, too, the founders of the Khalji and Tughluq dynasties acquired their fame as defenders of the faith, fighting off the Mongol attacks many times. At the end of the fourteenth century, however, Multan, like Delhi, was devastated by Timur. When he retired to Samarqand, Timur left Multan in the hands of Khizr Khan, his devoted servant and founder of the Sayyid dynasty. Khizr Khan was too worried about events in his own household and was unable to prevent the head of a Baluchi dynasty, the Langahs, proclaiming independence from Delhi (1437). The Langahs governed the city and its dependencies, defending them from the assault of the Lodis, with whom they managed in the end to establish neighbourly relations. The Langah dynasty in its turn was then overthrown by the Arghuns, sovereigns of Thatta, in 1527: in a short space of time they destroyed all that their predecessors had created in about 90 years of peace and prosperity. After some time, the Arghuns were supplanted by the Mughals; in 1654 Humayun occupied the Punjab and entrusted its government to a devoted courtier.

From the artistic point of view, the proximity of southern Persia, easily accessible by sea, river and land, meant that Punjabi art always seemed closer to Iran than to India. Lahore, too, gravitated towards Persia although not directly, but rather through Afghanistan. In the tenth century, Lahore became one of the main seats of the Ghaznavids and, after the destruction of Ghazni by the Ghurids, it became the refuge of the last descendants of Mahmud.

Practically nothing of the early architecture of these cities has survived. Presumably, at least in Lahore, it was similar to the architecture of Ghazni, which is known to us only through a few fragments.[2] It is also probable that many structures were at least partially of wood, similar to the Friday mosque of Mansura which had teak pillars. It may well be that there are still buildings to be discovered. Whatever the case, it is certainly true that although the buildings in Multan were Arab-Persian in origin, and the buildings in Lahore were Ghaznavid-Saljuq, they still had much in common. Indeed, together they can all be considered as forming part of the one Punjabi style. To judge from the buildings that have reached us from subsequent periods, we can deduce that the pre-medieval architecture of the Punjab was built mainly in brick, stone being almost unobtainable on the alluvial plain of the Five Rivers. These were bricks of top quality, wide but thin, and they could be reinforced with wooden beams inserted in the walls. The buildings were without arches as the dominant method of construction was to use beams and brackets. To ensure their greater stability, the walls were inclined. Decoration was provided by other wooden elements, especially the gates, which were surmounted by windows and protruding balconies that lent a most pleasing aspect to the façade. Parts of the building were then decorated with painted plaster and panels of glazed tiles in bright colours.

In some remote quarters of Lahore there are still remains of wooden constructions which, although of a much later date, display systems of building and ornamentation of the Saljuq period.[3]

MULTAN

Apart from these examples, however, Lahore has retained nothing of the art of this first period. But at Multan, a group of five tombs dedicated to local saints has survived; these can help throw some light on the style that followed immediately after the architectural beginnings. The original nucleus is rather ancient and extends from the first half of the twelfth century to the beginning of the fourteenth. The majority of the tombs have been damaged at different times and restored; although in many cases the structure is relatively modern, it seems that the original design has for the most part been respected and that these tombs therefore do not differ tremendously from their former aspect.

The Khalid Walid mausoleum at Kabirwala is believed to be the oldest Islamic funeral structure on the Indian subcontinent and dates from the Ghaznavid era (977–1186).

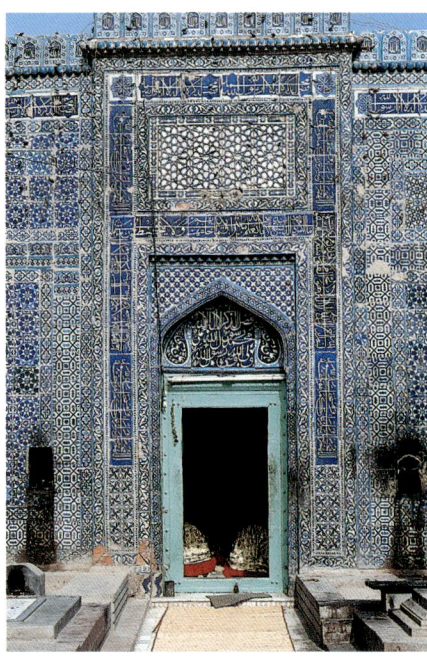

The Punjab and Sind
(1150–c.1550 and 1053–c.1592)

Although it is said that the first large mosque in Multan was built by Muhammad bin Qasim at the time of the first Arab conquest, it was replaced at the end of the tenth century by another building when a new, Ismailian, dynasty converted the population to Shiism. Neither of the two buildings has survived, just as the Tughluq mosques have disappeared together with those of the first Mughal governors.

Kabirwala: Khalid Walid mausoleum

Not far from Multan is the tomb of Khaliq or Khalid Walid. The oldest funeral structure known on the subcontinent, dating from the Ghaznavid epoch, it consists of a brick structure with a rectangular plan of about 21 x 27 m with semi-circular bastions at the corners and in the centre of three of the perimeter walls. On the fourth wall the bastion is replaced by a rectangular projection that marks, on the exterior, the niche of the *mihrab*. The entrance on the north side is situated off centre and is preceded by a flight of stairs that leads, through what must have been an imposing gate, to the floor of the funeral hall, which is raised some 4.5 m from the level of the surrounding land. The tomb chamber, covered by an exaggeratedly pointed dome, is flanked to the north and south by two smaller rooms, which in turn are enclosed in a series of galleries forming an ambulatory. The *mihrab* is adorned with reliefs in cut tiles embracing a trefoil arch, pillars and capitals of the Hindu type and foliated Kufic inscriptions. Although the present state of the monument is somewhat decrepit, it clearly served as a model for three subsequent buildings in Multan erected over a period of fourteen years from 1262 to 1276: the tombs of Baha al-Din Zakariya, Shadna Shahid and Shams Sabzawadi. To the same early period (the eleventh and twelfth centuries) can also be assigned the mausoleums of Lal Mahra Sharif in the Gomal valley (Dera Ismail Khan district) and that of Daud Gardizi at Bahawalpur (Punjab), which has recently been restored.

Multan: Shah Yusuf Gardizi mausoleum

The oldest Multan tomb is that of Shah Yusuf Gardizi, said to have been built shortly after his death in 1152. However, it has been largely restored and the original epigraphs are lost, so it cannot be dated with certainty. It is a rectangular brick construction, placed originally at the centre of a closed courtyard of which there remains very little today. Its peculiarity lies in the fact that it has only one floor, covered by a flat roof. The entrance is marked by a projecting rectangular panel in which there is a cuspidate arch framing the doorway. On the western façade is a projecting niche that marks the position of the *mihrab* from the exterior. Inside, along the profile of the

Above The entrance to the Shah Yusuf Gardizi mausoleum at Multan. The oldest tomb at Multan, it is said to have been built shortly after 1152.

Above left Detail of the decorative brickwork on the exterior of an early (eleventh–twelfth century) mausoleum at Lal Mahra Sharif in the Gomal Valley.

mihrab, as well as geometric decoration there is also a frieze of Koranic inscriptions that is repeated externally on all the walls below the cornice and around the door posts of the main entrance. The rest of the decoration on the exterior consists of dazzling blue tiles with an almost exclusively geometric design, apart from a few stylized floral motifs. This decoration is almost certainly later than the construction of the building.

Multan: Shaikh Baha al-Din Zakariya mausoleum

The second tomb in chronological order is that of Shaikh Baha al-Din Zakariya, also called Baha al-Haqq. It rises on the northwestern edge of the high hill that is the site of the ancient fort of Multan. The shaikh was a famous exponent of a religious community, who lived for almost a century and died at Multan in December 1262. Much respected for his political authority, he helped Iltutmish establish his power in the region and received from him the title of Shaikh al-Islam. In 1246 he succeeded in deflecting a Mongol siege of Multan by offering them 10.000 *dinars*. His mausoleum occupies the centre of a huge elongated area enclosed by a brick perimeter wall, badly restored, which was perhaps the wall of the celebrated *khanqah* (convent). It has two main entrances, one each to the east and west, and a series of small rooms to the south used as quarters for the sick and for visitors. During the British siege in 1848 it was much damaged, but was repaired soon afterwards with funds from a public collection. The tomb is built in fired brick, with a wooden infrastructure, and is on three floors of diminishing height and width. The first floor is a rather wide parallelepiped with very steeply inclined walls. The second floor is formed of a smaller octagon with cuspidate arch windows enclosed within rectangular mouldings, on which the dome is imposed. If the dome is original, it has corner squinches similar to those found in the mausoleum of Iltutmish of 1230 (see p. 26). In the centre of the slightly projecting part of the façade is the entrance which is framed by an ogival arch. The only decorative elements are the escutcheon-shaped mouldings that run along the border of the parapets and recall those on the tomb of Ismail at Bukhara, together with the miniature minarets rising at each corner which are purely decorative in function. According to some, these minarets led to the decorative *chhatri* of later Indo-Islamic buildings. This structure is perhaps the result of a fusion between the Saljuq tomb-tower and the square domed tombs (*imamzade*) of the Iranian region.[4] On the façade of the eastern gate is a monumental inscription executed in glazed tiles and displaying Saljuq or Ilkhanid taste.

Multan: Shadna Shahid mausoleum

The third tomb is locally referred to as the tomb of Shadna Shahid – also known as Shah Dana Shahid – disciple of Baha al-Haqq, who was killed by the Mongols in 1270. Inspired by the mausoleum of his master, it was built in fired brick held together with mud-plaster and reinforced with wooden beams placed horizontally in the walls. It has perpendicular walls with three floors and is covered by a dome. Originally the exterior was without decoration, with the bricks left visible, but later stucco and plaster were added and have disfigured the entire outer surface. Similarly, decorative panels of various sizes have been fixed into niches inside. Later, modern restorations have turned the first floor into a rough, unfinished cube. The second floor is octagonal with a niche on each wall. The lower floor carries a rectangular opening on the southern wall, against which an oblong verandah has

Above The Shams-i Tabrizi mausoleum at Multan. Built around 1329 and reconstructed in 1780, it is noteworthy for its stucco and glazed-tile decoration.

Top The mausoleum of Shaikh Baha al-Din Zakariya, who died in 1262, at Multan. It has been suggested that the miniature minarets at the corners of the building were the forerunners of the decorative *chhatri* on later Indian Islamic buildings.

been created in order to house various modern tombs. The dome, which rests on pendentives, is covered with stucco on the outside and is crowned by a round lantern and a pinnacle.

MULTAN: SHAMS-I TABRIZI MAUSOLEUM
The tomb known commonly, but erroneously, as that of Shams-i Tabrizi dates from a little later.[5] In actual fact this is the tomb of Shams Sabzawadi, an Ismailian missionary who died in about 1276. His mausoleum seems to have been erected about 1329 but was reconstructed in 1780 by a disciple of the family after it had fallen into complete ruin. It follows the usual three-storey design with a square base, an octagonal second floor and the hemispheric dome terminating with a high pinnacle rising from an upside-down corolla of lotus flowers. All the corners are decorated with small minarets with various storeys. The exuberant decoration is of stucco and glazed tiles with geometric, floral and naturalistic designs. The gratings that close the window spaces are especially vibrant and it is doubtful if they are the originals.

MULTAN: RUKN-I ALAM MAUSOLEUM
The mausoleum of Rukn-i Alam (1251–1335) – grandson and spiritual successor of Shaikh Baha al-Din Zakariya according to popular legend – was built by Ghiyas al-Din Tughluq as his own tomb during the period of his governorship at Depalpur and subsequently abandoned with his transfer to Delhi as sultan; it was then given by Firuz Shah Tughluq to the descendants of Rukn-i Alam as the tomb of their relative. The saint had in fact been buried temporarily in his grandfather's tomb. However, the Pakistani archaeologist Nabi Khan has put forward the theory that the mausoleum was planned by Rukn-i Alam who died before it was completed and therefore the members of his *silsila* (fraternity), Suhrawardiya, saw to its completion. If, in fact, as Nabi Khan maintains, the resources of Ghiyas al-Din, who was not yet sultan, were inadequate for the magnificence of the building, then the powerful *silsila* was able to sustain the burden of the construction instead. The building was widely imitated throughout the region in later periods. Examples include the Abdi al-Walid mausoleum at Daira Din Panah (*c*.1500), the Tahir Khan Nahar Mausoleum at Sitpur in Sind (*c*.1530) and the last one, again in Multan,

The mausoleum of Rukn-i Alam (1251–1335) at Multan is considered the finest example of ancient Muslim architecture in Pakistan. The building was later widely imitated in the Punjab.

the Sultan Ali Khan mausoleum (late sixteenth century).

The tomb of Rukn-i Alam is also built like a fortress and is in the brick characteristic of the region. It has two floors which slope towards the top and is covered by a fine dome. The tomb is 35 m high and sits on a 17 m high rise that makes it the highest and most conspicuous building in the city. It is reached through an elaborate entrance porch with a flat roof and two openings, to the east and south, which was probably built at a later date. The octagonal lower floor of the monument is 27 m in diameter but appears larger because of the steep batter of the walls, accentuated by eight bulky corner buttresses, markedly tapered towards the top and terminating in small domed pinnacles. The second floor, also octagonal, forms a type of high drum for the perfectly hemispheric dome above. This last, measurably solemn, completes the whole with rhythmic grace. The exterior decoration is very rich: on the base section there are alternate horizontal bands of wood, patterned or smooth bricks and tiles glazed in a vivid turquoise arranged so as to form geometric or floral designs. On the second floor, panels of tiles frame the windows that open on each side of the building and are arranged in a continuous row along the upper border, creating a pleasant contrast with the light-red bricks of the structure. The circular base of the dome is also ornamented with a ring of glazed tiles in the form of palmettes which alternate with a band of cut bricks in diamond shapes. Inside, the squinches of the dome are impressive, as is the decoration on the walls using beautiful *shishan* wood, most of all in the *mihrab*, where extremely refined epigraphic friezes alternate with exuberant floral volutes. Taken as a whole, the Rukn-i Alam mausoleum can be considered the masterpiece of ancient Muslim architecture in Pakistan in the same way that the tomb of Sher Shah Sur represents the apogee of the art of the Delhi sultanates, and the Taj Mahall (see p. 240) is the culmination of Mughal art.

Uchchh Sharif: Bibi Jawindi mausoleum

Another interesting building directly derived from the Rukn-i Alam tomb is found at Uchchh, an important centre for both religious and political activity situated about 100 km to the south-west of Multan. Among numerous remains, Uchchh still preserves the tomb of Bibi Jawindi in particular. Famous for her piety and devotion to God, she died in about 1404 and was buried on the northwestern edge of the hill of Nasir al-Din Qubacha's fort. It is said that the current beautiful structure was built in 1493 by a prince of Khurasan, one Muhammad Dilshad. Nevertheless, the building is the creation of a local talent who had already built another two tombs nearby and was steeped in the traditions of the Multan style.[6] Unfortunately, the terrible flood of the Chenab in 1817 destroyed almost half

The Punjab and Sind
(1150–c.1550 and 1053–c.1592)

Above A view of the Baba al-Halim and Bibi Jawindi mausoleums at Uchchh, showing the extent of the damage caused by a flood in 1817.

Opposite top Detail of the exterior decoration on the Bibi Jawindi mausoleum, which consists of bands of glazed tiles and six-pointed stars.

Opposite bottom The mausoleum of Bibi Jawindi (died c.1404) at Uchchh is derived from the influential Rukn-i Alam mausoleum at Multan (see p.67).

of the monument and the nearby tomb of Baba al-Halim.

Built in small, finely burnt bricks joined together with pointed mortar, the mausoleum is an octagon with a diameter of some 12 m and inclined walls some 9 m high to the first floor and some 4 m thick. The walls are reinforced at the corners with tapered buttresses and are crowned with pinnacles. The second floor is also octagonal, but is smaller with an exterior diameter of some 8.5 m, which allowed for a circular ambulatory at the top level. The second floor consists of a tall drum that is lavishly decorated with an application of glazed tiles around the projecting openings on all sides of the octagon; these are also decorated with turrets. On the top of the second floor is the round base of the hemispheric dome, decorated with a series of oblong glazed tiles with a floral motif, while the rest of the dome is covered in white glazed tiles. Each side of the lower part of the octagon has a projecting rectangular structure which is both functional and decorative and is divided into two arched oblong panels arranged one on top of the other. The lower oblong serves as the entrance to the mausoleum, where the upper part is an ornamental niche with a flat border decorated in the upper area with denticulations.

The tomb is completely covered in glazed ceramic tiles to the edge of the parapet, which is decorated with a false battlement in tiles with the word 'Allah' on the upper part. The gables and the borders of the arches are also decorated with glazed tiles of various shapes and floral designs. The fifth white band from the bottom has a row of six-pointed stars which is repeated both on the body of the small towers and in the main panel of the octagon. Inside, the mausoleum is dressed in stucco except for the centre of each side where there are blind niches with receding double-pointed arches that are partially decorated with glazed tiles. Other courses of star-shaped tiles with a six-petalled flower run along the entire surface of the first floor and at the junction with the dome.

Uchchh Sharif: other mausoleums

There are many other tombs and mosques at Uchchh of uncertain date, often

69

Left The Abu Hanifa mausoleum at Uchchh. Though restored in the nineteenth century, it retains its original flat roof, a characteristic of many tombs at Uchchh.

Opposite The Great Mosque of Thatta (1644–7). It is the most significant brick building erected in this area by Shah Jahan.

completely restored or rebuilt in the nineteenth century or at the beginning of the twentieth; they are thought to retain the aspect of the thirteenth and fourteenth centuries, when they were built. Many had flat roofs (Jalal Din Surkh Bukhari, Abu Hanifa, Jahaniyan Jahan Gasht, Rajan Qattal). Wood was much used in these tombs, especially in the ceilings, which were divided by beams supported by round, square or octagonal wooden pillars, with elaborately carved capitals and corbels. The ceilings were painted or lacquered with floral designs executed in brilliant yellow and white on a vivid red or orange background. Wood was sometimes used to reinforce the external perimeter walls, which were made up of fired brick held together with mud and lime; often they were cut and arranged to produce a great variety of geometric designs. The entrances to some tomb buildings, such as that of Jahaniyan, which also includes a mosque, are characterized by strongly projecting wooden porticoes with wide cornices.

Lahore

Not much is known of the history of ancient Lahore. In the Muslim epoch it was founded by Sultan Mahmud of Ghazni in 1022. Indeed, its name at first was Mahmudpur. The golden age of the Ghaznavid epoch coincided with the reign of Zahir al-Daula Ibrahim (1059–99), during which there lived both the first great Persian poet of the Indo-Pakistani subcontinent, Masud Saad Salman, and the famous saint Hazrat Data Ganj Bakhsh, who was also buried at Lahore. In 1186 Lahore was conquered by the Ghurids who destroyed the Ghaznavid empire and set out to attack Delhi. In 1206, on the death of Muhammad Ghuri, Qutb al-Din Aibak was crowned in Lahore as the first Muslim sovereign of the subcontinent; he died here four years later. Lahore was then contested by the sovereigns of Multan, Ghazni and Delhi, until Iltutmish succeeded in taking it definitively in 1217. It underwent various Mongol incursions – 1241, 1246, 1285, 1298 and 1301 – and was often devastated, to the point where it nearly became a rural locality. The Khukaz, who invaded Lahore in 1342 and 1392, caused further damage, as did Timur who extracted a ransom in 1398. Under the Sayyids it was rebuilt and repopulated (1421), and thereafter the Lodis elevated it to the rank of capital, a role that it was to enjoy again under the Great Mughals as an alternative to Delhi and Agra. Because of the extensive destruction the city suffered over the course of time, from an architectural point of view Lahore is essentially Mughal.

Only some mausoleums of famous saints (with extensive alterations) and a couple of not particularly significant mosques survive from earlier periods. The Niwi Mosque falls into this last category. A sixteenth-century Lodi era building by Zulfikhan Khan, it is situated between the Lahori and Shah Alam gates. Its dimensions are huge and it has massive inclined walls. The prayer hall is open to the courtyard with large arches, and it is well illuminated and covered by remarkably wide domes. Today the mosque is below road level, but at the time of its construction they must have been on the same level. The mausoleum of Hazrat Data Ganj Bakhsh, the 'saint donor of treasure', who came to Lahore with the Ghaznavids, was built by the successor of Masud, Sultan Ibrahim, at the time of his death in 1072. The current aspect of the tomb was imposed by Akbar and Aurangzeb at the height of the Mughal period: a building with a ribbed dome and expensive fine marble panelling. The Sikhs, too, sought to embellish the mausoleum, and so it retains virtually nothing of its original Ghaznavid nucleus. The small mosque attached to the tomb, built by the saint, has been rebuilt in Mughal style with bulbous, ribbed cupolas.

The mausoleum of Hazrat Yakub Sadar Diwan Zinjani, who died at Lahore in 1208, was built by Qutb al-Din Aibak who wanted it to be richly magnificent and placed in the most central area of the city. The sovereign's own mausoleum, which has now disappeared, was built nearby. The saint's tomb is now without any embellishment and has been reduced to a sad ruin. The Mughal buildings of Lahore will be discussed in Part 3.

THE PUNJAB AND SIND
(1150–c.1550 AND 1053–c.1592)

SIND (1053–c.1592)

The medieval architecture of Sind represents an interesting example of provincial taste which could be defined as Sind-Islamic and which lasted even into the Mughal period. After having been conquered by Mahmud of Ghazni in 1026, Sind was governed by a weak vizier, resident in Multan. But in 1053 it became independent under the Sumras, a local dynasty of Rajput origin who were initially Hindu but were soon converted to Islam. In 1333 the Sumras were succeeded by the Sammas, another dynasty of Islamicized Rajputs, who – not without contention – became independent of the sovereignty of Delhi. Muhammad bin Tughluq died close to the banks of the Indus while he was pursuing a rebel who received protection from the Sammas. Muhammad's successor, Firuz Shah, took revenge on the local sovereigns, but without destroying their independence.

The capital of the realm, Sammanagar, was situated a short distance to the northwest of present-day Thatta, close to the Makli Hills. Along these hills there are about one million Muslim tombs. In 1520 the Sammas were replaced by a descendant of Chingiz Khan who had been chased from Kandahar by the Mughal Babur. The new sovereign, Shah Beg Arghun, established himself in the fortress of Sukkur that he rebuilt on the ancient Hindu capital of Aror. His brief dynasty survived until 1554 when it was replaced by the Tarkhanids, who in their turn were defeated by Akbar in 1592, and Sind became part of the Mughal empire. In the seventeenth century, nevertheless, the Dandputras and after them the Kalhoras resisted Mughal dominion from a new capital which was established by the Dandputras at Shikarpur; in 1701 Aurangzeb formally recognized the jurisdiction of the Kalhoras over part of Sind. Furthermore, between 1783 and 1843 the Talpur sovereigns maintained their independence from Hyderabad before being absorbed into British dominion.

THATTA: DABJIR MOSQUE AND *JAMI MASJID*

The oldest mosque in Thatta, the Dabjir Mosque, was built in 1588 and had to function as a Friday mosque until 1644 when Shah Jahan built the present-day *jami masjid*. It is now in a state of ruin, but its ancient beauty can still be discerned. It is made up of a prayer hall with three archways, each surmounted by a low dome on a double octagonal drum, fronted by a court with a low wall. The building is of brick, in some cases trimmed with an imitation of white mortar, a widely diffused technique both in this and subsequent centuries. The *mihrab* is of stone carved delicately in bas-relief, but the determining characteristic of the building is its rich interior tilework. This decoration is pure Persian in style, with floral designs on the architraves of the two arches in front of the *mihrab* and on the borders that frame the niche itself. The dominant colours are white, dark blue and light blue. The façade, too, must also once have been decorated with tiles.

The most significant brick building is the Great Mosque of Thatta, built by Shah Jahan between 1644 and 1647, when he was in exile from the court of his father, Jahangir: the east wing, with its large gate, was added in 1658–9. The building is arranged on a stone plinth, but is built in solid brickwork. The prayer hall, covered by a large dome, is balanced on the opposite side of the oblong courtyard by an entrance passage with two slightly smaller domes. The courtyard is enclosed by a double arcade surmounted by cupolas, which, together with the larger domes, total 93 in number. Externally, the façade is dressed in tiles, but the rear is of plaster and there are some modern paintings on the drum of the main dome. Inside, the building presents the most complete existing example, in all the Indo-Pakistani subcontinent, of Persian-style dressing in glazed tiles. The main dome is a superb stellate vault with blue and white tiles arranged in a mosaic and the entrance domes are equally elegant. The spandrels of the main arches are filled with conventional floral designs from seventeenth-century Iran, while the main spaces are enhanced with a great variety of geometric and floral designs on square tiles arranged in panels.

Makli Hills: cemetery

There are other fired-brick buildings, of different periods, in the large Makli Hills cemetery nearby. The oldest seems to be the mausoleum of Mubarak Khan, Jam Nizam al-Din's general, who died in 1490.[7] A simple quadrangular enclosure on a high plinth, its high stone walls have magnificent decoration consisting of arabesques and floral designs, which demonstrate the existence of an independent artistic tradition in lower Sind as early as the end of the fifteenth century.

Another of the oldest buildings, dating from the Tarkhan period, is the brick mausoleum of Sultan Ibrahim, son of Isa Khan Tarkhan the Elder, who died in 1558. This is a solid octagonal structure with deep arched openings on each side, surmounted by a rather pointed dome which rests on a high drum. The entire edifice was originally covered in turquoise-blue tiles, of which there are still some traces on the dome, and had two small lines of Koranic inscriptions traced in white letters on a dark-blue background.

Dating from some decades later is the mausoleum of Mirza Jani Beg Tarkhan, who had to succumb to Akbar in 1591 and died ten years later.[8] It is picturesque and colourful in appearance with its wall structure of alternate courses of dark-blue glazed brick and plain red brick. It rests on a terraced sandstone platform at the centre of a courtyard surrounded by a wall which has an exquisitely carved *mihrab* on the western side. The tomb is on an octagonal plan with semi domed niches on four sides and arched doorways with richly carved slabs with geometric motifs. The Arab inscriptions on the doorway panels are very delicate, again traced in white paint on dark-blue tiles. The interior of the building is covered with wall tiles decorated with floral designs, the most beautiful in all Sind.

The later tomb of Diwan Shurfa Khan, who died in 1638 at the height of the Mughal epoch, is among the best preserved and most colourful in the Makli Hills. An open mosque with the same kind of decoration is annexed to it. On a square plan, surmounted by a Persian-style dome once covered in light-blue tiles, the tomb has a tower at each corner, each equipped with a stair that leads to the roof. The walls are of plain red brick, alternating with glazed blue brick in the joints which creates a lively note of colour. The same taste in colour is found inside where bands of tiles have been arranged near the springing line of the dome. This last is decorated with a radiant design of glazed bricks in a zigzag pattern.

Among the stone buildings in the Makli area of the Samma period worthy of note is the tomb of Jam Nizam al-Din, one of the most important sovereigns of the dynasty. The sovereign, known also by the name of Jam Nindo, reigned from 1461 to 1509. His tomb is a fine square structure carrying beautiful carved decoration of Hindu inspiration – lotus flowers, sunflowers, geese motifs (*hamsa*), and spires (*shikhara*) – alternating with Islamic motifs – arches, inscriptions, geometric designs – as well as on the beautiful *mihrab*.

Other stone monuments date from the Mughal period, such as the tomb of Jan Baba, who died in 1570 but whose tomb was not built until 1608. It is a quadrangular building originally covered by three domes of which only the central one survives. Finely carved decoration, similar to lacework, covers both the external and internal walls and is particularly rich in the *mihrab*.

The most impressive and remarkable monument of this type, however, is the mausoleum of Isa Khan Tarkhan the Younger, son of Jan Baba, who died in 1644. He was governor of Thatta and contributed to the building of other tombs besides his own and his father's. The tomb of Isa Khan Tarkhan is at the centre of a square courtyard surrounded by high stone walls with an *iwan* at the centre of each side, one of which constitutes the entrance. The domed funeral chamber is surrounded by a pillared gallery on two floors, interrupted in the central zone by a group of three tall, narrow and pluri-cuspidated arches surmounted by a wide parapet. The decoration carved on the building is refined and full of variety, almost the transposition on to stone of the glazed tile designs of other buildings.

To the right of the mausoleum of Jani Beg Tarkhan stands the small pavilion tomb of Beg Tughril.[9] This consists of 12 pillars supporting a dome pointed at the top and slightly narrowed at the base, all of which rests on a high platform. The pillars are decorated with carved designs and have stalactite capitals such as those of Isa Khan Tarkhan's tomb, while the interior of the dome presents zigzag

The Mughal-era mausoleum of Diwan Shurfa Khan (died 1638) is one of the best preserved and most colourful examples in the Makli Hills.

The Punjab and Sind
(1150–c.1550 and 1053–c.1592)

One of the carved stone arcades in the mausoleum of Isa Khan Tarkhan (died 1644) in the Makli Hills. It is the most remarkable Mughal-period monument in this area.

motifs in stone, similar to those made with coloured tiles in the mausoleum of Diwan Shurfa Khan. On the western side of the platform on which the pavilion stands there is a carved *mihrab* with three arches of which the central one is wider than the others with a crenellation that runs along the upper part, terminating at the top with a minaret.

On the whole the tombs of Makli represent the work of a provincial school of great ability which, even if it never attained a very high level of fulfilment, is nevertheless interesting as a synthesis of indigenous traditions with imported styles.

Chaukhandi: necropolis

Twenty-seven kilometres from Karachi, in a slightly raised area, is the necropolis of Chaukhandi (see p. 74). It contains an enormous number of ordinary graves together with a certain number of tomb buildings, unremarkable in size, which can be dated between the fifteenth and the nineteenth centuries. They are all built of a fine yellow sandstone that comes from the Jungshahi quarries near Thatta and they vary in their proportions. Most of them are simple tombs built on a platform with a surrounding balustrade, while others stand inside a pillared pavilion with a low dome. The most interesting thing about these tombs is the rich decoration: the whole surface is covered with intricate designs that look as though they have been carved in soft wood. In the tombs that were built for men the geometric or floral designs are further embellished by the addition of drums, horses, warriors and weapons, while the tombs built for women have designs of jewels, necklaces, bracelets, anklets and pendants. They are evidence of a local art of a pleasing and delicate nature, which also finds expression in Sind through other media, such as textiles, wood-carvings and jewellery.

Other sites

In central and northern Sind there are some towns, such as Sehwan, Hyderabad, Khudabad, Larkana, Sukkur and Chitori, some of them still unexplored, where there are a number of mausoleums and mosques dating from the seventeenth and eighteenth centuries that are all profusely decorated with faience tiles of a beautiful turquoise-blue. In all these monuments the Persian influence is clear – in the design of the structures as well as in the use of bricks and glazed tiles for decoration. This influence resulted in part from the region's geographic isolation from the rest of India and its accessibility both by land and sea from the Iranian plateau. Indeed, the art of these centres could be considered a provincial form of contemporary Persian art, although it is not without its indigenous element, which is comparable to that of the Punjab and to some extent Gujarat.

Sehwan

Worthy of note at Sehwan is the tomb of Shaikh Usman Marwandi (also known as Kalandar Lal Shahbaz), the most revered saint in Sind. It is said that this tomb was begun by Maliq Ikhtyar al-Din in about 1356, but was later enlarged by Mirza Jani Beg Tarkhan and Mirza Ghazi Beg and finally completed by Nawab Dindar Khan in 1639.[10] It has therefore become impossible to follow the evolution of this structure and understand its original design. Nevertheless, like other tombs in the area, it has a square plan with a low pointed dome on a polygonal drum whose faces are completely dressed in vivid turquoise faience tiles. The body of the mausoleum is decorated on three sides by pointed arch panels inserted between horizontal bands which in their turn are bordered by stuccoes. The main façade forms a large *pishtaq* (monumental entrance) which contains another pointed arch flanked by rectangular blind niches, all filled with blue, ochre and black tiles with floral and stylized designs like the interior of the arch and its extrados. Graceful pinnacles complete the outline of the façade and the dome; it seems that they were originally in silver (a generous donation from a Talpur sovereign to the saint's memory), as were the door of the tomb and the balustrade that surrounded it.

At Sehwan there is also the Lal Shahbaz Kalandar religious complex, said to have been founded in 1356. Today, surrounded by many tombs, are three bigger mausoleums in the typical later style of Sind.

Sukkur

The earliest phase of the provincial architectural style of upper Sind is best represented by a group of monuments at Sukkur connected with the Sayyid Masum family whose most important member, Mir Masum, was an artist, poet, historian, alchemist, sculptor, calligrapher and, above all, architect. His inscriptions decorated the doors of the fort at Agra and the Great Mosque of Fatehpur Sikri, and his constructions include bridges, rest homes, hotels, mosques and cisterns.[11]

At Sukkur, he built a cylindrical tower (see p. 76) to allow the inhabitants of the city to observe the surrounding countryside. It is an extremely simple brickwork structure, slightly tapered towards the top, which terminated with a lantern surrounded by an iron balustrade. It is not much if compared with the great towers of Delhi (the Qutb Minar; see p. 23) or the minarets of Daulatabad and Ahmedabad, but it is architecturally successful if we consider the utilitarian and leisure purpose for which it was built in 1594. In front of it, in a pavilion tomb of the Mirza Tughrul type of the Makli Hills, lie the remains of Masum; another domed building (Aram Gah), a sort of hostel for occasional visitors, can be discerned. Built towards the end of the sixteenth century, this building presents many of the characteristics that were to become common in upper Sind over successive centuries: the greater height; the façade divided into various storeys by means of panels in the form of blind arches; ornamental merlons; and decoration in glazed tile.

Khudabad

One of the most successful examples of the later architecture in the region is the Great Mosque of Khudabad (see p. 76), a small city not far from Sehwan, which was for some time the capital of the Kalhoras before it was moved to Hyderabad. It was the headquarters of Mian Nur Muhammad and, although flourishing at the time, it fell into ruin as soon as the court left. The *jami masjid* has suffered much from the vandalism of those who scavenged the glazed tiles that decorated it. Nevertheless, it still appears as an imposing building within a perimeter wall, with a fine gate and a main façade with three arches, once completely covered with splendid panels of white and blue tiles. The central *pishtaq* consists of two receding pointed arches, beyond which the actual entrance opens up. The lateral archways, which are lower than those of

Above The necropolis at Chaukhandi, near Karachi. The tombs are remarkable for their intricate carved sandstone decoration.

Opposite The tomb of the saint Shaikh Usman Marwandi at Sehwan. Said to have been begun around 1356 by Maliq Ikhtyar al-Din, it was later enlarged and finally completed by Nawab Dindar Khan in 1639.

the entrance, were highlighted by panels of tiles with beautiful patterns: a flowering shoot of white lilies on a dark blue background which sprout from a central stem, surrounded by buds, lanceolate leaves and large open flowers, all represented realistically and not at all conventionally. There is no doubt that this façade displays one of the most beautiful tile decorations in all Sind. The lateral façades are divided into three storeys by panels containing blind arched niches, the extradoses of which are also decorated with blue and white tiles. Similarly, the interior, covered by fine domes of moderate height, was dressed in panels of startling colours, but has suffered greatly from vandals.

Also at Khudabad is the tomb of Yar Muhammad, the first Kalhora sovereign of Sind, who died in 1718. This tomb continues the architectural and decorative development that is typical of the region. The funeral building is square, imposing, surmounted by a fine, slightly pear-shaped dome and is opened on the front by a grandiose entrance. This last has a deep archway surmounted by two short terminals which are emphasized by two oblong lateral bands divided into three zones by blind ogival niches. These niches are lined with glazed tiles in various colours, with a vivid blue predominating. The upper niches also have open work. The three outer sides of the mausoleum are divided into two zones by a row of arched windows filled with open-work terracotta panels in a delicate geometric design, and by a series of large blind niches lined with blue tiles. Above the entrance is a panel of coloured tiles forming a beautiful rose pattern, to the sides of which are huge panels in the shape of multifoil arches. Four large corner *chhatri* surround the dome.

Other mausoleums

A minimal variation on these architectural and decorative characteristics of upper Sind is represented in the tombs of Shah Baharo at Larkana, Shah Ilah Khair al-Din at Sukkur, Nur Muhammad at Moro and the Tahims' tombs at Drakhan. The variation consists of a small lantern arranged on top of the dome, which in the tomb of Shah Baharo – Nur Muhammad Kalhora's commander who died in 1735 or 1736 – is octagonal in shape with a small cupola surmounted by a high terminal. The sides are filled with open-work slabs and were once framed by glazed tiles in vivid colours. Otherwise, the tomb displays no other innovations: it has a square plan and the walls are slightly inclined at the corners, which terminate at the top with turrets with pyramidal roofs, while the façade has a somewhat recessed arched entrance. It is decorated very soberly with rectangular panels in glazed tiles and is divided laterally, as on the outer sides, by two series of arched blind niches. The slightly pear-shaped dome rests on a high polygonal drum, which is also decorated with panels that have niches without decorative tiles.

Very similar to these, but much more profusely decorated on the façade, is the tomb of Shah Khair al-Din who died at Sukkur – the precise date is not known – after having travelled for a long time in Arabia and Mesopotamia. His mausoleum was built between 1752 and 1761 and has, apart from the usual characteristics, a small octagonal lantern similar to that on the previous tomb. The same features apply to the other tombs which date from some years later (*c.*1781), but which are more or less in ruins.

Hyderabad: Kalhora mausoleums

The tradition already established in Sind found its fulfilment in the tombs of the royal families of the Kalhora and the Talpurs (see p. 78), built at Hyderabad in

Above The tomb and observation tower built in 1594 by the architect Mir Masum Bakkhari at Sukkur.

Below Though the *jami masjid* at Khudabad has suffered from neglect and vandalism, it is still imposing. It was once completely covered with panels of blue and white tiles.

the last decades of the 1700s and the early decades of the 1800s. The former are more ruinous and are distinguished by being large, isolated buildings, while the latter, better preserved, are in two groups and vary greatly in their dimensions. The surviving Kalhora mausoleums are those of Ghulam Shah, who died in 1772, and his brother Nabi Khan. The former is a large, square building standing on a broad platform that is surrounded by an openwork balustrade with a large *iwan* entrance on the eastern side. The large archway, decorated with the usual arched niches and blue ceramic panels, is flanked in the upper area by two small windows with open-work screens which are repeated on the upper zone of the lateral walls, alternated with blind niches. Another two levels of blind niches decorated with blue and white floral motif panels divide the exterior of the perimeter walls, while on the inside these walls have just one storey which is elaborately painted and gilded. A large dome on a high polygonal drum once crowned the building, but it has collapsed, partially ruining the white marble tomb below. Four corner *chhatri* on pillars with segmented domes are still in place. The mausoleum and the surrounding courtyard were once protected by a mud wall which has also now partially collapsed. The tomb of Nabi Khan, not far from his brother's, is also a massive structure, but with an irregular octagonal plan outside and a square plan inside. It is covered by a large dome on a polygonal drum surrounded by heavy *chhatri* placed at the centre of the shortest sides of the octagonal base. The external walls are dressed with a continuous covering of pale blue tiles in geometric designs. The extradoses of the large arches that open on the main façades carry graceful floral motifs interwoven into sinuous spirals. Within the perimeter wall of Ghulam Shah's mausoleum there is another square tomb: this is simpler in shape, being square with a dome, and is much less ornate than the tombs mentioned previously.

Hyderabad: Talpur mausoleums

The oldest Talpur tombs, both in the northern group, are those of Mir Karam Ali, who died in 1812, and his two wives. These were built very close together.

THE PUNJAB AND SIND
(1150–c.1550 AND 1053–c.1592)

The mausoleum of Ghulam Shah (died 1772) at Hyderabad, Pakistan. It is one of two surviving monuments built by the Kalhora royal family in the eighteenth and nineteenth centuries.

In terms of plan, Mir Karam Ali's tomb closely resembles Ghulam Shah Kalhora's, but in contrast with the latter it still has the dome on its polygonal drum, surrounded by corner turrets. All the external walls are divided into three storeys by blind ogival niches decorated in the extradoses by blue tiles with floral motifs. On the entrance façade, with its large arch inside a rectangle bordered in white marble, the tiles are of various colours and patterns – yellow, brown and ochre – with a general effect that is somewhat trite and clearly displays the repetitiveness and decadence of the formula. These defects are even more accentuated in the nearby tomb which was apparently for the sovereign's wives. It is smaller and without domes but more vividly decorated in assorted colours and motifs.

Even poorer in aesthetic effect are the mausoleums of Mir Muhammad Khan and Mir Shahdad Khan. These are not far from each other and both have a square plan with large domes on high fenestrated drums which constitute the most successful element of the whole. Other minor tombs, reserved for the wives and children of the sovereigns, or of their ministers, have a different structure, for the most part rectangular. These tombs are decorated with niche panels lined with glazed tiles and they are covered with attractive oblong barrel vaults.

HYDERABAD AND KOT DIJI FORTRESSES

The Kalhoras also built two forts at Hyderabad: a larger one, built in 1768 by Ghulam Shah, and a smaller one not far to the south-west, built in 1772 by the same sovereign. Both were decorated with slender *kanjura* (merlons) along the top of the walls and with deep vertical embrasures in the walls. Inside, the buildings were partly dismantled by the British or used for other purposes. Another fine fort was built by the Talpurs at Kot Diji in the first decades of the nineteenth century. It rises on a high hill and is in fired brick with three gates and imposing semi-circular bastions with crenellations. It also includes a residence for the royal family of the builder, Mir Suhrab Khan, which is known as Miran Haram.

CHITORI

A large group of tombs located at Chitori (see p. 79) – some 150 km to the north-east of Karachi – are of a similar architectural type. The decoration here, however, is very different and seems to echo that found in the best stone mausoleums in the Makli Hills. Indeed, these buildings are in a fine pinkish-yellow sandstone which has been worked with great skill. Their plans vary from a square covered by a large dome on a high drum, to an open pavilion with a dome on pillars, to a domed pavilion where the spaces between the pillars are filled with beautiful slabs decorated with fine inlay work and even in some instances with open work. The external walls of all the closed mausoleums are almost always divided into two or three levels by panels with blind niches which are deeply set and decorated like windows and have a false balustrade with geometric open work on the lower part and an ogival arch above decorated with lotus buds. The inner part of the panels is generally decorated with vases of flowers with long stems heavy with buds and large leaves which interweave in spirals and spread widely to fill the decorative field. Plaited motifs, rosettes, stellate polygons

Left The funerary complex of the Kalhora and Talpur families at Hyderabad, Pakistan.

Opposite A tomb in a funerary complex from the Talpur period at Chitori. The sandstone carvings on the building have been finely worked by skilled provincial craftsmen.

and scrolls with epigraphs complete the design, the general effect of which is extremely pleasing. Much simpler is the decoration of the open-work slabs which complete the pavilion tombs – severely geometrical and continuous squares or polygons – while the entrances of the same buildings display unusual spirals or concentric circles. Many of the domes have collapsed, but the interiors clearly reveal extremely skilful brickwork in the transitional area forming 'honeycomb' *muqarnas*. They appear to display a decided Gujarati influence, which after all is also to be found in the tombs of the Makli Hills.

1. The Fatimid caliphs of Egypt were Kutama Berbers, converted to the Shiite sect by the Syrian Abu Abd Allah, who had presented the Ismailite leader Ubayd Allah to them as the long-awaited Mahdi, the descendant of the Prophet's daughter Fatima and her husband Ali. Having settled in Mahdiya (in modern Tunisia), they rapidly succeeded in conquering all of the Maghreb and then spread into Egypt (969) where they founded al-Qahira ('the Victorious One', Cairo), which they provided with magnificent buildings. Their caliphate vied in splendour with the caliphates of Baghdad and Córdoba.

2. At Ghazni the palace of Masud III is still standing, though in a very ruined state. It was quadrangular in plan and the central courtyard had four *iwan*, their size varying according to their function: the one at the entrance and the one opposite that led into the throne room were larger than the two at the sides. The private area also centres around courtyards with four *iwan* which are built of mud and unfired bricks, with fired bricks used in the facing and where greater strength was required. The decoration consists mainly of fired-brick panels with geometric patterns, inscriptions and arabesques, all painted in bright colours, while marble is used mainly in the skirting of the outside walls and the courtyard where the decoration is formed of arabesques deriving from the Tree of Life, inside a frame of arches bordered by a Kufic inscription in Persian glorifying the Ghaznavid sultans. The palace also included a hypostyle mosque, with a minaret that is no longer standing. There are also two more mosques that have not yet been explored, with the bases of two minarets that bear inscriptions naming Masud III and Bahram Shah.

3. Brown, *op. cit.*, p. 32.

4. Tower mausoleums, on a square, round or octagonal base, came into use throughout Iran from the beginning of the eleventh century onward. They are domed, though the dome is sometimes concealed by a cone- or pyramid-shaped roof. They have an imposing appearance and can reach as much as 50 m in height (Gumbad-i Qabus, Lajin, Pir-i Alamdan). The *imamzade* is a funeral monument dedicated to a Shiite saint and usually consists of a square base with a dome on top. Some of the most venerated ones are the four mausoleums near Qumm, in which the 444 descendants of Ali are supposed to be buried.

5. Shams-i Tabrizi, who probably died at Konya during an uprising, is also buried at Konya. He was the spiritual master (*pir*) of the famous mystic Jalal al-Din Rumi (died 1273); Nabi Khan, *op. cit.*, p. 204.

6. Nabi Khan, *Uchchh: History and Architecture*, Islamabad, 1980, p. 59.

7. Mubarak Khan was the adoptive son of the sultan Nizam al-Din and had taken the royal name of the Darya Khans. Going by an inscription over the southern entrance to his tomb, it seems that it was completed in 1519 by his son Ahmed. A.H. Dani, *Thatta: Islamic Architecture*, Islamabad 1982, pp. 43-8, pls. 11-13.

8. The last of the Tarkhan sovereigns, Mirza Jani Beg was defeated and subdued by Abdur Rahim Khan-i Khanan, Akbar's famous general. He died in 1601, as is attested by an inscription on the mosque in his funerary enclosure. Dani, *op. cit.*, pp. 173-4, pls. 52-4.

9. It contains a tomb dated AH 1059 (AD 1649). Dani, *op. cit.*, pp. 128-9, pls. 28-9.

10. K. Khan Mumtaz, *Architecture in Pakistan*, Singapore 1985, p. 102.

11. *Ibid.*, p. 103.

The Punjab and Sind
(1150–c.1550 and 1053–c.1592)

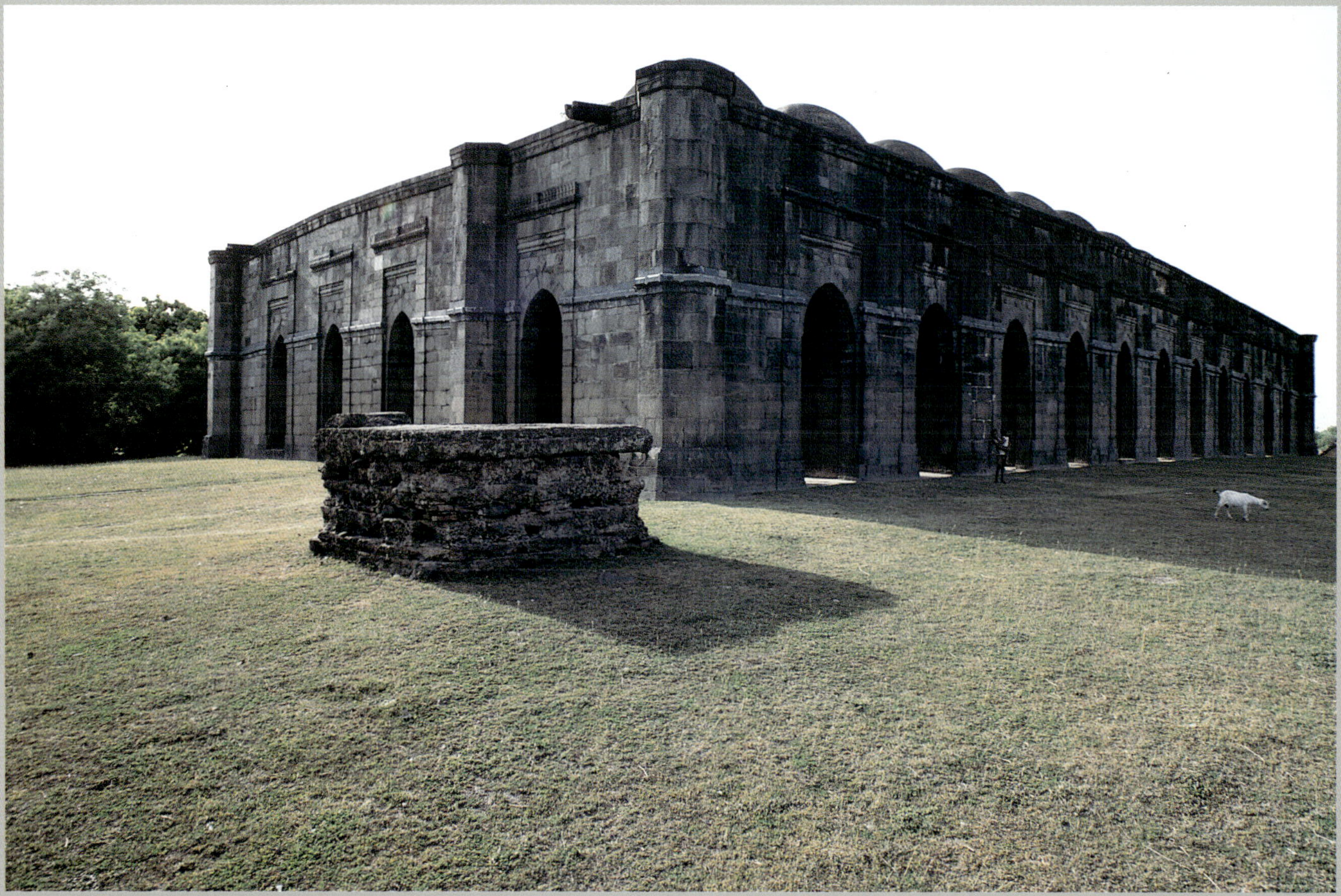

Bengal (c.1300–c.1550)

7

With its façade of eleven entrances, spacious courtyard, two buttresses and four corner towers, the Bara Sona Mosque is the largest building in Gaur.

Bengal was conquered early on by the sultanate of Delhi (c.1204), and became independent after the death of Balban in 1287. It was some decades, however, before Bengal recognized the nominal sovereignty of the Tughluqs. Since its damp climate and frequent floods did not appeal to the majority of Arabs, Turks and Persians (who came from dry countries), invasions were limited; eventually, converted Hindus came to constitute the Muslim aristocracy. The first religious buildings were constructed as early as the thirteenth century, but more than a century passed before it was possible to identify a sufficiently characteristic style. Once developed, this style lasted for about two-and-a-half centuries.

The principal construction material found on the vast Bengal flood plain was brick. The only stone available was black basalt from the hills of Rajmahal in the Malda district. Very rarely granite and sandstone were imported from Bihar. Stone was therefore used principally for the pillars that supported arches or domes and to dress external walls; it was often cut into slabs and skilfully decorated. Walls, held together with finest lime, were often dressed with terracotta worked in relief with patterns inspired by the exotic flora of the jungle that was typical of this region. Later, but without much imagination, Turco-Persian majolica was also used.

For climatic reasons, the line of the Bengali roof was modelled on the indigenous bamboo cabin that was always curved with two (*do chala*) or four slopes (*char chala*). For the same reasons, Bengali mosques were built as enclosed spaces, without *sahn* (apart from a notable exception) and with rather narrow entrances, designed to prevent rain coming in. Vaults and domes were massive, the latter without drums, and were supported by arches or spherical triangles that were emphasized with fancy brickwork.

Although various monuments are to be found in different parts of the province, the majority of the buildings are grouped in the district of Malda, which was the strategic centre of the region because of its situation at the confluence of two rivers, the Ganges and the Mahanadi. The capitals of the sultanate were Gaur and Pandua, the first from 1211 to 1354 and again from 1442 to 1576; the second in the interval between 1354 and 1442. Both were large cities, the one measuring 12 km north to south and about 2 km east to west; the other 10 x 1.5 km. Both were surrounded by high walls and deep ditches connected to the Bhagirathi and Mahanadi rivers.

Tribeni

Between Gaur and Pandua are to be found the ruins of Malda and Lakhnauti, the last Hindu capital and the first Muslim capital. Here in the nearby village of Tribeni (perhaps the site of the first Islamic outpost in Bengal) are the most ancient ruins of the region. This is because those at Gaur are lost, apart from the walls and the winding roads built by Ghiyas al-Din Iwaz Husain (1211–27), first sultan of Bengal. There is a mosque and a tomb at Tribeni. In the former there is still an Arab inscription with a record of the year 1298, but the mosque itself was rebuilt at the beginning of the sixteenth century, even although the original rectangular plan with two bays divided into ten spans, covered with domes and today for the most part collapsed, was probably not altered. The inscription records the building as a *madrasa*, as too was the tomb: it would seem that in the early days of the Islamic conquest much importance was placed on conversions and therefore all buildings were used to diffuse the doctrine.

In the tomb, dedicated to Zafar Khan Ghazi, conqueror of southern Bengal, there remains a *mihrab* – Saljuq in conception, but Hindu-Bengali in detail – which is probably even older. The entire building was built with the remains of a basalt Krishna temple with brick walls and pointed arches which, if they are original, are the oldest of this kind in Bengal. It is the oldest existing example of a mausoleum in eastern India. The plan comprises two communicating rooms, which perhaps reflects the structure of the Hindu temple from which the building is derived, with its large open hall (*mandapa*) and a shrine (*garbhagriha*).[1] In Deccan, too, there are twin-roomed tombs, but it is difficult to identify the origin of this type with certainty.[2]

Chota Pandua: Bari Mosque

Not far from Tribeni is a small village also called Pandua, or rather Chota (Little) Pandua, where there are the ruins of a huge mosque with walls and arches of brick with basalt pillars that certainly came from a dismantled Hindu temple. These pillars divide the hall into three bays parallel to the *qibla* wall and 63 spans; it was once covered by the same number of small domes on brick pendentives. In the central bay, less ruined than the others, a beautiful stone *minbar* still survives alongside the central *mihrab*. This domed structure in carved basalt functioned as a prototype for the *minbar* in the Adina Mosque at Pandua. In the north-western corner of the prayer hall stands a solid raised platform (*takht*), which faces the *qibla* wall. Surrounded by carved stone screens, it is equipped with small *mihrab*. This is the oldest existing example of a

Above A *minbar* in the Adina Mosque at Pandua. The dome over this area of the mosque has since collapsed, leaving it open to the sky.

Opposite The exterior of the Adina Mosque at Pandua. Begun in 1364 by Sikandar, the enormous building could hold thousands of worshippers.

takht in Bengal, but this feature, the function of which is still the subject of discussion among scholars, would later became common in the region in mosques with many bays.

Near this ruin is a victory tower erected, according to legend, by a Muslim saint, Shah Suri al-Din, to commemorate his conquest over the Raja of Pandua around 1340. It has been restored several times and is of some architectural value. Nevertheless, although some 40 m high, it is somewhat out of proportion because of its excessive width. The decoration of its façades, divided according to various floors, was clearly inspired by that of the much more famous Qutb Minar erected some 150 years earlier (see p. 23); as well as a victory tower, it must have functioned as both a minaret and an observation tower.

Pandua: Adina Mosque

The second phase of Bengal art began with the sultan Shams al-Din Ilias (1345–57), whose son Sikandar (1358–89) founded Pandua, where in 1364 he started the construction of the great Adina Mosque that was able to hold thousands of the faithful. Now the area is almost totally deserted and the mosque itself is largely destroyed. Of grandiose proportions, measuring 154.5 x 87 m, it was built on orthodox lines, in as much as the courtyard (some 130 x 45 m) is contained between the usual pillared bays: five arches deep on the west, where the shrine was, and three on the other side, with a total of 260 pillars. The entire complex is surrounded by a wall that makes the external dimensions almost the same as those of the eighth-century Great Mosque of Damascus, to which Adina has been likened. The interior of the courtyard is made up of a windbreak of 88 arches forming a continuous façade which is surmounted with a parapet, beyond which are to be seen the 306 domes of the roof. The main entrance of the mosque is made up of three arches that open on the south-eastern corner, an unusual position which is out of balance with the bulk of the sanctuary to the west.

Another three small entrances are to be found in the north-western wall, two of which lead to a higher floor known as the *badshah-ka-takht*, a private chapel for the king and the ladies of his house. This area and the vast central transept are the most successful parts of the mosque. The upper part of the building is supported by a series of arches mounted on short, powerful pillars with square plinths and weighty block capitals, which although sharing some similarities with other Bengali buildings, are unique and not at all in keeping with the architecture of the rest of India. The columns that support the hall of the *badshah-ka-takht* are of more normal proportions, with graceful tapered shafts and capitals in the shape of open lotus flowers, which derive from Hindu structures. The central bay of the sanctuary is a rectangular hall of approximately 24 x 12 m and is almost 18 m high from the ground to the line where its enormous, slightly pointed and now ruined vault begins. This central bay runs east–west and is therefore perpendicular to the five bays that extend from its sides. The façade must have been very imposing, with five large pointed arches on each side of the great central arch. Above the parapet there were stairways up which the *muezzin* could reach a high platform. On the rear wall of the prayer hall there is a beautiful central *mihrab*, as well as a smaller, additional one and a *minbar* in stone. A line of other *mihrab* runs along the whole western wall and upper level of the mosque. The 32 *mihrab*, and the *minbar* below, are truly magnificent, rigorously Islamic in their general conception, but Hindu in almost all the details: small scalloped columns, plinths in the shape of lotus flowers, corbels, trilobate arches each cuspidated with a vase of flowers, volutes representing leaves, rhomboid lozenges, friezes of lotus petals and so on. The main *mihrab* is a niche with a trilobate arch placed within a double rectangular frame decorated with arabesques and calligraphy. Both the shape and the ornamentation display their descent from the ancient niches containing images of the Buddha or Hindu gods. The vase of flowers at the apex of the arch is nothing less than a barely disguised *kirtimukha* (a type of ornamental mask), while the *hamsa* motifs usually placed at the opening of the arch have been transformed into conventional representations of leaves. The interior of the niche is divided into panels containing the Islamic motif of the 'hanging lamp', which is very common in Bengal.[3] Even in its grandiose vastness, the Adina Mosque is well proportioned with a dignified appearance which is both noble and austere.

Almost all the upper part of the building – including the arches and the domes – was of brick, while much of the base of the façade was of finely worked basalt taken from the earlier Hindu building at Lakhnauti or other areas nearby. Proof of this is to be found in the many stones embedded in the walls of the mosque and even in the *minbar* and the walls of the *badshah-ka-takht* that display carved figures. It seems also that the 300 pillars that divide the bays were recycled from Hindu buildings. The arch adopted for the mosque, and further utilized, with variations, in other mosques, is the so-called 'drop' arch with the centre at the level of the impost and a span greater than its radius. The arched openings are covered by small domes topped with a particular type of pendentive, made of bricks laid in diagonal courses so that their corners protrude. This technique had also been used in some buildings in Delhi and in the brick tombs of Multan. If it is difficult to believe that the Adina Mosque was the only important building erected during the fourteenth century in Pandua, nothing else remains to suggest otherwise.

Gaur

At Gaur the mosque and the tomb of Akhi Suraj al-Din survives from this period, although they have been much altered through restoration. The Kotwali Darwaza is a gate built at the southern entrance to Gaur which, although seriously ruined, displays similarities with the creations of Firuz Shah Tughluq: for example, the protruding turrets alongside the arches that resemble buttresses and taper towards the top are like those of the imperial capital. Today the Kotwali Darwaza marks the border between western Bengal and the Rajshahi district of Bangladesh. To the south is the suburb known as Chota Sona which includes the Chota Sona Mosque, the Darashari Mosque and other buildings. The area to the north, still called Gaur, is in the district of Malda, belonging to India.

A more advanced phase in Bengali architecture began in about 1400. This prevailed during the fifteenth century and the first half of the sixteenth and was greatly conditioned by the climate and the nature of the land. As it had been established that a curved surface was the most efficient in coping with the excess of water during the rainy season, a form of curved roof adapted from the local bamboo structures was adopted. This roof quickly became a standard for all buildings, irrespective of the materials used.

Pandua: Eklakhi mausoleum

An early example of this new regional style is a Pandua mausoleum known as the tomb of Eklakhi, which is thought to have belonged to Sultan Jalal al-Din Muhammad Shah (1414–32), and therefore dates from about 1425. About eight metres high and built entirely in brick, it consists of an almost square base (25 x 23 m) and is surmounted by a beautiful hemispheric dome. Turrets with octagonal bases dominate each corner, while the bulk of the building is finished with a triple curved cornice decorated with a frieze of small arches, an open-work border and some glazed tiles, used here for the first time in Bengal. All four façades

BENGAL (c.1300–c.1550)

Opposite The interior of the Adina Mosque at Pandua. The 300 pillars dividing the bays were taken from Hindu buildings.

Below The Eklakhi mausoleum (c.1425) at Pandua exemplifies a new phase in Bengali architecture that began around 1400. It is the first building in the region to have the curved cornice derived from local bamboo and hay structures.

are crossed horizontally with a stringcourse that gives the appearance of there being two floors: below there are ornamental relief brickwork panels while above there are blind niches in the shape of windows with the same exuberant decoration as the principal *mihrab* of the Adina Mosque, carved in hornblende. At the centre of each side is an aperture containing a stone portal of Hindu derivation, but with an arch above the architrave that is reminiscent of the Firuzian buildings of Delhi. The tomb chamber in the interior is an octagonal room more than 15 m wide, without windows; light enters only via the doors. This building, the first to display the curved cornice inherited from the bamboo and hay buildings, became the prototype of most of the Bengali Islamic architecture that was to follow.

GAUR: CHIKA BUILDING

An interesting building which is more or less of the same period as the mausoleum of Eklakhi is the so-called Chika Building. Some think it is a mosque, while others take it to be a prison or administrative offices (if so, it would be one of the few surviving administrative buildings). It seems to have been included in a quadrangle which also contained the Gumti Darwaza. All that is left of it now are the foundations of a pillared structure on the southern side and the cubic main part of the building with bastions at the corners and the characteristic domed roof without a drum. There are few openings in the walls: four on what must have been the façade and one in the centre of each of the other three sides.

GAUR: DAKHIL DARWAZA

Another splendid brick building was erected at Gaur about 40 years later (c.1465) at the time of Rukn al-Din Barbak (1459–74), according to some scholars; according to others, it dates instead from the first decades of the sixteenth century when the Husain Shahi ruled. This was the Dakhil Darwaza (see p. 86), the main northern entrance to the citadel, built as a triumphal arch or reception gate (Salami Darwaza). It is at once imposing and harmonious, flanked by two powerful towers five storeys high, tapered and measuring some 18.5 m in width at the front façade and almost 40 m at the rear. It is 18.5 m high, with an archway at the centre flanked by grandiose watchtowers. The true entrance opens between two large protruding buttresses connected with a large arch. Inside is a huge and deep arcade which forms a sort of vaulted central passage with thick walls, each with four doors. The façade – apart from the alternation of turrets and ramparts – was enlivened with a number of terracotta ornaments, mostly rosettes, hanging lamps, flaming suns, relief borders, blind niches in frames and pointed and multi-pointed arches together with other, well-distributed designs.

In the following decades numerous mosques and tombs were built, the latter following the example provided by Eklakhi's mausoleum. But the Adina Mosque did not serve as a prototype; the majority of mosques were built without the traditional courtyard because of the long rainy season in the region that tended to favour the covered and closed hall. The traditional form is represented by a rectangular plan, mostly oblong, with an open façade with a series of pointed arches that number sometimes as many as ten or twelve and two or three on the minor sides, with protruding towers at the corners. The interiors are divided by aisles supported by brick pillars, or stone if they come from a pre-existing Hindu building. The roofs are made up of small hemispheric domes whose circular bases rest on angular pendentives of brick, forming a sort of stalactite vault. On the western wall various *mihrab* with arched niches are aligned and decorated with very elegant carvings and designs. The *mihrab* facing the main entrance is the most important and is therefore the most elaborately decorated. The decoration of the exterior of the entrance comprises rectangular panels often enclosing blind niches and decorated with filigree designs which are repeated around the entrances and the gables. On the high edge of the walls run curved cornices, and the corner turrets are topped with small pointed domes similar to the Firuzian domes of Delhi.

BAGERHAT: SATH GUMBAD MOSQUE

A building of this type which dates from *c*.1440 is the Sath Gumbad Mosque – The

Above The Dakhil Darwaza (*c*.1465) at Gaur. This was the main northern entrance to the citadel, built as a triumphal arch or reception gate.

Opposite The richly decorated exterior of the Tantipara (Weavers' Quarter) Mosque (*c*.1475) at Gaur. The mosque takes its name from the area of the town in which it is built.

Mosque of Sixty Domes, although there are 77 in reality – which is to be found at Bagerhat, far south of Gaur, currently in Bangladesh. Its establishment is attributed to Khan Jahan Ali, governor of Bagerhat in that period, who died in 1459 according to the inscription on his tomb, erected a short distance from the mosque and displaying Tughluq-Lodi characteristics. The mosque is the largest in Bengal, measuring over 50 x 35 m. Its façade contains eleven entrances with pointed arches while each of the sides contains seven entrances. The corners are finished with four circular towers, two storeys high, massive and tapered towards the top where they are surmounted by small domes. On the roof rise numerous hemispheric domes that are interrupted in the middle by the four-sloped *char chala* roof. The interior is divided by means of stone and brick pillars into seven longitudinal bays and eleven deep spans which correspond to the same number of lightly decorated *mihrab* in the far walls. The general aspect is similar to Adina, while the countless small domes supported by arched bays, like the corner towers, recall the Khirki and Kalan Tughluq mosques built in Delhi over 60 years earlier and certainly very influential in Bengali architecture. The use of multiple vaults to cover the central part of a prayer hall would later influence the Darashari Mosque at Gaur.

Gaur: Tantipara Mosque

Another similarly ancient mosque is Tantipara, built at Gaur in about 1475. Its name means Weavers' Quarter and appears to have been adopted precisely because the mosque was built in that area of the town. According to a historic source, the name used locally was Umar Qazi, but the current name was always preferred. The Tantipara Mosque has a rectangular plan, measuring externally 25 x 15 m. Low octagonal towers close each corner while five archways open in the façade, which is set off with a double-curved cornice. Another curved edge divides the exterior façades into two: these are decorated with blind windows filled with small multifoil arches and a luxuriant floral motif in terracotta. Similar motifs, yet more exuberant, are repeated in the gables of the entrances, the frames for the doors and the corner towers; the general effect is perhaps too rich, but nevertheless rather pleasing. The prayer hall is divided internally into two bays by means of stone-faceted pillars on square pedestals which form ten spans, covered by domes which have now disappeared. The *mihrab* are delicately ornamented in the same style as the exterior façades and are among the most beautiful in Bengal. There is a small *takht* in the northern corner of the *qibla* wall.

For about 50 years after the construction of the Tantipara Mosque, various mosques of a similar type were built in quick succession. Many of them are found in Gaur, for example the Daraz Bari of 1480, the Gunmant of around 1484 (see p. 90), the Chota Sona dating from around.1510 and the Bara Sona of 1526. Another mosque from 1523 is to be found at Bagha, in the district of Rajshahi. Examples of mosques of a different type are the Chamkatti Mosque of around 1475, the Nattan Mosque of 1480 and the so-called Qadam Rasul Mosque dating from 1530 (see p. 91).

Gaur: Bara Sona

Some mosques are of considerable proportions, for example the Bara Sona (Great Mosque of Gold; see p. 80), the largest building in Gaur. Its façade has eleven entrances, four corner towers and two buttresses in addition to a spacious courtyard almost 70 m in diameter. The doors were once framed in stone and decorated with a mosaic of glazed coloured tiles in floral patterns. Various green, blue, orange, yellow and white fragments have been found at the foot of each door. The true prayer hall, which is divided into three bays parallel to the *qibla* wall and supported by pillars of stone, is preceeded by a 50 m verandah that is perhaps the most beautiful part of the interior, with a series of pointed arches that are stacked like the wings of a theatre. In three of the spans of the sanctuary there are women's galleries, accessible by means of a series of steps on the north side. The domes of the prayer hall, originally 33 in number, have collapsed, while those of the corridor still exist. Given the mosque's name, its domes must have been decorated in gilt work that presumably softened the darkness of the interior. In each of the 11 spans there is a *mihrab* on the western side, whose forms and ornament are not, however, of great significance.

Pandua: Qutb Shahi

A mosque that is very similar in its construction is the Qutb Shahi, built in 1582 by Makhdum Shaikh in honour of Nur Qutb Alam. It has a fine façade with five portals surmounted by a triple cornice, and corner turrets which are ornamented with borders in relief. The prayer hall, with two aisles parallel to the *qibla* wall, still has the fine pillars and a stone *minbar* with the characteristic canopy. The corner arches bear traces of the spherical triangles for the domes, which were built with a brick facing. On the *mihrab* wall, besides the elegant multifoil niche, large rosettes formed of lotus blossoms catch the eye.

Gaur: Daraz Bari Mosque

The Daraz Bari Masjid (mosque of the 'teaching hall', or rather of the *madrasa* that was once apparently attached to the mosque) is another large building in brick but with stone pillars. Its roof and its corner towers have collapsed; of the

Above The Tantipara Mosque at Gaur. Detail of the floral motif terracotta decorations on the *mihrab*.

Top A view of the prayer hall in the Tantipara Mosque at Gaur, showing the remains of the faceted stone pillars.

subject, although carved in marble, is found in the Sidi Sayyid Mosque (see p. 123) at Ahmedabad in Gujarat, which is more or less of the same period. Although it is hard to imagine contact between the designers of the two buildings, this fact offers material for study and speculation.

GAUR: GUNMANT MOSQUE

Of a similar aspect, but without the verandah, is the Gunmant Mosque (see p. 90), an oblong building, with hexagonal towers at the exterior corners and minarets on pillars flanking the central entrance. The stone finishing was stripped away in 1912, and used for the restoration of the Chota Sona Mosque (see below). The prayer hall, in imitation of the Adina Mosque, is divided into three sections, of which the central one is covered with a ribbed vault supported by massive, octagonal stone pillars on square pediments. The lateral wings are divided longitudinally in three sections by means of stone pillars and are each covered by twelve hemispheric domes. It seems that the walls and the bases of the arches were once finished in blue and white glazed tiles. An arched window helps illuminate the interior of the brick vault, and render more visible the terracotta decoration.

GAUR: CHOTA SONA

The Chota Sona (Small Golden Mosque) was so-called by local people, who compared it with the Bara Sona's ornamental gilt work. Very little of this decoration remained when Cunningham saw it at the beginning of the twentieth century.[4] The mosque is of the usual oblong type with octagonal towers at the corners and a richly decorated stone façade. Each of the five entrances on the façade has a sharp multi-pointed arch enclosed in rectangular borders profusely decorated with rosettes and vegetal and epigraphic motifs. The same decoration recurs on the sides which each contain three entrances. On the towers are chain and bell motifs derived from examples in terracotta. A triple, gently curved cornice finishes the walls, while the roof is covered with 12 small hemispheric domes and three *char chala* in the centre. Inside, these last are

latter there remain only the pediments at the corners of the prayer hall and the front-facing verandah to the east. In the eastern façade are seven arched entrances, of which the central one is wider than the others. The hall is divided into three sections – a central nave and two aisles – divided in their turn into three further aisles by means of two rows of stone pillars which support nine domes on each wing. Over the central nave there must have been a barrel vault along the lines of that of Adina, or perhaps the Bengali vault, already noted in the Sath Gumbad Mosque. On the verandah there must have been domes, of which the central one was probably again in the *char chala* style. In the north-west corner of the sanctuary there was a women's gallery accessible by steps from the exterior. On the western wall there are nine multi-cuspidated *mihrab* in heavily decorated brick. The mosque makes use of a great variety of ornamental motifs executed in terracotta, among which is an unusual floral design representing a parasitic climbing plant that comes out of the trunk of a palm tree and fills all the available space. This same

Above The Qutb Shahi Mosque at Pandua, built in 1582 by Makhdum Shaikh in honour of Nur Qutb Alam. It has the curved cornice characteristic of the region.

Top left The corridor alongside the prayer hall inside the Bara Sona Mosque at Gaur. While the domes over the prayer hall have fallen in, those over the corridor survive.

Left The Gunmant Mosque at Gaur. The original stone finishing was stripped away and used for the restoration of the Chota Sona Mosque in 1912.

Opposite The building bearing the misnomer Qadam Rasul Mosque at Gaur, built by Sultan Nusrat Shah in 1531, shows early signs of the decline of the Bengali regional style.

decorated with a motif taken from woven bamboo. The hall is divided into three bays parallel to the *qibla* and in five spans supported by stone pillars; again here in the north-west corner is a special entrance to the women's gallery which leads to the second floor on stone supports. There are five *mihrab* on the *qibla* wall and a supplementary one in the gallery above. Their decoration with stone slabs has for the most part been removed, but the central *mihrab* does retain traces of glazed tiles.

GAUR: QADAM RASUL AND JHANJHANIYA

The so-called mosque of Qadam Rasul (the name of which recalls the footprints of the Prophet which, according to legend, are conserved in its interior) demonstrates the first signs of the decline of this style. Built by Sultan Nusrat Shah and dating from 1531, it consists of a square hall bordered on three sides by a verandah which on the eastern side is much decorated and is opened by three arches resting on short and massive stone pillars. At the exterior corners are octagonal towers profusely decorated with stylized motifs and capped with pinnacles. The verandah, which permits entrance to the hall through three entrances on the northern, southern and eastern sides, is covered by barrel vaults, while the central hall – closed at the west and without *mihrab* because this structure is not, in fact, a mosque – is domed. In the centre is a small pedestal in black stone which carries a stone reproduction of the Prophet's footprint. The exterior decoration, based on the division of the façade into two equal parts, consists of rows of panels with the repeated motif of a hanging lamp, which renders the whole effect flat and lacking in character.[5] In the same area is the tomb of Fath Khan, though this dates from the late seventeenth century and was built by one of Aurangzeb's generals.

Of particular interest for its decoration is the Jhanjhaniya Mosque, a six-domed building dated 1535 and built by Bibi Malti. The interior is divided into two aisles of three bays, each corresponding with the three entrances.

GAUR: NATTAN MOSQUE

The Nattan (known locally as Lattan) Mosque was erected in honour of the king's favourite dancer, the famous Nattu. Another legend has it that it was built by the dancer herself with money earned by the benevolence of the sovereign. Cunningham dated it to 1475–80; more recently, Dani placed it at the beginning of the sixteenth century because of the great number of glazed tiles that adorn both the interior and the exterior. Such tiles came into fashion in the more mature phase of Bengali art. The mosque is lacking, however, in true creativity. Like the Chamkatti it consists of a square room of little more than 11 m with a corridor to the east and octagonal towers at the corners. The main entrance is also to the east, with three sharp arched entrances alternated with deep vertical panels which are superimposed in three rows carrying pointed-arch niches on decorated pillars. The final cornice is gracefully curved and above it the three domes of the verandah stand out; the central dome is of the usual *char chala* type. Much in evidence is the largest dome, which covers the prayer hall and rests on a low tambour decorated with blind merlons. The corner towers are also elegantly decorated with mouldings divided into three sections with vertical scalloping. Similar scalloping is to be found on the western wall at the sides of the *mihrab*'s overhang. Virtually nothing remains of the polychromatic tile coverings (green, yellow, blue and white) which, in the original design, covered both internal and external walls.

GAUR: FIRUZ MINAR

It seems the pretentious Firuz Minar (see p. 92) was built by the Abyssinian Saif al-Din Firuz in 1488, the period in which African tyrants ruled the country (1487–93).[6] This is a victory tower five storeys high – approximately 28 m – with the base portions approximately 6 m in diameter and terminating, originally, with an open, domed room which today has disappeared but is evidenced in Creighton's drawings of 1817.[7] Today the tower rises from an embankment which on the west side has a series of steps leading to the entrance. Perhaps originally there was a dodecagonal plinth which is now lost. From the base of the door the tower rises for three storeys in a polygonal shape, each floor decorated with chain motifs. There then follow two circular floors which diminish in diameter and are adorned with three parallel borders in relief. A protruding stone awning separates the two sections of the tower, and the polygonal floors are also divided by stone borders that protrude from the surface of the brick. Each floor has a door to the west, and an internal spiral staircase of 73 steps leads from the base to the top of the tower. The glazed tiles painted in white and blue that contributed to the ornament and the tower's name have all but disappeared.

Other buildings

During the Mughal and post-Mughal periods Bengali architecture, although adapting to suit imperial directives, maintained its own regional identity that is clearly shown in many monuments in its succession of capital cities: Rajmahal, Dhaka, Murshidabad and Calcutta. Nevertheless, in contrast with the pre-Mughal buildings, they display much less invention and poorer forms, deficiencies that were not made up for with additional ornament.

Among the first Mughal buildings is the Kusumba Mosque (1558–9), with two naves covered by six domes and the square domed tomb in Burdwan belonging to Pir Bahran (1562–3); both have the typical curved cornice.

A few years after the conquest by Akbar, the Afghan rulers of Bengal, together with some Mughal turncoats, returned to power. In 1581 Ma'sum Khan Kabuli assumed the title of sultan, as can be seen on an inscription in the mosque at Chatmohar (Pandua). A year later two mosques were built – the Qutb Shahi (see p. 89) at Pandua and the Kherua at Sherpur (Bogra district). The first mosque, in honour of the saint Nur Qutb Alam, is a pre-Mughal structure with two naves and a stone façade. The second mosque was built by the Afghan Murad Khan Qaqshal and was in bricks with one nave. Nevertheless the plan is not traditional, displaying many similarities with the mosque of Habash Khan at Rohtas.[8]

Rajmahal: *jami masjid*

Rajmahal (today in the state of Bihar) was the capital of Bengal between 1595 and 1606 under the Mughal rule of Raja Man Singh, and again between 1639 and 1659 when Shah Shuja, son of Shah Jahan, governed the region. The grandiose *jami masjid*, now much ruined, dates from the first Mughal period and in its design forms a link between the Mughal imperial style and the Bengali style. Its eastern façade, opened by seven large pointed arches, of which the central one is a high *pishtaq* covered by a barrel vault, is similar to that of the Adina Mosque at Pandua and the *jami masjid* at old Malda. A drawing of 1810 shows that the ornament of the upper façade, now totally destroyed, was similar to that of Akbar's Great Mosque at Fatehpur Sikri, built in about 1570. Fluted corner turrets close the corners of the building and frame the main entrance, as in the *jami masjid* at Malda. For the first time on the entire structure *kanjura* appear, an element that had previously been used in other areas of Islamic India. The interior has a long central zone covered with a barrel vault, flanked by two wings divided into the same number of bays by massive brick pillars; the resulting spans are domed, following an arrangement already well established in Bengali tradition. Only the most northern and southern extremities of the spans display an innovation: they are raised over two floors, each containing four individual rooms. Although no precedents of this kind exist in Bengal, a similar arrangement is found in the Great Mosque at Fatehpur Sikri.

Malda: *jami masjid*

The *jami masjid* at Malda (1595–96) suggests in its central vaulted zone the style of the Adina and Gunmant mosques. Nevertheless the interior spaces are closer to examples in northern India, as well as the stucco decoration of the façade, which is like that of the Kachpura Mosque of Humayun at Agra.

On a hill overlooking the *qibla* façade of the mosque is another interesting Mughal structure, the Nim Serai Minar, which resembles the Hiran Minar at Fatehpur Sikri (see p. 221) with the same decoration imitating elephant tusks. The building lies at the confluence of two rivers and suggests a watch tower or a Kos Minar, being midway (the name means 'half') between Gaur and Pandua.[9]

Rajmahal: Sanji Dalan

The Sanji Dalan, built by Shah Shuja (1639–59), belongs to Rajmahal's second Mughal period and is today for the most part ruined and partially occupied by government offices. Its rectangular structure, which dominates the Ganges from above, is divided internally into three spaces of which the central one has a large cuspidated opening, rests on six black basalt pillars and is covered by a curved vault. The lateral spaces have similar archways, but of stucco. The building's function is unknown, and the suggestion that it was part of the harem seems improbable because the areas facing the river are without *jali*.

Dhaka: Lalbagh Fort

The design of this building is found again in the *diwan-i khass* of the Lalbagh Fort at Dhaka, where the capital was moved in 1608 for logistic purposes and where it remained until Shah Shuja returned to make Rajmahal the seat of the governor in 1639. In 1659 Dhaka resumed its role as capital, and maintained it until 1717, when Murshidabad officially became the new administrative centre of the region. One of the most interesting secular buildings in the city is the Lalbagh Fort, built in the late seventeenth century by two successive Mughal governors. It seems the fort was never completed and what remains today – a mosque, a tomb, a reception hall, a bath, a pool and an entrance – constitutes just a fragment of the original plan. A two-storey building with an area to the north, which resembled the Sanji Dalan of Rajmahal, is thought to have been a *diwan-i khass*. On the western side is a small building thought to be a *hammam* (Turkish bath), while the splendid three-storey entrance on the southern side of the fort is purely Mughal in tradition and seems to have been the main entrance to the unfinished citadel. The mosque, traditionally held to date from the foundation of the citadel, carries an inscription that dates it to 1649. Designed according to a typical Bengali model of the Mughal period, it presents a rectangular structure divided internally into three spans covered by fluted domes of which the central one is larger and less bulbous than the others. The shape of the domes seems to be owed to a restoration of 1770. Turrets with characteristic horizontal ribs mark the four corners. The entrance façade is decorated with small rectangular niches which surround the three pointed-arch entrances. Similar decoration was seen previously in the Jhanjhaniya Mosque at Gaur of 1535 and also became common at Rajmahal (for example in the so-called Akbari Mosque attached to Shah Shuja's palace). The internal walls of the Lalbagh Mosque are decorated with horizontal panels that repeat the pattern on the façade and even the three *mihrab* are adorned with similar stucco faceting.

In an unusual position, between the mosque and the *diwan-i khass*, stands the tomb of Bibi Pari, the favourite sister of the Mughal governor Shaista Khan, who built it in the late seventeenth century in imitation of that built some decades earlier at Gaur by Shah Shuja for his spiritual leader, Nimat Allah. Internally, both buildings repeat the planimetric arrangement of the mausoleum of Itimad al-Daula at Agra (1622), with a square central room surrounded by corridors, off which are eight secondary spaces. The ceilings of Bibi Pari's tomb are not vaulted internally but have Hindu-type coverings with recessed corbels which were also used in Mughal buildings, such as in the Shish Mahall at Rohtasgarh, in Bihar. From the outside, the tomb appears as a massive flat and square structure with a small central dome – once gilded – and corner turrets which push beyond the level of the roof. These elements have fluted coverings but do not succeed in lending the building a vertical thrust. Each façade has three openings in the shape of a slightly lowered pointed arch: the central arch is flanked by slender fluted pillars which sprout from foliated bases, a detail that indicates the tomb was built more recently than the mosque.

Murshidabad: Katra and Muni Begum mosques

In 1717 the dynamic and powerful governor Murshid Quli Khan transferred the region's capital to a city that he called Murshidabad. As early as 1724 or 1725 he

The Firuz Minar, a rather pompous five-storey victory tower, was built in 1488 by the Abyssinian ruler Saif al-Din Firuz.

had a congregational mosque built there, the Katra Mosque, which also contained his tomb, so that it is thought that he conceived of it as his own commemorative monument. The large mosque rests on a high square plinth and is surrounded on four sides by a row of two-storey domed cells which, according to some scholars, must have contained a market, while according to travellers and chroniclers of the eighteenth and nineteenth centuries it was a *madrasa* and a Koranic school. The prayer hall reproduces the characteristic plan of Bengali mosques with five spans divided by lateral arches, each containing three *mihrab*. Outside, the usual faceted turrets finish the corners, while the eastern façade of the mosque, with five low openings with full-centred and multi-lobed arches, is decorated with rows of rectangular panels like those of the Jhanjhaniya Mosque at Gaur. Three slightly pointed domes surmount the roof but the central one has now collapsed. The same fate has befallen two of the four heavy octagonal minarets that towered over the mosque from the corners of the cloister, perhaps in imitation of those of the Badshahi Mosque at Lahore, built by Aurangzeb in 1674.

Another large mosque was built at Murshidabad in 1767 by Muni Begum, the influential wife of the nawab Mir Jafar. This differs slightly from the traditional plan with two series of *char chala* domes at the extremities of the prayer hall rather than in the central area. In this area there are five fine domes which increase in height towards the centre. The mosque is flanked by two high, slender minarets with graceful balconies which support domed terminals. The eastern façade – opened by seven arched, multi-lobed entrances that increase in height towards the centre and have upper parts that are shell shaped – is heavily decorated with floral motifs, scrolls, arabesques and small stucco niches, as well as slender, tapered columns. The interior of the building is also profusely decorated with stuccoes which echo the ornament on the façade and are repeated on the *mihrab*.

Many other mosques in Murshidabad present similar façades, although in much reduced proportions and with less ornament. With the passing of time the domes acquire an evermore bulbous shape and sprout from a series of lotus petals which emphasize the fluting of the shells above.

Among the tombs is the picturesque mausoleum of Khwaja Anwar-i Shahid, built in the late seventeenth century at Burdwan (western Bengal) by Aurangzeb's nephew, Azim al-Shan, the governor of Bengal. Khwaja Anwar, a valiant emir of the governor, had met his death in an ambush, for which the governor wished to dedicate him a sumptuous funeral monument. The tomb stands at the northern end of a huge complex, which is entered on the southern side through a wide gateway, flanked by a mosque to the west and a *madrasa* to the east. The mausoleum is unique in India, on account of both the originality of its ground plan and its general appearance. It is composed of a square, central domed hall with two lower rectangular rooms on the east and west sides and with *do chala* roofs reminiscent of the ones on the contemporary tomb of Fath Khan at Gaur. The façade, which is contained between slender domed towers, is enlivened by blind ogival niches, portals with polylobate arches and deep sunken panels which are all carved in stucco. The interior is also marked by niches of varying depth within scalloped arches. Similar stucco decoration is found in the mosque annexed to the tomb of Hajji Khwaja Shahbaz, a rich merchant from Dhaka, who had it built some decades earlier, in 1679, and so it probably served as a prototype for the Burdwan tomb. The resemblance between the two buildings is accentuated by the fact that, in the southern part of the mosque of Shahbaz, there was a lower rectangular room with a *do chala* roof, though it has now fallen in.

In conclusion, the Islamic architecture of Bengal, although original and full of invention, lacks an effective style and grand proportions – excluding, of course, the Adina Mosque and the Dakhil Darwaza. Nevertheless, the architecture of the region is strong in character, strong enough for the style to be diffused towards the east, beyond the borders with Assam. Here, on the site of the ancient capital of the Kachari Raja, is a doorway, probably from the sixteenth century, which is identical to the façades of the mosques at Gaur and Pandua. It is characterized by the same pointed archways, the low octagonal corner towers and the characteristic curved cornice.

[1] The *mandapa* is a large open hall, sometimes with columns; the *garbhagriha* is the most sacred part of the temple to which entrance is permitted only to priests.

[2] See, for example, the Bahmanid tombs of Dawud I, Ghiyas al-Din and Firuz at Gulbarga. G. Michell, ed., *Islamic Heritage of the Deccan*, Bombay 1986, s.v. Gulbarga, by E. Merklinger, pp. 27–41, pls. 9–11.

[3] The lamp placed inside the niche of the *mihrab* was meant to call to mind a passage from the Koran, namely verse 35 of the Sura of the Light (XXIV).

[4] A. Cunningham, *Archaeological Survey of India Reports*, vol. 15, pp. 73–6.

[5] Shah Shuja added the Lukochori Gate, in a typically Mughal style.

[6] Originally the tower was connected with a mosque, as is indicated by the mound of earth nearby, which is all that remains of it.

[7] H. Creighton, *The Ruins of Gaur*, London 1817, vol.1.

[8] Some Hindu statues were built into the eastern façade of the mosque, but they were turned round so that only the back could be seen and Persian inscriptions were engraved on them. As the re-use of Hindu materials in such large quantities is unusual in Bengal after the fourteenth century, we must suppose that the Afghan rebels had had their access to the stone quarries cut off and were thus compelled to use whatever stone they could find. In addition, there was the natural disgust that the Muslims felt for the Hindu images, hence the custom of turning them round. It is interesting to note that, out of contempt for the Mughal sovereigns, it was these rebels who diffused the characteristics of their architectural language in Bengal. Asher, *op. cit.*, pp. 93–4.

[9] According to Asher this structure is similar to the older Chor Minar in Delhi, used for hanging the heads of those put to death. Peter Mundy, the English traveller who made a journey across the Mughal empire in 1631, reported that in the most important cities there were several towers or minarets on which were displayed the heads of thieves.

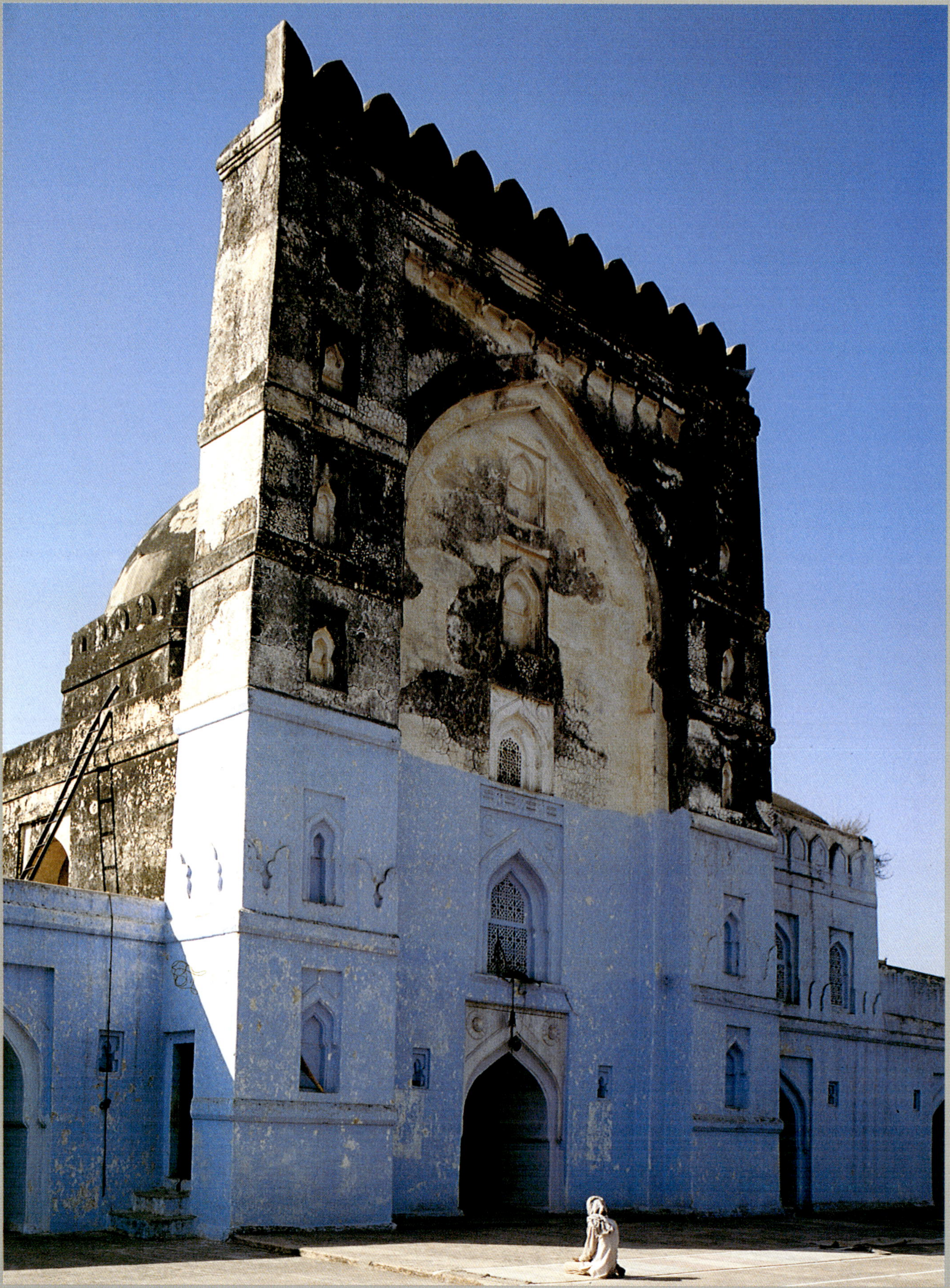

Jaunpur (1394–1483)

8

The congregational mosque at Etawa is one of several buildings in areas neighbouring Jaunpur to reflect the influential style of the Sharqi rulers.

Jaunpur was founded in 1358–9 by Firuz Shah Tughluq. It is about 60 km northwest of Benares on the banks of the river Gumti, on an ancient Hindu site rich in beautiful temples, and became one of the most strategically important capitals of the dynasty in that it formed the eastern bulwark for the emperor of Delhi. The governor of Jaunpur, the African eunuch Maliq Sarwar, was honoured by the Tughluqs with the title of Maliq-i Sharq (King of the East) so that his independent dynasty, which he founded in 1394 and lasted a little less than a century, came to be known as that of the Sharqis (Easterners) of Jaunpur. Legend has it that the name of the city was suggested to Firuz Shah by his cousin Jauna Khan and predecessor Muhammad Shah Tughluq, but it is more probable that Jaunpur is the Islamic version of the ancient Hindu name Yavanpur. This small kingdom, which for a time was more powerful than Delhi, flourished from the second half of the fourteenth century up to 30 years after the middle of the fifteenth. During this time the style went through three phases of architectural development. Firstly came preparation, secondly the release from the influence of Delhi; and finally full stylistic maturity. The Tughluq influence is predominant, even though it was interpreted locally with triumphant and monumental taste. The most important sovereign of the dynasty was Ibrahim Shah Sharqi (1401–40) and the best buildings are from his reign.

Unfortunately, very few architectural remains are extant. One myth has it that Sikandar Lodi wanted to punish the Sharqi sovereigns for their ambitions towards the sultanate of Delhi by systematically destroying their religious and civic buildings. But even accepting that this is a myth, and that Sikandar Lodi was too good a Muslim even to conceive of demolishing holy buildings, it remains true that apart from five mosques, nothing remains from this dynasty that governed the area for 90 years and gave it a reputation as being a 'refuge for scholars and men of letters' and as the 'Shiraz of India', evidently because of the great number of palaces, colleges and mosques that enriched it. Whatever the reality, the few mosques that escaped ruin are important examples of a provincial artistic expression that, although influenced by contemporary Tughluq art, is considerably more energetic and imaginative.

All the Sharqi buildings are grouped in the state capital. Those dating from the fourteenth century consist of a fort, destroyed by the English in the 1800s and now reduced to its imposing eastern gate, and a rather bland mosque within the fort, both constructed by Ibrahim Naib Barbak, brother of Firuz Shah, between 1376 and 1377. This sanctuary is in three sections with pillars and flat roofs of various designs taken from Hindu buildings. The *lat*, or stone minaret, is more interesting; it is almost 9 m tall and stands at the centre of the southern wing. It is square at the base, with the shaft first octagonal and then round, and is crowned with *amalaka* and *kalasha* motifs. It is purely ceremonial and carries an Arab inscription from Ibrahim Naib Barbak.

At more or less the same time, Firuz Shah Tughluq laid the basis for a congregational mosque, which for a variety of reasons was completed only in 1408 by the sultan Ibrahim Shah Sharqi and was called Atala Mosque. The name derived from the fact that the mosque was built on the site of the Hindu temple of Atala Devi which, together with other temples in the region, provided materials for its construction.

ZAFFIRABAD: SHAIKH BARHA MOSQUE

According to Percy Brown, the oldest building of this period is, however, a short distance outside the city, in the village of Zaffirabad, site of an early Muslim settlement.[1] This is the Shaikh Barha Mosque, built in 1311 using Hindu *spolia*. It consists of an unusually large hypostyle hall roughly 20 m square; the flat roof is formed by stone beams supported by over 60 pillars. The general appearance is rather rough and unattractive although it is not lacking in the solidity that became a distinctive element in later Jaunpur mosques.

Another mosque, probably later, is the Char Angli, where the central dome of the prayer hall is taken up by the large entrance arch, just as in the Begampuri Mosque in Delhi. (see p. 44) This is a forerunner of the propylons in the more important mosques of later periods. An interesting detail is the crenellation on the upper edge of the gate, which gives it a distinct Tughluq flavour.

At the beginning of the fifteenth century, with the occupation of Delhi by Timur, Jaunpur was presented with an opportunity to proclaim itself capital. Under the enlightened leadership of Sultan Ibrahim the city not only emulated the renown of Delhi, but actually overtook it. Exiled from Delhi and other regions threatened by the Timurids, many artists and men of letters established themselves in Jaunpur, thus conferring cultural leadership on the city. It became famous for its many and various schools of theology, to the point where it was considered the queen of university cities and equal to Shiraz, which was thought of in India as being the capital of education. In a short time architecture and the other arts were established there and the city soon enjoyed all those glories that go to make a capital, particularly palaces, mosques and tombs.

JAUNPUR: ATALA MOSQUE

The principal structure was the beautiful sandstone and granite Atala Mosque, which Ibrahim built on foundations prepared 30 years previously by Firuz Shah Tughluq and never completed because of the strong Hindu opposition to transforming an existing temple into a mosque. Although this is the most ancient building erected by the sovereign, it displays the salient characteristics of the architecture of the period and also constitutes the prototype of all later mosques in Jaunpur.

The design is traditional, consisting of a square, central courtyard with a diameter of some 60 m bordered on three sides by *riwaq* and with the prayer hall on the

Above The Ibrahim Naib Barbak Mosque (1376–8) inside Jaunpur Fort was built by the eponymous brother of Firuz Shah. Its ceremonial *lat* can be seen in the foreground.

Top left The fort at Jaunpur was destroyed by the British in the nineteenth century and now all that survives is its imposing eastern gate.

The fifteenth-century Atala Mosque at Jaunpur. This building was the prototype for all subsequent mosques in Jaunpur, and many of those in neighbouring areas as well.

western side. The arcades are spacious, consisting of five bays on two floors; two of the lower naves have a series of cells and a pillared verandah which face the road so as to provide an exterior space for visitors or merchants. At the centre of each of the three sides the *riwaq* are interrupted by a beautiful structure forming a door; those on the north and south are surmounted by domes and are hence the most imposing. The shrine consists of a central, rectangular nave covered with an eight-hemispheric dome with oblong transepts on each side, which are also partly covered by a dome. The transepts have pillars with two superimposed shafts which support Hindu-style ceilings resting on beams and corbels that protrude from the capitals. At the far end there is a second floor surrounded by stone open-work windbreaks which is reserved for the *zenana*. The central bay is covered by a high hemispheric dome resting on a series of angular corbels and arcades which transform the square ground plan into a 16-sided polygon. The ribbed dome is 25 m tall on the interior and is constructed with circular courses of stone, while the exterior is covered with a thick layer of cement which outlines the simple hemispherical curve. The three *mihrab* of the *qibla* wall and the beams are sumptuously decorated with stylized lotus flowers and elegant geometric designs. By contrast the *minbar* is made up of a simple series of stone steps.

The most striking characteristic of the entire complex is the immense propylon that makes up the façade. This is a stupendous archway, in truth an *iwan* flanked by grand oblong panels which protrude, are inclined and are divided into two floors decorated with blind niches and small arches. This large structure recalls the propylon of an Egyptian temple, being some 23 m tall, 17 m wide at the base and 14 m wide at the top. The real entrance is made up of an opening delineated by beams and corbels and smaller, lateral archways. Above this entrance are numerous arched windows spread over various floors. The great archway and the other archways are decorated with borders in the 'spear-point' style. Beyond this principal entrance are also two smaller entrances on the transepts corresponding to the domes. The entrances on the *riwaq* are decorated in the same way so that the entire effect is balanced and rhythmic, arranged with precision. Although not original – the prototype, in fact, is to be found in the Tughluq-era Begampuri Mosque of Delhi (see p. 44) – there is no doubt that this great archway is considerably more elegant and refined than its precursor. The tapered corner turrets of the original have been replaced by oblong pillars with ornamental niches and the spear-head border of the archway renders the aspect more pleasing and decorative.

This improvement in the general effect is also due to the building's grand proportions, the beautiful grey sandstone and the granite of which the propylon is made. From reading the inscriptions on the building, it seems possible that local artists contributed to the planning and the construction of the mosque. They were certainly masters of technique with an excellent, over-all vision, and knew how to combine the various elements to great and imaginative effect. The rear wall of the mosque is interesting for its special architectonic treatment. Like the domed area, the surfaces protrude strongly towards the exterior and are further emphasized with tapered turrets that are repeated in larger proportions at the principal corners of the building. The only weak point is the lack of harmony between the propylon and the main dome; from behind and from the side the dome appears diminished by the disposition of the façade.

Jaunpur: Khalis Mukhlis and the Jhanjiri mosques

The Khalis Mukhlis and the Jhanjiri mosques, now for the most part in ruins, date from 1426–30. The former was built by order of the two governors of the city, Maliq Khalis and Maliq Mukhlis, on the site of a Hindu temple. It is based on the style of the Atala Mosque with an extremely simple, functional structure free of ornament and with a large propylon before the main domed hall and its two columned wings.

Of the Jhanjiri Mosque, only the central part of the façade propylon remains, which because of its rich ornament contrasts strongly with the sober austerity of the Khalis Mukhlis Mosque and certainly must have been a true architectural jewel. Decoration featuring open-work stone screens, pillars and corbels, not to mention calligraphic elements reproducing the Hadiths of the Prophet, suggests the collaboration of Hindu craftsmen, perhaps more concerned with the treatment of the surfaces than with the construction or the proportions of the various parts of the whole. Anyway, this mosque, whose propylon casts a shadow over a screen of arches – from which comes the name Jhanjiri or 'screen' – although incomplete, remains the most beautiful and elegant mosque of Jaunpur.

Jaunpur: Lal Darwaza Mosque

About twenty years later, in about 1447, Bibi Raji, wife of Mahmud Shah (1440–57), ordered the construction of the Lal Darwaza Mosque (Mosque of the Red Door), which seems to have been the royal chapel of a palace that was later destroyed. The name derived from the fact that entry to the palace itself was via a high door painted in vermilion, although it is more likely that the name came from the particular colour of the sandstone from which it was built.

The plan of the mosque reproduces on a reduced scale that of the Atala Mosque; it is positioned on a high plinth, accessible by means of a series of steps at the eastern entrance. Much of the Lal Darwaza Mosque was built with Hindu *spolia* and, although simpler in its detail, it is more refined. The *riwaq* are only two bays deep and one floor high; in the prayer hall, four bays run parallel to the *qibla* on pillars positioned in such a way as to provide high, flat ceilings. Only in front of the *mihrab* is there a dome, which rests, however, not on spherical supports, but on massive pillars arranged in diagonals which transform the square room into an octagon, following the usual design of Jain temples. The entire construction is of red sandstone and granite; the carved decorations reproduce Hindu motifs, such as lotus flowers, or geometric patterns, such as a curious design of seven angles carved within a circle on a panel of the main *mihrab*. Some ornamental niches on the secondary *mihrab* display the pattern of Islamic talisman, symbol of strength and victory. The area reserved for the women on the second floor of the prayer hall is arranged around the two sides of the central nave and is not relegated to the extremes of the wings as it is in the Atala

JAUNPUR (1394–1483)

The Lal Darwaza Mosque (begun c.1447) at Jaunpur is a scaled down version of the Atala Mosque. The building may have acted as a royal chapel for a palace that has since been destroyed.

Mosque. Perhaps in this we witness the influence of Bibi Raji, who enjoyed a pre-eminent role in the history of the dynasty and who always favoured women.

The courtyard of the Lal Darwaza Mosque is a square of approximately 40 x 40 m; at the centre of each of the *riwaq* a monumental entrance foreshadows the propylon of the prayer hall, some 16 m tall and 13 m wide at the top. This is certainly the most successful part of the mosque even though, as in the Atala Mosque, it hides the dome. The ornamental *iwan* has a lancet arch and an interior spear-point border. The triple entrance is made up of a Hindu 'beam and corbel' structure supported by double pillars with an imposed shaft.

The indigenous elements seem to have the upper hand in comparison with other Jaunpur mosques, so that if we ignore the dome and some arches, the entire building seems to be Hindu. Indeed, an inscription on a pillar of the north-western *riwaq* displays the name of a Hindu architect, Kamau, son of Visadru, who could have overseen the construction or at least the general planning of the mosque. The building was completely restored in 1990, while work on the other mosques is still ongoing.

JAUNPUR: *JAMI MASJID*

The *jami masjid* is the last, the largest and the most ambitious of the mosques of Jaunpur. Begun by Mahmud around 1438, it was enlarged and completed in 1478 by Husain Shah, the last sovereign of the dynasty according to the inscription on the eastern entrance. Shortly after, Jaunpur ceased to be an independent state and was absorbed within the empire of Delhi. In several ways, although on a larger scale, this building repeats many of the principal characteristics of the Atala Mosque. It differs, however, in some important details. The entire structure is built on a 6 m high terrace reached by means of three entrances equipped with steep but imposing flights of stairs, similar to those of some Delhi mosques of the period of Firuz Shah Tughluq.

The entrances, a foretaste of the great central propylon, are situated at the centre of each side of the courtyard and are each covered with a fine dome. The eastern entrance, slightly larger than the others, is now ruined and the southern entrance functions as the main one. The courtyard is 61 m square and the *riwaq* with only two bays are two floors high and covered with flat roofs. The most remarkable part of the mosque is the propylon preceding the prayer hall that rises almost 26 m from a base that is more than 23 m wide. It projects from the bay by approximately 3 m and completely hides the dome behind it. On each side of the central hall and connected by arched apertures, lateral aisles are arranged at right angles to the long axis of the shrine. These rise to a second floor with open-work *jali* screen walls to allow light to enter; this floor was a sort of private chapel for the ladies of the royal family. Beyond the lateral aisles the builders introduced a different organization of space, adding to each side a large vaulted hall corresponding to a transept, each measuring 15 m in length, 12 m in width and about 13 m in height. The interiors of these halls are not obstructed by any supports and receive adequate illumination from the three arches that open on to the courtyard. The wide, pointed vault is similar to that of the nave of the Adina Mosque at Pandua in Bengal (see p. 84), built a century earlier but today in ruins perhaps because it was built of bricks. Although much more solidly built, these immense vaults are not in harmony with the imposing structure of the façade and give the impression of being 'military barracks rather than wings of a Congregational Mosque'.[2] This sense of a fortified building is increased by the conical bastions at the corners of the mosque and by the remarkable inclination of the propylon: the *jami masjid* thus displays signs of decline in its experimental forms.

Its imperfections – almost entirely in the upper regions of the façade – seem to declare the shortcomings of its designers. Although they conceived of the idea of two great vaulted halls forming the transepts, they then failed to reconcile them satisfactorily with the exterior elements. Consequently the aspect in this important area of the design is of something unfinished and incoherent that does not allow the building to attain the status of a work of art. The value of this and the other Jaunpur mosques is to be found not so much in the architecture as in the sculptural decoration, for example in the niches of the *mihrab* which are luxuriously decorated with exquisitely made geometric and floral motifs, or in the ceiling panels with elaborate patterns derived from lotus flowers and floral arabesques. Here is an elegance yet more refined than that which, years later, would be found in the Fatehpur Sikri of Akbar.

It seems that the Sharqis built no monumental tombs. Indeed, they are all buried in an enclosed, open-air area measuring some 36 x 18 m and situated not far from the northern door of the Great Mosque. The sarcophagi of white marble are beautifully sculpted.

JAUNPUR: MAUSOLEUMS

Also at Jaunpur is the tomb attributed to Firuz Shah. It has a characteristic appearance that recalls the tombs of the Tughluqs of Delhi. The square base, however, resting on a low plinth, is opened by three archways on each side, of which the central one is slightly higher than the others and stands out by means of a frame of azure glazed tiles. Other interesting motifs include the small ornamental columns decorated with tiles in herringbone patterns, which terminate above with subtle and gracefully worked points. A fine hemispheric dome rests on a high octagonal drum, which is also decorated

Jaunpur (1394–1483)

Above The tomb thought to be that of Firuz Shah at Jaunpur. Its style recalls that of the Tughluq tombs in Delhi.

Opposite The *jami masjid* is the last and most ambitious of all the mosques in Jaunpur, and, fittingly, was completed in 1478 by the last ruler of the dynasty, Husain Shah.

with a frieze of glazed tiles and terminates with an upside-down lotus flower. In the intradoses of the arches there are *muqarnas* motifs in stucco, probably dating from a later period. Good examples of later mausoleums are those of Shah Zaman Khan and Kalich Khan.

According to Nath, the Sharqi did not build any public works such as dams or bridges on the River Gumti, so that in 1564 Akbar had to build a bridge when he came to visit the city.[3]

The style of the Sharqi buildings influenced a number of structures in neighbouring areas, for example the Arhai Kanjura Mosque of Benares and the congregational mosque of Etawa (see p.94) where there is a propylon with the arch motif at the centre of the façade.

KANAUJ

Kanauj, some 90 km from Jaunpur, has a mosque that is today much changed from its original appearance; this is due to the collapse of the two rows of pillars that formed the *riwaq* inside the courtyard. The mosque is made up almost entirely of the prayer hall, a space some 36 x 9 m, with its roof supported by 60 pillars arranged in four rows. The roof is flat, except for the centre and the extremities where there are Hindu-type domes formed of superimposed circles of stone which diminish in size until they disappear. Five doors in the front of the building open on to the courtyard. According to an inscription the mosque was remodelled in 1406 by Ibrahim Shah of Jaunpur because, according to tradition, it was originally a Hindu building. This latter was known locally as Sita-ka Rasui and stood on a raised hillock in the heart of the citadel. It is now completely whitewashed, inside and outside, and has lost its Sharqi characteristics.

A fine mausoleum also survives at Kanauj, erected in 1470 during the reign of Husain Shah of Jaunpur. It is situated on a small hillock just outside the citadel, but it, too, is surrounded by walls with turrets at the corners and an entrance on the northern side. This is the tomb of Said Shaikh Makhdum Jahaniya Jahangasht, alias Jhanji. It is a severe, square building in well-cut red stone and measures some 12 m each side. It has

Above The Said Shaikh Makhdum Jahaniya tomb complex (late fifteenth century) at Kanauj.

Opposite The Akbar bridge at Jaunpur, built by Mun'im Khan in 1564 when the Mughal ruler came to visit the city.

three small openings on the façade, is covered by an imposing dome on an octagonal drum and is surrounded by *chhatri* resting on four slender pillars. To the rear, the only ornament consists of panels decorated with small tablets suspended by stone ropes and carrying the name of Allah. Seriously damaged by an earthquake, it was restored in 1794 by Abbas Ali, as an inscription testifies. Alongside the tomb of Shaikh Makhdum there stand another two anonymous tombs, both also square and domed. Other mausoleums of revered personages date from the Mughal period, as indeed do some mosques which stand isolated on the plain.

Civic buildings

In 1567 Akbar appointed Khan-i Khanan Muhammad Mun'im Khan, one of his most loyal supporters, as governor of the captured city of Jaunpur. Besides restoring a great many buildings that had been destroyed by the Lodis, Mun'im Khan built the fine bridge that bears his ruler's name and encouraged his nobles to construct a number of mosques in the city. The imposing east gateway in the city wall, with its decoration of blue and yellow tiles, is also attributed to him, as is the palace called Chehil Sutun, which we know from nineteenth-century drawings. It was two-storeyed, with a pillared verandah resembling the Iranian and Central Asian *talar*, but which in India is known as an *iwan*. Even though there are no similar buildings at Agra or Fatehpur Sikri, the Chehil Sutun nevertheless has an air of Mughal imperial building about it and we cannot rule out the possibility that it provided the model for the palace of Raja Man Singh which was built about 20 years later at Rohtas, in Bihar. Not far from Chehil Sutun there is a large *hammam* with a number of vaulted or domed rooms, similar to the baths at Fatehpur Sikri. With its hot and cold water system it is a rare example, still intact, of provincial baths and bears witness to the speed with which this type of building, which was introduced into India by the Mughals, spread throughout various parts of the empire. Under the patronage of Mun'im Khan, the Chunar Fort, southeast of Jaunpur, which Akbar had taken in 1561, was fortified. A portal that Muhammad Sharif Khan, possibly the son of the famous painter Abd al-Samad, erected in 1573-4, has as its only ornament four inscriptions in Persian, while there are other fine doors decorated with blind niches, rosettes and intricate geometric patterns that are reminiscent of Suri structures (the fort at Shergan, not far from Chunar) and are evidence of the survival of local motifs, even in the Mughal period.

[1] Brown, *op. cit.*, p. 42.
[2] R. Nath, *History of Sultanate Architecture*, New Delhi 1978, p. 104.
[3] The bridge, which is still in use, was built under the supervision of Munim Khan, one of Akbar's most loyal nobles, and is considered one of the most important works of Mughal engineering. It consists of ten spans with pointed arches carried on massive piers. On either side of the upper part is a row of attractive domed *chhatri*. According to the inscriptions on the bridge, it was begun in 1564-5 and completed in 1568-9.

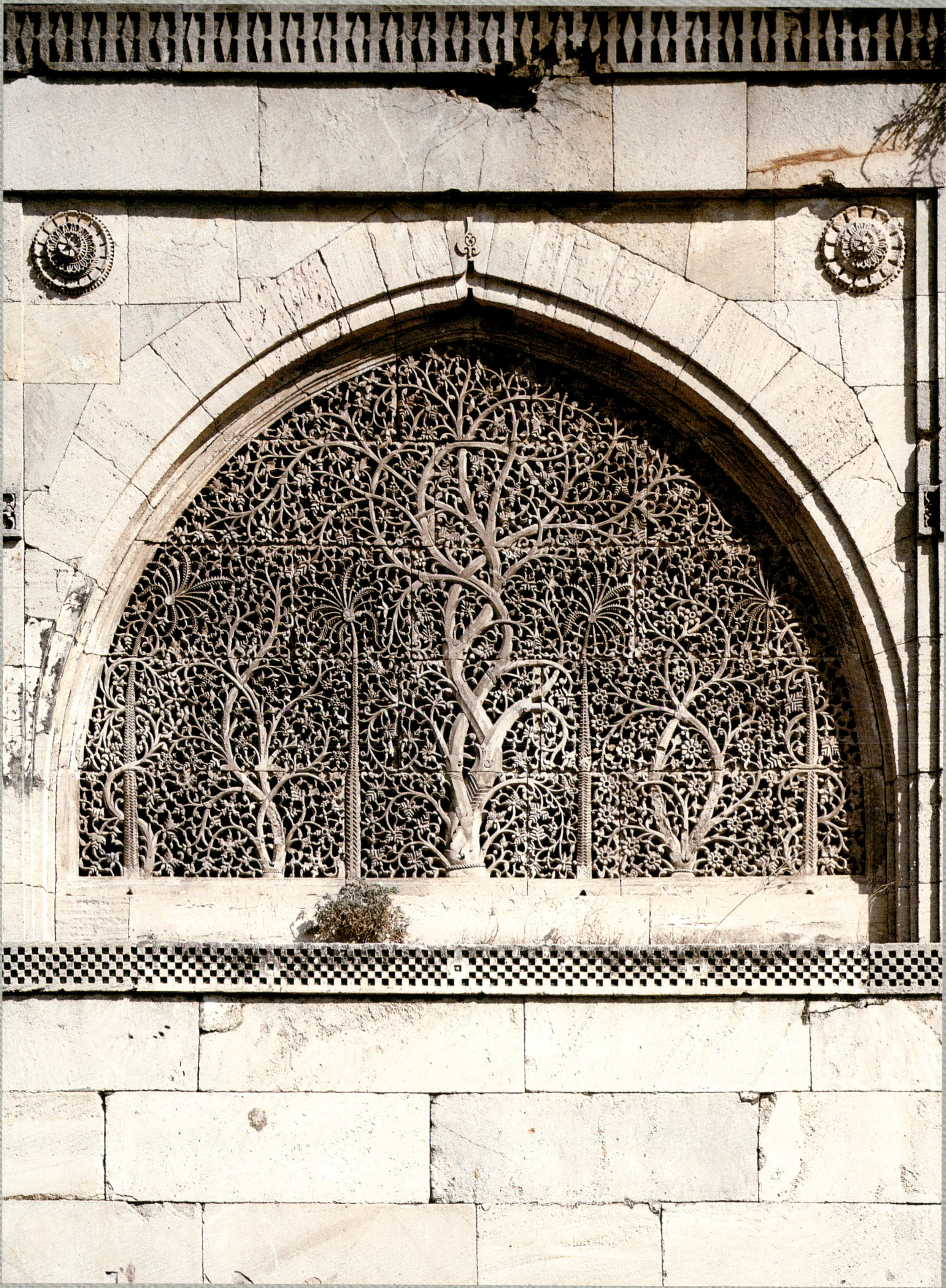

Gujarat (c.1300–c.1550)

9

A carved openwork window in the Sidi Said Mosque (1572) at Ahmedabad. Such remarkable windows are not found anywhere else in the Indian subcontinent, and consequently they became famous even outside India.

Although Gujarat was probably the object of several Muslim incursions from Sind during the eighth century, it suffered its first true invasion at the hands of Mahmud of Ghazni in 1025 while it was governed by the Saivite sovereign Bhimadeva (1021–63). Mahmud destroyed the renowned temple at Somnath (home of a famous golden idol and great riches), killed over 50,000 men and abandoned Anhilawada, the ancient capital, to retreat to Multan. A further wave of invasions took place a century and a half later under Bhimadeva II (1178–1241), led by Mahmud Ghuri and his successor, Qutb al-Din Aibak. The former was chased from the country; the latter succeeded in sacking it, but then had to retreat to face the Chauhans at Ajmer. Under Ala al-Din Khalji, Gujarat was dominated by his brother-in-law, Ulugh Khan, but the Muslim domination became long-lasting only with Ghiyas al-Din Tughluq, who appointed Taj al-Din Jafar governor of Gujarat. This last installed himself at Cambay. After a series of upheavals Muzaffar Khan assumed the governorship and, exploiting the occupation of Delhi by Timur in 1398, first declared himself an independent prince and then proclaimed himself king in 1404. Ahmad Shah, his grandson, who seems to have been involved in Muzaffar Khan's death, became sovereign in 1410–11 and founded Ahmedabad on the site of an ancient Hindu city. Ahmedabad was destined to become the capital of the realm for many years in the future, famous as 'the most beautiful city in Hindustan and perhaps the world', according to a historian of the Mughal court at the end of the sixteenth century. The greatest Muslim sovereign of Gujarat, however, was Fath Khan Mahmud, known commonly as Baiqara, Begra or Begarha (1459–1511), who expanded and reinforced his realm in all directions, destroyed the Malabar pirates, defeated the Portuguese with the help of the Turks and occupied Champanir, making it his new capital city.[1] After his death the realm declined until, in 1572, it was occupied permanently by Akbar and ceased to be an independent country.

Gujarati style
The art of the sultanate of Gujarat was without a doubt the most important of the

regional styles because of the quantity and richness of the monuments and the technical ability with which they were executed. Indeed, for centuries Gujarat was the centre for the most skilful craftsmen in all India, who for generations had passed on the construction techniques of countless superb Hindu and Jain temples, until they were called upon to put their skill to use for their Muslim masters. In this way Gujarati Islamic art can be considered the most 'indigenous' of all India. Indeed, the sultans of Ahmedabad did not have much of an artistic culture so that it made sense for them to turn the genius of Gujarati artists towards their own ends. These artists translated the strictly Muslim requirements of the buildings they were entrusted with into their own language.

It is not surprising therefore, that many of those Islamic monuments, including even some of the most beautiful, are adaptations or even 'reproductions' of Hindu and Jain temples. Imitations of these sanctuaries, built one above the other without figurative decoration, functioned as minarets; the entrance of the pagan temple became the niche of the *mihrab*; a series of *mandapa* (rooms of the cult) were joined together to form the main bay of the mosque; a Hindu *kunda* (sacred pool) was transformed into an area for ritual ablutions. Pillars, architraves, corbels, open-work slabs, ceilings and balconies, all with rich decoration, were generally used. The Islamic element, however, was represented by heavy pointed arches which alternated with trabeated Hindu constructions, small, light arches used as simple decoration, doorframes cut from slabs of stone and mounted between the Hindu-style pillars and architraves, or even by floral volutes that decorated the niches once destined for images of the pagan divinities. The inscriptions, arabesques and Islamic geometric designs alternate and fuse with the Hindu motifs, as in the oldest Mamluk buildings of Delhi.

This architectural style flourished in Gujarat for some 250 years, from when the governors of the Khalji sovereigns established themselves in the cities of the west coast at the beginning of the fourteenth century, to the time when the government of Ahmad Shahi ceased to be independent and the country was absorbed by the Mughal empire in the second half of the sixteenth century. To aid study, this style can be divided into three periods. In the fourteenth century, above all during its first half, there was the usual phase consisting of demolition of buildings attached to the indigenous cult. Many of the idols were taken to Delhi, such as the *linga* of the Somnath temple, which was thrown to the ground so that the people could walk over it as they arrived in the mosque. This was followed by the conversion phase. The buildings of this period display an experimental approach, and even though some of these mosques do not lack a certain architectural dignity, it is evident that the style had still to reach its distinctive character. The finest example of the first stage is the *jami masjid* of Cambay, which dates from *c.*1325. The second period dominated during the first half of the fifteenth century when the style, although still displaying some experimental characteristics, began to acquire increased confidence and autonomy. The most interesting monument of this epoch is the *jami masjid* of Ahmedabad (see p. 112), which although carrying some trace of the freshness and the ingenuousness of the previous examples, is nevertheless an almost complete example of architectural maturity. The third period developed in the second half of the fifteenth century under the patronage of Mahmud Begarha and his successors. The most typical example of this phase is the *jami masjid* of Champanir, certainly one of the most beautiful and representative monuments of Gujarati art.

Bhadreshvar: Dargah Lal Shahbaz

In 1988 some Gujarati buildings were identified as the oldest Islamic constructions in India. Indeed, although as early as 1875 Burgess had remarked on their presence at Bhadreshvar in the Kachchh Gulf, only in 1965 did Desai establish that some of these buildings dated from 1159-60 by reading inscriptions. This dates the constructions some 35 years before the foundation of the Quwwat al-Islam (see p. 20) and some 150 years before the occupation of Gujarat by the sultans of Delhi. In 1988 Shokoohy published plans and photographs of these buildings, gathered during his survey of the site which began in 1977. The complex is a mausoleum-cum-sanctuary with two mosques, one of which is slightly later, but both of which are much ruined. There are also two less important buildings: a domed pavilion known simply as Chhatri and a ruined cistern-well, known as the Dudha Waw, along the lines of later Gujarati stepped wells.

The mausoleum, which carries the name of Ibrahim, is called Dargah Lal Shahbaz by the local Islamic community. Ibrahim was a famous Shiite saint, revered in both Sind and Gujarat, but who died in Sehwan in 1274-5. In 1929 Cousens demonstrated that the saint is actually buried at Sehwan in a fine local tomb. The Bhadreshvar building rises within a closed perimeter with relatively recently constructed walls and consists of a square space fronted by a portico on columns and pilasters. The hall, which has no cenotaph,

Left The base of one of the carved stone minarets at the entrance to the *jami masjid* at Ahmedabad. Built in 1423, the mosque exemplifies the confidence of the second period of Gujarati architecture in the first half of the fifteenth century.

Opposite The *jami masjid* at Champanir typifies the third period of Gujarati architecture that developed in the second half of the fifteenth century.

although there are 11 tombs spread throughout the complex, is covered by a dome of the Jain and Hindu type: pyramidal on the exterior, conical inside with courses of concentric, finely worked and superimposed stone. These last are supported by 12 pilasters on the surrounding walls with corbel capitals similar to the portico supports and, like these, are decorated with foliate motifs. The shafts, on the other hand, have geometric and floral motifs arranged over three registers similar to those used traditionally in Jain temples. The flat ceiling of the portico was originally divided into 27 squares with a large lotus flower in the centre. The *mihrab* has a semi-circular plan, sits on the same axis as the entrance and is almost without any decoration, but some elements suggest that it was dressed in wood as in many examples from Afghanistan, Iran and Egypt. It projects towards the exterior in a shape that would later become common in Gujarat, and is flanked by two windows.

BHADRESHVAR: SOLA KHAMBA AND CHOTI MOSQUE

The local inhabitants call the larger of the two Bhadreshvar mosques Sola Khamba. It sits on a lower level than the mausoleum of Ibrahim, which is not far off, and is now partially submerged in the sand, as well as being much ruined. It is built of blocks of stone and has an Arab-type plan with a colonnade that runs around a central courtyard. Although many of the roof columns and architraves are still in place, the roof itself is almost totally collapsed; it is obvious, however, that it was flat. The prayer hall was formed of two bays parallel to the *qibla* wall, while the *riwaq* had just one single bay. An unusual portico, formed of four rows each consisting of eight columns, was arranged at the eastern extremity of the building, in front of the main building, and perhaps was derived from similar colonnades in the Jain and Hindu temples of Gujarat; this area of the mosque was also covered with a flat roof. In contrast with the great quantity of ornament on Ibrahim's mausoleum, the Sola Khamba Mosque appears to be completely bare, with just a few simple mouldings on the capitals and, originally, some lotus leaves over the only entrance. The *qibla* wall, much ruined, no longer carries the *mihrab*, but it seems that the latter had a semi-circular plan inside and rectangular outside. This form of *mihrab* is very similar to that of the Fatimid mosques in Libya and Tunisia and the *jami* mosque of Jibla in the Yemen dating from 1088–9. An extra *mihrab*, in the form of a semi-circular arch but not projecting towards the exterior, appears in the portico outside the eastern wall of the mosque and it seems that it, too, like Ibrahim's Dargah, was dressed in wood. The date of the Sola Khamba Mosque must be between 1166 and 1177–8; it therefore represents the oldest type of Indian mosque still standing.

Not far off, on a platform 45 cm high, stands a smaller mosque known as the Choti (Small) Mosque. It, too, is built with blocks of stone and consists of a courtyard that is now for the most part blocked by a secondary space with a double colonnade in front of the *qibla* wall and a prayer hall with two bays parallel to it. The hall is held up by a row of columns which are obviously Hindu in manufacture – both the shafts and the capitals. They are all richly decorated as in Ibrahim's mausoleum, even with the same motifs, which suggests the same craftsmen and therefore the same date of construction for the two monuments. Between the colonnades of the prayer hall are two doors opposite each other: inside, these present a profile of semi-circular arches elegantly decorated with spiral and leaf motifs. This arched profile does not appear in Hindu architecture but was common in the twelfth century in Islamic buildings in Syria and North Africa and would later become common in those Indian architectural styles influenced by the Iranian and Central Asian style. The diffusion of this arch in the buildings of Bhadreshvar suggests a link between the Arabs and the Muslim communities of the site. The *mihrab* of the sanctuary, semi-circular in form, projects towards the exterior and like the others is lacking in decoration even if it was probably dressed in wood. Once again it is evident here how indigenous traditions influenced the rise of Islamic architecture in India even before it developed in the sultanates of Delhi. The recycling of Hindu and Jain materials, as well as the use of local craftsmen, would make the Indian creative influence persist for centuries, above all in Gujarat. This was so even in the face of the deep-rooted Islamic faith, which in this period was represented by a small minority of traders who lacked effective power.

Junagadh Mosque

Another mosque dating from before the conquest of Gujarat by the Delhi sultanate, even if a century and a half later than the buildings of Bhadreshvar, has been identified at Junagadh on the Saurashtra peninsula. The city, situated between Somnath and Bhadreshvar, had been conquered by Mahmud of Ghazni who built a fort there. The mosque was built from 1286 to 1287 by the head of a traders' community who was also a local religious leader, Abu al-Qasim bin Ali al-Iraji, of Iranian origin. Fronted by an entrance to the north formed by a *chhatri* at the top of a stairway, the mosque consists of a prayer hall three spans wide and three spans deep with four columns at the centre and four pilasters against the walls. A long, narrow space is attached to the southern side of the sanctuary, but this was a later addition, perhaps reserved for women. At the front of the hall is a wide colonnaded portico. The *mihrab* has a semi-circular plan, which projects towards the exterior with the same contour. It is decorated with small Hindu-type columns which support a stone architrave carved with a triple-arched motif; but it would seem that the whole is from a later period since it contrasts with the rest of the decoration in the mosque, which is very similar to that of the buildings at Bhadreshvar. This Arab-type plan, but with the portico perhaps inspired by Hindu temples, was not repeated in the Gujarati mosques built after the conquest by the sultanates of Delhi. The plans of these buildings followed other schemes although they were always influenced by indigenous examples.

Patan

The first buildings of the initial period, which runs from *c.*1300 to 1411, can be seen in the city of Patan, which stands on the site of ancient Anhilawada, a place of considerable importance under the Hindu dynasty of the Solanki (tenth to thirteenth centuries). The mausoleum of Shaikh Farid (*c.*1300) is virtually a Hindu temple transformed into a Muslim tomb by means of a few additions and alterations.

Another Patan building was the Adina Mosque, or *jami masjid*, which was put together rather chaotically with over a thousand richly decorated pillars stripped from existing temples. Only the foundations remain, sufficient, however, to show the building's enormous dimensions.

Broach: *Jami Masjid*

The next stage, when new buildings were first erected, is represented by the *jami masjid* at Broach, a Gujarati maritime city (the ancient Barukhacha, known by the the Greeks as Barugaza) which was built very early on during the incursions begun by Ala al-Din Khalji in 1297, so that the mosque itself is probably datable from the beginning of the fourteenth century, as is confirmed by a ruined inscription on the entrance that dates the building from 1302. Although it was built for the most part with spoil material, this is not an improvised structure but is designed according to the conventional mosque plan. The courtyard, now much ruined, had entrances on three sides while on the western side stood the prayer hall, which was of the so-called 'open and pillared' variety. Indeed, it looks like a verandah in contrast to those with a wall opened by arcades to the front. In some of the Indian provincial styles, façades consist essentially of two types: the first has an open colonnade that leaves the pillared interior visible, as in this case; the second type has the front closed by a screen of arches. Both types were used more or less freely according to personal taste. The 48 pillars of the Broach Mosque are elaborately carved and are arranged in two rows on the front. Inside, they are arranged in such a way as to divide the sanctuary into three compartments, resembling the same number of *mandapa* in Hindu temples, the ceilings of which are profusely decorated with geometric patterns. The pillars certainly came from indigenous religious buildings and support three large domes and ten smaller cupolas. Although the perimeter walls came from Hindu and Jain temples, they have been remodelled according to Muslim requirements and could be considered original. Inside the *qibla* wall there are three *mihrab* and a series of arched windows with stone open-work screens which, although Islamic in concept, are designed in a totally indigenous manner. The *mihrab*, too, although making use of the

Muslim pointed arch, below the architrave are practically copies of the niches in Hindu and Jain temples, but without the conventional symbols.

Cambay: *jami masjid*

In about 1325 the Muslim government of Gujarat moved to the ancient port of Cambay (Khambhayat), known to Marco Polo as Cambaet. At more or less the same time a Great Mosque was erected there, which displays greater artistic maturity on the part of its builders. Indeed, these builders perhaps came from Delhi since they show considerable knowledge of Mamluk and Khalji structures. The façade of the mosque is reminiscent of that of the Quwwat al-Islam (see p. 20) and the Arhai-din-ka Johmpra, but above all of the Jamaat Khana of Ala al-Din, due to both its general appearance and the use of alternate, wide and narrow courses of brick. The mosque opens with three large archways; the central one is a little higher and projects more. The uprights, in imitation of minarets, rise to a height of almost 13 m and terminate in a very sharp point. The three arches are screened in the higher sections by elegant open-work slabs. The prayer hall, and the *riwaq* that surround the courtyard of the mosque, are made up of pillars that come, as usual, from local temples. In the sanctuary there are 100 pillars arranged to form two rows parallel to the *qibla* wall and 14 square spans with architraves above, which transform the spaces into octagons and easily support domes. The front of the main bay, on the other hand, has a flat ceiling of stone slabs. At the two extremities of the sanctuary are two enclosed galleries for women which are covered by domes. The pillars close to the central arch are decorated with a notched arch derived from temples, a feature that would later be much used in Gujarati mosques. The *riwaq* have flat roofs to the front and domes to the rear with windows in the wall aligned with each of the 21 domes. In the courtyard there is a small baldachin supported by four pillars and to the east is a large cistern, or perhaps two, covered by two platforms with openings to allow water to be drawn for ritual ablutions. One of these platforms has on one side a baldachin supported by ten pillars, now whitewashed. An inscription on this baldachin states that the cistern was repaired in 1621. In the prayer hall there are only three simple *mihrab* on the western wall, aligned with the main entrances. These project to the exterior with semi-circular buttresses, of which the central one is a little larger than the others. On the southern side of the mosque is a huge mausoleum, once domed, called Khtyar al-Daula (1316–17). This has rows of pillars arranged over two floors; inside are two tombs which were seriously damaged by the collapse of the dome. Connected to the mausoleum is a small funeral mosque also equipped with a gallery for the *zenana* and screened by stone open-work windbreaks which are much ruined.

Dholka: Hilal Khan Qazi and Tanka mosques

Some years later at Dholka – an area some 40 km south-west of Ahmedabad – the small mosque of Hilal Khan Qazi was built and named after the local governor who promised its construction. It appears simpler than, but with the same characteristics as, the Cambay Mosque. On the façade, however, is a pair of ornamental towers to the sides of the central arch; these are not minarets even if their appearance vaguely suggests that they are.

Another Dholka mosque, known as the Taka or Tanka Mosque because of the water well enclosed in the eastern entrance, dates from 1361. This is of the so-called 'open' variety in as much as its sanctuary is made up of some 100 pillars from Hindu temples, arranged into three rows which are not preceded by a brickwork wall. The ceilings, too, come from earlier indigenous temples and the *mihrab* are unusually deep niches (1.5 m). At the northern extremity is a small area reserved for women, separated from the rest by a screen of open-work stone with an autonomous entrance in the northern wall. Although not of great architectural importance, this mosque is one of the last buildings of this type in fourteenth-century Gujarat.

Ahmedabad

The political situation became increasingly uncertain due to the growing instability of central power in Delhi and hence

The *jami masjid* at Cambay (c.1325) is the best example of the first period of Gujarati architecture. The pillars in the courtyard were, as was often the case in this period, taken from local Hindu temples.

did not encourage the constructive arts. Building prospered only with the succession to the independent throne of Gujarat of Ahmad Shah (1411–42), who impressed his powerful character on the architecture of the first half of the fifteenth century. Ahmad Shah founded the city that took his name, Ahmedabad, in AH 813 and completed it in AH 820 (1417). It stands on the right bank of the Sabarmati river and the citadel containing its palace, as usual, occupied a raised position within a rectangular wall at the side of the river. Towards the centre of the city and outside the citadel, Ahmad Shah built the Great Mosque which was attached to his fortified palace by means of a wide processional road which started from the main gate of the citadel itself. Over this 'royal mall' a sort of triumphal arch was built, the Tin Darwaza (Triple Gateway), arranged in such a way as to form the main entrance to the exterior courtyard of the citadel. The king would sit in a throne on a terrace in front of the gate and watch contentedly the pomp and circumstance of his court. After the construction of the city Ahmad Shah inaugurated an era of unequalled architectural activity that prompted the officers of the court and other eminent personalities to follow his example. Indeed, within a short space of time Ahmedabad was enriched by a number of monuments that were superior to those of many other cities. Within the city's walls are over 50 mosques, small and large, and the same number of tombs; together they form a remarkable complex of Indo-Muslim architecture.

Among the main buildings erected in the capital during the first part of the reign of Ahmad Shah – the first half of the fifteenth century – four mosques can be taken as examples of the evolution of the style. These are the founder's mosque in the citadel (Bhadr), the mosque of Haibat Khan, the mosque of Sayyid Alam and the *jami masjid*.

AHMEDABAD: AHMAD SHAH MOSQUE
The mosque of Ahmad Shah, also known as the old *jami masjid*, stands in the Bhadr against the southern wall and on its central *mihrab* is the date 1414. Like the *jami masjid* of Cambay, it has a façade opened by five pointed arches, of which the central one is much wider and higher than the others and is flanked on both sides by two towers that project about a metre from the wall. On these towers it would seem that there rose two slender pinnacles which reached the height of about 6 m but which collapsed many years ago. The four minor arches of the façade alternate with eight open-work stone windows which are aligned with the same number of windows on the rear wall of the mosque and four on the northern side. The external wall decoration consists of three relief borders and a cornice, all in pure Hindu style. Inside, the sanctuary measures some 52 x 18 m and is covered by ten large domes arranged in two rows and interrupted by smaller domes. All these are supported by 152 columns and by pilasters on the perimeter walls aligned with the rows of columns. The supports were pillaged from Hindu temples and indeed many of them still carry reliefs with figures, the faces of which have been chiselled away; on one support is the trace of a Sanskrit inscription dated 1250. The 25 pillars that support the Gallery of the Princesses – the erroneous but popular name for this space, which is actually a *muluq khana*

Above The sanctuary in the Ahmad Shah Mosque (1414) at Ahmedabad. The supports were taken from local temples and still bear Hindu reliefs.

Top The Ahmad Shah Mosque at Ahmedabad. Its façade, opened by five pointed arches of which the central one is much higher and wider, echoes that of the *jami masjid* at Cambay.

(king's private room) – are richly worked and carry traces of a *linga* and other Hindu art forms. The gallery is surrounded by slabs of open-work stone with a great many patterns. The great dome and the 16 small rectangular areas that cover the roof are particularly rich in decoration. The columns are usually formed out of two shafts superimposed without any regard for the coherence of the design, and occasionally blocks of stone were inserted between the bases of the higher shafts and the terminals of the lower shafts to reach the required height wherever two shafts alone were not sufficient. The majority of them are in red, white and yellow sandstone. Behind the main entrance and aligned with the first dome there runs an open-work screen, a not uncommon arrangement in Gujarati mosques, the primary purpose of which is to adjust the positioning of the main archway at the centre of the façade. There are five *mihrab*, one for each span, while a sixth is found in the royal gallery. All are of white marble and in an elaborate style, apart from the central *mihrab*, which is more severe and comprises several colours of marble: white, yellow, dark grey and black. The *minbar*, which is made up of nine steps and covered by a baldachin supported by four small pillars, is of white marble and its sides are decorated with foliate motifs. On a low platform, still visible on the floor of the mosque, there stood a large baldachin under which Ahmad Shah would make his daily prayers, but it was dismantled illegally in 1870 and no trace of it now remains. The floor of the mosque is almost totally in white, dark grey and yellow marble.

Ahmedabad: Haibat Khan Mosque

The second mosque of Ahmedabad is that of Haibat Khan, situated at the southeastern extremity of the city. It seems that it was built on the site of a Hindu temple, desanctified and dismantled, naturally using the spoil material available. It is a little smaller and much rougher looking than the previous mosque discussed. It measures 26 x 10 m inside and is covered by three fine domes imposed on irregular octagons of which the lateral ones are a little smaller than the central one. The latter is higher than the others in that it is supported by pillars double the height of the rest. The façade is opened by three very pointed arches and has a bare aspect, like many Hindu works. The central part is higher than the rest and is crowned by two very slender turrets some five metres tall, which are imitation minarets. On the far wall open-work windows alternate with massive, projecting circular bastions similar to those in fashion in Delhi at the time of Firuz Shah Tughluq. The interior pillars, having been taken from various temples, present great variations in style and ornament. Part of the roof, which is formed of small cupolas or square and oblong panels of stone, is richly decorated and certainly came from Jain temples. The entrance from the southern side of the courtyard is a true Hindu *mandapa* with the characteristic square form imposed on a small stepped platform. Eight columns connected by architraves support a slightly pointed dome which constitutes the only Islamic element of the architectural whole. Low walls decorated with geometric patterns and floral wreaths delimit the structure below, while it terminates above with a projecting cornice and large merlons.

Ahmedabad: Sayyid Alam Mosque

The third mosque of this period, built perhaps in 1412 according to an inscription carved on the main *mihrab*, seems to anticipate some of those characteristics that would later find a more complete and mature expression in the subsequent *jami masjid* of Ahmad Shah. The mosque of Sayyid Alam, also known as that of Alam Chishti, stands near the Khanpur Gate and has at its front a wide courtyard which must have been used as a burial place since it is dotted with tombs. The building is small in size with two smaller, open and pillared lateral wings that were perhaps built later. The façade resembles that of Ahmad Shah's mosque, but the three entrances with pointed arches are of the same height, even if the central one is wider than the others and is flanked by two minaret towers, the upper parts of which, however, collapsed some time ago. According to Fergusson, these are merely unhappy imitations of Hindu structures:

One floor is superimposed on another with no apparent reason, the small balconies are used without windows and the building terminates suddenly without joining the balcony that should have functioned as a base for the minaret.[2]

On each side of the other two entrances rise slender pillars which support the gutter above the arches and continue further up, perhaps originally terminating in pinnacles. These mark progress in the design of the façade, but they find no echo in later buildings. The prayer hall is 20 x 9 m and is formed of five square units each of twelve columns, eight of which support the dome. Laterally, the main dome rests on pairs of pillars while in front, apart from the main entrance, there are two high columns formed out of two superimposed shafts. The frontal bay rises to the height of the entrances and is surmounted, in alignment with each entrance, by as many small cupolas, while the areas adjacent to these last are covered by carved slabs in the Jain style. The main dome does not rest directly on the base of the octagon but on an additional, intermediate floor: a sort of 'triforium', enclosed within an open-work stone screen with small arch motifs and geometric and vegetal patterns. The two end walls of the mosque, each over six metres wide, are completely open and connected to the hall itself by two open-work windows and a door. On the far wall of the sanctuary are five elegantly decorated *mihrab*, of which the central one is particularly fine, ornamented with a hanging lamp and chain (the motif that symbolizes the Sura of the Light).[3] This *mihrab* projects towards the exterior through a buttress with an elaborate design.

Ahmedabad: *Jami Masjid*

The *jami masjid* (see p. 112), the largest and most splendid of the Ahmedabad mosques (over 120 x 79 m), was built by Ahmad Shah in 1423, some 150 m to the east of the Tin Darwaza. It is generally considered to be the masterpiece of mosque design in western India, if not the entire country. Here, in truth, all the earlier experimental techniques reach fulfilment in the most complete and harmonious manner. The great courtyard that precedes the prayer hall is accessible on the northern side by an entrance which leads to the road, but the main entrance, on the same lines as that of the Dholka Mosque, is to the south. On the eastern side, another porch leads to an enclosure containing the mausoleum of the founder, built some years later by his son, Muhammad Shah. At the centre of the courtyard, which measures 83 m from east to west and 66 m from north to south, is the usual device for ritual ablutions. The *riwaq* are made up of 102 square pillars to the front and as many again on the internal walls and are arranged on three sides, while on the fourth, the western side, is the large prayer hall (34 x 99 m), with a height in the central area of some 15 m. The architectural effect of this mosque is concentrated above all in the façade of the sanctuary, in which the architect has combined the arched screen and the pillared portico, situating the former in the centre and the latter on the wings. This arrangement, which had already been tried in the mosque of Sayyid Alam, was here realized with greater intelligence, achieving complete success. The three principal entrances are well balanced and excellently proportioned, with the great central arch emphasized by lateral bastions in their turn harmoniously flanked by airy colonnades. As a whole, the façade is a superior composition of features and spaces in subtle and successful contrast, almost 'a silent fusion in stone of the spirit of two religions that were apparently as contradictory as day and night'.[4] The upper part of the two heavy minarets collapsed following the earthquake of 1819, but what remains gives us an idea of their solid and elegant appearance. These last were known in the region as the 'swinging minarets' because if one was shaken, the movement was transferred to the other. A drawing by James Forbes of 1781 provides us with evidence of their original form, which rose to four floors above the roof, terminating in a small open pavilion surmounted by *amalaka*.[5] The interior of the mosque is a hypostyle hall with some 300 high and slender pillars arranged so close to one another as to suggest a 'thick wood of silver trunks of pine trees'.[6] Here, for the first time, Hindu spoil material was not used, but the shafts were created specifically for this mosque out of fine sandstone from the region north of Kathiavar, some 115 km to the west of Ahmedabad. These,

Above The *jami masjid* at Ahmedabad. Built by Ahmad Shah in 1423, it is generally considered the best example of mosque design in western India.

Opposite Detail of a decorative panel, one of four flanking the secondary arches on the front of the *jami masjid* at Ahmedabad.

however, were worked in the Hindu manner with fluted faces and relief borders. This forest of columns was not arranged in monotonous rows, but is articulated over several superimposed floors covered by domes of varying dimensions. From east to west there are three domes and from north to south there are five, alternating with smaller domes and indigenous flat roofs. Despite his rigorous orthodoxy, Ahmad Shah did not realize that his mosque basically followed the layout of a Hindu temple, with the central area higher than the others in a vertical thrust that was unknown in the Islamic world. Indeed, in correspondence with the great central archway, the middle bay rises over three floors, the lateral arches over two floors, like the other arches, while the pillared wings are only one floor high, apart from a small area to the north where there is a suspended gallery for the *zenana*, supported by four pillars.

Where the central arch crosses the transept, a wide central space is created that has a platform at the height of each floor surrounded by a balcony equipped with seats with inclined backrests as in the *asana* (seat or throne) of the temples. This double gallery, which is covered by a dome, could be called a rotunda even though it is not circular in shape but is square in the lower area and octagonal above. Around each gallery are pillared verandahs, and the arcades between the pillars are screened by stone open-work screens through which pass a diffused light and fresh air, both very much necessary in the hot, humid climate of Ahmedabad. Behind the main entrance are two slender pillars some 8 m in height, which rise directly to support the third floor. The shafts of these seem to have been formed out of eight extremely slender columns, a local characteristic. On the capitals, a purely ornamental trilobate arch is imposed: this is an echo of the arch that, in the local temples, was necessary to spread onto the columns the weight of the architrave on which the pyramidal dome rested. The same arrangement was repeated on the two lower pillars in front of the central *mihrab*. As well as drawing inspiration from Hindu temples, this part of the mosque would seem to have been influenced by the *waw* or *baoli*, the large stepped wells that were very common in western India.

The builders of the *jami masjid* at Ahmedabad succeeded in resolving the problem of the vertical growth of their building and providing it with better illumination. The three central domes are richly decorated inside with a taste that was typical of Gujarat and was already very old. Even the smaller domes and the ceiling panels are profusely decorated. There are five *mihrab*, corresponding to the number of spans, and they are all decorated in various colours of marble. They are approximately 1 m deep, and project to the exterior with massive quadrangular bastions which are decorated with mouldings. On the perimeter walls and on the far wall of the mosque are open-work windows with elegant designs. On the façade, to the sides of the two secondary arched entrances, are four skilfully decorated panels with conventional leaf work combined with shoots. The execution of the work displays such naturalistic taste and such ease of conception that it leads us to think the work must be much older, having been created originally for some indigenous building. At the entrance, under the central archway, is a slab of black marble which is believed to be the upturned plinth of an image of Parshvanatha, the twenty-third Jain Tirthamkhara; it was taken from a temple that Ahmad Shah had destroyed and is in this position so as to allow the faithful to trample it as they entered the mosque.

Ahmedabad: Ahmad Shah Rauza and Rani-ka Hujra

To the east of the courtyard of the *jami masjid* is the *rauza* (mausoleum) of the sultan, which was probably begun by Ahmad Shah but completed after his death by his son Muhammad Karim (1441–51). It consists of an imposing square mausoleum with projecting porticoes at the centre of each side. Inside is an octagonal central area and four square rooms at the corners, connected by pillared verandahs. The frontage of the central area is formed of open-work slabs of stone. All the spaces are covered with domes: the central one, resting on a higher base, towers over the lateral domes, which are arranged symmetrically over the corner rooms. Although this building has no special architectural importance because it is an adaptation to Islamic needs of indigenous temple buildings, the tomb functioned as a model for later Gujarati structures.

Not far from the king's *dargah* was the Rani-ka Hujra (Tomb of the Queens), much simpler in design and dating from more or less the same period. It is reached by means of four stepped entrances that lead to the interior by means of a pillared corridor. The exterior perimeter is made up of a wall some 3 m high decorated with a series of columns and a projecting awning. In addition to the porticoes is a gallery made up of open columns; this is divided from the perimeter within which the tombs sit by a closed surface that is interrupted, however, by doors and windows. Beyond this gallery is another pillared verandah. Hugely imaginative geometric and floral decoration is arranged in panels in the doors and the windows. At the centre of the open courtyard is a platform on which the black-and-white marble cenotaphs rest, displaying highly refined work, almost like stone lace, with inlays of metal and mother-of-pearl. It would seem that the introduction of this fine elegance was the work of the Rani Rajputs and the eunuchs of the royal harem.

Ahmedabad: other buildings

The Tin Darwaza, a fine monumental gate 12 m high and some 27 m wide, dates from the epoch of Ahmad Shah. It has three vaults, of which the central one is a little wider and is flanked by two fluted bastions which are divided into various floors by means of relief borders. Above the arches, which are almost 8 m high, are three small balconies supported by corbels, a characteristic of Hindu architecture. The upper terrace was once covered by a tile roof (the present roof does not belong to the original structure). The entrance was the main gate in a wide perimeter wall in front of the *bhadr*, constituting the *maidan shah*, or royal square, at the centre of which was a fountain and a raised terrace from which the sovereign viewed military displays or parades by foreign emissaries.

However, Ahmad Shah's *jami masjid* represents the most significant monument of the second period of Gujarati art. The buildings erected during the reigns of Muhammad Karim (1442–51) and Qutb al-Din Shah (1451–8) did not add much to the evolution of the style, which is characterized by harmonious forms and measured decoration.

Two types of building developed alongside each other, one based on the Islamic arch, the other on pillars and architraves in the Hindu tradition. Buildings of both types were often covered with domes. As well as his father's mausoleum and the queens' cemetery, Muhammad Karim built Sakar Khan's tomb at Ahmedabad (1450) and contributed to the construction of a very large complex at Sarkhej which was finished by his son and successor, Qutb al-Din.

Sarkhej: Shaikh Ahmad Khattu Ganj Bakhsh complex

In the village of Sarkhej, some 10 km south-west of Ahmedabad, a famous Muslim saint retreated into hermitage. This saint was even credited with the foundation of Ahmedabad since he had been the spiritual counsellor of Ahmad Shah following his conversion from a dissolute life. He was Shaikh Ahmad Khattu Ganj Bakhsh, who died in poverty in 1446 at the age of 111 lunar years after having refused all the honours offered to him by the sovereign. In the year of his death, Muhammad Shah began building a splendid tomb and mosque for him, remarkable for its purity of design and elegance of detail. Subsequently, the area became one of the favourite retreats of the sultan Mahmud Begarha, who had a large artificial lake dug there, on the banks of which he built splendid palaces as his own residences. He also built two mausoleums, one for himself and the other for his family, opposite the saint's tomb. Other tombs were added later, transforming the area into a sort of imperial necropolis.

Some of the buildings have disappeared completely – pillaged for building materials – while just one remains in a reasonable state of conservation. It is on two storeys with projecting porticoes to the front and rows of elegant pillars which support the flat roofs.

The most interesting building of the complex, however, is the majestic tomb of the saint, completed in 1451 by Qutb al-Din Shah. It stands on a low platform in front of which, aligned with the main entrance, there is an elegant, square-based pavilion made up of 16 slender pillars carrying nine small cupolas. The mausoleum, 32 x 32 m, is the largest of its kind in Gujarat. It is made up of a square central hall, of some 10 m each side, covered with a large dome supported by double pillars and surrounded by another four rows of pillars which form an unusual hypostyle space. Smaller cupolas, thirteen along each façade, surround the principal dome. The square interior that holds the tomb is screened by open-work and chiselled brass panels with varied patterns. The external walls – divided into two floors and opened by arched doors – carry fine stone grates, also in delicate openwork, which introduce a pleasantly diffused light to the interior.

The mosque connected to the tomb is also very large – including the courtyard it measures some 80 x 60 m – while the sanctuary itself is 23 m deep. The *sahn* is surrounded by pillared corridors that support small cupolas or flat roofs. On the southern side is a projecting portico

Above The mosque at Sarkhej was constructed as part of a complex of buildings dedicated to the saint Shaikh Ahmad Khattu Ganj Bakhsh, who died in 1446.

Opposite The tomb of Muhammad Begarha at Sarkhej, southwest of Ahmedabad, is part of a family complex of tombs.

which reaches the level of the water in the large cistern. The hypostyle prayer hall faces onto the courtyard with 16 pillars and is covered by 10 larger domes arranged in two rows and 40 smaller domes arranged symmetrically between the others and alternating with flat roofs. The only ornament in the mosque, which is a perfect example of elegant simplicity, is found in the five fine *mihrab*, three of which have niches with rectangular profiles and two with semi-circular profiles, all projecting towards the exterior. Despite the absence of a traditional façade (this fact itself would seem to proclaim the triumph of local trabeated structures over Islamic arched structures) the whole is very convincing.

The later tomb of Sultan Mahmud Begarha is an almost square building (25 x 23 m), its façades dressed in slabs of open-work stone, except for the eastern façade which is in brickwork. Inside are two domed bays in which there is a square of 20 columns connected by open-work screens which include the burial chamber covered by a dome some 6.5 m in diameter. Of similar design, but smaller, is the Queens' Tomb, also decorated inside and outside with stone slabs worked with a great variety of open-work patterns, that even include the birds that symbolize heaven and immortality.

Ahmedabad: Darya Khan
Mausoleum and other buildings

During the brief reign of Qutb al-Din Shah (1451–8) the large Kankariya tank on the south of Ahmedabad was created. Various mosques and mausoleums were also built, among them the tomb that carries his name (which is nevertheless of little architectural interest), the much-ruined mosques of Maliq Alam and Maliq Shaban, and the much more important mosque in the suburb of Rajapur which included a tomb dedicated to the wife of Sayyid Budha bin Sayyid Yaqut, known as Bibiji.

Of great interest from a structural point of view are two buildings erected under Qutb al-Din, but perhaps commissioned by an official of his court. In terms of both design and technique these buildings are so different from any other of their time as to suggest the involvement of outside constructors, perhaps from the south of

Persia. These are the sepulchral monument of Darya Khan at Ahmedabad and the mosque of Alif Khan at Dholka. Both are built in brick, in contrast with all the other buildings of Gujarat, and are therefore completely lacking in pillars and architraves which were replaced by arches and brickwork piers. The mosque is much ruined, while the tomb is still in good condition. Quadrangular in form (some 40 m each side), each external façade has five openings with pointed arches, of which the central one is wider than the others, and all are enclosed within a rectangular frame with projecting moulding along the top. The funeral chamber at the centre measures some 15 m each side and is covered by a fine pear-shaped dome set on a high drum. The apex of the dome reaches almost 26 m from the ground. Four openings, one at the centre of each side, allow access to the chamber. Around this space are 16 communicating cells covered by small cupolas and forming a sort of open corridor corresponding to each of the external entrances. The bases of the domes are imposed on octagons formed out of four triangular arches which are filled with receding arches and display great constructive ability, reminiscent of some Iranian buildings that date to pre-Islamic times.

Dholka: Alif Khan Mosque

The mosque of Alif Khan at Dholka is a severe rectangular structure whose façade seems to have fallen into ruin long ago, but the two massive minarets with their vertical mouldings are still standing, even though their summit, in the form of a domed lantern, is missing in part. The prayer hall is made up of three square units, each covered with a fine hemispherical dome, with massive walls between them. In each of these walls are three archways, the central one larger than the other two. The façade in its present state is simple in form: the three doorways are of equal size with pointed arches, with three windows above them. The three deep *mihrab* project on the outside and their surface is decorated with geometric and floral motifs in stucco. Next to the *mihrab* there are pretty *jali*-filled windows. Between the two minaret towers, which jut out sharply from the façade, there was a row of arches whose supports can still be seen between the doors. These formed a sort of triple-arched screen which concealed the domes.

Rajapur

The *rauza* (funerary complex) of Rajapur dates from 1454, according to an inscription that attributes it to Qutb al-Din, and is clearly of great refinement. The mosque is very large, measuring almost 50 m in length by almost 18 m in depth and is covered by five wide domes. The façade is extremely imposing, with the central area framed by two large multi-storey minarets, one of which is partly collapsed as a result of a lightning strike in the 1800s. These minarets carry a rich decoration of floral motifs, above all on the bases and the small balconies that divide the various floors. The lateral sections of the mosque have respectively a pointed arch and a sort of portico made up of an arched entrance flanked by windows. The windows were also arched but a little lower and narrower than the central opening, with a richly decorated balustrade. The pillars that frame both sides of the windows are elegantly carved and support S-shaped corbels on which rest projecting awnings. Flanking these openings are two small windows crowned by a triangular motif and divided into 12 sections by open-work panels, each decorated with a different graceful pattern. Similar windows are also found on the lateral walls and the far wall of the mosque.

The central arrangement of the façade recalls that of the later mosque of Bibi Achyut Kuki (1469) while the external wings are very similar to those of the sanctuary of Miyan Khan Chishti (1465). Inside, the mosque measures some 46 x 10 m and is made up of five domed square spaces, while to the front and rear run two parallel bays, covered alternately by small cupolas and flat Hindu-style roofs. The central part of the mosque, as usual, rises above the rest of the building forming a gallery underneath the high central dome. At the northern extremity is the ladies' gallery, enclosed between screens of open-work stone and supported by 25 free-standing pillars and 11 pilasters. These, like all the other supports in the mosque, are square with moulded bases and capitals, but the two situated inside the main entrance are octagonal with slightly chamfered corners derived from a type of purely Hindu origin. The five *mihrab* projecting towards the exterior have different shapes, but are all decorated with fine mouldings.

Ahmedabad: Azam-Muazzam Mausoleum

On the road to Sarkhej is another unusual monumental tomb built in brick and known popularly as Azam-Muazzam. It is a massive square structure, with semi-circular bastions at the four corners tapered towards the top and a dome lower than that of the Darya Khan but arranged as in the Dholka Mosque, without a drum. Each façade is opened by three large and deep blind arches and has a continuous series of arched windows in the upper part. It resembles later Tughluq or Lodi buildings of Delhi and, more than the two monuments discussed above, seems foreign to Gujarati architecture.

Although, as Havell maintains, the style of these buildings may have exercised a certain influence on the later structures of Bijapur, Gujarati architects were too used to their pillared and trabeated system to accept unconditionally the curvilinear Islamic style. The two methods therefore continued to coexist even if, in the third and most mature period of Gujarati art (identified with the reign of Mahmud Begarha, 1459–1511), the arcuated style enjoyed more favour. Animated by a great passion for monumental architecture, Mahmud went on to enrich Ahmedabad with mosques and mausoleums and founded the cities of Mahmudabad and Champanir, embellishing them with noble and splendid buildings. Other cities, such as Baroda, Junagadh in Kathiavar and Jalar in Malwa, were also rebuilt and had many new buildings added.

Building activity continued under Muzaffar II (1511–26) and Bahadur Shah (1526–37), but it declined under their successors, who were involved in bloody struggles both internally and against neighbouring states. Nevertheless, the style continued to make its influence felt even after the fall of the sultanate (1573) and even in various works built outside Gujarat.

The most numerous and significant monuments are nevertheless those of Mahmud Begarha: usually complexes that include a mausoleum and a funeral mosque, known as a *rauza*. The mosques are of two types, with either an open or a

The Bibi Achyut Kuki Mosque (1465) at Ahmedabad. The perimeter wall surrounding the mosque has round corner towers not seen elsewhere in Gujarat.

closed façade. In the first case it is made up of a row of pillars, at the extremities of which are the minarets that constitute an essential part of the façade. In the second case, the frontage of the sanctuary is made up of a wall opened by arches with the minarets arranged to the sides of the main archway, which is wider than the others. The corner minarets lost their functional utility with the passing of time to become simply slender ornamental towers, as can be seen in the mosques of Rani Sipari (1514) and Shah Khub Muhammad Chishti (1538).

Ahmedabad: Sayyid Usman complex

The tomb and the mosque of Sayyid Usman (1460) at Usmanpur, a suburb of Ahmedabad, both have a domed hypostyle arrangement; the sanctuary is one of the oldest examples with minarets at the extremities of the pillared hall. Although the minarets are well proportioned with their six floors interrupted by projecting mouldings, they are perhaps a little too tall for the mosque which appears slightly out of proportion. Each section taken separately, however, is designed successfully. The tomb has a similar plan to that of the funeral site of Shaikh Ahmad Khattu at Sarkhej, with a domed square hall at the centre of a double row of pillars.

Ahmedabad: Dastur Khan Mosque

The Dastur Khan Mosque, which carries an inscription from 1463, is almost square (c.30 x 34 m) and rises on a high plinth. The courtyard is surrounded by *riwaq* that are just one span deep and completely domed. These lead directly into the prayer hall, which faces onto the courtyard with a series of pillars. It is separated from the exterior by a series of open-work screens with extremely refined motifs.

Ahmedabad: Miyan Khan Chishti and Bibi Achyut Kuki mosques

The mosques of Miyan Khan Chishti and Bibi Achyut Kuki (see p. 117), both at Ahmedabad, share similar designs and dimensions (33 x 15 m). The façades are opened by a large central archway, flanked by imposing multi-storey minarets divided by small balconies on elaborately carved corbels. To the sides of the balconies in the first mosque are three arched apertures with balustrades, similar to those of the Bibiji Mosque at Rajapur; in the second mosque are two smaller arched entrances. In both buildings the prayer hall is divided by pillars into three domed compartments, the central one of which rises on a double floor. The Bibi Achyut Kuki Mosque, along with its mausoleum in the form of a small pillared pavilion, stands inside a large rectangular enclosure, with round towers at the corners, which are unknown elsewhere in Gujarat.

Ahmedabad: Shah Alam mausoleum

The mausoleum of Shah Alam (c.1475) is made up of three successive enclosures and displays the first use of the arched elements that became more popular later, for example in the tombs of Vatva, Mahmudabad and Champanir. The funeral chamber, covered by a dome and with open-work walls, is made up of a series of pillars arranged in a circle and in their turn surrounded by an exterior arch made up of pillars connected by pointed arches filled with stone open-work slabs. Within the complex there is also a mosque of a type later than the 'open' variety with two high multi-storey minarets at the extremities of the hall, a pool for ablutions, a large underground water cistern, another domed monumental tomb, hundreds of free-standing tombs, various houses for the pilgrims and, naturally, an imposing entrance gateway.

Vatva: Qutb Alam mausoleum

At Vatva (also known as Batva or Batwa), about 8 km south-east of Ahmedabad, there are several tombs dating from about 1480: the main one is dedicated to Shaikh Burhan al-Din, the grandson of a famous saint from Uchchh who moved to the court of Ahmad Shah and died there in 1452. The mausoleum, also known as Qutb Alam, is a grand building, which, although greatly ruined, still carries notable traces of its ancient beauty. It represents a definite step forward in the evolution of the style because, as Fergusson states:

The arch replaces the architrave and consequently makes the building much larger ... with improved beauty and correct effect; [but] here the arch is used liberally everywhere: these are not windbreaks of arches that hide a columned interior, but a uniform design in all its parts.[7]

The large two-storey tomb rests on a platform of some 35 squ. m with a projecting portico on the southern side supported by four pillars and covered at the centre by a dome. This then leads to a verandah with arcades set on a double row of pillars which support vaulted ceilings. The central room is surrounded by 12 pillars and rises above the rest by means of another row of arches; it is crowned by a projecting cornice supported by corbels. Above the cornice is the wide central dome that had four corner *chhatri* on small slender pillars. The open-work slabs of marble that once connected the upper arches and perhaps even the lower arches have disappeared. Still surviving, however, is the elegant open-work balustrade arranged around the tomb and covered with a richly carved baldachin. The monument is said to date from the reign of Mahmud Begarha, but this is uncertain. The collapse of the lateral arches was probably due to lack of skill on the part of the builders, who were not used to working with arcuated forms. In fact the smallest tomb, and the mosque attached to the complex, are entirely in the trabeated style that local craftsmen of the time were used to. A smaller tomb, dedicated to the saint's son, was built in the Sarkhej style.

Sojali: Sayyid Mubarak Bukhari mausoleum

Even more successful from an architectural point of view is the tomb of Sayyid Mubarak Bukhari, built after 1588 in the village of Sojali, 3 km from Mahmudabad (now Mehmedabad). It is a striking example of the arcuated style, even although its lower floor is in the same style as that of the tomb of Shah Alam. Nevertheless, the external row of pillars is made of simple open arches without open-work screens, which appear instead around the internal burial chamber. Its square plan of 29 m each side includes a great number of pillars arranged in such a way as to support, every four pillars, a small cupola. These are arranged around the burial chamber, 11 m in diameter, which is delimited by 12 columns connected by panels decorated with *jali* upon which is set an elegant dome more than 21 m high at the keystone and surrounded externally by four *chhatri*. This happy arrangement of all the

GUJARAT (c.1300–c.1550)

The Qutb Alam mausoleum (c.1480) at Vatva, south of Ahmedabad. The sophisticated use of arches represents an advance in Gujarati regional style.

various parts of the monument and the increased strength in construction that it demonstrates are explained by the considerable influence exercised on Gujarati architecture by the contemporary Lodi period. Due to the decline of the sultanate of Delhi, many artists were drawn to Gujarat by its renown. It is not improbable that an artist from the capital – expert in the dictates of Islamic architecture which by that time were well developed in Delhi – guided the work of Gujarati craftsmen whose only contribution to the design of the Muslim tomb is to be found in the domed, stepped portico that precedes the perfectly square ground plan of the tomb.

OTHER MOSQUES

As well as funerary buildings, there was also increased activity in the building of mosques of various types, often of smaller dimensions, but always modelled exquisitely and decorated with a refinement that was sometimes luxurious. Among these mosques are the Muhafiz Khan of 1485, together with the Bai Harir at Asarva and the Rani Rupavati (see p. 120) in the neighbourhood of Mirzapur, both erected about 1500. The first is almost a family chapel, measuring inside only 15 x 8 m. The roof is supported by eight columns and by as many pilasters on the perimeter walls, which together divide the hall into square areas arranged in three rows by depth and five by width. At each corner is a small cupola – three in the middle area – in line with the *mihrab*. The first two of the square spaces, slightly different in their proportions, rise on a second floor supported by double pillars connected by open-work stone slabs which rest on a richly carved frieze. The other eight square spaces have flat roofs. The façade is opened by three pointed arches of equal height surmounted by extremely graceful small balconies on corbels, typical of Gujarati secular architecture, which are repeated on a larger scale in the lateral façades of the mosque. Two splendid four-storeyed minarets, divided by alternately octagonal and circular balconies and with pointed terminals, enclose the extremities of the façade and provide it with unity and grace.

The mosques of Bai Harir and Rani Rupavati have minarets that are arranged centrally and present an effective synthe-

Above The Rani Rupavati Mosque (c.1500) at Ahmedabad represents a synthesis of the earlier local 'trabeated' style and the more modern arched form.

Opposite The small, jewel-like Rani Sipari Mosque (1514) at Ahmedabad shows a distinctive advance in the decorative refinement of Gujarati architecture.

sis between the arcuated and the trabeated styles. Indeed, at the lateral extremities of the façade of the prayer hall, to the sides of the great entrance arch, there are small balconies that are very similar to those of the old Hindu temples. The splendid minarets, partly collapsed, carry extremely complex decoration that substantially lightens the mass of the building which is otherwise rather heavy. Connected to the mosques are the tombs, which are domed and have verandahs supported by pillars. In the Bai Harir complex there is also a beautiful *waw*. In this same style are two minarets, called Sidi Bashir, attached to a tomb that looks rather like a triumphal structure.

Some beautiful buildings date from the reigns of Muzaffar II, Bahadur and Mahmud III, although their architectural vitality gradually diminished as their decorative refinement increased. Among them the 1514 mosque and tomb complex of Rani Sipari (more correctly Rani Sabrai) is outstanding. This has been called 'the most exquisite jewel of Ahmedabad'. The mosque is small and has a pillared façade set between two slender minarets which are fluted and decorated with work that displays all the delicacy of a goldsmith. The tomb is square, with a domed upper floor that corresponds to the central space. The lower floor is enclosed by open-work slabs of superior production with extremely delicate designs.

Another small mosque, the Gumti, at Isanpur, is similar in appearance, with minarets at the extremities of the façade, which opens towards the exterior with four pairs of coupled columns. Compared with the Rani Sipari it has a more robust appearance and less refined ornament.

Similar in style are the Ibrahim Sayyid Mosque on the road that leads to the Shah Alam Mosque, and the so-called Bawa Ali Shah at Paldi-Kochrab with its stupendous stone corbels that support the projecting awning and its merlons worked as fine as lace in countless geometric and floral patterns. Likewise the Shah Khub Sayyid Muhammad Chishti, with an inscription that dates it from 1538 and the delightful Darwish Ali, built by Bibi Khonja in 1504. This last, connected to a tomb, is precious in every detail both in its structure and in its decoration: despite its limited proportions (little more than 10 m in length), it is a true architectural jewel. Of the same type, but much larger (some 38 x 8 m) is the Fateh Mosque at Daryapur, dating from the first half of the sixteenth century.

ISANPUR: IMAD AL-MULK MALIQ ISAN *RAUZA*

The *rauza* of Imad al-Mulk Maliq Isan, near Isanpur, on the other hand, has completely different characteristics. It includes a mosque and a tomb at the centre of a perimeter surrounded by pillared corridors covered by domes. Imad al-Mulk was one of the greatest nobles of the court of Mahmud Begarha and of Muzaffar II, and it seems that during the latter's reign he built Isanpur, one of the most beautiful suburbs of Ahmedabad, and his tomb with its adjoining mosque. The tomb's front has paired pillars, the central part rising above the rest with a series of pointed arches, the middle one of which is wider and higher than the lateral arches and has a festooned border. Above this raised floor is a central dome surrounded by three smaller cupolas, but there is no minaret on the façade or its wings. The elegant tomb, of the trabeated type with a large dome, fills the centre of the courtyard.

AHMEDABAD: MALIQ SARANG MOSQUE

The Maliq Sarang Mosque in the Sarangpur neighbourhood is stylistically similar to the mosques of Bai Harir and Rani Rupavati: an enormous façade dominated by two imposing minarets. It was founded by a nobleman from the court of Muzaffar II in the first decades of the sixteenth century. The mosque is accompanied by a mausoleum that is known locally as the *rauza* of Rani Bibi, because of which the mosque is also sometimes known locally as the Rani Mosque. Its façade is opened by five arches, of which the central one is much higher than the lateral arches and is more sumptuously decorated. To its sides stand two imposing minarets covered with magnificent carved decoration. Unfortunately, both minarets were truncated in the nineteenth century, partly because of vandalism, partly because of clumsy restoration work. The beauty of the northern minaret is preserved in a nineteenth-century photograph that shows its various floors divided by small balconies on curved and gracefully carved corbels. The mausoleum, too, standing not far from the mosque, has suffered much damage, but it would seem to have been one of the most splendid examples of the 'pillared' type.

The mosque connected to the mausoleum of Shah Alam, probably dating from 1550, instead presents a completely arcuated façade. It opens with seven pointed arches, alternately narrower or wider, which create different spaces even within the sanctuary. The widest spans are covered by huge domes, the narrowest by small cupolas; the oblong spaces between the wide and narrow spans have pyramidal covers. The high projecting minarets at the two extremities of the façade, which complete the whole majestically, are perhaps a little later than the mosque and carry four galleries supported by fine corbels.

AHMEDABAD: MUHAMMAD GHAUS GWALIYORI

Another unusual mosque, dating from the same period, is that of Muhammad Ghaus Gwaliyori, which has an imposing aspect due to the enormous central propylon. This last is similar to those of the Jaunpur mosques, but it has been disfigured by restoration work carried out in the nineteenth century. At its extremity rises a robust minaret over six storeys above the level of the parapet, with the same number of small balconies supported by fine corbels. Its ground plan is octagonal – unique among Gujarati buildings. At the southern extremity of the façade is a wider, simpler octagonal bastion that seems incomplete. The interior of the mosque is remarkable for the beautiful pendentives of the arches that support the domes.

Ahmedabad: Shaikh Hasan Muhammad Chishti Mosque

The mosque built in the Shahpur neighbourhood in 1565 by Shaikh Hasan Muhammad Chishti – also known as the Qazi Mosque – is imposing, with a façade opened by nine high arches. The two arches that flank the central arch are narrower than the others so that they align with the internal pillars that support the dome. Over the five central spans, for the entire depth of the prayer hall, there is an upper floor with five pillared openings and a central arch from which there projects a balcony supported by heavy corbels. At the extremities of the façade are the massive bases of two robust minarets which were never completed, but nevertheless display exuberant, rich and extremely refined decoration. Taken as a whole the mosque is very similar in design to that of Baba Lului, probably built in the same period at Berhampur. The latter, however, is more harmonious because its upper domed floor has just three pillared apertures on each side and is surrounded by four small cupolas. The bases of the minarets carry the same extraordinary richness of decoration as the Shahpur Mosque.

Ahmedabad: Sidi Said Mosque

The last great building in the Gujarati style, before the Mughal conquest, was built by the head of a faction of African slaves who had claimed power in some regions of the country. The Abyssinian Sidi Said had the homonymous mosque built in 1572, a little outside the northeastern corner of the citadel of Ahmedabad. Its façade is opened by five large arches of equal height enclosed within two octagonal buttresses that reached the level of the roof, which is covered by 15 small cupolas. It would seem that the buttresses once carried minarets. Inside, eight pillars arranged in two longitudinal rows divide the space into 15 units of varying dimensions further divided by arches supporting almost flat ceilings that rest on the base through a combination of the usual architraved system, corbels and a series of small arches that cut the corners. The most remarkable part of the mosque consists of a series of ten pointed windows (see p. 104) some 3 m wide and 2 m high, four of which are arranged on the far wall and three on the lateral walls. Eight of them are divided into small squares of openwork stone with extremely stylized geometric and floral patterns. The two most internal windows, which have spread the fame of this small mosque even beyond India, are decorated with the 'palm and parasite' motif, a common phenomenon among eastern plants. The designs of the two windows, however, are not the same. In the first there is only one palm with an extremely slender trunk that is trying to flee from the sinuous coils of the parasite. The parasite spreads over the surface with a series of curved lines that are repeated to endlessly, seeking to strangle the palm in its leaves. In the second window there are four palms being attacked by four parasites, the shoots of which envelop and spread, creating a splendid fabric of flowers and leaves which fills all the available space with an obsessive and fascinating rhythm. It could be said that in these windows there appears the miracle of conciliation between the indigenous artists' direct observation of nature and the Muslims' typical tendency towards stylization which arose out of their fear of copying the creative powers of God. In no other part of India, not even in the splendid Mughal *jali* of Delhi or Agra, are similar wonders to be found. As we have already mentioned, only in the Bengali mosque of Daraz Bari, among the terracotta decoration on the walls, does this motif of the climbing plant slowly killing the palm appear. This concomitance in representation has led to some theories on the passage of ideas across the subcontinent.

Champanir

In the first decade of the sixteenth century Mahmud Begarha completed the creation of his new capital at Champanir,

Above The Sidi Said Mosque (1572) at Ahmedabad, built by a former Abyssinian slave of the same name, is the last great example of the Gujarati style before the arrival of the Mughals.

Opposite An entrance gate in the city wall of Muhammad Beghara's new capital Champanir (begun 1486), which was built on the site of the Hindu fort of Pavagadh.

which he had begun in 1486 shortly after his capture of the fort of Pavagadh, torn from the Hindu leader Jai Singh Patai Rawal. It seems that the sovereign was fascinated by the high fortified hill surrounded below by forests and he decided to build his city there. However, after 23 years of construction, the city was actually inhabited for just a little over 23 years.

Champanir was planned, according to the usual scheme of Indian capitals, with the citadel surrounded by walls enclosing a central square, while the city outside spread across a wide area – given that some buildings have been found in the nearby forest some 5 km away. We know that the city had fine roads and a square with stone houses, but little remains of the civil and religious buildings, above all the former, which were pillaged and dismantled when the city was abandoned. The citadel walls survive with their bastions and well-proportioned gateways, as does the *mandvi* (toll-house) and the guards' quarters. The palace is very plain, almost square, is open at the two extremities and has façades carrying six windows. The interior is made up of five rows of arches that delimit a colonnaded space with five almost equal bays. The roof is flat, massive and without ornament. Naturally, because of their sacred nature, the mosques and the tombs were spared the pillaging and more of them have survived.

The most important of the Champanir monuments is the *jami masjid* (see p. 124), which stands some 40 m from the eastern gate of the city. Although derived from the Ahmedabad gate, it presents substantial differences both in its exterior aspect and in its internal arrangement. Even though it is of remarkable size, it occupies only three quarters of the area of the Great Mosque of Ahmedabad. The courtyard is surrounded by a series of arcaded cloisters just one bay deep. The perimeter walls are more richly decorated than any other buildings of this type, with windows carrying beautiful patterns.

The façade is made up of five arches, of which the central one is almost 5 m wide, while the lateral arches are exactly half that. The main arch is flanked by ponderous minarets 36 m high and patterned at regular intervals by horizontal cornices and mouldings, in their turn decorated with niches and small multi-lobed arches; it is also framed within a rectangular wall 17 m wide and more than 9 m tall on the lateral wings which rise in their turn to some 8 m. Above the apex of the arch and at the sides of the minaret are windows with small balconies supported by elaborated corbels of a clearly Hindu type. Another four smaller minarets rise at the corners of the perimeter of the mosque: the southern one was partly ruined by cannon fire in 1812. The interior of the mosque measures 66 x 27 m and contains 176 pillars arranged in such a way as to provide 11 large square spaces, of which there are four to the front and back and three to the centre. In the north-western corner is a ladies' gallery which has a raised octagonal bench under the dome. The middle bay rises over three floors above the others and reaches a height of 22 m. It assumes the form of a Latin cross with short arms, at the centre of which is the 'rotunda' covered by the dome. The 'rotunda', like a square well, is encircled on its two upper orders by splendid openwork balconies along which is an arrangement of seats for rest and meditation. The main dome has a profusely decorated

Above The *jami masjid* (1508–9) at Champanir. Although derived from the Ahmedabad gate, the mosque is smaller and more richly decorated.

Opposite left The highly decorative southern side entrance to the *jami masjid* at Champanir is the best preserved.

drum; inside it is divided by ribs into 16 sections, which are also decorated with refined patterns. Access to each floor is by means of stairs in the minarets, the first floors of which are common to the rest of the sanctuary. The second floors communicate with the balconied window that is above the main arch of the façade. The seven *mihrab* of the *qibla* wall are embellished with various floral motifs and, at the centre, with hanging lamps. Above the cornice is a graceful multi-lobed arch which, in the central *mihrab*, contains a slab with an inscription that carries the date AH 914, corresponding to 1508–9. The *mihrab* project to the outside with fine carved and modelled spurs. Among the larger domes there are smaller cupolas and flat roofs with rich ornament. Along the perimeter walls are windows, some of which, on the northern and southern sides, have balconies. The three gateways that led into the courtyard (measuring some 50 m from north to south by 40 m from east to west) were beautiful pavilions projecting from the centre of the northern, southern and eastern walls. The best preserved and most decorated is on the southern side, reached from outside by some steps: it has a fine central arch and two lateral blind niches filled with finely worked slabs of stone. The pediment, which protrudes considerably, is supported by beautifully designed S-shaped corbels and was surmounted by a dome, now collapsed, on an octagonal drum surrounded by corner *chhatri* on four pillars. The general impression given by this mosque is of an extremely refined structure in which the art of construction has reached its peak.

There are other, smaller, mosques at Champanir built in the same style. Among these, the graceful structure known as Nagina Mosque presents, in a much reduced form, a very similar plan to that of the Great Mosque. The minarets that flank the main entrance are decorated with unequalled elegance and refinement, as is the balustrade of the central bay under the collapsed dome.

More interesting than the mosque are the tombs, often nameless and in ruins. The ground plan typically consists of a domed central room surrounded by an arcade covered by smaller domes with a

Gujarat (c.1300–c.1550)

Above Dating from about 1525, this tomb near the Nagina Mosque at Champanir is one of the finest in the area.

Opposite The late fifteenth-century Shaer-ki Mosque at Champanir, one of the smaller mosques in the area.

pillared portico projecting on each side. The growing use of arches in these tombs is noteworthy; these add grace and allow greater height in the structures. The carved ornament is arranged over the surfaces with much care and is excellently designed, even although some details display signs of an incipient mannerism and a certain mechanic execution. Among the finest examples of these tombs is that known as the Nagina Mosque, dating from about 1525. Small and made up of a square space once covered by a dome fixed on a drum, it is open on each side by a pointed arch, flanked by two blind arches decorated with balconied windows and stylized floral motifs. A series of beautifully designed projecting corbels decorates the cornice, which carries geometric motifs at regular intervals. These motifs are repeated on the base, both inside and outside.

The Shaer-ki and Kamani mosques have different structures, of an entirely horizontal type, in spite of their tall minarets.

CIVIL BUILDINGS

We have already mentioned the remains of some buildings in Sarkhej that date from the time of Mahmud Begarha. Other public buildings of great architectural elegance include the locks of various artificial lakes, such as that at Kankariya, and the *waw* or *baoli* (the stepped wells), true oases of freshness which take the form of extended underground galleries. The *waw* are made up of two parts: a vertical well shaft, from which water was taken in the usual manner by means of ropes, and an inclined passage that led along flights of stairs on various floors to the level of the water. A few of the most elaborate of these stepped wells are the Bai Hari *waw* of Ahmedabad of *c*.1499; the *waw* at Adalaj, a village some 16 km to the north of the city, more or less of the same epoch; and the *waw* at Bhamaria near Mahmudabad. In the first (which is the most typical example of the genre), at each extremity of the plan above ground level, are two pillared cloisters, and the remainder is underground. Below ground level there extends a series of pillared galleries connected by stairs which descend for three floors. Each gallery forms a compartment with small balconies, creating a peaceful retreat similar to the 'rotundas' in the mosques and, like those, carrying profuse decoration on pillars, capitals, rails, wall surfaces and so on. The dimensions of these stepped wells are considerable. The Bai Hari, for example, is some 45 m long, 6 m wide and 10 m deep. The Bhamaria one was situated at the centre of a pleasure garden. According to local tradition, the emperor had built it as a summer refuge and the two stone arches that were erected on it acted as supports for the king's swing. As well as the four circular rooms built around the octagonal well at ground level, four flights of stairs led to eight underground rooms. From here four spiral stairways descended again to the spaces closest to the level of the water in the well. The courtiers and their consorts obviously must have spent much time here observing the waters of the well from the balconies and windows.

INFLUENCE OF GUJARATI ARCHITECTURE

Gujarati architecture exercised a remarkable influence in the areas around the Indian Ocean, for example the state of Jodhpur in Rajasthan where we find at least three mosques very similar to those of Ahmedabad.

In the Shams Mosque of Nagaur, which is said to have been built by the governor Shams Khan at the beginning of the thirteenth century and restored by Firuz Shah, there are in fact high turrets in the Firozian style at the extremities of the façade. Nevertheless, with its high, narrow arches – together with the interior of the prayer hall and its multi-storey gallery open under the central dome – the general concept of the façade itself reveals a decidedly Gujarati influence.

At Jalor there are two mosques, probably built in the first half of the sixteenth century, which mirror Gujarati forms of the late Begarha period. These are the mosque of the Fort and the Topkhana Mosque in the city. The first seems derived from the more graceful structures diffused in Ahmedabad at the end of Mahmud Begarha's reign. The second, although presenting a rather original aspect, with a façade dominated at the centre by three unequal arches surmounted by a gallery with small arches, and enclosed between two powerful, projecting towers, suggests a Gujarati influence in various elements; for example, the pillared wings covered by low cupolas, the arrangement of the arches (the central one is higher and wider, the lateral ones are lower and narrower), but above all the special use of the open-work screens that decorate the central structure. These *jali*, characteristic of Gujarati art and exported to various parts of India, especially in the Mughal period, were

Below The Shams Mosque at Nagaur, Rajasthan. Said to have been built by the governor Shams Khan at the beginning of the thirteenth century and restored by Firuz Shah, it has various elements that suggest Gujarati influence.

Opposite The Topkhana Mosque (first half of the sixteenth century) at Jalor in Rajasthan seems to have been inspired by late Ahmedabad and Gujarati structures.

inserted into panels and decorated the windows, the arches and the blind niches, to the point where the façade became as delicate as lace work.

A monumental *idgah* outside Jalor also has an interesting structure, with a deep *mihrab* niche surmounted by two small ornamental towers with several storeys.

In other places in Gujarat, such as Mangrol and Halol, buildings have survived that are of some architectural interest, though they are rather provincial interpretations of the great art of the cities. In this connection we may mention the Jami, Rahimat and Raveli mosques at Mangrol and the tomb of Sikandar Shah at Halol, with its extremely irregular ground plan. The surviving minaret of the Ek Minar-ki Mosque, which is all that is left of the building, has a structure that closely resembles that of the minarets of Bhurhanpur and is particularly interesting because it seems to have stood detached from the mosque, like the Qutb Minar in Delhi (see p. 23), which had so far been thought to be unique.

1. The nickname Begarha has been explained in various ways. The most likely seems to be that it refers to the *vegado* of Gujarat, a steer with very wide horns, this being an obvious allusion to his moustaches which were so long that he could have tied them behind his head. J. Burton-Page, 'Historical Contest', in *Ahmedabad*, ed. G. Michell and S. Shah, Bombay, 1988, p. 11.
2. Quoted in J. Burgess, *The Muhammedan Architecture of Ahmedabad*, Part i, A.D. 1412 to 1520, London, 1900, p. 23.
3. Koran xxiv, 35.
4. Grover, op. cit., p. 93.
5. J. Fergusson, *History of Indian and Eastern Architecture*, 1910, vol. 2, p. 232 and Burgess, op. cit., p. 30. The *amalaka* is a sort of ribbed stone ring which gets its name from the local fruit that it resembles.
6. Grover, op. cit., p. 93.
7. Fergusson, op. cit.

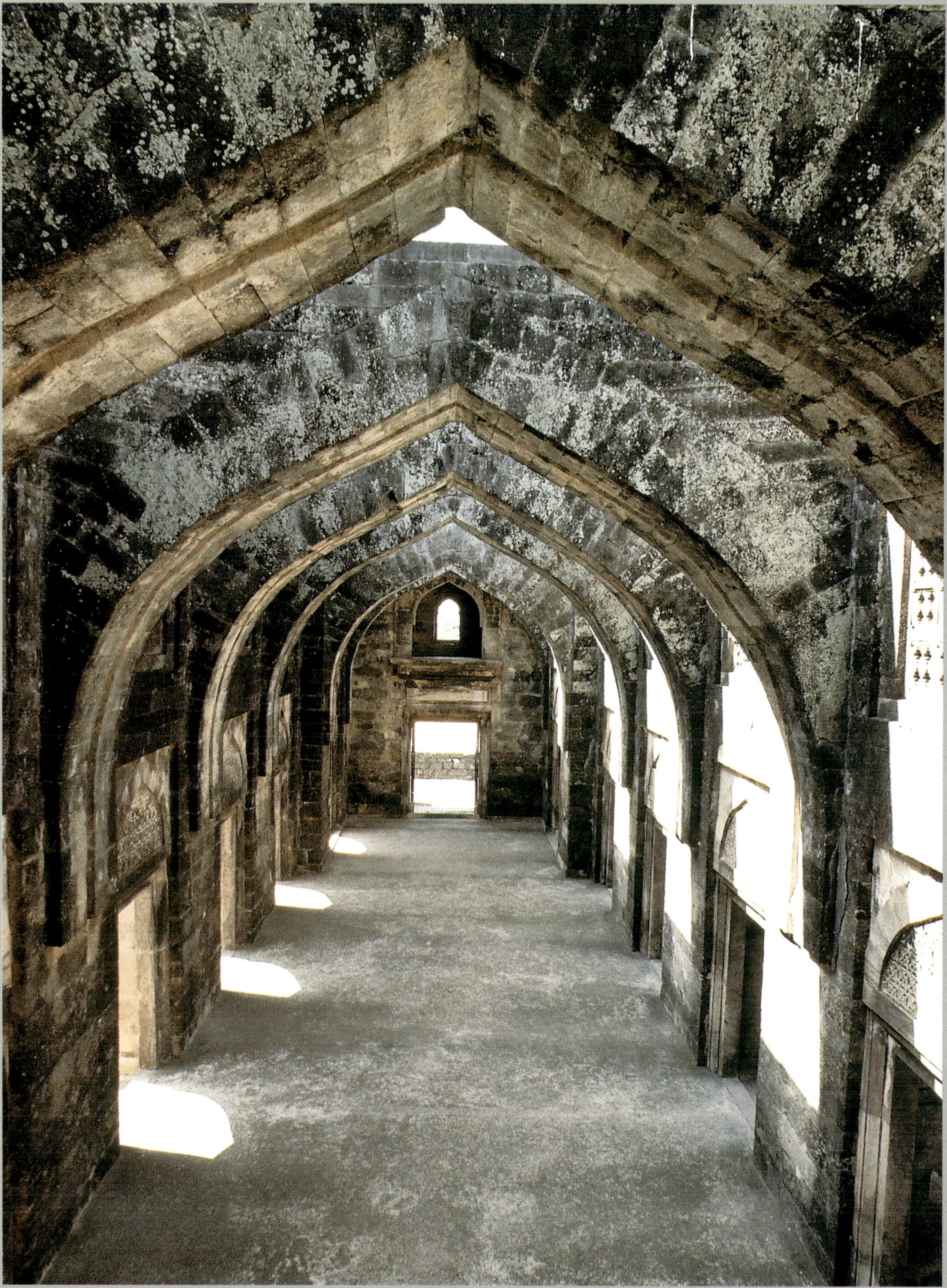

Malwa (c.1400–c.1550)

10

The fifteenth-century Hindola Mahall, an enormous meeting hall at Mandu. The name means 'Swinging Palace' and refers to the building's angled buttresses.

Malwa is situated towards the central south of the country and its architectural style is displayed fully in two cities, Dhar and Mandu. For some centuries the former had been the capital of the Paramaras, a powerful Hindu dynasty (eighth–thirteenth centuries AD) remembered in history as great protectors of literature. Mandu, too, 35 km from Dhar, was part of the Paramara realm when, in 1293, Jalal al-Din Khalji invaded, devastated it, and returned to Delhi loaded with spoil. In 1305 Ala al-Din Khalji definitively took possession of Malwa and the dominion came to form part of the sultanate of Delhi. In 1401 the governor of Malwa, Dilawar Khan Ghuri, made the most of Timur's invasion of Delhi, declared independence from the Tughluqs, and assumed the royal title. He made his capital at Dhar, but even while he reigned his son Hushang established a large fortress at Mandu on a plateau in the Vindhya mountains. Hushang moved the capital here in 1406 when he officially succeeded to his father's throne. Hushang Shah governed for almost 30 years (1406–32) and managed to expand the realm towards Kalpi in the north and Kharla in the south. Much loved by his subjects, he proved to be a great sovereign and was a prolific builder. With his son Muhammad Shah, who was poisoned in 1436, the Ghurid dynasty came to an end and the Khalji dynasty began. Mahmud, the founder, reigned for 33 years, making war on Gujarat, Deccan, Jaunpur and even the sultanate of Delhi. Under his government, nevertheless, the country prospered and became so famous that it received many emissaries from other Muslim realms, such as Sultan Abu Said, grandson of Timur, and the caliph of Egypt, Adil al-Mustaid Billah Yusuf. Mahmud was a great patron of knowledge and founded many colleges in various parts of his realm for the diffusion of literature. The philosophers and wise men of Malwa were able to hold their own with their counterparts from Shiraz and Samarqand.

Mahmud's passion for architecture was amply displayed in a great number of buildings at Mandu. However, these were built in a rush by incompetent architects and collapsed shortly after his death; now they are simply imposing ruins. Under Mahmud's successors the realm became weak, and in 1526 Bahadur Shah of Gujarat succeeded in invading and annexing it into his dominions until 1534, when he himself had to concede it to the ambitions of the Mughal Humayun. After some years a new, independent sovereign, Baz Bahadur, assumed the title of Sultan of Malwa and kept it until Akbar invaded the region in 1561 and caused him to flee. From then onwards Malwa came under Mughal domination and felt its artistic influence too. Being a meeting point between northern India, Gujarat and Deccan, Malwa was always open to various influences. It did manage, however, to amalgamate these influences into a characteristic style: simple, bold and well proportioned. Many elements of the Delhi styles are to be seen in its reinforced walls and the pointed arches with spear-point borders which were typical of the early Tughluqs, and in the 'boat keel' domes and the pyramidal roofs of Lodi taste. Local artists knew how to combine skilfully the two structural systems: the arch together with the pillar and the beam which was inspired by local temples. Their buildings are characterized by majestic stairways which lead to the high plinths on which they are built. Much of the decorative effect derives from the use of colour, both from coloured stone and marble and from encaustic tiles. These last, however, are largely lost because of climatic conditions. The principal construction material was a sandstone of a pleasing red colour which came from the nearby quarry at Bijawar, but the land was rich in marble and other stones of various hues and grains – yellow, slate black – of which the builders made liberal use. If marble was used above all in the roofs, in the interiors it was used together with semi-precious stones such as jasper, agate and carnelian. Blue and yellow glazed tiles – now for the most part lost – were arranged in panels and borders that rendered the buildings more lively. It is probable that the beautiful, brilliant turquoise produced at Mandu in the fifteenth century came from Multan, where it had arrived from Persia.[1]

Dhar: Kamal Maula and Lat-ki mosques

The first phase of Malwan architecture, which began about 1400 under the sovereign Dilawar Khan Ghuri, is represented in three mosques: two in Dhar and one in Mandu. The Kamal Maula (c.1400) and the Lat-ki Mosque (c.1405) are found in Dhar. The latter takes its name from the iron pillar in the Hindu style that stands in its courtyard as in the Quwwat al-Islam of Delhi (see p. 20). The Diwan Khan Mosque (c.1405) is found in Mandu. The three buildings make use of all the elements of Hindu architecture, although they are often used in an original way. For example, in the Lat-ki Mosque there is a series of pointed arches on pendentives decorated with open-work designs inserted between the pillars. The structures of the buildings are very similar: a central court is enclosed by a colonnade just one bay deep on the northern, eastern and southern sides and four bays deep in the prayer hall to the west. Both the *qibla* wall and the principal entrance are richly ornamented.

Mandu: Maliq Mughlis mosque

A mosque of this type, but built in Mandu in 1432, is the Maliq Mughlis, named after the father of Mahmud Khalji. It rises on a high plinth measuring some 50 x 40 m and has a series of arched rooms on both sides of its base, probably for use by the pilgrims or the mosque staff. The arched portico, once covered by a dome, is reached by means of a wide flight of stairs. Two domed turrets mark the corners of the façade and recall similar forms in Delhi, as seen in the mosques of Firuz Shah Tughluq. Inside, the courtyard measures some 33 m each side and the sanctuary, as in all buildings of this style, has a façade of the open, pillared variety on top of which rise three identical 'boat keel' domes supported by octagonal drums and surrounded by a marble parapet. The prayer hall is four bays deep and made up of groups of eight pillars which come from earlier Hindu temples and create three open, octagonal spaces. The spaces between the pillars are filled with pointed arches and are covered by the three domes that alternate with flat, stellate compartments. This arrangement into three areas lends the sanctuary a varied and graceful air. On the western wall the *mihrab* are elegantly ornamented with azure tiles and bands of floral designs.

The transfer of the capital to Mandu, known by its Muslim rulers as Shadiabad (City of Joy), coincided with the second

Above The *jami masjid* at Mandu was begun by Hushang Shah and completed (c.1452) by his successor Mahmud I Khalji. It is said to have been inspired by the Great Mosque of Damascus.

Opposite The Lat-ki Mosque (c.1405) at Dhar comprises Hindu materials, but these have been re-used in an original way.

phase of Malwan architecture. In addition to the fortified walls of the city, the Delhi and Tarapur gates were added in 1406–7 along the lines of Khalji and Tughluq constructions. In the Delhi gate, which consisted of a series of five archways which today are badly ruined, 'spear-head fringes' embellishing the austere profile are still visible.

It was under the strong personality of Hushang Shah that Mandu art really developed. Apart from erecting many buildings in the capital, he also invigorated Chanderi, in northern Malwa, along with other cities: Udaipur, Nilkhanthesvar, Sighpur, Ujjain and Mandasor, beautifying them all with fine monuments. Unfortunately the chronology of the buildings of Malwa has been studied very little, so that there are notable differences of opinion over the architectural development of the region.

MANDU: *JAMI MASJID*

Although Hushang Shah began the Great Mosque of Mandu, it was completed by his successor, Mahmud I Khalji, in about 1452. This is the most majestic building in the city and it is said that its builders were inspired by the Great Mosque of Damascus. It is 97.4 m square and is fronted by an imposing domed arcade which projects from the eastern façade and is accessible by means of a wide set of some 30 steps. Another two entrances are found on the northern side – one reserved for the mosque staff, the other for the *zenana* – and both are elegant structures that pleasingly divide the uniformity of the exterior wall. The whole building rests on a high plinth that rises some 5 m from ground level, so that on either side of the entrance portico there is a series of arched spaces reserved for the mosque staff or assigned to public use. The interior still carries some traces of borders and panels in glazed, exquisitely coloured tiles. The fine dome harmonizes perfectly with the three similar domes belonging to the shrine on the opposite side of the courtyard. These last lend the complex a rhythmic balance. The courtyard of the mosque, a square measuring over 50 m each side, is completely surrounded by arcades: two bays deep to the east, three to the north and south and five to the west in the prayer hall. Above the latter, as well as the three domes, are some 158 small cupolas arranged symmetrically over each interior section. The solemn bays of the sanctuary, supported by sober pillars lacking in ornament and severe pointed arches, evoke a mystic atmosphere. At the extremes of the colonnade there are raised compartments for women and royal visitors. The austere simplicity of the interior offers a remarkable contrast with the 17 niches of the *mihrab* that are aligned on the base wall, carved with fine crenellations along the edges of the arches and with Hindu-type pilasters worked in polished black stone. The main *mihrab* is much better designed than the others and is decorated with an elegant epigraphic band carrying verses from the Koran. The beautiful *minbar* alongside is a clear adaptation of a Hindu *chhatri* with S-shaped brackets resting on a stepped platform.

Mandu: Hushang mausoleum

The nearby mausoleum of Hushang was planned and begun by this sovereign, but completed by Mahmud I Khalji in about 1440. It stands at the centre of a square enclosure adjoining the western wall of the *jami masjid*. Access is by means of a domed portico on the northern side of the enclosure, which to the west had a pillared cloister reserved for the pilgrims. The mausoleum is a square structure which stands on a wide plinth over 30 m in diameter, with walls almost 10 m high terminating in series of 'elephant trunk' brackets which support a wide *chhajja*, on which is spread a band of small arches in relief. An elegant central dome with four small corner cupolas crowns the whole structure. The building, massive and severe, is completely sheathed in slabs of white marble which are made to stand out

Above Interior view of the *jami masjid* at Mandu. The delicately ornate *minbar* is an adaptation of the traditional Hindu *chhatri*.

Opposite The austere and monumental Hushang mausoleum (c.1440) at Mandu served as a prototype for several later tombs in the area.

with occasional touches of colour. The entrance to the mausoleum is on the southern side and is made up of a portal with a projecting double-pointed arch the extradoes, of which are decorated with lotus flower buds and flanked by two smaller pointed arches, filled with panels of open-work stone in geometric motifs. The interior is a 15 m square which transforms itself above, by means of arches, first into an octagon and then into a 16-sided polygon. The dome sits on this structure, its edge decorated with a row of small ornamental arches filled with a shining blue colour. Over the entrance is an inscription that recalls how, in 1659, the tomb was visited by some architects of Shah Jahan, among whom was the famous Ustad Hamid, who had taken part in the construction of the Taj Mahall at Agra. The mausoleum of Hushang functioned as prototype for numerous other tombs nearby that are distinct from the original because of the greater height of the drum on which the dome is positioned. These are the tomb of Darya Khan and those known as the Dai-ka Mahall and the Chappan Mahall.

Mandu: Hindola Mahall

According to some scholars, Hushang also planned the Hindola Mahall (see p. 130) about 1425. Others date this enormous meeting hall or *durbar* from the last years of the reign of Ghiyas al-Din, towards the end of the fifteenth century. Hindola Mahall (Swinging Palace) is named for the exterior buttresses which are inclined in such a pronounced way – they form an angle of over 77 degrees – that the entire structure seems to oscillate. Architectonically, it stands out from the other buildings of Mandu because of the extreme simplicity of its style of construction. Its ground plan is in a T-shape with the vertical mast constituting the main hall, while the crossbar is a transverse projection to the north, probably added later, as an examination of the variation in the external walls suggests. The main hall, which is an oblong structure of some 36 x 18 m and 12 m high, has on the exterior of each of its long sides six recessed arches carrying doors in their lower sections. The upper sections carry windows with three slabs of open-work stone for the flow of air and light. The lateral walls are some 3 m thick, but they are also reinforced by massive inclined buttresses which neutralize the thrust of the five massive ogee arches on the interior that once held the immense flat roof. This last rested on wooden beams of which the joints are still visible although the beams themselves have disappeared. The shortest part of the palace has practically the same dimensions as the main hall, but it differs as it is on two floors. The ground floor contains a cruciform gallery, a short arm of which ends with an arched opening in the main room. Some subsidiary passages are served by a separate entrance. The upper floor, which looks over the main hall through an arched opening consists of two rooms: one is longitudinal, divided in three bays by two rows of pillars; the other is transverse, much smaller, and may have been a retreat. The entire structure of the Hindola Mahall was therefore a continuation of the reception hall with royal apartments, but the incongruous volume and the robustness of the walls lend it an enigmatic character, almost like a 'folly' of the builder. It has been suggested that the imposing arrangement of the walls was originally prepared for the addition of a massive superstructure – for example the *zenana* apartments – which was never realized. Even if this were the case, the proportions of the base would have been exaggerated and incongruous. Despite these defects, many details in the construction of the Hindola Mahall are full of dignity, for example, the interior and exterior archways; the layout of the main hall; and the well-designed and ornamented windows.

An almost exact copy of this building, perhaps by the same architect, is to be found in the fort of Warangal in Deccan. This is the eastern region of the dominions of Nizam of Hyderabad and the building is known as reception hall of Shitab Khan, a rebel leader of the then declining Bahmanid empire who was killed in 1516 at Warangal. Although built on a reduced scale, it does have the same pointed arches to support the flat roof (which has now collapsed). The only difference is the addition of a capacious water cistern at the centre of the main hall. This influence can be explained by the frequent and recurring relationships between the Malwa sovereigns and the Deccani sovereigns, as confirmed by much historical evidence.

Mandu: Ashrafi Mahall

The later epoch of Mahmud I Shah saw the building of another immense structure known as the Ashrafi Mahall (Palace as Beautiful as a Golden Coin), which stands in front of the eastern entrance to the *jami masjid*. When it was complete it occupied a square measuring over 100 m each side and consisted of three distinct constructions which must have been built over a period of many years (1436–69). The first building was a school of theology, a single-storey structure articulated in a series of halls and compartments around a large rectangular courtyard with a circular tower at each corner. Parts of this building now constitute the ground floor of a second structure that was built later, but the rooms of the *madrasa*, together with a corridor with double arches, are still visible along the front of the building. There are also some fine ceilings which are beautifully designed pyramidal vaults. The building imposed on the college is the mausoleum of the emperor and was perhaps built about 1450. To this end the courtyard of the *madrasa* was filled so as to form a plinth some 9 m high, at the centre of which stands the royal funeral chamber. The entrance to the tomb is made up of a pillared portico with galleries on each side that rises on a large flight of stairs projecting from the front of the *madrasa*. Of the mausoleum itself only a few ruins remain, but it was an imposing hall. Its internal measurements reached 20 m each side and it was covered by an immense dome. The building had three openings on each side, of which the central was the highest. The walls were dressed in white marble while the windows, the doors and the cornices were elegantly carved and occasionally decorated with insets of different stone and blue and yellow glazed tiles. The calligraphic ornament, beautifully executed, seems to have been carried out by Persian artists summoned specifically for the purpose. Because of its impressiveness and the quality of the architectonic decoration, there is no doubt that, had it survived, the mausoleum of Mahmud would have appeared as one of the most impressive monuments of Muslim architecture in India. It has been noted that its large dome was perfectly aligned with that of the portico and the other dome at the centre of the *jami masjid*, thus creating a magnificently striking visual effect.

The third building within the Ashrafi Mahall was a victory tower which was added to the original scheme perhaps after 1443 and positioned on the site already occupied by the north-eastern turret of the *madrasa*. This may once have been the most spectacular building in all Mandu. It was built by the Khalji sovereign to commemorate his victory over Rana of Chitor. Some time earlier, to celebrate one of his victories over Mahmud, Rana of Chitor himself had another famous tower built in his city, the very beautiful Jaya Sthamba, still standing after five centuries and testimony to the better techniques of indigenous builders. Mahmud's monument, on the other hand, is represented today only by the base section which stands almost 10 m high. However, it must have towered over the mausoleum, reaching a height of over 50 m. Its seven floors in red sandstone were each divided by a strip of marble on which projected a small balcony supported by pillars covered by an awning. Polychromatic marble insets were arranged at intervals around the curved surface.

Mandu: Jahaz Mahall

Although the majority of scholars attribute the construction of the pleasing Jahaz Mahall (Ship Palace) to Mahmud, others consider it to be from the time of Ghiyas al-Din who succeeded his father in 1469 and whose 30-year reign was dedicated to the search for peace and the amusement of the court. It is said that his harem consisted of 15,000 women of various classes and professions and that 500 beautiful young Turkish women in men's clothes, together with as many Abyssinian women, accompanied him as bodyguards, arranged respectively to his right and left.[2] He had many pleasure domes, baths, barracks for female soldiers and palaces built, all of which reflect the romantic beauty and the joyous gaiety so characteristic of the palace life of the Muslim sovereigns of India. The Jahaz Mahall was in this vein when it was erected in the second half of the fifteenth century, at a moment when the style began to assume the pleasing

Above The lakeside Jahaz Mahall at Mandu, built in the second half of the fifteenth century, characterizes the elegance of the last phase of the Malwa style.

Opposite The immense Ashrafi Mahall (1436–69) at Mandu actually comprises three distinct structures: a school of theology, a mausoleum (shown here) and a victory tower.

and elegant aspect that was to become characteristic of its last phase. The palace stands on a narrow strip of land between the waters of two small lakes, Kaphur and Munja Talao. It is some 122 m long, just over 15 m wide and the façade is almost 10 m high. Despite its size, its aspect is not massive or excessively solid, but rather is lively and pleasing and its surfaces brilliant because of the glazing of the bright colours. The lower body of the building has a front of continuous arcades which are protected by a wide awning on which there is a series of built-in arches with a wide parapet decorated with glazed tiles. The plan of the ground floor consists of three huge halls separated by corridors and small enclosures at the extremities. In a room to the north is a beautiful cistern surrounded by a colonnade on three sides. To the rear of each hall a pavilion projects into the Munja Talao, of which the central one is the largest and has a domed ceiling decorated with a band of azure and yellow tiles. The other pavilions are smaller and still display the stone frameworks from which the curtains were hung when the women of the harem were inside. The room at the southern extremity of the building has a channel from which the cistern was filled. The cistern is elegantly designed and has a sort of shelf under the upper edge for the comfort of those who could not swim. On the spacious terrace, reached by means of a long series of steps, are various open pavilions, kiosks and suspended balconies arranged together with a variety of domes and turrets. The reflections of these structures in the calm waters of the lake presents a picture of uncommon beauty. The two pavilions at the extremities are larger and are divided into three compartments of which the central one has a dome higher than the pyramidal roofs of the surrounding rooms. Immediately above the central pavilion that projects from the rear of the ground floor there is a very similar pavilion covered by a dome. Both inside and outside it carries traces of bands of blue and yellow glazed tiles with paintings with floral motifs. The small *chhatri* on the opposite side, which rises on the front of the terrace, has a graceful pyramidal cover that offers an interesting contrast

Left The stepped *baoli* inside the Jahaz Mahall at Mandu.

Opposite The Baz Bahadur palace at Mandu. According to an inscription on the main entrance it was built in 1509 during the reign of the sultan Nizam al-Din.

with the other pavilions of the roof. The building was much appreciated by Jahangir who recalls in his memoirs having spent time there with his beloved wife, Nur Jahan, during a visit to Mandu. The empress loved to organize feasts, during which 'the lanterns and the lamps cast their reflection on the water, and it appeared as if the whole surface of the tank was a plain of fire'.[3]

MANDU: OTHER PALACES

A certain number of buildings erected on the north side of the Munja Talao, now reduced to a mass of ruins in which it is difficult to discern the original plan, date from the last phase of Malwa art. Among these is a well called Champa because of the sweet perfume of its waters which seem to smell like the Champak flower. An underground passage leads to the base of the well and there joins a labyrinth of vaulted rooms (*tah khana*). This is almost at the level of the lake with which it is connected by means of a gallery that leads to a pavilion situated on the west bank. From the *tah khana* steps descend to the base of the well which has arched niches in its walls while the roof is left open to allow light and air to enter. The *tah khana* was built so ingeniously and is so successfully connected to the well and the pavilion on the bank of the Talao, that even during the warmest weather the rooms remained fresh and comfortable. This was thanks to the gentle breeze that ran from the pavilion to the rooms along the gallery and crossed over the top of the well. Not far from this was the *hammam*, in the ceiling of which graceful stars were carved to provide light. On the western side of Munja Talao stood the Hawa Mahall (Palace of the Winds). This was sumptuous in its aspect with imaginative balconied windows, domes with merlons, pyramidal roofs, attractive stairways and unusual columns with circular shafts.

Once the space round the Munja Talao was used up, the last sovereigns of Malwa constructed their buildings in other picturesque areas of the city and in pleasant places where the resplendent side of court life could be enjoyed privately even when carried out publicly. The buildings created for this purpose took the form of summer houses, palaces and pavilions, the ground floors of which usually comprised a series of compartments built around a graceful central courtyard embellished with fountains and pools. Above there were usually arcaded galleries covered by fluted domes with surfaces dressed in gaudy painted tiles. The buildings, known as Lal Mahall, the Palace of Baz Bahadur, the Pavilion of Rupmati (named after the famous lovers, celebrated in poems and miniatures of the time, the sultan Baz Bahadur (1556–61) and the Hindu singer Rupmati who preferred to kill herself rather than surrender to his enemies) and the palace of Chishti Khan, are all pleasing but lacking in any particular architectural worth.

MANDU: BAZ BAHADUR PALACE

The palace of Baz Bahadur, which an inscription in Persian on the main entrance in fact assigns to the sultan Nizam al-Din (1500–11) and to the year 1509, stands on the slope of a hill in the midst of a beautiful natural landscape east of the Riwa Kund, a lake in which the foliage on the bank is reflected. The entrance is reached by means of 40 wide steps with landings at intervals. The main part of the palace consists of a spacious open courtyard with halls and rooms on all four sides and with a beautiful cistern in the middle. On the upper floor is a wide terrace on which two fine open pavilions (*baradari*) are arranged; from here there is an enchanting view of the surrounding countryside. On the high ridge of the hill, beyond the palace of Baz Bahadur, stand the pavilions associated with the romantic name of Rupmati. An accurate examination of the structure of the palace complex shows that it was built over two or three different periods. The original part consisted of a low, massive hall with two rooms at each end. The walls have a steep batter towards the base and the arches are rather heavy in proportion to their width. The rest of the building was built along the western side of the plinth to form a base that later had two long extensions added in the form of corridors, one towards the west, the other towards the east. On the last terrace there are two pavilions with a square plan and a

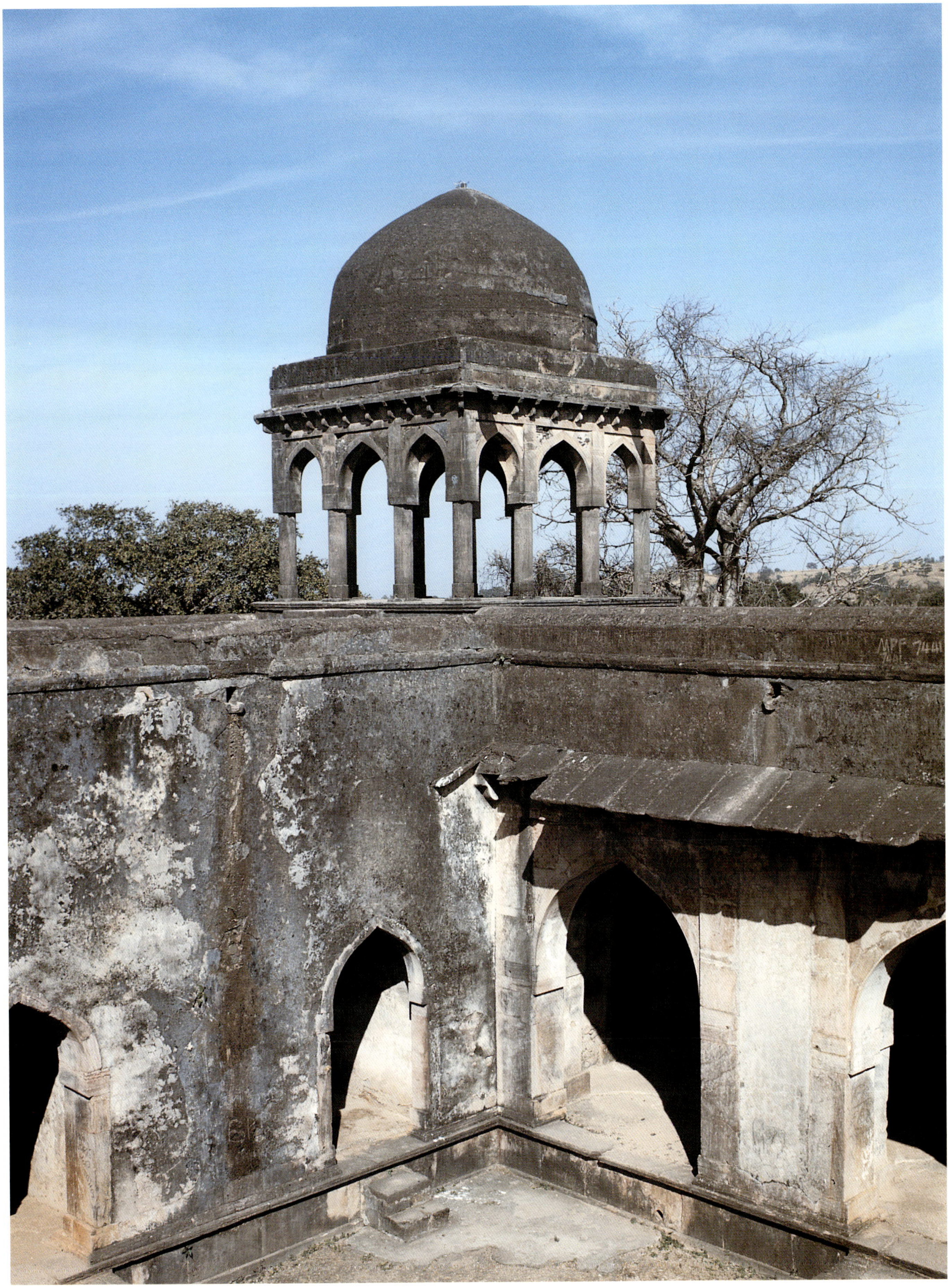

dome fluted both inside and outside, and resting on pillars and arches which, because of their style, have been dated to almost a century before Rupmati's time.

Mandu: other buildings

Two buildings date from the time of Mahmud II (1511–31), a drunken tyrant and weak puppet: the huge and badly built 'shop' and the 'house', both known as Gada Shah. The first was in reality the reception hall of the Rajput ruler Medini Rai, who for some time (1512–17) was the true leader of the realm and was called contemptuously by the Muslims 'the beggar king' (Gada Shah). The 'shop' was a pretentious imitation of the Hindola Mahall, planned on a larger scale with a yet grander hall where huge arches had to balance the thrust of the massive buttresses that are now nevertheless reduced to a wretched state. The 'house' is a building on two storeys, of which the ground floor has arched openings and lateral apartments. The upper floor consists of a huge hall and two lateral spaces. At the centre of the hall was a fountain, the water from which entered a network of small channels and pipes worked into tiger- and elephant-head shapes, a typically Hindu characteristic that can be associated with Medini Rai. In a niche in the south-western corner of the hall are two pictures, now ruined, representing a man and a woman, perhaps the Rajput leader and his consort. On the exterior of the building are traces of decorated panels and other designs in plaster.

More or less of this period is the Jal Mahall (Palace of Water) built at Kalyada on the Kshipra with canals arranged in a double spiral.

Chanderi: Kushk Mahall

Perhaps at the time of Ghiyas al-Din, between 1489 and 1499, a minister of the sovereign had various monuments built at Chanderi. Among them is the palace known as Kushk Mahall, built in the suburb of Fatehabad and now partially ruined. Because of the mistaken interpretation of some sources, it was once said that this building had seven storeys, of which four had collapsed. A more careful examination of the surviving structure has established, however, that it must have been planned over three floors. It has a square plan, with a diameter of over 35 m, and a high pointed entrance at the centre of each side. Graceful balconied windows are arranged at regular intervals and interrupt the otherwise plain surface of the exterior walls. The entrance structure is decorated with blind niches and lotus rosettes arranged inside larger pointed arches. The interior arrangement is rather unusual: the Kushk Mahall is in effect a complex of four buildings of equal dimensions that stand at equal distances from each other, and they are both separated and united by the open passages that run along the sides. Indeed, along the entire length of the building, both north–south and east–west, wide open passages run from the centre of each side, cross at right-angles and divide the whole into quadrants, within each of which is arranged a series of spaces that rise over three floors. Each floor opens towards the internal 'corridor' with a series of superimposed arches. In all four buildings, built in the fine local sandstone, the first floor is divided into rooms and corridors for residential purposes. The ceiling is formed of splendid cross-vaults resting on climbing arches supported by massive pillars. The rooms on the second floor are simpler and are covered by slabs of stone arranged diagonally for their entire length. The third floor had a flat roof supported by pillars and brackets. The final covering has collapsed, but it seems it was not a dome, while it is possible that angular *chhatri* were used. The buildings were connected on the upper level by four majestic pointed arches which were raised in the central area and were sufficiently wide to allow the men, and the women of the harem, to move easily from one quarter to another.

CHANDERI: *JAMI MASJID*

The Great Mosque of Chanderi is a notable building that dates from just a little later than the Kushk Mahall. In the arrangement of its three large domes over the prayer hall and the disposition of the arches that make up the façade, it displays its derivation from the *jami masjid* of Mandu. Nevertheless, there are various elements that lead us to think of local influences, above all the appearance of curious snake-like corbels which decorate, rather than support, the *chhajja* that cover the pillars along the entire courtyard of the mosque.

CHANDERI: SHAZADI-KA *RAUZA*

This same motif is found as ornament in a fine tomb known as the Shazadi-ka (Princess's) *rauza* (see p. 142) which was built probably about 1470. This is a square-planned building in grey sandstone which was once covered by a dome and the exterior of which is designed to give the impression of a two-storey structure. Each side is in fact divided by a double series of blind pointed arches supported by pilasters with brackets from which protrude *chhajja*. These last are decorated with graceful stanchions in a double S-shape that add a note of light elegance to an otherwise austere whole. These brackets, here more elaborate, already existed as prototypes at Dhar, under the awnings of the Lat-ki Mosque and at Mandu in the tomb of Hushang Shah and the *minbar* of the *jami masjid*. Later they are found in the Mughal architecture of Fatehpur Sikri, particularly in the mosque of the Stone Masons and in the tomb of Shaikh Salim Chishti (see p. 219).

CHANDERI: OTHER MAUSOLEUMS

Another tomb at Chanderi is of simple but elegant design and has been called a *madrasa* because it was used as such at some period. This is a square building surrounded on each side by a verandah opened with five archways. The funeral chamber is enclosed, apart from the entrance, with perforated slabs of stone which terminate in a pointed arch. The cover was a dome, now collapsed, surrounded by four corner towers which were probably originally surmounted by *chhatri* which must have supported the drum. Inside, the dome rested on squinches of receding arches which also formed an elegant decorative feature. A similar system is found in the Shazadi-ka *rauza*.

Other tombs situated in the cemetery of the family of Nizam al-Din are simpler structures, but are carefully decorated with panels of stone worked into finely designed geometric motifs.

Left The early fifteenth-century *jami masjid* at Chanderi shows influences from the *jami masjid* at Mandu as well as from local architecture.

Opposite The late fourteenth-century Kushk Mahall at Chanderi is actually a complex of four buildings that are both separated and united by the open passages that run along the sides.

Chanderi: civil buildings

Among the civil constructions of Chanderi are many monumental gates in the walls of the city. The majority of them are in ruins, but the Faqir Darwaza and the Delhi Darwaza are in a reasonable state of preservation and both are characterized by an extremely high pointed arch combined with Hindu corbels and beams. In the Delhi Darwaza, on both sides of the arch, the figure of a lion fighting with an elephant is carved in high relief, while in the Faqir Darwaza only the lion appears. This is a typical Hindu motif which here appears for the first time in Muslim decoration. In a different form it appeared later in the northern entrance of the ancient fort of Delhi, the Din-Panah of Humayun, built in about 1535, and on the carved panels decorating the Delhi Gate of the fort at Agra, built by Akbar about 1565. Other monumental gates were connected to palaces and tombs and they too have for the most part been destroyed, like those in front of the Kushk Mahall and the Shazadi-ka *rauza*. In reasonable condition is a gate that stood next to the Pathani Muhalla, a grand palace on seven floors, of which numerous rooms still survive.

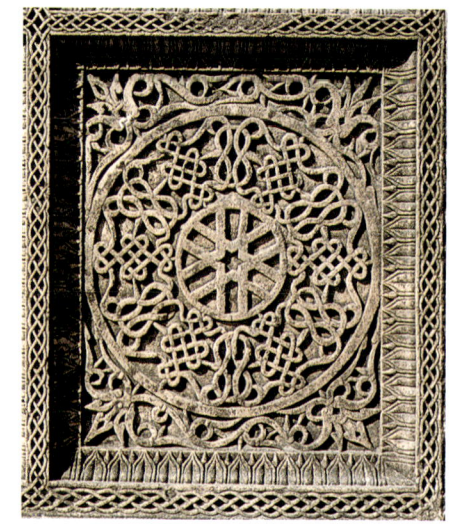

Above The Shazadi-ka *rauza* (c.1470) at Chanderi has distinctive snake-like corbels, a motif also found on the *jami masjid*.

Left Detail of a carved stone panel on one of the tombs in the Nizam al-Din family funerary complex.

Opposite The Badal Mahall Darwaza at Chanderi is the somewhat bizarre result of a combination of influences from Delhi, Gujarat and Malwa.

Chanderi: Badal Mahall Darwaza

The best preserved, however, is the Badal Mahall Darwaza that was long considered a triumphal arch because it seemed to stand alone. In reality the ruins of many buildings are dispersed nearby and it is therefore presumable that it was the monumental entrance to a building called Badal Mahall (Palace in the Clouds). The *darwaza*, a structure over 15 m high and just over 7.5 m wide, consists of two large lateral bastions of the Firuzi type at the sides of an entrance archway. This last, with scalloped edges, has an extremely pronounced point and is surmounted by a high band of ornaments which, rather than embellishing it, seem to oppress it. Another, higher pointed arch with a 'spear-head fringe' completes the middle area and is filled with stone slabs perforated in geometric designs. The bizarre character of the whole would seem to be the sum of various influences that reached a confluence in the art of Chanderi: from the Delhi of the Tughluqs, from Gujarat and partly from Malwa. These influences, rather than melting into the local taste, superimposed themselves one on the other, creating a curious and interesting amalgam. Like the architecture of Malwa, Chanderi architecture was destined to join and mingle with Mughal architecture during the reign of the emperor Akbar (1556–1605).

Shah Budagh Khan, the governor of Mandu under Akbar (1674–75), was responsible for the building of Nil Khant, a pleasure ground on the mountainside with a magnificent view over the valley below. The structure consists of a U-shaped court with three wide *pishtaq*, one in the middle of each side. The central one leads into a domed room dug out of the rock, above a fountain that is fed by a tank placed higher up. The Nil Khant is the clearest example of local motifs being combined with various elements of Timurid-Mughal expression. Of the same period is an octagonal domed structure placed near an artificial lake.

[1] Brown, *op. cit.*, p. 60.
[2] G. Yazdani, *Mandu: The City of Joy*, Oxford, 1929, p. 20.
[3] Quoted in Yazdani, *op. cit.*, p. 35.

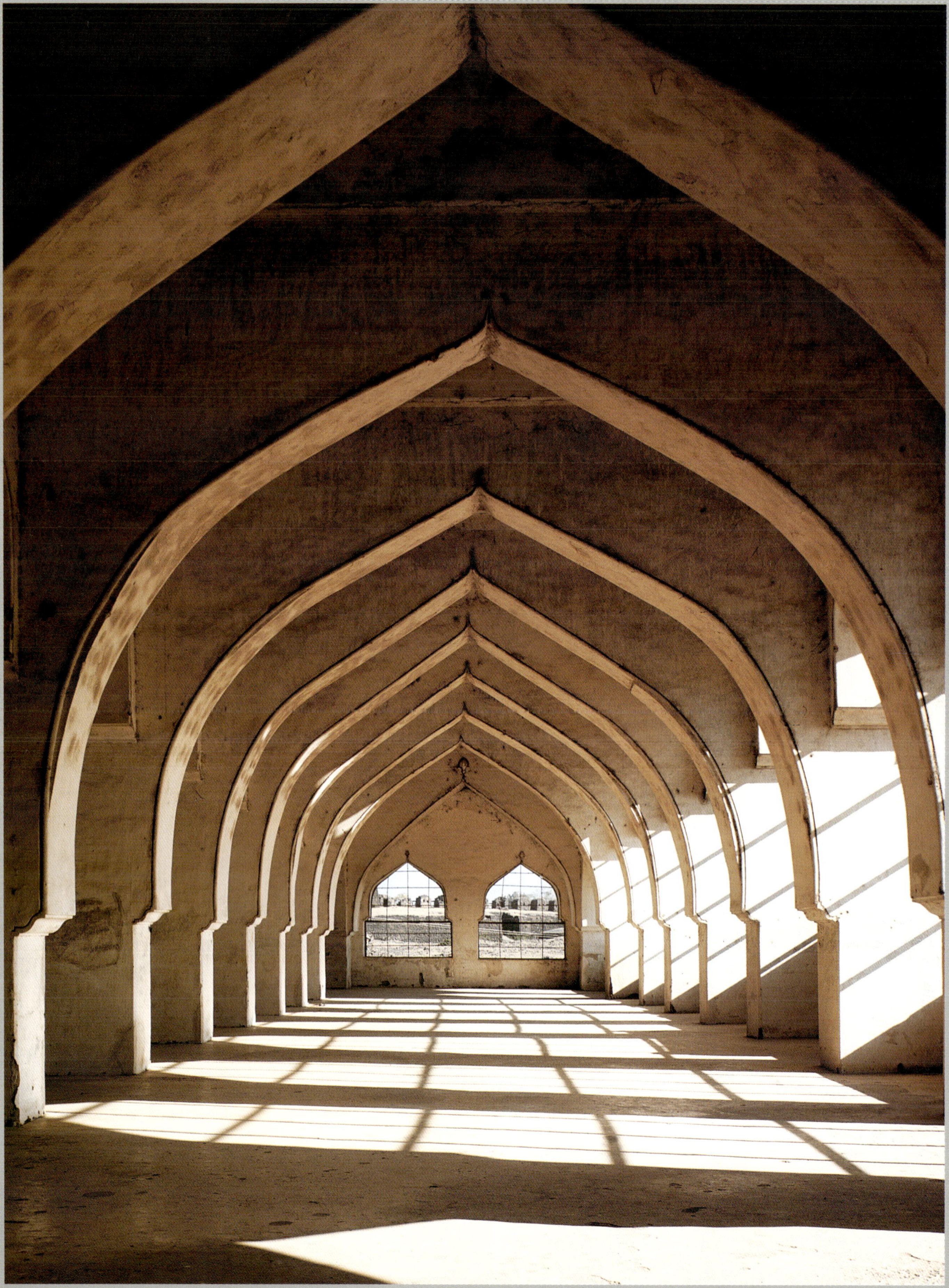

DECCAN (1347–1687)

11

Interior of the *jami masjid* (1367) at Gulbarga. The unusually wide spans of the arcades later became a characteristic of Deccani architecture.

The vast region of the country that lay towards the south of the peninsula, known as Deccan, liberated itself from Tughluq domination relatively early. This came about with the foundation of a truly independent dynasty by a Persian adventurer from the Delhi court who was an officer of Muhammad Tughluq, Ala al-Din Hasan Bahman Shah (1347–58). The Tughluq capital of Daulatabad proved problematic for the Bahmanids, because of friction with both the neighbouring Muslim states to the north and the neighbouring Hindu states. In 1347 he moved his residence towards the south, to Gulbarga – then in the state of Karnataka – which remained the capital of the Bahmanid realm until 1429. In that year the capital was transferred to Bidar and finally, in 1612, to Golconda, where it remained until 1687 when the sultanate and its art were reabsorbed by the Mughal empire.

In contrast with all the other regions of India, Deccani architecture did not exploit indigenous models, but created its own original and independent style which was nevertheless affected by influences from Persia and far-off Turkey. The rapid spread of the Muslim faith had facilitated relations with the West. Indian ports, for example, previously somewhat isolated, were visited by people from other Islamic countries who often, once installed at the Bahmanid court, succeeded in attaining prestigious positions. Apart from military adventurers, there arrived traders, craftsmen, builders and skilled workers who came to constitute a strong nucleus of foreign influence – especially Persian – in the capital. This was the main factor in the creation of the special architectural character of the region. Many monuments of the region often appear so Iranian that they could be straightforward transfers from their native land. The style was developed with some differences in the three successive capitals of the sultanate. In some cases the influences of the Delhi style was felt, above all in the Tughluq period, traces of which were left at Daulatabad and Badhan, near Hyderabad.

DAULATABAD: *JAMI MASJID*
The buildings of the pre-dynasty phase, dating from the first half of the fifteenth

century, were improvised, using material from existing temples. The *jami masjid* of Daulatabad, for example, although designed in the orthodox manner, is considerably lacking in originality in that all the material came from earlier buildings in the area. It is a huge building 63 m square, with entrances at the centres of the southern, eastern and northern sides. The sanctuary, to the west of the border walls, and five bays deep, contains 106 pillars which divide the space into 25 spans and is covered by a dome slightly pointed at its keystone. The front colonnade is finished at the corners with slightly leaning scalloped buttresses in pure Tughluq style.

Bodhan: Deval Mosque

At Bodhan (also known as Nizamabad) the Deval Mosque is a building of some interest because it is simply a Jain temple in a star shape – typical of Chalukya architecture of the ninth and tenth centuries – transformed into a mosque by closing the western side. This simple technique created the *qibla* wall of the shrine and was completed with the addition, inside, of a *mihrab* and a small *minbar* and, outside, of some brick domes on the flat roof.

The Bahmanids (1347–1542)

Fortresses

Ala al-Din Bahman and many of his successors, such as Muhammad I, Muhammad II, Ahmad I and the minister Mahmud Gawan, dedicated themselves to building a great number of fortresses, the greatest that were ever built in India. It seems that in fulfilling these plans they were able to call upon the solid help and experience of Syrian architects together with those Christians of Palestine who, following the failure of the Crusades, had been sold in great numbers in India as slaves. The majority of these forts remain unexplored. The most famous are those of Parendra, with its picturesque but deadly corner towers; Naldrug, with an imposing but graceful tapered bastion and pavilions on the water; Narnala, with its beautiful, richly decorated Mahakali portal; Raichur, with its simple yet daring Nawrangi Darwaza (Gate of Nine Colours); and then the forts of Nalgonda, Gawilgarh, Mahur, Ellichpur, Jalna, Naghai, Bhingar, Rajkonda, Warangal, Purandhar, Satara, Panhala, Akola and Mudgal. At Gulbarga, Ala al-Din built a citadel of which only the border walls remain. Nevertheless, these remains are sufficient to demonstrate that this is a remarkable example of military architecture. The fort is not of great proportions – its perimeter extends just over 3 km – but it was immensely strong with a double wall over 15 m thick and largely surrounded by natural rock that in places is 30 m wide. As in all the other fortresses, there is no symmetry in its ground plan, which follows the contours of the rocky outcrop on which it is built. Solid semi-circular bastions of Cyclopean construction protrude at brief intervals along the entire length of the walls. Many of these bastions are equipped with turning platforms for heavy artillery and gigantic crenellated parapets. Some of these are so large as to contain a room inside capable of housing two or three defenders; others have embrasures and other devices designed to allow attacks to be met with missiles of molten lead. There are four entrances to the fortress, the principal one at the north-east corner being the most impressive. This is equipped with a drawbridge which leads to an entrance with a sharp arch; beyond is a large but tortuous passage which snakes through many fortified doors, each protected by high guard towers, until the perimeter of the fort itself is reached. Here, however, almost nothing remains of the buildings, pavilions and royal environs that were once protected by the huge bastions. To the north-east stands a formidable rectangular structure known as the Bala Hisar. It has semi-circular turrets and is almost without apertures. It is reached by means of a single door situated in the high part of the northern wall, reached in its turn by means of a long row of steps, now for the most part collapsed. It must have functioned as a fortress or keep. Towards the western part was a road through the bazaar flanked by rows of small rooms, clearly the market shops with small arched door openings and covered with pyramidal vaults.

Above The *jami masjid* at Gulbarga. Built by Muhammad I in 1367, it is one of the most interesting Islamic monuments in southern India.

Opposite The fort at Naldrug is one of the most famous examples of the programme of fortress building instigated by many of the Bahmanid rulers from the fourteenth to the sixteenth century.

GULBARGA: *JAMI MASJID*

The only building that is preserved intact – obviously because of its sacred nature – is the *jami masjid*. This is one of the most interesting Islamic monuments of southern India, rising strangely alone in the midst of a scene of ruinous devastation. It was built in 1367 by Muhammad I (1358–75) under the direction of an architect from Qazvin, Rafi bin Shams bin Mansur. Nevertheless, the architect seems to have been inspired less by a Persian mosque and more by an example of a Western basilica that perhaps had influenced a Muslim religious building in some country of eastern Europe. According to Desai it was completed later, during the reign of Firuz, at the beginning of the fifteenth century.[1] Indeed, traces of later restoration work would seem to confirm this thesis.

The Great Mosque of Gulbarga is an unusual building. It lacks a courtyard and a minaret and has a prayer hall that is totally covered with domes and vaults supported by wide arches built on low pillars. The ground plan measures some 66 x 54 m and on three sides of the rectangle are wide vaulted cloisters with domes at the two extremities. The central hall is covered with 63 small cupolas while the sanctuary, to the west, is made up of a spacious bay covered with a high dome surrounded by twelve smaller and lower domes. From the exterior the main dome appears more imposing because it is set on a series of arcades, forming a sort of square cloister. Inside, the main dome is supported on the 'cloister' by means of very strange 'stretched' triangular arches, some of which are gracefully foliated. This means of supporting the dome was destined to become a characteristic form of Deccani architecture. The most remarkable aspect of the interior, however, is found in the extremely wide spans of the arcades, with unusually low imposts, that create an unusual, but not unpleasant, effect (see p. 144). This feature would also become a keynote for many of the later Deccani monuments. The principal entrance is at the centre of the northern side – a tall arched passage on small columns that majestically shatters the otherwise austere symmetry of the whole. The *mihrab*, too, is a narrow arch on columns, crowned by the splays of the dome. Although the arrangement of this mosque had many advantages over the usual open type, it did not find success in India and was never again repeated, perhaps because it did not respect tradition. It is nevertheless possible that its plan exerted a certain influence on the two Tughluq mosques of Delhi built just a few years later; Kalan (1370) and Khirki (1375; see pp. 36, 45). Both of these were largely covered, even if there was a compromise here with four open spaces left at the cruciform meeting of the pillared aisles. Since the building also lacks a *minbar* (the present *minbar* was added later) and devices for ritual ablutions, Schotten Merklinger has suggested that the mosque was perhaps not reserved for prayer, but was a building used for other purposes, for example public audiences, which would also explain the unusual arrangement of the entire structure.[2]

GULBARGA: SHAH BAZAAR MOSQUE

To the north of the fort is the area of the Shah Bazaar, dominated by a mosque from the late fourteenth century which is connected to the *dargah* of Shaikh Siraj al-Din Junaydi – situated to the north-west – by means of a road. The mosque is the oldest built at Gulbarga and dates from the time of Muhammad I. It was used as a model for subsequent Deccani mosques. The prayer hall with the walls that enclose it has an almost square plan, the form of which resembles a tomb, consisting of a domed room opened by an arch at the centre of each side. The courtyard is without *riwaq* and the sanctuary has 15 spans, each divided into six spaces covered by small domes supported by simple brick pillars.

GULBARGA: HAFT GUMBAZ AND OTHER MAUSOLEUMS

The last Bahmanid monuments of Gulbarga are the seven royal tombs of these sovereigns, the construction of which covers a period of almost 50 years. The first group, made up of three tombs, includes that of the founder of the dynasty, who died in 1358, and that of Muhammad I, who died in 1375, which reproduces Tughluq effects in its leaning walls, low arches, heavily fortified parapets, the fluted corner terminals and the low dome. Only in the tomb attributed to Muhammad Shah II, who died in 1397, is the dome slightly raised at the base in imitation of the *jami masjid*. The second group, known as Haft Gumbaz (Seven Domes), contains the mausoleums of the four kings of this dynasty, the oldest of which is that of Mujahid Bahman Shah, who died in 1378; this tomb displays the same characteristics as the earlier ones, but with slightly larger proportions. Three of the tombs of this group present unique double structures – two connecting burial rooms, both domed, in a single building, one containing the king's cenotaph, the other that of his family.

The most beautiful example of this type of monument is the mausoleum of Taj al-Din Firuz, the last Bahmanid of Gulbarga, who died in 1422. Although derived from a Tughluq prototype, it presents some original characteristics, above all in its decoration. Externally it measures some 48 x 24 m, with walls that reach almost 14 m including the parapets. Above the walls the two identical hemispheric domes rise a further 10 m. The mausoleum is on two floors: on the exterior these are indicated by pointed arcades

Left The mausoleum of Saint Chishti Gesu Daraz (died 1422) in the complex at Gulbarga constructed especially for him.

Opposite The mausoleum of Taj al-Din Firuz, the last Bahmanid ruler of Gulbarga, forms part of the Haft Gumbaz funerary complex.

Below The Chor Gumbaz (Bandit's Tomb) north-west of Gulbarga is the most monumental single tomb in the area.

formed by two receding arches, of which some are decorated with perforated slabs of stone. At the corners there are fluted terminals with small cupolas, while the cornice and the drum of the dome are decorated with foliage motifs. Inside, the walls of each burial chamber are divided into two floors by arcades which on the upper floor support the dome through triangular beams, similar to those of the tomb of Firuz Shah Tughluq built at Delhi some 30 years previously. The so-called Chor Gumbaz (Bandit's Tomb) to the north-west of Gulbarga constitutes the most monumental example of a single tomb. It is a cube decorated with two orders of niches with keel arches, surmounted by an almost hemispheric dome on a low drum, and four corner towers surmounted, in their turn, by domes and miniature towers. It seems that this mausoleum was built by a rich merchant for the revered Hazrat Gesu Daraz, but the building was abandoned and soon fell into the hands of thieving vandals.

Taj al-Din Firuz had been a great follower of Saint Chishti Gesu Daraz, to the point where he invited him to live in the Gulbarga citadel. Later, tired of his presence at court, he invited him to reside elsewhere and began the construction of a huge complex that was to become larger and larger for the two centuries that followed the death of the saint and the sovereign. The whole includes tombs, mosques, schools of theology, rest houses, courtyards and imposing entrances which together demonstrate the importance of this saint in the religious history of Deccan. Even today, the *dargah* constitutes one of the most revered Islamic sanctuaries in the region. The mausoleum of the founder dates from the year of his death (1422) and is a square building with a façade divided into two floors patterned with blind niches with pointed arches. The sober decoration is limited to a frieze of indentured lozenges on the high part of the walls, which are surmounted by a crenellated parapet with domed turrets at the corners. The fine hemispheric dome is decorated inside with sumptuous paintings. The baldachin that covers the tomb was added later and has rich decoration in mirror and mother-of-pearl. Many other buildings of the *dargah* were added under the Adil Shahs in the sixteenth and seventeenth centuries, such as the small mosque of Afzal Khan, a general of these sovereigns, with its typical Bijapur aspect. The impressive arch that rises from the two high towers in the southern corner of the courtyard was added in the fifteenth century. It is decorated with large stucco medallions containing figures of heraldic animals, which seem to be supported by strange corbels in the shape of fish.

Not far from this complex is the *dargah* of Shah Kamal Mujarrad, another revered saint who settled in Gulbarga in the fourteenth century. It is made up of a small, simple tomb of the late 1300s, a mosque, perhaps built a little later, and two other structures without ornament, probably used as a caravanserai or rest house. The mosque has five spans in three rows, all domed, and is highly decorated with stuccoes both inside and outside. The entrance arches are emphasized with multi-lobed bands of stucco and medallions in which lively geometric and foliate forms are mixed. Near the tombs of the first Bahmanid sovereigns is another *dargah*, dedicated to the saint Shaikh Siraj al-Din

Junaydi who was the spiritual counsellor of the sultans. It is divided into various courtyards, in the first of which is a simple tomb and a small mosque, both in the style of the late fourteenth century. At the beginning of the 1500s Yusuf Adil Khan, the founder of the realm of Bijapur, added a monumental gate to the complex, enclosed within two imposing circular minarets and flanked by two floors of arcades. To the north of Gulbarga is a fine mosque from the beginning of the 1400s, the Langar-ki Mosque, with an adjacent tomb. The main characteristic of the prayer hall comes from its extremely pointed vault, divided by ribs in imitation of wooden supports, evidently an influence from indigenous building techniques. The entrance openings consist of receding pointed arches in three profiles, a detail that is repeated inside in the decoration of the *mihrab*.

Firuzabad on the Bhima

Outside Gulbarga, Taj al-Din Firuz built another residence, today reduced to a pile of ruins – Firuzabad on the Bhima – where the buildings display a further enrichment of forms including double- and triple-pointed arches, ribbed vaults and pyramidal roofs set alongside the domes.

Bidar

In 1429 Ahmad I Wali (the 'Saint', 1422–36), ninth sovereign of the Bahmanid dynasty, took the capital of the region to Bidar, some 96 km to the north east of Gulbarga on a fertile plain nearer the more developed centre of the dominion. Other reasons for the change of capital certainly included the internal leadership conflicts that tormented Gulbarga and, above all, the external conflicts with the bellicose Hindu realm of Vijayanagar. Indeed, Bidar offered the Bahmanids a period of relative peace, and the development of the Deccani architectural style received a new thrust. Tughluq influence ceased altogether, to be partially replaced by Iranian and Central Asiatic influences which were reworked in the most beautiful monuments erected in the new capital.

Bidar: the fort

The major architectonic undertaking of the Bahmanid dynasty at Bidar was the construction of the fortress with its palaces, two mosques, a *madrasa* and various royal tombs. The Bidar fort, larger than that in Gulbarga, was, however, built along the same basic lines. Completed in 1532, it is surrounded by a triple moat partly dug out of the natural rock and has laterite walls 15 m thick. There are 37 bastions and seven entrances, each of which was equipped with a drawbridge and designed to keep any aggressor at bay. On the south-eastern side of the citadel are three entrances in a row which connect the fort to the city. One of these is called the Sharza Darwaza because it has two tigers carved on the façade. The main surviving buildings, although very much ruined, are still recognizable and both their style and their purpose can be discerned. In keeping with the Persian tradition, apart from the buildings there are ponds and fountains in ornamental gardens, within which running water was an essential element, as well as *hammam*.

Bidar, fort: Takht Mahall

One of the first buildings to be built, at the behest of Ahmad Shah al-Wali, was the so-called Takht Mahall (Throne Palace)

Above One of the seven entrance gates to the fort at Bidar (1532), the most ambitious architectural achievement of the Bahmanid dynasty.

Opposite The Takht Mahall in Bidar Fort. The palace, one of the first buildings to be constructed inside the fort, was built for Ahmad Shah al-Wali.

– contemporaries, although often full of praise for it, knew it as simply the 'building with a courtyard in front'.[3] It has an imposing entrance towards the east. The façade is greatly damaged, but the arches that remain intact combine strength and beauty in their architectonic style, differing both in their opening and in their shape, demonstrating their creator's love of variety. Persian influence can be noted here, and is also evident in the decoration of the palace. The royal apartments occupied the southern, eastern and western sides of a huge paved courtyard. The entrance portico is accessible via a flight of seven steps and is of a circular design, which is somewhat unusual among Islamic buildings in India. The façade of the portico is ornamented with a beautiful large arch, within which is the much smaller true entrance and a window. Blind niches are distributed to the sides of the arch, the extradoses of which are filled with tiles with geometric designs, among which the figures of two tigers and the rising sun stand out: a suitable transposition of the Persian royal emblem – the lion and the rising sun – to correspond with Deccani fauna. This could mean that Persian craftsmen were employed, since they were accustomed to using this emblem in their own country and adapting it to suit local conditions. The interior is animated with projections and recesses decorated in glazed tiles. Beyond this entrance is a rectangular hall with niches on the western wall and two small cisterns opposite, which, combined with the fact that at one time the hall opened on to the courtyard with three arches, suggests a palace mosque. From the mosque, one passes into a square area animated by niches and arches that transform it into a star-like octagon. On each of the principal sides there are arches with traces of encaustic tiles. From here there is access to the rectangular bedchamber of the sovereign, flanked by two vestibules which perhaps were for his bodyguards. The room overlooks a large paved courtyard with a beautiful pool in the centre and alcoves on both sides which in its turn leads to the royal hall, square in plan and articulated with arches and niches and crowned by a large beautiful dome. The niches were decorated with Chinese porcelain and blue Persian majolica, numerous fragments of which have been found. The walls of the hall were also covered with exquisite glazed tiles embellished with designs in pure gold. Here the Bahmanid sovereigns granted audiences to the dignitaries of the court. The hall was connected with a room equipped with cisterns and perhaps a fountain, and with a spacious pillared hall that looked over the main courtyard of the building. The wooden shafts of the pillars, once gilded and painted, were destroyed by a fire following an explosion. Other quarters have been found to the sides of this hall and opposite the entrance pavilion. Behind the large pool is a *hammam* two storeys high and the ruins of an open-air summer bath.

BIDAR, FORT: TARKASH MAHALL
Other palaces were built by later sovereigns, above all by Ahmad III (1461–3) and Muhammad III (1463–82). Among these buildings it was the Tarkash Mahall – built over several storeys – which although begun by Bahmanid sovereigns was certainly renovated by the Barids.

These last were ministers of Turkish origin who practically ruled the empire from 1487 onwards but only assumed the imperial title in 1542, maintaining it until 1619 when they were absorbed by the Adil Shahs of Bijapur. The palace has undergone many alterations over various periods according to the whims of various builders, to the point where it is now difficult to determine its original ground plan. At the centre of the upper apartments was a huge hall with an arched entrance and beautiful ornament in stucco and glazed tiles. In the walls is a series of small ornamental niches – built to hold porcelain and toilet objects – such as are to be found in the Mughal palaces from the Jahangir epoch and those of Shah Jahan in northern India. Other small antechambers have identical decoration with glazed tiles and carved stucco. Facing these apartments is a large terrace in the centre of which is a hexagonal fountain. On the ground floor there are spaces that rise through four floors or more and have barrel vaults.

To the east of this palace is another building that is also called Tarkash Mahall, now in ruins. It seems to have had two storeys with the upper floor probably occupied by the royal ladies, while the lower floor was used by the guards or perhaps was used as a store. Since the stucco decoration of the western wall includes designs and motifs found frequently in Barid architecture, it is probable that the palace is of this epoch. Indeed, contemporary accounts tell us that the Barids allowed ample space for their harems because they were never short of women of various nationalities: Persian, Georgian, Circassian and Turkish.

Bidar, fort: Gagan Mahall

The Gagan Mahall (Palace of Paradise) was also originally built by the Bahmanid sovereigns, but the Barids made additions and alterations, even to the ground plan. The building has two courtyards, of which the exterior one was used by the male staff and the guard of the palace. The entrance to the exterior courtyard is at the back of the Sola Khamba Mosque. On the south side of the mosque is a series of rooms and halls built in line, one after the other, which open on to the courtyard through arches. Stone pillars support the arches that divide the ceilings of these rooms into a number of vaults, decorated with elegantly designed stucco inserts.

Bidar, fort: Diwan-i Amm

Another interesting palace in the Bidar fortress is the Diwan-i Amm, which remains intact up to a considerable height on its southern side, but is reduced to little more than its plinth on the other three sides. The building had two entrances on the eastern and western sides, beyond which was a great courtyard divided into two sections along north–south lines. The main hall of the palace, probably used for public audiences, was divided into three spaces by rows of pillars – possibly wooden – which are now gone but were arranged in rows of six. The walls of the hall were decorated with panels of glazed tiles with epigraphic, stylized motifs and more naturalistic floral designs of a delicate manufacture which resembled Persian carpets or book-binding and were coloured in various shades of blue, green, yellow, brown and red. Like the pillars, the ceiling of the hall must have been in painted and gilded wood. In the hall stood the Takht-i Firuza (Turquoise Throne), which, according to the historian Firishta, 'surpassed in splendour and intrinsic value every other throne in the world'.[4] In this hall the coronations of Bahmanid sovereigns were celebrated with a magnificent display of their opulence and power. Here, too, foreign ambassadors brought the sovereigns the rarest and most precious gifts of their respective countries. At the back of the hall are the ruins of three rooms, of which the central one must have been the room where the king paused before arriving in the reception hall. It has a square plan and a floor with a mosaic design including geometric motifs such as hexagons and stars, while the walls, like those of the main hall, were richly decorated with tiles. The side chambers, perhaps reserved for ministers, were spacious and also adorned with coloured glazed tiles.

Bidar, fort: Rangin Mahall

From as early as the times of Ahmad Shah Wali there had been a royal tower (*shah burj*) near the Gumbad Darwaza. From this tower the Bahmanid sovereigns inspected their troops. Mahmud Shah

Bahman took refuge here to escape the Abyssinian and Deccani rebels who intended to kill him and, being subsequently successful in crushing the insurrections, came to consider the refuge offered by the *shah burj* as particularly auspicious. He decided to have a great palace built nearby, the southern part of which was rebuilt by Ali Barid (1542–80) and adorned with carving in wood and mother-of-pearl. The palace was called Rangin Mahall (Coloured Palace) because its external walls were originally decorated with tiles of various colours, some traces of which still remain on the façade of the eastern halls. One verandah and some dividing walls were added in modern times. The halls of the palace are organized in various fashions and include arches and colonnades in both Hindu and Islamic styles. The walls are covered with panels forming a mosaic of glazed tiles, with arabesque designs in the style of Kashan, the most important Persian production centre for this type, from where these tiles were almost certainly imported. The entrance arch of the main hall and some panels of the side walls are decorated with mother-of-pearl mosaics, while the pillars and the beams that support the ceiling are of richly carved wood in pure Hindu style.

BIDAR, FORT: SOLA KHAMBA MOSQUE AND *JAMI MASJID*

Compared with the lively and imaginative style of the palaces, the two mosques of Bidar, one in the fortress and one in the city, are bare and severe almost to the point of austerity; as if to underline, in contrast with the colourful display of the court, the simple solemnity of the Faith. Within the fort is the Sola Khamba (Sixteen Pillars) Mosque, so called because of the number of supports situated in the central area of the prayer hall. The *jami masjid* is in the centre of the city. Both are of the same serene and natural style of Gulbarga, but without the enclosed plan, in order to revive the more orthodox design of a building within an open courtyard, on one side of which is the pillared shrine, and with the central bay leading to the domed *mihrab*. In the *jami masjid* the dome ascends on the exterior from an octagonal base built on the roof of the building. In the Sola Khamba the

Above The Sola Khamba (Sixteen Pillars) Mosque in Bidar Fort was built in 1327 during the Tughluq era, making it one of the oldest mosques in the Deccan.

Opposite The Rangin Mahall (Coloured Palace) in Bidar Fort. Begun by Mahmud Shah and later rebuilt by Ali Barid, the palace is a combination of Hindu and Persian styles.

dome is fixed on a high, 16-sided drum that is opened by archways and resembles the dome at Gulbarga. In both mosques the supports for the arches are rather low and rest on stout cylindrical pillars, again like those of Gulbarga. Due to an erroneous reading of an inscription that was used again during a restoration, it was thought that the Sola Khamba was built in 1423-4 for the prince Muhammad, son of Ahmad Shah Wali and governor of Bidar, before the city was made the capital. It actually dates from 1327 in the Tughluq epoch – making it one of the oldest mosques in Deccan – and was probably rebuilt later. It is therefore the oldest Bahmanid monument in the city. The *jami masjid*, as evidenced in its exterior aspect and its decoration, dates from some decades later.

Bidar, Mahmud Gawan Madrasa

One of the most exotic and interesting buildings of Bidar is the *madrasa* founded in 1472 by Mahmud Gawan, Persian minister of Muhammad Shah III. Mahmud Gawan came from Gilan on the Caspian Sea and was a great statesman in the Bahmanid court between 1466 and 1481. It is probable that, due to the protection offered by his sovereigns who were patrons of culture and building, he was able to bring engineers and craftsmen to Bidar from his own country to work on this building. From the general aspect and infinite detail, from close by this *madrasa* greatly resembles the imposing university buildings that grace many Persian cities or Timur's Samarqand. According to some sources it is very similar to the *madrasa* of Khargird near Mashad, built 28 years earlier in 1444 and which enjoyed the fame of being the most beautiful building of its type in Khurasan. Apart from reproducing the magnificent lines of the Iranian Central Asian prototypes, the Bidar Madrasa had a library of over 3,000 precious manuscripts and could call on the teaching skills of eminent theologians, philosophers and scientists. It seems that Mahmud himself was a great scholar and that, particularly in mathematics, he had few equals, according to the historian Firishta. The building rises on a high base reached by means of two stepped terraces. It covers a rectangular space of some 68 x 60 m which encloses a central quadrangle. At the centre of the three sides of the exterior perimeter project semi-octagonal keeps, reaching a considerable height. These are covered by slightly bulbous or 'Tartar' domes, as in Timurid or Safavid architecture, even if here they would seem to have been in an experimental phase of their evolution. The main entrance, now lost, led to a huge courtyard with a dodecagonal cistern in the middle and surrounded by residential quarters for teachers and students. These were arranged over three

Above The Mahmud Gawan Madrasa (1472) at Bidar. The school was founded by the Persian minister of Muhammad Shah III, and as a result it comprises many Persian elements.

Opposite top The Chand Minar (1436) at Daulatabad, a cylindrical four-storey minaret that seems to have been influenced by similar Turco-Ottoman or contemporary Baghdad buildings.

Opposite bottom The Persian-influenced mausoleum of Ala al-Din Ahmad II (died 1458) is one of a group of tombs of the last Bahmanid rulers and Shiite saints at Ashtur.

floors around four grand reading halls on the centre of each side with open façades like the typical *iwan* structure. The front of the building was enclosed by two slender, three-storey minarets (one has now collapsed) dressed in green-azure majolica arranged on the shaft in zigzag motifs. Other bands of azure tiles dress the lateral walls of the *madrasa* and make the beautiful brick structure stand out by contrast. Apart from the floral designs and the arabesques, the tiles carry many expertly executed inscriptions, also probably done by Persian hands. With its dominating presence over the city, the *madrasa* of Mahmud Gawan displays the influence that the Persian Afaqis (new immigrants) had over the Bahmanid court compared with the Dakhnis (the old Sunnite class who arrived in Deccan at the beginning of the fourteenth century). It also shows the importance at that time of the Shiite doctrine.

BIDAR: OTHER MONUMENTS

In the city, at the centre of the junction of two roads which meet at a right angle, is a massive cylindrical tower called Chaubara. This was perhaps built by Shihab al-Din Ahmad I as an observation post. An important building is the Takht-i Kirmani, a gate which once led to a building erected around 1430, the façade of which still carries much of its original stucco decoration. The arched entrance is flanked by openings with smaller arches arranged over two floors and is surmounted by shamrock merlons. The bands and medallions with exquisite decoration in foliate and arabesque motifs constitute one of the most elegant and elaborate examples of stucco decoration from the Bahmanid epoch.

DAULATABAD: CHAND MINAR

Another exotic Bahmanid building is found outside Bidar at Daulatabad and was built some decades before the *madrasa* of Mahmud Gawan by Ahmad II (1436-58). This is the beautiful Chand Minar (1436), a cylindrical minaret on four floors which seems inspired by similar Turco-Ottoman or contemporary Baghdad buildings, although there is no lack of indigenous elements, such as the brackets supporting the small balconies that divide the various floors. The Chand Minar rises to a height of some 35 m with three circular shaft sections and one fluted, each divided by simple ornamental borders in relief. The whole, slender but stable, is extremely balanced.

ASHTUR: MAUSOLEUMS

Not far from Bidar, at Ashtur, is an impressive group of tombs belonging to the last Bahmanid sovereigns, as well as various mausoleums of Shiite saints. Their style differs from that of the tombs of Gulbarga owing to the increased influence of structural and decorative Persian forms. In general, these tombs have higher, more bulbous domes with straight walls. One of the oldest tombs is also one of the finest and belongs to Shihab al-Din Ahmad I (died 1436). The façade is decorated with three floors of blind arches: four on each façade in the middle and lower registers, seven in the upper register. The decoration, exclusively epigraphic, is arranged in bands alternating with stucco medallions. Inside is beautiful painted decoration with geometric, floral and arabesque motifs which is Persian in inspiration with lively colours augmented with gold.

Also Persian in appearance is the mausoleum of Ala al-Din Ahmad II (died 1458; see p. 155), its façade decorated by five blind arches, decreasing in size from the centre to the sides, and rhomboid panels above these.

The tomb of the Shiite saint Khalil Allah (died 1406 and known as Chaukhandi) is situated about 1 km to the west of the main group of tombs at Ashtur. Preceded by a large gateway, the mausoleum is made up of a domed square space within a two-storey octagon opened by deep niches on all sides, which are flanked by rectangular, rhomboid and pointed arch panels. These niches were probably filled with glazed tiles in bright colours, which have not survived.

The later tomb of Mahmud (died 1518) recalls the older tombs with its arcaded three-storey façade, the heavy hemispheric dome and the complete absence of decoration. Alongside this monument are two small tombs, unusually covered with pyramidal vaults.

HOLKONDA

As well as the *dargah* of Shaikh Muhammad Mashyakha, whose saint's tomb is the oldest of the complex and dates from the mid-fourteenth century, there are other Bahmanid funeral monuments at Holkonda in the district of Gulbarga similar to those at Gulbarga itself and those at Bidar, such as the ones said to be of Allu and Mallu and the tomb of Azam Khan.

Nevertheless, the tomb of Dilawar Khan – a high, octagonal domed building with narrow pointed arches inserted within rectangular panels on each side of the octagon – remains unique, not only within Deccan, but in all India. Its tomb-cum-tower design in fact appears purely Persian and follows a style diffused in Iran from the eleventh to the fourteenth centuries. It is still a mystery how it came to arrive in Holkonda, or who brought it. The tomb can be dated from the mid-fifteenth century because some of its details are similar to those in fashion during the reign of Ala al-Din Shah Bahmanid, such as the black stone borders that mark the contours of the arches and the panels within which they are inserted.

Some interesting remains are those of an elegant *jami* mosque which had three aisles parallel to the *qibla* wall, though only the bases of the pillars are left. The inside walls on all sides have receding ogival arches which are highlighted by striking stucco decorations featuring floral borders and rosettes on the extradoses. The roof, which was perhaps domed, has fallen in, but the outer courtyard is still preserved, as well as the outline of a small pool.

After the unjust execution of Mahmud Gawan, ordered by Muhammad Shah in 1481, the political and artistic decline of Bidar was inevitable. Regretting his extreme action, the sovereign survived his minister by only a year and died at the young age of 28. His 12-year-old son, Mahmud Shah (1482–1518), succeeded him and lived practically as a prisoner of the disputes among the nobles. Even before his death the realm was divided between the independent sultanates of Ahmadnagar, Berar, Bijapur and Golconda, governed respectively by the Nizam Shahi, the Imad Shahi, the Adil Shahi and the Qutb Shahi. Furthermore, after the death of Mahmud, Bidar was in reality governed by the Barid ministers rather than the Bahmanids themselves. In 1542 the Barids proclaimed independence when Ali Barid assumed the title of shah. To these five sultanates can be added the small principality of Kandesh, a region a little to the north-west of Deccan that had declared itself independent in 1382.

The small sultanate of the Imad Shahi of Berar did not have a rich artistic output and soon disappeared. The artistic output of Kandesh was rather interesting but somewhat ephemeral, while the more important Ahmadnagar survived for several decades. The true heirs of the Bahmanid tradition, however, were Bijapur and Golconda, in which Deccani Islamic art reached its apogee before being absorbed into the Mughal empire. Indeed, Bijapur and Golconda often equalled Mughal architecture in value, and in many aspects proved more interesting.

BIDAR: THE BARID MAUSOLEUMS

The tombs of the Barid sovereigns rise to the west of Bidar and their architecture displays the further evolution of the style following the Bahmanid prototypes. The buildings are always square and covered by domes. However, the use of openings and niches was increasingly important; they usually had a much wider four-centred arch at the centre of each side which was profiled with strips of brick. The upper part of the tomb always carries a parapet with shamrock motifs decorated at the corners with turrets. The dome, narrower at the base and accentuated in its bulbousness, sprouts from a border of petals, a characteristic that was destined to become dominant in later Deccani architecture. The oldest mausoleums are even closer to the Bahmanid style. The tomb of Barid I (died 1504), close to that of his son Amir Barid (died 1543), has a simple conical dome of a type that is unusual at Bidar, but inside for the first time superimposed arches appear, a type which reached stylistic perfection in the Gol Gumbaz of Bijapur (see p. 169). The tomb of Amir Barid is incomplete because of his sudden death: on each frontage it carries a large pointed arch at the centre, flanked by smaller arches on two storeys, but it is without a dome.

THE BARID SHAHI OF BIDAR (1542–1609)

The art of Bidar under the Barids was rather insignificant and lacking in originality. Apart from the buildings that they restored or added to the fort, the only structures that are worthy of mention are the last tombs of their sovereigns, situated to the west of the city.

BIDAR: ALI BARID MAUSOLEUM

The masterpiece of this group of tombs is the mausoleum of Ali Barid (died 1580), which rises at the centre of a huge square enclosure that once must have been a

Opposite The fourteenth-century *dargah* dedicated to the saint Shaikh Mashyakha at Holkonda.

Below The richly decorated Ali Barid (died 1580) mausoleum is the finest example from the group of Barid family tombs to the west of Bidar.

garden and of which there still remain a few sections of the perimeter walls. There were four monumental entrances, one at the centre of each side, three of which have now disappeared. The only one still standing is the southern entrance, a fine square building on two floors, with a double order of arches on the exterior and lozenge-shaped niches and friezes inside. The funeral chamber, imposed on a wide plinth, is opened on four sides by large central archways flanked by two superimposed blind niches with extradoses decorated with medallions carrying flowers with eight petals. Above run five horizontal bands which were probably supposed to have been decorated but which have reached us as plain specimens. The parapet has a shamrock motif and two slender terminals at the corners. The imposing hemispheric dome sprouts from a double border of elaborately worked leaves and is decorated at its apex with an octagon within two cylinders and a star. The arches seem to date back to Central Asiatic examples, the prototype of which is found in the mausoleum of Ismail at Bukhara, dating from before 943 and in its turn derived from the Iranian *char taq*, the tetrapylon of the Sassanid temple of fire. The interior decoration of the building is very rich, with glazed tiles arranged in bands and panels around the contours of the arches, the extradoses of which are decorated with medallions with Koranic inscriptions in tile mosaics. The *muqarnas* of the dome joints are decorated with stucco arabesques. The sovereign's sarcophagus is in beautifully polished black basalt. In the garden, reached by means of a wide entrance, there is a small mosque with three wide arches on three receding floors and decorated with stucco medallions with elaborate arabesques and enclosed within two minarets with small bulbous cupolas.

Very similar, but in a smaller format, is the tomb of Ali's son Ibrahim (died 1587), which remains incomplete.

The tomb of Qasim Barid II (died 1591) is again of the type with blind niches on two floors, but is remarkable because of its elaborate parapet and the bands of leaves at the base of the dome.

THE NIZAM SHAHI OF AHMADNAGAR AND DAULATABAD (1490–1634)

AHMADNAGAR

The first capital of the sultanate, Ahmadnagar, was founded in 1490 by Maliq Ahmad Barhi and was equipped with a fort which, although lacking in natural protection, is one of the most famous works of military engineering in all India. It was attacked and damaged more than once by the Mughals from the beginning of the 1600s. There is a most beautiful building here, the richly decorated small Damari Mosque. Its flat roof rests on pilasters which are supported by the capitals of octagonal, Hindu-type columns. The perimeter walls are opened by two pointed arches within a rectangular border and surrounded by three similar niches. All the borders are decorated with Islamic geometric motifs or flowing Hindu floral elements while the gables carry elegant rosettes in lotus-flower shapes.

Two Mughal-style buildings stand just outside the city: the tomb of Salabat Khan and the building called Faria Bagh (Garden of the Fairies). The first, known locally as the Chand Bibi Mahall, is in fact the tomb of a famous minister of Murtaza Nizam Shah I (1565–88). The building, in a raised position, has an octagonal plan and three rows of pointed arches on the walls. The second was built for the sultan Burhan Nizam Shah I (1508–53) and was demolished by him because it was not well built. Thirty years later it was rebuilt at the centre of a lake with an octagonal plan, two storeys high and with a flat roof. The external walls are decorated with a large central arch with two rows of smaller arches on either side that are faced with stucco. The palace is now mostly in ruins.

Daulatabad

The second capital of the sultanate, Daulatabad (1600–33), was originally the seat of the Yadava Rajas, then the Tughluqs of Delhi and finally became a Bahmanid fortress. Later, the Mughals made it their capital of Deccan. The buildings built by the Nizam Shahi are arranged between the entrance gate of the exterior fort and the deep moat cut into the rock of the volcanic cone. In a strategic position at the summit of the cone stands the Deogiri Fort which can only be reached across a dangerous underground passage which was equipped with poisonous gas devices. The royal palace is of modest dimensions and is articulated over various enclosures, within which Bahmanid pillars and arches mix with wooden corbels and beams of the Hindu type, while the stucco decoration is akin to that found in the royal palace of Bijapur.

Another secular building, beyond the road to the fort, is the Chini Mahall (Porcelain Palace); it is a rough imitation of the Hindola Mahall of Mandu (see p. 130), and must have been attractive once because of the almost total dressing in glazed majolica tiles. Nizam Shahi mosques, tombs and fortifications are found in various places, above all in hilly areas where the last sovereigns of the dynasty had to organize their resistance against the Mughals. Although not of great architectural value, they are distinguished nevertheless by a certain elegance arising from their careful construction.

The city of Khirki (destined to become Aurangabad at the end of the seventeenth century, the capital of the Mughal emperor Aurangzeb) was founded in 1610 by the talented black minister Maliq Ambar. He built the Kala Mosque and began the *jami masjid* there, both in the

Opposite The imposing main gate of the fort at Golconda, built during the reign of the Qutb Shahi (1512–1681).

Below The small but ornate Damari Mosque at Ahmadnagar, the first capital of the Nizam Shahi sultanate, founded by Maliq Ahmad Barhi in 1490.

ornate Bijapur style. In the city there are also numerous tombs which in part display the late Bahmanid style and in part the Bijapur style – characteristic lotus-shaped domes, graceful small balconies and small windows on the façade.

In the neighbourhood of the city are some tombs, the most notable being that of Nizam Shah, which has a quadrangular ground plan with three blind arches in each of the walls (except for the archway that serves as an entrance on the eastern side) and a fine cornice consisting of triple-bordered arches surmounted by corbels bearing *chhajja*. The pleasing hemispherical dome is surrounded by low terminals, four on each side. There are also two small mosques, the Mecca and the Kotla, but these are of little artistic value.

THE QUTB SHAHI OF GOLCONDA (1512–1681)

The last phase of the style initiated in Deccan by the Bahmanids flourished in Golconda under the dynasty of the Qutb Shahi, founded in 1512 by Sultan Quli Qutb Shah, a Turkoman adventurer from Persia. He was fervently Shiite but was nonetheless known for his loyalty to the Bahmanid Sunnites, fighting on their orders against the Hindu forces of Orissa and Vijayanagar and rival Muslim generals. On the sultan's death in 1543, the territories controlled by him were equivalent to those of the contemporary sovereigns of Bijapur, and Shiia was declared the state religion. Golconda had a strongly fortified citadel and the city was graced with numerous military and civil buildings.

The monuments of the dynasty, especially from the end of the seventeenth century onwards, display very pronounced characteristics. Examples include flared or 'stool leg' pillar and minaret bases, together with elaborate cornices, bulbous domes emerging from lotus petals, polygonal minarets interrupted by open galleries surmounted by bulbous cupolas, and galleries on the roof sometimes two floors high.

GOLCONDA: THE FORT
The most interesting remains are found in Golconda itself, in the surrounding area and in nearby Hyderabad, founded by Muhammad Quli in 1589. Golconda was built on a picturesque granite hill over 100 m high and fortified with 87 imposing bastions and a moat. The defensive plan is tripartite and culminates with the Bala Hisar, or acropolis, some 130 m from ground level. The outermost circuit of the walls that protect the city has a circumference of 2.5 km in an oval shape within which is the rectangle formed by the Naya Qila (New Fort), built in 1624 on the highest point of the northern area of the fortifications. The defensive wall reaches 18 m in height and has eight imposing entrances, four of which are open. These are: the Fath Darwaza (Victory Gate), through which Aurangzeb entered the city victoriously; the Mecca Darwaza, completed in 1590; the Banjara Darwaza, which leads to the tombs of the Qutb Shahi; and the Moti Darwaza (Pearl Gate). The Fath Darwaza still has its massive teak doors decorated with spikes to repulse elephant attacks. The Bala Hisar Darwaza is preceded by a high triumphal arch and leads into the second line of the fortifications that surround the hill. This gate is connected to the previous one by a wide road on the sides of which are workshops and homes, and the remains of baths, warehouses, bazaars, barracks, temples and mosques. Here lived the merchants, the officers, the nobles, the administrators and the rest of the inhabitants of the city.

Not far from the gate rises the *jami masjid*, built by Quli Qutb Shah in 1538 on the site where he was assassinated 5 years later. The stucco decoration of the Bala Hisar is interesting because of its Hindu motifs (mythical animals and lions) which alternate with medallions carrying floral arabesques on the extradoses of the arches. From this gate the road rises towards the citadel along hundreds of steps with insets every so often to allow for rest. Halfway from the summit of the hill runs the double wall that constitutes the third defensive line, to the left of which are the ruins of palaces, women's apartments, arsenals, offices, mosques, warehouses and grain stores, while to the right is an open space with parks and woods. Particularly interesting is the three-storey granite palace known as the Sila Khana (Armoury), which still contains many old rifles from

Aurangzeb's time; the Ambar Khana (House of the Royal Treasure) built by a governor of Abdullah Qutb Shah in 1642; the Naqqar Khana (House of the Drum); and the small Masjid al-Safa, again in the Bahmanid style.

A new development began under Ibrahim (1550–80) who between 1550 and 1559 enlarged the fort to make space for his huge palace, much of which was taken up with the *zenana* with wide courtyards, gardens, cisterns and rooms with walls decorated with arches and niches. The buildings, built in the area below the fort without natural protection, were equipped with a double line of robust fortifications, now ruined.

The mosque, however, which faces on to the courtyard with three pointed arches with double borders, is in good condition. It is without a dome, but it has two characteristically shaped minarets made up of polygonal shafts at the extremities of the prayer hall, together with a small corbelled balcony along the cornice and another high and narrow balcony from which sprouts a small bulbous cupola. To the left of the mosque is a flat-roofed building on which a stone throne is arranged with steps; here the king was able to enjoy fresh air while admiring his city. Not far from here is a small Hindu temple partially quarried out of the granite and still in use. In the penultimate fortification there is a small gate which is very interesting for the ornament on its huge stone architrave. These are medallions with delicate lotus flowers flanked by mythical animals: half-dog half-lion, swans with worms in the form of snakes in their beaks, as well as lion cubs, peacocks and parrots arranged around a simple pointed-arch niche.

Another series of wide steps joins the lower buildings with the Bala Hisar. To the sides there was a system of cisterns on various levels designed to carry water to the highest part of the citadel by means of pairs of oxen which hauled heavy leather buckets with ropes and pulleys. The water was then poured into the higher cisterns. The spilled water was taken down again by means of terracotta pipes, which are still extant.

Under the acropolis is a Great Mosque, built by Quli Qutb in 1518 and conceived according to a more robust style than that of the Bahmanids. The prayer hall is opened on the façade by five large pointed arches and is preceded by a courtyard enclosed by walls with an imposing domed entrance on the eastern side. The interior is five spans deep and three spans in width, all covered with domes. The *mihrab* is decorated with the characteristic chain motif.

GOLCONDA: QUTB SHAHI MAUSOLEUMS
However, it is the intact tombs of the Qutb Shahi sovereigns that best represent the style. Situated to the north-west of the city, these comprise seven royal tombs and others reserved for personages of the reigning family or courtiers of imperial rank. Almost all are of the same design as the Bahmanid tombs of Bidar, but with the addition of numerous characteristic architectonic and decorative – especially floral – details. These are rather showy ornaments in stucco which sometimes alter the contours of the buildings and confuse their surfaces. They range from richly modelled pinnacles to crenellated parapets. The domes are extremely characteristic, with an accentuated bulbous form that sprouts from a chalice shape at the base. The corner minarets terminate with arcaded galleries in miniature, which are characteristic of the Qutb Shahi style. As well the tombs there are various funeral mosques, mortuaries and entrances, all arranged within a series of well-kept gardens. Some tombs are on two floors, where the lower floor is made up of a wide arched verandah with projecting cornices on brackets.

One of the most characteristic is the tomb of Abdullah Qutb Shah, who died in 1672. This is an immense two-storey monument, the upper part of which is surrounded by a suspended balcony with open-work panels, merlons and many terminals.

More compact in its design, perhaps because of its earlier date (1612), is the tomb of Muhammad Qutb Shah, under whose reign building activity in the region reached its apogee.

The mausoleum of Jamshid (1543–50) is a rather unusual shape, but it was probably not erected before the beginning of the seventeenth century. It is an octagon on two floors with blind ogee niches in which smaller doors and windows have been inserted. It has a sumptuously decorated balcony on the upper floor and a most ornate cornice-parapet from which turrets protrude. The whole is covered by a large dome with a very accentuated bulbous profile.

Also interesting are the mausoleums of Muhammad (died 1626) and his wife, Hayat Bakhshi Begum (died 1667), whose connecting mosque has a parapet of open-work bricks with geometric motifs and lateral minarets with arcaded balconies on two levels.

HYDERABAD
Muhammad Quli (1580–1612) was the founder, in 1589, of Hyderabad, a city that from being a place of amusement moved

Left The tombs of the Qutb Shahi funeral complex (seventeenth century) at Golconda provide the best examples of the robust style favoured by the Qutb Shahi rulers.

Opposite The unusual Char Minar, a triumphal arch with four minarets built in 1591 at Hyderabad.

quickly to become the civil and commercial capital. The ancient city is surrounded by bastioned walls with 13 entrances which were built by Nizam al-Mulk after his proclamation at Nizam of a new, independent Deccani realm in 1724. The city is connected to the northern suburb by means of four bridges, the oldest of which, the Purana Pul, was erected by Muhammad Quli in 1593. This sovereign also had another complex of royal and ceremonial structures built which form the focal point of the city, starting from the Char Minar and the monuments connected to it around the crossing point of the four roads that lead to the four quarters.

Many of Muhammad Quli's buildings have disappeared, apart from the Ashur Khana, which is still in use for the ceremonies of Muharram and Dar al-Shurfa, and a large building for the treatment of illnesses, once also used for the teaching of medicine.

The Char Minar (Four Minarets) is in truth a triumphal arch along the lines of the Triple Gate (Tin Darwaza) of Ahmedabad. Built in 1591, the Char Minar has a square plan measuring over 30 m each side and the four minarets, one on each corner, are over 55 m high. Each is decorated with a double arched balcony; two other small balconies surround each shaft above roof level and terminate in a bulbous cupola with a foliated base, all characteristic of the Qutb Shahi style. The ground floor consists of four wide arches, one on each side, above which are diminishing arcaded storeys. On the upper part of the building is a little mosque, flanked by four minarets; at the eastern extremity of the courtyard of the mosque is a gateway surmounted by a bulbous dome with characteristic petals on the base. Near the Char Minar are the Char Kaman (Four Arches), four heavy arches built on the four roads and near which there extends a large cistern. The Dad Mahall (Palace of Justice) once stood here, but it was destroyed by an explosion in 1771.

In 1598 the *jami masjid* was built in the city. In this building the pointed arches of the façade are surmounted by a second floor of blind cuspidated niches. The minarets that flank the extremities of the façade terminate with the usual bulbous domes that sprout from flower petals. The famous Badshahi Ashur Khana (1593–97) is completely decorated with glazed tiles in a manner very similar to that of the Turco-Ottoman mosques.

The Mecca Mosque, begun by Muhammad in 1617, but completed many years later (1693) by Aurangzeb, is considered to be among the best buildings of the Qutb Shahi. It has a prayer hall with five spans and three bays deep, all domed, apart from the central one which is covered by a pointed vault. The arched façade is surmounted by a cornice on corbels and is enclosed between two rather stout minarets with arcaded balconies and bulbous domes. Alongside the mosque is an enclosure containing the tombs of various sovereigns, princes and princesses of the Asafiya sovereigns (the Nizams of Hyderabad); in the courtyard are the remains of a bath.

Many palaces, mosques and mausoleums were built under successive sovereigns both at Golconda and at Hyderabad using a yet more elaborate style but without substantial changes. In particular, the minarets and the roof parapets of the mosques became ever more bizarre until the Toli Mosque at Hyderabad, which, according to Goetz, 'reached the maximum degree of contrast between the vertical thrust upwards and horizontal pressure, between lightness of individual forms and the massive effect of their whole, between maximum simplicity and exaggerated ornament'.[5]

At Baghnagar, between Golconda and Hyderabad, some buildings were erected for the favourite Hindu women of the sultan, such as the Baghmati Mosque and the *baradari* (garden pavilion) of Taramati.

The Adil Shahi of Bijapur (1489–1686)

The Adil Shahi, who declared independence from the Bahmanid realm in 1489, were very proud of their Turkish origins – to the point where the crescent adorns all the buildings of Bijapur. Following various events, they became the most powerful sultans of Deccan. With them the Shiia was introduced into the country and Persian became the official language of the court. The Adil Shahi also welcomed the Hindu elite – poets, artists, men of

The Mecca Mosque at Hyderabad (1617–93) is considered one of the best buildings of the Qutb Shahi era.

letters, theologians and philosophers – and they admired the *sannyasin* just as they admired the Sufi. Ibrahim II, an expert musician, even knew the Hindu pantheon and especially admired Sarasvati, god of eloquence and music, and Ganesh, the symbol of knowledge and literature. Known as a just and impartial sovereign, he was called Jagatguru (Tutor of the World) by the Indian officials and administrators of the state, but he himself preferred to use the Sanskrit title, Navarasa (New Essence of the Time), which he felt was more appropriate to describe his new artistic and intellectual ideas. Architecture, however, was the chosen field of Adil Shahi patronage and their buildings are the most satisfying in Deccan, from both the structural and the aesthetic point of view.

Early Bijapur art was derived from Bahmanid art, but it displays a technical maturity that probably came from its contact with other, older schools that were possibly Ottoman, together with the skill of Hindu craftsmen who were certainly used in the construction of the buildings. In the more mature style of Bijapur architecture, the shape of the dome is unique – almost spherical and blossoming from a band of lotus petals that rise from the base of the dome. This form is found on a smaller scale on the turrets resembling slender minarets that are almost always present in the buildings as corner decoration. The arch lost the excessively pointed profile it had in the Bahmanid prototypes and assumed more graceful contours with the four-centred variety. There are still traces of the low impost arches, derived from Gulbarga, but here they have acquired a more beautiful line. The pillar was somewhat rare and was replaced by solid brickwork pylons, usually rectangular in section. The large *chhajja*, strongly projecting and supported by fine decorated brackets, appear as architectonic ornament in the majority of the buildings. In the gables of the arches there is often a corbel with volutes including a medallion, and above the arches a foliated terminal of singular beauty. Also present are the usual rosettes, the conventional hanging lamps and various intertwined symbols carved into the stone or modelled in stucco. The type of the buildings remained more or less the same, while ornament increased.

Each Adil Shahi sovereign forced himself to surpass his predecessor in the number, dimensions and splendour of his architectural projects. In this way they also transmitted their enthusiasm for construction to their subjects – in few other cities in India is there such a profusion of beautiful buildings. Despite the Maratha destruction of the eighteenth century, which resulted in the stripping of the various buildings of all movable material and speeding up the process of dilapidation, today some 50 mosques still survive, as do 20 tombs and the same number of palaces. In appearance they are now a little dilapidated because of the basalt stone with which they were usually built.

BIJAPUR

In contrast with the majority of large cities in Deccan, Bijapur does not dominate the surrounding countryside from on high but stands, with no natural protection, on lightly rising ground in the middle of the territory it controlled. Construction of the citadel, a fortress with an irregular, round plan containing a palace, various other buildings and two small mosques adorned with Hindu spoil material, began in the first half of the sixteenth century. With the growth of the Adil Shahi's power, the number of buildings surrounding the citadel also grew, and they were all enclosed within fortified walls completed by the end of 1565. The line of this urban wall has an irregular circumference of some 10 km and is broken by six gates through which pass roads that run to the centre of the citadel. At the beginning of the 1600s, when the dynasty was at its height, there was a notable expansion of the city with the construction of the peripheral areas of Shahapur to the north and Ainapur to the east. Both of these areas have monuments of particular architectural interest.

Nevertheless, it was to the west that Ibrahim II (1580–1627) founded Nauraspur, a second and larger city linked to the capital by a wide road. But building work was abandoned before completion and therefore the city has no buildings worthy of note. Hence the most important buildings are to be found within the confines of the original city which reached its maximum size in the first half of the seventeenth century.

Some monuments still survive from the pre-Adil Shahi period. Among these is an ancient mosque, dated 1320 from an inscription, which is built with Hindu spoil material; in the central area of the prayer hall – raised above the other areas – it is structurally reminiscent of the Gujarati mosques. This is the Karim al-Din Mosque which rises near the southern part of the citadel. Another later mosque, but again of the Bahmanid epoch (*c.*1485), is that belonging to the vizier Khwaja Jahan near the northern gate of the citadel and also put together with Hindu pillars. The two high brick minarets with ruined wooden galleries that are found in the much later complex of the Mecca Mosque in the citadel are also Bahmanid. A large bridge with a low, wide opening on the eastern side of the citadel moat must also be from this period. The characteristic low imposts on which the arch rests are very similar to those of the lateral bays in the Gulbarga Mosque. This fact increases the likelihood of a true dating being pre-Adil Shahi.

According to legend the founder of the dynasty, Yusuf Adil Shah (1489–1510), was the cadet of Sultan Murad II of Turkey and escaped death with the help of his mother when his father ordered the death of all his sons except the heir. After various adventures he reached Bidar and fell into favour with the Bahmanid court. When independence was gained he established himself in Raichur, in a massive palace that was later transformed into a prison. His successor, Ismail Adil Shah, lived instead in the Arg Qila of Bijapur and perhaps built the Old Mint, with a wide and low arched entrance. The oldest Adil Shahi building would appear to be the ancient *jami masjid* named after Yusuf, but in fact it dates from 1513, three years after the death of the sovereign. It presents many of the characteristics that became typical of the style, such as the prayer hall with three spans, of which the central one is wider than the others, covered by a single hemispheric dome resting on a circular drum the base of which is surrounded with vertical leaves. The whole resembles a bud surrounded by petals. The ancient *jami masjid*, on the other hand, dates from the time of Ibrahim Adil Shah I (1534–57). This is a rather small mosque with three arcades with low imposts in the Bahmanid tradition, externally simple but well finished inside. The most remarkable characteristic is the two minarets (one has now collapsed) that rise on the central pillars of the façade while four much smaller minarets crown the corners of the building. The Ikhlas Khan Mosque is later (1597) and is basically similar to the *jami masjid*. In both mosques the open arches in the façade and those around the *mihrab* are shadowed by cuspidated arches; in the Ikhlas Khan Mosque there are rectangular zigzag motifs between the two types of arches, while the central arch is lower and is even scalloped.

BIJAPUR: GAGAN MAHALL

Vigorous building activity began with the succession to the throne of Ali Adil I Shah (1557–80) who had rid himself of the Hindu threat with the victory at Talikota. The construction of the assembly hall of the Gagan Mahall of about 1560 is attributed to him. This building is remarkable because of the immense 20 m long arch, almost 17 m high, that dominates the façade and is flanked by two narrower, very high archways. At the rear there was a huge central hall with a smaller room at each side. The ceiling has collapsed, but it seems to have been of wood and supported an upper floor by means of massive wooden pillars. This upper floor must have contained the sovereign's private apartments and must have had projecting balconies from which the ladies of the palace could see, through screens, what happened in the hall below or in the square in front of the great arch. On the extradoses of the arches there appear 'medallion and corbel' decorative motifs. The corbel is in the form of an upside-down fish, with its eyes, gills and scales clearly visible; this supports the round medallion between the flukes of its tail. (Flags bearing fish are flown during the celebrations of Muharram at Hyderabad, an important event in the Shiia of Bijapur.) A palace similar to this, the Sangat Mahall, is found at Tarweh-Nauraspur, 6 km to the west of Bijapur. When it was discovered it still had part of its roof intact; study of it has also allowed us to make some deductions about the roof structure of the Gagan Mahall.

Above The *jami masjid* at Bijapur, built in 1576 by Ali Adil I Shah. Though similar to Bahmanid examples, this mosque has a more sumptuous style.

Opposite The simple but impressive interior of the *jami masjid* at Bijapur. Wall decorations were added in the seventeenth century that are not entirely in character with the austerity of the building.

BIJAPUR: *JAMI MASJID*

Ali Adil I Shah had many fortifications built in the city, including the *jami masjid* (1576) which is considered the finest example of architecture from the classic Adil Shahi period. The mosque is close to Bahmanid examples but reinterprets them in a more sumptuous manner. It was never completely finished. Two minarets that should have adorned the eastern façade are missing and it also lacks the usual merlons on the parapets of the *riwaq* that surround the courtyard and on the façade of the prayer hall. Despite these defects, the building has a noble and imposing aspect. The ground plan shows a large rectangular structure some 150 x 80 m with a square internal courtyard of over 50 m each side. The perimeter walls are adorned outside by two orders of superimposed arches, of which the lower one is purely ornamental while the upper one forms an open gallery that runs along three sides around the mosque and the *sahn*. The prayer hall faces on to here through seven fine archways of equal width of which the central one is decorated with a foliated motif. The lateral *riwaq* also face on to the courtyard through seven arches and are opened at the centre by doors that lead to the exterior. Another doorway, more or less in the same style, was built later on the eastern side by the emperor Aurangzeb. A deep and wide cornice on corbels projects over the arched façade, and above the centre of the sanctuary there rises a square, arched structure that supports the large dome and lends it an appropriate setting. The dome is hemispheric, blossoms from a floral motif and is crowned by a massive metal terminal that carries the symbol of the crescent. The interior of the mosque, impressive but not pretentious, is made up of a vast hall of some 70 x 36 m, divided into five bays parallel to the *qibla* and 45 spans by means of pointed arches supported by massive brick pillars. The central bay consists of a square space 25 m in diameter including nine spans delimited by twelve arches, three on each side, which intersect above and create an octagonal cornice on which the base of the dome rests. The remaining spans are covered by low cupolas carved in the same thickness as the flat roof which do not project on the exterior. The treatment of the interior surfaces is simple and severe and every piece of ornament is architectonic in character, tending to accentuate lines and spaces rather than create embellishments. In a later epoch, perhaps under Sultan Muhammad (1627-57) an elaborate mural decoration in relief and brilliant colours was added near the *mihrab*. This represented tombs and minarets, censers and chains, niches containing books, vases with flowers, medallions and epigraphic bands. Although not totally without merit, this decoration is out of character with the simple and dignified sanctuary that is complete in itself and therefore without the need for superimposed ornament.

Also from the reign of Ali Adil I are the mausoleum of the sovereign, the Chand Baori and the palace and mosque of Mustafa Khan. The first is a linear structure without much artistic worth. The Chand Baori is an artificial lake that the queen, Chand Bibi, had built in 1579 with a border wall, platforms and stairways. The palace of Mustafa Khan is in ruins; the mosque is a small building with three

BIJAPUR: *JAMI MASJID*

arches of different widths, as in the Gagan Mahall, and with a large dome which rises from a square structure opened by archways, as in the *jami masjid*.

The following reign of Ibrahim Adil Shah II (1580–1627) saw the construction of the Anand Mahall, today used as a government office and originally very similar to the Gagan Mahall but altered in modern times; the Jal Mandir, a small water pavilion on several floors with a bulbous dome; and the Anda (Egg) Mosque, a curious building on two storeys where the mosque itself only occupies the upper floor while the ground floor is a hall or an alms house. The name of the mosque refers to the shape of the dome which is ribbed on the exterior. Construction of the Malika Jahan Begum Mosque is also to be attributed to Ibrahim II, indeed it was built in honour of his wife. It is a small building with a façade opened by three fine pointed arches, covered by a bulbous dome and flanked by four slender ornamental minarets. The ornament on the awning and the cornice is extremely refined and is certainly one of the most beautiful examples of the genre in Bijapur. During restoration work, however, hanging chain motifs in stone that had earned the building the local name of Zanjiri Mosque and contributed to its elegant ornamentation were lost.

Bijapur: Ibrahim *rauza*

The same sovereign began and carried forward the construction of the Ibrahim *rauza*, planned as a tomb for his wife, Taj Sultana, but including his own mausoleum and those of the family which were all positioned within a square walled area with a beautiful gate. The complex is not very large, indeed the entire exterior wall is only 137 m each side and the tomb, also square, measures less than 35 m each side. Mosque and mausoleum rise on an oblong terrace (120 x 50 m) at the western and eastern extremities respectively, while at the centre there is an ornamental cistern and a fountain. Although different in shape and purpose, the two buildings are perfectly balanced in both style and volume so as to create a symmetrical composition. The mausoleum is most certainly the more splendid of the two, with a central room surrounded by a double verandah with arches, two of which on each exterior façade are narrower than the others so as to create a subtle variety in the spaces. The whole is surmounted by a bulbous dome which blossoms from a series of lotus petals and is fixed on a square structure supported by corbels. Along all the walls above the arches runs a parapet supported by beautifully designed corbels with a cornice above that is interrupted regularly by decorative terminals. From each corner of the building rise turrets in the form of minarets. Beyond the arched verandah, which was added later by Muhammad Adil Shah, is a row of pillars that forms a second arcade around the central room, the exterior walls of which are decorated in a way that clearly reveals the influence of Turco-Ottoman art. Each wall is divided into three large arches, enclosed by borders and panels with a pillar at each corner of the building. Everywhere there is decoration consisting of arabesques, Koranic inscriptions on a blue background and friezes of refined elegance. The total effect is perhaps a little excessive, but taken individually each element is of exquisite beauty. The interior of the funeral chamber has a skilfully curved casement ceiling on which the dome stands. The mosque, less deep than the mausoleum although in perfect harmony with it, is also distinguished by the precious quality of its ornament which in the brackets for the awning 'give the impression of countless petrified drops of rain water'.[6] The slender ornamental minarets are surrounded at the base by a series of graceful miniature minarets and more domed terminals decorate the façade above the parapet. An inscription states that the building's date of completion is 1626. Inside, the *mihrab* is inserted into a deep domed niche – almost a room.

Bijapur: Mihtar Mahall

A yet more refined building, which by its style dates from about 1620 (once again the epoch of Ibrahim Adil Shah II), is the Mihtar Mahall (see p. 168). Although called 'Mahall', this is not a palace but rather an entrance to the interior courtyard of a mosque which in itself would have attracted much attention if it had not been eclipsed by its annexe. This is not a building of exceptional design, but the elegant treatment of every part and the careful decorative details make it one of the most graceful buildings in Bijapur. In truth it is not simply a portal since above the entrance way is a balconied room, from which it was possible to enjoy the pleasant view of the city. Above this room is an open terrace surrounded by a wall on which balconied windows open; the terrace is covered by an open-work parapet. The exterior aspect of this building is of a square tower some 8 m each side with a façade enclosed between two slim buttresses that terminate in bulbous domes. The most noteworthy characteristic of the Mihtar Mahall is found in the window of the second floor, the balcony of which is supported by beautifully made corbels with rows of tear-shaped buds which recall those of the cornice on the Ibrahim *rauza* mosque. The balcony is in the shadow of a strongly projecting *chhajja* which rests on very fine corbels with superb intaglio work in which Hindu animal figures – *hamsa*, lions, elephants, peacocks, parrots and others – appear next to floral arabesques. An elegant frieze, now disappeared, adorned the cornice and it seems that stone chains once hung from the corners of the building as in the Kali Mosque of Lakshmeshwar.[7] Lotus roses and delicate floral friezes complete the decoration of the façade, and become most dense around the three arches of the entrance. The final frieze on the terrace was an extremely fine work of interlacing and palmette volutes executed in open

Above The mosque in the Ibrahim *rauza* complex at Bijapur. The complex was planned around the tomb of Taj Sultana, wife of Ibrahim II, but it also includes his own mausoleum and those of his family.

Opposite The Jal Mandir, a small water pavilion at Bijapur, was built during the reign of Ibrahim Adil Shah II (1580–1627).

work with the care of a goldsmith. The casement ceiling of the ground-floor room in the Mihtar Mahall also has lovingly carved and chiselled work of such refined taste that it recalls the work of Italian artists of the 1400s. It is not known who commissioned the portal. In an ancient hand-drawn map it is called the *chhajja* of Mihtar Gada Wazir (Minister), but such a name is not found in the history of Bijapur. According to legend the portal was built by a sweeper (*mihtar*) who unexpectedly became rich thanks to a present from the king. Not knowing what to do with so much money, he used it to build this portal and called it the Mihtar Mahall (Sweeper's Palace). Another legend, again rather improbable, attributes the building to a certain Mihtar Gada, a fakir or beggar of Ibrahim II's time. Perhaps the gateway and the mosque were built privately and therefore, because the gate was more often than not closed, the mosque was out of sight and the gateway assumed the dignity of a palace.

Although it does not compare with the gateway, the mosque is a small, graceful building with a triple-arched façade from which projects a beautiful cornice supported by finely worked corbels. Strangely, the minarets are not of the same quality as the rest but have a rather inelegant and primitive aspect; they are not crowned with the usual bulbous cupolas, but rather a small ball and a trident. During a rushed restoration, the minarets even lost the small balconies that interrupted their shafts at various heights. The roof of the building is flat without a dome.

Other buildings of this period worth mentioning are the elegant mosques of Batulla Khan, similar to the Golconda ones, and the Mustafa Khan and Mecca Mosque, which have a more traditional layout, though the former is erected on a high platform with arches along the front.

Bijapur: Gol Gumbaz

One of the most representative monuments of Bijapur dates from the time of Muhammad Adil Shah (1627–57) and is the mausoleum of the sovereign himself which was known as the Gol Gumbaz (Round Dome). Muhammad understood the impossibility of equalling the plastic architectural beauty of the *rauza* of Ibrahim and so decided to surpass it in size, creating one of the largest and most remarkable buildings in all India. The tomb is only one part of a complex that includes a mosque, a *naqqar khana* that functioned as a gateway, a *dharmshala* or inn for travellers and other buildings associated with the sovereign's funeral construction. All were contained within a walled enclosure. This grandiose idea began towards the mid-seventeenth century when Muhammad's reign was coming to a close and it was never totally carried out. The sepulchral building itself never reached the state of completion its designers had intended.

The wall surfaces of this immense building are very simple, both inside and out. The plan of the mausoleum is simply a large cube with a tower on each corner and covered by a majestic hemispheric dome. In this building the detail contributes to the harmony of the whole, above all the fine projecting cornice fixed on closely spaced corbels with the joints raised in relief by the lengthening of the curved shapes. A row of well-spaced small arches runs on the cornice, and above are massive merlons which, together with the terminals, break the line of the horizon with their graceful forms. At the base of the dome, elegant curved leaves subtly cover the joint with the drum. Below, on each perimeter wall, are based three great blind arches. These are elegant and rhythmic in form and the central one, wider than the others, is dressed with wooden panels and functions as an entrance. On the northern side the central arch has been opened at a later date to form the entrance to a room which projects to the exterior and – following examination of the walls – also seems to have been added after the construction of the mausoleum. The corner towers, octagonal in section, are not totally in harmony with the rest of the composition: they are divided into too many floors (seven) and resemble Chinese pagodas more than minarets.

The interior of the Gol Gumbaz consists of a single room, but is of majestic proportions like the Pantheon in Rome or Saint Sophia in Istanbul. This is one of the largest single-chamber buildings ever constructed. The most remarkable architectural characteristics of this great hall are the high pointed arches that form the corners; on them rests a high circular platform 29.5 m wide which in its turn supports the base of the dome. The interior surface of the dome overlaps the edge of the circle by some 4 m so that part of its weight falls on the four exterior walls while the remainder falls on the intersecting arches that bear and neutralize any other exterior forces. The dome has six small openings in the base and a flat section at its crown. It is built with horizontal courses of brick cemented with substantial layers of lime that reach the considerable thickness of over 3.5 m. The system of

Above The Gol Gumbaz, one of the most representative monuments of Bijapur, is the mausoleum of Muhammad Adil Shah (1627–57). It is remarkable for its system of intersecting arches, a feature not seen elsewhere.

Opposite The Mihtar Mahall (1620) at Bijapur. Despite its name, this refined building is not a palace but is actually an entrance to the courtyard of a mosque.

support using intersecting arches, which seems to have been so familiar to the builders of Bijapur, was in fact almost unknown elsewhere; one other example is found – in the Great Mosque at Córdoba dating from some 600 years earlier.

The mausoleum of Muhammad Adil Shah, despite the imperfection of the corner towers, is a majestic construction built with the aim of provoking wonder and awe. The total width of each of its four square sides is equal to the entire height of the building, some 70 m. The exterior diameter of the dome is almost 43 m. The interior of the hall from one side to the other measures some 41 m and is about 60 m high, while the gallery from which the dome rises is about 35 m from the floor. The entire area covered is more than 1,672 squ. m and is therefore larger than the Pantheon which measures some 1,393 squ. m. There must also have been an acoustic gallery that reverberated with echoes around the base of the dome, as found in other buildings such as the Pantheon, the tomb of Cecilia Metella and St Paul's. Naturally this depends on the size of the dome – the larger it is, the more pronounced the acoustic effect. At the centre of the mausoleum is a platform on which are arranged the tombs of the sultan Muhammad, his youngest wife, Arus Bibi, his favourite, Rambha, his daughter and a grandson. Over the main tomb is an elaborate wooden baldachin. According to some, the room added to the north side of the mausoleum was destined to shelter the remains of Jahan Begum, wife of Muhammad Shah, but this is not possible because, by tradition, the wife is always put to rest alongside the husband. Instead it may be that the room was reserved for the sultan's spiritual mentor. Above the main entrance, hanging by a chain from the cornice, is a meteorite (*bijli patthar*) which is said to have fallen nearby during the reign of Muhammad. On the southern side of the Gol Gumbaz, not far from it, rises the great exterior gate, the upper floor of which was used as a *naqqar khana* where music was played on special occasions. Like the tomb, it does not seem to have been completed. Above the corbels that run to the edge of the roof there should have been a cornice and then a parapet with minarets at the corners. In modern times the building was transformed into a museum. To the west of the mausoleum is the mosque which adjoins the tomb. For many years this was used as a temporary residence for travellers. It is a well-proportioned structure with slender minarets and a deep, rich cornice which is badly damaged.

The mausoleum of Jahan Begum, Muhammad's wife, is at Ainapur and must have been similar in plan to the Gol Gumbaz. Only the foundations and the pillars survive, but it seems that the façades were opened by three archways and that the dome was only half as wide as that of the larger mausoleum.

BIJAPUR: CIVIL BUILDINGS

Not far from the Gagan Mahall stands the Sat Manzil (Seven-floored Palace) which is partly ruined so that now it only has five floors. Originally it was probably built with three levels and terminated with a terrace of which the *kanjura* around the walls remain; the other floors were added later. At the time of Muhammad the Chini Mahall (Palace of Porcelain) was also built and dedicated to the sultan's favourite, the Indian dancer Rambha. It is equipped with ornamental bathing pools in many of the rooms, and has beautifully decorated ceilings and figurative frescoes in which images of the sultan and Rambha appear. Another palace, built perhaps at the time of Ibrahim II, but rebuilt by Muhammad Shah in 1646, is the Asar Mahall, connected to the citadel by means of a wide single-arched covered bridge. It faced on to the artificial lake and was originally a garden pleasure palace with a high hall supported on four wooden pillars. To the rear it had rooms arranged over two floors in which there are some frescoes which, according to eighteenth-century sources, were executed by Italian artists in Muhammad's service and which, in a 'rough imitation of the manner of Paolo Veronese', represent in the technique of dry fresco some scenes from the life of the *zenana*.[8] In later years Aurangzeb ordered that the faces of the figures should be blanked out because, after having functioned as a court of justice, the building was then dedicated to preserving some hairs from the beard of the Prophet and thus became a most sacred sanctuary.

Other frescoes, but oriental in style, are found in the palace built on a little lake at Kumatgi, some kilometres to the east of Bijapur. Various scenes from the game of polo are represented above an archivolt; elsewhere there are scenes of tiger-, leopard- and deer-hunting, which are divided by graceful pictures of birds. There are also representations of two characters who, judging by their clothes and general appearance, are upper-class Europeans, probably ambassadors to the Bijapur court. On another wall there is the figure of a musician in Persian clothes who is playing a guitar while a queen and her maid sit and listen. Another, more lively scene shows a wrestling match in front of various people both seated and standing. Two men appear with tiger skins over their shoulders and heads as they sit alongside two horses under a tree full of birds. It is not known who built this palace on the water, but it is certain that all the sovereigns appreciated it, coming here often during the dry season to enjoy the fresh play of the sparkling fountains and the peace of the lake.

BIJAPUR: OTHER BUILDINGS

Other Bijapur buildings worthy of note are the Adil Shahid Pir Mosque, the façade of which is of exemplary design; the Chinch Diddi Bukhari and Rangin mosques, together with others in the suburb of Shahpur; the tombs of Shah Nawaz Khan and Yaqut Dabuli; and the Taj Bandi *baoli*, a large artificial pond surrounded by a series of apartments and terraces that Taj Sultana, wife of Ibrahim II, had built in 1620. The unfinished tomb of Ali II (1656-72) is also very interesting. It was planned on a large scale, but never progressed beyond the majestic arches of the ground floor – Ali II was buried in the Gol Gumbaz alongside his father and Rambha. Under Ali II and his successor Sikandar (1672-86) the realm disintegrated as a result of the frequent sieges of the Mughals that made necessary the reinforcement of the walls with robust bastions such as the Sharza Burj (1671) which was equipped with the powerful gun known as Maliq-i Maidan (Sovereign of the Field). Some Adil Shahi buildings are also found outside Bijapur, such as the mosques of Ausa, Bir and Hirapur, or

Above The tomb of Ali II (1656–72) at Bijapur. It was planned on a large scale, but work never got beyond the majestic arches on the ground level.

Top The Taj Bandi *baoli* (1620) at Bijapur. This complex of apartments and terraces around an artificial pond was built for Taj Sultana, the wife of Ibrahim II.

Opposite The Asar Mahall, connected to the citadel at Bijapur, was originally a garden palace. It may have been built at the time of Ibrahim II, but was rebuilt by Muhammad Shah in 1646.

the parts added to the *dargah* of Gesu-Daraz Banda Nawaz at Gulbarga in 1640.

The last buildings that Aurangzeb had erected at Bijapur included the mausoleums called Jod Gumbad (Twin Domes): one of them contains the remains of Khan Muhammad and his son Khawass Khan and the other the remains of the important man of religion Abd-al Razzaq Qadizi. The first is octagonal with a large bulbous dome, while the second is larger, square in plan, and also has a large dome. On the inside both of them have a gallery beneath the dome, like the Gol Gumbaz. Another building, which is even later in date but just as elegant, is the mausoleum of the local saint Shah Karim, which is shaped like a two-storey pyramid with a graceful bulbous dome on top. It seems that the mausoleum was erected *c.*1731, although the saint died in 1693.

Kandesh (1382–1601)

Not truly in Deccan, but in an area slightly to the north-west, reigned the Faruqi dynasty. They obtained independence from Delhi in 1382 and maintained it until the end of the sixteenth century when Akbar united the realm with the Mughal empire. The two capitals of the country were Burhanpur, where the sovereigns lived, and Thalner on the River Tapti which was the Faruqi family stronghold. At Asirgarh, on a hill, was the main citadel where they took refuge in case of danger. It still has, on its highest point, a beautiful mosque from the period of Shah Jahan which is typical of the style of the area: a long arched façade repeated on the *riwaq* and very high corner minarets over three floors divided by balconies in the Iranian style and capped with cupolas. Inside there are numerous pointed archways resting on rather massive pillars and the singular peculiarity of a series of *mihrab* at the sides of the principal one, dug out of the *qibla* wall and functioning as windows which provide a view of the splendid surrounding countryside. At the foot of the fortress stands a small but graceful *idgah*.

Burhanpur

Burhanpur was founded in 1401 and about this time the great citadel and the palace, or Badshahi Qila (King's Fort), were built. Known locally as Lal Bagh, they occupy a high site on the banks of the River Tapti. It seems that the fort was once a sumptuously decorated structure, but it is now too ruined to give an exact idea of its architectural value. In excellent condition, however, is a beautiful *hammam* of white marble, made up of a single space that includes the cistern and is characterized by delicate polychromatic floral decoration in typically Persian style arranged on the high sections of the perimeter walls.

Not far from the city are some tombs, including that of Nadir Shah (1399–1437), the first independent sovereign, and the adjacent tomb of Adil Shah. The mausoleums consist of an octagon resting on a platform covered by a dome fixed on a high drum; they recall the forms of Malwa, Gujarat and Bahmanid Deccan and present an aspect similar to, although less ornate than, some Thalner tombs.

The mausoleum dedicated to Shah Shuja, Shah Jahan's unfortunate son who died in 1660, is an elegant building in the Faruqi style although it belongs to the late Mughal period. The building, which is

Left The *jami masjid* in the Faruqi family citadel at Asirgarh, north-west of the Deccan. The mosque typifies the regional style of Kandesh.

Opposite The tomb of Shah Shuja (died 1660) at Burhanpur, the capital of the Faruqi dynasty of Kandesh. Though dating from the late Mughal period, the monument is in the local style associated with the Faruqi rulers.

enclosed by a wall with a gate in it, has a multifoil ground plan and is topped by an umbrella vault which blossoms from a wreath of tall miniature cupolas. The curved segments of the main part of the building are separated by slender pilasters, while cable mouldings run transversally. The dome is ribbed and topped by an ornament in the shape of three balls rising from an upside-down lotus blossom.

Towards the end of the sixteenth century two mosques were built at Burhanpur: the *jami masjid* of Adil Shah IV in 1588 and the Bibi-ki (Lady's) Mosque at about the same time. Both are Gujarati in style. The first has a façade opened with 15 arches supported by striking black basalt pillars which are, however, very low in comparison with the two imposing minarets. The second, now unfortunately badly ruined, is of the closed variety with a great central arch once enclosed between elegant three-storey minarets crowned with hemispheric cupolas. One of them has now fallen down. Original features are found on the upper part of the shaft which is decorated with highly ornamented balconied windows.

The tomb of Shah Nawaz Khan – one of the seventeenth-century provincial governors – is of this period and seems to combine various influences. Its square two-storey design recalls the royal tombs of Gujarat, with pinnacles similar to those of the Tughluq buildings of Delhi and a Lodi-style dome, while the foliated decoration owes much to examples from Bijapur. Despite this multiplicity of influences, the general effect is not displeasing, even if it does firmly display the general lack of spontaneity in Kandesh art. At Burhanpur also exists a huge *idgah*, locally known as Sanwara *idgah*.

Thalner

A group of tombs at Thalner show a close affinity with those of Hushang Shah (see p. 135) and Darya Khan at Mandu, built just a few years earlier, although there are some structural and ornamental differences introduced by indigenous artists. The main innovations are recognized in the arrangement of the openings, in the wider spaces reserved for doors and windows, the emphasis given to the parapet on the *chhajja* and the elevation of the dome which rests on an octagonal drum. The tomb of Miran Mubarak, who died in 1457, despite the fact that it is somewhat ruined, is still extremely beautiful – it has no parallels either in Malwa or in any other Faruqi monument. Its eight sides are separated by pilasters and carry doors and windows alternately under Khalji-style arches, while the walls are adorned with a refined series of blind niches, intertwined polygons, fine arabesques, stars, medallions and small ornamental corbels.

---

[1] Z. A. Desai, 'Architecture: The Bahamis', *History of Medieval Deccan*, Hyderabad 1974, vol. 2, pp. 240–43.

[2] E. Schotten Merklinger, *Indian Islamic Architecture: The Deccan, 1347–1686*, New Delhi 1981, p. 32.

[3] G. Yazdani, *Bidar*, Oxford 1947, p. 29.

[4] Yazdani, *op. cit.*, p. 10.

[5] H. Goetz, 'Arte dell'India musulmana e correnti moderne', *Le civiltà dell'oriente*, vol. 4, Rome/Venice 1970, p. 810

[6] H. Cousens, *Bijapur and its Architectural Remains*, ASI. New Imperial Series, XXXVII, Bombay 1916, p. 74.

[7] Burgess, *op. cit.*, p. 85.

[8] Goetz, *op. cit.*, p. 809.

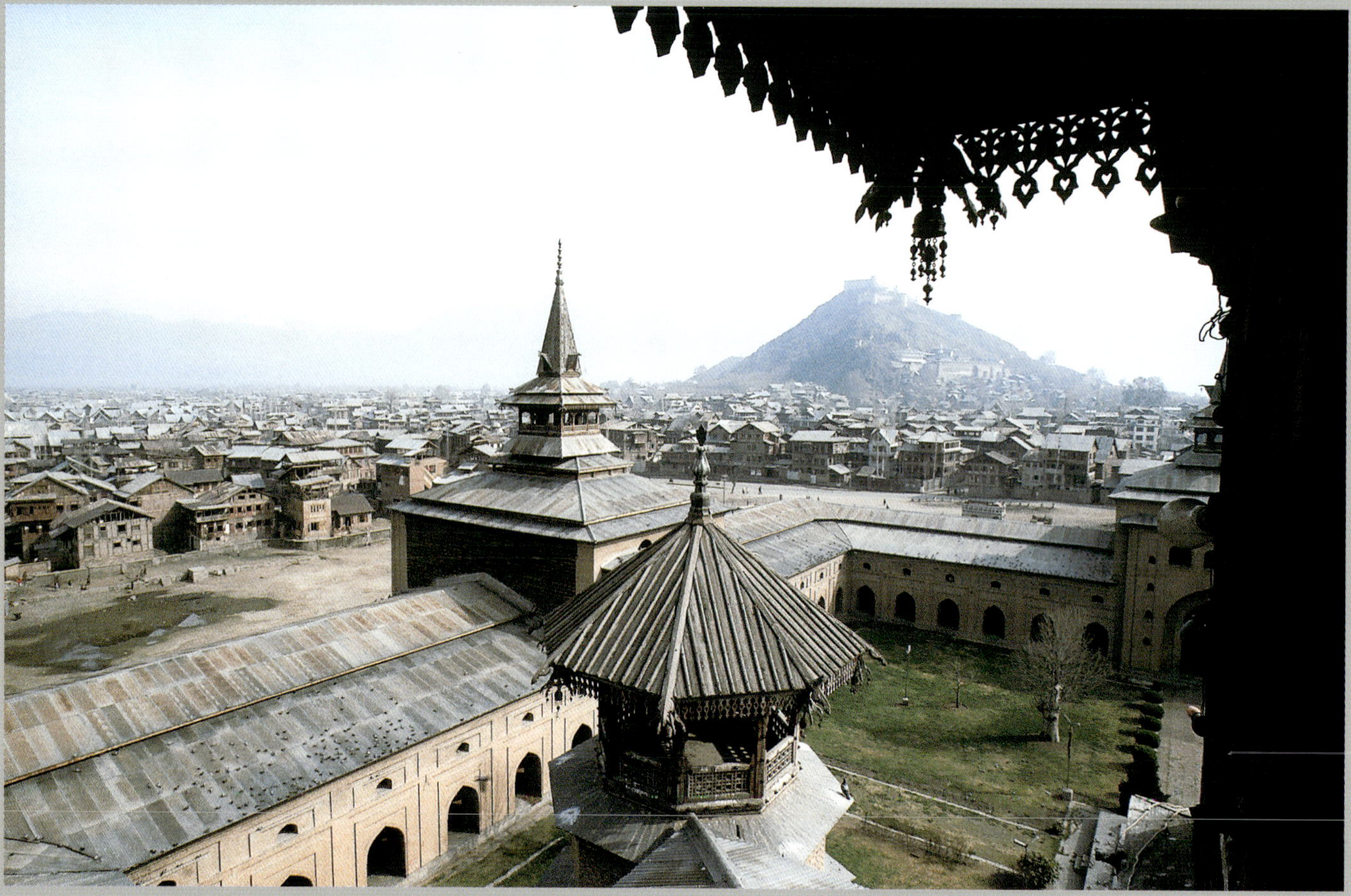

Kashmir (1346–1586)

12

The *jami masjid* at Srinagar was founded by Sikandar Butshikan in the fifteenth century, but was enlarged by his son Zain al-Abidin and underwent reconstruction by the Mughals in the seventeenth century.

Kashmir fell under Islamic domination when it was seized by Shah Mirza Swati, a Muslim adventurer. He had been minister to the Hindu *raja* Sinha Deva, and lately married his widow, Kota Devi (1339). Shah Mirza murdered Kota Devi and proclaimed himself sovereign under the name of Shams al-Din. His four children in turn succeeded him to the throne which then passed on to his grandchild, Sikandar Butshikan (1393–1416), who remained neutral during Timur's expedition against Delhi. Sikandar was dubbed Butshikan ('iconoclast') because of the many idols and temples he destroyed and looted. He vigorously Islamicized the country, offering the idolaters the alternatives of either conversion or exile from Kashmir. Sikandar's eldest son continued with this religious policy, but while preparing on one occasion to leave for Mecca, he was supplanted by his brother, Zain al-Abidin (1420–70), who proved to be indisputably the best sovereign of his dynasty. Zain worked towards a conciliation between Muslim and Hindu and – unique in all Islam – allowed those forced into conversion to return to Hinduism. He was a patron of the arts and sciences and established the use of the Persian language at the court and in the country's administration. The decline of his lineage began immediately on his death: his successors were weak and inept, mere puppets of various factions. After civil wars, attempted invasions by the sultan of Kashgar and a brief reign by Mirza Haidar of the house of Humayun, Akbar incorporated Kashmir into the Mughal empire in 1586.

The Islamic art of Kashmir was influenced by three factors: ancient stone architecture, both Buddhist and Hindu, which was adapted with slight alterations; the indigenous practice of building in wood, which was in abundant supply in the region; and the architecture of Persia and Turkestan, which was predominantly in brick and often decorated with majolica. The wood most commonly used in building was a variety of cedar, the deodar (*Cedrus deodara*). This was also used in building bridges over the River Jhelum which bisects Srinagar, the state capital.

The most typical structures in the region are mosques and tombs, these last

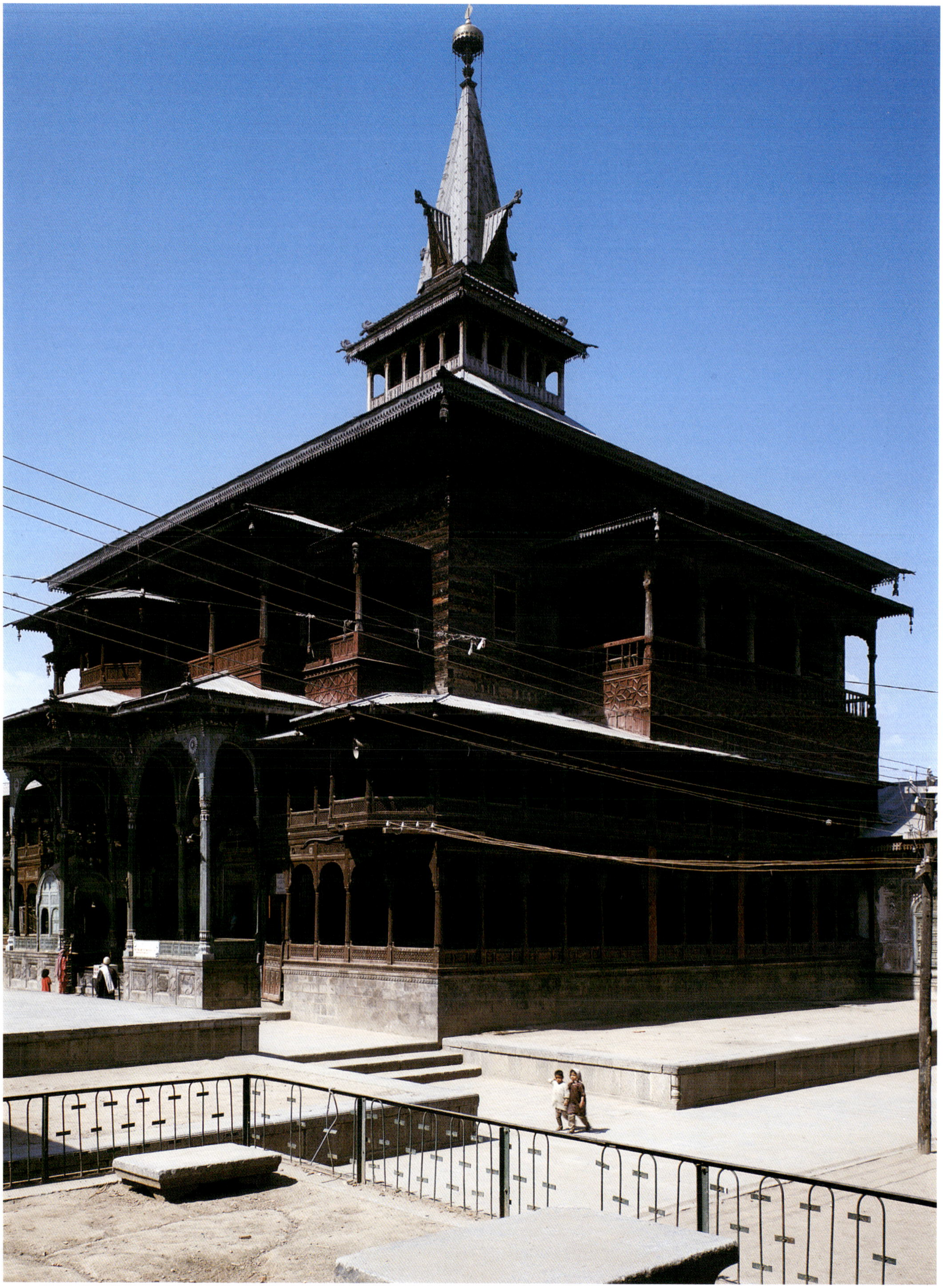

The Shah Hamadan Mosque, on the bank of the Jhelum river at Srinagar is a typical example of Kashmiri wooden architecture.

known by the name *ziyarat*, and usually dedicated to local noteworthies or local saints. Both in the mosques and in the *ziyarat* there are three principal architectonic elements which are arranged in the same way. A low, cubic space constitutes the prayer hall or the burial chamber. A pyramidal roof with a delicate peak, often supported on pillars, was the cover. In the mosques, above all in the larger mosques, between the apex of the roof and the base of the peak there is a third element in the form of a square, open pavilion, a *mazina*, which constitutes a minaret and from which the *muezzin* issues the call to prayer.

SRINAGAR: SHAH HAMADAN MOSQUE

A typical example of the wooden architecture of the country is the beautiful mosque of Shah Hamadan at Srinagar, which underwent some alteration in later periods, such as the addition of a small subsidiary temple and a row of cloisters. Built on the right bank of the Jhelum river on an irregular walled base of materials culled from ancient temples, the mosque has a square plan of approximately 23 m each side and its two storeys reach a height of 16 m. The cover consists of a low pyramidal roof with a mild slope from which the open pavilion for the *muezzin* rises, crowned by a peak with protruding triangular sections at its base. The lower part of the building is made of logs which have been squared and are arranged in alternate courses that create an attractive exterior design. Under the eaves is a heavy cornice, also in wood. The arcades and verandah, the openings of which have been covered with grilles (*pinjra*), characterize the base, while the pyramidal roof, in three terraces, is covered with grassy sods that are coloured with flowers at certain times of the year. The interior of the hall on the ground floor is the only area of the mosque with any architectural pretension. It is on a rectangular plan of approximately 21 x 14 m. On the northern and southern sides a series of small rooms have been created. In the centre are four solid wooden pillars almost 7 m high which form a square space. Around this space are walls made of wooden panels with a skirting of stone. The *mihrab* are arched niches and the ceiling is pleasantly painted.

SRINAGAR: *JAMI MASJID*

The *jami masjid* of Srinagar was founded by Sikandar Butshikan in the early 1400s, but was enlarged by his son Zain al-Abidin and was subsequently restored more than once following fire damage, a common problem in Kashmiri buildings. Nevertheless, it seems that the reconstructions of 1503, the Mughal reconstructions of 1620–37 and 1674 (this last Aurangzeb's work), those of the end of the eighteenth century and that of 1913 were all reasonably true to the original plan, although with some concessions to the taste of later periods. Partially built in brick, much of the *jami masjid*'s structure is wooden, with halls with tall pillars, colonnades and ceilings in the indigenous style derived from log cabins. The ground plan, however, is that of an Iranian mosque with four *iwan*, and the façade, the windows and the arches are also entirely Persian. The mosque comprises a square courtyard roughly 80 m wide, surrounded by wide colonnades on all sides and closed by an exterior quadrangular perimeter wall over 95 m long each side and approximately 10 m high with three entrances protruding from the centres of the northern, southern and eastern sides. These entrances correspond to the same number of *iwan*, and form separate buildings along the lines of the *ziyarat*, to which we can add a fourth on the west side which constitutes the prayer hall. This last has a great central bay flanked by a double row of high wooden pillars, while a *mihrab* with a pointed arch is set on the far wall. The remaining pillared aisles extend through the interior of the building and are distributed in four orders on three sides and three orders on the fourth side. They are made up of a series of pillars, each carved from a single trunk of deodar and vary in height from 8 to 18 m; they total some 380 in number, lending an extraordinary effect of vertical movement to the interior.

Various buildings, above all from the early Islamic period, were adaptations of existing Hindu structures. The *ziyarat* of Bamzu on the Pahlgam road, for example, together with that of Madin Sahib at Zadibal, near Srinagar, fall into this category. These were built in 1444 and 1483 respectively, on the ruins of temples from the ninth and eleventh centuries, with beautifully carved doors and a *mihrab* in pure Persian style. The tile panels that decorate the wooden walls were added during the Mughal period. There are also beautiful ceilings painted with geometric and floral motifs.

Srinagar: mausoleum of Zain al-Abidin's mother

The mausoleum of Zain al-Abidin's mother, built in the middle of a cemetery by this sovereign at the beginning of his reign, provides a similar example. It is a brick building, decorated with carved and glazed tiles and topped with five ribbed domes resting on as many drums. The central dome is larger and the other four are attached to its sides. The unusual shape of the plan is owed to the cross-like layout of the Hindu temple of the eighth century, on the ruins of which the mausoleum is built. The original base was raised to form the burial chamber by means of a brick superstructure. On each façade there is an entrance with a pointed arch, while the entrance inside seems to have been an attempt to create a rare type of horseshoe arch. The design of the domes and the use of encaustic on the tiles demonstrate a Persian influence.

Other buildings

Numerous mosques and minor *ziyarat* were built with logs, often hidden behind a casing of plaster. Examples include the Shah Makhdum, the Khanazad Sahib, the

Opposite The mausoleum of the mother of Zain al-Abidin at Srinagar is built on the ruins of an eighth-century Hindu temple, which accounts for its unusual cross-shaped ground plan.

Below The fifteenth-century *jami masjid* at Srinagar derives its style from the indigenous log cabins of Kashmir. The pillars in the aisles are each carved from a single tree trunk.

Naqshbandi Sahib and other mosques in Srinagar. The mosque of Pampur also conforms to this type and has only its base made from the ruins of a temple while the upper sections are in wood and brick. Most of these examples date from the fifteenth century, but practically all of them have been rebuilt more than once, although respecting the original plans. Decoration was at times altered according to contemporary taste during the various renovations. Zain al-Abidin was also responsible for the creation on Lake Dal of two small pleasure islands – Sona Lanka and Rupa Lanka – not to mention the island of Zaina Lanka on Lake Wular. He also commissioned a complex network of canals in the surrounding area and blessed the River Jhelum at Srinagar with six log bridges, which until fairly recent times preserved the same structures he had planned and were modernized simply out of a desire for modernism. Kashmir also had Zain to thank for the introduction of gunpowder and all the industries that brought fame to the country from Timur's Samarqand: xylography, lacquerwork, *papier mâché* and so on. The art of weaving shawls, on the other hand, had already been introduced into the country from Central Asia in the Hindu epoch under Sahadeva (1301–20) and subsequently flourished under the Mughals and the Afghans. Not even one building remains of the late period of the sultanate, which was blighted by civil war and invasions. In 1586 Kashmir was occupied by Akbar; the Mughal period has left several beautiful buildings in stone as well as the famous gardens.

Part 3: The Mughals

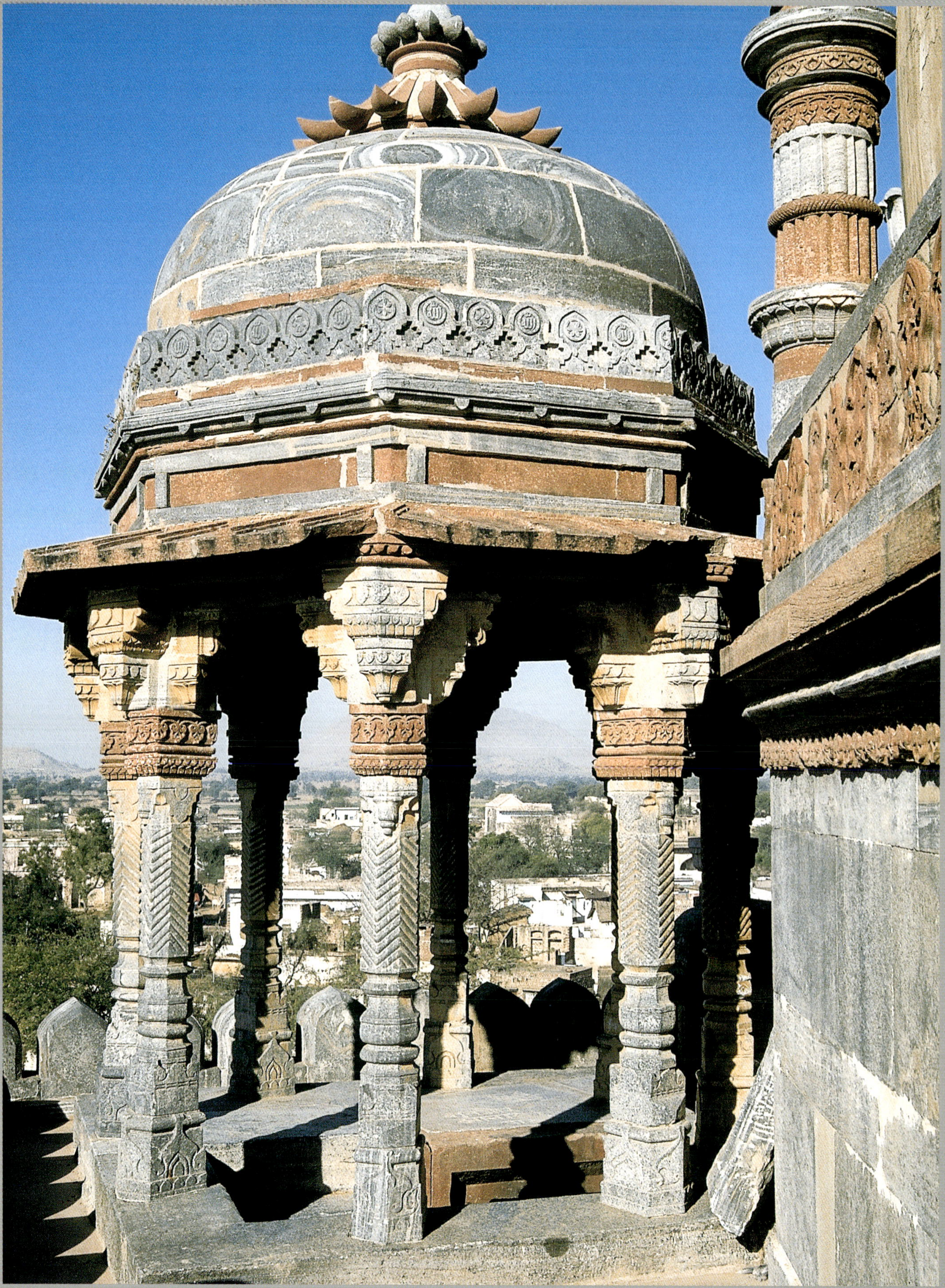

The Arrival of the Mughals

13

The Ibrahim Khan mausoleum at Narnaul, built around 1540 by Sher Shah for his grandfather, recalls the style of tombs built during the reign of the Lodi dynasty.

While the power of the Lodis was weakening in Delhi – ensnared by rebellions in Bihar and in the Punjab – Babur (1483-1530), a descendant of Timur, began to turn his gaze towards India. Babur had taken refuge first in Kabul and then in Bukhara and Samarqand after having been chased out of his small realm of Ferghana to the north of present-day Afghanistan by the Uzbeks. He quickly made his influence felt in the Punjab and marched against Delhi with a small but modern and well-organized army. His cavalry and riflemen were without equal, his artillery was efficient and thus he was able to beat the Lodi army easily at the battle of Panipat, 26 April 1526, although the opposition were ten times his strength in number. Ibrahim Lodi fell on the field and Delhi and Agra were occupied in rapid succession, leaving Babur free to start the great dynasty of the Mughals. This marked the beginning of the most brilliant period in the Muslim history of India and at the same time eliminated the states founded on Indian soil by invaders from bordering countries. However, his first challenge was to inculcate in his own officers the ideal of the foundation of an Indian empire. They were northern people who longed to leave the heat of India to return to the fresh climate of Kabul. Babur convinced them by the force of his own personality and dedicated himself to taming the revolt of a confederation of Rajputs who attempted a revolt in the north; he defeated them definitively and then went on to rout the Afghans of Bihar. Finally, he sought to organize his dominion, but was cheated by death on 26 December 1530 at the young age of 47. His character is remembered, as though reflected in a mirror, by his lively, interesting and amusing book of memoirs entitled *Babur Nama*, an accurate and enjoyable account of all his deeds.

His eldest son, Humayun (1530-40, and then 1555-6), succeeded him to the throne. Humayun, although valiant and, like his father, a gentleman, was lacking in any quality as a man of state and was certainly Babur's inferior in strategy and mediocre as a general. After a rapid and victorious campaign against Gujarat, which won him possession of Malwa in 1535, he remained inert at Mandu until he was called again to the north with the news of the rebellion of Sher Khan Sur, a minor Afghan nobleman who had taken Bihar and begun the conquest of Bengal. In 1537 Humayun tried to regain Bihar and Bengal, but he did not know how to take advantage of the victory and tarried in the deadly Bengali climate which withered his troops. When he confronted Sher Shah in 1540 (who in the meantime had assumed the royal title) he was defeated disastrously and was forced to flee, first to the Punjab, then to Sind and Afghanistan, to find refuge in the Persian court of the Safavid Shah Tahmasp. Only after many years, with the aid of the Persians, did he managed to reoccupy Kabul and tear it from his brother Kamram (1547). He settled there and awaited an opportunity to return to India.

After his victory over Humayun, Sher Shah (1540–45) had become lord of India from the Indus to the mouth of the Ganges; soon he defeated the Rajputs and also captured Malwa. He displayed exceptional abilities, above all in his organization of the realm. Indeed, later financial administrations of the Mughals based themselves on principles he promulgated, the effects of which are still felt today.

Sher Shah died of burns from the explosion of a powder barrel at the siege of Kaliya just five years after taking the throne and his dynasty (the Suris) did not survive much longer. Under his son, Islam Shah (1545–52), there were continuous rebellions and finally ruin: Bengal declared itself independent and three Suri princes contested the remains of the empire (1555). Humayun understood that the moment had arrived to retake the throne of India. He defeated the Suri pretender in the Punjab and returned to Delhi in July 1555, but his reign lasted only six months. On 24 January 1556 he died falling from the stairs of a building that still carries the name Humayun's Library. His death opened the way to the reign of his son, Akbar, who was destined to become the first true Mughal sovereign, and the greatest. Indeed, his predecessors' reigns had been too short to allow us to speak of a real empire or even an autonomous artistic style.

The Baburi Mosque (1527–8) inside the Kabuli Bagh at Panipat. The mosque is named for its founder, India's first Mughal ruler.

Babur (1526–1530)

Gardens

Among the most important of Babur's creations are the numerous gardens he discusses in his memoirs, above all those built around Agra. He was gifted with a real, as opposed to a literary, sense of nature and was steeped in Persian culture with its exaltation of the ideal landscape and of the 'paradise' with plants and flowers arranged in elegant geometric order around water. Immediately he felt uneasy in the often arid and suffocating climate of India. 'Three things', he wrote in his memoirs, 'oppressed us in Hindustan: its heat, its strong winds and its dust.' All this increased the longing for the green prairies of his native land, the freshness of Ferghana with its babbling waters, and pushed him to recreate the memory if only in the enclosed magic of a garden. Among his constant concerns – even in the midst of difficult conquests – was the thought of bringing the blessing of water to his new country by means of canals. Water was the fundamental material required for building an oasis and was seen as the great restorer of the body and the spirit. Another passage from Babur's memoirs documents his genuine joy in having succeeded in cultivating a garden near Agra: 'Thus, in unpleasant and inharmonious India, marvellously regular and geometric gardens were introduced. In every corner were beautiful plots, and in every plot were regularly laid out arrangements of roses and narcissus.'[1]

The master plan of the *paradeisos* was a crossing of two channels that divided given areas into grids which were in their turn divided into eight parts, according to the plan of the perfect garden of Paradise promised to the faithful in the Koran.[2] The channels ran into a central cistern that on occasions measured ten cubits by ten, an allusion to the religious significance of these dimensions in Islam – those prescribed for the cisterns used in ritual ablutions. The gardens were enclosed by high walls with the purpose of keeping away the sand lifted by the wind, but above all to maintain secrecy and protection. Along the water channels cypresses and fruit trees were preferred: the former were a symbol of immortality, the latter, with their spring blossoms, represented the renewal of life. Furthermore, the climate and the vigorous Indian flora offered an infinite variety of plants and flowers of every species which rendered these gardens truly luxuriant versions of paradise. Water was the fundamental component in the garden and was the physical and symbolic source of life. Babur had acquired his taste for gardens in Timurid Samarqand and at Herat, seat of Sultan Husain Baiqara, a descendant of Timur and also creator of a great many gardens. The gardens planned by Timur in his own city had seductive names such as 'Heart's Delight', 'The Perfect Garden', 'The Garden of the Plain', and Babur was inspired by these when in Kabul he created the Bagh-i Vafa (Garden of Faith), the Bagh-i Banafsha (Garden of the Violets), the Bagh-i Padshahi (Imperial Garden) and the Bagh-i Chinar (Garden of the Plane-tree).

In India he created numerous gardens: at Agra the Bagh-i Hast Bihisht (Garden of the Eight Heavens); at Dholpur the Bagh-i Nilufar (Lotus Garden); and at Fatehpur Sikri the Fateh Bagh (The Garden of Victory). At Agra today only the Ram Bagh (Happy Garden) is left, later called Aram Bagh (Garden of Rest). Babur had called it, more romantically, the Bagh-i Gul Afshan (Garden of the Flower Planter), perhaps because of the great number of flower beds there. It has been much altered, however, in successive demolitions and restorations, so that very little remains as evidence of its original magnificence and ingenuity. According to some sources Babur actually died in the Ram Bagh on 26 December 1530 and was buried in the Bagh-i Zar Afshan (Garden of the Sower of Gold), in the pleasure pavilion that was converted into a tomb and is still partially preserved. Records of the time mention that Kamram, son of the emperor, who arrived in 1539, paid his respects at this tomb before having his father's ashes transferred to Afghanistan. But E. Koch maintains that the Ram Bagh was built under the instructions of Nur Jahan.[3] Indeed, Babur's current tomb is to be found in Kabul, in one of his most splendid gardens which was further improved by all of his descendants from Akbar onwards who made it their duty to go there and pay homage to him.

Agra: Chauburj

At Agra, in what was the Bagh-i Zar Afshan, there still exists a square building with four corner towers known as Chauburj. According to Nath it was originally covered by a dome and must have contained the remains of the emperor and his principal wife, Maham Begum, mother of Humayun, until it was profaned and destroyed by vandals in the eighteenth century.[4] The plan of Chauburj presents remarkable similarities with that of the later mausoleum of Itimad al-Daula, built between 1622 and 1626 nearby by the wife of Jahangir, Nur Jahan, for her father, Mirza Ghiyas Beg Itimad al-Daula. Clearly the earlier tomb was a source of inspiration, but it is impossible that it was Babur's *superdgah* (temporary grave).

Apart from the creation of gardens, the brief reign of Babur also saw the construction of mosques in various places: Sambhal, Panipat, Rohtak, Maham, Sonepat, Palam (Delhi), Pilakhna, Agra and Ayodhya. But in his memoirs Babur mentions only one mosque, at Dholpur, so it is possible that the majority of them

The interior of the Baburi Mosque at Panipat. In this building Babur may have tried to recreate the style of his Central Asian ancestors.

were built not by him, but only during that period. They are for the most part in the Lodi style with wide four-centred arches, high single domes and profuse decoration in stucco as well as pillars from earlier Hindu temples.

PANIPAT: BABURI MOSQUE

Nevertheless, the Baburi Mosque (see pp. 184, 185) inside the Kabuli Bagh at Panipat does show one innovation: the rectangular prayer hall (53.75 x 16.50 m) has a very wide, domed, central area with three aisles on either side, all of them parallel to the *qibla* wall and divided into three bays with a dome over each one. They open on to the courtyard through an arcade of ogival arches on heavy pillars, while the central area is remarkable for the high *pishtaq* that is reminiscent, in a way, of the ones in the mosques at Samarqand, such as the Bibi Khanum of Timur. It is quite likely that Babur wished to commemorate the dearly loved art of his predecessors but that his architects were not capable of reproducing it. At the north-west and south-west corners of the mosque there were octagonal towers topped with domed pavilions, but one of them has fallen into ruin. There is a stone gate in the north wall of the courtyard, which must have been surrounded by other walls with gates in them, but now nothing is left. An inscription on the *mihrab* dates the Baburi Mosque to 1527–8.

SAMBHAL: MIR HINDU BEG MOSQUE

At Sambhal, about 140 km east of Delhi, there is another mosque, which was built in 1526 by Mir Hindu Beg, an important nobleman of Babur and Himayun's court. It is the oldest Mughal monument still standing, although some changes were made to it in the eighteenth century. The entrance is on the eastern side where a gateway leads into a spacious walled *sahn*. The prayer hall, like the one at Panipat, is rectangular with a large central domed area, into which leads a tall *pishtaq* that resembles the ones in the Sharqi mosques at Jaunpur. The wings of the building, like the ones in the slightly later mosque at Panipat, have two aisles which are each divided into three bays covered by low domes. They open on to the courtyard through an arcade of ogival arches on heavy pillars.

DELHI: JAMALI KAMALI MOSQUE AND MAUSOLEUM

The Jamali Kamali Mosque of Delhi, situated near Qutb, was built about 1528–9 by Shaikh Fazl al-Allah, also known as Jalal Khan Jalali. It represents a multiple advance on the Moth Mosque (see p. 56) in Delhi. The sanctuary is divided into the usual five areas which correspond to the openings of the façade. The façade itself has been treated in a special way by the architect. The central *iwan* is contained within a frame in light relief and projects somewhat from the wings. At the sides, instead of the panels and the niches of a Lodi mosque, there are four-storey turrets with angular and rounded flutes as in the Qutb Minar (see p. 23). These turrets may have been crowned by pinnacles in the form of lotus flowers. The intrados of the *iwan* has a spear-point border while on the extrados there are stone rosettes in high relief. The entrance to the main bay, formed by two receding arches, is surmounted by a graceful balconied window. The lateral entrances each have three receding arches and their pillars are ornamented by arches within oblong panels. Other stone rosettes in high relief sit in the extradoses of the lateral arches and decorate them in a much more appropriate manner than the stucco medallions of the Moth-ki Mosque. The ornamentation of the wings also makes use of arched niches filled again with rosettes in high relief, all made of stone in various colours and hues (grey and whitish sandstone, greyish quartzite) as well as white marble arranged in complicated interlacing in the pure Mamluk tradition.[5]

This is explained by the arrival in India at that time of many skilled Egyptian marble masons who, about a decade earlier, were left without work following the occupation of Egypt by the Ottoman Selim I. Indeed, the finest and most expensive buildings in their country, which had characterized the Mamluk period, were suddenly abandoned in favour of plainer, less demanding buildings that rendered the use of many marble craftsmen unnecessary. They were forced to look for work in more welcoming courts. The mosque is covered by a single dome which was perhaps once flanked by pinnacles which crowned the turrets of the façade. Other turrets adorned the corners of the rear side of the building, but later restorations have greatly altered their shape and have stripped them of their original elegance. The Jamali Mosque is the most beautiful of those built in Babur's time and is also the best preserved.

Adjacent to the mosque stands a monument with a square plan, a flat roof and a deep *chhajja*. The façades are decorated with blind niches and trilobate arches. Graceful decoration in the form of glazed tiles also survives. In the mausoleum are the tombs of Jamali Khan and an anonymous Kamali, from which the mosque has earned a double name. It seems

Opposite left The Jamali Kamali Mosque at Delhi, built around 1528–9 by Shaikh Fazl al-Allah.

Below The mausoleum (c.1530) of Jamali Khan and Kamali, adjacent to the Jamali Kamali Mosque at Delhi.

possible that it dates from 1530 and that it was Jamali Khan himself who had it built. In the Bagh-i Zar Afshan, on the left bank of the River Jumna, is the Baburi Mosque, although it has been completely changed over the course of the years. Indeed, it maintains little of the style of the sixteenth century, in common with the homonymous mosque at Ayodhya near Fayzabad, and the other mosques that carry inscriptions in the name of the emperor.

HUMAYUN (1530–1540 AND 1555–1556)

Humayun came to the throne on 29 December 1530. Like his father, he was an art lover, but unlike him he was much more of an idealist and enjoyed the study of astronomy and astrology. Indeed, his actions were regulated in strict accordance with the movements of the heavens. According to Khwand Amir, a contemporary historian who wrote the *Qanun-i Humayuni* for the emperor, Humayun divided all the officers of his state and the inhabitants of his dominions into three classes: the Ahl-i Daulat, which included brothers, sisters and relations as well as princes, ministers and soldiers; the Ahl-i Saadat, which covered the shaikhs, the sayyids, the *qadi* and the philosophers, the intellectuals of the realm; and the Ahl-i Murad, those gifted with beauty and elegance – musicians, singers and artists, the entertainers.[6] Each class was further divided into 12 divisions and to each one an arrow of a different type of gold was allocated. The main reason behind this sub-division into 12 classes was astrological. Even the days of the week were divided into three categories and assigned to each of the three classes: Saturday and Thursday to the Ahl-i Saadat; Sunday and Tuesday to the Ahl-i Daulat; Monday and Wednesday to the Ahl-i Murad. Everyone assembled together on Friday. Khwand Amir records how Humayun also divided the affairs of state into four departments which corresponded to the four elements: Atashi (Fire), which included the military and war machines; Hawai (Air), covering the wardrobe, the kitchen, the stables and so on; Abi (Water), concerning canals, wine and syrups; and finally Khaki (Earth), relating to agriculture, land, building and the treasury. A *wazir* was appointed in charge of each of these departments.

Humayun enjoyed peace and preferred to expend his energies in creating amusements rather than organizing war campaigns. According to Khwand Amir, he created a floating market on wide boats which was called the *char taq*; very little trade was carried out there, however.

He also had a three-storey wooden building constructed which could be dismantled, transported and reconstructed at will. According to Khwand Amir, this building was decorated wonderfully in various colours by the most skilful painters, and the ingenious goldsmith had made a golden dome that shone like the sun. The chamberlains of the throne, the nest of religion, had covered it with curtains of seven colours made of fabrics from Khotan, Turkey and Europe. Khwand Amir also records how Humayun invented a colourful wide tent divided into 12 compartments which corresponded to the 12 signs of the zodiac. Like the building, this tent was mobile and could be set up whenever he wanted. Long poles divided it into compartments and when the supports were brought together the tent rose up on them; 'its top rose higher than the Ayyuq star'. The emperor dedicated much time to choosing his clothes and wearing the colours that matched the reigning planet of the day, for example, a yellow suit for Jupiter on Sunday; a green suit for Venus on Monday; red clothes for Mars on Tuesday; and blue for Mercury on Wednesday. The emperor's most curious innovation was the commissioning of the Carpet of Happiness (Birat-i Nishat). This was a large circular carpet, divided into astronomic circles which were each assigned to a planet. Guests were seated on the carpet according to their rank: for example, officers of Indian extraction and the sheikhs in the circle of Saturn, which was black; the sayyids and the learned in the circle of Jupiter, which was light brown; and so on for the other circles. Humayun sat in the middle – corresponding to the position of the sun – and when everyone was seated they took turns at throwing dice on which human figures in various positions were painted. Some positions were possible to attain, others were impossible, but all guests were obliged to try to assume the positions they threw: if the figure shown was on its feet, you had to rise, if it was stretched out, you lay down, if it was sitting, you sat. Consequently the group created new and unusual positions and this gave life to a continuous stream of liveliness and gaiety. Apparently on one occasion the minister for finance had to relate his budget measures standing on his head. Humayun dedicated himself to these pursuits while Sher Khan Sur was consolidating his position in Bihar and preparing himself for the definitive conquest of Hindustan.

Khwand Amir also describes the buildings erected by Humayun at Gwalior, Agra and Delhi. The buildings of Gwalior were dominated by a palace in polished stone, profusely decorated with glazed tiles that have now disappeared, as they have in the magnificent Imarat Tilism of Agra.

Agra: Kachpura Mosque

The only building in Agra that undoubtedly belongs to Humayun's reign and that still has its original form is the mosque of the village of Kachpura, on the left bank of the River Jumna, the side opposite the Taj Mahall. Lacking *riwaq*, monumental entrances and minarets, this mosque has a façade with five arches, of which the central one is twice the width of the others and forms a large *iwan*; this precedes the main bay which is covered by a large dome. The lateral rooms, each divided into two parts, were once covered by eight cupolas. The southern wing of the mosque has collapsed completely. The sanctuary is in brick and lime dressed with stucco and resembles the Begampuri Mosque of Muhammad bin Tughluq (see p. 44), which in its turn was inspired by the mosques of Jaunpur. The great propylon carries traces of decoration in glazed tile. An inscription in the main bay carries the date 937/1530, the year of Humayun's accession to the throne, and the name of the commissioning client, Shaikh Zain of Khaf, who was a scholar as well as an important nobleman and friend of Babur. This mosque was built according to a traditional design and it is unlikely that it was planned or influenced by Humayun's taste, which was certainly more refined and innovative, as we are able to attest from later works.

Delhi: Din-Panah

Humayun's most ambitious architectural project was the building of the city of Din-Panah at Delhi which, according to Khwand Amir, was intended to include grand palaces, gardens and orchards and to provide 'exile for the scholars and refuge to the vigilant and prudent people, so that it will be known as Din-Panah (Refuge of the Faith)'. Construction of the city began in August 1533, and by the middle of May 1534 'The walls, the bastions, the fortifications and the doors ... were almost finished and ... the high buildings of the great city will soon be completed.'[7] According to to Nath it seems likely that the city is today's Purana Qila (Old Fort), situated between the tomb of Humayun and the Kotla Firuz Shah, which had traditionally been attributed to Sher Shah together with its three gates, the beautiful Qila-i Kuhna Mosque and the Sher Mandal.[8]

A closer study of historic documents on the one hand and a consideration of stylistic elements on the other, as suggested by Nath, allow us now to revise the attribution on more concrete grounds and to assign it to Humayun. In the brief early period of his reign, between 1540 and 1545, Sher Shah had been so preoccupied in looking out for a return of the Mughals, in suppressing the Rajput revolts, in reoccupying the territories of the sultanate of Delhi, in reuniting the Afghan tribes, in establishing the solid political bases of his government and above all in reorganizing its administration, that he could never have had the time to dedicate himself to the art of construction. Furthermore, he considered Agra, rather than Delhi, the centre of his government. Indeed, he returned to Agra after every campaign and from there built the roads that connected Burhanpur, Jodhpur and Lahore, as well as building there the *jami masjid*, which is now known as Kali Mosque, a corruption of *kalan* ('large').

Nevertheless, Sher Shah had a city built at Delhi, the location of which has been much debated owing to the imprecise nature of historic references to it. Abbas Khan Sarwani wrote a biography of Sher Shah in 1579 on Akbar's orders: this document is reliable enough given that, as well as being a distant relative of the Suris, the author also gathered information from original sources. According to

The Talaqi Darwaza, the entrance gate to the Purana Qila at Delhi. The style of the Persian inscriptions on the gate suggests that it dates from 1533–4.

this biographer Sher Shah, before building his new capital near the River Jumna, destroyed the previous capital that was some distance from the river. Some have identified this last city as Humayun's Din-Panah, others as Ala al-Din Khalji's Siri. The latter would seem more probable because historians of Akbar's and Jahangir's time reaffirm that Sher Shah built a city situated between Din-Panah and Firuzabad. The only remains of it are the two gates known as Kabuli Darwaza and Lal Darwaza which led to the fortifications; these, according to Sarwani, were never completed because of the death of the sovereign. The Great Mosque – decorated with much gold, lapis lazuli and precious stones – and the multi-storey palace, both mentioned by Sarwani, have disappeared. The Qila-i Kuhna Mosque and the so-called Sher Mandal, part of the Purana Qila, would therefore seem to belong to Humayun's reign, even though they have been attributed traditionally to the sovereign Sur. If the Sher Mandal is now more often dated to the Humayun epoch, the attribution of the fine Qila-i Kuhna Mosque is still controversial. Indeed, a study by Catherine Asher in 1981 attributed it to Sher Shah.

Delhi: Purana Qila

The Purana Qila has an irregular oblong plan, with its principal axis running parallel to the River Jumna, which seems to have flowed at one time along the eastern wall. The other three sides were reinforced by a continuous moat of which some parts still exist. The access points to the river have now been closed and even the steps leading to the boat moorings have gone completely. The high protective wall has circular bastions which project at regular intervals. Ornamental windows with screened *jharoka* and balconied windows alternate here and there to break the monotony of the wall, which is built in unfinished stone without plaster. There is a remarkable batter on the exterior side which recalls the earlier Tughluq style that remained influential to a greater or lesser extent for the entire first half of the sixteenth century. If the building – constructed in crushed stone and mortar – is extremely massive, rough and lacking ornament, this is not the case with the three doors that open on the northern, western and southern sides. Aesthetically these are very beautiful because of the use of finely chiselled red and grey stone together with black and white marble and various ornaments.

Delhi: Talaqi Darwaza

The Talaqi Darwaza (see p. 189) is a three-storey gate protected on each side by a circular bastion. In essence this is a very high oblong *iwan* in which there is an arched gate that constitutes the true entrance together with another arch that gives access to the second-floor apartments. Among the interesting white marble decoration set into red sandstone panels there are two stylized lotus flowers with eight petals containing eight-pointed stars, but even more interesting are two *shardula* arranged under the pediment. The *shardula* is an element characteristic of Hindu mythology and is formed out of a union of a lion and a horse, or occasionally other animals. It was used widely in Hindu architecture as an ornament – in the reliefs of Khajuraho, for example – but here it would seem to fulfil a precise role as a good-luck charm. Certainly for Humayun it must have been important, as strict Muslim orthodoxy was against figurative representation.

The superstructure of the gate is made up of two square *chhatri* and an octagonal *chhatri* which is placed slightly behind the others. They are all in red stone and are decorated with green, turquoise and yellow glazed tiles in a combination of colours and shapes that recalls the nearby art of Gwalior. Stylistic examination of the Persian inscriptions on the gate has allowed scholars to date the Talaqi Darwaza from 1533–4.

Delhi: Bara Darwaza

The Bara Darwaza, built, like the Talaqi Darwaza, in red sandstone, white marble and black slate in order to emphasize outlines, has a more simple structure and is without *chhatri*. These are moved instead to the circular bastions that flank the door. A significant characteristic is the presence of a six-pointed star on the extradoses of the main arch. This star contains a lotus flower in high relief at its centre and therefore cannot be likened to the Seal of Solomon, generally so common in Muslim decoration. The lotus, however, had acquired strong symbolic values of good fortune.

Delhi: Humayun Darwaza

The Humayun Darwaza, similar to its antecedents by virtue of style, structure and design, is differentiated from them by some details. Above the balconied windows there are two panels, one each side, and each containing a white elephant in high relief, again an unorthodox element but favoured by Humayun. Above the parapet at the two extremities are the

The Sher Mandal at Delhi. The sixteenth-century two-storeyed octagonal tower has been generally identified as Humayun's famous library.

remains of two octagonal turrets with fluted shafts and two hexagonal *chhatri*. The interior of the gate is on three floors, each containing a series of halls, rooms, pavilions, corridors and stairs. An inscription in *nastaliq*, written on the gate in Indian ink, records that it was built in 1543-4 by order of Ghazi Khan Lahori during the reign of Sher Shah Sur. But it is most probable, according to Nath, that this inscription, which is not carved in the stone but only painted, refers to a restoration carried out on the rear of the gate. The style of the gate, similar to Humayun's other two, and above all the presence of the elephants, testify that it must have been completed before 1534.

Delhi: Sher Mandal

The Sher Mandal, more than once identified as the palace of Sher Shah, is really only a two-storey octagonal tower in red sandstone resting on an octagonal plinth and surmounted by a wide *chhatri* on the terrace. The lower floor is completely closed, and we do not know why. On the exterior walls there are eight niches, alternately square and semi-octagonal. A stairway on the south-western side and another on the opposite side lead to the upper floor and the terrace. The granite steps are extremely steep, narrow and irregular because of the relative lack of horizontal space compared with the height. The *chhajja* that must have covered the lower floor has disappeared completely while the final *chhajja*, resting on carved corbels, is still preserved. The upper floor also has eight niches, deeper than the previous ones, rectangular in design and with stalactite coverings. The extradoses of the arches are each adorned with two six-pointed stars in white marble against a background of red stone. The intradoses of the arches have geometric designs, executed in mosaics with white marble. On the corners are small columns flanked by square slabs of red sandstone decorated with geometric patterns in white marble and bordered by black slate. The decorative motif consists of a 12-petalled flower with a 12-pointed star at its centre. Evidently these refer to the signs of the zodiac and, according to Nath, this was Humayun's preferred lucky number. The interior is made up of a single square room which opens on four sides into as many niches that are connected by an exterior passage. The covering is a semi-vault on profusely coloured stucco stalactites dressed in glazed tiles. The wall decoration consists mostly of carved stucco, with a beautiful interplay of light and shadow and glazed tiles, the colours of which are somewhat faded. The effect is nothing less than exquisite and is perfectly homogeneous. The terrace is surrounded by a cornice and an ornamental frieze and contains a 6.5 m wide octagonal *chhatri* at its centre. The ceiling of the hemispheric dome has an arabesque design and was originally painted.

The Sher Mandal has generally been identified as Humayun's library, where he fell from the stairs on 20 January 1556 and died a few days later from his injuries. Witnesses from Akbar's time state that Humayun had gone on to the roof of the library to see Venus rise that night. On hearing the call to prayers of the *muezzin* he hurried to reach the mosque next door but tripped on a hem of his robes, lost his stick and fell, hitting his head violently. He never recovered from the blow and died a few days later in agony. On the basis of his observation of Venus and the fact that Humayun that day had called all his mathematicians and astronomers to see him, Nath has suggested that Sher Mandal was in fact the Mughal emperor's observatory. It stands on the highest point of the fort and its decoration is inspired by various symbols from astronomy. The name itself could be the corruption of the original Saur Mandal, connected with the study of earthly bodies, and this would constitute further proof of the purpose of the tower. After all, both from the functional and the stylistic point of view, it could hardly be considered the palace of Sher Shah as it has been described by historians. The building's complex decorative symbology in particular is totally in contrast with the pragmatic and rigorous character of the Afghan Sher Shah's orthodoxy. Nath also excludes the possibility that the building could have been Humayun's library by pointing out that the narrow spaces in the tower do not lend themselves to collecting books. Other Indian scholars have put forward an interesting hypothesis, suggesting that the lower room was walled up because for some time it held the body of the dead emperor while a more fitting mausoleum was built for him.

Delhi: Qila-i Kuhna Mosque

The best-preserved building in the Purana Qila is the Qila-i Kuhna Mosque (see p. 192), situated on the eastern side of the Old Fort, very close to the Sher Mandal. Entering from the Bara Darwaza, the rear part of the building is visible first. The *qibla* wall is of grey quartzite and is divided into two floors by means of a stone cornice above which runs a wide band of patterns carved in white marble above a background of red sandstone. The central area, corresponding to the back of the main bay, projects markedly to the exterior and is emphasized with tapered stone turrets which are surmounted with simple pinnacles. If the lower floor is plain, the second floor is decorated with three balconied windows supported by graceful corbels and covered with a small semi-pyramidal roof. At the corners of the back wall there are three-storey octagonal turrets, the lower parts of which are surmounted by two orders of blind arched niches, while the two upper floors carry

The *mihrab* in the Qila-i Kuhna Mosque at Delhi are splendidly decorated with coloured stone and marble.

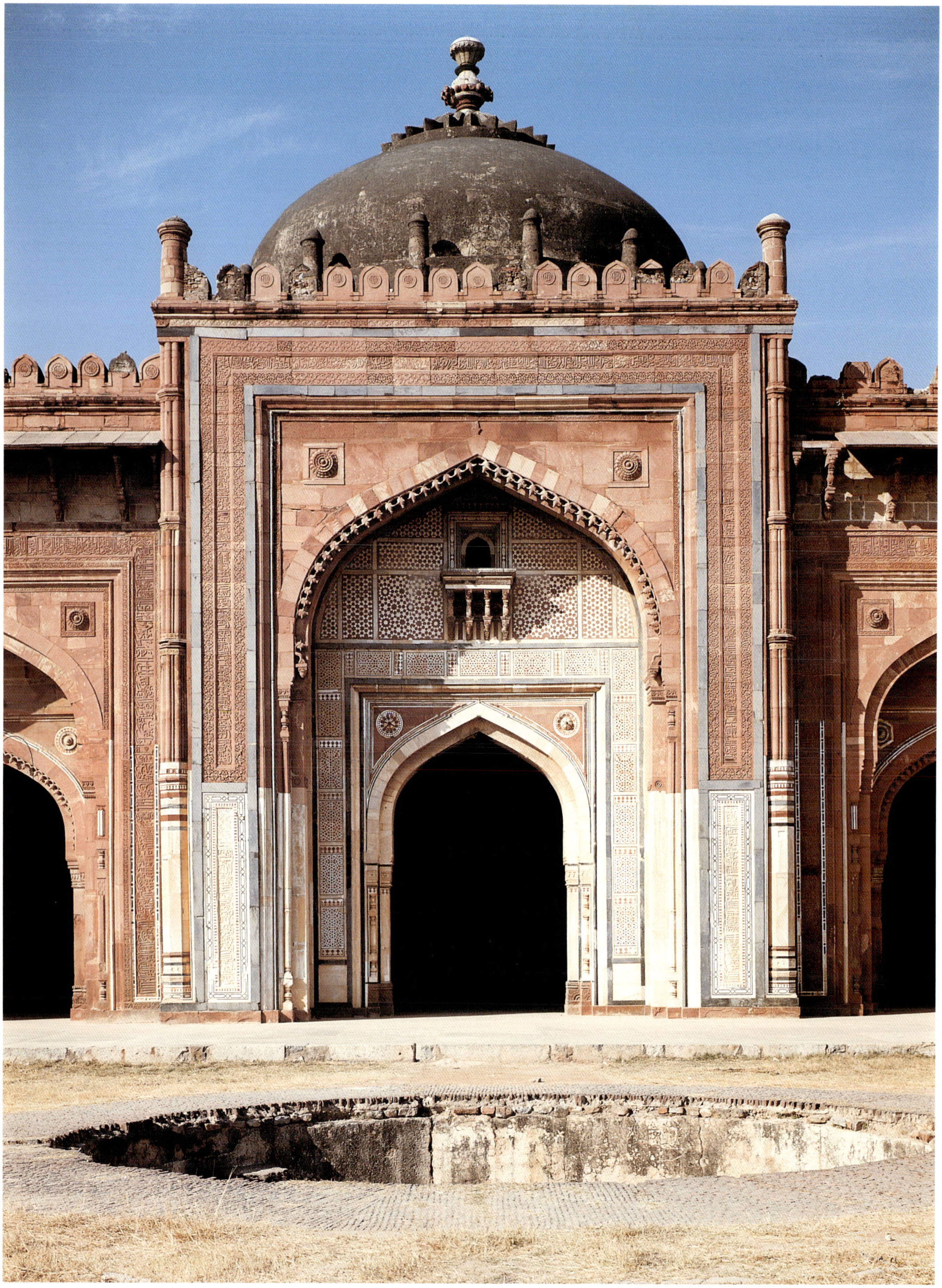

Above The simple Gate of Sher Shah at Delhi is also known as the Lal Darwaza (Red Door) because of the red sandstone used.

Opposite The Qila-i Kuhna Mosque is the best preserved building in the Purana Qila, the fort at Delhi thought to have been built by Humayun.

an order of small single arches. It is not impossible that these terminated with octagonal *chhatri* which have now disappeared. The red sandstone alternates with the local grey stone and each floor is protected by elegant *chhajja* on finely worked corbels. Even if the inspiration for these turrets can be traced back to the Moth Mosque, they are used here in a much more elegant and effective manner than in the Lodi prototype. Even the northern and southern walls are divided externally into two floors by a band of patterns in red sandstone; in the upper area they have a small balconied window and in the lower part a graceful, sharply arched door which served as a private entrance for the royal family. The façade of the mosque presents five fine double arches of differing widths – the central one is the largest – and all five correspond to the same number of spans within of differing dimensions. The decoration with stone inlays of various colours is truly magnificent and alternates with small carvings, such as the border of lotus flowers that runs along the intrados of the central arch and a miniature window above the entrance.

The bands of Koranic inscriptions carved in relief along the panels around the arch are also worth noting. The middle span is square and is flanked by two identical rooms while at the extremities there are oblong rooms. The only dome rests on a 16-sided polygon adorned with niches and glazed tiles. The *mihrab*, too, especially the main one, are enriched with splendid decoration in which colour is much exploited by the use of stones and marbles in various tints. Also in evidence is an extraordinarily elegant epigraphic decoration. The motif of a lamp hanging within a trilobate niche also appears inserted into the widest lancet arches. Both the *mihrab* and the façade of this mosque present obvious similarities with the later mosques of Khair al-Manzil of Delhi and the *jami masjid* of Fatehpur Sikri. Six-pointed stars (*satkona*) filled with garlands of lotus in relief appear on the extradoses of the four principal arches of the main bay which support the dome. Ornamental *muqarnas* fill the corners of the bays adjacent to the lateral rooms. The mosque has no courtyard or minarets, like other similar mosques in Delhi. The Qila-i Kuhna

Mosque marks the beginning of a new, rich architectural style and is the first fulfilled expression of the aesthetic ideals that later came to characterize the great art of Fatehpur Sikri and Agra.

On the basis of two vague historic sources this mosque has always been considered to be that built by Sher Shah in his city of Delhi. Nevertheless, it presents none of the characteristics that the documents attribute to it, such as the use of gold, lapis lazuli and other precious stones. Furthermore, it is stylistically completely different from the more genuine works of Sher Shah, the tombs of Sasaram. It is therefore evident that, like his palace, the mosque described by the historians has not survived. The Qila-i Kuhna could instead be the mosque begun by Humayun in 1533 at the same time as he began Din-Panah. Indeed, the mosque was designed as the crowning glory of Din-Panah. It remained incomplete during the time of the sovereign's exile and was completed by Akbar immediately following the death of his father, making use of indigenous craftsmen, as displayed by the many details in the Gwalior style. Nevertheless, a comparison with the tomb of Ibrahim Suri, grandfather of Sher Shah, at Narnaul, would seem to undermine this theory; the similarities that it displays with the Delhi Mosque, although not numerous, are evident and undeniable.

THE SURI INTERVAL (1540–1555)

DELHI: KABULI AND LAL DARWAZA

The only surviving works of Sher Shah in Delhi would therefore seem to be the two gates to the city, which were not completed after his death. The Kabuli Darwaza is a simple and austere gate, built for the most part of grey stone, a local quartzite. Red sandstone is used in some places: the elaborate corner columns, the balcony corbels, the high relief rosettes in the extradoses of the main arch and alternate decorative strips. The crenellated parapet has covered trap doors that are not found in Humayun's buildings. The Red Gate (Lal Darwaza; see p. 193), commonly called the Gate of Sher Shah, is also a simple and functional structure in which red sandstone has been used more widely, hence the name. Its higher pavilions are in rough stone and the ruined areas display much use of rubble construction. Only the façade was given artistic treatment and, in accordance with the taste of the time, glazed tiles were inserted into the panels and ornamental friezes.

PATNA: SHER SHAH MOSQUE

The so-called Sher Shah Mosque at Patna is a square brick building with one triple-arched façade. It measures just over 19 x 19 m and has a hall with 12 pillars, four on each side, covered with a semi-circular dome. Although the *qibla* is outlined on the exterior of the western wall, the building resembles a tomb more than a mosque and has no particular characteristics that allow us to ascribe it a precise architectural style.

ROHTASGARH: *JAMI MASJID*

The *jami masjid* of Rohtasgarh, a stone sanctuary built in 1543, according to a Persian inscription, also has a triple-arched façade with a central *iwan* archway that seems to have been inspired by

Right The mosque (1647) in the complex of buildings dedicated to Isa Khan at Delhi.

Opposite The mausoleum (1647) of Sher Shah's powerful Afghan minister, Isa Khan, at Delhi.

the mosques of Jaunpur. Like the earlier building at Patna, however, this mosque also lacks any striking characteristics in its construction.

Delhi: Isa Khan complex

More successful, on the other hand is the slightly later complex (1647) built at Delhi that includes the mausoleum and mosque of Isa Khan, the powerful Afghan minister of Sher Shah and his son Islam Shah. The tomb is of the usual octagonal variety with an arcaded verandah, inclined corners, deep *chhajja* and a fine dome surrounded by *chhatri*. The whole is in perfect harmony and the monument has an elegant and decorous aspect. The mosque, which seems to have been built contemporaneously with the tomb, has three spans and as many arches of equal width on the façade. The central arch is held within a rectangular frame of red stone, adorned on three sides by deep niches filled with azure and green glazed tiles. The lateral arches in grey stone are adorned with stuccoes and covered by *chhajja*. A large dome on an octagonal drum crowns the whole and is flanked by stone *chhatri* which are also octagonal.

Rohtas: fort

The fort that Sher Shah had built at Rohtas, some 20 km to the north-west of Jhelum, in the Punjab, is an imposing architectural project, emblematic of his vigorous style. It was an outpost built to contain the wild tribes in this part of his dominion. The walls are immensely robust – 10–15 m thick – because of the military nature of the project, but some of its 12 gates are exceptionally beautiful examples of the architecture of the period. Among these is the Sohal Gate which is still in good condition in the south-western wall. It is on a huge scale, more than 32 m tall, and consists of a central arch within a wider arched niche with a balconied window projecting from the wall on each side. Each part of the structure, executed in simple and plain lines, combines to form a whole that is aesthetically extremely strong.

Narnaul: Ibrahim Khan mausoleum

The tomb that Sher Shah built about 1540 at Narnaul for his grandfather Ibrahim Khan (see p. 182) refers to the style of Lodi tombs, a square plan divided into two floors both inside and outside. The oblong frame at the centre of each façade contains an *iwan* and has vertical panels decorated with arched niches and horizontal panels on the frieze. The intrados of the *iwan* has a spear-point border while the true entrance is surmounted by a beautiful balconied window. The dome is flanked by beautiful corner *chhatri* and is surrounded by pinnacles, all elements that are found in the Qila-i Kuhna Mosque of Delhi. In terms of beauty there is no doubt that in some details this building surpasses many earlier examples of the type, including even the Shish Gumbad.

Sasaram: Hasan Khan Sur and Sher Shah mausoleums

Nevertheless, it was only at Sasaram, his place of birth where he spent his youth and began his career, that Sher Shah erected his most significant buildings, above all the tombs. It seems that in nearby regions he was able to find materials and craftsmen expert in the traditional styles of Delhi. He also left his projects in the hands of his talented architect, Alawal Khan, who was left free to develop the design as best he thought; Sher Shah was unable to follow the work closely for lack of time.

Alawal Khan built the tombs of Hasan Khan Sur and Sher Shah and began the tomb of the son, Islam Shah. The first of these buildings, with an octagonal plan, is situated in the inhabited area of Sasaram within a square wall which is opened with stone gates at the centre of each side and is adorned at the corners with turrets with closed octagonal pavilions. The tomb, extraordinarily massive, is built for the most part in grey sandstone and has three arches of equal width, each on two receding floors, on each façade. These arches rest on heavy stone pillars, while thick stone walls are found at the corners. The walls, however, do not have the inclination that is characteristic of the Sayyid and Lodi tombs of Delhi. A *chhajja* supported by beautifully worked corbels runs round the arches and is crowned on each side by three domes. A very high stone drum rises on the terrace; it has an opening at the centre of each side that seems to form a second floor and it supports a wide dome, surrounded by hexagonal *chhatri*, and culminates in an elaborate pointed terminal on which are arranged various Hindu motifs. The ornamentation on the verandah that surrounds the burial chamber, and on the interior of the chamber, consists of alternating epigraphic and geometrically patterned friezes. Although not without defects, such as the lack of a base plinth, this tomb nevertheless signals an advance on other examples from Delhi in the evident emphasis that the architect has given to the vertical axis of the building, creating a structure of great aesthetic effect.

By way of contrast, Sher Shah's tomb was planned at the centre of a lake that has stone banks and stepped moorings on all sides. The lake is surrounded by palm woods and small hills covered in blossoming trees. This is a new approach which recalls the arrangement of some Hindu temples and confers on the mausoleum a special fascination and the impression of extraordinary beauty. The islet on which the tomb stands is connected to dry land by means of a wide stone bridge supported by pillars; on the northern side it is even equipped with a domed entrance pavilion. The high square platform that supports the building is built entirely in stone and rises from the water on eight shallow steps. The perimeter wall is interrupted at the centre of each side by a double stairway and is adorned with two balconied windows supported by graceful chiselled corbels. At the end of the bridge there is a long row of steps which lead to the platform; this has domed octagonal pavilions at its corners which – almost like embryonic minarets – elegantly complement the great central dome. The placing of the mausoleum in the middle of an artificial lake is a reference to Paradise with its plentiful waters, as described several times in the Koran. The inscription on the tomb, with verses 1–3 of Sura 108, refers to the Kautar, a river in Paradise.

The octagonal tomb, like that of Hasan Khan, has three pointed, double and receding arches of some 2.75 m in width on each of its façades. Adorned with lotus medallions on the extradoses, they rest on heavy stone pillars and are surmounted by a *chhajja* which runs all round the tomb and preserves some traces of decoration in glazed tile. Above this verandah a simple wall forms a second floor without windows interrupted by corner *chhatri* which function as a prelude to the great final dome, resting on a drum which is also emphasized with pillared kiosks that divide its circular base and carry the eye along the ascending curves to the massive lotus terminal that crowns the whole. The general effect is of an immense pyramid with five stages reaching over 45 m high with a diameter of about 75 m.

The funeral chamber, reached from the verandah except on the western side where it is closed in order to carry the *mihrab*, is a large room of about 22 m in diameter and over 31 m high from the floor to the keystone. This is the largest covered space of its kind in northern India, since the Taj Mahall reaches only 24.35 m in height inside. The movement from the square base to the circumference of the dome is managed by means of the 'beam and bracket' technique with the addition of a pendentive at each corner. This gives three rows of superimposed arches that diminish in height as the number of arches increases. The base row is made up of eight arches, the middle row of 16, the upper

The Arrival of the Mughals

Above The mausoleum of Humayun at Delhi was built some years after his death at the instigation of his wife Hajj Begum, and stands out as one of the most important buildings to be erected between the end of Humayun's rule and the great building programmes of Akbar.

Opposite Sher Shah's mausoleum, which sits on an islet in the middle of a lake at Sasaram, was completed just after his death in 1545 and is the most significant building erected by the ruler.

row of 32. The corners of each floor are surmounted by a beam with its centre supported by a projecting bracket. In the middle zone of the dome, beautiful windows with perforated screens ensure the circulation of air and light and give the interior a sober and tranquil atmosphere. The stone *mihrab* has some parts dressed in stucco and blue-turquoise glazed tiles. An inscription records that the complex was completed on 16 August 1545. Since Sher Shah died on 13 May 1545, the building was almost completely erected during his reign, and three months after his death was carried to completion by order of his son Islam Shah.

The entire monument is built of a beautiful grey sandstone which came from the historic caves of nearby Chunar. The walls are made up of large blocks arranged in rather irregular courses, but the stone is held together with good joints. Although it now appears as a uniform mass of grey, some remains of glazed decoration have been found and indicate that colour played an important role in the decorative scheme. Furthermore, the great dome was painted in brilliant white, while the high terminal was in red-gold. The dramatic effect, especially if we consider that the whole must have been reflected in the placid waters of the lake, must have been sumptuous and imposing. Indeed, more than a few scholars consider this mausoleum more successful even than the Taj Mahall.

A careful study of the structure of the complex reveals that it was not built on a perfectly symmetrical plan, but during the course of works a correction to its orientation was carried out. In fact, compared to the platform, the mausoleum has been rotated by eight degrees; evidently this was to perfect the alignment with Mecca which is required in a tomb and which initially must have been badly calculated.

Although very little of Sher Shah's architectural work during his reign has survived, historians of the time refer to his great wish to build on a large scale, cut short by his early death. It is said that on his deathbed he recalled his desire to erect a great number of buildings, 'with such beautiful architecture that friends and enemies alike will have to pay tribute and applaud and that my name will be honoured on earth until the day of the Resurrection'. But apparently he concluded disappointedly, 'God has granted that none of these wishes be fulfilled and I must carry this disappointment with me to my tomb.'[9]

SASARAM: ISLAM SHAH AND ALAWAL KHAN MAUSOLEUMS

Islam Shah planned his own tomb on a much larger scale than his father's, probably during the last part of his reign in about 1550. It remains incomplete because of his death and the civil war that followed. This tomb too was planned in a mirror of water and, as far as we can judge from the plinth, the bases of the pillars and the skeleton of the arches that remain, it was to develop more in width than in height. At each corner of the structure stone turrets were planned, again octagonal, but with alternately rounded and angular shafts as in the Qutb Minar (see p. 23). It is probable that they were to end in *chhatri*, so as to provide vertical lines capable of balancing the solidity of the structure on its horizontal axis. The remains of the arches and the unfinished *mihrab* show that the architect aspired to accentuate the architectonic effect to the detriment of the sculpted and decorative ornament, and it is a pity that this inspired structure should not have got beyond this basic stage. The tomb of Alawal Khan, the architect of these tombs, also remained unfinished because of the death of Islam Shah; only the entrance and the *mihrab* remain. Both structures are in yellow sandstone and include an *iwan* with niches and ornamental arches at the sides and two square *chhatri* on the covering which project on wide corbels over the entrance.

The incomplete mausoleums of Islam Shah and Alawal Khan signal the end of the Suri building activity. The last years of the reign, tormented by foreign and civil wars, were totally unproductive from an architectural point of view.

DELHI: HUMAYUN MAUSOLEUM

Between the death of Humayun and the imperial creations of Akbar there are some buildings which are of aesthetic importance, including the tomb of the emperor himself. Contrary to tradition, Humayun's mausoleum (see p. 197) was built some years after his death, thanks to his principal wife, Hajj Begum. According to the historian Badaoni it called for eight or nine years of work and was finished in 1569–70. The building was attributed to an architect of Persian origin, Mirak Mirza Ghiyas, although he appears in the memoirs of Babur as a mere foreman of the stone masons. The monument displays many innovations compared to those of Delhi and many Timurid Iranian elements, not least of which is the garden that frames it. This leads us to conjecture – as Abul Fazl and Father Monserrate suggested – that Akbar was instrumental in its planning, given his eclectic taste and his use of craftsmen from various places.[10]

The building can in fact be defined as an Indian interpretation of a Persian concept. The long sojourn of the Mughals at the Safavid court must have influenced this, as well as their common Central Asiatic origins. The tomb is situated at the centre of a *char bagh*, a Persian garden, closed on all sides by a high rubble wall and divided into square quarters divided in their turn by paved pathways crossed by water channels on which cisterns and basins are arranged at regular intervals. Originally the River Jumna ran along the eastern wall where a reservoir was situated, but now the river has changed its course and deprived the monument of the beautiful natural feature that the architect had planned as a border.

At the centre of each side of the perimeter stand pavilion gates: the southern gate, which once constituted the main entrance, but is now closed, is a spacious structure on two floors made of grey quartzite finished in red sandstone and white marble.

The present entrance to the west is again in grey quartzite, red sandstone and white marble, but is a much smaller building with a high central arch flanked by four smaller archways arranged one on the other with a more modelled than monumental effect. The corners are crowned by fine square *chhatri* with perforated balustrades and marble cupolas while the extradoses of the central archway, as in the entrance discussed above, are adorned with six-pointed stars with a lotus garland in the centre. The mausoleum rises on two stone bases, the first of which, 1.5 m in height, has lightly bevelled corners and is equipped with shallow steps. Another short stairway is found at the centre of the main side. A second and more important plinth, 6.1 m high and 99 m wide, and opened on all sides with arched niches that lead to a small room, forms a huge square platform with bevelled corners in keeping with the design of the tomb above and has deep stairways at the centre of each of the sides. On this platform rests the funeral chamber itself, with a square plan 47.54 m each side which becomes octagonal as a result of the light bevelling of the corners.

Each façade is made up of an *iwan* flanked by protruding wings, opened by arched entrances with lateral decoration in the form of blind niches which flank other sharply pointed arched niches arranged over two floors. The lively surfaces provide a pleasing movement of space and architectonic elements; equally attractive is the combination of colours with alternating red sandstone and white marble, which culminates in the noble marble dome with its pyriform profile.

The dome has a double skin and rises to a height of 42.67 m. The interior cover is lower, rests on a series of *muqarnas* and is divided from the exterior by a skeleton of bricks. The double bulbous dome is realized here in its most advanced form, and even though it appeared at Delhi some years earlier in the nearby tomb of Sabz Burj, it clearly derives from the Central

THE ARRIVAL OF THE MUGHALS

Opposite The Shams al-Din Atgah Khan mausoleum (1566–7) at Delhi. It is one of the finest tombs in a large necropolis.

Below The Afsarwala Gumbad and accompanying mosque (second half of the sixteenth century) sit atop a large platform on the western side of Humayun's mausoleum complex at Delhi.

Asian domes of Samarqand, the most notable examples of which appear in the Bibi Khanum Mosque and Timur's tomb.

The interior plan of Humayun's mausoleum comprises a central octagonal hall containing the cenotaph of the emperor and the corner spaces, again octagonal. These are connected to one another by means of corridors radiating in an intricate network that seems to correspond in some way to the plan of the Hindu temple known as Hemakuta. All the exterior openings, with the exception of the entrance, are screened by elegantly patterned *jali*. In the central hall are eight niches arranged over two floors. The third floor is opened by windows with perforated slabs of stone above which are the *muqarnas* that support the dome. Outside, the dome is surrounded by four spacious octagonal *chhatri* that form the roofs of the corner rooms. In addition there are eight smaller square *chhatri* arranged two by two on the entrance of each façade. Along the parapet run 24 graceful pinnacles in white marble, capped with lotus flowers.

The general impression of the mausoleum is of an elegant, sober and harmonious building, even though its total length (47.54 m) is a little excessive compared to its height (approximately 43 m) and the large *chhatri* are arranged too far from the main dome to create a truly balanced composition. However, with the border of the splendid garden, certainly derived from Babur's gardens, Humayun's tomb is without doubt the most beautiful sepulchral monument of this first phase of Mughal art, in the same way as the Qila-i Kuhna is the best mosque.

Although many of the most remarkable characteristics of Humayun's mausoleum, such as the imposing mass, the symmetrical plan and the dressing in red stone and white marble, are pre-Mughal in origin and have counterparts in other regions of Islam and India, their combination in the same monument is nevertheless original and completely unique. Akbar probably intended to make his father's tomb a dynastic tomb for the sepulchres of many princes. This had already happened in the Gur-i Amir in Samarqand, the mausoleum of Timur and members of his family, which the Mughals must have known of and decided to imitate.

Above The Lal Gumbad (Red Tomb) at Delhi (c.1570) takes its name from its red sandstone façade.

Opposite A detail from the interior of the Muhammad Ghaus mausoleum (c.1565) at Gwalior showing the perforated panels on the verandah – the building's most remarkable feature.

DELHI: KHAIR AL-MANZIL MOSQUE

The small mosque of Khair al-Manzil, built in 1561–2 by Akbar's nurse, Maham Anga, under the supervision of Shihab al-Din Ahmad Khan, belongs to a period of transition in the style. It is a mosque with a rectangular *sahn* surrounded by two-storey arcades that originally housed a *madrasa*. The monumental entrance, in the form of an *iwan*, is in red stone, while the rest of the building is of rubble construction dressed in stucco. The prayer hall, with five spans and covered at the centre by a dome, opens on the courtyard with only three archways, of which the central one is wider and taller than the others. It is flanked by octagonal turrets, the pinnacles of which have collapsed. The dressing was in the form of polychromatic glazed tiles together with Koranic inscriptions in stucco, of which there are still evident traces on the inside, too, above all in the *mihrab*.

DELHI: SHAMS AL-DIN MUHAMMAD ATGAH KHAN MAUSOLEUM

Other buildings that by date or by style can be considered contemporaneous with Humayun's mausoleum are some funeral buildings located in the large necropolis that hosts the tomb of the sovereign and was formed after 1325 around the site of the life and death of the great Sufi saint Nizam al-Din Auliya. Among these the beautiful tomb of Shams al-Din Muhammad Atgah Khan, dating from 1566–7, stands out (see p. 198). With a square plan, it is covered by a double marble dome and is opened on all sides by arched entrances screened by *jali*. The white marble has been used profusely for the ornament both outside and inside, occasionally mixed in worked slabs with azure and green glazed tiles in mosaics, or alternated with geometric motifs in stucco. In the funeral chamber all the skirtings are dressed with marble mosaics on slabs of red sandstone, according to a design that was later used widely both at Fatehpur Sikri and at Agra.

DELHI: AFSARWALA GUMBAD

Of the same period is the tomb popularly called Afsarwala Gumbad (see p. 199), situated near the so-called Arab Serai, on the western side of the complex which includes Humayun's mausoleum. It stands on a spacious platform that also contains a small domed mosque with a triple-arched façade. The plan, originally square, has strongly bevelled corners that make it appear octagonal. All the sides carry deep niches of varying dimensions. The cover is made up of a double hemispheric dome, resting on a high octagonal drum.

DELHI: NILA GUMBAD AND SABZ BURJ

A little older, and datable by their style to about 1560, are the tombs known as Nila Gumbad and Sabz Burj. Both have square plans but with highly bevelled corners. The first is covered by a single, almost hemispheric dome resting on a cylindrical drum and owes its name of Azure Tomb to the external sheathing in lively glazed tiles of various colours with turquoise azure dominating. The second has pointed, arched entrances that project from each of the four principal sides and deep blind niches on the others. The dome, double and bulbous, is imposed on an extremely high cylindrical drum – both are dressed in azure and green glazed tiles that have contributed to the tomb's elongated aspect and its name, Green Tower. The Sabz Burj, being a little older than Humayun's mausoleum, is also the first example of a square-planned building with bevelled corners. The so-called Tartar dome, which had already appeared in an experimental phase in the *madrasa* of Mahmud Gawan at Gulbarga (1472; see p. 154), appears here perfectly developed for the first time.

Delhi: Lal Gumbad

The Lal Gumbad (Red Tomb) dates from about 1570 and is known locally as the Barber's Tomb. Built, as its name suggests, in a fine red sandstone, with decoration in grey stone, it has a square plan and rests on a high plinth. Opened by arches on each side, it has ornamental niches and windows screened by *jali*. The beautiful double dome rests on a high 16-sided drum and is surrounded by four high, square *chhatri*. It rests inside on four intersecting arches on a principle that was taken up on a larger scale almost a century later in the Gol Gumbaz of Bijapur (see p. 169).

Gwalior: Muhammad Ghaus

There is another tomb datable from about 1565 which stands, however, not in Delhi, but near the fort of Gwalior and seems to be the final example of the square tombs from the epoch of the sultanates, even though it does display noteworthy innovations. Dedicated to the Sufi saint Muhammad Ghaus, it has a square plan of large proportions (30.4 m each side) with four hexagonal towers at the sides crowned by domed *chhatri*. The two-storey towers are opened by pillared arches. A square area projects at the centre of each side and supports a square *chhajja* resting on elegant corbels; this creates a fine effect of light and shadow. The funeral chamber is surrounded by a high and spacious verandah, the ceiling of which is painted with conventional patterns. The northern and eastern sides of the verandah are closed by perforated panels with beautiful geometric patterns while the southern side, which constitutes the entrance to the mausoleum, and the western side are open, and the *jali* simply form a low balustrade. The high dome that covers the room rests on a raised square drum surrounded by four hexagonal domed *chhatri* which harmonize perfectly with those of the structure below. It seems that both the dome and the *chhatri* were dressed in glazed tiles. The major point of beauty in this building, however, is found in the perforated panels on the verandah, which seem to be inspired by the Gujarati panels in the tomb of Shaikh Ahmad Khattu at Sarkej and which soon spread to the Akbari buildings of Fatehpur Sikri and Sikandra.

1. Trans. W.M. Theakston, Oxford 1996, pp. 359–60
2. Koran, *passim*, but especially Suras XLVII, 15; LV, 46–76; LVI, 12–22.
3. A. Petruccioli, ed., 'The Garden as a City – The City as a Garden', *Journal of the Islamic Environmental Design Research Center*, 2nd issue (1986), p. 107
4. R. Nath, *History of Mughal Architecture*, vol. 1, New Delhi 1982, pp. 118–19.
5. Goetz, *op. cit.*, p. 703.
6. Muhammad Khwand Amir, *Qanun-i Humayuni* (translated by Baini Prasad), Calcutta 1940, pp. 59–60.
7. *Ibid.*, p. 62.
8. Nath, *op. cit.*, p. 136.
9. Nath, *op. cit.*, p. 142.
10. Lowry has also maintained that Akbar played a part in the designing of his father's tomb: G. Lowry, 'Humayun's Tomb: Form, Function and Meaning in Early Mughal Architecture', *Muqarnas*, 4 (1987), p. 136.

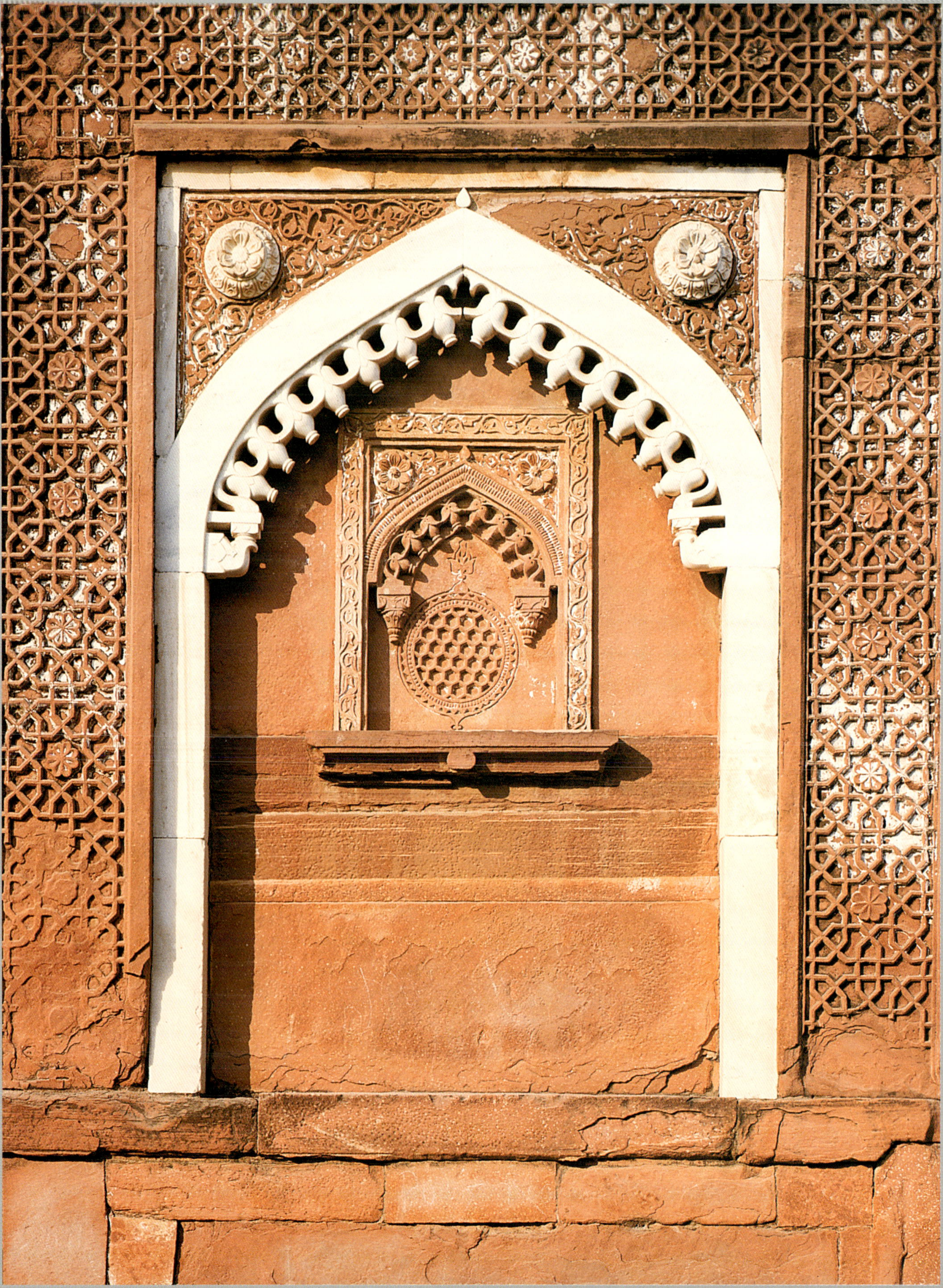

The Classic Mughal Period I
Akbar (1556–1605)

14

A detail of the elaborate carved decoration on the exterior of the Jahangiri Mahall at Agra Fort. The palace is one of the few buildings constructed by Akbar inside the fort to escape demolition.

Akbar, the greatest of the Mughal sovereigns, was born in Umarkot in Sind in 1542 while Humayun was escaping to Iran. Akbar succeeded his father in 1556 and governed initially under the regency of the general Bairam Khan, who managed to complete the restoration of the empire just begun by Humayun. When Bairam Khan fell in 1562 as a result of plots within the imperial harem, Akbar grasped the reins of government firmly and kept hold of them until his death in 1605. He was an attractive figure of great human interest and historical importance who revealed himself to be a building genius and a unifying force previously unimagined in India's history. In a few short years he succeeded in conquering one after another all the provinces of northern India, even those which previously were not part of the empire: Malwa (1562), Gondwana (1564), Bundelkand (1569), Gujarat (1572), Bengal and Orissa (1576), Kabul (1585), Kashmir (1587), Sind (1591), Kandahar, torn from the Persians, and Baluchistan (1595). Finally his expansion turned towards Deccan, annexing Berar (1596), Ahmadnagar (1600) and Kandesh (1601). At the same time he sought reconciliation with the Rajputs, the most important Hindu community in his empire both from the religious and the military points of view. This was in keeping with his constant concern to be sovereign of all his people, not merely by the dominant Muslim class. Once his supremacy over Rajasthan had been established through various victorious campaigns, Akbar succeeded in cementing personal relations with the Rajput princes, many of whom entered his service and were honoured and promoted to the highest ranks of the military hierarchy. These relations were further consolidated with opportune matrimonial alliances. The same trust was extended to other Hindu communities until he even abolished the *jizia*, the personal tax to which non-Muslims were liable.

Furthermore Akbar attempted to resolve the religious problem of his empire, made up of Sadhu, Hindu and Jain, Mobed Parsi and representatives of the Catholicism of Goa. From the discussions that took place between scholars of the various faiths in the Ibadat Khana

(House of the Cult) at Fatehpur Sikri, and by dint of a subtle political calculation coupled with a sincere spiritual commitment, the idea of the Din-i Ilahi was born. This was a new religion in which various influences mingled, above all Zoroastrian, and which was supposed to constitute a type of bridge between Hinduism and Islam. Akbar, by now far from the Sunnite orthodoxy of his youth, took the position of God's vicar on earth. Although officially proclaimed in 1582, Din-i Ilahi never reached beyond the court and ended with the death of its creator. Akbar never attempted to impose the new religion through force. Indeed, tolerance was the basis of his policy right to the end.

Once he had reorganized the administration of the realm, based on the institutions already created by Sher Shah, Akbar dedicated himself to an intense patronage of arts and letters. He was personally responsible for the plans and the supervision of many architectural projects, not least the design of Fatehpur Sikri, the new imperial city that rose not far from Agra, near the hermitage of the saint Salim Chishti who the emperor felt had interceded positively in the birth of his first son. Indian music went through a golden age under Akbar's reign and was best symbolized in the famous court musician, the Hindu Tansen. Akbar's coins are perhaps the most beautiful in Indian numismatics. Mughal painting was born under Akbar through two Persian artists brought to India by Humayun, and even early on this art form began to show the first signs of the excellence it would soon reach. Court literature in the Persian language had its major exponents in two brothers: Faizi, a great poet, and Abu al-Fazl, writer, general, minister and author of *Ain-i Akbari*, the true manual of the Mughal administration. But Indian literature also flourished greatly during the period of religious peace instigated by Akbar with *Ramcarit-manas*, the work of Tulsi Das.

In line with his policy of embracing the cultures of all his peoples, Akbar favoured their many and varied artistic expressions which combined to give his architectural creations a highly characteristic stamp. Initially Akbar eschewed Delhi as imperial capital, preferring Agra where from 1564 onwards, according to historical sources, he built 'over 500 red stone buildings in the refined styles of Bengal and Gujarat' in his fortress-cum-palace. For the most part these were demolished 65 years later by his grandson Shah Jahan to erect his more sumptuous marble pavilions. Agra became the Dar al-Mahall (Seat of the Palace); later Lahore was considered the Dar al-Sultanat (Seat of the Sovereignty), and Delhi finally became, under Shah Jahan, Dar al-Khalifat (Seat of the Empire).

Agra: fort

The fort at Agra was just one of the many, large fortified residences that the emperor wanted to have built in various strategic points of his realm: Allahabad, Lahore, Nagarcain, Ajmer. Like almost all these buildings, it was built on the bank of a river, which formed a natural barrier on one of its sides. Its plan has the form of an irregular semi-circle with a radius, some 800 m long, which runs parallel to the right bank of the River Jumna. The massive perimeter wall consists of a solid, squared bastion of red sandstone almost 20 m high and some 2.5 km in length. Contemporary accounts affirm that 'from top to bottom the fired stones are so tightly united that not even a hair could pass between the joints'. Despite its imposing structure, the bastion does, however, have considerable aesthetic value because of its crenellated parapets, the embrasures for cannons and the other military devices cleverly designed and similarly well arranged. Two entrances opened in this fortified wall: one on the southern side, used as a private entrance, and the other on the western side known as the Delhi Gate, which functioned as the main entrance and was designed to harmonize in the best possible way with the many bastions that flanked it. Altogether the plan is simple enough, in as much as the frontal aspect is formed of two great octagonal towers linked by a vaulted passage, while the rest has an elegant façade articulated with arcaded terraces and surmounted by domes, kiosks and pinnacles. Its dimensions are spacious enough to contain several rooms for the guards. The decorative elements, rich and various, make use of white marble inlays which stand out against the warm red of the sandstone background. Along the edges the conventional representation of a bird is repeated; this certainly goes against the Koranic guidelines regarding living beings, but is characteristic of the spirit of tolerance which motivated the emperor. Two panels even present the opposed figures of two composite animals which are formed of parts of elephants, horses, lions and birds. These animals are winning a battle over seven elephants.

Agra: Jahangiri Mahall

The many buildings erected by Akbar inside the fortress originally occupied the southern corner and ran along the parapet of the eastern wall in a strategic position which dominated the river. At least one of Akbar's buildings has escaped demolition and can give us an idea of the whole. This is the Jahangiri Mahall (see p. 202), a huge and rather complex arrangement of rooms that were perhaps destined for the rightful heir, hence the name. The rooms are freely arranged around two courtyards aligned along a central axis. The courtyard that looked over the river was obviously reserved for the harem, while the reception courtyard was near the entrance. Although it is uncertain, this building seems to have been inspired by the Hindu type of residence, exemplified in the Man Mandir built at Gwalior 75 years earlier and already considered by Babur the only Indian building worthy of note. Nevertheless, the façade is original when compared to the model and presents a frontage over two floors with a central pointed arch opening which protrudes slightly, and deep horizontal *chhajja* above a wall of blind arches flanked by octagonal turrets covered by *chhatri*. The interior halls and the courtyards evoke more strongly the spirit of the Hindu prototype with typical Jain *torana* (free-standing portals) which spring from the trabeated openings, richly carved stone pillars and corbels, and inclined stanchions which support *chhajja* and roofs. Although built completely in stone, the building seems to derive many of its elements from typical wooden construction; the position and the shape of the corbels under the awnings suggest this, as do the inclined struts that support the beams of the ceiling in the northern hall and the pillars of the portico. Opposite the façade is a large stone bowl which was added to the palace by Jahangir and which, according to some, once formed part of an original Bengali Mahall and included another palace, the Akbari Mahall, with the same plan as the preceding palace, the Akbar Mahall, but more ruined.

Ajmer: fort, pillared hall

In almost the same period as the Agra fortress the fort at Ajmer was built. This was reserved purely for brief visits by the emperor and was destined to function as a frontier outpost. It is comparatively small and fortified with double walls, giving it an impenetrable appearance. At the centre of the ample courtyard is a two-storey pillared hall (see p. 206) in the characteristic palatial style of the Akbar period. The façades are opened, in the centre, by three pointed high arches. Inside there is a chamber and rooms in each of the angles.

Another palace of the same period at Ajmer is the so-called Badshahi Mahall.

Lahore: fort

A few years later (1575) Akbar built the fortress at Lahore, which is very similar in many respects, but is much smaller. Because of the lie of the land, the fortress at Lahore is less irregular and forms a parallelogram of some 400 x 350 m contained within a high fortified wall. The interior arrangement is symmetrical with the entire rectangular area divided longitudinally into two more or less equal sections: towards the south are the public and service buildings, towards the north the royal palaces. Between these two sectors a series of buildings were arranged which separated the public and the private areas. The buildings of Akbar's time that survive in this fort are similar in style to those at Agra – built in red sandstone with the indigenous system of the architrave and corbel – although in the wall decorations local craftsmanship perhaps displayed a superior imagination and ability.

Allahabad: palace-fortress

The palace-fortress of Allahabad was built between 1583 and 1584 at the confluence of the River Jumna with the Ganges, so that its plan takes the form of a wedge or an irregular segment of a circle. At its widest point it measures about 1 km and is therefore the largest built by Akbar. It has, however, been demolished for the most part and stripped of much of its architectural interest. There is still a fine *baradari* or pavilion, known as the Rani-ki Mahall (Palace of the Zenana), evidently one of the many buildings that formed the fort's royal quarter. Here, too, the trabeated system of building has been largely maintained and is particularly clear in the organization of the pillars around an interior hall. The pillars are arranged in pairs, except at the corners of the building where they are grouped in fours, and they support a terrace roof, delimited by a perforated parapet and surmounted by kiosks with perforated wind breaks.

Fatehpur Sikri

The most ambitious of Akbar's architectural projects was nevertheless the creation of an entirely new capital on a site some 37 km from Agra. Here, in the village of Sikri, stood the hermitage of Shaikh Salim Chishti, whom the emperor chose to meet in 1568-9 to request the birth of an heir, an event that the saint accordingly prophesied as being imminent. The Prince Salim, later known as Jahangir, was in fact born on 30 August 1569. In recognition, two years later, Akbar decided to build a city on the site and to transfer the seat of the Mughal empire to it.

Naturally there were also precise political considerations that affected Akbar's choice. Fatehpur Sikri, even more so than

The fort at Agra, on the bank of the Jumna river, was one of several fortresses Akbar planned to build at strategic points throughout his kingdom.

Agra, was of strategic importance to Rajasthan. The sovereign did seek the support and the consensus of the valiant princes of this land, the Rajputs, but Rajasthan constituted a bridgehead into Gujarat, the new goal of Akbar's expansionist policy. The Gujarati ports of Surat, Broach and Cambay offered a route to the sea and steady trade with the Arab countries. It is also possible that Akbar sought to transfer his court in order to remove potential dissidents from the power struggle. Louis XIV did exactly this with the creation of Versailles. Finally, it must be remembered that the village of Sikri had for some time been an auspicious place for the Mughal dynasty. Babur himself had renamed it Shukri, which means 'thanks', as a sign of gratitude for his victory there over Rana Sanga of Mewar. Indeed, Babur found a garden there that was, according to him, badly designed and he immediately ordered another one to be designed and had some buildings erected, the remains of which are still visible in the outskirts of the present-day city. Akbar's city rose extremely quickly on an isolated rocky plain. It runs lengthwise along the bank of a seasonal river, the Khari Nadi (Saltish Waters), which was dammed in order to form a huge artificial lake that supplied water for the city. The complex, with its religious and secular buildings, forms a rectangle some 2 x 3 km and is surrounded on three sides by 6 km of non-fortified wall, originally opened by nine gates flanked by semi-circular bastions, one of which is permanently closed. The wall is now collapsed in various points. On the fourth side is the artificial lake, now reduced to swamp. The defensive apparatus was for appearances' sake more than anything else because the proximity of Agra, with its powerful fortifications, would have allowed shelter to all the court within its well-armed bastions in case of internal revolt or outside attack.

Apart from the public and private buildings commissioned by the emperor, the city is furnished with services. Chronicles of the time mention the building of villas with gardens and guards belonging to the various categories of residents, such as the Rajput nobles, the ministers, the artists and the men of letters, all dependent on the patronage of the sovereign or other personages. As well as these more luxurious dwellings spread around the centre of the city, there were also more modest homes reserved for the civil servants, the cooks and the quartermasters, the state messengers, the stable keepers, the eunuchs, the harem maids and, naturally, the officers and soldiers of the imperial guard. According to official statistics of the time, the city had some 200,000 inhabitants, a figure that is probably rather exaggerated.

In the central area of the city, as is the case at the nucleus of every Islamic city, is the mosque, the palace (or rather the complex of imperial palaces), the caravanserai and the *hammam* (again usually built as a complex). The services are found in a peripheral area, but often their precise function remains unknown as a result of demolition, collapse or the superimposition of later villages which are still inhabited. The most important buildings are all set at about 45 degrees to the lie of the land, while the gardens and the other, marginal buildings take the north-east/south-west lie of the land.

Above The monumental Buland Darwaza at Fatehpur Sikri was built by Akbar in 1596 as the entrance to the Great Mosque.

Opposite The pillared hall at Ajmer Fort, a frontier outpost built around the same time as the fortress at Agra.

The entire city is built in the beautiful red sandstone of the plain on which it stands and, for the most part, makes use of the traditional Hindu trabeated building system. Essentially the buildings are arranged in groups on three different levels. The largest of these, called Sahn-i Ibadat (Sacred Complex) by Nath, includes the majority of the religious buildings of Fatehpur Sikri: the Sangtarashan (Stone Masons') Mosque, which is the oldest Mughal building on the plain, the Great Mosque with its monumental door (Buland Darwaza) and the tomb of Shaikh Salim Chishti.

The second group of buildings, defined by Nath as Sahn-i Khass (Royal Complex), includes the so-called palace of Jodh Bai, two bazaars, until now considered horse and camel stables, and the palaces of Raja Birbal, Maryam and the Turkish Sultaness. All of these were attributed by nineteenth-century guides without regard to the buildings' true functions. Today's scholars have attempted a different and more precise identification, although even they are not in agreement among themselves. The Rang Mahall must be added to these buildings, although it stands far away from this area, to the east of the Great Mosque, not far from the Sangtarashan (Stone Masons') Mosque. Like this last, the palace was one of the first buildings constructed by Akbar in the new capital; his wife was probably here just before giving birth since it was close to the hermitage of the saint shaikh. The Palace of Pleasure, or more literally, Coloured Palace, is today mostly a ruin and is inhabited by the descendants of the shaikh.

The third group of buildings, called Sahn-i Rayyat (the Public Court) by Nath, contains diverse structures arranged in receding terraces which also have controversial names and functions: the Panch Mahall, over five diminishing floors; the Khwabgah, or private apartment of Akbar, with the so-called bath of the Turkish Sultaness connecting with it; the Anup Talao pavilion; Abdar Khana (the Girls' School); the Ankh Michauli, or Michoni; the Diwan-i Khass; the Diwan-i Amm; the imperial workshops; and other buildings connected to them.

In addition there are other constructions which have been variously interpreted, such as the Hiran Minar, the supposed homes of Abul Fazl and Faizi, the Elephant Gate, the Naqqar Khana, or rather the Naubat Khana (Drum House), from which came the drum roll that announced the emperor's appearances in the Diwan-i Amm and subdivided the day and night into sections. As well as the main buildings there are the gardens, the ornamental cisterns and the baths which were fed by an extremely efficient channelling system, a true masterpiece of hydraulic engineering based on the principle of the 'Persian wheel' driven by oxen.[1]

Both in the design of the buildings and in the town planning, at Fatehpur Sikri Akbar intended to express those principles of universality and eclecticism that underpinned his deep desire to amalgamate Islam and the vast, variegated Hindu world in a firm union. From close by the planimetric arrangement of the buildings recalls that of the Mughal encampments (and those of Central Asiatic Islam). The structures and the decoration were strongly influenced by the indigenous taste of Gwalior, Rajasthan, Gujarat, Malwa and other regions of the empire. Indeed, even the workers who contributed to the creation of Fatehpur Sikri were recruited from various Indian provinces, both because of their specific skills and because of the desire to bring the entire country together in the construction of the new capital. The building work continued for 15 years and, as Jahangir recorded in his memoirs, 'Over the course of fourteen or fifteen years that hill, full of wild beasts, became a city containing every type of structure and garden, noble, elegant buildings and delightful places.'[2]

Father Antonio Monserrate, who lived in Fatehpur Sikri from 1580 to 1582, recounts in his commentaries: 'In the past nine years the city has been marvellously laid out and beautified, the bill being met by both the royal treasury and the great nobles and the courtiers who passionately follow the example and the wishes of the king.' He adds that the public baths and the bazaar are of extraordinary elegance. He describes the bazaar as:

more than half a mile in length and full of a surprising amount of merchandise of all types and countless people all on their feet in a compact mass. To provide water for the city a reservoir two miles long and one mile wide has been built with much effort and skill. The king goes down to the lake on holy days and enjoys its many beauties.[3]

The English traveller Ralph Fitch visited Fatehpur Sikri in 1610 and wrote that it was larger than London and Rome. Even if this were an exaggeration, it is nevertheless evident that Akbar must have built many buildings in his capital – perhaps even too many: according to legend, Shaikh Salim Chishti was exasperated at seeing his peaceful hermitage transformed into a busy city and one day said to the emperor that either Akbar or he himself would have to leave Sikri. Akbar agreed to leave and in 1586, just 15 years after beginning the construction of his capital, he abandoned it for ever. Obviously the reason for his departure could not have been as the legend states, or at least not purely this reason. Some have attributed the abandonment of Fatehpur Sikri to the sovereign's unhappy spirit; he could not bear to feel attached to one place for too long. Others have attributed the departure to the exhaustion of the water supply brought about by the ever-increasing demands of the court and exacerbated by the collapse of a dam in the artificial lake. However, modern criticism has reassessed these theories. The great Mughal was indeed a despot, but was intelligent and enlightened and certainly was not subject to irrational fluctuations in mood that motivated the foundation and the abandonment of a city out of a simple whim. As far as the drying up of the water supply goes, it is important to remember that the present-day villages around Fatehpur Sikri are supplied from the artificial lake, the cisterns and the wells planned by Akbar. It is therefore evident that the second transfer of the imperial capital, this time to Lahore in the north, must have been brought about by political reasons much more serious than a 'changeable state of being'.

In fact, in those years Akbar increasingly reinforced the northern frontiers of his immense empire in order to move nearer to Kabul, which he conquered in 1585, and Kandahar, which he occupied in 1595. It was therefore necessary that his political and administrative base was nearer to the theatre of operations than Fatehpur Sikri. The capital's strategic function had ended. Nevertheless, it is important to remember that the sudden change of capital and the foundation of a city were common practices among Islamic sovereigns. They abhorred the concept of imposing their mark on a captured city and preferred to celebrate victories by creating a new city. Abandoned by its creator and by the court, the city was for some time the refuge of the elderly queen mothers. Later it would experience a few days of glory. Jahangir became emperor in 1605 and spent three months at Fatehpur Sikri in 1619, when Agra was struck by a terrible plague. Shah Jahan visited the city just once. In 1709 it rose to new splendours when the coronation of Muhammad Shah (1709–48) was celebrated there with much ceremony; some maintain that the design of the 'Pachisi Board' on the platform in front of the Abdar Khana dates from this time. After this Fatehpur Sikri was left to its fate until the British government decided to restore it to its ancient beauty. Lord Curzon, Viceroy of India from 1898 to 1905, was responsible above all others for the restoration of various buildings and for entrusting them to the Archaeological Survey of India.

Fatehpur Sikri: Tansen's *baradari*

The most traditional of the entrances to the city is to the north-east, through the Agra Gate which leads immediately to the caravanserai, the remains of the gardens and the nobles' homes, the bazaar and a well-preserved pavilion known as Tansen's *baradari*. Tansen, Akbar's greatest musician, is buried in a small tomb at Gwalior. The *baradari* consists of a space surrounded by a verandah covered with slabs of stone arranged so as to resemble tiles on a flat roof. Although this simple and graceful building was possibly used for musical entertainment, it is simply by popular tradition that it is linked to the famous Tansen. One theory is that since it is connected with a huge *hammam* and a two-storey house, the remains of which can still be seen, the *baradari* could have been one of the apartments reserved for Prince Salim when he was still a youth. Numerous fragments of glazed ceramics and Chinese porcelain have been found on this site. Under the pavilion are some vaulted rooms that probably functioned as *tah khana*, cool places or cellars where it was possible to pass the time during the ferocious summer heat. A similar structure survives in the Jahangiri Mahall of the fort at Agra.

Fatehpur Sikri: Naubat Khana

Continuing towards the Diwan-i Amm there is a building with three barrel-vault openings and an upper gallery covered by a terrace and surmounted laterally by two square *chhatri*. It is known commonly as the Naubat Khana, or Naqqar Khana, which refers to the fact that the imperial band, who rolled the drums for every appearance made by the sovereign, lived there. However, chronicles of the time, and even some miniatures, place the Naubat Khana near the Hathi Pol (Elephant Gate), which stands on the steep north-western side of the rocky plain and overlooks the imperial palaces on the one side and the Hiran Minar on the other. It seems that the true name of the so-called Naubat Khana was Chahar Suq – a market-place arranged round a square and derived from the Persian *char su* which in its turn comes from the Turkish *çarshi*, the crossing of four trade roads, often covered by a dome and therefore a type of market. It also seems that for festivals and parades this building was sumptuously decorated, like the bazaar, because illustrious guests were welcomed here.

Fatehpur Sikri: mint

Further on still there is a remarkable single-storey construction with rubble-filled perimeter walls and an entrance to the south. This is popularly known as Taksal (the mint), but some think that it contained the royal stables. Instead it seems that at the time of Akbar it was the Kar Khana (workshop) where, under direct imperial control, the objects necessary for the court, both run of the mill and luxury, were prepared. In the words of Father Monserrate, the emperor had 'built a workshop near the palace, where there are studios and laboratories for all the most beautiful and prestigious arts, such as painting, goldsmith's art, tapestry, carpet, curtain and arms manufacture'.[4] According to the Jesuit Akbar often came to visit his workshops to relax while watching his craftsmen concentrating on their work. The master painter in the imperial Kar Khana was the famous miniaturist Abd al-Samad, whom Humayun had brought from the Safavid court of Persia, together with Mir Sayyid Ali, giving him the title of Shirin Qalam (Sweet Pen). Akbar, in his turn, after having taken painting lessons from him, nominated Abd al-Samad director of the Fatehpur Sikri mint in 1576, and at the end of his public career made him Diwan (superintendent of taxes) of Multan. The workshops are made up of a series of wide square spaces, each formed by four arches, covered by a flat or domed roof and arranged regularly at the four corners of a huge courtyard.

Opposite the entrance there is another building in red stone which also has pillared verandah around an open courtyard and a complex of five rooms. Its proximity to the Kar Khana has led to the theory that it could have been a store for working materials or a warehouse for the finished goods awaiting the superintendent's instructions. Petruccioli maintains that 'as it is an extremely flexible type' the building could have fulfilled another of the proposed functions, as a stables for animals. But neither can we exclude the possibility, 'given the arrangement of the archaeological strata, that this was a building erected very quickly by Jahangir or Shahjahan in order to host the royal court during a later stay.'[5]

Fatehpur Sikri: Diwan-i Amm

The Diwan-i Amm is made up of a wide oblong courtyard (112 x 65 m) surrounded on all sides by verandahs with pillars which form 111 spans with ceremonial entrances to the east and the south, although these have perhaps not reached us in their original form. At the centre of the western side, on a platform divided into three sections, rises the throne pavilion, which faces on to the courtyard with five apertures articulated by pillars terminating in corbel capitals which support a wide *chhajja*. This is covered by a *khaprel* (a characteristic ceiling with stone tiles) on which there is a terrace bordered by a high frieze of small arches. At the base of the pillars runs a series of perforated balustrades (*jali*) with geometric motifs. From the central area of this pavilion, sitting on cushions and carpets, Akbar showed himself to the people each morning about three hours after sunrise. Here, too, he sat among his ministers and officials to administer justice with severity and impartiality, as emphasized by Father Monserrate, but always without bitterness or malice. An executioner stood by among the onlookers, complete with torture equipment, which was more to inspire terror than for practical use. In fact those sentenced to capital punishment, by hanging, impaling or crushing by elephants, were taken elsewhere for execution. In the afternoons, again in this pavilion, Akbar inspected the animals of the imperial stables, giving rewards or punishments to the keepers according to the condition of their charges. Sometimes he concerned himself with the administration of the Kar Khana and the court. To the back of the pavilion was a door which allowed the emperor to retire directly to his private apartments, collectively called Daulat Khana (Fortune's Home).

The place where Akbar appeared for the *jharoka darshan* (literally the audience from the balcony), a ceremony of Hindu origin, is unknown. Shortly after sunrise and awakened by the music of the *naqqar khana*, the sovereign completed his toilet and prepared himself for prayers. At the sound of the royal drum, which alerted the people who had gathered below the palace during the night, the king showed himself at a window or a balcony. The ceremony was not designed simply to confirm his majesty, but also to forestall any attempts at sedition by displaying his perfect efficiency. During the ceremony of *darshan* Akbar used to accept the worship of his subjects and then retire for a short rest. Three possible sites for the *jharoka* are the small gallery projecting from the Daftar Khana (archive), the terrace of the Khwabgah near the Daftar Khana, or one of the façades of the so-called Palace of Jodh Bai that faced east.[6]

Fatehpur Sikri: Khwabgah

Some of the most interesting buildings in the city rise in a very large area spread out over various receding terraces. On the southern side rises the imperial Khwabgah (literally, bedroom) complex. On the whole this is extremely sober compared with the sovereign's other residences, but it nevertheless includes various halls circled by verandahs to ensure maximum shadow and ventilation: terraces, pavilions and screened passages, all built in the beautiful local red sandstone.

The bedroom itself – screened by a porch and with wall decoration of paintings representing hunting and fishing scenes – is on the first floor, on a raised platform supported by pillars which today are inaccessible since the wooden or marble stair that connected it to the ground floor is lost. Here there are two rooms, one of which measures some 13 x 8.76 m; it is from its southern wall that the Khwabgah platform rises. The other room, 8.3 x 5.18 m, has three doors which open towards the interior; the lower parts of the walls are carved to form niches, which were closed by sliding slabs of stone.

It seems that the books which Akbar loved to keep to hand for daily reading were kept here. Others maintain that this room was part of the imperial Kutub Khana (library), which amounted to 25,000 manuscripts on an immense variety of subjects reflecting the wide-ranging interests of the emperor. The remainder of the manuscripts were kept in the small, graceful pavilion erroneously called House of the Turkish Sultaness, or Hujrai Anup Talao. The supposed Kutub Khana still preserves the outlines of tulips, poppies and roses, traces of a rich pictorial decoration that certainly covered all of it.

On the terrace of Akbar's apartment is a square pavilion, consisting of a single room surrounded by a wide verandah, open on each side with five barrel vaults of unequal width and covered with the characteristic roof of stone slabs in imitation of tiles already seen in the Diwan-i Amm and in the so-called Tansen's *baradari*. This technique seems to have been the transposition into stone of the clay tile roofs of the local village cabins, and was therefore of local origin.

All the pillars, the corbels and the walls of the verandah and the room were originally painted directly on the surface of the stone, without rendering. Alongside floral subjects there is a series of representations of Mughal court scenes, as well as events that are difficult to identify, as for example in the painting of many people on a sailboat against an architectural background; or a man sitting alongside two headless figures, one on top of the other, with crossed legs. The lower part of this painting is full of damaged fragments of naked men and women, all painted in gold, red, black and white. Another painting represents the entrance to a cave, inside which is a winged figure, probably a fairy, with a baby in its arms. This is a possible allusion to the birth of Salim by divine intervention at Fatehpur Sikri. Presumably these paintings, which represent the transposition of Mughal miniatures to mural form, have a symbolic meaning which is a mystery to us now, but must have been very clear to Akbar who commissioned them.

On the pillars of the verandah of this pavilion, and on some external and internal walls, numerous Persian inscriptions in pleasant colours have been found. These are written in fine *nastaliq* characters and for the most part sing the praises of the palace, comparing it to heaven. One inscription says, 'Rizwan, the custodian of heaven, made the floor of this palace as clear as a mirror and the *Huri* use the dust of this palace as a salve for their eyes.'[7] The presence of many paintings suggests that Akbar used this small pavilion as a study (*citra shala*), a common feature in royal Hindu homes since the earliest times. Covered passageways connected the Khwabgah with the harem and the Panch Mahall, buildings reserved for the sovereign and his women: the first is lost today, while the second survives. The possibility that this site hosted the painting studio is not to be excluded. Akbar supervised the studio personally, and it is possible that the *mahtat khana*, the translation service instigated by the emperor to provide him with Persian versions of Sanskrit classics, was situated in the ground-floor rooms. Behind the library with its frescoes is a room measuring 12.97 x 8.76 m, dominated by a raised platform that projects from the southern wall. Light comes from a small window and the room had a door, today bricked up, which connected it directly to the courtyard of the Daftar Khana. According to Petruccioli this would have been the Diwan-i Khass from which Akbar, sitting on his throne, directed the discussions of his 20 ministers.

The imperial apartment overlooks a fine square swimming pool with a seat at its centre (*char chamand*), called 'incomparable' (Anup Talao) by Abu'l Fazl, and 'camphor swamp' by Father Monserrate. It measures just over 29 square metres and is currently 1.37 m deep because the floor was restored and raised in about 1840 by Sayyid Ahmad Khan. According to contemporaries it was much deeper and the water arrived here through a channel system situated to the north. According to the historian Badaoni it was completed in 1575; three years later Akbar, who had undergone a strange mystic experience while hunting in the Punjab, filled it with copper, silver and gold coins which were then distributed as gifts to the population.[8]

Fatehpur Sikri: House of the Turkish Sultaness

In the north-eastern corner of the Anup Talao stands a small structure measuring 3.96 x 1.37 m which to the west has a portico almost as high as the ceiling of the principal room and supported by pillars at the corners with octagonal shafts. It is connected to the ground floor of the Daulat Khana complex and to the building known as the Girls' School by a rough colonnade that was added later. Originally the verandah and the portico were screened by slabs of perforated stone. This small building was called the House of the Turkish Sultaness by local guides and some scholars have deduced from this that it was the home of a wife of the emperor who also owned the connecting bath known by the same name. The decorative richness and the elegance of this small building have led to its being defined as a superb jewel casket. In fact it does seem to be more the work of a craftsman's chisel than a bricklayer's trowel. Both outside, on the verandah, and inside, each stone slab is decorated differently and all seem to be competing among themselves for the fine design and refined details. The arabesque friezes alternate with sinuous strands of vines or spirals within which are enclosed flowers, pomegranates and melons. The geometric designs display semi-hexagonal borders and herringbone bands. The skirtings are dressed in slabs with motifs of small cypresses, palm trees and trees with branches rich with intertwined leaves and trunks. On the verandah the bell-shaped corbels which support the architraves of the ceiling are similar to those of other monuments in Fatehpur Sikri, but the original sculptures which decorated them make them unique. It seems that Gujarati craftsmen, highly specialized in inlay work, contributed actively to the decoration of the building. The interior of the house is completely decorated from the floor to the ceiling. There is an incredible variety of motifs, among which are even Hindu swastikas and human or animal figures whose faces, however, are often mutilated, perhaps as a result of Aurangzeb's unfortunate religious intolerance. The scenes represented take place in the jungle, and the Indian flora and fauna reproduced stand out with grace and exquisite taste.

The name 'House of the Turkish Sultaness' seems not to reflect historical fact, as Akbar had no wife of Ottoman origin. Some have hypothesized that the sultaness of the legend must have been Salima Sultan Begum, initially the wife of Bairam Khan, Akbar's tutor, who married the emperor after the death of Bairam in 1561. Salima, however, was a Mughal, niece of the emperor himself. Another wife, Ruqayya Sultan Begum, according to legend, was the daughter of Hindal, uncle of the emperor, and became his first wife. According to Banerjee the two ladies, being cousins, lived in the same house in

Above and right Details of the delicately carved decoration on the pillars of the so-called House of the Turkish Sultaness at Fatehpur Sikri. Although traditionally known by this name, the building's true function is widely disputed.

apartments separated by stone screens of which no trace is left.⁹ Modern critics have rejected this theory, above all because the house is too small for two people. According to Rizvi it is simply a pleasure pavilion (Hujra-i Anup Talao) connected to the swimming pool where the women of the imperial harem could find rest and refuge, reaching it by means of a covered passage connecting the royal apartment with the Hujra.¹⁰ This idea is based on a statement made by the historian Badaoni. Here, on more than one occasion, important religious disputes were played out which were destined to reinforce the political and religious power of Akbar. According to Nath, on the other hand, the small building constituted an adjunct to the imperial library, to which it was connected by means of a covered passage screened by curtains which he called *saraparda*.¹¹ In truth, both interpretations of the building's function could be correct. Certainly it must have been closely linked to the emperor, a fact which would explain its profuse and refined decoration. The connecting bath could also have been a private *hammam* for the emperor.

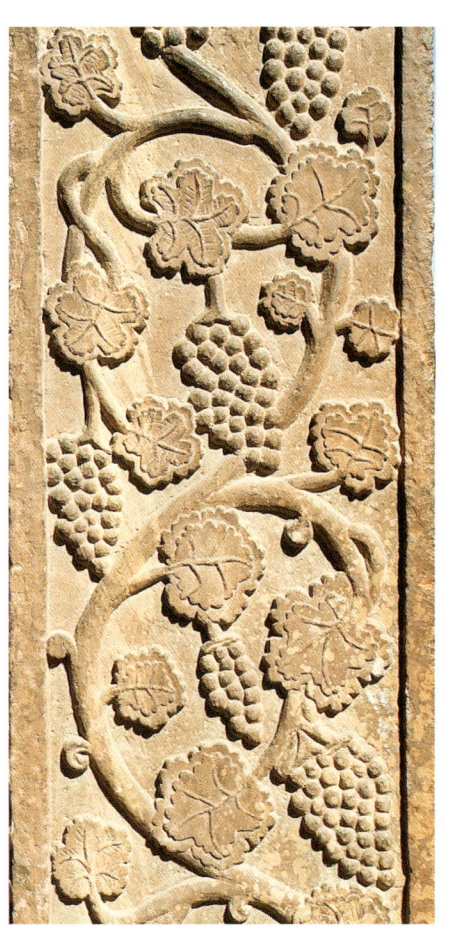

FATEHPUR SIKRI: GIRLS' SCHOOL

On the northern side of the Anup Talao stands a large pillared building surrounded by a verandah covered with slabs of stone and called the Girls' School, which according to Banerjee was supervised by Salima Sultan Begum, the supposed Turkish sultaness. Rizvi maintains instead that it was a sort of dispensary for Akbar's drinking water (*abdar khana*) and a store for fine fruits such as melons, mangoes and grapes. Akbar used to drink only water from the Ganges, which he called 'the water of immortality'. More recently Nath suggested that this was the Ibadat Khana, which Badaoni described as a hall surrounded by spacious open galleries. According to the Indian scholar this could easily have been divided into four parts, each of which was reserved for one of the theological categories quoted by contemporary historians, and with whom Akbar preferred to discuss matters separately. It would seem, however, that after 1576 the business of the Ibadat Khana was transferred to the Anup Talao, the symbolic throne from which Akbar could quench his thirst for knowledge and which on cold winter nights was kept instead in the room preceding the Khwabgah.

The building overlooks an immense courtyard (66.29 x 46.93 m) called Pachisi because of a cruciform platform which reproduces the game of that name. Pachisi means 'twenty-fifth', alluding to the highest number that could be scored at each throw of the shells with which the game was played. Popular legend has it that the emperor was wont to sit at the centre of the platform and play with young slaves dressed in different colours who functioned as living pieces. This is probably why the platform for Pachisi, known in ancient India as the game of *chaupar*, is too large to be able to use the usual wooden pieces. Abul Fazl speaks of it as one of Akbar's amusements, but makes no reference to living 'pawns'. The grand court's board probably had only symbolic aims, or had been monumentalized deliberately in order to display the game to the people and foreign visitors.

FATEHPUR SIKRI: DIWAN-I KHASS AND PANCH MAHALL

In the same large courtyard, but once set apart by a wall that has now been demolished, stands the most singular and mysterious building of the entire city. This is the so-called Diwan-i Khass, a square building in the inevitable red sandstone, measuring externally 13.18 m each side with four façades over two floors separated by a *jali* balcony supported by two large worked corbels. On the northern and southern sides the lower floor has an oblong central area flanked by beautiful windows screened with *jali*. On the third side there is only one *jali* window while the last side is closed to allow for an internal stairway. The upper floor has three apertures on each side protected by an extremely wide *chhajja* which creates a fine *chiaroscuro* effect. Four bold *chhatri*, square in shape, complete the corners of the building, terminating in a lotus and a *kalasha*. It is not known whether there was a central dome, as implied by a miniature of the time. As no traces of a dome remain at the site, its presence in the painting may derive from the imagination of the miniaturist.

The internal arrangement of the building lends itself to various interpretations. It presents itself as a single square room measuring 8.74 m each side and occupies the entire height of the building; the room therefore appears as though it were a single floor. From the exact centre of the floor rises a pillar with a square base and an octagonal shaft (see p. 214); this is decorated with beautiful and finely carved

The red sandstone Diwan-i Khass (Hall of Private Audience) is the most mysterious and certainly the most distinctive building at Fatehpur Sikri.

stylized designs. Near the capital the shaft takes on first a hexahedral shape and then becomes circular. From the capital 36 splendid tripartite corbels start which recall the work of Gujarati craftsmen. Together these constitute one of the most imaginative capitals ever designed. On the corbels rests a circular platform from which four narrow passages radiate diagonally to the corners where there are the same number of quarter-circle platforms supported by nine corbels identical to those of the central pillar. From these corner corbels there extends a balcony which runs all round the room and which, like the central platform and the suspended bridges, has an open-work balustrade.

The ceiling is of a particular type of barrel vault with panels and ribs called *ladao* which is to be found in a more or less identical form in the Jahangiri Mahall of the fort at Agra and in the Man Mandir of Gwalior, as well as in the buildings of Fatehpur Sikri.

The building in its entirety is very simple, but is enhanced by the extraordinary central structure and the elegant open work of the balustrades. For years, given the name by which the building was known, it was held to be designed for the private audiences of Akbar who would have sat at the centre of the platform to listen to his ministers arranged in the narrow diagonal passages. But modern criticism has destroyed this theory and proposed various others. The restricted and uncomfortable space of both the platforms and the corridors would not have allowed the emperor and his ministers to stay there for long. Above all the conditions would have forced Akbar to turn continually to face speakers who were behind him and in the meantime his personal guard could not surround him – no sovereign could do without that protection.

For the same reasons this room cannot be the Ibadat Khana where, according to contemporary writers, the emperor and the theologians he invited to discussions would spend entire nights. Rizvi has sought to identify the building as the Treasure House where Akbar kept the crown jewels and inspected them from the height of the platform. Nath has criticized this theory, maintaining instead that the building is a symbolic representation of Akbar's belief in the cult of the sun. The central column represents the *Ekastambha* (the Unitary Pillar), the axis of the cosmic order measured from the *Surya Purusa* (Body of the Sun). It seems, on the other hand that a central column supporting four galleries, although unique in Islamic art, was known in Indian art from the earliest times, above all in Gujarat where it occurred in wooden examples before being created in stone. It was used in secular buildings at Patan, Ahmedabad and elsewhere. Again in Gujarat it is also found as an independent structure with a varied number of corbels supporting a platform which can be an open terrace or covered by a *chhatri*; in this last case the structure is a *parabadi*, a bird rest.[12] These were functional structures, with no symbolic character, while the example at Fatehpur Sikri is quite the opposite. The column has no utilitarian value but serves purely to represent Akbar's faith in the doctrine of solar supremacy, which he had given such an important place in his new religion, the Din-i Ilahi, in which, naturally, even his own solar-divine nature was eclipsed. Petruccioli carries Nath's suggestion even further and maintains:

This is certainly a symbolic building. Indeed, it is a place in which two symbolic functions converge to represent the act of reintegration in the Hindu Brahman, or the union of micro and macrocosm, which in Sufi thought is represented by the Supreme identity, expressed as the Universal Man ... The supposed Diwan-i Khass is above all the Kaaba with its four corner pillars (arkan) marked by four chhatri and the four corners ... which correspond in the superior order to Universal Intelligence and Universal Material ... the Kaaba built by Akbar on the Fatehpur Sikri plateau is the allegory of a pilgrimage to the sacred places that he was never allowed owing to his state duties.[13]

According to Nath, the real Diwan-i Khass is the building called curiously Ankh Michauli, the venue for 'hide-and-seek', where, according to legend, the emperor played with the women of the harem. It is composed of three oblong halls of equal dimensions arranged in an E-shaped plan, where the lateral sections flanking the central hall project from it at right-angles, leaving space in front for an open courtyard. The three spaces are connected by narrow passages. Each room measures little more than 7 x 5 m and has rather wide openings (1.47 m) between the stanchions so that they appear very airy. In the walls there are deep niches and secret safes. These led Rizvi to suggest that the copper, gold and silver coins of the imperial treasure were kept here, while Nath maintains that they contained seals and important documents for the sovereign's private meetings with his ministers. Akbar would in fact have sat in the central room and his ministers in the lateral rooms, all of which were well connected with their wide openings and made extremely comfortable by plenty of carpets, cushions, cupboards, curtains, chairs and so on. The central area is covered by a flat roof divided into 15 compartments by means of beams supported by oblique corbels in the form of *makara* (crocodile-like creatures), as in the ceiling of the Jahangiri Mahall in the Agra fort. In the lateral rooms the ceilings take the form of barrel vaults, with the usual system of panels and ribs already seen at Agra and Gwalior. The decoration of all the three rooms is very sober and contained, in contrast with the House of Maryam or the Palace of Birbal. On the eastern side there are two stairways that lead to the roof; the entire structure is almost 9 m high, including the plinth of some 1.1 m on which it rests, but it has no superstructure and therefore lacks any vertical momentum. A wide *chhajja* protects the whole façade, creating deep shadows and conferring a fine horizontal rhythm to the marked vertical lines of the wide entrances. Naturally, the legend that the building was dedicated to the game of hide-and-seek has no substance in contemporary documents. Certainly if Akbar spent time in such frivolous ways the austere Badaoni would not have missed an opportunity to record the fact.

At the south-western extremity of the Ankh Michauli is an elegant square *chhatri* in red stone. This is rendered very original by eight extremely graceful snake-like corbels, exquisitely made, which seem to form four *torana*. The prototype of this feature is to be found in Jain architecture, in particular the temple of Vimala Sah on Mount Abu and in the Girnar temple in Kathiavar. In Hindu ceremonial architecture it is found on the façade of the palace of Man Sing Tomar at Gwalior. This small

The highly unusual central pillar in the Diwan-i Khass at Fatehpur Sikri boasts 36 carved corbels, and recalls the work of Gujarati craftsmen.

building is known by the imaginative name of the Astrologer's Seat, a theory that is not given much credence by modern scholars. Some have thought that it was dedicated to a yogi, because they were held in great esteem by the emperor. Rizvi has suggested that it could have been the place where the principal treasurer of Akbar, the eunuch Phul Maliq, distributed money to the officials, his subordinates and the servants. But this supposition, too, has been dismissed by Nath as being overly imaginative.

To the south-east of the so-called Diwan-i Khass is the strange building called Panch Mahall (see p. 216), so named because it is built over five floors (*panch* means 'five'). This is an extraordinary structure in red sandstone, entirely in columns (176 in all) and composed of four floors of diminishing size arranged asymmetrically above a ground floor containing 84 columns. It seems that this is a cabalistic number obtained by multiplying the seven known planets by the 12 signs of the zodiac, a lucky number according to the Hindus. The pillars are coupled at the points where support for the upper floors is most needed, and they are quadrupled in the north-eastern corner for the same reason. An open-work balustrade with geometric designs surrounds the perimeter of the upper floors.

The first storey is formed of 56 pillars (again a cabalistic number), each different, beautifully designed and finely decorated, perhaps because they are connected to the Khwabgah and the other royal apartments by means of a covered passage. The floor is protected by a strongly projecting *chhajja* which carries a carved frieze on top. The second storey, much smaller, is composed of 20 pillars situated on the exterior side. It is also protected by a *chhajja* with a carved frieze. The third storey is formed of 12 pillars, also situated on the eastern side, and ends with an open-work balustrade supported by graceful corbels. The building is finally crowned by a square *chhatri* with a domed roof. Apart from this terminal section the Panch Mahall is a trabeated building which resembles the temple of Vaikuntha Perumal at Conjeeveram (710–20), arranged over five floors, a fact that would therefore suggest it was inspired by indigenous models. It is a very balanced building, its total height being equal to the length of the ground floor. Because of its complete openness and lack of barriers, it has been suggested that Akbar and his ladies used it as a *hawa mahall*. Indeed, Rizvi has given it the Persian name *badgir* (wind-tower). But others, Nath for example, believe it to be the *jharoka darshan*, the most appropriate place for the emperor to show himself daily to the worshipful people, due to the elevation of the building and its connection with the sovereign's private apartments. Fergusson compared this building to the Ratha of Mahabalipuram; Smith compared it to the Buddhist monastery; Ebba Koch has referred to the Nagina Mahall in the Khimlassa Fort, datable from the fifteenth century; others have compared it to the Hawa Mahall (Lat Pyramid; see p. 42) of Firuz Shah at Delhi of 1365. For his part Petruccioli sees in the pyramid of the Panch Mahall 'a third possibility as well as the Anup Talao and the supposed Diwan-i Khass, connected with the divine cult of Akbar'. Furthermore, he maintains that on the highest point there was an astronomical observatory (*rasad khana*), the graduated wood and metal instruments of which – some of considerable size – were kept in the lower rooms.[14]

Fatehpur Sikri: Jodh Bai Palace

The buildings that Nath grouped in the so-called Sahn-i Khass stand on a slightly higher level. The largest and the best preserved of these is known as the Palace of Jodh Bai. This extends for 211.3 m from east to west and 196.5 m from north to south and in its plan recalls the Akbari Mahall and the Jahangiri Mahall at Agra. It has a single entrance that faces east across a wide paved courtyard. The aspect is graceful: a three-centred arch decorated with lotus garlands which border the portal itself, deep blind niches to the sides and wide covered balconies crowned with *chhatri* surmounting it. Such an entrance, with a small outer room to the exterior for guards, is fitting for the building that must have contained Akbar's *zenana*, not for the residence of one of Jahangir's wives, Jodh Bai, whom he married in 1586. The building is on two floors and its perimeter walls are very simple, solemn and massive, although they are interrupted by *jharoka* windows, characterized by four slender corbels, open-work balustrades and *chhajja* which project from the eastern side of the rooms on the upper floor. These are covered by hemispheric domes which rest on octagonal drums. The building has a spacious courtyard inside (54.9 x 49.32 m) around which various two-storey apartments are arranged with living spaces at the corners and ceremonial rooms at the centre of the four spaces. These are connected by single-storey corridors. The corner suites are made up of a closed room on two sides with two deep verandahs open on the other two and a closed inner room where various objects could be kept. The ceremonial rooms are identical on the northern and southern sides. On this latter side there is a rectangular room with a spacious colonnaded verandah with *torana* niches and a small raised platform at the centre which, according to Nath, must have served as a temple since it faces east. According to Rizvi it could have been the throne on which the emperor sat when he went to visit the women in his *zenana*. The eastern side is for the most part taken up with the entrance and there is just one verandah there.

The upper floor is made up of four square and domed rooms at the corners, two pavilions with columns and triangular gable roofs on the eastern and western sides, and two triangular pavilions with *khaprel* ceilings and *chhatri* on the southern and northern sides, corresponding to the lower apartments. The domed corner rooms are extremely simple, but on their ceilings traces of paintings with arabesque designs have been found. Even the domes were originally dressed in glazed tiles from Multan in a magnificent azure colour which reflects brilliantly on the sea of opaque and discoloured kiosks, domes and flat plastered roofs of the city.

The pavilions to the east and west are made up of verandahs with three barrel vaults, with square pillars and corbels with a pyramidal roof supported by eight pillars and resting on each side at a right-angle. This is in keeping with the corresponding lower apartment: the entire two storeys are excellently homogeneous and unified so that the building appears as a composition of rare architectonic beauty. The pavilions to the north and south have triangular *khaprel* ceilings, which are

The Panch Mahall at Fatehpur Sikri. This extraordinary structure is supported by 176 pillars.

dressed in blue glazed tiles similar to those of the royal palace at Gwalior. This palace seems to have been the inspiration for the pavilions.

The decoration of the columns, the pediments and the capitals is much varied throughout the building and sometimes draws on Hindu models as well as more strictly Islamic canons, above all in the central rooms. Motifs used include small lozenges, balls, lotus-petal rosettes, chains and bells; in the northern room of the upper floor there are snake-shaped corbels, figures of geese in various positions and even *gajamukha* – a triple corbel similar to an elephant's head with the trunk held back to the head and then pushed forwards. The refined execution of these features reveals that considerable use was made of the extremely skilled Gujarat craftsmen; the same craftsmen were probably responsible for the extraordinarily fine designs carved into the square stucco panels of the corner rooms on the ground floor and the superb medallions, again carved in stucco, under the keystone of the ceiling vaults in the four corner domes.

The northern apartment extends on the upper floor into a small double-storey extension building which has been identified correctly as a *hawa mahall*. The lower floor, resting on a double row of columns, is open; the second floor is closed with beautiful slabs of open-work stone with highly refined patterns which provide fresh air and shade for the interior, and at the same time guarantee privacy by the use of a stone *pardah* (screen).

From the eastern and western sides of the northern central room two stairways lead to the first floor and provide access to a screened viaduct which leads beyond the harem garden to the Elephant Gate and then towards the Sangin Burj, from which other covered passages lead to the Hiran Minar. This passage allowed the women of the imperial harem to reach the lake – on the other side of which stands the Hiran Minar – and the pleasure domes on its banks.

The viaduct, 8.23 m high, is supported by arches and surmounted at intervals by *chhatri*. It is wide enough to allow for simultaneous passage of several people and originally its sides were embellished with open-work slabs that provided the necessary secrecy. A similar viaduct united the palace with the Khwabgah, but it has been destroyed. These viaducts were inspired by the *saraparda* (covered passageways) of the Mughal fields, which provided security and privacy. The first use of such an arrangement was found, although in a simpler form, between the four sections of the Kushk Mahall at Chanderi (see p. 140). The so-called Palace of Jodh Bai, which would be better called Haram Sarai, Raniwas or Zenani Dyodhi, could have been built between 1569 and 1572, according to Badaoni's testimony: 'In the year 979 (1571–2) the royal palace at Agra and another palace in the new city of Fatehpur were completed.'[15]

FATEHPUR SIKRI: BIRBAL PALACE

In the north-western corner of the royal complex, adjacent to the so-called Palace of Jodh Bai, stands a beautiful building of more modest proportions than the previous one and known commonly as the Palace of Birbal. It, too, is on two floors, again in warm red sandstone of the highest quality. On the ground floor are four square spaces measuring 5.13 m each side and connected by open entrances and two oblong entrance porches on the northern and southern sides, each preceded by a platform, a *chabutra*. While the square rooms are covered by flat roofs, the entrances have triangular ceilings, *chhappar*, which culminate in pyramidal roofs on the first floor. An extremely wide *chhajja*, supported by abundantly decorated triple but unified corbels, shades this floor on all the exterior sides.

The first floor has only two rooms, arranged diagonally to those of the floor below. The other spaces are occupied by terraces and stairways. Each space is covered by domed ceilings made up of panels and ribs which rest on hanging supports carried by two fine corbels at the corners. On the eastern and western sides attractively designed *jharoka* windows open over the courtyard below. This floor is surrounded by a narrower and simpler *chhajja*. The final domes rest on octagonal drums and seem to have been originally dressed in turquoise-blue, green, yellow or milk-white glazed tiles which harmonized well with the ruddy gradation of the sandstone.

However, the single most important characteristic of this building is the profuse decoration carved both inside and out. Not only the walls, but also the pillars, their pediments and capitals, the corbels and the architraves are decorated with motifs carved in low and high relief with an infinite number of motifs, both Hindu and Islamic. *Kirtimukha* (ancient ornamental masks) on the pediments alternate with geometric and floral arabesques on the shafts, and lotus petals on the capitals to which stalactite forms and spear-point friezes are attached. Although the whole construction is trabeated, arches appear as an ornamental motif; they are always bordered by lotus-garland friezes, as in the Jahangiri Mahall at Agra, and are sometimes paired with peacock, parrot, goose and elephant figures. Some empty spaces emphasize the decorative richness which extends with inexhaustible vigour and fantasy without ever falling into trite virtuosity or monotonous repetition. Here, too, the work of Gujarati craftsmen was important even though it was under the direction of the best Muslim designers. An inscription in *devanagari* (a kind of Indian script used in Sanskrit and Hindi) on the western entrance of a room on the ground floor confirms that the building was built in 1572 (or 1582: one letter is almost unintelligible) for the initiation ceremony of Din-i Ilahi, which indeed took place in 1582. It would therefore seem likely that Akbar erected this building in order to carry out his own religious matters there, and in particular those regarding the foundation of his new religion, destined to be practised at the court alone. In any case it could not have belonged to Raja Birbal who, although dear to Akbar and a follower of Din-i Ilahi, would never have been allowed to live alongside the women of the harem – Akbar did not even allow his son Salim this liberty. According to Rizvi this could have been the home of two women of high rank, the queen Ruqayya Sultan Begum and Salima Sultan Begum.

The 'stone palaces' dedicated to Birbal of which Abul Fazl speaks were perhaps arranged gardens on some part of the plain, but they cannot now be identified. The present construction, according to Rizvi, is the northern part of the Haram Sarai, while Nath maintains it should more correctly be considered the Mahall-i Ilahi (Palace of the Divinity).

Fatehpur Sikri: the Stables

Directly in front of this, and adjacent to the Raniwas, there opens a spacious rectangular courtyard known locally as the Stables. This is made up of two distinct parts: a closed and covered interior with columns and a courtyard with a verandah on three sides. The fourth side, to the north, is now destroyed, even though it must have been the main entrance. The closed area is divided into 17 spans by simple and rough slabs of stone and by columns which separate each section. The few openings on the 3.81 m high flat roof leave the interior practically in the dark. It was thought that this space was for 17 camels, but there would have been no need to keep them here in such small numbers when much larger spaces in the city allowed for 5,000 to be maintained in optimum conditions. Furthermore, proximity to the harem would have discouraged the use of stables in this position because the traffic of people and animals would have been at the very least inconvenient. The open area originally had 24 spans on each long side and seven on the short side to the south. This was connected with the closed area by means of two entrances and also had two secondary exits to the east and the west. Each span has a simple oblong niche at the centre of the wall and rings of stone parallel to the columns which divide each section. This has led to a theory that these are horse stables, but this seems impossible because the stone rings are not at the centre of each cubicle so they could have been used only to divide one section from another by means of curtains, and not for tying horses to. There is not even space for arranging foraging or other material for the horses. Indeed, the floor has no slope, necessary for cleaning stables. However, the fact that the verandahs are divided uniformly in recesses and that each of them can be separated from the others by means of curtains hung between the rings of stone attached to the walls and the respective pillars has led Nath to conclude that the complex represents a series of stands for a bazaar, with the central niche used for displaying wares.

Nath also suggests that the interior of the complex constituted the Mina Bazar (Fantasy Bazaar), which, according to Abul Fazl, took place every third holy day of each month and was reserved for the ladies of the imperial harem and the women of other men who were able to acquire the wares of all the best merchants in order to show their wondrous things to the emperor.

The exterior complex was the Shahi Bazar (the Emperor's Bazaar) which was also held periodically for the guests of the harem. This would explain the vicinity of the entire complex to the palace itself. It is not impossible, however, as Rizvi maintains, that the Stables might actually have been the homes of women of lower social rank, each residing in individual cubicles separated by means of a curtain attached to the rings, or even the *tosha khana*, the clothes, cloth and furniture warehouse. However, examples of stables alongside the harem, which were inspected daily by the king, are to be found in Persian and Mughal buildings.

Fatehpur Sikri: Maryam House

Not far from the entrance to the harem in a north-easterly direction stands a small single-storey building surmounted by a beautiful *chhapparkhat*, a small pavilion supported by corbelled pillars and with a pyramidal roof, known as the House of Maryam. It is not connected with any other structure by means of a covered passage, but it rises majestically and independently in its own small courtyard which faces north. Its plan is singular, being made up of an oblong central hall surrounded on three sides (east, north and west) by a high colonnaded verandah, and three small quadrangular spaces on the southern side. The central hall has a high ceiling, wide openings to the sides and niches on the perimeter wall, and it opens pleasantly on the verandah which is organized on a lower level; on the upper level there are another three rooms, while on the northern side of the terrace is a pavilion covered by a curtain roof, which follows a set type of the period as is confirmed by a miniature of the *Babur Nama*, now in the State Museum of Oriental Art in Moscow. Outside, a wide oblique *chhajja* surmounted by carved corbels provides pleasant shade all around the building.

The most striking characteristic of this graceful building is that originally it was completely painted both inside and out with figurative scenes directly on the surface of the stone, without plaster, as in the Khwabgah, apart from the floral motif frieze that surrounds the Persian verses of Faizi arranged all round the room. These figurative paintings are traced with strong and lively designs and seem like enlargements of typical Akbari miniatures. The preferred subjects are fights between elephants, hunting and battle scenes, tournaments and architectural landscapes. There are also some mysterious scenes, such as in the emperor's bedroom, with Akbar in the jungle and some winged figures, similar to angels, which led nineteenth-century guides to identify it as representing the Christian annunciation and original sin. Instead it seems very probable that these are episodes taken from the *Hamza Nama*, a poem of Persian origin which was extremely popular in the Mughal court and for which Akbar had commissioned illustrations more than once. The dominant colours are deep blue and red, invariably used with gold and creating an extremely rich effect. In fact because of these large expanses of gold the building is popularly known as the Sunahra Maqan (Golden House) or the Rangin Mahall (Painted House). As well as the paintings, the building has a series of drawings carved on the corbels and the beams of the *chhajja* including rows of goslings, *kirtimukha* and elephants. Surprisingly, some small figures which were extremely important in Hindu mythology seem to have escaped the attention of the Muslim supervisors – Rama and Hanuman are found on the corbels of the northern façade of the building. Nevertheless, it must be remembered that Akbar had great respect for the Hindu epic, so much so that he ordered the translation into Persian and the miniature illustration of the *Mahabharata* and the *Ramayana*. Rama and Hanuman were the heroes of the latter epic.

The presence of these reliefs and the paintings excludes the possible use of this building as the private home of a queen such as Maryam al-Zamani (Mary of the Times), mother of Prince Salim, who could never have lived in a place so lacking in protection and secrecy. Nevertheless, Rizvi thought that this was the private residence of Maryam Maqan, Akbar's mother and equal in rank to Mary, who retired here perhaps with Akbar's daughter, Gulbadan Begum. Nath maintains on the other hand that the small building must have been a *baithak* (sitting room) which Akbar used when he received his painters, poets and musicians. Indeed, this building would have been used for cultural purposes in the same way that the Diwan-i Khass was used for affairs of state.

Fatehpur Sikri: Rang Mahall

The Rang Mahall, another building in the royal complex, was built some distance away, to the west of the *jami masjid*, some time between 1565 and 1570. For much part ruined, it was constructed of red sandstone with five interior courtyards, of which just one survives with apartments arranged on four sides and an arched portal with two pedestals (*chowki*) in the northern corner. There are fine verandahs with three apertures (*tibara*) which open on two-storey sitting rooms (*duchhatti*) and on internal closed rooms (*kotha*). Sculpted corbels and extremely simple *chhajja* complete the complex which, from as much as can be discerned, must have been extremely functional and equipped with all the annexes necessary for a residential building. It is possible that Akbar's wife spent her confinement here while pregnant with Prince Salim, or perhaps with the second-born, Shahzada Sultan Murad, born in 1570.

Fatehpur Sikri: Stone Masons' Mosque

The Stone Masons' Mosque (Masjid Sangtarashan) is the oldest building in the 'Sacred Complex' (Sahn-i Ibadat) of Fatehpur Sikri. Built in red sandstone on a part of the rock where, originally, in a semi-natural cave, the pious Shaikh Salim Chishti lived, it is made up of an open courtyard measuring some 24 x 17 m and a prayer hall almost 17 x 6 m. It is without *riwaq* and minarets and has a modest entrance porch on its eastern side. The sanctuary is made up of an oblong hall divided into two bays parallel to the *qibla* wall with a flat roof supported by both octagonal and square pillars. The only decoration inside is represented by the *torana* shape of three of the seven *mihrab* that mark the *qibla* wall, similar to those of many Gujarati mosques which obviously were the inspiration for the workers from that region who probably worked on the mosque.

The extreme simplicity of the interior contrasts with the rich decoration of the façade, comprising a series of snake corbels decorated with *jali* slabs in geometric and floral designs which support a wide *chhajja* and provide the façade with a majestic and lively aspect. These corbels, characteristic of the *mandapa* of Hindu temples, were also widely diffused in Gujarat, executed both in wood and in stone, and it is from them that examples such as this mosque and the tomb of Salim Chishti are derived. Nevertheless, their most direct prototypes can be traced to the Great Mosque and the Shazadi-ki *rauza* at Chanderi (see p. 142), both from the end of the fifteenth century. Even if the Masjid Sangtarashan was commissioned by Akbar before he decided on the construction of Fatehpur Sikri, and was not erected by the stone masons as the guides maintain, there is no doubt that its builders must have come from Gujarat because the building 'both in spirit and in form is a Gujarati mosque in miniature'.[16]

The Salim Chishti mausoleum at Fatehpur Sikri is built completely in white Makrana marble, in contrast to the rest of the buildings in the complex which are red sandstone.

FATEHPUR SIKRI: *JAMI MASJID*

The nearby *jami masjid* is, by contrast, the largest and most majestic religious building in the city. Built, according to the sources, over a long period, it was certainly completed in 1571-2, as the inscription on its door attests, which goes on to praise it for its elegance, 'second only to the mosque of Mecca'. Contemporary authors wrote that there was no equal to it in the inhabited world and travellers of the time confirmed that it was the most wonderful mosque in all the East. Jahangir himself, known as an art lover, called it one of the greatest monuments of his father's reign. Again, as is stated in the inscription, Akbar built this mosque for the shaikh, like the previous one, and as a monastic school for the disciples of the saint (*khanqah*).

The site on which the mosque stands is higher than the rocky plain on which the city sits, and since the site is so steep a high plinth supported by arches had to be built to provide a level surface. On this platform the beautiful mosque was placed – one of the largest and most fully ornamented in the world, measuring 165.20 x 133.60 m externally. Only at the end of the nineteenth century was it surpassed in size, by Taj al-Masajid (Crown of the Mosques), built at Bhopal by Shah Jahan Begum.

Completely in red sandstone, it has a *sahn* 130 m long from north to south by 165 m from east to west, surrounded by pillared porches which support wide cuspidated arches. These are surmounted by wide *chhajja*. The massive whole is lightened by a series of *chhatri* arranged rhythmically on the parapet. The prayer hall, which measures 87.8 x 19.8 m and is divided into various sections, of which the central one is 12.5 m square, is covered by a huge dome, flanked by two cupolas and with ribs inside similar to those of the great mosque of Champanir and has on its *qibla* wall a splendid *mihrab*, richly decorated on the borders by an inlaid mosaic of stone and glazed tile with engraved and painted inscriptions in azure and gold. It is flanked by two smaller *mihrab* with the same splendid decoration. The intradoses of the arches of the *mihrab*, the squinches of the dome and all the other arches in the sanctuary have lotus-bud borders that decorate them like floral garlands. The lateral sections of the prayer hall *iwan*, each measuring 28.91 × 19.02 m, are made up of a colonnaded salon covered by a flat roof, apart from one square section against the back wall which is domed. The supports of the rest of the ceiling have gracefully worked capitals and corbels. The *qibla* wall is filled with a series of 18 *mihrab*, nine for each section, of which the central ones have a slightly larger and taller arch than the others, but they are all equally ornate in their decoration with mosaic inlay and glazed tiles as well as carved and painted inscriptions. The interior of the prayer hall is lushly painted with stylized floral drawings, traced directly on the stone without plaster so that this mosque is in fact one of the most richly decorated Muslim places of worship in the world. At the two extremities of the sanctuary there is a series of five rooms where the ladies' galleries were arranged.

The façade of the prayer hall is dominated by a large central *iwan* flanked by two arches shaded by a wide *chhajja* supported by fine corbels and crowned by a series of small *chhatri*. If the large *iwan* recalls the Atala Mosque of Jaunpur, the exteriors of the domes echo Lodi designs, while the internal ribs are reproductions of those in the *jami masjid* at Champanir.

At the centre of the spacious courtyard there is a huge pool for ritual ablutions while at the north the tombs of Shaikh Salim, Islam Khan, the Chishti family and the ladies (Zenana Rauza) are all lined up.

There are two entrances to the mosque: the oldest, called the Emperor's Gate (Badshahi Darwaza) is at the centre of the eastern side of the courtyard and was used by Akbar to reach the shrine. It is a simple structure dominated by a central *iwan* with lateral niches and two heavy *chhatri* on the crenellated crown. Built in red sandstone, it is decorated with simple squares of cut mosaic. The southern gate, originally probably similar to the northern gate, was rebuilt by Akbar in 1573 to celebrate his victory over Gujarat, as the commemorative inscription records. Imposing, grandiose and over several floors with wide halls, small rooms, passages and stairways, all arranged on the two sides of the majestic *iwan*, this is a complete monument in itself. The Magnificent Gate (Buland Darwaza; see p. 207) is 40.84 m high and rises from a stepped platform 12.8 m high which takes the total height to 53.64 m. The southern façade is dominated by an immense *iwan* within a rectangular 'panel' crowned by 13 *chhatri* in front of three larger *chhatri*. The two lateral wings are lower and receding and are opened by deep niches broken in their turn by bands of small arches and finished at the corners by extremely slender turrets terminating in pinnacles. The interior part of the portal presents three arched entrances and a two-storey parapet designed in such a way as to harmonize with the arches and colonnades of the mosque with which it is joined. In truth, the Buland Darwaza impinges somewhat on the surrounding buildings and upsets the balance of the sacred complex. However, its grandiosity was without a doubt the intended effect. Similarly, its positioning on the southern side of the *sahn* – however open to criticism, because it was out of alignment with the shrine – is in order for it to face Gujarat, the conquest of which was the reason behind the construction of the gate. At the same time, the gateway had to represent the magnificence of its creator and the greatness of the state and the epoch to which it belonged. The Persian inscriptions in *nastaliq* that are inscribed on the northern side include this one near the courtyard: 'Said Jesus Christ, blessing upon him, the world is a bridge so pass over it and do not build on it ... It is also that the world is but for a moment, so spend it in worship, the remainder of life is worthless.' Curiously, in this fairly long inscription there is no mention of the name of the Prophet Muhammad and, equally curious, the saying attributed to Christ comes not from the New Testament but is a precept of Sufism of which Akbar in later life professed to be a follower. Perhaps in order to calm any suspicion of heterodoxy attached to the mosque, some years later Shah Jahan had a plaque fixed to the western wall which carries an inscription with the names of Allah, Muhammad, Abu Bakr, Umar, Uthman, Ali, Hasan and Husain.

Fatehpur Sikri: Salim Chishti mausoleum

The small but very beautiful tomb of Shaikh Salim Chishti (see p. 219) is situated in the quadrangle of the *jami masjid* near the Zenana Rauza, in front of the Buland Darwaza. It has a square plan (14.63 m each side) with an entrance on the southern side and is built completely in Makrana white marble which contrasts notably with the rest of the complex in red sandstone. The main hall, which contains the sarcophagus of the saint closed within an ebony structure inlaid with mother-of-pearl, is also square, measuring 4.88 m each side, and is covered by a slightly pointed dome. Around the tomb chamber is a spacious verandah divided on each side into square spans, each resting on pillars and covered by slabs arranged to form a 'lantern' roof. The spaces between the pillars on all the external sides, except for the entrance to the south, are filled with fine *jali* with geometric designs which lend the verandah a peaceful atmosphere and beautiful silence which is perfectly in harmony with the sacred nature of the space.

Outside, a spacious *chhajja* runs round the building, lending it a soft and pleasant shadow. The wide cornice rests on snake corbels of delicate and elegant manufacture and refined detail. The spaces between the sinuous curves are filled with extremely fine *jali* in geometric or stylized floral designs with a small teardrop pendant at the upper and lower extremities, and a *semichakra*, a wheel-shaped ornament, on the crown. The soft luminescence of the marble seems to transform these motifs into gently carved ivory and there is no doubt that they were created by extremely skilled Gujarati craftsmen who had already given such a good account of themselves in making the beautiful open-work slabs for the mosques of Sidi Sayyid and Shah Alam at Ahmedabad. Similar snake corbels of a more simple style, but with the same purely ornamental function, had been used in the Shazadi-ka *rauza* at Chanderi and were again derived from Gujarati originals. The tomb of Shaikh Salim Chishti includes other Hindu motifs, such as the *padma* (lotus flowers) that appear on the pinnacles of the arches, and the *kirtimukha* on the base of the pillars. A corbel in the north-western corner of the building has a curious *satkona* (six-pointed star) design made out of six interwoven serpents which are joined in a complicated but harmonious fashion around a central point. The animals' coils are curved in such an elegant way that they reveal a perfect understanding between the artist and the subject represented. There is no doubt that this *naga-pasha* motif was made by an indigenous artist and that – more than a mere ornamental motif – it represents a Tantric symbol used by Akbar as a good-luck charm. Simplified *satkona* are found in other of the sovereign's monuments such as Humayun's mausoleum (see p. 197), the Delhi Gate at the Agra Fort, the Jahangiri Mahall, on a door leading to the *zenana* at Fatehpur Sikri and even on a *mihrab* on the north aisle of the *jami masjid* in the city itself. This feature on the tomb of the shaikh, however, is unique in Indian Muslim art and is much more valid for its own vigour and the perfection of its manufacture than for 'the symbolism which Akbar wanted to inscribe in stone for posterity'.[17] The decoration of the mausoleum is completed by a great number of inscriptions, many in Arabic, with quotations from the Koran and the Prophet's Hadiths. These are inscribed into the marble in *naskhi* characters and occasionally are painted in gold on a blue background or in green and a chocolate colour. They are intertwined with garlands of leaves and flowers, almost in imitation of the illuminated pages of a manuscript Koran.

The interior of the tomb chamber is also profusely decorated from the skirting to the domed ceiling with paintings executed on a layer of plaster thrown on to the surface of the stone. These represent naturalistic and stylized floral motifs traced with much vigour and painted in pleasant, lively colours. In terms of style, it would seem to belong to the period of Shah Jahan. Indeed, not all of the mausoleum can be attributed to Akbar's time. We know that the shaikh died in 1571 and that within a decade his mausoleum had been completed. But the rich marble decoration of the verandah and the exterior cannot be dated to 1581. In that period marble was used parsimoniously, purely as a decoration on red sandstone, as seen in Humayun's mausoleum and the Jahangiri Mahall. The burial chamber has a brick skeleton frame and interior finishing in stone with marble only on the skirtings. We can therefore hypothesize that Akbar had it built completely in red sandstone and that only later were the verandah, the entrance porch and the exterior walls covered in marble. Jahangir's memoirs speak expressly of this change which was carried out under the artistic direction of Qutb al-Din Kukaltash Kuban, his foster brother and grandson of the shaikh. It must have taken place between 1605 and 1607 when Kuban was killed by Sher Afkun, first husband of Nur Jahan. It is not improbable that similar snake corbels, but in red sandstone, decorated the exterior of the monument (an earlier example is found in the Stone Masons' Mosque) but were removed and replaced by the much more refined corbels that we can admire today and with which Jahangir sought to improve his father's work. However, it is also possible that Shah Jahan contributed to the project, especially given the ornate work in hard stone which decorates the base panels.

The nearby tomb of Islam Khan, much more modest in construction than that of the Sufi saint, stands on a platform of red stone and is enclosed by perforated slabs of stone, partially open at the front. It is surmounted by a hemispheric dome which in its turn is surrounded by 36 small, domed kiosks.

Among the buildings not included in the three principal groups are the houses attributed to Abul Fazl and Faizi. The first is on one floor with a verandah with three barrel vaults, the second is over two floors, again including a verandah, this time with five spans. The caravanserai is also outside the three main groups, as is a building with four terraces, together with the Hathi Pol and the Hiran Minar.

The Hathi Pol owes its name to the two elephants that formed a sort of triumphal arch (*torana*) with their intertwined trunks. It constituted the official gate to the royal complex and allowed access to the Hiran Minar. Now the trunks and the heads of the elephants are lost and only the lower parts of the sculptures on their pedestals remain. Since keeping elephants was a royal prerogative, to decorate gates with their representation either painted or carved was common practice in Rajasthan, from where Akbar must have taken the idea.

FATEHPUR SIKRI: HIRAN MINAR
The Hiran Minar (Tower of the Antelope) rises to over 21 m on a massive octagonal plinth which rests on a square platform measuring some 22 m each side and 3 m

The Hiran Minar (Antelope's Tower) at Fatehpur Sikri is decorated with elephant tusks. Suggestions as to the building's function range from a lighthouse to a road marker.

in height. It is octagonal to 3.9 m and thereafter is circular and is interrupted by a platform supported by stalactite corbels on which an octagonal *chhatri* rests crowned by a graceful dome which was entirely decorated with paintings in stylized designs. The minaret is built entirely in red stone with decoration in grey stone and is ornamented with a unique fixture of elephants' tusks in stone which protrude from the cylindrical shaft and are arranged vertically in 15 rows. It is not impossible that originally these were in fact in ivory and came from elephants that died fighting or in battle.

Opinion is divided on the function of this building. Some have suggested that it is a type of lighthouse which shone at night with hundreds of flares hanging from the tusks. Others believe it to be a special *kos minar* (pillars that mark the sections of principal roads). Yet others consider it to be a look-out tower over the area below where polo was played and elephant fights took place. Akbar was particularly fond of this last pursuit. Indeed, regarding the *kos minar* Abul Fazl states that they were usually decorated with antelopes' horns, which could give substance to the theory that the Hiran Minar was in fact a Hathi Minar, or rather a *kos minar* dedicated to elephants, given that it was decorated with elephants' tusks. Its name was perhaps given later by Jahangir who made the nearby polo field a sanctuary for antelope which he caught.[18]

Fatehpur Sikri: other buildings

Among the buildings that have disappeared, the mythical nine-storey Nau Mahall should be mentioned. Together with various pavilions and kiosks along the banks of the lake, it was taken apart and sold piece by piece by quarrymen over the centuries.

Water was very important at Fatehpur Sikri, both as a necessary feature of life and from the symbolic point of view, as it signified well-being, life and happiness. Great feats of hydraulic engineering were achieved under Akbar, among them rose gardens, kiosks and pavilions, baths of various sizes, together with the Gujarati-designed *baoli* which provided this precious element to all the buildings.

Akbar's building activity did not end with his leaving Fatehpur Sikri. He built forts and gardens in Kashmir (Nasim Bagh) and in the Punjab (Alan Khas Bagh), palaces, mausoleums and hydraulic works at Lahore and Agra and in many other places in his immense empire. All of these buildings reflect his eclectic taste which spread and became in turn a classic style.

Gardens and hydraulic works

The Nasim Bagh of Srinagar was the first of the terraced gardens built by the Mughals in Kashmir, but it is no longer extant. At Sirhind, on the other hand, there survives one of the oldest gardens in the Punjab, the Amm Khass Bagh, planned by one of Akbar's superintendents, Sultan Hafiz Rakhna of Herat, between 1556 and 1580. As well as the garden this includes a palace and a caravanserai. Divided into three parts and surrounded by a high wall with fine entrances, it reproduces the classic plan of the Persian *char bagh* and is enriched with fruit trees, bathing pools with central platforms, fountains and waterfalls, all supplied with water from various wells which are still in place. It was visited by Father Monserrate and then by other Western visitors such as Ralph Fitch and Father Manrique. Jahangir had it restored in 1617 and ordered that the trees that did not provide shade should be replaced with others more suitable for that purpose. He also had various baths, kiosks and graceful pavilions built. The most beautiful buildings, however, were added by Shah Jahan who stayed there for the first time in 1628 and on other occasions after that. The magnificent Shish Mahall dates from Shah Jahan's time, with its small Bengali vaults (*bangaldar*), dressed inside with bright glazed tiles. So, too, do the Daulat Khana-i Khass and the Khwabgah, private apartments containing the bedroom of the emperor; the *jharoka mubarik* (open-work balcony) and various *mehtabi chabutana* (platforms on the bathing pools to enjoy the moonlight). Another garden, now disappeared, was at Kalanaur, where Akbar was crowned emperor. All that is left is a brickwork platform known as Takht-i Akbari (Akbar's Throne).

Other hydraulic works of Akbar's time include the *baoli* of the Haryana, one of which was built at Narnaul by Ali Jan and is at the centre of a complex called Mirza Ali Jan Ka Takbat. At Narnaul there is also a palace, the Jal Mahall, a fine structure over two floors and picturesquely situated at the centre of a huge artificial lake. With a square plan (17 m each side), it consists of a central space surrounded on the four sides by a deep verandah and with two-floored square rooms at the corners. The parapet is enriched by a deep *chhajja* which, as usual, serves to shade the strong light from outside. On the roof there are four fine corner *chhatri* which are square, while at the centre there is an octagonal platform covered by a dome resting on eight red sandstone pillars. It is accessible by means of steps and must have been used to enjoy the fresh air and the view of the lake. The external walls are decorated with *iwan* which are deep at the centre and carry traces of *muqarnas* and niches to the sides. Inside can be seen the remains of graceful painted decoration. An inscription attributes the palace to Shah Quli Khan, with the date 1590.

Narnaul: Shah Quli Khan mausoleum and pavilion

Shah Quli Khan, governor of Narnaul for 42 years, was considered in Akbar's time as second only to his guardian Bairam

Above The mausoleum of Shah Quli Khan, governor of Narnaul. The inscription over the entrance dates the tomb to 1574–5.

Opposite A pavilion in the middle of a dried up artificial lake near the Shah Quli Khan mausoleum at Narnaul. The area was originally designed as a pleasure complex.

Khan. His tomb stands within a wide enclosure preceded by a gate, known locally as Tripolia, erected approximately a decade after the tomb itself, in 1588-9. The gate is a three-storey structure with sharply tapering rubble walls covered with a thick layer of plaster. Two wide flights of lateral steps lead directly to the third floor, which consists of a central room surrounded by a verandah and decorated with paintings, together with four smaller spaces at the corners.

The mausoleum has an octagonal plan and rises to the north-east of the gate on a huge platform which is also octagonal and each side of which measures 11.5 m. Each façade is opened by a niche culminating in a pointed arch together with windows adorned with *jali*. Red sandstone panels and blind arched niches complete the exterior decoration even on the high octagonal drum, which is decorated by merlons with representations of flowers; this in turn supports the fine, slightly compressed dome which terminates in an upside-down lotus flower. Inside, the tomb is dressed with marble on the walls while the dome has painted red and green floral designs. The inscription over the entrance dates the tomb to 1574-5. Built 25 years before the death of Shah Quli, it was conceived of as a pleasure pavilion, like the Iranian ones, and likewise it had a garden all round it. Near by, in the middle of an artificial lake, now dry, is an elegant pavilion with a projecting *chhajja* which runs all around it.

Another similar tomb is the one built for Mirza Muzaffar Husain (died 1603) in Delhi, known as Bara Batashewala Mahall.

Other buildings at Bahlolpur, Jhajjar and Thanesar

The tombs of Husain Khan and his son, Bahadur Khan, at Bahlolpur, some 200 km to the south-west of Lahore, are also considered to be from Akbar's time. These two structures are similar, with octagonal plans and covered by domes supported by drums. In the first tomb the dome has now collapsed; the façades are divided by deep arches arranged over two floors. In the tomb of Bahadur Khan, on the other hand, there is just one large arch which occupies the entire surface of each side of the octagon, surrounded by arched blind niches.

A group of seven tombs connected with funeral mosques or *idgah* is to be found at Jhajjar, not far from Delhi. These have a severe aspect that relates them to earlier Lodi examples. Almost all these tombs are built in local stone known as *bichhwa kankar* and have red sandstone decoration on their façades with elegant medallions in the shape of lotus flowers on the extradoses of the ogival arches and elsewhere. The oldest tomb, belonging to Mian Raib, son of Pyara, dates from 1593-4 and carries inscriptions in Arabic and Persian. The connecting mosques are later (1611 and 1629-30) but maintain the same severe and somewhat rigid aspect as the tombs.

The Chiniwali Mosque of Thanesar, north of Delhi on the road to Lahore, by contrast, owes its name to its lively decoration in glazed tile with floral designs. This has now been lost for the most part. The mosque is set at the northern extremity of the main bazaar and stands on a high platform containing various cells used as workshops to help in maintenance. The prayer hall, divided into three spans, is covered with low domes, and the façade is enclosed within two short octagonal minarets, one of which still carries an inscription that dates it to 1565–6.

Among the palaces that Akbar built, his contemporaries Abu-al Fazl and Nizam al-Din noted the palace at Nagarcain (City of Rest), near modern-day Kakrauta, not far from Agra. Described as a place of pleasure, rich in elegant buildings and with a field for playing polo, the king enjoyed going there to hunt or rest in its natural beauties. However, it has completely and mysteriously disappeared. Indeed, Badaoni, one of the court historians, after having defined it as 'one of the wonders of the world', says, 'Of the city and its buildings there remains no trace, its site has become a level plain.'[19] It is probable that the city, once destined to become Akbar's capital, was abandoned shortly afterwards for the construction of Agra and that its buildings were used as building material for the new enterprise. In this way the buildings that remained soon disappeared, as in many other abandoned cities, including, in part, Fatehpur Sikri.

BAYANA

At Bayana, too, there are some Mughal constructions including a graceful Jajri (Water) Pavilion and a tomb known as Kale Khan Gumbad. These are markedly Akbarian in character.

FORTS

Much more long-lasting, however, were the forts that the sovereign built in a perfect chain of defences for his huge empire, stretching from Attock on the western frontier, to Allahabad and Cuttack on the eastern side. They include the forts at Gwalior, Chittorgarh, Ranthambor, Mandu, Champanir, Chunar, Kalinjaor, Rohtas and others; all heavy structures and unassailable thanks to their position. In 1578 Habash Khan built a mosque in the Rohtas fort similar to that built by Haibat Khan, a general of Sher Shah Sur. The plan of the mosque has three spans, covered by three domes; the façade is opened by three *pishtaq*, the central one being higher. Not far away there are some small tombs, one of them belonging to Saqi Sultan (died 1579) which is virtually laid out as a large *chhatri*.

In the nearby city of Hajipur, Makhsus Khan built a mosque dated 1586–7. It was badly damaged by an earthquake in 1934, but the interior seems to have maintained more or less its original form. That it follows the local Suri-Afghan building tradition is evident from its design, but there is also evidence of Bengali influence, due to the close ties between Hajipur and Bengal under the Husain Shahi sovereigns.

MUGHAL INFLUENCE IN HINDU BUILDINGS

There were some Rajput nobles at the court of Akbar who played an important part in the construction of palaces, mosques and even Hindu temples that were clearly inspired by Mughal models. One of them was the powerful Raja Man Singh of the Kacchawahas, whose daughters had become the wives of Akbar. Man Singh, who was governor first of Bihar and then of Bengal, had palaces built in the capitals of these provinces, namely Rohtas and Rajmahal. The palace at Rohtas, which was completed in 1596, equalled the imperial palaces in its grandeur: it measured 200 x 185 m and, like the palace at Fatehpur Sikri, was composed of two distinct areas, the administrative quarters and the private quarters. In the former, besides the various public and private buildings, was the *jharoka* overlooking the quadrangle in front of the main administrative building. The style of the Hall of Private Audiences, and of all of the other buildings, resembles the style of the main buildings at Fatehpur Sikri. The part that was reserved for the governor's private use includes the residential quarters, the *zenana* and several *hammam*.

The Hindu temples that are reminiscent of Mughal constructions are the Govinda Deva at Brindavan and the Jagat Shiromani at Amber.

RAJMAHAL: *JAMI MASJID*

At Rajmahal in Bengal, first named Rajanagar and then Akbarnagar, as we are told by Farid Bhakkari,[20] Man Singh built the grandiose *jami masjid*. Instead of repeating the local building types, this mosque is inspired by the one at Fatehpur Sikri, though the large *pishtaq* in the prayer hall and the arcades facing on to the courtyard are more reminiscent of the Baburi Mosque at Panipat (see p. 184).

NAGAUR: HUSAIN QULI KHAN MOSQUE

Another very powerful *raja*, Husain Quli Khan, built a large mosque at Nagaur, dated 1564–5. Unlike the mosque at Rajmahal, this one makes greater use of local styles, for example in the *minbar* which closely resembles the ones in the *jami masjid* at Mandu (see p. 133) and Chanderi (see p. 141).

At Ajmer, where Akbar had gone on 14 pilgrimages to the *dargah* of Muin al-Din Chishti, several dignitaries built houses and gardens for themselves, as well as gates in the city walls and a mosque, named the Akbari Mosque, near the southern entrance to the *dargah*. The large *pishtaq* that dominates the entrance to the prayer hall and the decorative inlay in

Akbar (1556–1605)

Left The Khale Khan Gumbad, a characteristically Akbarian tomb at Bayana.

Opposite The domed Jajri (Water) Pavilion at Bayana.

coloured stones remind us of the mosques of Humayun in Kachpura and of Akbar at Fatehpur Sikri. In 1570–71 Ismail Quli Khan had a large portal (19.5 m high and 5 m wide) built at the entrance to the sanctuary of Sayyid Husain Khing Sawar, on a hill overlooking the *dargah* of Muin al-Din. The excessive height of the portal compared to its width makes it look somewhat out of proportion as it stands out austerely above the sanctuary with its single, pointed archway and its two small *chhatri* on top.

1. A. Petruccioli, *Fatehpur Sikri: città del sole e delle acque*, Rome 1988, p. 92.
2. *Tuzuk-i Jahangiri*, cf. S.A. Rizvi and V.J. Flynn, *Fatehpur Sikri*, Bombay 1975, p. 14.
3. Father Antonio Monserrate, *Commentary on his Journey to the Court of Akbar*, translated by J. S. Hoyland, London 1922.
4. Monserrate, *op. cit.*, p. 201.
5. Petruccioli, *op. cit.*, p. 47.
6. Asher maintains that Akbar held the *jharoka darshan* from the balcony of the Daftar Khana: Asher, *op. cit.*, p. 62.
7. R. Nath, *History of Mughal Architecture*, vol. 2, New Delhi 1985, p. 234.
8. *Ibid.*, p. 171.
9. S. K. Banerjee, 'Turkish Sultana House of Fatehpur Sikri', in *A Historical Outline of Akbar's Dar-ul-Khalifat, Fatehpur Sikri, Journal of Indian History*, 21 (1942), pp. 198–215.
10. S. A. Rizvi and V. J. Flynn, *Fatehpur Sikri*, Bombay 1975, p. 34.
11. Nath, *op. cit.*, p. 232. *Saraparda* is a Persian word meaning the floor of carpets on which the royal tents stood. Amongst the Mughals it referred to the screen of embroidered brocade or velvet which was used to separate the private quarters of the royal palace.
12. A more significant example of corbels of this type can be found in the minarets of the mosque of Sidi Beshir at Ahmedabad, dated to the late fifteenth century, cf. E. Koch, '(The) Influence (of Gujarat) on Mughal Architecture', in *Ahmedabad*, ed. by G. Michell and S. Shah, Bombay 1988, pp. 168–85, fig. 182.
13. Petruccioli, *op. cit.*, p. 119.
14. Petruccioli, *op. cit.*, p. 122.
15. Nath, *op. cit.*, p. 218.
16. Nath, *op. cit.*, p. 291.
17. Nath, *op. cit.*, p. 210.
18. Hunting towers were perhaps imitated from Iran, where they were quite common even in very early times. One of them can be seen in a drawing of the 'Amoenitatum Exoticarum' done in 1712 by E. Kaempfer, now in the School of African and Oriental Studies in London. It is the Kallam Minar (*Turris Cornuta*) in Isfahan. Other towers like the one at Fatehpur Sikri are the Chor Minar at Delhi, and the Nim Sarai Minar at Malda, in modern Bangladesh; Koch, *op. cit.*, p. 67.
19. Nath, *op. cit.*, p. 273.
20. Farid Bhakkari, *Dhakhirat al-Khawamin*, 3 vols., Karachi 1961–74, vol. 1, p. 106. It seems that Akbar had ordered the *raja* to change the name of the city because he had understood that his Rajput subject was inclined to claim too much power for himself.

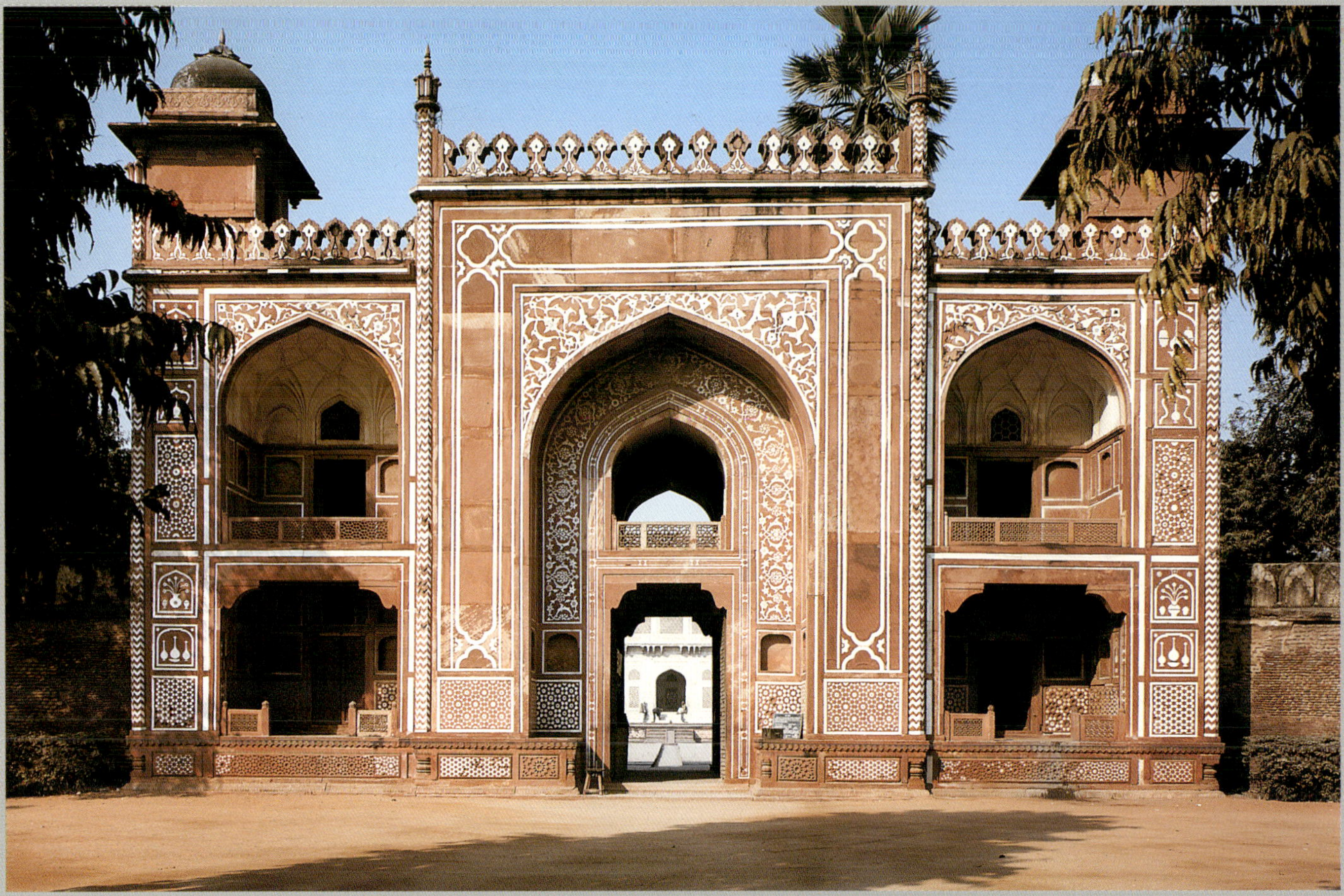

The Classic Mughal Period II
Jahangir (1605–1627)

15

The monumental entrance to the Itimad al-Daula mausoleum at Agra. The tomb could almost be said to represent a direct link between the styles of Akbar and Shah Jahan.

In contrast to his father, Prince Salim, who was elected emperor on 24 October 1605, was not a great builder. His aesthetic predilections in fact took him closer to painting and miniatures. He preferred the creation of gardens and peaceful ornamental follies to palaces and architectural monuments. Nevertheless he encouraged the nobles of his realm to have buildings constructed and gardens laid out, so that he himself could enjoy them. But his favourite wife, Nur Jahan, was a great promoter of public buildings for charitable, religious and funerary purposes. For this reason, in spite of the fact that Jahangir preferred other art forms, architecture was given a substantial boost during his reign, with results of great aesthetic value.

As soon as he reached the throne Salim changed his name to Jahangir (Conqueror of the World) because, as he wrote in his diary, 'The [name] I had recalled an emperor of Rum'.[1] He was alluding to Istanbul, over which a sultan by the name of Salim had just reigned. For several years Prince Salim had made his father's life a misery with continuous rebellions stemming from his impatience to succeed to the throne. In 1601, although not daring to meet Akbar on the battlefield, he rose against him openly and the women of the imperial family had to work hard to establish peace between father and son (1604). On his deathbed Akbar asked his dignitaries to pass the sword of Humayun to Salim and bestow the imperial turban on him, although he probably would have preferred to nominate Khusrau, Salim's son, as his heir. Jahangir was then 37 years old.[2]

Intelligent and refined, energetic in the moments that mattered, devout but without fanaticism, Jahangir was not interested in politics but knew intuitively how to find the most talented people to administer the affairs of state while he escaped the weight of these duties and concentrated on his hobbies. He was curious about everything and wanted to be kept informed scrupulously on all experiments. He wrote about the philosophy of this approach in his diaries: 'I don't want to believe that which I cannot see and which lies beyond my own experience.' He was also a passionate observer of nature, particularly flowers and birds. He had rare examples of birds captured so as to be able to examine them closely and describe them so that others could share his wonder and admiration. Indeed, he commissioned some court painters, Mansur in particular, to paint these birds in miniature and insert them into his diary so that they were immortalized.

The painting studios were Jahangir's favourite place, where he spent days scrupulously checking that reality was being reproduced carefully and exactly. Seventy artists worked for Mansur in the section known as 'Nature and Reality', with the job of reproducing all that the sovereign deemed worthy of being recorded. Another section was directed by Bichtir and Abu al-Hasan and concerned itself with 'imperial jollities': Jahangir was never satisfied with it. A third section was charged with copying 'the most beautiful portraits from the entire world'. Soon, under Jahangir's guiding hand and his incessant spur, Indian painting reached the heights of expression with subtle realism and lively use of colour.

However, this sovereign's good qualities were often overshadowed by the hereditary vice of the house – alcoholism. At times this made him commit cruel and sadistic acts, as unpredictable as they were merciless. From boyhood, as his diary testifies, he drank wine and soon progressed to strong spirits in addition to two grammes of opium daily in pill form. To this clear contravention of Koranic laws, Jahangir added yet another: he had his own image placed on his first coins which show him raising a cup of liquor.[3]

Jahangir had the good fortune to marry, in 1611, the beautiful and cultured Persian, Nur Jahan. She was able and full of energy and took upon herself the affairs of state when her husband was under the influence of opium and alcohol. Nevertheless, Jahangir never totally relinquished supreme control of the government with all final decisions in matters of great importance going before him.

After the rapid territorial expansion under Akbar, Jahangir's reign represented a phase of consolidation and reorganization. The campaign against Mewar was concluded victoriously in 1604 thanks to Prince Khurram, and for the first time in history a Maharana bowed to worship the emperor. In Deccan, on the other hand, despite Khurram's successes – he was even granted the title Shah Jahan (Lord of the World) by his father – Nizam Shahi, reinforced by the Abyssinian Maliq Ambar, offered insurmountable resistance (1617). To the north Kandahar was conquered by Shah Abbas (1622). On the whole, however, Jahangir's reign was peaceful. The empire was governed solidly for ten years by a competent cabal: Nur Jahan, her father Itimad al-Daula, her brother Asaf Khan and the prince heir Shah Jahan. (The first born, Khusrau, had rebelled years earlier and had been partially blinded and subsequently held prisoner by the emperor, while the second born, Parviz, had been a disappointment from infancy.) When the precarious agreement between the members of the government fell apart, Shah Jahan was afraid that he would be disinherited by another prince and so for four years he fought against his father.[4] This weakened the empire and prevented the reconquest of Kandahar. Only in 1626, once again in Deccan, did he accept defeat and his father's rule, but this did not prevent a coup at the court under General Mahabat Khan. This was overturned, however, some months later thanks to the able politicking of Nur Jahan; the general was forced to flee. The following year, on 28 October 1627, during the return voyage to Kashmir from Lahore, Jahangir died. He had been ill for some time. Asaf Khan, loyal to the dynasty, had his sister arrested and put Dawar Bakhs, an under-age son of Khusrau, on the throne. This move allowed Shah Jahan to arrive from Deccan and have himself crowned as emperor. The coronation took place on 31 December 1627, but not without a bloodbath which began a painful tradition. From that point onwards successions to the Mughal throne were disputed with arms.

ALLAHABAD: SHAH BEGUM MAUSOLEUM
Despite Jahangir's predilection for painting, his era saw the creation of several remarkable architectural monuments, in particular the mausoleum of his first wife, Shah Begum, the sister of Raja Man Singh and mother of Prince Khusrau. She had commited suicide at the defeat of her rebel son and was buried at Allahabad in a fine tomb designed by Aqa Reza, one of Jahangir's leading artists, in 1606-7. It stands in a pleasant garden, later called Khusrau Bagh, with an imposing bastioned portal in front of it. The tomb itself has three storeys, practically terraced plinths, surmounted by a large *chhatri* under which stands the queen's cenotaph. At the present time the lower level is plain and austere, but in eighteenth-century drawings it and the upper level have fine openwork stone slabs on them. The inscriptions on the tomb, which are entwined with delicate floral arabesques, were carved by Jahangir's greatest calligrapher, Mir Abd Allah Mushkin Qalam, who had previously designed the inscriptions on the king's black throne at Allahabad and on one of Ashoka's pillars, which Jahangir had set up in his father's fort. From that time onwards, the place was called Behistabad (Dwelling of Paradise).

SIKANDRA: MAUSOLEUM OF AKBAR
Jahangir's most important architectural project, however, was the mausoleum of Akbar, at Sikandra near Agra. This building is so grandiose that it took many years to build. Indeed, it was not finished until 1613, eight years after the succession to the throne of the new emperor. Although the site of the building and its general plan were chosen by Akbar, there is no doubt that a large part of the imposing structure was finished under the close supervision of Jahangir. Like Humayun's mausoleum, Akbar's is also situated at the centre of a *char bagh*, surrounded by a perimeter wall opened by four portals, of which the southern one constitutes the main entrance while the others have false doors and were added simply to provide symmetry. Although they are all imposing, the southern entrance is the most impressive and is realized in a hybrid style which includes Persian motifs (the great central *iwan* and the superimposed wide lateral niches) and Hindu motifs (the graceful *chhatri* at the top). The red sandstone of which the building is made is dressed in a fine mosaic of white marble and coloured stone forming elegant geometric and floral designs. The entrance is also equipped with four graceful minarets in white marble that seem to be precursors of those of the Taj Mahall at Agra and which, according to some, precisely because of their close resemblance, were later additions by Shah Jahan to his grandfather's tomb.[5] Beyond the entrance the garden is paved at

The mausoleum of Akbar at Sikandra (completed 1613). Jahangir closely supervised the building of this, his most important architectural project.

the centre, with platforms that widen at the sides of fountains and cisterns distributed at intervals; from these run water channels according to the classic plan of the *char bagh*. The mausoleum itself, in the shape of a truncated pyramid some 30 m high, is composed of five levels, of which the first one, square in plan with sides 105 m long, forms a base for the four upper storeys. The emperor's sarcophagus is contained in a dome-covered central chamber. A vaulted, domed gallery runs all round the top of this huge chamber, the arcades on its outer side have fine *pishtaq* at their centre with a magnificent panelled decoration inlaid with white marble in geometric and arabesque patterns which provide a pleasant contrast to the red sandstone of the rest of the building. The four *pishtaq* lead into vaulted rooms which, according to Father Sebastian Manrique who visited the mausoleum in 1641, housed the 200 readers of the Koran whose job it was to keep watch on the sanctity of the tomb. The most ornate of these rooms is the southern one, from which a long narrow corridor leads to the central burial chamber. The lower part of the walls is inlaid with yellow, black and brown stones, and the rest of the walls and the low, domed ceiling are covered with elegantly carved stucco work painted with floral arabesques. Some beautiful Koranic inscriptions, in gold on a deep blue background, glorify the might of God and describe the gardens of Paradise, a just reward for the true believer.[6] The square room containing Akbar's sarcophagus is almost 18 m high and reaches the level of the third storey. Today it is whitewashed all over, but once it was decorated with paintings which included Christian subjects, such as the Virgin Mary and various angels, according to the testimony of some European travellers.[7] Other chronicles from the end of the seventeenth century praise the richness and beauty of the interior, which was subsequently ravaged by the fury of the Jats when they defiled the tomb of the great Mughal, symbol of the power and prestige of the hated dynasty.[8] Precious stones, silver and gold objects and valuable carpets were all seized and dispersed, and yet the imposing mausoleum-palace still has much of its structural and decorative beauty intact.

Each of the next three storeys that are built on the plinth is smaller than the one below and they have graceful *chhatri* of red sandstone placed at close intervals. The last storey consists of a simple enclosure surrounded by white marble arcades with openwork decoration. At each of the four corners there is a large domed *chhatri*, also of white marble. In the middle of the enclosure there stands a cenotaph of snow-white marble on which the 99 names of Allah are carved within intricate floral patterns to form a marvellous design. Alongside the cenotaph there is a small pedestal where it is said that Shah Jahan, once he had become emperor, had set the Koh-i Nur diamond that he had bought back after Humayun had used it in Persia to pay his army. Legend apart, it is most likely that the pedestal held a lamp. According to Fergusson the terrace must have had a dome over it, which would have formed an apex to the pyramid as well as protecting the delicate fineness of the cenotaph from the elements.

However, according to orthodox practice, the tomb of the believer should be left open to the sky and this is perhaps the reason why there is no roof over Akbar's cenotaph. Asher has advanced an interesting hypothesis concerning the importance that all the Mughals attached to the symbolism of light, suggesting that the exposure of the cenotaph to the light of the sun and moon followed the wishes of Akbar and Jahangir. According to this interpretation, the same wish is expressed in the last verse of the Persian inscription over the entrance to the tomb, which reads: 'May your soul shine like the rays of the sun and the moon in the light of Allah'.[9] Many of the fine inscriptions in this mausoleum were done by one of the greatest calligraphers of the time, Abd al-Haqq Shirazi, better known by the title of Amanat Khan, who was also the author of the inscriptions in the Taj Mahall.

The typology of Akbar's tomb is both unusual and controversial; it also differs from the Timurid models. Although it has quite a lot in common with the Panch Mahall (see p. 216) at Fatehpur Sikri, we must take into account that the function of the two buildings was completely different, as the latter was a palace. Some resemblance can be seen in the contemporary tomb of Shah Begum at Allahabad, or in Sadik Khan's tomb at Dholpur (1596–7), now in ruins but with the same arcaded substructure, a raised platform that once had openwork walls all round it, and *chhatri* at the ends.[10]

Allahabad: Khusrau and Sultan Nisar Begum mausoleums

At Allahabad, not far from Shah Begum's tomb, there is the tomb of his son Khusrau who died in 1622, at the hand, it is generally thought, of his elder brother, the future Shah Jahan. The tomb was probably begun by Khusrau's sister, Sultan Nisar Begum, who had just begun the construction of her own tomb at that very same time. It is a two-storey building with arcaded walls, surmounted by a large hemispherical dome on an octagonal drum, with small *chhatri* at the corners. The interior consists of a single room whose walls are painted with a design of floral patterns, cypresses and verses in Persian expressing the sorrow brought by death. On the dome there is a painted medallion with stars and geometric patterns, similar to the ones in the contemporary tomb of Itimad al-Daula.

The tomb of Sultan Nisar Begum (1624–5), which was never used, is much more impressive. Similar to Khusrau's, it stands on a high plinth which is adorned with panels containing a scalloped arch motif. Inside the plinth there is a small room whose ceiling is painted in vivid colours with stars arranged in concentric circles. This decoration is repeated on the domed ceiling of the main room, while the walls are painted with Persian cypresses, bottles of wine, plants and flowers taken from the European herbals that were very much in vogue at that time, and verses proclaiming that Allah is the only refuge.

Ajmer: pavilions and palace

Further constructions of Jahangir's include the three hunting pavilions (of which only two are left) on Lake Pushkar, near Ajmer. They were built between 1615 and 1616 to celebrate the victory over a Hindu *rana*. They stand facing one another on a large rectangular plinth and consist of a single room with a flat roof and a wide verandah all around it. They resemble the pavilion that Jahangir had built in the Lahore Fort, a sure sign that the prototype was a traditional one.

Another small palace of a similar type, the Chashma-i Nur (Fountain of Light), was built in 1615 near Ajmer. Jahangir was very fond of it and went there often during his three-year stay at Ajmer. In the vicinity of the city the sovereign began to build some other fine pavilions on the Ana Sagar, a lake with a perimeter of 13 km, on whose shores he was wont to spend his nights, by lamplight, in the company of the ladies of the palace. The pavilions were subsequently completed or rebuilt by Shah Jahan, to whom they are now attributed.

The gardens

Jahangir was a great lover of gardens and he greatly admired the ones at Agra, especially Babur's Gul Afshan, nowadays known as Ram Bagh. It was also Nur Jahan's favourite and she had pavilions built there, two of which face each other at the sides of a large pond. The pavilions have pillared verandahs at each end; on the inside, the rooms are decorated with the figures of birds, including the Persian *simurgh*, angels and geometric patterns, all in bright colours. On one wall the figure of a lady in European dress is visible, as is often the case in miniatures of this period. In about 1619–20, at Agra, the emperor also had the Nur Manazil garden built and adorned it with beautiful dwellings, ponds, canals and flowerbeds.

Jahangir's most beautiful gardens, however, were in Kashmir. At Srinagar, where Akbar had built the Hari Parbat Fort overlooking Lake Dal, he had a garden built, as well as restoring part of the city walls and various palaces. The garden was planned by Muhammad Khan on three different levels and the pavilions that embellished it were decorated by the leading court artists. It was given the name of Nur Afzar (Increasing Light) as a tribute to the Mughal fondness for the symbolism of light. In 1620 the sovereign ordered his son, the future Shah Jahan, to dam up a course of water on the banks of Lake Dal. The garden that was built there, one of the most famous of the Mughal period, is, however, the work of Shah Jahan. Other gardens that can be attributed to Jahangir or to his more powerful courtiers are situated not far from Srinagar, near natural springs or watercourses, and they are embellished with plants, flowers and dwellings.

Detail of the front exterior of the Itimad al-Daula, built in 1626 by Jahangir's wife Nur Jahan in honour of her father. The white marble exterior is inlaid with hard and semi-precious stones to form geometric designs.

The Garden of Joy (Nishat Bagh) is one of the gardens on the shores of Lake Dal that were not built by the king. It is attributed to Asaf Khan, Nur Jahan's brother, who is said to have donated it to his brother-in-law since the latter envied it. But it could also have been built by another Asaf Khan, a former governor of Kashmir who was a great botanist and garden-lover. However, the refined nature of its design makes us suspect the hand of Nur Jahan and Jahangir.

It is conceived on a monumental scale and is meant to be viewed from the level of the lake, rising in a continuous progression of terraces to the picturesque backdrop of the mountains behind. The waters flow in an almost continuous play right down to the lake over 12 different levels, one for each sign of the zodiac. Since the Nishat Bagh was not a royal creation with all the connected requirements of court protocol and ceremony, there are only two divisions: the pleasant garden and the terrace of the harem. The main feature is the central watercourse, about 10 m wide. It is formed from a number of canals, each fed by a waterfall from the terrace above. The canals are full of jets of water and each change of level is accentuated by flights of steps, pools with reflections or, a peculiar feature of Nishat Bagh, a number of stone or marble seats on the water's edge. These seats are the perfect complement to the watercourses: they do not block the view, even if one sits on them, while the water running below them refreshes the air and enhances the feeling of peace. This area is flanked by avenues of tall *chenar*; the garden reaches the height of its beauty in autumn when the red and gold of the trees forms a contrast with the blue of the surrounding mountains.

Jahangir had another two gardens built outside the capital of Kashmir, Achabal and Vernag. Both were rich in waters and fruit trees, though today for the most part nothing is left of either of them. When mentioning Achabal, which had still not been completed in 1626–7, Jahangir recalled the charming pavilions, the luxuriant foliage of the trees and the cascades of crystal-clear water that flowed into the canals below and that can still be admired today. Vernag above all, secluded and difficult to reach at the foot of the hills under the Banihal Pass, was much loved by both Jahangir and Nur Jahan. An inscription testifies that it was created in 1609 following a suggestion by the Angel Gabriel: 'Constructed by Haidar, by order of the King of the World, the Paramount Lord of his Age, this canal is a type of the canal in Paradise, this waterfall is the glory of Kashmir.'

Agra: Itimad al-Daula mausoleum
The fame of Nur Jahan – apart from her political energy – ties in to the construction of various works and in particular to a small artistic masterpiece which almost constitutes the link between Akbar's and Shah Jahan's styles.[11]

This is the tomb of her father Ghiyas Beg, bestowed with the title of Itimad al-Daula (Emperor's Pillar) by Jahangir. Ghiyas was first treasurer and then prime minister of the realm and died in 1622. Four years later his daughter built a splendid mausoleum (see pp. 226, 231) for him at Agra with an extremely graceful and exquisitely feminine plan, enclosed within a garden surrounded by walls some 165 m long on each side with entrances in red sandstone.

The building is of modest proportions with a plan some 21 m square and a central structure enclosed within four octagonal towers in the form of minarets and a small pavilion on the summit covered by a harmonious *bangaldar* roof completed by a wide *chhajja*. On each façade of the mausoleum there are three arched openings, while a cornice on fine corbels supports a *jali* balustrade with geometric patterns. The minarets are completed by small hemispheric cupolas resting on small arches supported by eight pilasters. The interior of the ground floor consists of a series of rooms and corridors arranged around a verandah which surrounds a central area containing the cenotaph. The upper compartment is square and is enclosed within grates of extremely fine marble which delicately shadow the two cenotaphs of yellow porphyry which are placed on the polished floor with its geometric patterns.[12]

The decoration of the lower floor consists of paintings with realistic motifs of plants (characteristic small Iranian cypresses) and flowers, bowls and vases, while on the skirtings there are geometric and arabesque designs. While these motifs are clearly inspired by Iranian ones (the family was of Perso-Safavid origin), the ceiling repeats the circles of stars and polychrome geometric patterns that appear in the mosque of Maryam al-Zamani at Lahore, one of Jahangir's works. Outside, the delicate white marble is inlaid with semi-precious stones (lapis lazuli, onyx, jasper, topaz, cornelian) which here, too, form geometric and arabesque designs.[13] The surrounding garden with its stone pavements, water channels (now dry), its plants and its flowers, increases the sense of tranquil serenity that pervades the entire complex.

If this work is to be credited entirely to Nur Jahan's taste, Jahangir is instead responsible for the glazed tile decoration on a part of the perimeter wall of the fort at Lahore.

Lahore: fort
The emperor's palaces in this fort are almost all lost, except perhaps those corresponding to the so-called Jahangir's Quadrangle, which nevertheless were altered during the Sikh era.[14] The sheathing in tiles with scenes of hunting, animal fighting, parades, winged figures and so on, which begins on the wall behind Jahangir's Quadrangle, in fact dates back to the first half of the seventeenth century when this ornamental art was flourishing in India. The decoration continues on the external walls of the Shah Burj, erected some months later by Shah Jahan, and reaches its zenith at the Elephant's Gate, splendidly dressed in tile mosaics, the colours of which are still brilliant and lucid today.

The most important structure built by Jahangir in the Lahore Fort is the Kala Burj, a tower that is not dated but can be traced to 1610 because of the similarity of its decorations with the ones done in the Maryam al-Zamani Mosque in 1611. These are paintings with European subjects (real and fantastic birds and angels) which are arranged in Islamic-type polygons. The angels would seem to refer to the heavenly procession of King Solomon, who is represented as the ideal monarch in the Koran and for this reason was often associated by Muslim rulers with their own kingship. On other occasions, for instance in an inscription in the same fort, Jahangir had compared himself with Solomon in Dignity, thus emphasizing his own role as a demigod.

Lahore: Anarkali mausoleum
Just outside the Lahore Fort there is a fine octagonal tomb, called the tomb of Anarkali, who was perhaps one of Jahangir's wives. Originally the building was situated in a *char bagh*, but later it was altered and changed into a church; later still it housed the Punjab Records Office. On the outside it is in the shape of an irregular octagon, with octagonal towers at its corners that are topped by *chhatri*. On the inside there is a central, domed room that is surrounded by smaller rooms, arranged so as to form a cross and an X-shape. The splendid marble cenotaph, which is inlaid with floral arabesques and the 99 names of Allah in black stone, bears an inscription in which Jahangir declares his great love for the dead woman.[15]

Srinagar: Pattar Mosque
In 1623 Nur Jahan had ordered the erection of a beautiful mosque at Srinagar, called Pattar Mosque (see p. 234) after the stone with which it was built. Apart from the building material, it distinguishes

itself from other Kashmiri buildings by the construction techniques used and its general plan, just like the fort at Hari Parbat which Akbar had built some years earlier, making use of Indian craftsmen because the natives were only skilled at working with wood. The mosque has a unified and severe style; although it maintains the characteristics of the architectonic creations of the capital of the dynasty, it does seem to represent a movement towards a more 'provincial' Mughal style. It has three aisles parallel to the *qibla* wall, each formed of nine bays supported by massive cruciform pillars, and arched or vaulted ceilings with the intricate designs that are typical of the period. This layout is a forerunner of similar buildings by Shah Jahan.

JAJJAR AND NAKODAR: MAUSOLEUMS

Another tomb from Jahangir's time is found among those at Jhajjar (Hasan Shahid, died 1625–6; see p. 235).

At Nakodar, too, on the road between Delhi and Lahore, there are two fine tombs known locally as the Master's (Ustad) and the Scholar's (Shagird), situ-

Above A building in the fort at Lahore. Towards the south are the public and service buildings, while towards the north are the royal palaces, very few of which survive.

Left A detail of the intricate tiled decoration on the walls of Lahore Fort.

ated next to each other and dating from 1612 and 1657 respectively. Both sit on an arched platform, but have different plans that attest to the difference in date of construction. The Ustad's Tomb is an irregular octagon, the Shagird's is square. Both are covered with domes on high drums surrounded by four *chhatri*. The Ustad's Tomb – an inscription allows us to identify the *ustad* as Muhammad Mumin Husain, drummer to Khan-i Khanan – has its wider façades opened with large pointed arches flanked by blind niches and decorated with glazed tiles as in Jahangir's palace at Lahore; the narrower façades are divided into two floors with niches that are smaller, but are equally deep.

CIVIL BUILDINGS AND CARAVANSERAIS
We know from Jahangir's memoirs that on his accession to the throne he ordered the construction of wells and caravanserais at regular intervals along the major roads of his realm, and later the arrangement of *kos minar* along these roads to mark every *kos* (3 km). Most of the buildings are now lost, but some remain and thus allow us to point out the most important features. Two fine caravanserais also belonging to Jahangir's time are situated on the road that once linked Agra and Lahore. This road once had some 20 caravanserais along a 1,030 km stretch, arranged some 32 km from one another. The Nur Mahall Serai is found in the district of Jullemdur and the Doraha in the district of Amritsar.

The best preserved is the caravanserai that carries the name of the wife of the emperor, Nur Jahan. It has a square plan 168 m each side including the octagonal bastions at the corners. The huge internal courtyard is overlooked by 128 rooms built within the arcaded perimeter wall. These small rooms were rented to travellers for a modest fee, although the majority of the caravans preferred to set up camp directly in the centre of the courtyard in the open air; some 2,000 travellers together with their camels and horses could be accommodated. Mughal caravanserais were usually built in brick, but the one named for Nur Jahan was an exception because its beautiful western gate, which is preserved in excellent condition, is entirely dressed with red sandstone from Sikri, over 480 km away. It opens with a fine arch

Above Massive stone pillars form the aisles of the Pattar Mosque (1623) built for Nur Jahan at Srinagar, in Kashmir.

Opposite A tomb at Jhajjar dating from Jahangir's reign.

pointed at the keystone which protrudes from the perimeter wall and dominates the true entrance, which also had a pointed arch. To the sides there are panels with various designs, surmounted by small balconies supported by corbels and covered with small cupolas. The smaller sides of the gate have a triple series of superimposed pointed-arch niches divided by small slender columns which terminate above the crenellated frieze in domed turrets. The extradoses of the arches are decorated with squares that intersect, forming eight-pointed stars filled with lotus buds. Above the gate, to the sides, and above a panel that carries an inscription in Persian with the date of foundation (1618–19 and 1620–21), there runs a frieze with animals in movement or fighting among themselves and floral motifs carved in low relief. This beautiful gateway, extremely unusual for a charitable work such as a caravanserai, is emblematic of the ambitions of Nur Jahan and her wish to imitate the power of her father-in-law, Akbar, by reproducing, in miniature, but in the same shape and with the same materials, the imposing Buland Darwaza at Fatehpur Sikri (see p. 207). The eastern gate is much ruined but still carries traces of painted decoration. Each corner of the caravanserai had three rooms, a larger one and two smaller ones, which are still intact in the south-western corner. The emperor, who visited the building on two occasions, had the three-floored apartment at the centre of the southern side reserved for him, with a huge oblong central salon and with semi-octagonal niches at the sides. Currently this section of the caravanserai is occupied by a school. In the courtyard there is still a well and a small mosque, covered by a dome.

The Doraha Serai, as its name suggests (*darha* means 'two roads'), stands at the intersection of two main roads and, although undated, seems to precede the Nur Mahall by at least a decade. It should therefore date from 1606–11. Like the others of this period, it is built in brick and decorated with coloured tiles (*kashi kari*), an important technique in the Punjabi zone of which Lahore seems to have been the main centre of production. The northern gate of the Doraha Serai has a rather simple design. The wide central arch is flanked by niches arranged on two floors, terminating in pointed arches. At the two extremities there are imposing octagonal keeps, divided into five floors by arched niches arranged within panels and covered by small cupolas. The façade terminates with a series of crenellations, typical in these buildings, but which disappeared after 1630. From close by the glazed tile decoration recalls that of the Ustad's Tomb at Nakodar, a few kilometres from here and very nearly of the same period (1612–13). The general aspect of the façade of the Doraha Serai is also very similar to the gate of the Fatehpur Sikri caravanserai, built by Jahangir between 1606 and 1611 to commemorate his victory over his brother Khusrau.

Shaikhupura: Hiran Minar

A building that was particularly dear to Jahangir, and about which he wrote at length in his memoirs, is the Hiran Minar (Antelopes' Tower; see p. 236), more precisely a complex of hunting buildings that stands at Shaikhupura, some 40 km to the west of Lahore.[16] This consists of a five-storey tower, a *daulat khana* and a *baradari* situated at the centre of a huge artificial pond surrounded by corner pavilions. Jahangir had the complex built between 1607 and 1620 to honour his favourite antelope, Mamsaraj. As Jahangir stated, this animal had no equal in battle with domesticated antelopes and in hunting wild antelopes. The complex was modified some years later by order of Shah Jahan. The high minaret must have served to spy the best areas for the king's amusement and the *baradari* to create an ideal place for peace and meditation. The minaret, circular in form, is tapered towards the top and terminates in a flat covering that carries no sign of a pavilion or lantern. Its base is octagonal, decorated with rectangular panels and arcuated blind niches, and has at its centre an arched entrance reached by means of some steps. The various floors are divided by a projecting border and are perforated with 210 square holes arranged regularly in 14 rows. The heads of hunted animals may have been hung from these holes, according to a strange practice of the Mughal sovereigns; other scholars maintain that they were arranged as nests for wild birds. Inside the minaret is a spiral staircase which is provided with light and air from 11 openings. On the third floor there is a small octagonal room. It is said that the minaret rises above the tomb of Jahangir's favourite antelope and in fact during the excavations at its base in 1959 an antelope's head in red sandstone was found. This was probably an effigy of the original Mamsaraj placed there by Jahangir. There are two other known portraits of antelopes which probably refer to the emperor's favourite animal: one is reproduced in the tile mosaic at Lahore Fort, alongside a keeper who holds it with a leash; the other is in a miniature by Manuhar, the court painter, now in the Victoria and Albert Museum in London.

In front of the large minaret is a huge rectangular pond bordered by a small wall; a raised road leads to the octagonal *baradari* at its centre. At each corner there are square pavilions with low pyramidal roofs and wide *chhajja*. To the north-west there is an arched portal with lateral niches which leads to the *baradari*. At the centre of each side of the pool there are wide inclined ramps with four flights of eight steps that lead into the water. It would seem that these were built to ease the animals' access to the water when they needed to drink. The corner pavilions carry traces of fresco painting in lively colours on the inside, especially on the dome which is decorated with floral motifs in red, yellow and green. The main entrance to the *baradari* is also decorated, both outside and inside. The raised road across the pool rests on 21 pillared arches with a high parapet; halfway along there is a square platform and the road terminates at the centre of the lake with another octagonal platform on which the *baradari* stands, built by Jahangir in 1620 but modified in 1634 by Shah Jahan. It is now a two-storey building with an octagonal pavilion opening on to the terrace, supported by eight arches on pillars and crowned with a graceful dome. At the centre of the ground floor is an octagonal room surrounded by eight communicating spaces, alternately square and oblong with flat or vaulted roofs and with openings above. The perimeter walls are finished in stucco, with small niches and panels decorated with frescoes in lively colours, while the floors are in slabs of red sandstone. A stairway leads to the upper floor, which is modelled after the lower floor but is completed by an arched verandah which runs all round the building. The rich painted decoration, inside and outside, was probably added by Shah Jahan.

SIKANDRA: MARYAM AL-ZAMANI MAUSOLEUM

One of the last buildings erected by Jahangir was a mausoleum for his mother, Maryam al-Zamani, built at Sikandra, not far from Akbar's tomb. This is a square structure, resting on a high plinth with short stairways on its northern and southern sides, at the centre of a fine garden. In each side of the building there is a slightly projecting central archway flanked by

Left The Hiran Minar (Antelope's Tower; 1607–20) at Shaikhupura, near Lahore. The tower formed part of a hunting complex and was one of Jahangir's favourite buildings.

three unequal arches (the central one is wider and higher than the laterals). At the corners there are double arched and pointed niches, superimposed one on the other, and the upper spaces are reached by means of internal stairways. The interior consists of series of compartments and corridors that intersect and are covered by vaults dressed in stucco with stalactite patterns. On the terrace there is the white marble cenotaph resting on a platform and surrounded by fine corner *chhatri* with octagonal plans in red sandstone. Other small, domed pavilions surmount the entrances while the wide *chhajja* that surrounds the entire building is supported by corbels in the shape of horses, but represented without mouths, perhaps for religious reasons. It seems that originally the domes shone with multi-coloured glazed tiles: the façades are decorated with exquisitely carved friezes with inlays of white marble. The tomb, with its relatively unusual interior appearance, is a readaptation of a Lodi-period *baradari*, ennobled through the fine aesthetic taste of Jahangir, who sought to honour his Hindu mother near his father's grand tomb.[17]

LAHORE: MARYAM AL-ZAMANI MOSQUE

In 1611-12 Jahangir also dedicated a mosque at Lahore to his mother. Crowned with a double dome, it is a massive structure in brick which represents the transitional phase between Lodi and Mughal architecture. The Maryam al-Zamani Mosque has two entrances formed out of deeply inset arched portals on the northern and eastern sides, which lead to the main courtyard through a series of steps.[18] The courtyard was once surrounded by a row of cells on the northern and southern sides, of which some traces remain. To the east is a wide platform on which a domed octagonal tomb stands together with some other cenotaphs. At the centre of the courtyard is the apparatus for ritual ablutions. The prayer hall is oblong, divided into five spans by massive pillars and covered by as many domes, of which the central, largest one has a double shell and is erected on a high cylindrical drum. The *mihrab* is decorated by stuccoes with geometric motifs. The façade of the mosque has five archways, of which the principal one is higher and wider than the others, and is decorated with a series of niches, some deeper than others. Both inside and outside, the mosque was covered with plaster, which had originally been decorated with paintings. The most interesting part of the mosque is the decoration inside the dome, with its lovely central medallion from which radiate polygons containing the names of Allah, all worked in stucco, giving the dome a very refined look. This type of decoration was to be repeated often by the Mughals.

DELHI: CIVIL BUILDINGS AND MAUSOLEUMS

Both in and around Delhi there are various buildings that were erected by Jahangir's nobles. One of these, Shaikh Farid Bukhari, even built a whole town, Faridabad, with a mosque and caravanserai. Probably the emperor stayed there sometimes, to devote himself to his beloved hunting parties. In 1608-9 a further embellishment was added to the *dargah* of the saint Chishti Nizam al-Din, in addition to the ones that Akbar had carried out, while the tomb of the poet Amir Khusrau had assumed its present appearance two years earlier. Shaikh Farid Bukhari donated to Nizam al-Din's funeral monument a fine wooden canopy inlaid with mother-of-pearl, borne by four pillars, which is a rare and exquisite example of this genre in Mughal India.

DELHI: CHAUNATH KHAMBA

In the last period of Jahangir's reign (1623-4), Mirza Aziz Kukaltash, the son of Akbar's minister Ataga Khan, had a tomb built for himself in Delhi. It is known popularly as Chaunath Khamba (see p. 238), on account of the 64 pillars of which it is composed: these divide the interior into 25 spans which are all covered with domes. The whole building is in white marble and, from the outside, it looks as though it has a flat roof. There are five pointed arches along each façade which are carried on square pillars, and these are joined by splendid *jali* similar to the ones in the tombs at Sarkhej in Gujarat, where Mirza Aziz Kukaltash had spent a long time as governor. The only decoration in this simple but refined tomb is the elegant *chhajja* that shades all the façades. The building seems to be the most direct *trait d'union* between the constructions by Jahangir and those by Shah Jahan.

DELHI: KHAN-I KHANAN MAUSOLEUM

The fine tomb of Abd al-Rahman Khan in Delhi (see p. 239) must date from 1627. This nobleman, son of Bairam Khan, guardian of Akbar, was a poet and man of letters who had served both Akbar and Jahangir. He bore the title of Khan-i Khanan and died in 1626-7. Although the mausoleum was stripped of its beautiful decoration in red sandstone, marble and other stones in order to build the mausoleum of Safdar Jang, it has a very noble appearance which leads us to suppose that it served as a model to the architects of the Taj Mahall even more than the mausoleum of Humayun did. It stands on an arched platform and the quadrangular main part has deep *iwan* on all four sides which are flanked by two rows of arched niches, one above the other. The fine dome, which is harmonious and well proportioned and narrows slightly at the base, is erected on a cylindrical drum and surrounded by domed *chhatri* on slender columns.

OTHER BUILDINGS

Besides Shaikh Farid Bukhari, there were other nobles who financed public works, in particular caravanserais, though a great many of these have not survived. One of them, at Chatta, a town north of Agra, still has a fine entrance-way in red sandstone in the form of a tall *pishtaq*, in which is set the arch of the actual gateway, with small balconies on either side. The upper edge is adorned with trilobate merlons, while at the very top there are beautiful *chhatri*. Its general appearance and the fine carved decorations, with motifs featuring bottles and pitchers of wine, suggests a date of about 1612.[19]

Another fine portal, the Kanch Mahall, can be seen at Agra, though this one belongs to a tomb. The elegance of its structure and its rich decoration seem to indicate that it belonged to a lady of the imperial family. It has two storeys and in the centre of the façade there is a deep ogival niche, with lower arches on either side and above them elegant balconies screened with beautiful *jali*. The extradoses of the arches are inlaid with white marble in a pattern of delicate vegetal arabesques, while the rest of the surface is decorated with rectangular panels containing wine pitchers, rosettes and geometric patterns.

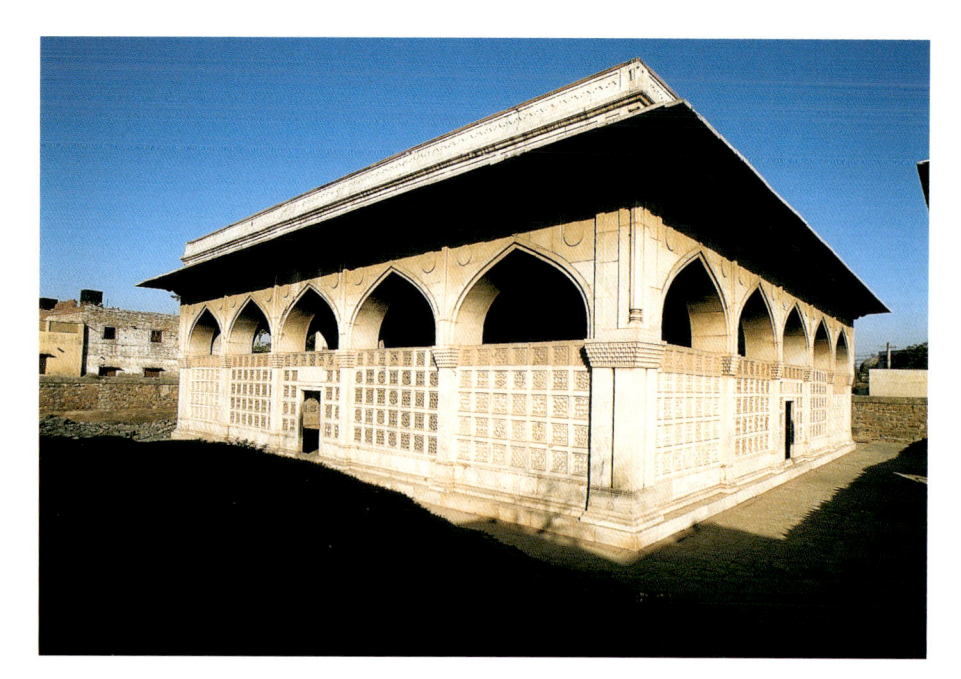

Left The Chaunath Khamba (1623–4) at Delhi is probably the most direct link between the architecture of Jahangir and that of Shah Jahan.

Opposite The Khan-i Khanan mausoleum (1627) at Delhi. The nobility of the building suggests that it may have influenced the architecture of the Taj Mahall.

Similar decoration can be found in the mosque of Mutammad Khan, also at Agra, which is built of red sandstone. The façade has three arched openings and a hexagonal tower topped with a domed *chhatri* at either end. The rectangular prayer hall is covered by three heavy domes on octagonal drums: the central one is slightly higher than the other two, but they all end in an upside-down lotus-blossom surmounted by a spike. The decoration, consisting of square and rectangular panels, covers the façade of the mosque as well as the minarets. This is typical of the late Jahangir period; it can also be seen in the Nur Mahall Serai (1618–20) and the Suraj Bhan-ka Bagh, which is also built of fine red sandstone inlaid with white marble.

[1] Jahangir wrote in his *Memoirs* that he had assumed this title because it was the king's task to control the world: his other title, Nur al-Din (Light of the Faith), suited him because his ascent to the throne 'coincided with the rising and the shining upon earth of a Great Light, the Sun' (*Tuzuk-i Jahangiri*, transl., 2 vols., Delhi 1968 repr., vol. 1, p. 23). With the assumption of this 'solar' title, Jahangir expressed his desire to perpetuate Akbar's concept of a semi-divine light, with which he identified himself. It was not by chance that he had himself portrayed in many miniatures with a huge solar disc behind him.

[2] H. G. Behr, *Die Moguln*, Dusseldorf 1979, p. 149.

[3] Other Islamic sovereigns had had themselves portrayed in the same way, as is evident from various scenes in miniatures or paintings (the *maqamat* by al-Hariri, paintings in the Cappella Palatina in Palermo, other fragments of paintings, cups of the Fatimid period, the stone reliefs at Akhtamar that show Abbasid influence, the Buyid silver plate in the Hermitage in St Petersburg, etc.).

[4] Up to that time both Jahangir and Nur Jahan had considered Shah Jahan as the legitimate heir to the throne, but when the empress's daughter by her first marriage was married to Prince Shariyar, the son of another of Jahangir's wives, Nur Jahan did everything she could to favour the nomination of her son-in-law, thus causing Shah Jahan to rebel.

[5] However, while Jahangir's memoirs, with reference to the date 1608, record the emperor's dissatisfaction over the work that had been done so far, they also mention a stately portal, with minarets in white marble that had already been completed (*Tuzuk*, I, p. 152).

[6] Koran, Suras XLVII, 12, 15; LII, 17–28, etc.

[7] These Christian subjects were not due to any adherence of the Mughals to Christianity, but simply to their aesthetic appreciation of Western art, with which the court had become acquainted through the visits of European diplomats, travellers and missionaries, from Akbar's time onwards.

[8] In 1691, during the reign of the gloomy fanatic Aurangzeb, the last great Mughal sovereign, a revolt of Jat peasants broke out in this area on account of the reintroduction of the *jizia*, the tax levied on non-Muslims, which reduced the farmers to poverty, oppressed as they were by countless duties, as well as by frequent famines and natural calamities. By defiling the tomb of the greatest of the 'foreign' rulers, the rebels meant to outrage the symbol of the oppression that Islamic rule represented.

[9] Asher, *op. cit.*, pp. 108–9.

[10] Koch, *op. cit.*, pp. 72–3.

[11] Nur Jahan, who as a wife outshone all of the emperor's numerous consorts, had such a strong personality that, at the death of her father, Itimad al-Daula, she managed to get herself appointed minister of finance and to mint coins with her name, something unique for a woman. Going by the reports of European travellers, too, the empress's economic policy was very shrewd: in a caravanserai near Agra, where all the caravans travelling with their merchandise from eastern India to the north had to pass, Nur Jahan charged fees which ensured her a considerable profit. The caravanserai is no longer there, but Peter Mundy, who stopped there twice, reported that it was large enough to accommodate two or three thousand people and more than five hundred horses at a time, and the caravans stopped there frequently. Nur Jahan's influence was very strong in every other aspect of court life. Her clothes set the fashion, and so did her jewellery and the perfume of roses that she herself had invented. Her taste in creating designs for carpets, gardens or buildings was particularly regarded, as was her skill in writing poetry. After Shah Jahan's revolt, Nur Jahan no longer managed to keep her hold on power, because many of the courtiers were against her. And so, after Jahangir's death, she retired to Lahore where Shah Jahan had established an income for her, and she died peacefully there in 1645.

[12] Besides the cenotaph of Ghiyas Beg, the tomb also contains that of his wife, Asmat Begum, Nur Jahan's mother.

[13] In the opinion of some scholars this 'mosaic' technique of semi-precious stones on marble was due to European influence on the Mughals in the seventeenth century, while others think it developed independently of Western influence, as marble inlaid with stone. The most reliable research nowadays tends to look to close associations with Italy, particularly Florence, on account of the affinities that have been shown to have existed between the Medicis and the Mughals (see E. Koch, *Lo specchio del principe*, Rome 1991, pp. 17–19).

[14] Jahangir himself tells how his architect, Khwaja Jahan Muhammad Dost, had taken only three months to prepare a palace for him to stay in when he went to Lahore in 1611. According to later historians, Jahangir had constructed three marble buildings, with pillared rooms, near the octagonal tower overlooking the River Jumna, then known as the Shah Burj and now as the Musamman Burj. From this tower hung the famous Chain of Justice, which could be rung by the subjects when they wanted the emperor to hear their complaints. In the neighbourhood there was probably the *jharoka* of Jahangir, under which in 1616 he had set up the marble statues of his defeated Rajput enemies, the *rana* Amar Singh of Mewar and his son Karan, in imitation of what Akbar had done at the Elephant Gate at Agra. Jahangir often refers to his beautiful residences in the Lahore Fort and to the paintings that adorned them. One of them can be identified as the Daulat Khana-i Jahangiri, which was built in 1617 by Mamur Khan, an architect who was also active under Shah Jahan. It is situated on the western side of the Diwan-i Amm and is composed of arcaded rooms built around a courtyard. Other buildings attributed to Jahangir are the small rectangular rooms of red sandstone with flat roofs supported by pillars inside Jahangir's Quadrangle. In appearance they are similar to Akbar's palaces, but the richer, more sumptuous decoration favours an attribution to Jahangir.

[15] Lahore, which some European travellers described as one of the greatest cities of the East, had many other constructions that are now no longer standing, such as a garden belonging to Asaf Khan, a caravanserai, a bazaar and the mosque of Shaikh Farid Bukhari. Authors writing at the time of Jahangir, e.g. Inayat Khan in his *Shah Jahan Nama*, tell us that the emperor had ordered his nobles to build a lot of caravanserais along the road leading from Lahore to his beloved Kashmir, because it was too cold to stay in tents (see Inayat Khan, *The Shah Nama of Inayat Khan*, transl. by A. R. Fuller, ed. W. E. Begley and. Z. F. Desai, Delhi 1990, p. 123).

[16] This locality is mentioned by Jahangir in 1606 as Jahangirpura (City of Jahangir) and in 1620 as Jahangirabad, which has the same meaning but in a Persian form.

[17] Asher, *op. cit*., p. 118, thinks that it was not part of the Mughal tradition to re-use an older building as a tomb for such an important member of the royal family. If the identification of the building is exact, she is inclined to take it as an *ex-novo* construction, also because its structure is in keeping with other Mughal funerary buildings. On the outside it resembles the plinth of Humayun's tomb, while on the inside the layout, with several rooms, is typically Mughal.

[18] Originally there were three entrances, all of them with inscriptions.

[19] This date is confirmed by the accounts of English travellers. W. Finch, who is always extremely scrupulous in his descriptions of monuments, does not mention the caravanserai of Chatta in the account of his journey in 1611, whereas it is mentioned by Steel and Crowther, who passed there in 1615.

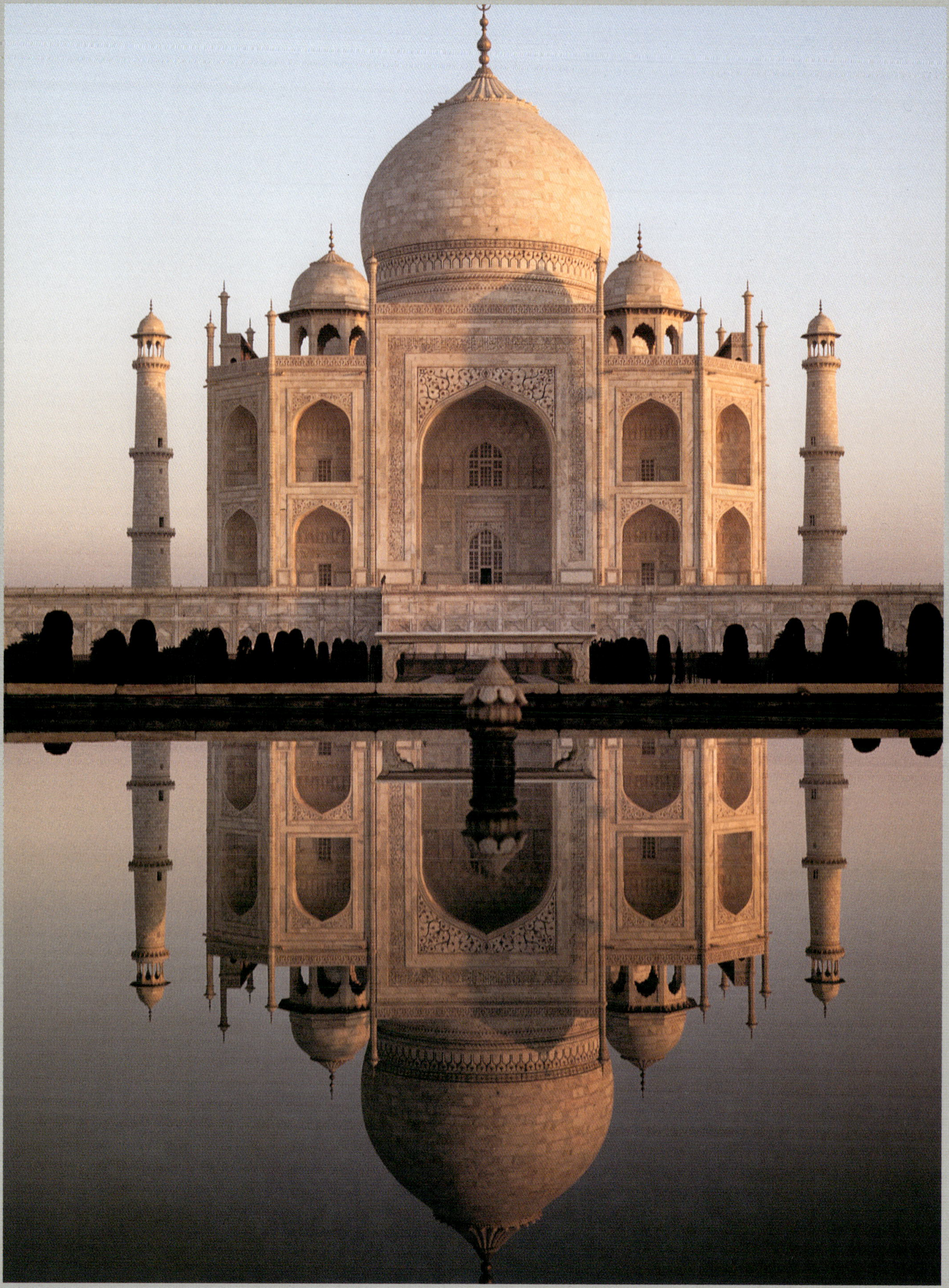

The Classic Mughal Period iii
Shah Jahan (1628-1657)

16

The Taj Mahall at Agra. Though traditionally admired as a symbol of Shah Jahan's love for his wife, who died in 1631, some believe that it is simply a monument to his vanity.

The reign of Shah Jahan, although darkened at the outset by the suppression of three brothers and two nephews, was the most splendid period in the Mughal epoch. European travellers who visited at that time have left enthusiastic and admiring descriptions. Unbridled ostentation and luxury dominated the court. Shah Jahan was a great aesthete, music lover (he had more than 2,000 full-time musicians at court from every corner of Asia) and above all a lover of architecture. He sought to surround himself with the almost veinless beautiful white marble from the quarries of the south-western Hindu Kush. Floors, walls, terraces, window grates, sometimes even doors, garden benches, kiosks, fountains, vases, flowerbed borders – everything had to be in marble. This was extremely expensive not least because of the lengthy transport operations with long convoys of ox-carts. The use of such huge quantities of this precious material eventually undermined the economy of the empire.

For much of his life Shah Jahan proved to be a just sovereign, mild but energetic, a pious Muslim, initially a good politician but much less so towards the end of his reign. His principal success was the conquest of Daulatabad in 1633 which led to the end of the reign of Nizam Shahi, but not to a solution of the Deccani problem. Indeed, Bijapur took advantage of this to extend its own dominion over the southern territories of Nizam Shahi, and the war that followed did not end with a completely favourable peace; Bijapur and Golconda were able to appropriate territories from the dying realm of Vijayanagar. Aurangzeb, the third and most able of Shah Jahan's sons, was placed as head of Mughal Deccan. He had to contain his own bellicose obsessions in order to satisfy his father's desire for peace. However, peace left the country in a precarious situation. Shah Jahan suffered a bitter defeat in the north-west where he strove to reconquer the Central Asian lands of his forbears. He was beaten in Badakhshan (1646-7) and also lost Kandahar, after ups and downs, because of the superiority of the Persian artillery which was organized along Turkish and European lines in contrast with the medieval Mughal formation. All told, however, Shah Jahan's good sense and balance assured three decades of peace for the empire.

The financial administration, however, was weakened by the reappearance of *jagir*, in practice a form of feudalism. The state's income diminished while corruption was widespread and indeed was fuelled by the example of the emperor himself, who called for an obligatory donation at every formal audience.

Towards the end of his reign he addressed the problem of succession and fooled himself that he had solved it by nominating his first-born, Dara Shikoh, as heir. Dara Shikoh was an educated gentleman, refined and with the same feelings as Akbar in religious questions, but he was without experience of government and in military matters. In September 1657 when Shah Jahan became gravely ill, his three youngest children – governors of great provinces and all envious of one another, but especially of the eldest brother – rose up against him. They did not stop their fighting even when Shah Jahan recovered miraculously. The emperor entrusted command of his army to Dara Shikoh, but he was defeated by the astute politics and superior strategy of Aurangzeb. One after another Aurangzeb eliminated his brothers and even imprisoned his father in the fort at Agra (1658). Shah Jahan died here in solitude eight years later with, as legend has it, the name of his beloved wife, Mumtaz Mahall, on his lips. She was buried on the other river bank in the wonderful white marble mausoleum which her inconsolable lover had built for her some decades previously.

Characteristics of the architecture

The critics are in agreement in judging Shah Jahan's era as the happiest in Mughal architecture: the art of construction reached the heights of perfection and at the same time assumed a refined aspect and an exceptional splendour. The use of marble naturally produced changes not simply in the techniques of construction, but also in the design of the buildings. Akbar's robust buildings were replaced by lighter, more delicate structures which some have even defined as 'voluptuous'. Trabeated construction made way for arched structures and sometimes domes with characteristic arches decorated with nine cusps which became special features of the style. The Persian dome, bulbous in profile and narrow at the base, was preferred to the hemispheric dome. This necessitated the use of a double skin, again a feature of Persian origin. The curved *bangaldar* roof was also adopted, as were ceilings with rosettes and lotus or banana leaves. Carved pilasters and corbels were replaced with tapered shafts resting on foliated bases which supported light volute capitals of extraordinarily fluid lines. The plans of the buildings became even simpler and more linear, at the same time acquiring elegance and lightness. If 'the art of Akbar was of exuberant vitality, rich in colour and full of interest due to the life and action it contained, Jahangir's again was lively and curious, although with the detachment of an observer and sceptical collector; Shah Jahan's art became reserved, not very communicative, dreaming and ceremonious almost to the point of ritual'.[1]

Agra: fort, Diwan-i Amm

Shah Jahan dismantled many buildings put up by his predecessors in the forts at Agra and Lahore in order to replace them with his characteristic marble pavilions. In the fort at Agra most of the buildings still standing today are from his time. From the western entrance, the Delhi Gate, with its elephant statues (erected by Akbar), the Mina Bazar led to a courtyard, south of which opened the great square of the Diwan-i Amm. This was a great hall in red sandstone painted white, open on three sides by a triple portico with festooned arches supported by columns in pairs on the façade, in fours at the corners and covered by a flat roof. The columns, the capitals with stylized leaves and the lobes of the arcades are underlined by borders which constitute the only decoration in the space, together with the six-petalled buds that mark the culmination of the festoons on the arches. On the back wall there is a *jharoka* balcony on which the sovereign appeared during public audiences. It has three mullions with each opening trilobated. The balcony leads to a private room with walls thickly decorated with niches.[2]

Agra: Fort, Moti Mosque

To the north of the courtyard is the extremely elegant Moti (Pearl) Mosque, named for the iridescent clarity of its marble. Built between 1646 and 1653, it has many elements similar to the *jami masjid* at Ajmer, built by Shah Jahan between 1637 and 1638 on the site of Muin al-Din Chishti's *dargah*. It has a most graceful façade opened by seven multi-lobed archways resting on rectangular pilasters, three bulbous cupolas of equal size alternated with small *chhatri* which at the corners become true small domes on eight pillars, and a deep *chhajja* on the front. Below this runs a Persian inscription in black marble. Inside, it is divided into aisles with many bays supported by 12-sided pilasters, typical

SHAH JAHAN (1628–1657)

Above The interior of the Diwan-i Amm (Hall of Public Audience) at Agra Fort.

Right The Moti (Pearl) Mosque (1646–53) at Agra Fort is named for its pale, iridescent marble facing.

Opposite The exterior of the Diwan-i Amm at Agra Fort. Shah Jahan replaced many of his predecessors' buildings at the fort with his own distinctive structures.

of the later buildings of Shah Jahan's reign. The prayer hall is preceded by a pool and is surrounded by an arcaded courtyard with high entrance openings at the centre of each side in the Persian manner. Behind the Diwan-i Amm stretches the marvellous panorama of buildings in white marble inlaid with precious stones.

Agra: fort, Macchi Bhavan

In the quadrangle, known today as Macchi Bhavan, where the treasure was guarded, there is a courtyard with a two-storey arcaded gallery running round three sides of it. At the centre of the upper storey on the southern side there is a small pavilion jutting out. It is formed of four columns with bulbous bases supporting a canopy which is decorated on the ceiling by a medallion with the disk of the sun. It is thought that this was the niche for the throne, since the bulbous columns and the sun's disk are connected with the symbolism of royalty. The historian Lahori reports that Shah Jahan had his golden throne placed here and he links it with the 'seventh heaven'. On the lower floor there are several vaulted rooms which served as the treasury. On the eastern side of the quadrangle, on a raised white marble platform, two pavilions face each other. The one to the north was the royal bath (*hammam*), which is divided into several luxuriously decorated rooms and once had a façade with a gallery supported by pillars that were adorned with delicate inlaid work. The southern pavilion was a small reception room for private audiences, with five polylobate arches opening along the front, whose columns, coupled at the corners, are amongst the most graceful ones produced in this period. An inscription in Persian, which is worked in black marble and dated 1636–7, compares this room to the highest heaven and Shah Jahan to the sun. As a matter of fact the ceiling of this delightful pavilion was once lined with gold and silver, to imitate the sun's rays and to emphasize still more the figurative allusion to Paradise.

Agra: fort, Musamman Burj

The private dwellings of the emperor were set out in another quadrangle, which was also raised on a plinth. To the north there stands a very fine octagonal tower of several storeys, with a dome of gilded copper at the top: it is called Musamman Burj and its decoration is extremely refined. Next to it there is a small pavilion, known as Shah Burj, which is perhaps the most ornate building in the whole fort. Polychrome marbles and semi-precious stones are arranged to form plant and flower motifs, interspersed by niches of various sizes that were perhaps used to hold vases of flowers, bowls of fruit, bottles of wine or lamps. A magnificent fountain in the shape of a stylized lotus, which is set in the floor in the middle of the room, helped to keep the room cool, though it already received fresh air through the portico that opened on to the outer gallery facing the countryside.

Agra: fort, Khass Mahall

The Khass Mahall, once called Aramgah (Place of Rest), was the emperor's bedroom. It stands at the centre of the platform, flanked by two almost identical, rectangular pavilions which have *bangaldar* roofs with deeply curved eaves. From the northern pavilion (Bangla-i Darshan) Shah Jahan appeared to salute the crowd that thronged the area below. The second pavilion (Bangla-i Jahanara) belonged to Shah Jahan's favourite daughter.

The Aramgah faced on to the Anguri Bagh (Grape Garden), which was designed according to the usual *char bagh* plan with four stone paths intersecting in the shape of a heart around a central fountain, with flower beds in geometric shapes, perhaps with the aim of creating splashes of contrasting colour with different flowers.

Agra: fort, Shish Mahall

In the north-eastern corner of the Anguri Bagh, on the western side of the Musamman Burj, is the Shish Mahall (Palace of Mirrors), one of the three with this name that Shah Jahan built during his reign. The others are found in the forts of Lahore and Delhi. The palace at Agra has very thick walls and ceilings to ensure freshness inside. Light penetrates only through two doors and some ventilation apertures in the southern wall near the ceilings. The structure was designed this way because only artificial light could produce dazzling special effects from the mirrors that dressed the walls. Another source of these special effects and freshness is the two fountains, connected by a canal and terminating in a cascade on the northern wall, which decorate the two halls of the palace. The skirtings of the halls are dressed with panels painted with floral motifs, while the high walls carry niches of various shapes at regular intervals; here on a layer of stucco fragments of green mirrors are inserted which form representations of leaves and flowers among racemes and arabesques in stucco. The vaulted ceiling is adorned at the corners with characteristic Persian stalactites. It seems that there were portraits on the walls executed on gold leaf; these have been removed, however, perhaps because of their intrinsic value. There are another two small mosques in the fort: a private chapel with only one nave and three bays – Mina (Gem) Mosque – and a slightly

SHAH JAHAN (1628-1657)

Right The Jahangir mausoleum at Shadera, near Lahore. The monument was built in the garden of Nur Jahan by Shah Jahan in honour of his father.

Opposite The Khass Mahall at Agra Fort, which was Shah Jahan's bedroom, has the multi lobed arches characteristic of many of the ruler's buildings in the fort.

larger one – Nagina (Jewel) Mosque – which has two aisles of three bays, parallel to the *qibla* wall. Both were completed in 1637. The second mosque, with three domes, has at the centre of the façade a curved *chhajja* of the *bangaldar* type, the first example of this kind in a mosque.

AGRA: FORT, JAHANARA BEGUM MOSQUE

Outside the fort, in the heart of the old town, stands the principal mosque of the city which is dedicated to Shah Jahan's favourite daughter, Jahanara Begum. Built on a high platform, it covers an area of 1,200 squ. m. Here the white marble is used only on the main opening of the façade, on the *chhatri* that frame the building and on the smaller ones that decorate the main door. The rest is in red sandstone but maintains the simple and sober lines characteristic of Shah Jahan's reign. Three large bulbous and pear-shaped domes surmount the building: they are all decorated with a herringbone motif and terminate in an upside down lotus flower and an elaborate point. The *sahn* is enclosed only on two sides by flat-roofed galleries (the front archways are missing), and has a pool at the centre for ritual ablutions. The mosque of Jahanara is also the *jami masjid* of the city. It is decorated with alternating reliefs and mouldings in sandstone inlaid with white marble, flat or in relief. This reaches maximum intensity in the panels of the *mihrab*, in the façade of the courtyard and in the fine zigzag decoration of the domes.

LAHORE: FORT

In the fort at Lahore, too, Akbar's red sandstone buildings were demolished to make way for marble pavilions in a more refined style. The new buildings rise mostly towards the northern side of the fort and include the Diwan-i Amm, the Khwabgah, the Shish Mahall, the Musamman Burj and the Naulakha. Some of these, however, destroyed or damaged by the Sikhs, were rebuilt or roughly reconstructed at the beginning of British domination in 1846. This is the case with the Diwan-i Amm, an open hall with 40 columns in the southern quadrangle. The Shish Mahall in the Shah Burj (today called the Musamman Burj), built in 1632 for the empress, makes use of various decorative techniques.[3] It has a carved marble skirting, stuccoes, hard and semi-precious stone inlays in floral designs inserted on a backdrop of marble and mosaic works with convex mirrors which lend the building its name. The same delicate and expensive decoration in hard stone is found in the elegant marble pavilion with the curved roof in the Bengali manner, therefore called *bangla* (bungalow) or *naulakha*, built in the same period. The curved cornice, associated with the typical roof, became a fashionable characteristic in the Mughal buildings of the first half of the seventeenth century. The upper part of the walls of the pavilion is a mediocre imitation from the Sikh period, together with the paintings and the glass work. The original roof was possibly in gilded metal.[4]

The small Diwan-i Khass is of contained and refined elegance; its hardstone frieze on the parapet derives from Lodi examples. It dates from 1645, the year in which the graceful Pearl Mosque was also built, the oldest of the three that carry this name. The façade of the Moti Mosque opens on to a small *sahn* with five arched entrances of which the lateral ones are multi-lobed while the central arch is cuspidated and is higher and wider than the others and framed by elegant and slender small columns. The three domes of equal size are slightly bulbous with a cavetto moulding which sits on top of the drum. Inside, simple frames in black marble mark the position of the worshippers on the floor.

SHADERA: JAHANGIR MAUSOLEUM

Soon after his ascent to the throne, Shah Jahan had the great mausoleum for his father built at Shadera, near Lahore, in the garden of Nur Jahan. The beautiful garden in which the tomb stands forms a square measuring more than 400 m along each side, and is situated a few kilometres north-west of the city, once on the bank of the River Ravi. The complex includes an outer courtyard, now known as Akbari Serai, with lodgings for travellers, who could spend the night in the row of niches along the brick boundary walls which have a high gateway in the middle of each side. The garden is divided into 16 equal sections by means of pavements with a star motif. At each intersection there is a pool and a fountain. All the beds have different flowers planted in them which produce, according to the season, a true feast of colour. At the centre of the composition stands the mausoleum: quadrangular, single-storey, enclosed by four graceful octagonal minarets over 30 m tall and in five stages interrupted by small balconies and crowned with graceful domed *chhatri*. It seems that a marble pavilion or a dome must have completed the central part, as in the similar monument at Itimad al-Daula, which must have served as prototype. Whether the dome or the *chhatri* was never completed or whether it was later destroyed is unknown. Currently the minarets, slender and elegant as they are, are out of proportion with the rest of the central mass of the building which is too flat. The interior arrangement is very simple, consisting of a corridor which leads to a row of rooms arranged along all the external sides of the building and a series of compartments which stretch from the centre of each side to the central vaulted space. Here there is a marble cenotaph exquisitely inlaid with semi-precious stones representing wreaths of cyclamens and tulips which must have reminded Jahangir of his beloved Kashmir. The 99 names of Allah also appear, traced in a calligraphy of consummate elegance. The decoration of the interior rooms comprises frescoed paintings on the walls and tile mosaics on the skirtings of the corridors. The external walls and the lower floor of the minarets are in red sandstone with geometric patterns in white and black marble, among them the characteristic Persian 'wine carafe'. The three intermediate stages of the minarets have herringbone designs in white and yellow marble; the terminal *chhatri* are in white marble with *chhajja* supported by finely worked corbels. Not far away there is a mosque that has a single nave with three bays and a façade with three archways, the central one exaggeratedly high compared with the other two. It is quite different from Shah Jahan's other buildings.

Lahore: Asaf Khan and Nur Jahan mausoleums

Not far from Jahangir's mausoleum are the mausoleums of Asaf Khan, brother of Nur Jahan, and that of the empress herself. Both are much simpler in plan and both, especially the latter, are largely ruined. The tomb of Asaf Khan was built by his son-in-law, Shah Jahan, with an octagonal plan and a pear-shaped dome which has lost its original facing of glazed tiles. On her plain and simple mausoleum Nur Jahan had an epitaph engraved which reads: On my tomb when I am dead/ No lamp will burn nor jasmine lie/ No candle with a flickering flame/ Will serve as reminder of my fame/ Neither will the sweet song of a nightingale/ Tell the world that I am gone.

Delhi (Shahjahanabad): Red Fort

On the right bank of the River Jumna at Delhi in 1639 Shah Jahan began to build a new city which he called Shahjahanabad. The fort is surrounded by walls in red sandstone from the quarries of Fatehpur Sikri and is therefore known as the Lal Qila (Red Fort) to distinguish it from Humayun's fort in grey quartzite. It has an elongated octagonal shape some 900 m from north to south and 540 m from east to west, and constitutes the citadel of the new city of Shah Jahan, the walls of which were completed while the fort was still under construction.[5] The main buildings stand along its eastern wall which faces the river and is some 18 m high. The walls rise to some 33 m above the level of the moat which surrounds them. There are two principal entrances as well as a small side gate. Currently the main gate is the western one, known as Lahore Gate, with an arch 12 m high flanked by imposing semi-octagonal towers surmounted by domed kiosks. Connecting the two towers is a series of graceful multi-lobed small arches crowned with marble cupolas and enclosed between two turrets, but the pleasing effect of the gate was ruined by Aurangzeb who after a few years added a defensive barbican to the front. It seems that Shah Jahan, deposed and imprisoned by his son, was upset enough to write to Aurangzeb: 'You have made the fort your bride and you have hung a veil over her face.'[6]

On the southern side opens the Delhi Gate, so called because it faces the ancient city of Delhi. It is similar in design to the Lahore Gate, but was flanked on both sides of the main arch by stone statues of two elephants which Aurangzeb had destroyed. The current elephants were erected by the enlightened viceroy Lord Curzon in 1903. The Lahore Gate constituted the royal entrance to the Great Mosque, built on a rocky outcrop of the Aravalli mountains to the south-west of the fort. To the west of the entrance runs the main road for Shahjahanabad, better known by the name Chandni Chowk (Moonlight Market). From the two entrances two roads lead inside the fort and intersect at a right-angle towards the centre of the complex. The roads provide access to a large rectangular area which occupies some two-thirds of the entire space and is contained within perimeter walls.[7] In this internal area all the private and royal apartments are arranged. Outside, but still within the remaining rectangular space, are the service quarters, servants' homes and other buildings of various functions.

The Lahore Gate entrance to the complex leads to a covered way – a two-storey vaulted arcade with arched spaces to hold workshops[8] – which in turn leads to the Naubat Khana (the bodyguards' quarters) where the royal band played five times a day, at each arrival and departure of the king and on other special occasions.

Detail of the black and white marble decoration on the red sandstone lower walls of the Jahangir mausoleum at Shadera, showing the Persian 'wine carafe' motif.

Delhi (Shahjahanabad): Red Fort, Diwan-i Amm

On the eastern side of the large quadrangle is the Diwan-i Amm. This was the hall of public audiences, built in red sandstone; it was once dressed in mother-of-pearl stucco and in some parts covered with gold and silver leaf decorated with reliefs. The space was supported by pillars and was open on three sides, to the north, south and west; it was divided internally into three arcades. All the arches are multi-lobed and rest on elegant octagonal pillars arranged in two rows on the external sides. On the back wall there is a marble baldachin, facing a niche which constituted the Nashiman-i Zill-i Ilahi (Seat of the Shadow of God). This rests on a beautiful square base in marble, richly ornamented with engraved floral designs and covered by a curved roof in the typical *bangaldar* form, richly decorated in semi-precious stones. Here during audiences the most impressive of Shah Jahan's peacock thrones was displayed. It was so richly decorated that the court poet wrote about it: 'The world became so poor in gold because of it, the purse of the earth was empty of treasure.'[9] Behind the baldachin the niche on the wall is dressed with a series of panels in hard stone and black marble with the figures of Orpheus with a violin and various birds among flowers and fruit. It is said that these were drawn by Austin de Bordeaux, a French jeweller who was a guest of the Mughals, but it is more likely that they were executed in a Florentine studio and then imported, suggested by the fact that Orpheus carries a violin rather than a lute. Nevertheless, the floral arabesques between the panels appear to be Indian in both style and manufacture.[10]

Beyond the Diwan-i Amm are the royal palaces, arranged in flower-filled courtyards and gardens within which runs, from north to south, a canal set into the earth in a shallow bed of marble. The Nahar-i Bahisht (Heaven's Canal) was an extension of the canal opened in 1350 by Firuz Shah Tughluq to bring water to Delhi from a site on the Jumna 90 km to the north. The palaces arranged on the canal are, from north to south, the Moti Mahall, a small pavilion from the last phase of Mughal architecture; the Hammam, with three main apartments, the floors of which together with the baths, the skirtings and the slabs of the walls are in the purest white marble inlaid with precious and semi-precious stones arranged to form delicate floral designs with arabesqued borders;[11] the Diwan-i Khass, situated in its own courtyard from which it could be separated by means of a red curtain; the Khwabgah, with a tower projecting out from the walls; the Rang Mahall (Painted Palace); and the Moti Mahall, then the apartments of the royal princesses and now the museum of the fort. Before reaching the main royal palace, Tasbih Khana, the canal passes through a marble screen with extremely fine *jali*. Above this screen is an arch decorated with a relief of a set of scales in the midst of tulip and daffodil arabesques which contrast with the fine, translucent slabs. This motif of the 'scales of justice' could suggest a Western influence.

Delhi (Shahjahanabad): Red Fort, Diwan-i Khass etc.

The Diwan-i Khass is a single-storey building with a flat roof surmounted by four small *chhatri*. The ceiling, decorated with gold leaf, is supported on massive quadrangular pillars which carry multi-lobed arches that divide the interior into 15 sections. The lower parts of the pillars, up to the imposts of the arches, are dressed in panels with refined floral decoration in hard stone, while the upper part is gilded and painted. In many ways the interior, illuminated by a soft diffused light, rivals the Rang Mahall in terms of exuberant grace. On the northern and southern walls are the most famous of all the Persian inscriptions which proclaim emphatically, but not without truth, 'If there is heaven on earth it is here, it is here, it is here.' The windows that overlook the river have finely carved openwork screens while the façade is made up of five equal arches; arches of various sizes are arranged on the short sides so the interior is fresh and airy, there being no closed wall. Here, too, the Peacock Throne was displayed; it was impounded and carried to Persia by Nadir Shah in 1739 where it was dismantled. The throne of Shah Pahlavi at Teheran was from the Qajar epoch. From descriptions of the time it seems nevertheless that despite its intrinsic value, the throne was a work of 'ostentatious and sumptuous vulgarity'.

The Khwabgah (today known as Khass Mahall), the walls of which were once inlaid with precious stones, is the central complex of rooms in the royal palace and leads to the octagonal tower, Musamman Burj, with finely perforated windows which overlook the old beach where animal fights were held. It contains the Zar Jharoka (Golden Balcony) from which the emperor, following the ancient Hindu tradition of the *darshan*, displayed himself to his subjects.

The Rang Mahall (also known as Imtiyaz Mahall) was also single-storey and was richly decorated using colour. It can be considered the jewel in the crown of Shah Jahan's seraglio. A contemporary chronicler proclaimed it, 'because of its light and colour far superior to the palaces of the promised Heaven'.[12] On the ground plan the building measures some 50 x 20 m and consists of a huge central hall with smaller rooms at each corner. The main space is subdivided into 15 square areas each 7 m in diameter, by means of heavy pillars and arches similar to those of the Diwan-i Khass, and it has a gilded silver ceiling decorated with golden flowers. The Nahar-i Bahisht runs here in a shallow bath with a marble floor sculpted in the shape of a flat but fully blooming lotus flower. From each delicately modelled petal of this flower spurts a jet of water, so that the petals and inlaid leaves seem to move with the rippling of the water. A contemporary observer wrote that the waving of the plants and the flowers under the dancing water was nothing less than a scene of magic.[13] Even though today the precious stones that adorned it are missing and the water no longer runs, the lotus fountain of the Rang Mahall is still a creation of great and refined beauty. South of this building is the Moti Mahall which formed a part of the *zenana*.

Shahjahanabad was a city in the true sense, capable of providing for its own needs by means of a whole army of artisans, whose sole aim was to meet the requirements of the emperor and his court. In the account of his travels in India, Bernier says that there were 400,000 persons living in the citadel, of whom 57,000 were in the emperor's service. Many of the people at court, including Dara Shikoh, Jahanara and some of

Shah Jahan's wives, had built gardens, mosques and houses for themselves, both inside and around the citadel. Jahanara's garden (Sahibabad) was situated north of the Chandni Chowk and included a *hammam* and a caravanserai. In the Chandni Chowk there is also the mosque built by Fatehpuri Begum, thought to have been the king's third wife, in about 1650. It bears a likeness to the mosque built by Jahanara at Agra. It seems that Akbarabadi Mahall, Shah Jahan's first wife, had also built an impressive mosque of a similar type, with an adjacent serai, though it is now lost. Still extant is the small mosque in red sandstone of Sirhindi Begum, an influential lady of the court. Shah Jahan was responsible for two religious buildings, an *idgah* (1655) with a red sandstone façade known as Purani Idgah (Old Idgah), now badly ruined, and the Great Mosque.

DELHI (SHAHJAHANABAD):
JAMI MASJID

Outside the fort, but connected to it by means of a wide processional road, stands the *jami masjid* that Shah Jahan himself called Masjid-i Jahanuma; its construction began in 1650.[14] Like the mosque at Agra this, too, rises on a high platform, but in contrast it is accessible by means of three entrances complete with imposing stairways. The public were admitted to the mosque only through the northern and southern entrances, the eastern entrance being reserved for the sovereign and his court when they came here in procession at midday every Friday.

The stone-floored *sahn* is a large quadrangle some 99 m each side with a pool at the centre surrounded by open arcades to the sides, connected by doors and kiosks.

The prayer hall projects towards the courtyard and is separate from the surrounding arcades. Like the rest of the construction it is in red sandstone with profuse decoration in white and black marble. Measuring some 61 x 27 m, it is characterized on the façade by a wide multi-lobed central archway flanked on each side by five smaller, festooned arches which form the wings, closed at the extremities by two elegant, four-storey minarets. Three fine bulbous domes in white marble with stripes of red sandstone sit on cylindrical drums and are arranged in such a way as to avoid, above all in the centre, any lack of balance caused by the close proximity of the *iwan* with the domes, such as happens in some Iranian mosques and in the first Indian mosques. The interior of the shrine consists of a great hall divided into bays by means of massive pillars which support lobed arches. The simple decoration is found in the numerous niches in the *mihrab* over the whole rear wall and in arabesque designs in white marble on walls of red sandstone.[15] Before the construction of the Badshahi Mosque at Lahore, the *jami masjid* of Delhi was the largest mosque in the whole subcontinent. Although it has an impeccable layout and sober ornamentation, this mosque is sometimes felt to be a little too academic, to the point of being a stereotype.

Outside the city walls there were numerous gardens that were highly praised by European travellers, such as the Shalimar Bagh of Akbarabadi Mahall, built in 1650 in the likeness of the gardens of the same name at Lahore and Srinagar. In the same period Raushan Ara,

Shah Jahan's youngest daughter, built another magnificent garden with her tomb in it, but only the latter still survives. It is in the shape of a rectangular pavilion with *chhatri* at the corners and stands in the middle of a small pond, where it can be reached by a causeway. The central burial chamber has no roof, but it is surrounded by flat-roofed galleries that open towards the outside through three pointed archways supported by bulbous columns, usually the royal prerogative of Shah Jahan.

Lahore: Wazir Khan Mosque

Considered much livelier, by contrast, is a totally different construction erected in Lahore in 1634 by the Wazir Khan, a physician called Hakim Ala al-Din Ansari of Chiniot, who became governor of the Punjab at the outset of Shah Jahan's reign. Inserted between crowded bazaars on the south-eastern side of the city, it is said to have been built on the tomb of a saint from the Ghaznavid era.[16] The mosque (see p. 250) is essentially Persian in type with four great *iwan* arranged in a cross around a central courtyard, but various elements of Hindu tradition are evident. It is built entirely in brick, the most diffused technique in the Punjab, and is dressed outside by a bright mosaic in small glazed tiles where geometric motifs alternate with floral and epigraphic motifs. Inside, however, decoration is obtained by means of frescoes painted on carved plaster, extremely delicate in their detail. The majestic main portal in the perimeter wall on the eastern side is in itself a treasure. It rises over the surrounding walls and is decorated with two domed balconies supported on richly sculpted corbels at the sides of the great central arch. Two slender arches delimit the external contours while blind niches and panels of tile mosaics dress the surface. Above the cuspidated arch runs an italic script with the Muslim credo. The inner hall is in the form of an irregular octagon. Inside the courtyard the arcades to the north and south are interrupted at the centre by great *iwan* halls. The shrine, further to the west, displays five imposing arches of which the central one is higher and wider

Right The *jami masjid* (1650) built by Shah Jahan just outside his new city of Shahjahanabad (now Delhi).

Opposite The Fatehpuri Mosque in the Chandni Chowk area of Shahjahanabad (now Delhi) was built around 1650 by Fatehpuri Begum, one of Shah Jahan's wives.

than those alongside. At its highest this arch is some 9 m above the courtyard, double the height of the interior arch behind it, and its width also hides the dome that sits behind. Another four smaller domes of the Lodi type cover the prayer hall, which is closed externally by four splendid octagonal minarets crowned by *chhatri* with high, slightly bulbous cupolas. The minarets are slightly inset at each corner and rise from high square skirtings the same height as the façade of the shrine and terminating in balconies supported by pairs of sculpted corbels. The mosaic decoration, which is arranged in panels, even extends under the curved support of the gallery at the top of each minaret which carries the eight-pillared kiosk. The small Persian cypresses alternate with Indian *chenar* (plane trees) and stylized floral motifs in lively turquoise, yellow, green, blue, white and black. Under the cupolas of the *chhatri* runs an elegant pattern of white bows on a blue background between geometric borders and small arches filled with intertwined floral motifs. Although architecturally the mosque is an extremely effective building, there is no doubt that the profusion of colours and the disposition of the decorative motifs notably increase its aesthetic value.

Lahore: other buildings

The Wazir Khan Mosque is certainly the most beautiful example of this phase in Mughal architecture, but there are numerous other structures inside and outside Lahore which are designed and built in the same way and which reach a high artistic level. The entrances to some lost gardens, such as the Gulabi Bagh and the Chauburji, are also extant, both remarkable for the rich and vivid mosaic of tiles arranged in panels on all the surfaces. The first garden (1655) was built by the Persian noble Mirza Sultan Beg, who was admiral of the fleet under Shah Jahan; the second seems to have been dedicated to Jahanara Begum (1646), the emperor's favourite daughter. This last owes its name to the four towers that decorate the entrance which is now partially ruined.[17] Other examples of mosaic decoration are found in the tomb of Ali Mardan Khan, who was governor of Kandahar under Shah Safi

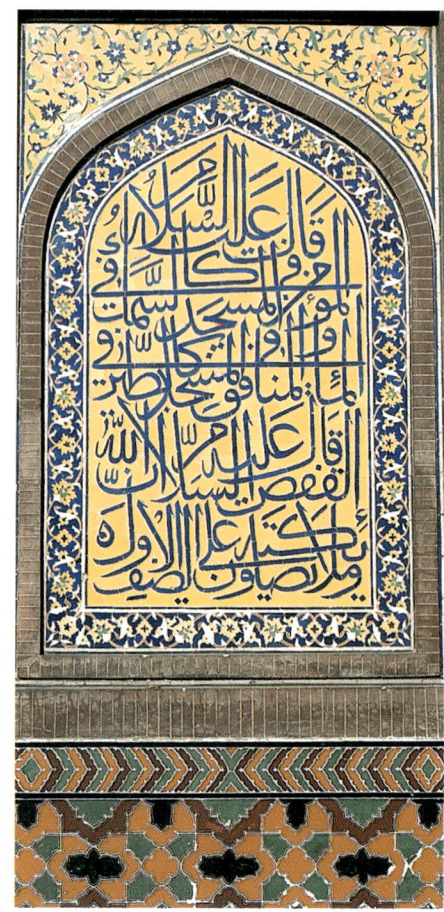

SHAH JAHAN (1628–1657)

(1629–42) and then transferred to the employ of Shah Jahan, to whom he delivered up the city and then subsequently became governor of Kashmir and the Punjab. His massive octagonal tomb in brick with a high dome and corner *chhatri* was profusely decorated with glazed tiles that were damaged by the Sikhs; little trace of them remains. The dome seems to have been covered in white marble with floral designs in black marble.

Another noteworthy example of this type is the beautiful mosque of Dai Anga (see p. 252), Shah Jahan's wet-nurse. Although used by the Sikhs as a military warehouse and then by the British as a private residence, it maintained its lively and elegant aspect after restoration thanks mainly to its tiled walls in shining shades of yellow.[18]

AGRA: TAJ MAHALL

The most famous of Shah Jahan's buildings is without doubt the most widely known of all Indian monuments, the Taj Mahall. This is the grand and solemn mausoleum that he had built in memory of his dear wife, Arjumand Banu Begum, known as Mumtaz Mahall (Jewel or Chosen of the Palace).[19] Daughter of Asaf Khan and therefore granddaughter of Nur Jahan, Arjumand was always close to her husband who preferred her to all his other wives. He even granted her the royal seal and she followed him everywhere, even on military campaigns without ever complaining of tiredness or the uncomfortable conditions. Exhausted by numerous pregnancies, she died at Burhanpur just three years after Shah Jahan's succession to the throne from an infection contracted following the birth of her fourteenth child. Her husband was busy at the time containing the rebel Khan-i Jahan Lodi. It was 17 June 1631 and Mumtaz Mahall was only 38 years old. Shah Jahan was shattered by his loss; according to the chronicler Lahori his beard became white overnight and as a sign of his mourning for two years he renounced flavoured food, coloured robes, music and any other form of entertainment. He dressed only in white. According to Lahori he was heard to say more than once that his pain was so great he wanted to renounce the throne itself and for an entire week he made no public appearances. Mumtaz's body was held temporarily in the Zainabad garden at Burhanpur until, six months after her death, it was transferred to Agra. There, on a plot of land belonging to the Raja Jai Singh, Shah Jahan had decided to bury her in the most beautiful mausoleum ever built, a symbol of both his love and the pain that had overwhelmed him on losing his wife.

The monument is actually a majestic complex within a stupendous garden where a large pool reflects the clear silhouette of the mausoleum. From the time of its construction this building has received all types of admiring praise. Considered by many as the 'Pearl of India', the Taj was most admired in the nineteenth and at the beginning of the twentieth centuries. Fergusson maintained that it was 'the most graceful and the most impressive of the sepulchres of the world'. Major Archer, similarly, asserted that it was 'the most gorgeous and magnificent mausoleum under the heavens', while W. H. Russell stated that it was 'a dream in marble ... a thought, an idea, a conception of tenderness, a sigh of eternal devotion and heroic love'. Percy Brown defined it as a 'materialized vision of loveliness'. Bayard Taylor noted, 'So pure, so gloriously perfect did it appear that I almost feared to approach it lest the charm should be broken.' Others have stated that it is a poem in marble; Rabindranath Tagore called it 'a teardrop on the cheek of time'. More recently Bussagli wrote that, 'More than an architectural miracle, it remains the translation into bright and luminous stone of the great and impassioned love of an emperor for his woman.'

To this chorus of praise only a few voices are raised in discordant criticism, such as Huxley who confounded all popular opinion on the supposed beauty of the Taj Mahall; or the philosopher Keyserling who held it to be a useless work of art lacking in expressive and spiritual force, and who thought that it was not even necessarily a funeral monument. In more recent times the Bengali writer Sarat Chandra Chatterji has the heroine of one of his novels say that Shah Jahan would probably have built the Taj Mahall even if Mumtaz Mahall had not died – he would have found another excuse to build it, perhaps in the name of religion, perhaps as a monument to his conquests.

Above The Chauburji gate at Lahore. Once the entrance to gardens that are now destroyed, the vivid tile mosaic decoration on the exterior of the gate survives.

Opposite top The Wazir Khan Mosque (1634) at Lahore. Though essentially Persian in structure, it does include Hindu elements.

Opposite bottom Detail of one of the decorative tile mosaic panels flanking the main arch of the Wazir Khan Mosque.

Begley started from this last supposition and proposed an original theory on the purpose of the Taj Mahall and its symbolic significance.[20] Based on some contemporary evidence which had been deliberately ignored by the monument's admirers, he provided proof of the not fully shattering pain that Shah Jahan felt at the loss of his wife, or at least not so long-lasting as to push him to erect for her a mausoleum of such 'silent and majestic beauty'. Rather Shah Jahan was prey to his limitless vanity and the high ideal of his own perfection, not dissimilar to those feelings which had led his grandfather Akbar to encapsulate his majestic divinity in the Din-i Ilahi axiom Allahu Akbar. Shah Jahan created the Taj for his own glorification. Indeed, having been born in the exact year of the end of the first millennium of Islam, he tended to identify himself with the Perfect Man, 'the distilled irradiation of God's Divine Essence'. According to some Muslim mystics this was the true instrument of divine Creation, God being totally transcendent and lacking in attributes while the act of Creation had to be an attribute by definition. According to the most orthodox Muslims the archetype of the Perfect Man would have been Muhammad who was nevertheless merely the first in a recurring series. Much evidence suggests that Shah Jahan believed himself to be the Perfect Man of the second millennium and not by chance did he choose among his titles the following: Auspicious Lord of the Age; King of the World; Shadow of God; August Representative on Earth of the Divinity. The form of the mausoleum itself, similar to the seats of eastern sovereigns, with the profile of the dome similar to that of the Mughal crowns; the arrangement of the supposed tomb at the end of the garden and not at the centre of it as in other Mughal examples; and all the inscriptions on the building seem to indicate that the entire complex must have represented symbolically 'an allegory of the Day of Resurrection when the dead shall arise and proceed to the place of Judgement beneath the Divine Throne'. This throne itself was the Taj true and proper, with the minarets representing the four 'pillars' of the divine throne supported by angels and situated in the Garden of Eden according to the description of a great mystic of the thirteenth century. The inscriptions in the funeral chamber – where, within an octagonal marble screen, stand the cenotaphs of Mumtaz Mahall and Shah Jahan – seem to allude to this symbolic representation. These inscriptions are in fact taken from Sura 40 of the Koran and carry the prayers of the angels who support God's Throne. The same balustrade recalls the shape of many Islamic thrones and was originally forged in gold and dressed with jewels, just like a royal throne.

Indeed, the true sepulchres of the sovereigns are found in the crypt below the hall, therefore under the symbolic representation of God's Throne, which, according to tradition, the inhabitants of Heaven will see on the day of Resurrection after the tombs are opened. Shah Jahan had himself buried there by his daughter Jahanara, who saw to the transfer of his corpse from the fort at Agra to the Taj Mahall alongside his wife's sepulchre. This underlined once again the superiority of Qalam – the Divine Pen, incarnation of the Perfect Man – over Mumtaz, Lawh al-Mahfuz, the Sacred Tablet which God used to transcribe the subsequent destiny of the world. The Taj was therefore 'less a romantic symbol of devotion, than a vainglorious yet profound attempt at defining God in Shah Jahan's own terms, perhaps even to rival him'.

Although this theory contravenes all our deep-seated notions on the sentimental beauty of the Taj, it does seem to be well documented and worthy of consideration, especially when Begley concludes:

The Taj, although in the final analysis without precedent, is perhaps one of the most powerful images of Divine Majesty so far created. Its architectural beauty constitutes the formal counterpart of our most exalted mental concepts of a formless Deity. Frequently praised as 'the most beautiful building in the world', the Taj in its relative beauty seems deliberately intended to mirror God's absolute Beauty. Of course the beauty and majesty of the Taj also reflect the glory of its earthly creator, who has certainly been immortalized by it, although perhaps for the wrong reasons ... It would be gratuitous, nevertheless, to dismiss Shah Jahan's reasons for building the Taj as mere impious vanity, just as it would be gratuitous to praise him for his supposed devotion to his wife.[21]

Whatever the reasons that justified the construction of the 'Crown of the Palace', according to Tavernier it called for the steadfast work of 20,000 workers for 22 years. The rich complex of buildings was begun, according to the testimony of the European traveller Mundy, in 1632 and was finished only in 1653. But some epigraphs found in various parts of the mausoleum have led to a reconsideration of this date, asserting that the exterior of the tomb was already complete around 1636 while the rest of the complex was completed in 1647.

SHAH JAHAN (1628-1657)

Above The Taj Mahall at Agra. The most famous of all Indian monuments, it was built by Shah Jahan as a mausoleum for his wife Mumtaz Mahall. The tomb itself was conceived as only a part of a larger complex.

Opposite The Dai Anga Mosque at Lahore, dedicated to Shah Jahan's wet-nurse. It is notable for its bright yellow tiled walls.

Although the monument has a totally 'oriental' aspect, more than a few scholars believed for a long time in its 'Western' design. This conviction was based on the affirmation of a Spanish Augustinian monk, Father Sebastian Manrique, according to whom the architect of the Taj Mahall was the Venetian Geronimo Veroneo who lived at Agra for several years and served the Mughals. Father Manrique stated in his *Itinerario de las missiones del India oriental*: 'The architect of these buildings was a Venetian by name Geronimo Veroneo who came in the Portuguese ships and died at Lahore shortly before my arrival.'[22] Both Hosten and Blunt lent credit to this statement, and supported the theory of the Taj's European origins. However, contemporary Persian sources which provide many particulars on the construction of the complex and carry names of various artists and craftsmen, make no mention of the supposed Venetian architect. On the contrary, all the European travellers who passed through Agra in those years remember Veroneo only as skilled jeweller. This was the case with Peter Mundy, who knew him personally, Tavernier and the Jesuit priest Corsi, according to whom Veroneo 'had beautiful hands and a great ability in creating curious pieces in gold worked with precious stones'.[23] It seems improbable that all these contemporaries could have neglected to mention such an important commission for a European – a noble and important building such as the Taj. Indeed, the Venetian is not remembered as the creator of any other work in India, neither was he an architect in Italy. There is no doubt that because of his abilities as goldsmith he was employed by both Jahangir and Shah Jahan in the creation of jewels, of which both sovereigns were fond. Perhaps he even worked on larger pieces such as thrones, the ceilings of residential apartments or even the original gold and jewel balustrade which surrounded the cenotaph of Mumtaz Mahall.[24] Modern critics maintain that he, like many artists, could have created a model or two, perhaps even those presented to Shah Jahan for final judgement, but he could not be considered the true creator of the Taj because he could never have known the traditional construction techniques of India, represented so clearly here in the monument which truly marks the high point of the evolution of the tomb on Indian soil. Bussagli suggested that because of his knowledge of Venetian villas, Veroneo could have provided the Taj with its illusory effect which is obtained through, among other features, 'chromatic effects, the quality of the materials used, proportion and the dimensions themselves of the work'. Other theories, above all from the nineteenth century, attributed the design of the mausoleum to a pupil of the Turk Sinan, Isa Muhammad Effendi; and an architect of Persian origin, Ustad Ahmad, creator of the Red Fort and in his son's memoirs of the Taj too. Ustad died two years after the completion of the Taj. Other works speak of another Ustad Ahmad, known also as Ustad Isa, who would seem to have been another goldsmith, the Frenchman Austin de Bordeaux who lived at Agra for many years and died in 1632. He is mentioned as *naqsh niwis*, 'creator of the project', and his identification is owed perhaps to the assonance of Isa with Isai which means Christian. In fact, a book entitled *Risala-i Rauda-i Taj Mahall* maintains that the most important member of the team that worked on the Taj Mahall was a Christian and 'a rare designer and artist'. Despite all these contradictory testimonies we must not forget that the Taj in effect, as Bussagli rightly maintains, is essentially 'the work of Shah Jahan himself, passionate coordinator of the suggestions and projects provided by his artists whether they were French, Turkish, Indian or Italian'.[25] The Taj represents the culmination of an evolutionary process, all the previous stages of which can be charted. But it is also a miracle of architectural balance that could only be realized with careful and accurate synthesis of countless designs and opinions.[26]

Although the funerary building represents the high point of the scheme, it occupies only a relatively small part of the architectural whole. The plan of the complex takes the form of a rectangle aligned from north to south, surrounded by a wall in red sandstone 567 m long and 305 m wide with the central area made up of a garden 305 metres square. On the southern side there are some areas used as stores, service quarters for guards, courtyards, stables and a small bazaar for provisions. On the northern side rise two large superimposed platforms which are almost on the right bank of the River Jumna. The first platform, reached by a few steps, functions as the base for two large and almost identical buildings situated at the sides of the tomb. The building to the west is a mosque, the other, very similar, has no religious function but was introduced to the scheme as a *jawab* (answer), a symmetrical copy used as a *mihman khana*, or 'guest house'. Both buildings are made of red sandstone and are topped with three elegant bulbous domes supported by cylindrical drums decorated with a sheath of black and white tiles. In their tones these drums emphasize the shining central outline of the Taj in white Makrana marble which reflects an incredible, subtle variety of tints and tones according to changes in the light. The tomb itself rises on a plinth over 7.5 m from the level of the garden and has a square plan with bevelled corners so as to form an irregular octagon like those in the tombs of Humayun (see p. 197) and Khan-i Khanan (see p. 239).

In the centre rises an elegant octagonal space measuring 24.35 m from the floor to the ceiling of the internal dome. A second bulbous dome, erected on an extremely high cylindrical drum, rises on the exterior to 45 m including the apex of the terminal, so that the total height of the central building is some 74 m. The empty space between the two domes is so great that it corresponds exactly to the total volume of the octagonal space. To the minor sides of the octagonal base there correspond the same number of smaller rooms, also octagonal, which rise over two floors. A series of corridors connects the various spaces with one another while spiral staircases lead from one floor to another. The general arrangement could be defined as being *in quincuncem*, as in Humayun's mausoleum, with rooms arranged like the points that mark five on dice. Such a plan is clearly Indian in conception.

On the exterior the less important rooms are finished with graceful *chhatri* which are very decorative. At the four corners of the plinth rise four slender, three-storey minarets crowned with small kiosks on small pillars which make the mausoleum appear like a 'lotus flower among a bunch of lotus buds'.[27] The square pool to the front with the usual channels set in a cross, and the flower beds divided into squares, add a touch of magic to the fine scene, so that the whole seems to 'rise above green glittering lotus leaves floating on crystal-clear water'.[28]

On the external façades of the mausoleum an immense central *pishtaq* niche stands out, the semi-vault of which is finished with *muqarnas*. The *pishtaq* is flanked by small double arches arranged one on another. Except for the entrance on the southern side all the other sides are closed with screens divided into small compartments filled with pieces of glass, both on the lower floor and on the upper floor. The glass is slightly milky so as to appear more translucent than transparent to reduce the strong Indian light which with the reflection from the white marble would have been intolerable. Each section of the façade is underlined on both sides by pillars which rise up from the level of the plinth to the frieze of the tomb and are crowned by graceful pinnacles with lotus buds and terminals. The pillars are decorated with a herringbone motif in black and yellow on the white marble background and are flanked at the base by panels carrying the same motif.

The majestic double dome terminates in a wide upside-down lotus flower surmounted by a high terminal. The lack of contrast between the surface of the façade and the curved line of the dome, derived from Persian prototypes, clearly demonstrates the attention with which the effect of the whole has been studied. The octagonal plan seems to create, at a distance, the illusory perspective of a compact, almost cylindrical mass that is nevertheless extraordinarily balanced and free of any structure that could possibly generate 'horizontal' tendencies, such as are found instead in the entrance to the garden, the mosque and the *jawab* that stands opposite it. On the other hand we cannot talk of a true tendency towards the vertical, despite the presence of the minarets. The height of the façade, indeed, is equal to the height of the dome, excluding the terminal in gold that completes it, while the width of the building is little less than its height from ground level to the summit of the dome, so that the construction could be contained within an immense cube resting on the more important sides of the base. But the thrust upwards is achieved firstly because the clarity of the marble negates the heaviness of the material and, secondly, through the contribution made to this effect by the deep and clear areas of shadow drawn on the burial structure by arches and galleries, together with the ascending note of the small pilasters which delimit all the structure's projecting surfaces.

The rather sober exterior decoration makes use of epigraphic elements taken from Koranic Suras, chosen for their precise symbolic meaning by Abd al-Haqq of Shiraz, the empire's best calligrapher. He had already executed the inscriptions on Akbar's tomb and had been honoured by Shah Jahan with the title of Amanat Khan (Noble Worthy of Praise), as well as an extremely high income. Other decoration, arranged over the surfaces of the building, include racemes, bouquets of flowers, zigzag motifs and series of small arches repeated several times and made in hard stone with occasional use of precious stones. Some of these decorations are already found in the mausoleum of Itimad al-Daula and in various Persian and Mughal miniatures in which finely decorated architectural structures appear.

Contemporary texts specify the stones used in the ornamentation and the artists who carried out the work. Lapis lazuli, various types of jasper, agates, carnelian, jade, amethyst, turquoise, onyx and Mediterranean corals together with yellow and black marbles were all used. Here and there even diamonds, sapphires and emeralds were used which were then looted by the Afghans of Ahmad Shah Durrani after the tragic defeat of the Marathas at the battle of Panipat (13 January 1761). In their turn the Marathas had already melted the massive silver doors of the mausoleum because of the necessities of war.

Inside, the mural ornamentation was equally sober and delicate. At the centre of the funeral chamber is a beautiful balustrade in perforated marble which surrounds the cenotaphs of Mumtaz Mahall and Shah Jahan. As early as 1643 it replaced the original balustrade in gold and precious stones that the emperor had commissioned. The joints of the delicate *jali* slabs are also decorated with floral motifs in hard stone.

Undoubtedly, however, much of the charm of the Taj Mahall is due to the splendid Makrana marble which with its pearly clarity acquires infinite shades of colour and soft, ethereal shadows which succeed in lending definition and depth. It appears shrouded at dawn, dazzling at midday, rosy at sunset and 'splendidly cold in the moonlight when the dome, thin in substance as the air, hangs suspended among the stars like a great pearl'.[29]

From a distance all the decoration disappears and the mausoleum, fixed between its minarets, appears like a tiny block of worked marble which increases in size until it dominates the vision as one moves closer to it. Without a doubt the water of the canals adds to this effect, together with the clear paving of the central pool and its cruciform branches with the cypresses, while the evergreen plants in rows suggest a perspective running to infinity.

From the Mughal epoch onwards Tavernier spread the news that Shah Jahan had started to build a tomb for himself on the other side of the river from the Taj, but that he had been prevented from completing it by the war that started with his son Aurangzeb who had no intention whatsoever of finishing it.

With this scant information the imagination of nineteenth-century chroniclers ran wild to the point of suggesting that the new tomb must have been in black marble in order to contrast with the clarity of the Taj and the two tombs must have been connected by a bridge that symbolized the indissoluble union between the two spouses. They even pointed out the remains of the foundations on the site. But in reality those ruins are part of the perimeter walls of the Mahtab Bagh with the plinths of some pavilions, traces of canals, pools, corbels, slabs of stone, all founded by Babur. Anyway, contemporary Persian histories make no mention at all of a second Taj. Furthermore, the Mahtab Burj, which rises alone on the other side of the river and is the south-eastern tower of the Mahtab Bagh, the others having collapsed, cannot be compared at all with the towers of the Taj. The former reaches a height of 3.66 m and has one single storey crowned by a *chhatri*, while the latter are over 13 metres high over several floors with a complex system of rooms and verandahs. One piece of evidence put forward in favour of the construction of a second mausoleum for Shah Jahan is the unusual position, almost an inferior position, of the emperor's cenotaph compared with that of his wife which occupies the centre of the funeral chamber. But this position is identical with that found in the tombs of Itimad al-Daula, both on the ground and upper floors. While the mausoleum of Asmat Begum occupies the exact centre of the tomb chamber, Mirza Ghiyas Beg's occupies a non-symmetrical position to the right. The reason for this is probably to be found in the fact that in both cases the wife died before the husband. Since according to Islamic law bodies must be buried with the face turned to Mecca and the legs pointing south, the husbands were arranged to the right of their wives. Thus fails the theory that the cenotaph of Shah Jahan was never supposed to be installed here, but in an independent mausoleum, and that only *force majeure* constrained him to be buried here, near his wife.

The Taj Mahall was also easily accessible from the river. Indeed, it seems that, early, approach by water was preferred. A state barge was used for the emperor and

One of four marble pavilions (1637) on the banks of Lake Ana Sagar at Ajmer.

Above The tomb of Afzal Khan at Agra, called Chini-ka Rauza becaues of its glazed tile decoration, now mostly lost.

Opposite The Akhund Mulla Shah Mosque (1649) near Fort Hari Parbat, at Srinagar.

his court and they would disembark on the ground-floor steps on the north-western corner of the terrace. The appearance of the building from the water was no less striking in the reflection of the river than it was from the fine arches of the entrance. It remained consistently clear yet remote like an opalescent painting. From any point of view the Taj seemed to confirm the emotional verses of Sir Edwin Arnold, according to whom in front of it, 'The blood runs quicker and the spirit rises, and the need to worship bends weak knees while breath, forgotten, stops.'[30]

Ajmer: marble pavilions
At Ajmer are four single-storey marble pavilions (see p. 255) on the bank of Lake Ana Sagar with fine *chhajja* supported by elegant worked corbels.[31]

Agra: Chini-ka Rauza
At Agra there is the beautiful tomb of Afzal Khan, called Chini-ka Rauza because it is decorated with glazed tiles, now for the most part lost.[32]

Srinagar: Akhund Mulla Shah Mosque
In 1649 Shah Jahan dedicated a mosque at Srinagar, near Fort Hari Parbat, to Akhund Mulla Shah. This mosque is worthy of note although modest in size and now for the most part ruined. The shrine, with one aisle and three spans, is enclosed within a courtyard which includes a fountain for ablutions and various spaces for the mosque staff or worshippers. The entire construction is in slabs of grey granite on a frame of bricks and in its simplicity of line and the elegance of its proportions it reveals the taste of Shah Jahan, although obviously more modestly than the Taj.[33]

Gardens
The Peri Mahall (Palace of the Fairies) with five terraces, built near Srinagar by Dara Shikoh, is lacking in cascades and pools, perhaps because water was brought there underground. It is thought that this was an astrology school for the tutor of the prince and heir, Akhund Mulla Shah.

Again in the vicinity of Srinagar stands the charming garden known as Chashma Shahi (Royal Spring) which an inscription of 1632 on the entrance attributes to Shah Jahan himself but which was perhaps really built by Ali Mardan Khan under the emperor's supervision. It is small and exploits the powerful jet of spring water that spurts from the high part of the garden and which was renowned for its purity. The water was made to gurgle through a marble basin in the shape of a lotus flower which is now missing. This was arranged on the floor of the upper pavilion and from there the water ran down a small cascade and a channel until it filled a wide rectangular pool in which the second and principal pavilion was reflected, erected on a magnificent supporting wall some 6 m high. Underneath this a second, extremely steep cascade ran from the centre of the wall to fill another water garden on the lower level. The pavilions, in the Kashmiri style with several slopes on the roofs, but with Mughal bases, dominate a splendid view of Lake Dal. Even though much altered and now diminished in size, this garden still has a sweet and romantic atmosphere, accentuated by the cloister of the mountains that surrounds it together with the richness of the flowers and the birds that adorn it.

Many of Shah Jahan's gardens were along the road between Agra and Kabul, so that they could be used as resting places when the king travelled to Kashmir or to Afghanistan. One of these gardens was at Ambala; it had been donated to Jahanara, who had beautiful pavilions built there for the women of the *zenana*.

At Sirhind, Shah Jahan had some additions made to the garden designed by Akbar. These included pavilions for public audiences and private structures. The Amm Bagh, as it was called, was divided into four sections, of which one, reserved for the sovereign, included an elegant two-storey building with a *bangaldar* roof. The other sections were used to grow flowers, vegetables and fruit trees. But the pride of Shah Jahan's gardens are the Shalimar gardens near Lahore and Srinagar.

The garden on Lake Dal is enriched with various rows of sparkling fountains and numerous shady trees which together manage to temper and make bearable the intense summer heat. Jahangir, who had a special predilection for Kashmir, had chosen the place: he was charmed by the area when he visited it as a child. Later, together with his wife Nur Jahan, he built many gardens there, of which some still exist. He wrote in his memoirs:

Kashmir is an eternal spring garden. Its pleasant lawns and charming waterfalls are above any description. There is no end to its babbling brooks and fountains. Wherever one turns there are cascades and greenery. Roses, violets and daffodils grow wild; in the fields there is every type of flower and sweetly perfumed herb, more than one could ever count. In this charming spring the hills and the plains are full of budding flowers while doors, walls, courtyards, roofs are all lit by tulip torches.[34]

The Mughal gardens of Kashmir are perhaps the most successful example of the adaptation of an existing gardening tradition to new environmental conditions. The basic form of the *char bagh* was maintained with channels crossing at right-angles and dividing the garden in quarters where beds full of flowers and trees bloomed between the channels. But the perimeter walls of Persian tradition were replaced by the surrounding circle of mountains; pavilions were added which introduced the charm of reflections in the water enlivened by fountains and jets.

The garden of Shalimar, the most secluded, but also the most famous of the Srinagar gardens, was reached directly from Lake Dal by means of a canal. This was about 1 km long, flanked on both sides by high trees, and led straight into the garden. Today an asphalt road crosses the entrance of the garden, cutting it off from its original approach. The flow of water leads to a huge basin in which stands a large black marble pavilion, surrounded on all sides by water and fountains. This was the Diwan-i Amm, where the emperor chaired public hearings sitting on a black marble throne under which ran water that then poured back into the large basin underneath in a small cascade. From here another, wider canal began which led to the most secluded part of the garden, reserved for the harem, where the gradients are more accentuated. The canal culminates in the beautiful marble pavilion that Shah Jahan had built. According to Bernier, in the mid-seventeenth century it was covered by a dome, like the Diwan-i Amm: today it carries a triple Kashmiri roof and the pictorial decoration which appears on the ceiling is of the mid-nineteenth century. Shalimar Bagh combines refined detail and proportions with an all-pervasive peace and calm that creates a sort of melancholy. The lake is invisible from here but it is always present in one's thoughts with its fresh, placid waters dotted with lotus flowers. The mountains are all around but are not overpowering and oppressive as in the other two gardens at Nishat Bagh and Chashma Shahi. The circular range is gentle, the mountains are glimpsed only occasionally through the branches of the trees, the changes in level are gradual and were kept as such to provide a sense of rest and reserve. The choice of the site was Jahangir's work, but Shah Jahan helped him plan it even from the days when he was still only a prince, and certainly Nur Jahan will have assisted. The original name of the site was Farah Baksh (Dispensary of Pleasure), because Shalimar seems to date from the Hindu Pravarasena II who in the sixth century built a house here called Shalimar (Home of Love). Shah Jahan, after having enlarged it, built the *baradari* of the *zenana* garden (1630), and having himself succeeded to the throne, called this area to the north the Faiz Baksh (Dispensary of Plenty).

Lahore: Shalimar gardens

But the crowning glory of Shah Jahan's gardens is found in Shalimar at Lahore (see p. 258), built by Ali Mardan Khan under the emperor's instructions between 1633 and 1642. The gardens consist of three large terraces arranged over various levels with canals, pools, pavilions, fountains and cascades (*abshar*), all in white marble in a huge complex and enlivened with flowering perfumed plants. Some writers recorded that originally there were seven terraces, corresponding to the seven stages of Heaven, but others consider the current garden to be complete in itself. Since it is of a considerable size and is surrounded by a high wall of bricks, this last theory seems more probable. Nevertheless, the entrance to the garden has been altered. Originally the entrance

Above The Shalimar gardens at Lahore were built from 1633 to 1642 by Ali Mardan Khan under Shah Jahan's instructions.

Opposite The tombs of Bala Pir and his son Shaikh Mahdi at Kanauj in northern India.

was on the lowest terrace, as is normal in Mughal gardens where one proceeded upwards and new delights appeared gradually as the observer passed each terrace until reaching the last, private, terrace which constituted the *zenana*. The upper terrace was known by the name of Farah Baksh (Dispensary of Pleasure), while the central terrace and the lower one, forming the most public area of the garden, were known together as Faiz Baksh (Dispensary of Plenty). Indeed, the central level is the most spectacular. The great cistern, over 60 m wide, once contained 152 fountains of which over 100 survive. At the centre there is a marble platform reached by means of a narrow raised pathway. The water flows down through the southern pavilion by means of a wide cascade in carved marble (*chadar*) and at the base, suspended over the water, is the white marble throne of the emperor where he used to sit and watch the fountains, while the air around him was freshened by the babbling waters.

The original number of the fountains has been estimated at 450, many of which survive. In the canals, the water rose in sprays more than 3.5 m high. Shah Jahan used to change the trees and the flowers, even having them brought in from Kabul and Kandahar. Planes and poplars were planted at intervals while under the trees there were grassy swards where one could lie comfortably in the shadow. Among the original trees were apples, mangoes, apricots, cherries, plums, almonds, oranges, quinces, mulberries and cypresses, all mixed with aromatic plants. Lahori describes the cascades with countless *chini khana* or holes dug for the doves underneath. In these, during the day, vases of golden flowers were displayed; at night perfumed candles were lit in them.

In the garden there were many buildings. There were four pavilions on the *zenana* terrace and some smaller buildings to the side. On the central level there were four more pavilions, two of which were once joined on the northern side. There were even baths to the east, with warm and cold areas and a dressing room. On the lower terrace in front of the central axis of the garden was the hall for private audiences. The pavilions were stripped of their marble and agate decoration by the

Sikhs in the eighteenth century in order to decorate the Ram Bagh and the Golden Temple at Amritsar. The pavilions are currently restored in brick and plaster; very little of the original work survives.

OTHER MINOR BUILDINGS

In addition to the gardens, Shah Jahan also had pavilions built in various places, including the reconstruction, in 1634, of the one that his father had built at Sheikhpura (Punjab). In 1637 the construction of the Lal Mahall (Red Palace) was completed at Bari, not far from Dholphur. This large palace, which got its name from the colour of the stone of which it was built, stood on the shore of a lake and was actually made up of a number of small buildings, including a *hammam* which was reached by means of a raised passageway adorned with *chhatri*. In one large pavilion there are three courtyards, of which the central one, reserved for the emperor, has a *jharoka* with a curved roof over it. All of the palace buildings are contained within a walled enclosure. A similar layout, though on a smaller scale, was also used for the hunting lodges at Rupbas and Mahal, not far from Agra. About 120 km from Delhi stand the ruins of Shah Jahan's summer palace, which was built for him in 1653. It was called Faizabad and was one of the sovereign's favourite retreats, as it afforded him shelter from the fierce summer heat of the capital. It also provided hospitality for the whole court when, towards the end of Shah Jahan's reign, Delhi was struck by a terrible epidemic of plague and cholera.

In various centres of population to the north of Delhi, along the Delhi–Lahore directrix – Jhajjar, Garaunda, Thanesar, Sirhind, Nakodar – there are many remaining monuments of the Mughal epoch. The oldest of these dates back to Akbar's last years while the most recent dates from the time of Dara Shikoh, Shah Jahan's son.

In this period various caravanserais were built, some 20 dotted along a route of some 1,000 km, each a day's walk from the next. Among these we should mention those at Begly, Garaunda and Gurgaon. At Alwar stands the mausoleum of a minister of Shah Jahan, Fateh Jang, remarkable for its bulk and its unusual architecture.

Other minor buildings include the tombs of Bala Pir and his son Shaikh Mahdi at Kanauj, once the ancient Hindu capital of northern India. The two harmonious stone structures have a square plan with low domes fixed on octagonal drums surrounded by corner *chhatri* and supported by slender pillars.

THANESAR: SHAIKH CHILLIE

The tomb of Shaikh Chillie (see p. 260) at Thanesar on the road between Delhi and Lahore is of great architectonic and decorative elegance. David Ross has classed it as second only to the Taj Mahall. It would seem that the shaikh was the spiritual guide of Dara Shikoh and Cunningham attributes the construction of this mausoleum to Shah Jahan's son, dating it about 1650. Built in red granite dressed in white marble, it rests on an octagonal platform, each side of which measures some 10 m, and was once surrounded by open-work balustrades. The platform rises at the centre of a square enclosure (53 m each side), originally paved in marble, which is built over 12 m above the ground level of the surrounding plain. The perimeter walls are adorned with 12 small cupolas dressed in glazed tiles, of which little trace now remains. The tomb itself has an octagonal plan, with each façade opened by a deep, multi-lobed, arched niche in which there are two windows, one on top of the other: the lower one is rectangular, the other is pointed arch in shape and is filled with *jali*. A wide *chhajja* runs all round the top of the building and terminates with a frieze of crenellations decorated at the corners by slender domed terminals; it is surmounted by a fine, slightly pear-shaped dome resting on a high cylindrical drum. Inside, the dome is decorated with pleasant paintings. It seems that the Sikhs transformed the building into one of their own sanctuaries after having taken away various slabs of open-work marble. In the western wall of the perimeter there stands another structure which is held locally to be the tomb of Shaikh Chillie's wife, but which S. Parihar considers to be a mosque. It, too, rests on a marble platform and is covered by a fine Bengali-type dome (*char chala*), again in white marble. Its red sandstone walls are divided into panels, with simple bas-relief patterns alternating with rectangular open-work windows. Inside the enclosure is a garden divided into squares with a wide central pool, and also a quadrangular brick *madrasa*, surrounded by an open court.

NAKODAR: HAJJI JAMAL (SHAGIRD) MAUSOLEUM

The tomb of Hajji Jamal (Shagird) at Nakodar, which we have already mentioned, also belongs to Shah Jahan's time. Square outside, with octagonal turrets at the corners surmounted by *chhatri* which frame a fine central dome on a high cylindrical dome, this tomb is octagonal inside, the opposite arrangement to that of the nearby Ustad's Tomb. Its four external façades are opened by deep, semi-octagonal pointed arch niches, flanked by much smaller niches and completely dressed with rectangular panels of tile mosaics in lively colours with motifs of bunches of flowers and leaves in vases.

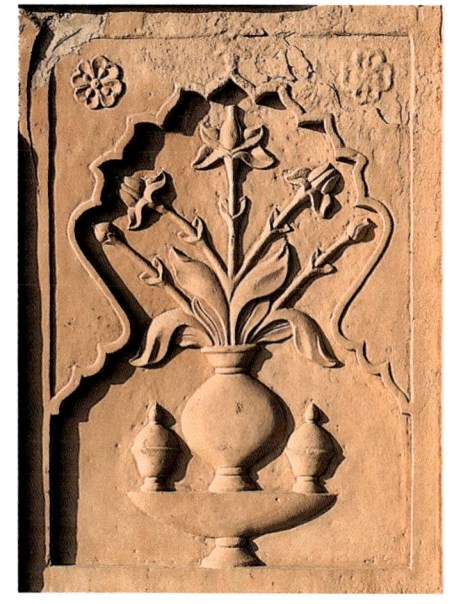

Caravanserais

Not far from Nakodar stands the Dakhni caravanserai which has not been dated, but because of the similarity of some of its structures and decoration with the Wazir Khan Mosque at Lahore and the mausoleum of Itimad al-Daula at Agra, it has led Begley to consider 1632–4 as a possibility.[35] The caravanserai presents an imposing façade without crenellations but enclosed between octagonal towers divided into five floors by ornamental panels terminating in a high cornice supported by arches and on which domed *chhatri* are fixed on pillars. Around the wide central pointed arch that dominates the true entrance there are rectangular balconies arranged on three floors: the lower one contains blind niches, the two upper ones carry triforia supported by slender pillars. The extradoses of the arches are decorated with glazed tiles that carry sinuous, vegetal arabesque designs.

Another beautiful caravanserai, much ruined by the structures of a modern village, is the Amanat Khan, dated 1640, a few kilometres from Amritsar, the sacred city of the Sikhs.[36] It has an almost square plan of some 180 m each side with corner bastions and is dominated by two enormous entrances at the centre of the eastern and western sides, through which once passed the Mughal road for Lahore. These display numerous stylistic innovations over the Serai Dakhni. Here the entrance archway is much wider and more articulated through the addition of a fluted intrados which accentuates the play of *chiaroscuro* with the more deeply inset entrance arrangement. The panels that articulate the octagonal corner towers with their *chhatri* are varied in format and are clearly different from the panels on the rest of the façade. On the façade the projecting balconies are much refined and their slender proportions emphasize even more the width of the central arch. All these details reveal the hand of a knowing architect, perhaps the very same who executed the Wazir Khan Mosque some six years previously. Given the ruinous condi-

Shah Jahan (1628–1657)

Opposite top The elegant mausoleum of Shaikh Chillie (c.1650) at Thanesar on the road between Delhi and Lahore. It has been classed by one scholar as second only to the Taj Mahall.

Opposite bottom Decorative red sandstone relief panel showing a bunch of flowers in a vase from the Shaikh Chillie mausoleum complex at Thanesar.

Below The red sandstone gate of a mid-seventeenth-century caravanserai outside Gurgaon, near Delhi on the road to Agra.

tion of the caravanserai, the exact number of rooms that were aligned on its four arcaded sides is not known, but we know that they measured 3.5 m each side and were covered with cupolas. The decorative detail is also extremely refined: the elegant floral and epigraphic designs in glazed blue and yellow tiles which fill both border panels and the extradoses of arches seem destined for a carpet rather than a work of architecture. The beautiful inscriptions were executed by the owner of the caravanserai, Amanat Khan – held in very high regard by Shah Jahan who showered him with honours – and who looked after the epigraphic decoration of the Taj Mahall. In the southern half of the courtyard is a small mosque with three spans, covered by three low domes; its façade is dominated by two pointed arches with lower lateral arches. Here, too, there is much floral and calligraphic decoration executed in multicoloured glazed tiles and dated 1640–41. Some hundreds of metres from the caravanserai is a domed tomb in the same style, which it is thought to be that of Amanat Khan, and was erected by him or by one of sons, Aqil Khan, who had attained a position of eminence at the court of Shah Jahan.[37]

Another beautiful but much ruined caravanserai rises at Garaunda, between Panipat and Karnal. Its courtyard is enclosed by a high wall with corner bastions and it had two beautiful porches on its northern and southern sides, practically the only structures that have survived. They are very similar and, although not of great proportions, have an extremely elegant aspect. On the outside a large pointed and multifoil arch frames the lower arch of the entrance, likewise multifoil and surmounted by three ogival niches, in their turn surmounted by another, central niche. The lateral panels are lightly traced with blind niches in various shapes and sizes on which there are two balconies, one on each side. The whole is enclosed by two cylindrical bastions with their shafts alternately triangular and rounded and tapering towards the top as in the Qutb Minar (see p. 23); they are divided into two sections by a relief border which is emphasized even more by cross motifs painted in white on the brickwork. The upper part of the shaft is decorated with a series of miniature balconies which protrude from the circular flutes. The bastions must have been covered by domes which are now lost. The interior of the porches is also very elegant, articulated by deep niche openings and by large domed balconies resting on extremely elegant corbels. It seems that this caravanserai was built by a certain Firuz Khan at the time of Shah Jahan, according to an inscription, now lost, which was still in place at the beginning of the nineteenth century.[38]

Another small caravanserai (see p. 261), built near the village of Gurgaon, not far from Delhi on the road to Agra, must be from more or less same period as the Amanat Khan serai. Here, too, the beautiful entrance in red sandstone is preserved: it is characterized by a large pointed and lowered arch which frames the entrance. It is flanked by two elegant domed balconies which face towards the exterior with three small, multi-lobed arches divided by small columns which reach to the level of the supporting corbels and are finely carved. The extradoses of the arch are filled with white marble and are decorated with lotus buds, while panels of various sizes and dimensions occupy the rest of the surface. The façade is enclosed by two elegant and slender keeps on two floors, which terminate in elegant octagonal and domed *chhatri* (one of which has collapsed). At one extremity of the caravanserai's perimeter there stands a small mosque carrying three openings with multi-lobed arches and as many small hemispheric cupolas, sprouting from a row of lotus petals and terminating in an upside-down lotus flower. The central arch projects strongly relative to the others, but they are all adorned with a wide, slightly inclined *chhajja*. The lateral walls of the mosque are also decorated with blind niches in arch or geometric shapes.

Other buildings

The Rang Mahall at Buria, dating from 1630, and the Chatta Rai Bal Mukand Das at Narnaul both date from Shah Jahan's time. The former is a simple construction on two floors resting on a platform, which on the ground floor includes a central hall and four oblong spaces at the corners, connected together by means of small arched openings. All the rooms have flat roofs; the ceiling of the great hall is supported at the centre by a solid pillar which could have been a later addition. From the north-western and south-western corners short flights of stairs lead to the upper floor, the rooms of which are arranged identically, but are covered with low domes. The roof, reached by means of two flights of stairs, is covered by cupolas and carries an octagonal platform. The external walls are articulated by deep niches and symmetrical designs; inside there are paintings with floral motifs and animals (especially elephants) executed in brilliant colours.

The Narnaul palace, known locally as the Birbal Ka Chatta, is a large four-storey residence erected by the *mansabdar* (rank holder) Rai Mukand. It sits on an elaborate *tah khana* and is arranged through a series of ingenious cloisters, courtyards with pools decorated by fountains, *hammam*, domed spaces and decorated entrances. A series of steps on the western wall leads to a first-floor terrace in front of which is the *chhatta* (literally the hive), a marble platform covered by a curved roof – typical of Shah Jahan's epoch – which is joined to the southern wall of the building and supported by S-shaped corbels. On the same floor is a large entrance with a multi-lobed horseshoe arch decorated inside with a fine stalactite motif. It leads to a courtyard surrounded on all sides by arcades, with a high platform at the centre. From the courtyard the other floors can be reached as well as the ground floor, which contains many dark, fresh and pure areas enlivened with pools and cascades. Many of the ceilings are in wood and some parts of the building carry traces of painted decoration.

Among the mosques that were built during Shah Jahan's reign we may mention the ones that were built by two women from Ajmer: one of them was the daughter of a famous musician and the other was Miyan Bai, to whom Jahanara had donated the Gulabi Bagh garden at Lahore. Both these mosques are on the road that leads to the tomb of the saint Muin al-Din. The more beautiful one is Miyan Bai's, which is modelled on the mosque that Shah Jahan had had built some years before in the *dargah* of the saint Chishti. The façade, on the eastern side, has five archways supported by slender pillars and, on the inside, a very fine ogival *mihrab* forming a deep niche which is divided into three sections.

Nevertheless, the most elegant mosque, and the one most closely connected with Timurid models, is the Great Mosque that Shah Jahan himself had built at Thatta between 1644 and 1647 (see p. 71).

In all of the buildings of Shah Jahan's reign, whether they were planned directly by the emperor or whether they were the creations of his sons, his wives or his nobles, there is an easily recognizable unitary design that builds on Akbar's and Jahangir's works, and also on Timurid and Safavid buildings (prevalently the Central Asian ones), but these are elaborated so as to be presented in a new aspect, perhaps simpler in design but more sumptuous in decoration, though this is never excessive or vulgar.

[1] Goetz, *op. cit.*, p. 817.
[2] In the ornamental design along the skirting of the walls, we come across the first representation of a row of bulbous-based columns that seem to stem from vases. According to Koch (*op. cit.*, pp. 251–62) these columns were taken from European prints, where they were shown on either side of the figures of kings or religious authorities. They would have been used by Shah Jahan in the rooms that were reserved for him personally, as for instance this room behind the *jharoka*, to emphasize his semi-divine nature in the eyes of the courtiers who assembled there.
[3] Asaf Khan, the emperor's father-in-law, was charged with the job of rebuilding the tower, though it was the emperor himself who made the final decision as to the design of the building. The entrance to the quadrangle, now known as the Elephant Gate, is a large brick structure with a tiled roof. It was the work of Mamur Khan, formerly Jahangir's architect.
[4] On the western façade there is an arched niche enclosed within exquisitely carved marble slabs, and three rectangular windows that perhaps served as the *jharoka*.
[5] Construction was begun by the architects Ustad Ahmad and Ustad Hamid, though both of them died before the work was completed. In 1647 Shah Jahan called in two more architects, Aqa Yusuf and Aqil Khan, as he was impatient to see his work completed. He had actively taken part in the construction, not only by choosing the design of the various buildings but also personally by urging on the workmen to do better and better. The work was supervised at first by the Governor of Delhi, Ghairat

Khan, and then by Makramat Khan who, by completing the work quickly in 1648, earned himself an important honorary title. The fort was inaugurated in great pomp and splendour in April of the same year, with generous gifts from the sovereign to all those who had helped make his city beautiful. The main buildings were draped with silken hangings embroidered with gold, silver and pearls. During the ceremonies Shah Jahan gave his nobles gifts of money, ceremonial garments, gem-encrusted swords and even parade elephants, to thank them for having built themselves luxurious houses, gardens and small mosques. Cf. S. P. Blake, 'Cityscape of an Imperial Capital: Shahjahanabad in 1739', in R. E. Frykenberg ed., *Delhi through the Ages*, Delhi 1986, p. 175.

[6] *List of Muhammadan and Hindu Monuments, Delhi Province*, 4 vols., Calcutta 1916-22, vol. 1, p. 4.

[7] These have now been removed. They divided the fort in quadrangles, as at Lahore and Agra.

[8] The roofed-over market, an Iranian tradition, was an innovation in Mughal palaces. The ones at Fatehpur Sikri and Agra are open-air markets. It appears that the idea of this new type had come to Shah Jahan after he had seen the one that Ali Mardan Khan, his most senior nobleman, had constructed at Peshawar (northern Pakistan). He had occasion to see it during his visit to that city in 1646 and later instructed his head architect, Makramat Khan, to build a similar one at Shahjahanabad.

[9] Brown, *op. cit.*, p. 104.

[10] Like the curved canopy and the bulbous columns, these were directly linked with the symbolism of royalty and thus served to emphasize the role of 'Lord of the World' that Shah Jahan felt he impersonated.

[11] The imperial baths were one of the most important parts of the palace: only the emperor's most trustworthy counsellors were admitted, in order to discuss delicate state matters.

[12] Brown, *op. cit.*, p. 104.

[13] *Ibid*.

[14] The supervision of the work was entrusted to the architects Allami Said Khan and Fazi Khan, who had received orders from Shah Jahan to reproduce the design of the *jami masjid* of Fatehpur Sikri, considered to be a model of perfection. The emperor named it Masjid-i Jahanuma (The Mosque that Shows the World). The interior bears a closer resemblance to the Agra Mosque, although, like the one at Fatehpur Sikri, it stands on a rise.

[15] In the *mihrab* and the half-domed niches that adorn the side walls can be seen columns with bulbous bases, connected with Shah Jahan's royal and semi-divine nature.

[16] The tomb of the saint, Miran Badshah, is situated on one side of the courtyard. In the area where the mosque stands there was also a *hammam*, the proceeds of which were used to finance the mosque, a caravanserai, various shops and private houses.

[17] The huge portal, which had ogival niches on all sides, is built of bricks faced with tiled panels, in the typical Punjab fashion. The inscription, which is dated 1646, states that Jahanara built the portal and donated the garden (now no longer there) to Miyan Bay, an unknown but evidently influential lady, who some years earlier had a mosque bearing her name built at Ajmer.

[18] The mosque has a slightly irregular groundplan, in order to adapt to a previously existing road, and the single nave is divided into three bays. The façade has three large, pointed arches in it. Above the central one there is an openwork frieze, while on either side there is a slender turret whose shaft is decorated in a herring-bone pattern. This arch is also taller than the others and is adorned with panels that are beautifully carved with inscriptions, arabesques and floral wreaths.

[19] In the Mughal chronicles the mausoleum is only called Rauza-i Manuwwara (Illuminated Tomb).

[20] W. E. Begley, 'The Myth of the Taj Mahal and New Theory of its Symbolic Meanings', *Art Bulletin*, 61 (1979), pp. 7-37.

[21] *Ibid*.

[22] Cf. Nath, *The Immortal Taj Mahal: the Evolution of the Tomb in Mughal Architecture*, Bombay 1972, p. 55.

[23] *Ibid*., p. 56.

[24] In actual fact, the design of the gold balustrades was the work of Bebadal Khan, Shah Jahan's chief jeweller, who had also completed the Peacock Throne (Asher, *op. cit.*, pp. 197 and 214).

[25] M. Bussagli, 'Il Taj Mahall', in *Oriente e occidente*, Florence 1970, pp. 55-63 (62).

[26] However, the artists who certainly worked on the Taj Mahal included Makramat Khan, Abd al-Karim and Amanat Khan, the famous calligrapher who attended to all the inscriptions and also chose the texts that were to be reproduced.

[27] Nath, *op. cit.*, p. 51.

[28] *Ibid*.

[29] Brown, *op. cit.*, p. 109.

[30] Bussagli, *op. cit.*, p. 62.

[31] These four pavilions, known as *baradari*, are all that is left of a palace built in 1637 by Shah Jahan at Ajmer, in the place where his father had previously built pleasure pavilions. Two of them, which are very similar, stand opposite one another on the shores of the lake. Their 'trabeated' structure, of a Hindu-Akbar type, is made up of faceted columns of white marble supporting multiple corbels with a characteristic curved form, which carry the flat roof with sharply sloping *chhajja*. Two more pavilions face respectively towards the water and towards the land: the latter, hypostyle one is divided into two concentric zones, following the design of Akbar's private buildings.

[32] Afzal Khan (died 1638) was Shah Jahan's minister of finance and the brother of the great calligrapher Amanat Khan. It must have been the latter who did the beautiful inscriptions in stucco all round the top of the burial chamber which is situated at the centre of the building. The tomb, which is also decorated with very fine paintings, once stood in a large garden. It is the only example at Agra of a decoration similar to that of the Wazir Khan Mosque at Lahore.

[33] Jahanara, like her brother Dara Shikoh, was a great devotee of the saint.

[34] H. Beveridge, ed., *Memoirs of Jahangir*, trans. A. Rogers, London 1909 and 1914.

[35] W.E. Begley, 'Four Mughal Caravanserais Built during the Reign of Jahangir and Shah Jahan', *Muqarnas*, 1 (1983), pp. 167-79.

[36] As is attested by its name, this was constructed by Shah Jahan's famous calligrapher.

[37] Amanat Khan is also attributed with having built the small mosque Shahi Madrasa at Agra (1636), in which he executed the Koranic inscriptions in the three *mihrab*.

[38] Firuz Khan had a fine tomb built for himself near Agra in about 1640. It is an octagonal building in red sandstone which stands inside a walled enclosure, with a pond on the western side and a fine, two-storey portal. Both the tomb and the portal are covered with beautiful panels which are finely carved with motifs such as vases of flowers, wine carafes, confronted animals and floral arabesques.

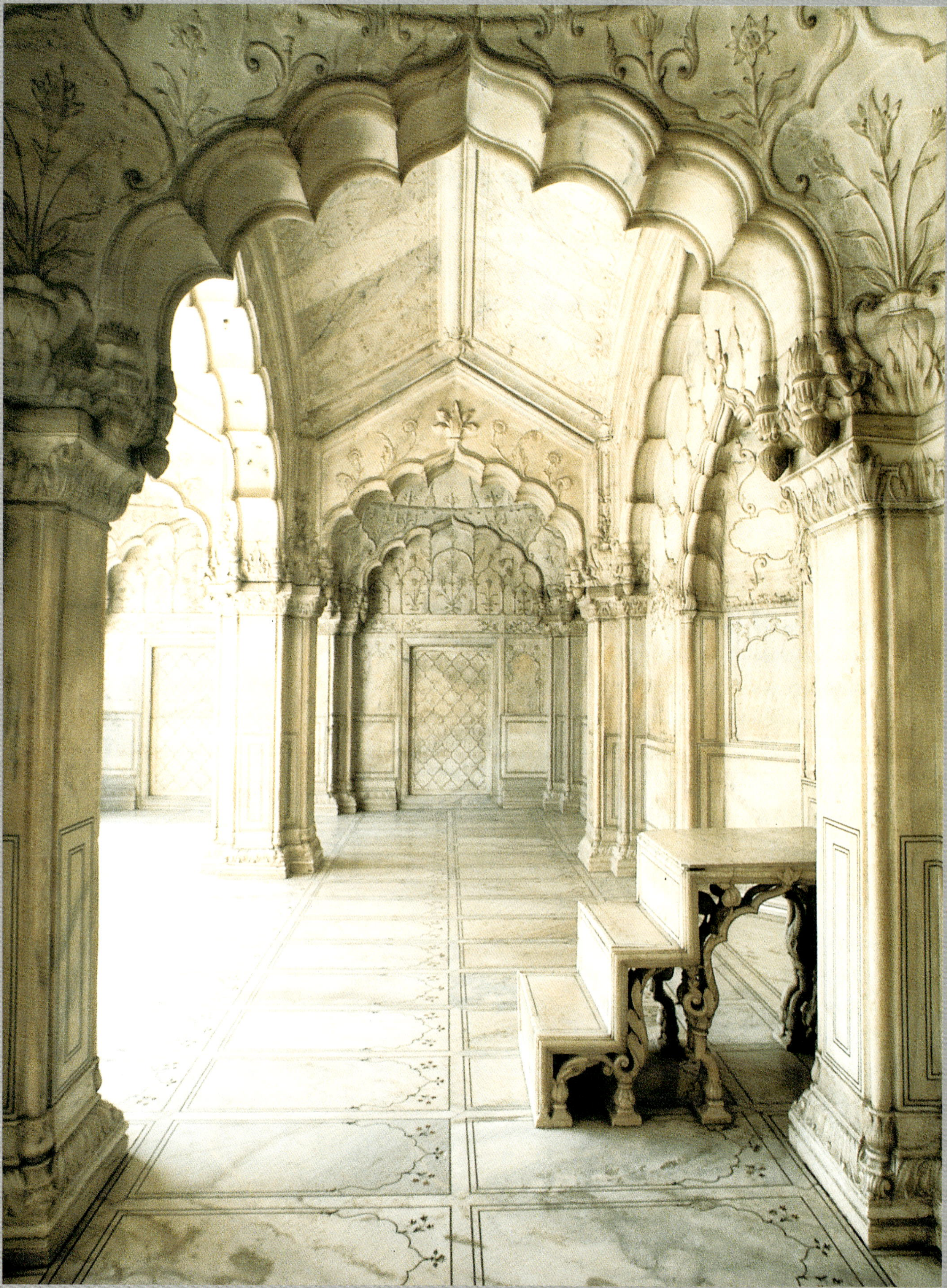

THE CLASSIC MUGHAL PERIOD IV
AURANGZEB (1658-1707)

17

Interior of the Moti Mosque, in the Red Fort at Delhi. The white marble mosque incorporates sinuous and exaggerated forms, unlike its rather severe namesake at Agra.

Aurangzeb came to the throne in 1658, having deprived his father of all authority and imprisoned him in the fort at Agra. His official coronation, however, took place on 5th June of the following year, three hours and fifteen minutes after sunrise, according perfectly with the astrologers' instructions and, in a certain sense, against the teachings of the Koran in which astrology has no place. The Koran was Aurangzeb's supposed inspiration. He took the name of Alamgir I (Lord of the World), but not even his court historians referred to him by this name; modern historians and critics prefer to call him Aurangzeb. His figure looms solitary, majestic, ominous and severe over the colourful background of Indian history. Deeply devoted and assiduous in his prayers, to which he dedicated from six to nine hours a day, Aurangzeb lived as a pauper in the midst of the luxury of his court; he disdained precious robes and wore only extremely simple white clothes. He was violently faithful to his duties, energetic to the point of cruelty, and governed his enormous empire with an iron fist, pursuing his doctrinaire vision of Islam until it brought about complete ruin. He had no desire to be the sovereign of the entire Indian people, who by that time had indeed become his people: he wanted instead to be champion of Islam. He consciously deprived himself of the Hindus' support and inverted the policy established by Akbar by persecuting the great majority of his subjects. In return he won hatred and rebellion. His army slowly lost its generals and its Rajput troops and was no longer able to provide real opposition to attacks, above all from the Sikhs and the Marathas. With Aurangzeb's reign began the decline of the Mughals' old military code.

His reign is divided into two almost equal parts of completely differing character: during the first (1658-81) he lived in the north, mostly at Delhi, completely depriving Agra of its role as capital. In those years there was relative peace. In the second part of his reign (1681-1707) he moved to Deccan where he was on campaign until his death without ever returning to the north. If the first period can be considered as one of apparent stasis, the second was characterised by a rapid and irresistible decline.

Aurangzeb eliminated his elder brothers through violence and cunning: Murad was tried and condemned in 1654, Dara Shikoh was executed in 1659, Shah Shuja was killed in 1660, probably by Arakanese bandits in central Burma where he had fled, pursued by Aurangzeb's troops. So, too, were his brothers' sons and the male relatives of his wife. Following this, together with his skilful minister and general, Mir Jumla, he began a campaign of conquest against Assam (1661–2), the results of which, however, were not long-lasting. In 1666, during an expedition against Arakanese bandits, he conquered Chittagong. But in the following year a revolt broke out between the tribes of the north-western frontier which lasted until 1676 and proved to be ruinous, costing the empire great losses in men and money. In 1669 Aurangzeb was driven by his conscience to begin his disastrous anti-Hindu policy and ordered the destruction of all the Hindu temples in the empire: Mathura and Benares fell victim to his iconoclastic fury, and the ultimate insult came with the construction of mosques in the two centres, a further affront to the indigenous heretics.

The *jizia*, abolished more than a century earlier by Akbar, was reintroduced and this provoked revolts even in the north where the Jat farmers in the area south of Delhi rebelled and even profaned Akbar's tomb, casting his ashes to the wind. The Sikhs, the religious sect founded in the sixteenth century by Guru Nanak, were deeply offended by the killing of their Guru Tegh Bahadur, who preferred death to conversion. They organized themselves into a warrior community that would provide problems for the Mughals themselves, and later the British. In Rajasthan the Rajputs rebelled – until then they had been loyal officers of the empire but they saw themselves threatened by a policy that called for their destruction and the institution of direct government of their land by the emperor.

Even if the rebellion ended with apparent peace in 1681, the Rajput aristocracy was by then an enemy of the empire. Prince Akbar also rebelled against his father and fled to the Maratha court in Deccan. Aurangzeb felt it was necessary to leave the capital in order to sort out the difficult situation that had been created. He could not have imagined that he would never return to Delhi and that Deccan was to be the tomb of the strength and prosperity of his empire, just as it would be his own sepulchre.

In addition to the two Muslim realms of Bijapur and Golconda, the small state of Maratha had emerged from the end of the Nizam Shahi reign. The Marathas acquired a true national consciousness under the leadership of Shivaji, who had struggled long against the sovereigns of Bijapur and the Mughal governors. On the death of Shivaji, following a final victorious campaign against the Mughals, Aurangzeb decided to destroy all the Deccani states and annexe their territories into the empire. He succeeded in this design: Bijapur surrendered in 1686; Golconda fell the following year through treason; in 1689 Shambuji, son of and heir to Shivaji, was captured and tortured to death. But the Maratha guerrillas continued to fight relentlessly. In vain Aurangzeb led his armies personally and stubbornly sought to root out the revolt by systematically conquering the Marathas' mountain fortresses. Once these fell, usually as result of the bribes offered to their governors, they were reconquered by the enemy. For eight long years the old sovereign was almost besieged in his own field by brigades of Maratha cavalry that captured his provision convoys and broke his communications with the north where for months on end the imperial officers waited without news of their leader.

In 1705 the Maratha resistance defeated Aurangzeb's obstinate perseverance. Ill and exhausted, at the end of his strength, he retreated to Ahmadnagar where he died at the age of 89 on 2 March 1707. He must have realized the extent of his total defeat because he wrote in his will, 'I am truly afraid that I have drowned the force of our lineage in blood. All my desires have ended in nothing.' With much humility, he had dedicated his entire life to the service of his God and his faith, but 50 years of strenuous, honest, energetic and laborious leadership managed only to bring the country to irretrievable ruin. His empire, nominally, included all of India, from Kabul to Bengal, from Kashmir to Mysore. But his army had disintegrated completely, the administration was in ruins, the treasury was empty, the economic situation was disastrous, his Hindu subjects were declared enemies, the Muslims were worn out. The relentless Maratha revolt gnawed at the southern provinces, while in northern India, bled dry by 26 years of war, the state machinery was broken down and the Jats continued their own rebellion. Arts and letters suffered because of the total lack of patronage from the puritan emperor who had closed the royal calligraphic workshops, banned music at court and interrupted the work of the historians.[1] Just as he had lived simply, Aurangzeb wanted to be buried at Khuldabad, near Aurangabad, 'under a small mound of earth, with neither a roof nor a canopy, out in the sun, wind and rain, without a name'.[2] Later a ruler Nizam of Hyderabad had the tomb encircled with an elegant stone balustrade.

Architectural style

Although the emperor's aversion to all forms of artistic activity did not extend to architecture, it is nevertheless undeniable that his zeal for orthodoxy led him to deny the use of luxury materials such as marble and red sandstone, which were replaced with rough stone and recovered bricks. Decoration in hard or precious stone was replaced with decorated and painted stuccoes which were rather unattractive in effect. Consequently, even the architectural style itself deteriorated, becoming often too charged, heavy and incoherent. The court's long sojourn in Deccan and the possibility of easy access to the work of local artists who were then unemployed, brought about an invasion of Deccani forms into the architects' and the stone masons' creations: pillars on stool or lotus-flower bases; columns and turrets terminating in lotus flowers and minarets with a heavy, projecting last floor sitting on a *muqarnas* cornice; domes and ceilings again in the shape of lotus flowers. Even the single forms lost their value: niches, panels, small arches are all amassed in regular monotony; *bangaldar* roofs and domes are fused into new units; Hindu corbels, where they still exist, have degenerated into wide volutes; domes become ever more bulbous and pointed and are decorated with vertical, horizontal and herringbone stripes; the floral motifs on columns, corbels and arches, and on decorative panels on the wall, are multiplied and intertwined into a virtual

The *jami masjid* at Benares, built in 1658 in the centre of the city near the banks of the Ganges.

jungle. 'All the forms have lost their harmonious balance ... the perfect taste of the reign of Shah Jahan gave way to a mixture of ostentatious display and ascetic mysticism, which recalls the spirit of Spanish art in Philip II's era with whom Aurangzeb and his era had much in common.'[3]

DELHI (SHAHAJANABAD): RED FORT, MOTI MOSQUE

During the first decades of the reign building activity was still intense. In the fort at Delhi the garden of Hayatbakhsh was built with a graceful pavilion in marble with tapered columns and flower-shaped bases, as was the Moti (Pearl) Mosque (1662; see p. 264), added to the buildings to enable the devout emperor 'at various times of the day or night to pay his devotions without the trouble of a retinue or long journey'.[4] It is situated near Aurangzeb's private bed-chamber and is small in proportion, truly like the sovereign's private chapel; it has two small aisles, divided into three spans each. Its exterior walls in red sandstone are aligned with the axes of the Red Fort which follow the cardinal points while the interior walls are arranged transversely so as to align with Mecca. As its name suggests, this mosque is also in shining white marble, but in contrast with the serenity of the Moti Mosque at Agra, it is characterized by the predominance of a sinuous contour – the curved Bengali cornice on the façade – and by the bulbous domes crowned with exaggerated upside-down lotus flowers with extremely high metal terminals. All the surfaces have curvilinear decoration, the themes of which tend to confound the distinction between the various elements and the forms of the building. On the curved cornice there is limited decoration in hard stone, while the marble floor is subdivided into rectangles, almost as though to determine the positioning of the worshippers.[5] The three marble domes were replaced by the British after the revolt, substituting those damaged during the siege, but they are too wide for the structure and they increase the imbalance between the small prayer hall and its cover. The internal decoration of the entrance reserved for ladies consists of a frieze of petals which resemble flames. This frieze continues the similar one arranged on the door surround and the top of the *bangaldar* roof. The hall and the exterior wall of the mosque are ornamented with slender towers in imitation of minarets. The façades and the walls of the courtyard are completely decorated with small arches and columns which are carved into the marble, slender and purely ornamental in their function.

BENARES: *JAMI MASJID* AND ALAMGIRI MOSQUE

The corollary to the systematic destruction of Hindu temples was an equally systematic construction of mosques, such as those at Benares and Mathura, two of the holy cities most revered by Hindus. There are seven such holy cities and these mosques were built more out of contempt for the Hindu religion than out of any need on the part of the Muslim faithful.[6] At Benares there are two, the *jami masjid* (see p. 267), built in 1658 at the centre of the city,[7] and the Alamgiri Mosque, built in 1666–7 on the *ghat*, almost on the banks of the Ganges. The *jami masjid* stands on the site of the destroyed temple of Vishvanath. Its façade is dominated by a high portal with an ogival arch, above which there are smaller arches shaded by a *chhajja* and covered by a row of miniature domes. At either end of the façade there is a slender tower topped by a domed *chhatri*, while at the sides there are two wings with pointed arches which also lead into the prayer hall. This is covered by three heavy domes, of which the central one is slightly pear-shaped. The second mosque dominates the Panchaganga *ghat*, for the very purpose of affirming the supremacy of Islam over the holiest of the Hindu cities. Although it is not huge, it still looms imposingly over the pilgrims who come to fulfil their ritual requirements. It no longer has the minarets that made it look more slender, but it still has a dignified appearance. The façade, which is almost uniform in height, features three rows of niches placed above the three arched entrance-ways. On the inside, the hall has a single nave divided into three bays, each covered by a well-proportioned, bulbous dome. The decoration in stucco and different coloured stone is finely executed and stands out against the background of red sandstone of which the structure is built.

Mathura: *jami masjid* and *idgah*

At Mathura three mosques were built, one of which, the *jami masjid* (1660–61), is very well proportioned. It stands on a low plinth in the highest part of the city and is built of the red sandstone that is typical of Mathura. It was sponsored by the governor, Abd al-Nabi Khan, who was later killed by Jat rebels. It is flanked by tall minarets soaring above the prayer hall, which is covered by three fine bulbous domes, the central one, as usual, being higher than the others. In the courtyard, which is occupied by a large pool for ablutions, there are some fine rectangular pavilions with ogival archways carried on bulbous columns and *bangla* roofs. During Shah Jahan's reign structures of this type were used only in the imperial palaces, as they were connected with the symbolism of royalty. Aurangzeb divested them of this meaning and used them mainly in religious buildings. The murder of the governor had aroused the anger of the king, who ordered the immediate destruction of the famous temple of Keshava Deva, to be replaced straight away by the construction of a large *idgah* (1669–70). This *idgah*, which is also built on a hill, has a monumental façade which is a forerunner of the one on the Badshahi Mosque at Lahore. The large central *pishtaq* is flanked by much lower ogival archways between towers topped by domed *chhatri* on either side. The prayer hall, with two aisles divided into several bays, has almost no ornamentation, just like the façade which is entirely in red sandstone. The only remarkable thing on the inside is the central *mihrab*, which consists of a deep niche divided into three sections, while on the outside the three fluted, pointed domes are the main attraction.

Above The Badshahi Mosque at Lahore was built from 1673–4 as an annexe to the fort. It is one of the largest mosques on the Indian subcontinent.

Opposite The *idgah* (1660–61) at Mathura in Uttar Pradesh, built by the local governor Abd al-Nabi Khan. The use of red sandstone is typical of the area.

Lahore: Badshahi Mosque

The great Badshahi Mosque of Lahore was built in 1673–4 as an annexe to the fort; it is one of the largest on the entire subcontinent. The elevation of the prayer hall is based on that of the *jami masjid* at Delhi, with some significant changes: the slender, three-storey minarets are here replaced by octagonal turrets crowned with *chhatri*, arranged at each of the four corners of the prayer hall, so that this became an independent structure from the arcades that enclose the courtyard. Other minarets are arranged at each corner of the *sahn*, visually framing and articulating the whole complex. The red sandstone of the prayer hall and the minarets is counterbalanced by the white marble of the bulbous domes, the cupolas of the *chhatri* and the delicate carved decoration. The façade of the sanctuary is dominated by a wide *pishtaq* which has five much lower arches on each side. More successful are the three large domes, accentuated in their bulbousness and superb examples of design and execution which clearly illustrate the gradual evolution of this form in the late Mughal period. Surprisingly, the decoration of this mosque is much richer than in Shah Jahan's. On the outside floral patterns, scrolls and ogival arches, highlighted by strips of white marble, stand out against the red sandstone, while on the inside sinuous designs with posies of flowers, foliate spirals, columns with bulbous bases and plant-shaped capitals are all created in stucco. The whole is made more attractive by a well-balanced use of polychromy, instead of the inlaid work with semi-precious stones that was used in Shah Jahan's buildings.

Even more than his predecessors, Aurangzeb put a lot of effort into restoring mosques and tombs of venerated saints, as well as encouraging the construction of buildings for religious worship by members of his family, ministers and princes of his court.

Lahore: Alamgir Gate

In 1673, on the side of the fort opposite the Badshahi Mosque, Aurangzeb built the gate known as the Alamgir Gate (see p. 270) to replace the one that Akbar had built. It is a huge structure with imposing towers on either side: these are fluted, with lotus petals at the base, crenellations along the upper edge and domed *chhatri*.

Other buildings

Zinat al-Nisa, Aurangzeb's second daughter who was well known for her devotion and her deeds of charity, had a fine mosque built at Shahjahanabad, near her tomb. The mosque, which is dated 1711–12, is situated on the southern side of the palace, towards the river. It stands on a high plinth and imitates the mosque of Shah Jahan in the high *pishtaq* on the façade, which is adorned with white marble, and in the marble domes, which are divided into lengthwise segments by bands of red sandstone. Here, too, there are slender turrets framing the *pishtaq* and soaring, three-storey minarets at each end of the façade, which has three polylobate archways on either side of the portal. A closer link with the aesthetic canons of Aurangzeb's reign can be seen in the marked bulbous shape of the domes, which have high upside-down lotus blossoms at their summit.

Another mosque, built between 1692 and 1693 at Ajmer near the tomb of the saint Sayyid Muhammad, is quite small, with only one nave, and three ogival archways on the front. Built over a row of workshops, it is adorned by numerous elegant inscriptions by Naji, a well-known poet and calligrapher of the time.

The mosque of Hajji Muhammad at Merta, about 100 km north of Agra, is similar. Built of the attractive local red stone, it features very tall minarets with *chhatri* at the top and three peculiar domes with a marked narrowing at the base, of which the central one has red and white stripes.

Some religious buildings were also constructed at Ahmedabad, Aurangzeb's birthplace, where he also had many mosques restored, even pre-Mughal ones. A rather unusual type of mosque is the one that Sardar Khan had built adjacent to his tomb. It has a single nave, divided into bays, and is covered by a large pear-shaped dome which narrows markedly at the base and is surrounded by a number of similar smaller domes. On the inside, though, there are some local features, such as the open-work walls around the burial chamber, which we have already come across in the famous tombs at Sarkhej.

Two mosques built over rows of workshops can also be found in Delhi: the Anarvali Mosque and the Khalil Mosque, which date to the last decade of the 1600s. Both of them are small, with a single nave and three domes over the bays.

A very large complex consisting of a mosque, a *madrasa* and a tomb, situated just outside Delhi, was founded by Mir Shihab al-Din of Bukhara, who had come to India in 1674. He was granted the title of Ghazi al-Din Khan Bahadur for his victorious campaigns in Deccan in 1683. The construction of the complex that bears his name would have to be between this date and the year of his death in 1709. The *madrasa*, which is now the Zakir Husain College, has an Iranian-type ground plan, according to the origin of its founder. The square courtyard has galleries all round it on two levels which house the lodgings for the teachers and students, and a large *iwan* at the centre of each side. The galleries on the eastern side have small balconies with curved roofs jutting out at intervals, a typically Mughal feature. The mosque stands on the western side of the *madrasa* and is completely independent of it, unlike the analogous Iranian examples. It is of the late Mughal type with bulbous domes, once decorated with red and white stripes. The adjacent mausoleum, which is roofless, is enclosed by attractive stone balustrades with fine open work.

At Gwalior, too, at the foot of the fort, there is a Great Mosque faced with stone, which was built in 1664-5 by Mutamad Khan, the commandant of the fort. The mosque, which is reminiscent of the *jami masjid* in Mathura in both ground plan and elevation, has at its entrance a fine

Above The Bibi-ka Maqbara (1660–61) at Aurangabad. Built as a tomb for Auragzeb's wife, it is an obvious and rather inferior scaled-down imitation of the Taj Mahall.

Opposite The heavy and imposing Alamgir Gate (1673) on the side of Lahore Fort stands opposite the Badshahi Mosque.

portal surmounted by a small pavilion with a curved roof.[8]

Mosques were built in Bihar by both Aurangzeb and some of his officers. The king himself is said to have been responsible for the Rauza Mosque in Patna, the capital of Bihar, which is dated to 1667–8. Connected with the tombs of two saints, it is a modest building with a single nave divided into three bays. In spite of its attribution, it is hard to believe that it could have been due to imperial patronage. Moreover, it seems that Aurangzeb had never been to Patna and was not in the habit of financing works in which he had no direct interest. By contrast, a mosque that was sponsored by the governor of Bihar, Daud Khan Quraishi, in 1660 is a small but attractive brick construction with a single nave divided into three bays and covered with low hemisperical domes. It was built in the fort of Palaman, a former fief of the *raju* of Bihar. The other mosque of Patna, which was ordered in 1688-9 by Khwaja Amber, coincides with imperial taste: it is especially noteworthy for the stucco decoration of the interior which resembles that in the *jami masjid* at Benares and is quite unusual in the buildings of Bihar, which are rather bare and austere.

Aurangzeb not only had a lot of mosques restored, but also several tombs of famous saints, for instance those of Gesu Daraz at Gulbara, Muin al-Din at Ajmer, and Khwaja Qutb Salub Bakhtyar Kaki in Delhi. Where there was no need for restoration, he had improvements made instead.[9] For himself, by contrast, not long before his death, he ordered an extremely simple tomb near the *dargah* of Shaikh Nurhan al-Din, at Khuldabad in Deccan, not far from Aurangabad. It is a simple stone cenotaph, like his sister Jahanara's, fully exposed to the sky, and earth was placed on top of it so that plants might grow there. At the beginning of the twentieth century it was enclosed with white marble slabs.

Aurangabad: Bibi-ka Maqbara

In 1660–61 Aurangzeb had ordered his son Azam Shah to prepare a monumental mausoleum for his wife, Rabia Daurani, who had died in 1657. The Bibi-ka Maqbara (Queen's Tomb), is an obvious imitation of the Taj Mahall (see p. 240) on a reduced scale, without its splendid majesty but not totally lacking in a certain charming simplicity, enhanced by the lovely garden in front of it. Some, however, take it to be a mere parody of its immortal prototype: it presents, in its smaller proportions, a confused cluster of pinnacles and domes crammed into its upper part, while the square pillars at its outer corners where, in the original, there were bevelled corners are an unsatisfactory innovation to the original plan. Similarly, the ornamentation above the parapets, the regular blind niches above the arches and the polished stucco decoration of the entire mausoleum are, generally speaking, mediocre. However closely stucco may imitate marble and however attractive and well rendered its bunches of flowers and leaves may be, it certainly cannot compete with the ornamentation in semi-precious stone in Shah Jahan's building. The domes too, although they are well designed, are far too near each other to create an effect of true elegance. Perhaps the most successful elements of the whole complex are the minarets: they are multi-storey and well proportioned, and tend to widen the central tomb rather than to enclose it. The *char bagh* that surrounds the mausoleum contains two very simple mosques, on either side of the tomb, just as in the Taj Mahall. The close resemblance in the layout of the two complexes is due to the fact that Ata Allah, the author of the Bibi-ka Maqbara, was the son of the Ustad Ahmad, Shah Jahan's architect, who is thought to have been one of the authors of the Taj. Unlike the mausoleum, the portals leading into its garden are ornately decorated with polychrome stucco work. This mausoleum of Rabia Daurani is the last Mughal one to be of large proportions and to have a garden round it. Subsequently, even royalty – and Aurangzeb himself set an example – preferred simple tombs in the open air, with open-work marble slabs around them. The tombs of the emperor's daughters, Zeb al-Nisa and Zinat al-Nisa, are of this type. They are both in Delhi, near the Red Fort.

Other mausoleums

A similar type of mausoleum, but with a flat roof, is the fine one belonging to Shaikh Ala al-Din at Ajmer. It was built near the *dargah* of Muin al-Din Chishti in 1659–60 and is known by the name of Sola Khamba, on account of the 16 columns that support the arches around it.

At Ajmer there is also another very fine mausoleum, of white marble, which is thought to belong to the wife of a high court official, Abd Allah Khan. It stands on a high plinth and is without a roof. The cenotaph is surrounded by very fine *jali* surmounted by a cornice with elegant floral decoration, whose corners terminate in slender, domed pillars. The tomb was placed in a garden and there was a mosque to go with it, both of them dating between 1702 and 1704. Subsequently the tomb of Abd Allah himself was added, under the patronage of his sons.[10] This latter tomb, which also stands on a plinth and has arches all the way round, is covered by a central dome with small *chhatri* at the corners.

Public works

Amongst the public works that Aurangzeb restored or created *ex novo* we may mention a great number of stepped wells (*baoli*), caravanserais (the serai Lashkar Khan, built between Lahore and Delhi in 1669–70), bridges, fortifications (especially in the Deccan) and defensive gates. The gates of the citadels of Delhi and Lahore masked the ones that Shah Jahan had already built, so that the latter, from his prison at Agra, wrote a letter of complaint to his son about it. In 1683 the city walls of Aurangabad were built, with 13 gates, of which only a few remains are extant. The massive Delhi Gate is almost intact, with its large double pointed arch flanked by mighty hexagonal bastions with huge *chhatri* on top of them. The imperial citadel that Aurangzeb had constructed at Aurangabad (Qala-i Arg), which also housed his nobles and officials, has practically disappeared.

Gardens

Before his accession to the throne, Aurangzeb had created gardens at Ujjain and near Bijapur. After he had defeated his brothers, he built one at Fatehabad, surrounding it with walls with corner turrets. In the middle of the garden a rectangular pavilion is still extant, built of bricks and red sandstone and composed of two blocks of three rooms each. These are enclosed within outer walls, but between them there is an area with polylobate arches. It was probably built in 1659 and in its layout it closely resembles Shah Jahan's Rang Mahall, in the Red Fort in Delhi. In Punjab, not far from Chandigarh, Fidai Khan Kuka, Aurangzeb's foster brother, had the beautiful garden of Pinjore built. It is set out on seven terraces, following the plan of the Shalimar garden, and makes use of the natural slope formed by the Ghaggar stream. The main door, on the eastern side, leads to a rectangular platform with seats on three sides. This is where the first terrace begins. Unlike the other Mughal gardens, this one is designed in descent, rather than rising upwards to the main canal. The natural slope of the site facilitates the cascading of the water from one terrace to another and also speeds up the impetuous rush of the main watercourse, but the mysterious and intimate charm that was typical of the older gardens is lacking here. At the canal's edge there stands a graceful *baradari* with a curved roof and small lateral domes. Alongside the *baradari* there is a wall with two doors in it that lead to the second terrace, once the *pardah* garden for the women. Continuing on its course, the water falls on to a projecting shelf, opposite which there is a wall with six rows of 15 small niches in it: these were used to hold terracotta lamps which would create wonderful effects on the water at night with their flickering light. Along the edge of the second terrace there stand the tall archways of the palace known as the Rang Mahall, which separates the two upper terraces from the rest of the garden. It is a great open hall, beneath which the main canal flows. Successive alterations have changed the upper part of the building by adding to it an asymetric structure that is lacking in taste. In the rooms on the lower floor there were a great many paintings, which gave the building its name, but these have been destroyed. The water that runs beneath the Rang Mahall falls into a large pool situated in the middle of a platform, then flows on into the garden below and cascades on to the third terrace. On the fourth terrace there is a large pool with a small pavilion at the centre, which is reached by means of a raised pathway. From it there is a fine view to be had over the main canal. Numerous fountains sparkle all around and once there were several small channels running in different directions. The large garden was once

The Dai Anga mausoleum (1671) at Lahore was built during the reign of Aurangzeb in honour of Shah Jahan's wet-nurse.

planted with flowers and fruit trees, and the whole was enclosed within a wall with octagonal turrets at the corners.

Lahore: Dai Anga mausoleum

Some buildings from Aurangzeb's time stand at Lahore. Among these we should note the tomb of Dai Anga, Shah Jahan's wet-nurse, who was buried on the site of the Gulabi Bagh in 1671. The tomb is of brick with a square plan and rests on a low platform, under which, in an underground chamber, the corpse is buried. The mausoleum consists of a central domed room and eight smaller rooms arranged around it, covered with flat roofs, but surmounted by square kiosks at the corners supported by slender brick pillars. The interior spaces were once elaborately decorated by a splendid mosaic of glazed tiles.

With the transfer of the capital to Aurangabad, Delhi, Agra and Lahore naturally began to be less important, even though Aurangzeb had given strict orders that the palaces were to be kept in perfect order and the religious buildings restored. Imperial buildings were no longer erected there, although several nobles continued to construct their own residences with gardens, tombs or mosques, at their own expense. The same thing happened in other regions, where some noblemen's residences were so rich and grandiose that they could compete with the princely ones. An example is the large complex known as Nauratan (Nine Jewels) which was built in 1688-9 at Bihar Sharif by Saikha, a noble Afghan who had settled in Bihar some time before. The main building, now used as a school, is a single-storey palace with the usual layout consisting of a domed central room surrounded by eight smaller ones. The other structures in the complex included a mosque, but most of it is now missing.

[1] Aurangzeb also abolished the *jharoka-darshan*, the sovereign's appearance in public on the balcony, because it was a custom that had been taken from the Hindus.
[2] Behr, *op. cit.*, p. 236.
[3] Goetz, *op. cit.*, p. 820.
[4] Brown, *op. cit.*, p. 112.
[5] The mosque bears a marked resemblance to the Nagina in the fort at Agra, though here the central dome is higher than the other two. All three domes were originally covered with gilded metal, but this was later replaced by the marble that still distinguishes them.
[6] This is controversial. Some historians believe that Aurangzeb destroyed the Hindu temples only when his political authority was threatened and not out of mere bigotry. As a matter of fact, many of those temples had been built with his permission and with state subsidies, by those very same rajas who, after having been in his service, revolted against him and killed many of his loyal officers.
[7] Now known as the Gyanvapi Mosque. The *qibla* wall was built on the site of the famous temple of Vishvanath, apparently constructed by Raja Man Singh. Aurangzeb had it destroyed to punish Jai Singh, the great-grandson of Akbar's nobleman, for having given protection to one of his mortal enemies, the Maratha Shivaji.
[8] According to an inscription in the prayer hall, this mosque was also built on the site of a Hindu temple that had been destroyed by Mutamad Khan.
[9] Both during his father's imprisonment and after his death Aurangzeb provided for the maintenance of the Taj Mahall, for which purpose the governors of all the provinces were obliged to pay each year the sum of 2,000 rupees.
[10] The sons of Abd Allah Khan, the Sayyid brothers, became famous after Aurangzeb's death, as it was they who actually held the reins of power during the reign of the weak Farukh Siyar (1712-19).

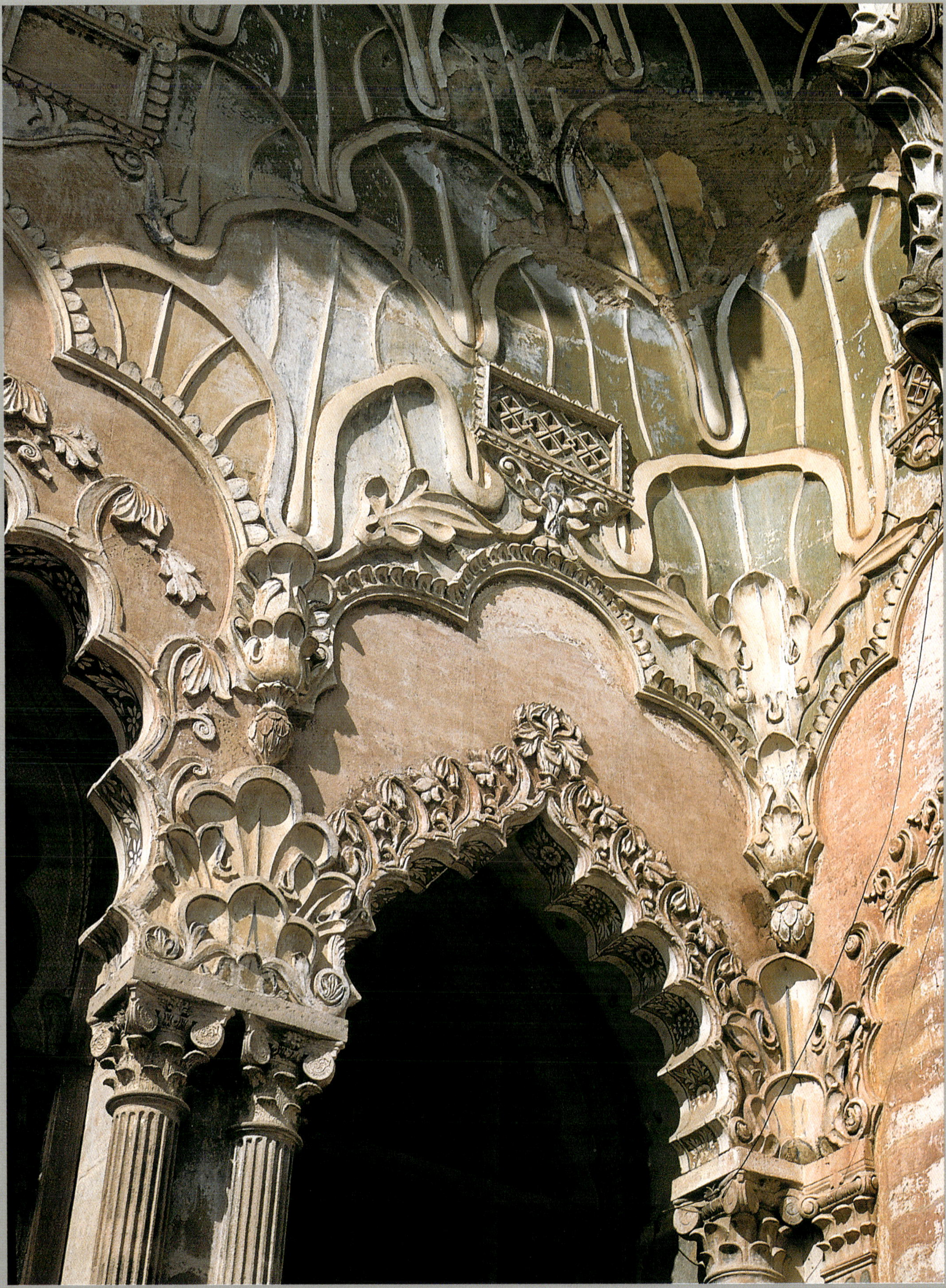

THE FINAL PHASE OF MUGHAL ARCHITECTURE

18

Detail of the exuberant and colourful decoration on the entrance to the *jami masjid* at Lucknow (1850).

After the death of Aurangzeb India underwent the most terrible century in its history as the Mughal empire disintegrated rapidly in an inglorious and bloody sunset. The brief reign of Bahadur Shah, old and tired (1707-12), amounted to no more than a series of useless battles to smother the rebellions that were breaking out all over the empire. His successors, who became instruments of the noble factions in their power struggles, passed their time in pointless intrigues to recapture power or in revelries and endless parties of excess in the *zenana*. Meanwhile, the provinces, left to their own devices and without checks from central government, became effectively independent. At the same time the army and the civil administration, lacking in funds, rebelled and disintegrated while the territory controlled directly by the emperors narrowed to the outskirts of the capital. Although reduced to a shadow of its former self, for almost all of the eighteenth century the empire did succeed, however, in covering these losses because it offered some semblance of legitimacy to the new ambitious dynasties. The sovereigns did not have the means to finance any sort of patronage and when they did have money they preferred to win favour from courtiers, finance parties and fireworks, and employ dancers, musicians and clowns.

Those who truly encouraged building activity in the eighteenth century, which for these times was intense, were the last great nobles of the imperial court, the independent governors (*nawab*) of the provinces, and the Hindu princes who had reacquired their independence.

DELHI: MOTI MOSQUE AND OTHER MONUMENTS

Shah Alam Bahadur Shah, who succeeded his father Aurangzeb in 1707, although he had never been to Delhi, gave orders that a tomb – a plain, roofless structure – and a mosque should be built for him there, near the *dargah* of Bakhtiar Kaki, behind the Qutb Minar. Later on many of his successors chose this area, which had been made famous by the saint Chishti, to build their own residences. The mosque of Shah Alam at New Delhi, known as Moti Mosque (see p. 276), is a small building of white marble (hence its name), with

The Moti (Pearl) Mosque at New Delhi was built in the early eighteenth century by Shah Alam Bahadur Shah, the son and successor of Aurangzeb. The slightly bulbous columns, seen here on either side of the entrance, became a feature of religious buildings from the time of Aurangzeb onwards.

a single nave and three scalloped archways in the façade, the central one jutting out slightly and contained within a higher, pointed arch. On either side of this arch there is a column with a foliate, bulbous base, a feature that became more and more typical of religious buildings from Aurangzeb's reign onwards. Three fluted domes, with a pronounced narrowing at the base, cover the prayer hall, which is entered through two rectangular doors at the sides.

The emperor's sister had the Zinat al-Masajid (Decorum of the Mosques) built in 1710 to the south of the Red Fort. It is a fairly representative example of the architecture in the later part of Aurangzeb's reign, in red sandstone with red and white stripes on the dome, just like those on Shah Jahan's *jami masjid*.

Farukh Siyar (1713–19) followed the example of his predecessor and embellished the tomb of the saint with gratings and portals of marble, decorated with arabesques, floral medallions and fine inscriptions. Later on he had the small mosque that completes the *dargah* and was originally in stucco rebuilt in marble. Muhammad Shah (1719–48) is thought to have commissioned the construction of a wooden mosque (Chobi Mosque) in the imperial palace in Delhi. His white marble tomb is inside the enclosure of the *dargah* of Nizam al-Din, next to Jahanara's tomb, of which it is an exact copy, except that its decoration is much more ornate.

In 1721–2 Muhammad Shah's powerful emir, Raushan al-Daula Zafar Khan, built the Sunahri (Golden) Mosque right in the heart of the Chandni Chowk. The mosque, which is reached by a narrow flight of steps, is dedicated to Shah Bhik, the emir's spiritual counsellor, who had died two years previously. It features three gilded domes which have a marked bulbous shape, and slender minarets which are also topped by small bulbous domes. The façade has three fine archways with a wide scalloped border set inside a square panel outlined with a spiral pattern. The stucco decoration, both inside and out, is very rich, unfolding in bunches of flowers, lotus petals or floral arabesques arranged in panels. The Fakhr al-Masajid (Pride of the Mosques), built in 1728–9 by the noblewoman Kaniz-i Fatima in her husband's honour, stands on a high plinth near the Kashmir Gate. It is built of red sandstone and faced with white marble, which is applied in stripes on the bulbous domes and on the extradoses of the three arches along the façade. Thinner strips of marble form a design on the slender minarets at either end of the façade. Other mosques of interest are the ones built by Nawab Sharaf al-Daula (1722–3) and Muhtasib (1723–4). Both have a single nave, with three bays covered by bulbous, ribbed domes.

A slightly different mosque is the one built by Tahawwur Khan, a rich Delhi landowner, who constructed it for his own private use. It is dated to 1728–9 and has only one nave with a flat roof. Along the façade there are three polylobate arches carried on columns with bulbous bases. During the reign of Muhammad Shah, *raja* and courtiers also constructed buildings for public use, such as gardens, caravanserais and bazaars. One of these, nowadays known as the Tripolia Bazaar, was built in 1728–9 by Nazir Mahaldar, who was supervisor of the royal harem. It was a huge construction, with a large triple-arched portal at either end.

In 1739 north-western India was occupied by the Persian Nadir Shah who, after having conquered Kabul, confronted and defeated definitively the old Mughal army in a decisive battle near Karnal. Delhi was conquered and most of the population was massacred, but Nadir soon retreated, like Timur before him, carrying with him huge quantities of loot, including the Peacock Throne and the famous Koh-i Nur diamond. He never appeared again in India, but Kabul, Peshawar, Baluchistan and Sind passed into the Persian empire. While the latter two regions soon became independent, after Nadir's death Kabul and Kandahar passed into the hands of Ahmad Shah Durrani, the creator of the Afghan state. From the moment that he decided neither to settle there nor to found an empire, Ahmad Shah Durrani immediately began a series of expeditions in India, mostly predatory. In 1752 his son, Ahmad Shah, succeeded in obtaining all of the Punjab and Kashmir from the Mughals; in this way practically the whole of modern-day Pakistan was lost to the Delhi court.

After the destruction by Nadir Shah, however, Raushan al-Daula built another Sunahri Mosque in Delhi, which was dedicated once again to his master Shah Bik. It is a massive construction with a single nave divided into three bays, which were once covered by three gilded, bulbous domes, though these are no longer to be seen. The three archways along the façade have a double scalloped edge, with a few stucco ornaments.

Delhi, complex of Qudsia Begum and other later buildings

Muhammad Shah was succeeded by his son Ahmad Shah, though in actual fact all the power was in the hands of Ahmad Shah's shrewd and ambitious mother Udham Bai, known as Qudsia Begum, and her prime minister and lover, Javid Khan. Just north of Delhi, in the garden that still bears her name, Qudsia Begum built herself a large palace. The palace, which overlooks the Jumna, has been almost completely destroyed, but some late eighteenth-century prints show us its immense size and splendid appearance. It was a two-storey building with polygonal turrets at either end and small balconies jutting out on the façade, sheltered by the typical *bangaldar* roofs. All that is left of the complex is a massive portal at the entrance, built of bricks coated with plaster, and a mosque with a large pool in front of it. Similar to many others of this late Mughal period, the mosque has three archways along its façade, in correspondence with the three bays in the single-naved prayer hall, and three ribbed domes with a marked narrowing at the base. It is faced with stucco in an elaborate polychrome design. At the sides of the portals there appear once again the slender columns with bulbous bases that are by now common in all buildings.

Qudsia Begum and Javid Khan were also responsible for the building of another attractive mosque, in 1750–51, to the south of the queen's palace. It is built of red stone with gilded domes, and therefore also bears the name of Sunahri Mosque. The mosque, with a portal of red stone in front of it and a very tall, slender minaret on either side, has three fine archways with double polylobate borders in its façade. Not far from Delhi, Udham Bai, a follower of the Shia, had a whole complex of buildings constructed near the tomb of the saint Shahi Mardan, including a meeting-room and a mosque. The mosque was perhaps contemporary with the one in the Qudsia Bagh as it is very similar in both ground plan and elevation, but it is not so ornate, probably as it was meant for public use.

In Delhi, in a walled garden, are three tombs that Shah Alam II (1760–88; 1788–1806) built for his mother and his sisters. They are all built of red stone, hence their name Lal Bangala (Red Pavilion), and each has three archways along the sides and a bulbous, ribbed dome. They were probably built in about 1780 and are now in the grounds of the Delhi Golf Club.

The palaces of the Delhi nobles occupied entire neighbourhoods, but now only a few ruins remain – for example the Phatak Tiliyan, near the Turkoman Gate. Among the public buildings still extant is the Tripolia Gate at the Sabri Mand (fruit market), built in 1729 by Nazir Mahalldar Khan to the north-west of the city. Among the religious buildings is the *madrasa*, later transformed into an Anglo-Indian college, just outside the Ajmer Gate. Nearby are the tombs of Ghazi al-Din, father of the first Nizam of Hyderabad, and of his son and grandson who were also imperial ministers. Other religious buildings include: the Gold Mosque of Raushan al-Daula in the Chandni Chowk (1721) which is not noteworthy but has gold domes; the Fahr al-Masjid (1728); the Khan Dauran Mosque of Nizam al-Din (c.1739), the graceful Gold (Sunahri) Mosque alongside the Red Fort, built 1750–51 by the emperor's mother, Qudsia Begum, and her confidant, the eunuch Javid Khan. The same empress had a large garden built outside the Kashmiri Gate, the Qudsia Bagh, which was for the most part destroyed during the siege of Delhi in 1857.

Both the Persians of Nadir Shah and the Afghans of Ahmad Shah Durrani (in 1761), like the Maratha, ransacked the imperial palaces of Delhi more than once, carrying off the gold and silver ceilings and transforming various buildings into barracks, so that when the last Mughals were forced to accept the protection of the British (in 1803), Akbar II (1806–37) had to refit the palace, which had been reduced to extreme ruin, in order to confer a minimum of decorum to it. The same sovereign also carried out a restoration of the Qutb Minar (see p. 23). Bahadur II (1837–57) erected various pavilions in the Hayatbakhsh garden of Aurangzeb – the Hira Mahall, the bath of Zafar Mahall in red sandstone and so on – but later he was forced to abandon the Red Fort and settle in a new palace, the Zafar Mahall (1847–8) at Mehrauli.

Most of the last emperors and their relatives were buried in this same area, or at Nizam al-Din, in plain tombs surrounded by marble balustrades, or even in the lateral vaults of Humayun's mausoleum. The endless wars between the Marathas and the Afghans, Mysore and the British, continually eroded the authority of the Mughal sovereigns, until they were practically reduced to hostage status by the contenders and later to British dependants. The only art that flourished again was painting: romantic, sentimental and often exaggeratedly erotic under Muhammad Shah (1719–48); again static in the first years of Shah Alam II's reign (1759–1803); and then renewed by Akbar II and Bahadur II in a rather superficial imitation of the style in vogue under Shah Jahan.

After the definitive disappearance of the dynasty, some of the painters emigrated to Kashmir, others preferred to concentrate on the production of city views and ugly pseudo-portraits of emperors and empresses for tourist consumption.

Nawab architecture

Those who truly encouraged building activity in the eighteenth century, which was quite intense considering the circumstances, were the last great nobles of the imperial court, the independent governors (*nawab*) of the provinces and the Hindu princes who had regained their independence.

Amongst the buildings that were erected by these nobles we must mention, in Delhi, the mosques of Qasim Khan (1779), Mubarak Begum (1822–3), which is known as Lal Kunwar, and Hamid Ali Khan (1841–2), the prime minister of the last Mughal emperor, Bahadur Shah II. This last-named mosque, the largest and most significant of the three, is built on a raised platform not far from the Kashmir Gate. Unlike the other two which, according to the fashion of the time, tend towards verticality, this one has a more horizontal aspect. The spacious, white-painted façade features a large central arch with a lobate border, surmounted by a high, curved cornice. On either side there is a smaller entrance with an ogival archway, above which runs a parapet with miniature domes.

Lahore: Sunahri Mosque

At Lahore in 1753 a Sunahri Mosque was built, yet another small mosque with gold domes, commissioned by Bikhari Khan, the favourite of Muglani Begum, last Mughal governess. Again in the Punjab, Governor Zakariya Khan, at the time of Muhammad Shah, had built the small but harmonious mosque of Begampur with a *bangaldar* roof and ornament in green glazed tiles painted with elegant floral designs. The governor's sister, Sharaf al-Nisa, is buried nearby in the Tomb of the Cypress (Sarwalla Maqbara); it has towers and ornament in painted tiles with cypresses on a white background.

Lahore: Sikh buildings

Under the Sikhs a great deal of building went on, especially with the marble taken from earlier Mughal buildings, and in the same style as them. An example of this is the *baradari* in the garden opposite the Badshahi Mosque, a square pavilion with elegant ogival archways along its four sides, entirely faced with delicate white marble. It was built by Ranjit Singh in 1818.

Delhi: Safdar Jang mausoleum

The most important building of the eighteenth century, however, is the large mausoleum of Safdar Jang, the second *nawab* of Oudh (1739–53). This imperfect imitation of the tomb of Humayun (see p. 197) and the Taj Mahall (see p. 240), built of red sandstone and marble by Safdar's son, Nawab Shuja al-Daula, is a remarkable example of the descending parabola of the art of construction in this period. Built in 1753, it stands in the middle of a large *char bagh* on a broad terrace measuring more than 33 m along each side and about 3 m in height, with arcades all along its sides. It is two storeys high and has turrets topped by *chhatri* at the corners. The funeral chamber is covered by a bulbous dome that comes to a point at the top, while the outside walls are broken up by large and small niches on either side of a larger arch that serves as an entrance. Although all the elements of its noble prototypes have been used, this building lacks that subtle balance of forms that made them masterpieces. The vertical thrust has been accentuated, as has the narrowness of the structure. This, combined with the inadequate width of the base and the absence of that pyramidal mass which gave the two classic examples that wonderful sense of rhythm, all make this monument architecturally inferior. On the inside, however, especially in the galleries of the lower floor, is the finest mural and ceiling decoration in the 'Mughal rococo' style.

Amongst the last works of the Mughal period we must include the fifth rebuilding of Nizam al-Din's mausoleum, which was done by the *nawab* Ahmad Bakhsh of Firuzpur (1808–9) and Akbar II (1828–9).

The Mughal style survived in the provinces until about 1780, but it ended by giving way to new, Persian-Afghan, French and British influences. The most prolific builders were the *nawab* of Oudh (Auadh), who first made Faizabad and then Lucknow their capitals, enriching them with countless monuments, both religious and civil, all erected in less than a century. The *nawab* Shuja al-Daula (1753–75) built a luxurious residence at Faizabad which is now completely in ruins; only his gigantic mausoleum and that of his consort, Bahu Begum (died 1816), are still standing.[1] His successor

THE FINAL PHASE OF MUGHAL ARCHITECTURE

Above The Safdar Jang mausoleum (1753) at Delhi. Built by Nawab Shuja al-Daula in honour of his father, it is an imitation of the tomb of Humayun at Delhi and the Taj Mahall at Agra.

Opposite The Sunahri Mosque (1753) at Lahore. The gold-domed mosque was commissioned by Bikhari Khan, the favourite of Muglani Begum, the last Mughal governess.

Asaf al-Daula (1775–97) settled at Lucknow where he built various palaces and gardens such as the Daulat Khana with Asafi Kothi, the Hurshid Manzil, the Char Bagh and the Aish Bagh.

LUCKNOW: GREAT IMAMBARA

The most important creation of the late Mughal style was the Great Imambara with its mosque, its courtyards and entrances, which are imposing and remarkable because of their grandiose proportions. The complex is accessible by means of two entrances, one on each side of a wide road of which the southern one constitutes the true entrance while the second was introduced purely for the sake of symmetry. Inside the southern entrance is a courtyard which leads to another triple passage, across which the main courtyard is reached. Here the Imambara occupies the southern extremity and the mosque the western. The Imambara, a building dedicated to the Muslim ceremony of Muharram, a celebration of the death of Husain at Karbala in 680, is a huge building on just one floor which has no particular architectural pretensions, but is remarkable above all for its dimensions and its interior construction. It is made up of a vaulted hall measuring 50 x 16 m, and over 15 m high. Its decoration, however, is very mediocre. The mosque, known as Asafi Mosque (see p. 280), has a more pleasing architectural aspect with a clear sense of space in its wide frontage and in the stepped platform on which it rises, and not least in its harmonious proportions which are logical and full of dignity. Nevertheless, here, too, the ornament is unsatisfactory; it is excessive and discordant, as for example in the open-work arch on the parapet which would later become a constant feature in the buildings of Lucknow, and in the shape of the domes with their leaf scalloping. More original is the great 'Turkish Gate' (Rumi Darwaza) which leads to the exterior area of this complex. The architects intended to surpass the Sublime Gate of Istanbul in beauty, but in reality they succeeded only in building a fantastic and hybrid creation, evidently destined to gratify a patronage totally lacking in refinement and reserve.

Lucknow: Martinière and other buildings

In the first half of the nineteenth century the number of large buildings in European styles increased. At Lucknow, in the last years of the previous century, there had already been built a large, pretentious building later used as the Martinière School, but originally intended as the country residence of Major General Claude Martin (1735–1800), a French mercenary in the service of the *nawab* of Oudh. Designed by Martin himself, in what could be described as a degraded Palladian style, this is an immense castle. But despite its bizarre aspect it is a creation of character and remarkable strength and is one of the first European-style buildings built in the north of India. Many other buildings in Lucknow were inspired by it. Indeed, the architectural character of the city is strongly hybrid (see p. 283), combining triangular pediments with Corinthian capitals, roman rounded arches with fluted domes, pointed arches and floral, arabesque elements, a mixture of Western and eastern forms, most of which were *spolia*.

These buildings could be defined as poor-quality Mughal structures, decorated with inappropriate classic motifs. They are for the most part civil buildings, such as the large and the small Chattar Manzil, two buildings built by Nawab Nasir al-Din Haidar (1827–37), together with the Sikandra Bagh entrance and the Chaulakha Darwaza of Kaisar Bagh, both built during the reign of Nawab Wajid Ali Shah (1847–56). The second entrance is characterized by two keeps in the form of bell towers, surmounted by bulbous domes and by three vaults with circular arches, multi-lobed above and with a curious ornamentation of dolphins in the extradoses and shagreened stripes on the pillars which support the towers.[2] Some buildings display characteristics that are more Italian than eastern and it is therefore likely that they were inspired by Western models. These buildings are: the Roshanwali Kothi, then used as the Court of the Assistant Commissar, and the Begum Kothi at Hazaratganji.

Religious buildings maintained more characteristically Mughal features: the mausoleum known as the Shah Najaf, built by Ghazi al-Din Haidar, first King of Awadh; the Qadam-i Rasul; the tombs of Nawab Saadat Ali Khan (died 1814) and his wife, which are found in Kaisar Bagh; the Husainabad Imambara (see p. 282); the Hazaratganji Imambara and the *jami masjid*, begun by Nawab Muhammad Ali Shah (1837–42) and not finished until

Left The late eighteenth-century Asafi Mosque in the Great Imambara complex at Lucknow. Though its proportions are dignified its decoration is rather excessive.

Opposite top Detail of the decoration on the front of the Martinière at Lucknow. The palace, one of the first European-style buildings in northern India, was built by Major General Claude Martin (1735–1800), a French mercenary in the service of the *nawab* of Oudh.

Opposite bottom The *jami masjid* at Lucknow, built in 1850 by Nawab Muhammad Ali Shah. It has fewer of the incongruous European elements that characterize many buildings in the city.

The Final Phase of Mughal Architecture

1850. This last building, although rather sophisticated, is one of the least incongruous creations in the capital of Oudh. In 1856 building activity in Lucknow ceased because the last *nawab* was deposed. The Husainabad Imambara complex was built by Muhammad Ali Shah in 1839 and a mosque and a tomb are to be noted among the other monuments. This last is the tomb of the king and his sister Janabasya, one of the countless inferior copies of the Taj Mahall.[3]

One of the buildings of the Rauza Kazimain is most unusual in its appearance. It has four minarets and two contiguous squat, pear-shaped domes that are erected on abnormal cylindrical drums.

Persistence of the Mughal style

During this time the Mughal style continued in other regions of the country. In Bihar the tombs of Shamsher Khan and Ibrahim Khan were built along the lines of those constructed in the time of Jahangir (Iftikhar Khan), though with more pronounced decoration. While these buildings display purely Mughal characteristics, the residence of the *nawab* Luft Ali Khan, Bawli Hall, of the nineteenth century, is exactly like the major British houses of the period. On the other hand, the mosque inside it is once again very similar to late Mughal models, for instance the Hamid Ali Khan Mosque in Delhi.

In Bengal Murshidabad, founded at the beginning of the eighteenth century by Murshid Quli (1704–25), became the residence of the *nawab*. Here the Katra Mosque, the Moti Jhil Palace, the Jafarganj Deorhi, the Compani Bagh, the Khush Bagh and the Chowk Mosque of Muni Begum (1767) were all built.[4]

At Patna the mausoleum of the *nawab* Haibat Khan was built in 1748. At Benares the tomb of Lal Khan was constructed in 1768–9 on a square ground plan, with a large hemispherical dome terminating in a tall spire and an unusual decoration in glazed tiles, just like the decoration in the contemporary mosque of Mir Ashraf (1773) at Patna, though here it is used on the floor.

At Bhopal the small and harmonious Islamnagar Fort (1709–22) was built before the castle of Fatehgarh. Qudsia Begum had the *jami* mosque and the Aish Bagh built

Above The Husainabad Imambara complex (1839) at Lucknow, built by Muhammad Ali Shah.

Opposite A palace at Lucknow. The building exemplifies the hybrid and highly decorative style that was common during the last years of Mughal rule.

at the beginning of the nineteenth century. Shah Jahan Begum commissioned the Bara Mahall and the gigantic Taj al-Masajid (Crown of the Mosques) at the end of the same century.

At Ajmer, in Rajasthan, the *nawab* Mirza Chaman Beg had a huge *idgah* built in 1773–4, in honour of the saint Muin al-Din Chishti, with a peculiar, curved façade resembling a *bangaldar*. The two-storey mosque built by Mir Saadat Allah, with an inscription done by Ghalib, dates to the mid-1800s. In 1793, again at Ajmer, the *nawab* Ali Jah had a white marble pavilion built, outside his province, for the *dargah* of Muin al-Din.

At Golconda the first Nizam had the graceful Moti Mahall built in wood, and at Hyderabad the Purani Haveli. In the later buildings echoes of Persian architecture of the eighteenth and nineteenth centuries can be detected alongside the Mughal style, as in the mosque of Afzalganj, the Lakkar Kothi and the *baradari* of Nawab Teg Jung.

At Arcot, where the *nawab* of Carnatic (Karnataka) had settled, the ruins of their palace are extant as well as three mosques (*jami*, Kala and Faqir Muhammad) and the mausoleum of Saadat Allah Khan (*c*.1732).

The sultans of Mysore (*c*.1761–99), Haidar Ali and Tipu Sultan, who at the end of the eighteenth century pushed aside the local Rajput rulers, installed themselves on the fortified island of Seringapatnam. Here there still stands a fine summer palace, richly painted and standing in the garden of Darya Dulat, together with the sultans' tombs in the Lal Bagh and a curious mosque (Ala Mosque) which has an entrance in a neo-classical style and two imposing minarets at the two sides. Haidar Ali's Lal Bagh at Bangalore also survives, and Tipu's palace in the fort, while the family tombs are at Vellore. The Mysore sultans' buildings present an interesting mix of contemporary southern Arabic (derived from the Mamluk-Egyptian style) and French characteristics.

In this last period the building material most commonly used is brick with richly modelled and painted plaster. All the innovations introduced in Aurangzeb's time were in common use and were fused with complicated play of lines, volume and colours. Increasingly common are: columns with lotus shapes, paired or inset into walls and dressed in leaves or scales with bases painted with naturalistic floral motifs; simple or festooned round arches with 11, 13 or more cusps flourishing from floral bands and framed by flaming petals and followed by climbing plants; and occasional low arches doubled with small *bangaldar* roofs or alcoves in concave niches or even surmounted by a dome in relief at the highest point of the dome itself. Light balconies rise from supports in lotus shapes and are covered by curved roofs, often combined with domes. Ceilings are decorated with volutes intertwined with banana leaves, lotus petals or floral arabesques in relief; cornices are concave and projecting and provide a substitute for single-sloped roofs; parapets are always crenellated, roofs curved and domes markedly bulbous; the *chhatri* are countless, reduced to minimal dimensions or incorporated in the galleries. Often decoration is reduced to pompous volutes, painted pink, pale yellow, or bright yellow. 'In its entirety an artificial paradise, illusory, gay, frivolous in a time of misery.'[5]

[1] The domes of both the mosque and the mausoleums have a marked bulbous shape, as in many other late Mughal examples. The tombs are very ornate and also display original features, such as the multiple entrances in the façades and the elaborate parapets on the cornices and around the domes. These motifs were all to become common in the Oudh style.

[2] The fish was the emblem of the *nawab* of Oudh.

[3] The architecture of Lucknow, as far as public buildings or the *nawab* residences are concerned, shows a great deal of European influence, whereas the religious buildings repeat the style of the earlier Indo-Islamic structures. On the outside of the palaces there are often Palladian style decorations, or even niches with statues instead of windows, and paintings in fresco with human figures. On the inside the European fashion did not catch on at all, which shows how superficial an impression it had made on the Indian clients. The first fortified palace, the Macchi Bhavan, was built by Asaf al-Daula in 1774, and the last, the Kaisar Bagh, by Wajid Ali Shah in 1848, with whom the *nawab* dynasty of Oudh came to an end.

[4] Some religious buildings that were dedicated to the Shiia, a sect to which the *nawab* of Murshidabad belonged, were erected by persons who were not members of the royal family but gravitated around the court. One of these is the *husainiya*, whose purpose was to commemorate the martyrdom of Husain, the grandson of the Prophet. It was begun by the eunuch Amber Ali Khan in 1804-5 and completed by another eunuch, Darab Ali Khan, in 1854-5. The Qadam Sharif complex, whose main building conserved a footprint of the Prophet, had also been built by a eunuch, Itwar Khan, in 1788-9. The sanctuary grew in importance after the mid-1800s, when an attempt was made to shed lustre on the city, though at the beginning of the 1900s it was overshadowed by Calcutta, which had become the seat of British power in India. Towards the middle of the nineteenth century a large *imambara*, which had been designed some years earlier by a European architect, was built by the architect Sadiq Ali at the command of the *nawab* Feredun Jah, opposite the latter's residence. It is interesting to note that in 1850 Sadiq Ali began to build a mosque that was completely without any European influence and was modelled on the Bengalese mosques of Shah Jahan's time. In fact, the Chotte Chowkki Mosque has narrow pointed archways along the façade and bulbous, ribbed domes.

[5] Goetz, *op. cit.*, p. 823.

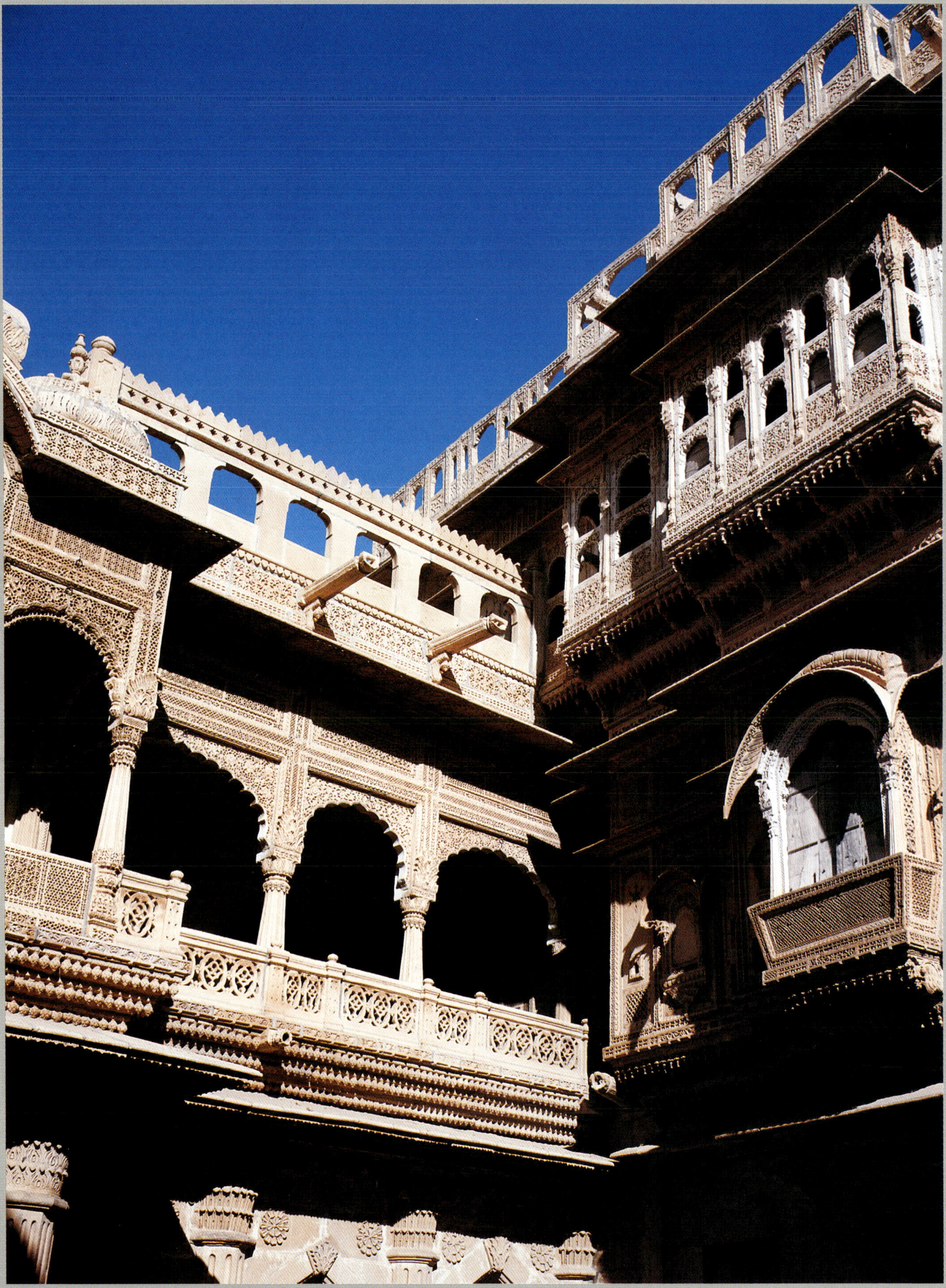

The Mughal Provincial Style

19

With its balconies, windows and carved decoration, this building is characteristic of the style of Jaisalmer, the twelfth-century city in Rajasthan built by the Rajput ruler Jaisal.

The Rajput princes were in close contact with the Mughal court for over a century and a half and inherited its architectural style. Indeed, they perpetuated it in their palaces built during the sixteenth, seventeenth and eighteenth centuries.

When the Rajputs regained their independence (1710–30), the adoption of imperial splendour became an expression of sovereignty and was facilitated by the immigration of Mughal artists from the provinces of the disintegrating empire. The Rajputs' secular buildings, freed from the strictures of religious construction, show great diversity of design and leave much to individual taste. The internal arrangement shows little sign of a set plan, but always features a huge reception hall (*durbar*) and a meeting hall, while the rest of the space is occupied by a labyrinth of apartments connected by poorly illuminated passages. These last do much to recreate the atmosphere of mystery associated with palace life of the time. The exteriors of the buildings are characterized by suspended balconies of various shapes and sizes or long open galleries supported by rows of elaborately carved corbels, clearly derived from Hindu styles. Also characteristic are columned kiosks with ribbed domes which rise from each corner on open-work stone parapets, while often the upper floors consist of endless arches with scalloped crowns and apertures filled with open-work windbreaks. There is always a curved or undulating cornice in the form of a strong, projecting arch; this creates an arched shadow which in falling and moving across the façade of the palace lends it life and charm.

Maharaja palaces

The most important palaces of the sixteenth and seventeenth centuries are those at Bikaner, Bundi, Jodhpur, Jaisalmer, Orchha, Datia, Udaipur and Amber, to which we can add the smaller, though elegant, ones of Samod and Kotah. In the eighteenth century Maharaja Badan Singh built the Bharatpur Palace; in about 1750 Maharaja Suraj Mall built the Dig Palace, while the Jaipur Palace, together with the city of the same name, was begun in 1728 by Maharaja Jai Singh who reigned from 1699 to 1744. Most of these palaces consist of groups of buildings which have been extended and altered with the passing of time, but they remain recognizable because of the architectonic features mentioned above.

The ancient palace of Bikaner consists of a great number of pavilions built on top of a high defensive wall. Along this wall there is a continuous line of balconies and round windows of various designs, interspersed with kiosks and small towers at regular intervals.

The palace of Jodhpur, which crowns a rocky hillock, is unrivalled in the grandeur of its conception. This grandeur is coupled with an extraordinary elegance of detail, as witnessed in the simple fortified bastions that support parapets decorated in relief, or in the open-work apertures and small gilded domes that cut into the skyline to pleasing effect.

At Udaipur, on the banks of an artificial lake, stands the largest palace in Rajasthan. It is distinguished by a graceful entrance with three arches (Tripolia Darwaza) in the foreground, against which in a back row there are countless fluted turrets which make this noble group of brick constructions a vision of grace. Inside there are many buildings, all connected in a vast labyrinth. Among the buildings are the Mor Chowk, the peacock court with shining glass mosaics, the Chini-ka Chita Mahall and others with fine marble inlays, coloured glass decoration and mural paintings. The Jag Niwas, built in 1746 and situated in an enchanting spot on the Jag Mandir isle of Lake Pichola, offers a spectacle of such exquisite beauty as to appear almost unreal.

Jaisalmer

Set apart stands Jaisalmer, a city of mystic beauty enclosed within the walls of an exterior fortress with 99 projecting bastions. Built by Jaisal in the twelfth century, it includes a palace and various groups of residences, all characterized by balconies, windows and entrances carved so exquisitely as to form a true jewel of Rajput craftsmanship (see p. 284).

Amber

One of the most beautiful medieval Rajput palaces is at Amber, one of the seats of the sovereigns of the state of Jaipur, until the capital was transferred in 1728 to the current city of Jaipur. Amber had been founded already in AD 928, but most of the buildings that still stand there date from the sixteenth century because they were constructed by Maharaja Man Singh (1592–1615), while substantial additions were carried out by Maharaja Jai Sing I in the seventeenth century. This large complex of royal buildings occupies a huge area at the front of a rocky gorge and alongside a beautiful lake. The whole is protected by a series of fortresses erected on the crest of the mountains that tower around. The royal palace itself is in a central position and consists of a large open courtyard reached by an imposing entrance and a fine stairway. On one side of the square is the fine Diwan-i Amm, on

Below left The Junagarh Fort at Bikaner in Rajasthan. The defensive wall is distinctively topped with balconies and arched windows.

Below right View from the top of the palace at Udaipur. Set on the banks of an articifial lake, it is the largest and most impressive palace in Rajasthan.

Opposite The medieval palace at Amber, once the seat of the rulers of Jaipur. The palace forms part of a large complex of royal buildings on a rocky gorge alongside a lake.

another side the entrance to the palace, clearly inspired by the Mughal architectural style. The Diwan-i Amm is a hypostyle hall with rows of double pillars with groups of worked corbels in typical Akbar style, wide awnings and open-work balustrades. Overall it recalls the pavilion known as the Palace of the Zenana in the fort at Allahabad. Indeed, it would seem that craftsmen from Allahabad built it. Almost directly in front of the *diwan* is the façade of the entrance hall to the palace apartments, built in brick with a lively decoration of vaulted niches, pointed arches and walls divided into painted tempera panels which all face the exterior with a lively and elegant movement.[1] Inside, both skirtings and ceilings are decorated with inlaid glass which produces a shining, if rather bizarre, effect. Beyond the square courtyard is a large group of structures consisting of smaller buildings: apartments for the women, courtyards, terraces and gardens which are arranged over a large space and are profusely decorated, often with inlays and coloured glass. Although these are graceful, they do not approach the architectonic harmony of the large buildings around the courtyard of honour. Among the most noteworthy buildings are the Jai Mandir (Shish Mahall), the Sohag Mandir and the Sukh Niwas. The last is in marble, with mosaics and mirrors, built by Maharaja Jai Sing I (1625–67). The two-storey Jai Mandir has a curved roof that closely resembles those on the pavilions built by Shah Jahan in the forts at Agra and Lahore. The interiors are decorated with floral patterns, while the ceilings are encrusted with mirrors, like those in the Shish Mahall at Lahore.

DIG

The most spectacular palace is perhaps the one at Dig, in the Bharatpur district, which was built in different stages by various Hindu rulers, in particular Suraj Mal (1756–63) and his successors. In spite of the difference in the date of the buildings, their style is fairly uniform. The garden, together with the palaces built in it, all follow the canons of Mughal style. The central *char bagh* has pavilions along all its sides, simply built but richly decorated, whose design is inspired by similar buildings in the imperial capitals. At the northern and southern ends of the complex there are large pools which recall the ones by Hindu temples, a concession to the taste of the *raja* builders.

The pavilions built by Badan Singh (1722–56) have a rectangular ground plan and markedly curved roofs with spires on top. The palaces overlooking the Gopal Sagar are the largest and most complex in design. The central one has a rectangular ground plan and is three storeys high, with its façade broken up by small jutting balconies with *bangaldar* roofs and polylobate arches carried on bulbous columns. At its sides there are smaller, single-storey pavilions with curved roofs which have a number of elaborate spires on top. The most attractive building in the complex, the Keshav Bhavan, is a pavilion overlooking one of the large pools. It is a one-storey building with polylobate arches along all its sides. These are supported by low, fluted columns whose bases rise out of large lotus petals.

JAIPUR

The city of Jaipur is famous for its huge palace and other pink-painted buildings, in particular the façade of the Hawa Mahall, with its most graceful rounded pyramid shape and row upon row of small balconies shielded by *jali* and surmounted by curved roofs and small, compressed cupolas, all of which combine to lend it the appearance of lacework rather than an architectonic structure. This palace was erected in 1799 by Maharaja Sawai Pratap Singh, who dedicated it to the Hindu deities Krishna and Radha. Six storeys high, with the multiplicity of its windows it almost reproduces a traditional Hindu concept, of which there are clear examples in mediaeval temples. The palaces of Galta, near Jaipur, the Anup and Rang Mahall in the Bikaner Fort, the palaces of Man Singh and Takhat Singh in the Jodhpur Fort and even many small funeral temples, were all inspired by a late 'Rajput baroque' – a style that was, in some ways, parallel to late Mughal architecture but more extreme in the richness of its intricate forms and abundant decoration. These were all decorated with murals carrying scenes from Krishna's or Durga's legends, royal processions, battles and erotic scenes, all executed in Mughal techniques and to Mughal taste.[2]

ASTRONOMICAL OBSERVATORIES

In 1725 an unusual complex was built in Delhi by the *raja* of Jaipur, Sawai Jai Singh Kachchwala, a renowned statesman, mathematician and astronomer. This was the astronomical observatory known as Jantar Mantar, which the *raja* erected at the command of the sovereign, a great lover of astronomy and mathematics, as well as of literature. Subsequently, Jai Singh had similar buildings constructed at Jaipur (see p. 290), Mathura, Benares and Ujjain. The best preserved is at Jaipur, with its many extraordinary buildings, with plastered brick walls; it combines the astrological instruments with circular and angular forms placed one on top of the other, achieving an amazing effect.

Rajput art strongly influenced Sikh and Maratha art. The Sikh confederation, which became very strong in the Punjab during the eighteenth and nineteenth centuries, could almost be considered a reformed Hindu sect because every building connected with the cult had to be designed according to Hindu ritual and practice. The architectural style adopted by the Sikhs therefore displays Mughal characteristics, through Rajput influences, but also presents its own individual character. Among its most typical traits are: the great number of *chhatri* which decorate the parapets, the corners and all projecting features; the constant use of the fluted dome, usually covered in brass or gilded copper; the frequent use of round or vaulted windows with shallow elliptical cornices supported on corbels; and the enrichment of all the arches by means of much ornament. This gives the buildings richness and pretension as well as animation and picturesque vivacity. Many cities in the Punjab, particularly Lahore, have examples of these buildings, such as the mausoleum of Ranjit Singh, a two-storey pavilion decorated with mural paintings, the Haveli of Nau Nihal Singh and numerous temples. But the most famous example of the type is certainly the Golden Temple of Amritsar, the sect's most important shrine.

AMRITSAR: GOLDEN TEMPLE

In this monument all the most obvious characteristics of the Sikh style are represented. The Golden Temple (Durbar Sahib or Hari Mandir; see p. 291) has a clearly

Above The Hawa Mahall at Jaipur. Built in 1799 by the Maharaja Sawai Pratap Singh, it has the graceful pink façade characteristic of the city.

Opposite The Suraj Bhavan, built by the Hindu ruler Badan Singh in the first half of the eighteenth century, is part of a complex of royal buildings at Dig. The pavilions of Badan Singh are distinguished by their highly curved roofs.

ancient base, but the present structure dates from 1764, while the most conspicuous section was added later, at the beginning of the nineteenth century. The remarkable visual effect of the temple is increased by the beauty of the main building which stands at the centre of a large pond, the 'Small Pond of Nectar'. Access is possible only by means of a causeway which crosses the water and is over 70 m long. Over the course of time the temple and the pond became the focal point of a complex of buildings that had developed nearby, most of which repeat the characteristics of the main building in their architectural detail, such as small balconied windows suspended on carved corbels, low fluted domes and pointed arches, elliptical awnings with multi-layered ceilings and so on. Ranjit Singh, the builder of the Golden Temple, used many slabs of marble stripped from Nur Jahan's mausoleum together with worked gold foils from the ceilings of Mughal palaces, late Rajasthani mural decoration and mural paintings in popular styles.

On the western side of the pond is a large archway over the causeway. The causeway itself is paved and bordered by open-work marble balustrades and lamps with elegant gilded lanterns arranged at short but regular intervals. At the centre of the pond the road opens into a square platform roughly 20 m each side and in the middle stands the temple itself, a square building some 17 m each side. Externally the shrine presents itself as a two-storey structure upon which rises a low fluted dome in gilded metal, while on each corner there is a *chhatri*, again with fluted metal domes. The interior is made up of a wide hall, richly decorated like all the rest with floral designs, tempera paintings or metal sculptures, the Sikhs being skilled craftsmen in brass and copper work.

At Benares, Ranjit Singh covered the temple of Shiva Vishveshvar, destroyed by Aurangzeb and rebuilt by the Rani Ahilya Bai of Indore, with gold leaf; it became famous as the Golden Temple because of the gold leaf which covered the spire. Other Sikh buildings include the *gurdvara* (temples) of Jwalamukh, Bhavan and Purmandal. Also noteworthy are the Ram Bagh of Amritsar and the palace of Bashohli, all with quiet charm, and often decorated with graceful mural paintings.

In 1818 the Sikhs, using white marble that was stripped from other Mughal buildings in Lahore, built the *baradari* pavilion in the middle of the Hazuri Bagh, which is opposite the Badshahi Mosque. Inside the fort the northern wall was added as well as some minor constructions, mostly tombs. One of these is the mausoleum of Ranjit Singh, a two-storey pavilion like the temple of Amritsar, covered with Pahari paintings.

The Marathas

The Marathas of Deccan were a race of peasants who rebelled against the Mughals in the second half of the eighteenth century and dominated India between 1730 and about 1818. Lacking artistic tradition, they were, however, patrons and dedicated themselves above all to restoring many temples and shrines. They took ancient Hindu styles such as the Chalukya as models, then the architecture of the Deccani Islamic provinces such as the Adil Shahi and Nizam Shahi, and then the Mughal style and late Rajput and finally European and Chinese art. Towards the end of the eighteenth century under various prime ministers (*peshva*), namely Madhav Rao, Savai Madhav Rao and Baji Rao II of Pune, they developed a personal style, a sort of Hinduized Mughal baroque, pompous and vulgar. Their temples were made up of elements of the Hindu medieval sanctuary reintroduced in a Mughal form, or a hall of the cult, vaulted and resting on Mughal festooned arches, the spire formed of superimposed *chhatri* and terminating with a Deccani Mughal dome in a lotus shape, while decoration consisted of Rajput wall paintings. Secular buildings developed from the Maratha farmhouse, consisting of a wooden frame filled with bricks on sandstone platforms and arranged around courtyards. The buildings were decorated with wall niches and windows of the Mughal type, rather rough wall paintings and rich wooden carvings influenced by Gujarat and China.

The most famous of the palaces belonged to the Peshva of Pune (Poona), the Shanwar Wada or Saturday Palace, once nine storeys high, built within a massive fort; it was destroyed by fire in 1827 and since then preserved as a national monument. There are many temples at Pandharpur, Trimbak, Dakor, Dwarka and Benares. In this last area the Scindia Ghat, commissioned by the Maharana Baija Bai, was also built, along with the temple of Vishveshvar and the Manikarnika Ghat, both commissioned by the pious Queen Ahilya Bai of Indore (1754–94).

A variety of Maratha art flourished at Tanjore, in southern India, which had been conquered in 1677–8. Here Mughal and Maratha styles fused with the late art of Madurai. The result was baroque and fantastic and in its way rich and cultured, a hybrid style but often full of charm.

In central India, more precisely in Bundelkand, during the sixteenth and at the beginning of the seventeenth centuries, a rather special architectural and artistic movement flourished which has been defined as the Bundela style. This was a development of contemporary Muslim creations which evolved under the sultans of Delhi, but was enriched by elements of indigenous Hindu extraction according to the Rajput sovereigns' taste. The buildings in this style have a square plan and are several storeys high with a square courtyard in the centre. Externally, each floor is marked by a wide projecting awning and suspended balconies; the walls carry kiosks on arcades which project from each parapet and each corner is capped with a graceful dome. The interior is made up of rows of apartments alternating with open terraces which communicate by means of passages and corridors.

ORCHHA AND DATIA PALACES

Examples of this type are found at Orchha and Datia. The former, begun by Raja Rudra Pratap (1501–31), was finished by his successor Raja Bharti Chand, who completed the walls of the city and erected the citadel and the first of the three buildings included in this group, the Ramji Mandir, which was inspired by the Kushk Mahall of Chanderi (see p. 140), built a century earlier by Mahmud Shah Khalji of Malwa. It consists of a rectangular central courtyard, around which rise the apartments, arranged on receding floors with the whole surrounded by a high perimeter wall. Around 1575 the Raj Mandir (Royal Palace) was erected. This is a solid square structure, divided into two wings. After passing through the first courtyard, one enters the main courtyard which is surrounded with five-storey buildings on three sides and a four-storey one on the other side. Some rooms have open terraces on which smaller rooms have been built, with domed kiosks on top of them.

However, the most important palace is the Jahangir Mandir (see p. 292), built by the *raja* Bir Singh Deo and named after the Mughal emperor who was his protector.[3] It covers a square of over 67 m along each side and rises in an immense rectangular mass topped by eight attractive fluted domes. One enters through a projecting portal on the southern side and passes through a hall on the ground floor into a square courtyard, around which the inside of the palace rises on three different levels. The rooms are grouped at the corners and at the centre of each side, with open terraces between them, along the lines of the so-called House of Jodh Bai at Fatehpur Sikri, but the Orchha palace is much larger and has a more complex design. Each group of rooms is connected

Right The Golden Temple at Amritsar (1764). Though the temple has all the characteristics of Sikh style, the builders used materials taken from Mughal structures.

Opposite The astronomical observatory at Jaipur. It is the best preserved of several observatories built in the eighteenth century by Jai Singh, *raja* of Jaipur.

by a continuous suspended balcony with a slanting balustrade and ornamental overhang and corbels, which has an overall effect of great variety. Many of the walls have paintings showing scenes of Hindu life and court personages dressed in the Mughal fashion. The main portal has very fine 'elephant trunk' corbels and sumptuous stucco decorations featuring floral patterns or figures of peacocks, Ganesh and Lakshsmi. Figures of elephants are carved in the round. At the foot of the palace are grouped the remains of numerous subsidiary buildings – pillared courtyards, pavilions, gardens, portals, all contained with a massive circuit wall with turrets.[4]

The Datia Palace, built by the same *raja* in 1620 some 30 km away from the previous palace, rises on an outcrop of rock and, although considerably smaller than the Jahangir Mandir in that its sides measure less than 50 m and the total height as far as the keystone of the central dome is some 40 m, its aspect remains imposing and majestic. It rises on an uneven crest of granite and its base rests on various levels so that much of its structure, like an iceberg, remains out of view below the ground floor, and its true height is illusory. The structures consist of a series of huge underground halls which descend over various floors, some of which are even carved out of the rocky base. The visible exterior of the palace is a square over five irregular storeys, each defined by a cornice and interrupted at intervals by projecting windows. At each corner and at the centre of each side rises a large dome flanked by *chhatri*, while at the centre, supported by a square gallery, rises the principal dome. The main façade is to the east and stands out thanks to a finely designed entrance; there was another door to the north, which probably served as a private entrance. Inside, the visible elevation rises over five floors of apartments which face on to a wide open courtyard at the centre of which there stands another five-storey building which makes up the nucleus of the royal apartments. This is connected to rooms around four raised corridors, almost two-storey bridges, which branch off in the form of a cross from the centre of each side. The structure is embellished by a pleasing play of

Opposite The palace at Datia. Built in 1620 by the *raja* Bir Singh Deo, it rests on an uneven crest of rock, so that the lower ground levels are invisible from the front.

Below The Jahangir Mandir at Orchha. The large and complex palace was built by Bir Singh Deo and named for the Mughal emperor who was his protector.

light and shadow because of the large number of balconies on worked corbels, wide awnings, small kiosks and round windows, some of which are supported by volute corbels which lend the interior an extremely animated aspect. For some reason, according to contemporary chronicles, this superb palace was never inhabited: no royal family ever lived within its walls, but it stands as a splendid although unused architectural achievement.[5]

VIJAYANAGAR (HAMPI): LOTUS MAHALL
In the south of India, too, a few buildings of the sixteenth and seventeenth centuries are to be found where the Muslim influence is more obvious, although diluted by the ancient Hindu architectural style. The oldest example is the Lotus Mahall (see p. 294), not much more than a garden pavilion, built at Vijayanagar (Hampi) in 1575. This is a small two-storey building, the base of which, erected on a stepped platform, is arranged in a series of receding, multi-lobed arches which recall those of the Lodi buildings of Delhi a generation before. Between the first and second floors is a strongly projecting awning supported by extremely simple corbels. The pyramidal roof, supported by pillars interrupted by multi-lobed arches, is an adaptation of the *shikara* of the Dravidic temple. At the beginning of the seventeenth century the sovereigns of Vijayanagar built a palace in the fort at Chandragiri: here, too, the fusion of the Hindu and Muslim styles can be seen, above all in the exterior where seven *shikhara* surmount the corners and the main hall, while pointed arches decorate all the openings on the façade.

MADURAI: TIRUMALA NAYAK PALACE
The palace of the powerful sovereign Tirumala Nayak (1632–59), built at Madurai around 1645, displays strong but badly integrated Western influences as well as a fusion of Muslim and Hindu styles which together render the building a curious hybrid. It is a grandiose construction, the main building of which measures 135 x 75 m and consists of a spacious internal quadrangle some 81 x 45 m, surrounded on three sides by columned bays and with the large *durbar* and the throne hall on the remaining side. On the northern side is another hall, 40 x 11 m. The arcades that enclose the internal courtyard like a peristyle are made up of massive granite columns over 12 m high; they recall a little the spirit of Greek temples, but are surmounted by multi-lobed arches in brick and stucco, which recall the plaster arcades of the Alhambra in Spain, while the domes and the vaults have, in Fergusson's words, 'all the structural properties and the character of a Gothic building'.[6]

Another palace of yet more decadent and eclectic architecture was built in the fort at Tanjore around 1700. Similar to the previous palaces, but even less coherent in the composition and decorative treatment, it consists of an eight-storey tower, fantastic but lacking in character, and has exuberant stucco decoration clumsily encrusting weak and shapeless arches and with classic moulding and clearly Hindu iconography. This palace can be considered as an expression of the cultural extravagance of Lucknow of around a century later, when the socio-political and economic conditions gave life to an architecture that was no longer an essential part of the life of the times, but had become simply the material expression of a whim.

Between the sovereigns' palaces and the humble homes of the majority of their subjects there is a considerable difference, but in some parts of the country ordinary people distinguished themselves with characterful architectural creations.

The Lotus Mahall (1575) at Vijayanagar (Hampi). The two-storey pavilion is the oldest example of Muslim-influenced architecture in southern India.

Examples of good domestic architecture are not distributed in equal measure throughout the entire subcontinent, but even where homes are very poor in terms of construction, such as in the painted cabins of Orissa, the influence of the decorator is very strong. In Bengal, for example, some rural cottages in woven bamboo display such a high technical quality that they can be classified as true works of art. Nevertheless, secular architecture reached its most refined expression in the central-western and northern regions of the country. In Rajputana and to the east near Agra, the material used for construction was stone, while towards the west, in Gujarat and in Kathiavar, wood was preferred, and in the north, in the Punjab and Kashmir, wood and brick were used. Naturally this domestic architecture is almost exclusively reserved for city buildings since the structures in villages, although interesting as examples of popular art, are much less permanent.

The cities were sometimes planned with four main roads (*char rasta*) aligned at right-angles, and the intersection formed the focal point of the city itself which had entrance gates at its extremities. Usually, however, centres of population were made up of a chance agglomeration of small narrow roads which were given shade by the height of the buildings aligned on each side, not unlike medieval European cities. In the main roads of the cities, built in stone, the homes of upper-class people alternated with the attractive façades of temples and with noble residences. But the most typical houses were found in the quieter, outer quarters of cities such as Bikaner, Jodhpur, Lashkar (Gwalior) and Ajmer. These homes were built over three floors, with flat roofs enclosed by a balustrade or an open-work parapet which transformed them into terraces to be used in the hot season. Externally, above ground level, a platform stretches from the house to the road; reached by means of steps, the householder would entertain his friends or carry out his business on this *chabutra* (seat). The openings on this floor are heavily barred and the only entrance, at the centre, is of solid wood, to ensure protection.

The middle floor of the home is usually the most ornate, often embellished with a wide, continuous balcony supported by fine, worked corbels; when arcades appear they carry open work with intricate designs traced in the stone. The ceiling of this projecting storey, contained within an ornamental balustrade, forms a small terrace for the attic above, the windows of which are also screened with stone grates. It was in the creation of these open-work stone slabs that the stone masons of Gujarat excelled; with their intricate geometric designs and floral arabesques of exquisite refinement they constituted the architectural glory of such homes. In Gujarat and in Kathiavar stone was often replaced with painted wood, but worked with the same ability and care. In the Punjab, too, the façades of houses are picturesque compositions in wood, in which arched balconies constitute a particular characteristic.

An ancient school of wood carvers existed in all the main centres of the Punjab, such as Lahore, Multan, Amritsar, Bhera and others, as is evidenced in the frontages of the houses or the interiors of apartments found in even the most remote streets of these centres, often dating from the sixteenth century or even earlier. The style of these buildings presents a fusion of Hindu and Muslim motifs, some of which are of uncommon character.

From the end of the eighteenth century onwards Mughal art began to be substituted by new fashions introduced from Europe. Contemporary Hindu taste and motifs went the same way. Practices changed and with them the traditional way of life: the old houses and palaces became uncomfortable, chairs and tables replaced rugs and cushions. Water-colour miniatures could no longer compete with European oils, which became extremely fashionable with all the courts.

Ancient crafts were threatened or even suppressed by imports of modern industrial products wherever the newly built railways penetrated the interior. As Goetz has written, 'The agony of the old world continued beyond the nineteenth century, and, departing from administrative and commercial centres, it pushed into even the most inaccessible districts. The old art died at the beginning of our century, but it did bequeath its heritage to the pioneers of modern national art.'[7]

As we have seen, the Islamic architecture of the immense Indian subcontinent displays extraordinary richness and variety, more than in any other region of Islam. Every Indian province contributed, with an independent style of its own, towards the realization of this versatile, multiform artistic expression, which is an integral, but quite original, part of Islamic culture as a whole. It is all the more interesting because it is the result of a fusion, or rather a sublimation, of the most diverse contributions: 'indigenous', but never the same in the various regions that were gradually conquered by Islam, and 'foreign', but of Timurid, Safavid and Ottoman schools, all fundamental to the formation of the Muslim style. They were all assimilated and then brilliantly presented in new forms that do not deny their roots but make them manifest. It is this refined and ingenious blending of 'Indianness' and 'Islamicity' that enables us to recognize, without hesitation, an Indo-Islamic religious building amongst all those inspired by the same creed in the rest of the Islamic world.

[1] The Elephant Gate gets its name from the painting of Ganesha, the elephant-headed god, on the façade, just above the polylobate arch of the entrance. His presence was considered to be a good omen.

[2] Jaipur, which is situated on the plain below Amber, was designed by Jai Singh. Its extremely regular plan is divided into quadrants, in which numerous straight roads intersect. This regularity reveals Jai Singh's interest in mathematics, just as the highly efficient astronomical observatory bears witness to his predominant interest in astronomy. Inside the city walls is the palace which, like all the important houses in Rajasthan, is designed with residential apartments and administrative offices taking up several storeys. The decorative elements consist of windows with openwork screens, pointed arches carried on slender columns and curved roofs.

[3] Bir Singh Deo was one of Jahangir's loyal princes. In 1602 Jahangir asked him to assassinate Akbar's minister, Abu al-Fazl. He was rewarded for this and in 1623 the title of *maharaja* was conferred on him. Bir Singh Deo died in 1627, almost at the same time as his protector.

[4] At Orchha Bir Singh Deo had built a grandiose temple, the Chaturbhuj, that was partly demolished by Shah Jahan. Even so, it is still quite an impressive structure, which was influenced stylistically by the temple of Govinda Deva at Brindavan, built by the same *raja* in 1590. The interior has a composite structure, with arcades, a domed area and another, Hindu-style, 'curved' one. According to the French traveller Tavernier, this massive red sandstone structure was visible from a long way off.

[5] Brown, *op. cit.*, p. 121.

[6] J. Fergusson, *History of Indian and Eastern Architecture*, vol. 1, London 1910, pp. 412–14.

[7] H. Goetz, *A History of Indian Art*, Baden-Baden 1958, p. 256.

Glossary

abshar
cascade in a garden

adhan
summons to prayer

amalaka
flat, ribbed, melon-shaped ornament

ambar khana
storehouse, house of the royal treasure

arg
fort, citadel

asana
seat or throne in a Hindu temple

ashlar
squared stonework

badgir
wind-tower

badshah-ka-takht
ruler's throne or gallery, private chapel for the king

bagh
garden

baithak
drawing room, reception room

bangaldar
curved roof derived from the shape of roofs on Bengali huts

bangla
Bengali hut

baoli
stepped well

baradari
open detached pavilion in a compound or on a terrace, with three arched openings on each side

bhavan
house

burj
tower with imposing superstructure

caravanserai
inn for boarding and lodging on caravan routes

chaitya
originally a tumulus (*chita*), but subsequently a sanctuary of any kind, Hindu or Buddhist

char bagh
garden divided into four compartments

char chala
Bengali roof form with crossed curved ridges and curved eaves, on a square or rectangular plan; also *chau chala*

char su
bazaar crossing

char taq
square domed structure supported on arches on all four sides; the tetrapylon of the Sassanid temple of fire

chaubutra
platform

chhajja
sloping projection from a façade, overhanging eave on brackets to protect from rain or sun

chhappar
triangular roof or ceiling

chhapparkhat
small pavilion supported by corbelled pillars and with a pyramidal roof

chhatri
kiosk, or small pavilion, acting as turret on the roof

chowki
pedestals

daftar khana
office, archive

dar
house, habitation; also palace

dar al-Khalifat
Seat of the Empire (Delhi, under Shah Jahan)

dar al-Mahall
Seat of the Palace (Agra)

dar al-Sultanat
Seat of the Sovereignty (Lahore)

dargah
tomb complex of a Muslim saint

darha
two roads

darshan
'beholding': the practice of viewing the emperor at a window or a balcony

darwaza
gate, monumental gate

daulat khana
palace, personal residence of the ruler

devanagari
a kind of Indian script used in Sanskrit and Hindi

dharmshala
inn for travellers

dhimmi
followers of a revealed religion

diwan
government department or royal reception chamber

diwan-i amm
hall of public audience

diwan-i khass
hall of private audience

do chala
Bengali roof form with single curved ridge, curved side eaves and gabled ends, usually on a rectangular plan

duchhatti
a two-storey room

durbar
court or meeting hall

Glossary

ertimukha
grotesque stylized animal mask

gajamukha
elephant trunk-shaped element of decoration

garbhagriha
adytum, shrine, the most sacred part of the Hindu temple

ghat
stepped embankment on a tank, lake or river to facilitate religious rituals or bathing

guldasta
slender ornamental minaret, often flanking a portal in pairs

gumbad
dome, but used for pre-Mughal mausoleums; also *gumbaz*

hadith
Islamic traditions, sayings attributed to Muhammad

hammam
baths, public or private

hamsa
goose-shaped decoration, a common Hindu motif

harem
women's quarter, private quarters of a house

haveli
residential building complex, often multi-storey, with profuse stone work

hawa mahall
wind palace, designed so as to catch the breeze

hisar
fort or fortress

huri
girls, lovely companions of the believers in the Muslim Paradise

ibadat khanah
place or house of worship of religious discourses, sanctuary

id
festival

Id al-Fitr
festival at the end of fasting

Id al-Kabir
festival of the sacrificed lamb, held on the last day of the pilgrimage to Mecca

idgah
praying place used during the most important Muslim festivals, often only a *qibla* wall

imambara
religious structure used for the Shiite Muharram festival

imamzade
mausoleum of a saint in the Persian world

iwan
roofed or vaulted hall opening on to a courtyard

jali
open-work, pierced screen, often of stone

jami masjid
congregational mosque, Great Mosque

jawab
identical building installed for sake of symmetry

jharoka
window, fully or partially closed by *jali*, to look over

jizia
tax reserved for the privileged infidels

Kaaba
sacred black stone housed in the courtyard of the Great Mosque at Mecca

kalasha
vase-shaped ornament found in finials and capitals, used to crown the domes of *chhatri* by Mughal builders

kanjura
stepped battlement, merlon

kar khana
house or department where various works for state use were produced

kashi kari
glazed tile-work for mural decoration

khamba
pillar or column; also *stambha*

khana
house

khanqah
convent for mystics

khaprel
roof covered by stone tiles

khass mahall
emperor's bedroom; once called Aramgah (Place of Rest); also personal palace, for the exclusive use of the emperor and his chief queens

khwabgah
sleeping chamber of the emperor

kirtimukha
ornamental mask of great antiquity in Indian art

kirtisthambha
Hindu victory or celebration towers

kos minar
tapering, massive pillars that mark the sections of the main roads of the Mughal Empire

kotha
internal closed rooms

kotla
citadel, royal citadel

Kufic
rectangular script used for monumental purposes; originally an epigraphic, lapidary script in ancient Arabia

kutub khana
library

ladao
barrel vault with ribs

lat
minaret; also *stambha*

linga
standing pillar based originally on the male reproductive organ, symbol of the god Shiva

madrasa
school, theological school

maidan
square

mahtat khana
writing room of the translation service instigated by the emperor to provide him with Persian versions of Sanskrit classics

makara
corbel in the form of a crocodile-shaped creature

mahall
palace, palace complex

mandal
wooden pavilion on pillars, generally covered on all sides to make a private room

mandapa
pavilion, columned temple hall

mansabdar
rank holder in the Mughal administrative system

maqan
house

maqbara
cemetery

maqsura
enclosure near the *mihrab* intended to protect the ruler against assassination; screen or arched façade of a mosque

masjid
small mosque

mazina
square pavilion instead of a minaret, mostly in Kashmir

mihman khana
guest house or assembly hall

mihrab
prayer niche, concave or flat, indicating the direction towards Mecca

minar
minaret, slender tower of the mosque from which the faithful are called to prayer

minbar
pulpit inside the mosque

muluq khana
private room of the king

muqarnas
stalactite or honeycomb ornament or vaulting made of small concave segments

musalla
open-air place of community prayer

naga-pasha
Hindu motif representing a Tantric symbol, used as a good-luck charm by Akbar

naqqar khanah
upper chamber over the gateway where ceremonial music was performed at fixed times

naskhi
cursive script

nastaliq
cursive script

naubat khana
see *naqqar khanah*

naulakha
see *bangla*

navarasa
Sanskrit title, 'New Essence of the Time'

nawab
title for vice-regents of the Mughals and later independent rulers

niwas
abode, used to refer to a small palace or to an apartment within a palace

parabadi
bird-roost, composed of a circular platform resting on a single central pillar; generally used in Gujarat

paradeisos
garden plan according to the plan of the perfect garden of Paradise promised to the faithful in the Koran

pardah
screen

pietra dura
inlaid mosaic of hard and semi-precious stones

pinjra
lattice work

pir
Muslim saint; Sufi teacher or spiritual guide

pishtaq
monumental entrance portal

pol
gate, gateway, fortified gate

pul
bridge

qala
fort; also *qila*

qibla
wall of prayer hall facing Mecca (in the Indian subcontinent facing west)

qutb
stake, axis or pivot

Ramadan
ninth month of Hijra era, the month of fasting

Ramayana
Sanskrit epic poem of great antiquity

raja
king

rani
queen

rauza
tomb, mausoleum, funerary garden

riwaq
portico, colonnade around mosque courtyard

Glossary

sagar
lake

sahn
court, mosque courtyard

saraparda
covered passage screened by curtains

satkona
six-pointed star ornament

semichakra
wheel-shaped ornament

shah burj
royal tower

shardula
Hindu ornamental motif including two animals, usually a lion and a horse

Shia
Muslim sect which accepts Ali as the true successor to Muhammad

shikara
curved tower in Hindu temples

shish mahall
palace complex, internally decorated with glass mosaics

sikhara
spires, carved decoration of Hindu inspiration

sila khana
armoury

silsila
fraternity which traces itself back to Muhammad

Sufi
mystic

Sunni
Muslim sect which believes in Abu Bakr as the elected successor to Muhammad

Surya Purusa
the Body of the Sun

tah khana
low, arched structure, basement; underground chamber or vault

takht
throne; also raised and screened platform within a mosque, either for ladies of the court or for the ruler and immediate entourage

taksal
mint

talar
building supported by pillars

tibara
verandah with three openings

torana
gateway of Indian design

tosha khana
clothes, cloth and furniture warehouse

tripolia
triple gateway

vahana
vehicle, the mythical bird that was the vehicle of Vishnu

vihara
Buddhist or Jain monastery

vilas
house, pleasure palace

waw
stepped well; same as *baoli*, in Gujarat and western India

zenana
women's quarters

ziyarat
tomb of holy personage, mostly in Kashmir

Table of Dynasties and Rulers

Northern India
The Delhi Sultans 1206–1555

1 Mamluks or Muizzi
- 1206–1210 Qutb al-Din Aibak
- 1210 Aram Shah
- 1211–1236 Shams al-Din Iltutmish
- 1236 Rukn al-Din Firuz Shah I
- 1236–1240 Jalalat al-Din Raziyya Begum
- 1240–1242 Muizz al-Din Bahram Shah
- 1242–1246 Ala al-Din Masud Shah
- 1246–1266 Nasir al-Din Mahmud Shah I
- 1266–1287 Ghiyas al-Din Balban
- 1287–1290 Muizz al-Din Kay Qubadh
- 1290 Shams al-Din Kayumarth

2 Khalji
- 1290–1296 Jalal al-Din Firuz Shah II
- 1296 Rukn al-Din Ibrahim Shah I
- 1296–1316 Ala al-Din Muhammad Shah
- 1316 Shihab al-Din Umar Shah
- 1316–1320 Qutb al-Din Mubarak Shah
- 1320 *Usurpation of Nazir al-Din Khusrau Shah*

3 Tughluq
- 1320–1325 Ghiyas al-Din Tughluq Shah I
- 1325–1351 Ghiyas al-Din Muhammad Shah II
- 1351 Mahmud
- 1351–1388 Firuz Shah III
- 1388–1389 Ghiyas al-Din Tughluq Shah II
- 1389–1390 Abu Bakr Shah
- 1390–1393 Nasir al-Din Muhammad Shah III
- 1393 Ala al-Din Sikandar Shah I
- 1393–1395 Nasir al-Din Mahmud Shah *first reign*
- 1395–1399 Nusrat Shah *disputing power with Mahmud Shah II*
- 1399–1413 Mahmud Shah II *second reign*
- 1414 Dawlat Khan Lodi

4 Sayyid
- 1414–1421 Khizr Khan
- 1421–1435 Muizz al-Din Mubarak Shah II
- 1435–1446 Muhammad Shah IV
- 1446–1451 Alal al-Din Alam Shah

5 Lodi
- 1451–1489 Bahlol Lodi
- 1489–1517 Nizam Khan Sikandar II
- 1517–1526 Ibrahim II

Mughal conquest under Babur

6 Suri or Afghans
- 1540–1545 Sher Shah Sur
- 1545–1554 Islam Shah
- 1554 Muhammad Adil Shah
- 1554–1555 Ibrahim Shah III
- 1555 Ahmad Khan Sikandar Shah III

Final Mughal conquest by Humayun

Bengal
1336–1576

1 Eastern Bengal
- 1336–1349 Fakhr al-Din Mubarak Shah
- 1349–1352 Ikhtiyar al-Din Ghazi Shah

Conquest by Shams al-Din Ilyas Shah

2 Western Bengal and then all Bengal
- 1339–1345 Ala al-Din Ali Shah

Line of Ilyas Shah
- 1345–1358 Shams al-Din Ilyas Shah
- 1358–1390 Sikandar Shah I
- 1390–1410 Ghiyas al-Din Azam Shah
- 1410–1412 Sayf al-Din *Hamsa* Shah
- 1412–1414 Shihab al-Din Bayazit Shah
- 1414 Ala al-Din Firuz Shah

Line of Raja Ganesha
- 1414–1432 Jalal al-Din Muhammad Shah
- 1432–1436 Shams al-Din Ahmad Shah

Line of Ilyas Shah, second reign
- 1437–1460 Nasir al-Din Mahmud Shah
- 1460–1474 Rukn al-Din Barbak Shah
- 1474–1481 Shams al-Din Yusuf Shah
- 1481 Sikandar Shah II
- 1481–1487 Jalal al-Din Fath Shah

Line of Habashi
- 1487 Sultan Shahzada Barbak Shah
- 1487–1490 Sayf al-Din Firuz Shah
- 1490–1491 Nazir al-Din Mahmud Shah
- 1491–1494 Shams al-Din Muzaffar Shah

Line of Sayyid Husain Shah
- 1494–1519 Sayyid Ala al-Din Husain Shah
- 1519–1532 Nazir al-Din Nusrat Shah
- 1532–1533 Ala al-Din Firuz Shah
- 1533–1539 Ghiyas al-Din Mahmud Shah

Line of Suri or Afghani
- 1539–1540 Sher Shah Sur
- 1540–1545 Khizr Khan
- 1545–1555 Muhammad Khan Sur
- 1555–1561 Khizr Khan Bahadur Shah
- 1561–1564 Ghiyas al-Din Jalal Shah

Line of Sulayman Kararani
- 1564–1572 Sulayman Kararani
- 1572 Bayazit Shah Kararani
- 1572–1576 Daud Shah Kararani

Mughal conquest

Jaunpur
The Sharqui Sultans of Jaunpur

- 1394–1399 Maliq Sarvar, Khwaja Jihan
- 1399–1402 Mubarak Shah
- 1402–1440 Shams al-Din Ibrahim
- 1440–1457 Mahmud Shah
- 1457–1458 Muhammad Shah
- 1458–1479 Husain Shah

Conquest by the Lodi Sultans of Delhi

Gujarat
The Gujarat Sultans

- 1391–1411 Zafar Khan Muzaffar I
- 1411–1442 Ahmad I
- 1442–1451 Muhammad Karim
- 1451–1458 Qutb al-Din Ahmad II
- 1458 Daud
- 1458–1511 Mahmud I Begara (Begra)
- 1511–1526 Muzaffar II
- 1526 Sikandar
- 1526 Nasir Khan Mahmud II
- 1526–1537 Bahadur
- 1537 *Miran Muhammad of Kandesh*
- 1537–1554 Mahmud III
- 1554–1561 Ahmad III
- 1561–1573 Muzaffar III *first reign*
- 1573 *Mughal conquest*
- 1573–1583 Muzaffar III *second reign*

Definitive Mughal conquest

Malwa
The Sultans of Malwa

1 Line of Ghuris
- 1401–1405 Dilawar Khan Husain Ghuri
- 1405–1435 Alp Khan Hushang Shah
- 1435–1436 Ghazni Khan Muhammad
- 1436 Mashud Khan

2 Line of Khaljis
- 1436–1469 Mahmud Shah I Khalji
- 1469–1500 Ghiyas al-din Shah
- 1500–1511 Nizam al-Din Shah
- 1511–1531 Mahmud Shah II

Conquest by the Sultans of Gujarat

Deccan
1347–1687

1 The Bahmanids and their successors
- 1347–1358 Ala al-Din Hasan Bahman Shah
- 1358–1375 Muhammad I
- 1375–1378 Ala al-Din Mujahid
- 1378 Daud
- 1378–1397 Muhammad II
- 1397 Ghiyas al-Din
- 1397 Shams al-Din
- 1397–1422 Taj al-Din Firuz
- 1422–1436 Ahmad I Wali
- 1436–1458 Ala al-Din Ahmad II
- 1458–1461 Ala al-Din Humayun Zalim
- 1461–1463 Nizam
- 1463–1482 Muhammad III Lashkari
- 1482–1518 Mahmud
- 1518–1521 Ahmad III
- 1521–1522 Ala al-Din
- 1522–1525 Wali Allah
- 1525–1527 Karim Allah

From 1518 the rulers were nominal sultans under the tutelage of the chief minister Amir Barid of Bidar. Dissolution of the Bahmanid sultanate into five local sultanates (see below)

2 The Barid Shahi of Bidar
- –1504 Qasim Barid
- 1504–1543 Amir Barid I
- 1543–1580 Ali Barid I
- 1543–1580 Ali Barid Shah
- 1580–1587 Ibrahim Barid Shah
- 1587–1591 Qasim Barid II
- 1591–1600 Amir Barid II
- 1600–1609 Mirza Ali Barid
- 1609–1619 Amir Barid Shah

Mughal conquest

3 The Nizam Shahi of Ahmadnagar
- 1496–1510 Ahmad Nizam Shah Bahri
- 1510–1553 Burhan Nizan Shah I
- 1553–1565 Husain Nizam Shah I
- 1565–1588 Murtaza Nizam Shah I
- 1588 Miran Husain Nizam Shah
- 1588–1591 Ismail Nizam Shah
- 1591–1594 Burhan Nizam Shah II
- 1594 Ibrahin Nizam Shah
- 1594–1595 Ahmad Nizam Shah
- 1595–1600 Bahadur Nizam Shah
- 1600–1631 Murtaza Nizam Shah II and III

Mughal conquest

4 The Qutb Shahi of Golconda and Hyderabad
- –1543 Quli Qutb al-Mulk
- 1543–1550 Yar Quli Jamshid
- 1550–1580 Ibrahim Qutb Shah
- 1580–1612 Muhammad Quli Qutb Shah
- 1612–1626 Muhammad Qutb Shah
- 1626–1672 Abdullah Qutb Shah
- 1672–1687 Abul Hasan Qutb Shah

Mughal conquest

5 The Adil Shahi of Bijapur
- 1490–1510 Yusuf Adil Khan
- 1510 1534 Ismail Adil Khan
- 1534–1535 Mallu Adil Khan
- 1535–1558 Ibrahim Adil Shah I
- 1558–1580 Ali Adil Shah I
- 1580–1627 Ibrahim Adil Shah II
- 1627–1656 Muhammad Adil Shah II
- 1656–1672 Ali Adil Shah II
- 1672–1686 Sikandar Adil Shah

Mughal conquest

6 The Faruqi Sultans of Kandesh
- 1370–1399 Maliq Raja Faruqi
- 1399–1437 Nasir Khan
- 1437–1441 Adil Khan I
- 1441–1457 Miran Mubarak Khan I
- 1457–1503 Adil Khan II
- 1503–1510 Daud Khan
- 1510 Ghazni Khan
- 1510 Alam Khan
- 1510–1520 Adil Khan III
- 1520–1537 Miran Muhammad I
- 1537 Ahmad Shah
- 1537–1566 Mubarak Shah II
- 1566–1576 Miran Muhammad II
- 1576–1577 Hasan Shah
- 1577–1597 Raja Ali Khan or Adil Shah IV
- 1597–1601 Bahadur Shah

Mughal conquest

Kashmir
1346–1589

1 Line of Shah Mirza Swati
- 1346–1349 Shams al-Din Shah Mirza Swati
- 1349–1350 Jamshid
- 1350–1359 Ala al-Din Ali Shir
- 1359–1378 Shihab al-Din Shirashamak
- 1378–1394 Qutb al-Din Hindal
- 1394–1416 Sikandar But-Shikan
- 1416–1420 Ali Mirza Khan
- 1420–1470 Zayn-al-Abidin Shahi Khan
- 1470–1471 Haidar Shah Hajji Khan
- 1471–1489 Hasan
- 1489–1490 Muhammad *first reign*
- 1490–1498 Farah Shah *first reign*
- 1498–1499 Muhammad *second reign*
- 1499–1500 Farah Shah *second reign*
- 1500–1526 Muhammad *third reign*
- 1526–1527 Ibrahim I
- 1527–1529 Nazuk *first reign*
- 1529–1533 Muhammad *fourth reign*
- 1533–1540 Shams al-Din
- 1540 Nazuk *second reign*
- 1540–1551 Haidar Dughlat *governor for Humayun*
- 1551–1552 Nazuk *third reign*
- 1552–1555 Ibrahim II
- 1555–1557 Ismail
- 1557–1561 Habib

Dethroned by Ghazi Khan Chak

2 Line of Ghazi Khan Chak
- 1561–1563 Ghazi Khan Chak
- 1563–1569 Nasr al-Din Husain
- 1569–1579 Zahir al-Din Ali
- 1579–1586 Nasr al-Din Yusuf
- 1586–1589 Yaqub

Submission to the Mughal emperor Akbar

The Mughal Emperors
1526–1858

- 1526–1530 Zahir al-Din Babur
- 1530–1540 Nasir al-Din Humayun *first reign*
- 1540–1555 *Suri sultans of Delhi*
- 1555–1556 Humayun *second reign*
- 1556–1605 Jalal al-Din Akbar I
- 1605–1627 Nur al-Din Jahangir
- 1627–1628 Dawar Bakhsh
- 1628–1657 Shihab al-Din Shah Jahan I
- 1657 Murad Bakhsh *in Gujarat*
- 1657–1660 Shah Shuja *in Bengal*
- 1658–1707 Muhyi al-Din Aurangzeb Alamgir I
- 1707 Azam Shah
- 1707 Kam Bakhsh *in Deccan*
- 1707–1712 Shah Alam I Bahadur Shah I
- 1712 Hasimash Shain
- 1712–1713 Muizz al-Din Jihandar
- 1713–1719 Farrukh Siyar
- 1719 Shams al-Din Rufud Darajat
- 1719 Rafi ad-Daula Shah Jahan II
- 1719 Nikusiyar
- 1719–1748 Nasir al-din Muhammad
- 1738 *Invasion of Nadir Shah*
- 1748–1754 Ahmad Shah Bahadur
- 1754–1760 Aziz al-Din Alamgir II
- 1757 *Invasion of Ahmad Shah Durrani*
- 1760 Shah Jahan III
- 1760–1788 Jalal al-Din Ali Jawhar Shah Shah Alam II *first reign*
- 1788 Badar Bakht
- 1788–1806 Shah Alam II *second reign*
- 1806–1837 Muin al-Din Akbar II
- 1837–1858 Siraj al-Din Bahadur Shah II

Direct British rule

Bibliography

Primary Sources

Abbas Khan, *Tuzuk-i Sher Shah*, trans. H.M. Elliot and J. Dowson, in *The History of India as Told by its own Historians: the Muhammadan Period*, London 1867–77, vol. 4, pp. 301–433

Abd al-Hamid Lahori, *Padshah-nama*, 2 vols., K. Ahmad, M.A. Rahim (eds.), 2 vols., Calcutta 1867–8

Abdullah, *Tarikh-i Da'udi*, trans. H.M. Elliot and J. Dowson, in *The History of India as Told by its own Historians: the Muhammadan Period*, London 1867–77, vol. 4, pp. 434–513

Abul Fazl, *A'in-i-Akbari*, H. Blochmann (ed.), 2 vols., Calcutta 1867–77 (reprint New Delhi 1977)

Abul Fazl, *Akbar-nama*, trans. H. Beveridge, 3 vols., Calcutta 1907–39

Afif, Shams-i Siraj, *Tarikh-i Firuz Shah*, trans. H.M. Elliot and J. Dowson, in *The History of India as Told by its own Historians: the Muhammadan Period*, London 1867–77, vol. 3 (reprint Calcutta 1953, pp. 1–143)

Aftabchi, J., *Tazkirat al-Waqiat*, trans. C. Stewart, 1832 (reprint New Delhi 1972)

Ahmad, Maulvi Bashir ud-Din, *Waqiat-i-Darul-Hukumat-i Dilhi*, 3 vols., Delhi 1919

al-Biruni, *Kitab al-Hind*, trans. E. Sachau, London 1914 (reprint Lahore 1962)

al-Moqaddasi, *Descriptio imperi moslemici*, M.J. De Goeje (ed.), Bibliotheca Geographorum Arabicorum, vol. 3, Leiden 1887

Amir Khusrau, *Khaza'in al-Futuh*, S. Mu'in al-Haq (ed.), Aligarh 1927

Amir Khusrau, *Tughluq-nama*, Aurangabad 1933

Asad, B., *Wikaya*, trans. H.M. Elliot and J. Dowson, in *The History of India as Told by its own Historians: the Muhammadan Period*, London 1867–77, vol. 4, pp. 150–74

Babur, *Babur-nama*, trans. A.S. Beveridge, 2 vols., London 1921

Bada'uni, 'Abd al-Qadir, *Muntakhab at-Tavarikh*, trans. G.S. Ranking, W.H. Lowe, T.W. Haig, 3 vols., Calcutta 1898–9 (reprint New Delhi 1973)

Badr, C., *Sharh-i Qasaid*, Lucknow

Barni, Z., *Tarikh-i Firuz Shahi*, trans. H.M. Elliot and J. Dowson, in *The History of India as Told by its own Historians: the Muhammadan Period*, London 1867–77, vol. 3 (reprint Calcutta 1953, vol. 14, pp. 1–196)

Biyat, B., *Tazkira-i Humayun wa Akbar*, M. Hidayat Hosein (ed.), Calcutta 1841

Firishta, M.A., *Gulshan-i Ibrahimi*, trans. J. Briggs, *History of the Rise of the Mahomedan Power in India, till year A.D. 1612*, 4 vols., London 1829

Firuz Shah, *Futuhat-i Firuz Shahi*, trans. H.M. Elliot and J. Dowson, in *The History of India as Told by its own Historians: the Muhammadan Period*, London 1867–77, vol. 3 (reprint Calcutta 1953, vol. 15)

Gulbadan Begum, *Humayun-nama*, trans. A.S. Beveridge, London 1922 (reprint New Delhi 1972)

Haidar, *Tarikh-i Rashidi*, trans. E. Denison Ross, *A History of the Moguls of Central Asia*, London 1895

Jahangir, *Tuzuk-i Jahangiri*, trans. A. Rogers, 2 vols., London 1909–14 (reprint New Delhi 1968)

Kambu, M.S., *'Amal-i-Salih*, G. Yazdani (ed.), Calcutta 1912–39

Khafi Khan, M.H., *Muntakhab al-Lubab*, trans. H.M. Elliot and J. Dowson, in *The History of India as Told by its own Historians: the Muhammadan Period*, London 1867–77, vol. 3 (reprint Calcutta 1959, vols. 1–3)

Khan, Shah Nawaz, *Ma'athir al-Umara'*, M.A. Rahim, M.A. Ali (eds.), 3 vols., Calcutta 1887–96 (reprint Patna 1979)

Khan, Zayn, *Tabaqat-i Baburi*, trans. Sayed Hasan Askari, New Delhi 1982

Khwandamir, *Qanun-i Humayuni*, trans. Baini Prasad, Calcutta 1940

Minhaj-us Siraj, *Tabaqat-i Nasiri*, trans. H.M. Elliot and J. Dowson, in *The History of India as Told by its own Historians: the Muhammadan Period*, London 1867–77, vol. 2 (1869), (reprint Calcutta 1953, 16 vols., pp. 1–155)

Niamatullah, *Makhzan-i Afghani and Tarikh-i Khan Jahan Lodi*, trans. H.M. Elliot and J. Dowson, in *The History of India as Told by its own Historians: the Muhammadan Period*, London 1867–77, vol. 5 (reprint Calcutta 1955, pp. 22–152)

Nizam ud-Din, A., *Tabaqat-i-Akbari*, 3 vols., trans. B. De and M. Hidayat Hosein, Calcutta 1927–39

Nizami, H., *Taj'ul Maasir*, trans. H.M. Elliot and J. Dowson, in *The History of India as Told by its own Historians: the Muhammadan Period*, London 1867–77, vol. 2 (1869) (reprint Calcutta 1953, pp. 56–99)

Qandahari, M.A., *Tarikh-i-Akbari*, Mu'in'ud-Din Nadwi, Azhar 'Ali Dihlavi, Imtiyaz 'Ali 'Arsi (eds.), Rampur 1962

Qane Mir Ali Sher, *Tuhfat al-Kiram*, trans. A. Rizvi, Karachi 1959

Sarwani, Abbas Khan, *Tarikh-i Shershahi*, trans. H.M. Elliot and J. Dowson, in *The History of India as Told by its own Historians: the Muhammadan Period*, London 1867–77, vol. 4 (reprint Calcutta 1952, pp. 14–157)

Tabataba Ali, *Burhan-i Ma'asir*, trans. J.S. King, *The History of the Bahmani Dynasty*, London 1900

Timur, *Malfuzat-i-Timur*, trans. H.M. Elliot and J. Dowson, in *The History of India as Told by its own Historians: the Muhammadan Period*, London 1867–77, vol. 3

Utbi, Abu Nasr, *Tarikh-i-Yamini (Kitab'ul Yamini)*, Ali and Sprengher (eds.), Delhi 1847

Yahya, Sirhindi, *Tarikh-i Mubarakshahi*, trans. H.M. Elliot and J. Dowson, in *The History of India as Told by its own Historians: the Muhammadan Period*, London 1867–77, vol. 3 (reprint Calcutta 1958, pp. 77–161)

Yazdi, Shaf al-Din, *Zaffar-nama*, Muhammad Allahdad (ed.), 2 vols., Calcutta 1885–6

TRAVELLERS

Abbas Shirazi, A., *Journal of a Tour through Parts of the Punjab and Afghanistan in the Year 1837*, Bombay 1843

Ansari, M.A., *European Travellers and the Mughals (1580–1627)*, New Delhi 1975

Archer, E.L., *Tours in Upper India and in Parts of the Himalayan Mountains*, 2 vols. in 1, London 1833

Aynsley, Murray J.C., *Our Visit to Hindustan, Kashmir and Ladah*, London 1879

Barr, W., *Journal of a March from Delhi to Peshawar and from thence to Cabul*, London 1844

Bernier, F., *Travels in the Mogul Empire: A.D. 1656–1668*, trans. A. Constable, London 1891 (reprint New Delhi 1979)

Coryat, T., 'Letters': *Early Travels in India: 1583–1619*, W. Foster (ed.), London 1921, pp. 234–87

De Laet, J., *De imperio magni Mogolis* (1631), trans. J.S. Hoyland and S.K. Banerjee, *The Empire of the Great Mogul*, London 1928

Della Valle, P., *Viaggi descritti in 54 lettere famigliari*, 4 vols., Rome 1650–58

Fane, H.E., *Five Years in India*, 2 vols., London 1842

Finch, W., 'Account': *Early Travels in India: 1583–1619*, W. Foster (ed.), London 1921, pp. 125–87

Fitch, R., 'Memoirs': *Early Travels in India: 1583–1619*, W. Foster (ed.), London 1921, pp. 1–47

Forbes, J., *Oriental Memoirs*, 2 vols., London 1834

Foster, C.W. (ed.), *Letters Received by the East India Company from its Servants in the East: 1602–1617*, 2 vols., London 1896–1902

Heber, R., *Narrative of a Journey through the Upper Provinces of India from Calcutta to Bombay: 1824–25*, 3 vols., London 1828

Herbert, T., *Some Years Travels into Africa and Asia the Great*, London 1638

Hodges, W., *Travels in India during the Years 1780, 1781, 1782 & 1783*, London 1783

Ibn Battuta, *Rihla: The Travels in Asia and Africa*, trans. H.A. Gibb, New York 1928

Ireland, J.B., *Wall Street to Cashmere*, New York 1859

Jourdain, J., *The Journal of John Jourdain: 1608–17*, W. Foster (ed.), Cambridge 1905

Madelslo, J.A., *Voyages and Travels into the East Indies*, trans. Davies, London 1669

Major, R.H., *India in the XV Century*, London 1857

Manrique, S., *Travels of Fray Sebastien Manrique*, trans. C.E. Luard and H. Hosten, 2 vols., Oxford 1927

Mildenhall, J., 'Letter': *Early Travels in India: 1583–1619*, W. Foster (ed.), London 1921, pp. 54–9

Minturn, R.B., *From New York to Delhi*, New York 1858

Monserrate, A., *Commentary on his Journey to the Court of Akbar*, trans. J.S. Hoyland, London 1922

Mooncraft, W. and Trebeck, G., *Travels in the Himalayan Provinces of the Hindustan and the Punjab*, London 1837

Mundy, P., *Travels of Peter Mundy in Europe and Asia 1608–1667*, Sir R.C. Temple (ed.), 5 vols., Cambridge 1907–36

Noer, *Kaiser Akbar*, vols. 1–2, (1880-1885), trans. Beveridge, Calcutta 1890

Orlich, L., *Travels in India*, trans. H. E. Lloyd, London 1845

Parks, F., *Wanderings of a Pilgrim in Search of the Picturesque during Four and Twenty Years in the East, with Revelations of Life in the Zenana*, 2 vols., London 1850

Pelsaert, F., *A Contemporary Dutch Chronicle of Mughal India*, trans. B. Narain and S.R. Sharma, Calcutta 1957 (reprint Lahore 1978)

Peruschi, G.B., *Informazione del regno e stato del gran re di Mogor*, Rome 1597

Pratas, C.R., *Early English Travelers in India*, Patna 1965

Roe, T., *The Embassy of Sir Thomas Roe to India, 1615–19*, W. Foster (ed.), London 1926

Sleeman, W.H., *Rambles and Recollections of an Indian Official*, London 1844 (reprint Karachi 1973)

Steel, R. and Crowter, J., *A Journal of the Journey of Richard Steel and John Crowter: 1615–16*, S. Purchas (ed.), 4 vols., Glasgow 1905

Tavernier, J.-B., *Les Six Voyages de Jean-Baptiste Tavernier, ecuyeur baron d'Aubonne qu'il a fait en Turquie, en Perse et aux Indes... seconde partie, ou il est parlé des Indes voisines*, 2 vols., Paris 1676, trans. V. Ball and W. Crooke, London 1925 (reprint New Delhi 1977)

Taylor, B., *A Visit to India, China, and Japan in the Year 1853*, New York 1855

Temple, R., *Journals Kept in Hyderabad, Kashmir, Sikkim and Nepal*, London 1887

Terry, E., *A Voyage to East India*, London 1777

Thevenot, J., *Voyages: relation de l'Industan, des nouveaux Mogols et des autres peuples et pays de Indes*, Paris 1684, trans. of the 3rd part, 'Indian Travels of Thevenot and Careri', in *India in the Seventeenth Century*, J.P. Guha (ed.), New Delhi 1984

Tieffenthaler, J., *La Géographie de l'Indoustan, écrite en Latin, dans le pays même*, in Jean Bernoulli, *Description historique et géographique de l'Inde*, vol. 1, Berlin 1786

Withington, N., 'Account': *Early Travels in India: 1583–1619*, W. Foster (ed.), London 1921, pp. 196–223

General Works

Barnow, F. and Shodan, M., *Notes on the Urban History of India*, Copenhagen 1977

Basham, A.L., *The Wonder that was India*, London 1954

Basham, A.L., *A Cultural History of India*, Oxford 1975

Batley, C., *The Design Development of Indian Architecture*, 1934 (reprint New York 1973)

Bedge, P.V., *Ancient and Medieval Town-Planning in India*, New Delhi 1978

Bedge, P.V., *Forts and Palaces of India*, New Delhi 1982

Bell, E., *Early Architecture in Western Asia*, London 1924

Brown, P., *Indian Architecture, (Islamic Period)*, Bombay 1975 (6th edn.)

Brush, J.E., 'The Morphology of Indian Cities', R. Turner (ed.), *India's Urban Future: Selected Studies from an International Conference on Urbanisation in India*, held at the University of California, 1960, pp. 57–70

Bussagli, M., *Profili dell'India antica e moderna*, Turin 1959

Chaghatai, M.A., 'What India owes to Central Asia in Islamic Architecture', *Islamic Culture* (1934), pp. 55–65

Chand, T., *Influence of Islam on Indian Culture*, Allahabad 1943

Chandra, J., 'Bibliography of Indian Art, History and Archaeology', *Dr Anand Coomaraswamy Memorial Volume, Indian Art*, vol. 1, New Delhi 1978

Coomaraswamy, A.K., *History of Indian and Indonesian Art*, London 1927

Craven, R., *A Concise History of Indian Art: Islamic India, Architecture and Painting*, London 1976

Cuneo, P., *Storia dell'urbanistica, il mondo islamico*, Bari and Rome 1986, 'L'India musulmana prima dei Moghul', pp. 299–320; 'L'India musulmana dei Moghul', pp. 323–37

Cunningham, A. (ed.), *Archaeological Survey of India Reports*, Annual Reports, 23 vols., Calcutta 1871–87 (reprint Varanasi and Delhi 1969)

'Delhi, Agra, Sikri', *Marg* (1967)

Deloche, J., *The Ancient Bridges in India*, New Delhi 1984

Desai, Z.A., *Indo-Islamic Architecture*, New Delhi 1987 (2nd edn.)

Desai, Z.A., *Mosques of India*, New Delhi 1979

Doshi, S. and Khandalavala, K., *An Age of Splendour: Islamic Art in India*, Bombay 1983

Elliot, H.M. and Dowson, J., *The History of India as Told by its own historians: the Muhammadan Period: The Posthumous Papers of the late Sir H.M. Elliot*, London 1867–77

Fergusson, J., *History of Indian and Eastern Architecture*, 2 vols., London 1910

Fischer, K., 'Form und Bedeutung indischer und islamischer Doppelkuppeln', *Kunstchronik*, 21/12 (1968)

Fischer, K., *Islam in the Indian Subcontinent*, Leiden 1980

Fischer, K. and Fischer, C.M., *Indische Baukunst islamischer Zeit*, Baden-Baden 1976

Fischer, K., Jansen, M. and Pieper, J., *Architektur des indischen Subkontinents im Überblik*, Darmstadt 1985

Forrest, C.W., *Cities of India, Past and Present*, London 1903

Gascoigne, B., *The Great Moghuls*, London 1971

Goetz, H., 'Persian Architecture in India', *Bullettin of the American Institute for Iranian Art and Archaeology*, 6 (1938), pp. 262–9

Goetz, H., *A History of Indian Art*, Baden-Baden 1958

Goetz, H., 'An Irruption of Gothic Style Forms into Indo-Islamic Architecture', *Artibus Asiae*, 22 (1959), pp. 53–8

Goetz, H., 'Arte dell'India musulmana e correnti moderne', *Le Civiltà dell'Oriente*, Rome and Florence 1970, vol. 4, pp. 781–882

Golombek, L., 'From Tamerlan to the Taj Mahal', *Essays in Islamic Art and Architecture in Honor of Katharina Otto-Dorn*, Malibu Cendena 1981, pp. 43–50

Gray, B., *The Arts of India*, Oxford 1981

Grover, S., *The Architecture of Islamic India (727–1707 A.D.)*, New Delhi 1981

Grube, E.J., *The World of Islam*, London 1966

Gutschow, N. and Pieper, J., *Indien*, Köln 1978

Harle, J.C., *The Art and Architecture of the Indian Subcontinent*, Harmondsworth 1986

Havell, E.B., *Benares: the Sacred City*, Calcutta 1933

Hill D., and Grabar, O., *Islamic Architecture and its Decoration, A.D. 800–1500*, London 1967

Hillenbrand, R., *Islamic Architecture: Form, Function and Meaning*, Edinburgh 1994

Hoag, J.D., *Islamic Architecture*, New York 1977

Holod, R. and Rastorfer, D. (eds.), *Architecture and Community-Building in the Islamic World Today*, New York 1983

Hourani, A.H. and Stern, S.M. (eds.), *The Islamic City*, Philadelphia 1970

Hurlimann, M., *India*, London 1975

Hurlimann, M., *Delhi, Agra, Fatehpur Sikri*, London 1985

Husain, A.B., *The Manara in Indo-Muslim Architecture*, Dacca 1970

Imperial Gazetteers of India: Agra, vol. 5, pp. 82–91; Ahmadabad, vol. 5, pp. 106–111; Ajmer, vol. 5, pp. 170–74; Banaras, vol. 7, pp. 189–93; Delhi, vol. 11, pp. 233–41; Gwalior, vol. 12, pp. 438–43; Jaunpur, vol. 14, pp. 82–4; Jodhpur, vol. 14, pp. 198–200; Mathura, vol. 18, pp. 72–4; Ujjain, vol. 24, pp. 112–15

Jairazbhoy, R.A., *Art and Cities of Islam*, New York 1964

Jairazbhoy, R.A., *Oriental Influences in Western Art*, Bombay 1965

Jairazbhoy, R.A., *An Outline of Islamic Architecture*, Bombay 1972

Joshi, S.K., *Defence Architecture in Early Karnataka*, New Delhi 1985

Kittoe, M., *Illustrations of Indian Architecture from the Muhammedan Conquest Downwards*, Calcutta 1838

Kühnel, E., *Islamic Art and Architecture*, New York 1966

Kuttiammu, T.P., *Splendours of Kerala*, Bombay 1979

Kuttiammu, T.P., 'The Mosques of Kerala: a Study of Adaptation and Re-adaptation of the Islamic Tradition', *Marg*, 32/2, pp. 111–15

Lalvani, H., 'Pattern Regeneration: a Form on Islamic Jalis and Mosaics (the Impulse to Adorn: Studies in Traditional Architecture)', *Marg* (1982), pp. 123–36

Majumdar, R.C., *The History and Culture of the Indian People*, 10 vols. (vols. 4, 5, 6, 8), Bombay 1951–69

Marshall, J., *Annual Reports*, Archaeological Survey of India, 1902–7, 1911–15, 1921–30

Marshall, J., 'The Monuments of Muslim India', *The Cambridge History of India*, vol. 3, Cambridge 1928, pp. 568–663

Mehta, R.J., *Masterpieces of the Indo-Islamic Architecture*, Bombay 1976

Michell, G., *Architecture of Islamic Word: its History and Social Meaning*, London 1978

Nasr, S.H., *Islamic Science: an Illustrated Study*, London 1976

Nath, R., *Monuments of Delhi: Historical Studies*, New Delhi 1979

Nilsson, S., *The New Capitals in India, Pakistan and Bangladesh*, London 1973

Petech, L., 'Subcontinente indiano (India, Pakistan, Nepal, Bhutan e Ceylon)', *Le civiltà dell'oriente*, Rome and Florence 1965, vol. 1, pp. 661–709

Qazi, A., *Indian Cities: Characteristics and Correlations*, Chicago 1965

Rajan, S.K., *Islam Builds in India: Cultural Study of Islamic Architecture*, New Delhi 1983

Salomon, W.E., 'The Art and Colour of Gwalior', *Islamic Culture*, 7 (1933), pp. 380–94

Sarkar, H., *Monuments of Kerala*, New Delhi 1978

Scarcia Amoretti, B., 'Qualche osservazione in margine all'ingresso dell'Islam nel Kerala', *Studi in onore di L. Petech*, P. Daffinà (ed.), *Indo-sino-tibetica*, Rome 1990, pp. 341–48

Scarcia, G. and Taddei, M., 'The Masjid-i Sangi of Larvand', *East and West*, 23 (1973), pp. 89–108

Scerrato, U., *Islam*, Grandi Monumenti, Milan 1972

Schmidt, K. and Khan, F.A., *5000 Years of Art in Pakistan*, Utrecht 1963

Shah, U.P., *Studies in Jaina Art*, Benares 1955

Sharma, Y.D., 'Delhi and its Neighbourhood', *Organizing Committee, XXVI International Congress of Orientalists*, New Delhi 1982

Singh, A.P., *Forts and Fortifications in India*, New Delhi 1987

Sivaramamurti, C., *The Arts of India*, New York 1977

Smith, E.W., *Portfolio of Indian Architectural Drawings*, London 1897

Spodek, H., 'Studying the History of Urbanisation in India', *Journal of Urban History*, 6/3 (1980), pp. 251–96

Stierlin, H., *The World of India*, New York 1978

Terry, J., *The Charm of Indo-Islamic Architecture*, London 1955

Terry, J., 'Background of Indo-Islamic Architecture', *Marg*, 11/3 (1958), pp. 8–14

Tillotson, G.H., *The Rajput Palace: the Development of an Architectural Style, 1450–1750*, New Haven and London 1987

Toy, S., *The Strongholds of India*, Melbourne 1957

Toy, S., *The Fortified Cities of India*, London 1965

Volwansen, A., *Islamisches Indien*, Freibourg 1969

Volwansen, A., *Living Architecture: Islamic-Indian*, London 1970

Wheeler, M. (ed.), *Splendours of the East*, London 1965

Wolpert, S., *A New History of India*, Oxford 1977

Gardens

Ahmad Shaikh, 'Gardens Architecture', *Pakistan Miscellany*, 2 (1958), pp. 56–62

Ansari, M.A., 'Palaces and Gardens of the Mughals', *Islamic Culture*, 33 (1959), pp. 61–72

Archer, M., 'Gardens of Delight', *Apollo* (1968), pp. 172–84

Bamber, C.J., *Plants of the Punjab*, Lahore 1916

Bazmee Ansari, A.S., 'Les jardins mughals' entry 'Bustan', *Encyclopédie de l'Islam*, new edition, Leiden and Paris 1975, vol. 1, pp. 1387–8

Berral, J., 'The Garden: an Illustrated History', *Gardens of Islam*, New York 1966, chapter 5

Brandis, D., *Indian Trees*, London 1906

Brookes, J., *Gardens of Paradise: the History and Designs of the Great Islamic Gardens*, London 1987

Brown, P., 'Moghul Gardens', *Marg*, 8/2 (1955), pp. 93-9

Chandra, K. and Chandra, R., *Ancient Monuments of Kashmir*, London 1933

Crane, H., 'The Patronage of Zahir al-Din Babur and the Origins of Mughal Architecture', *Bulletin of the Asia Institute*, 1, (1987)

Crowe, S. and Haywood, S., *The Gardens of Moghul India: a History and a Guide*, London 1972

Dar, S.R., *Historical Gardens of Lahore*, Lahore 1982

Dunn, T., 'Kashmir and its Moghul Gardens', *Calcutta Review*, 288 (1917), pp. 148-56

Ettinghausen, R. and Mac Dougall, E.B., 'The Islamic Garden', *Dumbarton Oaks Colloquium on the History of Landscape Architecture*, 1976

Gotheim, M.L., *Indische Garten*, Munich 1926

Huegel, C., *Travels in Kashmir and the Punjab, with notes by T.B. Jervis*, London 1845

Jairazbhoy, R.A., 'Early Garden Palaces of the Great Mughals', *Oriental Art*, 4 (1958), pp. 68-75

Kheiri, S., 'Indische Garten', *Washmuth Monatshefte der Baukunst*, 7 (1922), pp. 1-11

Kheiri, S., 'Jardin de la India', *Arquitectura*, 5 (1923), pp. 260-62

Kheiri, S., 'The Pleasure Gardens of India', *Architectural Review*, 56 (1924), pp. 140-47

Lehrman, J., *Earthly Paradise-Garden and Courtyard in Islam*, London 1980

Moynihan, E.B., *Paradise as a Garden in Persian and Mughal India*, London 1980

Moynihan, E. B., 'The Lotus Garden Palace of Zahir al-Din Mihammad Baburi', *Muqarnas*, 5 (1988), pp. 135-152

Petruccioli, A., *Dar al Salam: architetture del territorio nei paesi islamici*, Rome 1985

Petruccioli, A., 'The Garden as a City – the City as a Garden', *Journal of the Islamic Environmental Design Research Center*, 2nd issue (1986)

Petruccioli, A., 'Urban Landscape and Hydraulic Architecture in 16th Century Moghul India', *Turkish and Islamic Science and Technology in the 16th century, 2nd International Congress of History of Turkish and Islamic Science and Technology*, Istanbul 1986, pp. 275-84

Petruccioli, A., (ed.), *Il giardino islamico: architettura, natura, paesaggio*, Milan 1994

Prabhakar, 'Gardens and Orientation', *Islamic Gardens, 2nd International Symposium on Protection and Restoration of Historical Gardens*, Paris 1976, pp. 145-54

Prawdin, A., *The Builders of the Mogul Empire*, London 1963

Pugachenkova, G.A., 'The Art of Gardens in Central Asia during the Reign of Timur and Timurids', *Trudy Sredneaziatskogo Gosudarstvennogo Universiteta*, 23 (1951), pp. 143-68

Rajaram, 'The Gardens of Agra', *Journal of the United Provinces Historical Society*, 4 (1928), pp. 12-27

Randhawa, G.G. et al., *The Famous Gardens of India*, New Delhi 1971

Randhawa, M.S., *Gardens through the Ages*, New Delhi 1976

Schoenfeld, D., 'Die Mongolen und ihre Paläste und Garten im mitteleren Gangestale', *Zeitschrift des Deutschen Morgenländischen Gesellschaft*, 66 (1912), pp. 577-88

Shafi, M., 'The Shalimar Gardens of Lahore', *Islamic Culture*, 1 (1927), pp. 58-66

'Shalimar (The) Garden', *Pakistan Quarterly*, 10 (1960), pp. 20-27

Smith, E.W., 'The Shalimar Gardens in Lahore', *Journal of Indian Art* (1895), pp. 95-6

Smith, E.W., *Akbar's Tomb, Sikandarah near Agra, Described and Illustrated*, Allahabad 1909

Ullmann, M., *Die Natur und Geheimwissenschften in Islam*, Leiden 1972

Vigne, G.T., *A Personal Narrative of a Visit to Ghuzni, Kabul and Afghanistan*, London 1840

Vigne, G.T., *Travels in Kashmir, Ladakh, Iskardo, etc.*, London 1842

Villiers Stuart, C.M., *Gardens of the Great Mughuls*, London 1913

Villiers Stuart, C.M., 'Indian Water Gardens', *Journal of the Royal Society of Arts*, 62 (1914), pp. 447-67

Villiers Stuart, C.M., 'Indian Paradise Gardens', *Journal of the Royal Society of Arts*, 79 (1931), pp. 794-808

Wali Ullah Khan, M., Saif-ur Rahman Dar, 'Shalamar Gardens', *The Cultural History of Pakistan* (1966), pp. 50-60

Wilber, D.N., *Persian Gardens and Garden Pavilions*, Rutland 1962

The Origins

Ashfaque, S.M., 'The Grand Mosque of Banbhore', *Pakistan Archaeology*, 6 (1969), pp. 182-209

Baloch, N.B., 'The Most Probable Site of Debal, the Famous Historical Port of Sind', *Islamic Quarterly* (1952), pp. 35-49

'Banbhore', *Pakistan Archaeology*, 5 (1968), pp. 176-185

Khan, A.N., 'Banbhore: a Probable Site of Debul or the First Landing Site in Sindh (now in Pakistan) of the Arab General Muhammad Ibn Qasim in 711-12 C.E.', *Islamic Revue*, (1966), pp. 19-23

Khan, F.A., *Banbhore: a Preliminary Report on the Recent Archaeological Excavations*, Karachi 1960

Pathan, M.H., 'The Ruins of Banbhore and its Identification with al-Daybul, the Arab Seaport of Sind', *Islamic Culture*, 43 (1969), pp. 297–304

Pathan, M.H., *Arab Kingdom of al-Mansura in Sind*, Hyderabad 1974

Delhi Sultanate

Ara, M., 'The Lodi Rulers and the Construction of the Tomb Buildings in Delhi', *Acta Asiatica*, 43 (1982), pp. 61–80

Ara, M. and Tsukinowa, T., 'Outline of Survey and Studies of the Architectural Remains of the Delhi Sultanate Period', *Acta Asiatica*, 43 (1982), pp. 92–109

Asher, C.B., 'From Anomaly to Homogeneity: the Mosque in 14th to 16th Century Bihar', in Bhattacharya, G. and Debala, M. (eds.), *Studies in the Art and Archaeology of Bihar and Bengal*, Delhi 1989

Banerjee, S.K., 'The Kutb Minar, its Architecture and History', *Journal of the United Provinces Historical Society*, 10/1 (1937), pp. 38–54

Banerjee, S.K., 'The Quwat ul-Islam or the Oldest Mosque in Delhi', *Journal of the Royal Asiatic Society of Bengal*, third series, 4/15, part 2 (1938), pp. 293–307

Beglar, J.D., 'Delhi', *Report for the Year 1871-72* (reprint Benares 1966), pp. 1–91

Blakiston, J.F., *The Jami Masjid at Budaun*, Archaeological Survey of India, Memoir 19, New Delhi 1926

Bukhart, Y.K., 'Mosque Architecture of the Sultans of Delhi', *Indo-Iranica*, 9/4 (1956), pp. 35–42

Bullok, H., 'The Architecture of the Delhi Sultanates', *Islamic Quarterly*, 1 (1954), pp. 144–151

Burton-Page J., 'Dihli Sultanate', *The Encyclopaedia of Islam*, new edition, Leiden 1962, vol 2, p. 274

Burton-Page, J., 'Dihli', *Encyclopédie de l'Islam*, new edition, Leiden and Paris 1965, vol. 2, pp. 454–68

Burton-Page, J., 'Indo-Islamic Architecture: a Commentary on Some False Assumptions', *Art and Archaeology Research Papers*, 6 (1974), pp. 14–21

Campbell, C.J., 'Notes on the History and Topography of the Ancient City of Delhi', *Journal of Asiatic Society of Bengal*, 35, part 1 (1866), pp. 199–218

Cole, H.H., *Preservation of National Monuments (Agra, Delhi and Gwalior)*, Madras 1884

Cole, H.H., *The Architecture of Ancient Delhi*, London 1884

Cope, H. and Lewis, H., 'Some Account of the Town and Palace of Feerozabad in the Vicinity of Delhi, with Introductory Remarks on the Sites of Other Towns', *Journal of Asiatic Society of Bengal*, 16 (1847), pp. 971–86

Cunningham, A., *Budaun*, Archaeological Survey of India Reports, vol. 11, Calcutta 1880

Digby, S., 'The Tomb of Buhlul Lodi', *Bulletin of the School of Oriental and African Studies*, 38 (1975), pp. 550–61

Fanshawe, H.C., *Delhi: Past and Present*, London 1902

Fanshawe, H.C., 'Dihli', *The Encyclopaedia of Islam*, Leiden 1913, vol.1, pp. 999–1000

Goetz, H., 'Eine alte Ansicht der Kajserburg von Delhi', *Ostasiatische Zeitschrift*, 12 (1925), pp. 306–10

Hasan-Mosul, 'Adjmer', *Encyclopédie de l'Islam*, new edition, vol. 1, Leiden and Paris 1975, p. 214

Hearn, G.R., *The Seven Cities of Delhi*, London 1906

Husain, A.M., *Tughluq Dynasty*, New Delhi 1976

Islam, M.S., *Jami Masjid of Sikandar Lodi, Delhi*, Dacca 1977

Lehmann, F., 'Architecture of the Early Sultanate Period and the Nature of the Muslim State of India', *Indica*, 15 (1978), pp. 13–31

Meister, M.U., 'The "Two-and-a-half-day" Mosque', *Oriental Art*, 18/1 (1972), pp. 57–63

Munshi, R.N., *The History of the Qutb Minar, Delhi*, Bombay 1911

Naqvi, S.A., 'Sultan Ghari, Delhi', *Ancient India*, 3 (1947), pp. 4–10

Nath, R., 'On the Identification of the Tomb of Muhammad Bin Tughlaq', *Indo-Iranica*, 26/2, 3 (1973), pp. 93–6

Nath, R., 'Chaturangana (Four Quartered) Mosques of the Firuzian Era', *Itihas Journal of the Andhra Pradesh Archives*, 3/2 (1975), pp. 29–33

Nath, R., 'Concept of the Qutb Minar', *Islamic Culture*, 49 (1975), pp. 42–62

Nath, R., 'Jami Masjid of Muhammad Bin Tughlaq at Jahanpanath, Delhi', *Indo-Iranica*, 29/1, 4 (1976), pp. 25–8

Nath, R., 'Panchmukhi Mosques of the Afghan Period', *Islamic Culture*, 50 (1976), pp. 33–9

Nath, R., *History of Sultanate Architecture*, New Delhi 1978

Nath, R., *Monuments of Delhi*, New Delhi 1979

Nath, R., 'The Jamat Khanah Masjid', *Studies in Islam*, 16 (1979), pp. 131–6

Page, J.A., *An Historical Memoir on the Qutb, Delhi*, Archaeological Survey of India, Memoir 22, Calcutta 1926

Page, J.A., *Guide to the Qutb, Delhi*, Calcutta 1927

Page, J.A., *A Memoir on the Kotla Firuz Shah, Delhi*, with a translation of *Sirat-i-Firozshahi* by M. H. Kuraishi, *Archaeological Survey of India*, Memoir 52, Delhi 1937, pp. 42 and 26

Petruccioli, A. and Terranova, A., 'Modelli culturali nell'impianto e nelle trasformazioni di Old Delhi', *Storia della città*, 31-2 (1984), pp. 123-44

Sanderson, G., *Archaeological Works at the Qutb Minar*, Archaeological Survey of India, Annual Report, 1912-13

Sanderson, G., *Delhi Fort: a Guide to the Buildings and Gardens*, Calcutta 1914

Sen, S., *Delhi and its Monuments*, Calcutta 1948

Sharp, H., *Delhi: its Glory and Buildings*, London 1921

Shokoohy, M., 'Bhadresvar the Oldest Islamic Monuments in India', *Studies in Islamic Art and Architecture*, supplement to *Muqarnas*, 2 (1985)

Shokoohy, M. and Shokoohy, N.H., 'The Architecture of Baha al-Din Tugrul in the Region of Bayana, Rajastan', *Muqarnas*, 4 (1987), pp. 114-32

Stephen, C., *The Archaeology and Monumental Remains of Delhi*, Simla 1876

Tremilett, J.D., 'Notes on Old Delhi', *Journal Asiatic Society of Bengal*, 34, part 1 (1870), pp. 70-88

Tsukinowa, T., 'The Influence of Seljuq Architecture on the Earliest Mosques of the Delhi Sultanate Period in India', *Acta Asiatica*, 43 (1982), pp. 37-60

Waddington, H., 'Adilabad: a Part of the "Fourth" Delhi', *Ancient India*, 1 (1946), pp. 60-76

Welch, A. and Crane, H., 'The Tughluqs: Master Builders of the Delhi Sultanate', *Muqarnas*, 1 (1983), pp. 123-166

Yamamoto, T., Ara, M. and Tsukinowa, T., *Delhi: Architectural Remains of the Delhi Sultanate Period*, 3 vols., Tokyo, 1967-70

Zafar Hasan, M., 'Guide to Nizamuddin', *Archaeological Survey of India*, Memoir 10, Calcutta 1922, pp. 1-38

Zafar Husain, H., 'Siri: a City of Delhi, Founded by Ala ud-Din Khalji', *Archaeological Survey of India, Annual Report*, 1935-6, pp. 137-43

The Punjab and Sind

Ali, A., *Historical Aspects of Town Planning in Pakistan and India*, Karachi 1971

Burton-Page, J., 'The Tomb of Rukn i-Alam, Multan', *Splendours of the East*, London 1965

Chughtai, M.A., *The Wazir Khan Mosque*, Lahore 1972

Chughtai, M.A., *Badshahi Masjid, Lahore*, Lahore 1974

Cousens, H., 'Brahmanabad-Mansura in Sind', *Archaeological Survey of India, Annual Report*, Calcutta 1903-4, pp. 132-144

Cousens, H., 'Antiquities of Sind', *Archaeological Survey of India*, Calcutta 1929 (reprint Karachi 1975)

Creswell, K.A.C., 'Excavations and Explorations', *Pakistan Archaeology*, 7 (1970-71), pp. 4-5

Creswell, K.A.C., 'Mansura', *Pakistan Archaeology*, 7 (1970-71), pp. 2-3

Dani, A.H., *Thatta: Islamic Architecture*, Islamabad 1402/1982

Feroze, S., 'Uch the Ancient', *Pakistan Quarterly*, 5/1 (1955), pp. 22-6

Forkl, H. *et al.*, *Die Garten des Islam*, Stuttgart 1993

Hasan, S.K., 'Origin of Chaukhandi Tombs', *Journal of Pakistan Historical Society*, 24/2 (1976), pp. 98-107

Hillenbrand, R., 'Turco-Iranian Elements in the Medieval Architecture of Pakistan: The Case of the Tomb of Rukn-i Alam at Multan', *Muqarnas*, 9 (1992), pp. 148-174

Irving, M., 'The Shrine of Baba Farid Shakarganj at Pakpattan', *Journal of Punjab Historical Society*, 1 (1911)

Jairazbhoy, R.A., 'Architecture of Sind', *Pakistan Quarterly*, 7/1 (1957), pp. 35-42, 65

Khan, A.N., 'Sehwan: its History and Monuments', *Journal of Pakistan History Society*, part 4 (1962), pp. 312-30

Khan, A.N., 'The Mosque of Wazir Khan', *Pakistan Quarterly*, 15/4 (1967)

Khan, A.N., *Maryam Zamani Mosque, Lahore: History and Architecture*, Karachi 1972

Khan, A.N., *Iran and Pakistan: a History of Cultural Relationship through the Ages*, Karachi 1973

Khan, A.N., 'The Mausoleum of Shaikh 'Ala al-Din at Pakpatan: a Significant Example of the Tughluq Style of Architecture', *East and West*, (n. s.), 24/3-4 (1974), pp. 311-26

Khan, A.N., 'Mausoleum of Sultan 'Ali Akbar at Multan', *Journal of the Research Society of Pakistan*, 12/3 (1975)

Khan, A.N., 'Uchchh Sharif: a City of Monumental Splendour', *Pakistan Pictorial*, 20 (1976)

Khan, A.N., *Uchchh: History and Architecture*, Islamabad 1980

Khan, A.N., *Multan: History and Architecture*, Islamabad 1983

Khan, A.N., 'The Dabgaran Mosque', *Honer va-Mardom*, 159-60 (1354 H. S.)

Khan, F.A., *Lahore and its Important Monuments*, Karachi 1964

Khan, F.A., *Architecture and Art Treasures in Pakistan*, Karachi 1965

Khan, F.A., 'The Dabgaran Mosque, Thatta: its Architecture and Architectural Decoration', *Sind Quarterly*, 7/3 (1979), pp. 50-56

Khan, F.A., 'A Group of Four Tombs in Multan Style Architecture at Lal Muhra Sharif', *Journal of Central Asia*, 7 (1984), pp. 29-48

Kahn, M.I., 'Muslim Architecture of Sind', *Journal Reg. Cultural Institute*, 2 (1967), pp. 51–60

Latif, S.M., *Lahore: its History, Architectural Remains and Antiquities*, Lahore 1892

Mumtaz, K.K., *Architecture in Pakistan*, Singapore 1985

Rajput, A.B., *Architecture in Pakistan*, Karachi 1963

Rajput, A.B., 'Muslim Architecture in Pakistan', *Pensé*, 1/5 (1965), pp. 78–87

Sanday, J., *Conservation of the Cultural Heritage of Pakistan*, Paris 1981

Siddiqi, N.J., *Thatta*, Karachi 1963

Wheeler, R.E., *Five Thousand Years of Pakistan*, London 1950

Zajadacz, H. S., *Chaukhandigräber: Studien zur Grabkunst in Sind und Baluchistan*, Wiesbaden 1978

BENGAL

Abid Ali Khan, M., *Memoirs of Gaur and Pandua*, Calcutta 1931

Ahmad, N., *Bagerhat Monuments*, Dacca 1980

Ahmad, N., *Mughal Dacca and the Lalbagh Fort*, Dacca n.d.

Asher, C.B., *Islamic Monuments of Eastern India and Bangladesh*, Leiden 1991

Ashfaque, S.M., *Lalbagh Fort: Monuments and Museums*, Karachi 1970

Aulad, H.S., *Notes on the Antiquity of Dacca*, Calcutta 1904

Chakravarti, M., 'Notes on Gaur and Other Places in Bengal', *Journal of Asiatic Society of Bengal*, n.s., 5 (1909), pp. 199–239

Creighton, H., *The Ruins of Gaur*, London 1817

Cunningham, A., 'Bengal', *Archaeological Survey of India*, vol. 15, New Delhi 1892

Dani, A.H., *Muslim Architecture in Bengal*, Dacca 1961

Dani, A.H., *Dacca: a Record of its Changing Fortunes*, Dacca 1962

Desai, Z.A., 'The Indo-Islamic Architecture of Bihar', *Islamic Culture*, 66 (1970), pp. 17–38

Desai, Z.A., 'Gaur and Pandua', *Asiatic Journal and Monthly Register*, 8 (1919), pp. 559–60, and 9 (1929), pp. 30–33

Goetz, H., 'Late Indian Architecture', *Acta Orentalia*, 18/2 (1940), pp. 81–192

Hasan, S.M., *The Adina Mosque at Hazrat Pandua*, Dacca 1970

Hasan, S.M., *Mosque Architecture of the Pre-Mughal Bengal*, Dacca 1979

Hasan, S.M., *Muslim Monuments of Bangladesh*, Dacca 1980

Hasan, S.M., *Dacca: the City of Mosques*, Dacca 1981

Husain, A.B., 'A Study of the Firozah Minar at Gaur', *Journal of the Asiatic Society of Pakistan*, 7 (1963), pp. 53–70

Karim, A., *Dacca: the Mughal Capital*, Dacca 1964

Khan, F.A., 'Muslim Architecture of East Pakistan', *The Cultural History of Pakistan*, 1966, pp. 41–9

Kuraishi, M.H., *List of Ancient Monuments Protected under Act VII of 1904 in the Province of Bihar and Orissa*, Archaeological Survey of India, New Imperial Series, vol. 51, Calcutta 1931

List of Ancient Monuments in Bengal: Revised and Corrected up to 31st August 1895, prepared by the Government of Bengal, Public Works Department, Calcutta 1896

Michell, G. (ed.), *The Islamic Heritage of Bengal*, Paris 1984

O'Malley, L.S., 'Murshidabad', *Bengal District Gazetteers*, 32 (1914)

O'Malley, L.S., 'Rajshashi', *Bengal District Gazetteers*, 33 (1916)

Patil, D.R., *Antiquarian Remains in Bihar*, Patna 1963

Ravenshaw, J.H., *Gaur: its Ruins and Inscriptions*, London 1878

Sanday, J., *Bangladesh: Conservation of Monuments and Sites*, Paris 1983

Sarawati, S.K., 'Indo-Muslim Architecture in Bengal', *Journal of the Indian Society of Oriental Art*, 9 (1941), pp. 12–36

JAUNPUR

Cunningham, A., *Jaunpur, Archaeological Survey Report*, vol. 11, Calcutta 1880

Fasih ud-Din, M., *The Sharqi Monuments of Jaunpur*, Allahabad 1922

Führer, A., *The Sharqi Architecture of Jaunpur*, Archaeological Survey of India, New Imperial Series, vol. 11, Calcutta 1889

Nevill, H.K., *Jaunpur*, District Gazetteer of the United Provinces, vol. 28, Allahabad 1908

GUJARAT

Burgess, J., *On the Muhammadan Architecture of Baroch, Cambay, Dholka, Champanir and Mahmudabad in Gujarat*, Archaeological Survey of India, New Imperial series, vol. 23, and Western India, vol. 6 (1896)

Burgess, J., *The Muhammadan Architecture of Ahmadabad: Part 1, A.D. 1412 to 1520. Muslim and Hindu Remains in the Vicinity*, Part 2, Archaeological Survey of India, New Imperial series, vols. 24 and 33, and *Western India*, vols. 7 and 8, London, Calcutta and Bombay 1900–1905

Burgess, J. and Cousens, H., *The Architectural Antiquities of Northern Gujarat, more especially of the Districts included in the Baroda States*, Archaeological Survey of India, New Imperial series, vol. 22, and *Western India*, vol. 9, London 1903

Desai, Z.A., *Indo-Islamic Architecture*, New Delhi 1987

Jain Neubaver, J., *The Stepwells of Gujarat in Art Historical Perspective*, New Delhi 1981

Michell, G. and Snehal, S., *Ahmadabad*, Bombay 1988

MALWA

Barnes, E., 'Mandu and Dhar', *Archaelogical Survey of India, Annual Report* (1903–4), pp. 30–45

Barnes, E., 'Dhar and Mandu', *Journal of the Bombay Branch of the Royal Asiatic Society*, 21 (1904), pp. 339–91

Campbell, J.M., 'Mandu', *Journal of the Bombay Branch of the Royal Asiatic Society*, 19 (1896), pp. 154–201

Creswell, K.A.C., 'The Vaulting System of the Hindola Mahal at Mandu', *Journal of the Royal Institute of British Architects*, third series, 25 (1918), pp. 237–245.

Crump, L.M., *The Lady of the Lotus: Rup Mati, Queen of Mandu*, London 1926

Nath, R., *The Art of Chanderi*, New Delhi 1979

Patil, D.K., *Mandu*, New Delhi 1975

Yazdani, G., *Mandu the City of Joy*, Oxford 1929

Yazdani, G., 'In Praise of Mandu: Architecture', *Marg*, 12/3 (1959), pp. 2–38

DECCAN

Alikhan, R., *Hyderabad: a City in History*, Hyderabad 1986

Bombay Gazetteer. Belgaum District, 21, Bombay 1884

Bombay Gazetteer. Satara District, 19, Bombay 1885

Bombay Gazetteer. Sholapur District, 20, Bombay 1884

Burgess, J., *Provisional Lists of Architectural and other Archaeological Remains in Western India*, Archaeological Survey of Western India, Bombay 1875

Burgess, J., 'Report on the Antiquities in the Bidar and Aurangabad Districts, in the Territories of His Highness the Nizam of Hyderabad, being the Results of the Third Season's Operations of the Archaeological Survey of Western India', *Archaeological Survey of Western India*, 3 (1875–6), London 1878

Burgess, J., 'Lists of Antiquarian Remains in Bombay Presidency', *Archaeological Survey of Western India*, Bombay 1885

Burgess, J. and Cousens, H., 'List of Antiquarian Remains in His Highness the Nizam's Territories', *Archaeological Survey of India*, new imperial series, vol. 32, and Western India, vol. 31, Bombay 1900

Burton-Page, J., 'Dawlatabad', *The Encyclopaedia of Islam*, new edition, Leiden 1962, vol. 2

Campbell, C.A., *Glimpses of the Nizam's Dominions*, Philadelphia 1898

Cantrell, A.M., *An Account of the Ruins of Beejapore*, Bombay 1872

Cousens, H., *Notes on the Buildings and other Antiquarian Remains at Bijapur*, Bombay 1890

Cousens, H., *Bijapur and its Architectural Remains*, Archaeological Survey of Western India, new imperial series, vol. 37, Bombay 1916

Cousens, H., *Bijapur: the Old Capital of the Adil Shahi Kings*, Poona 1923

Cousens, H., *The Architectural Antiquities of Western India*, London 1926

Desai, Z.A., 'Architecture of the Bahmanis', H. K. Sherwani (ed.), *History of Medieval Deccan*, Hyderabad 1974, 2 vols., ch. 4, pp. 240–43

Fergusson, J. and Taylor, M., *Architecture at Bijapur*, London 1866

Fischer, K., 'Firuzabad on the Bhima and its Environs', *Islamic Culture*, 29 (1955), pp. 246–55

Gazetteer of Bombay State. Dharwar District, Bombay 1959 (rev edn.)

Goetz, H., 'Ottoman-Turkish in India: the Architects of the Gol Gumbad at Bijapur', *Studies in the Foreign Relations of India, H. K. Sherwan Felicitation Volume*, Hyderabad 1975, pp. 522–6

Haig, T.W., *Historic Landmarks of the Deccan*, Allahabad 1907

Khan, M.A., 'Excavation of a Medieval Site near Qutb Shahi Tombs (Golconda)', *Islamic Culture*, 44 (1970), pp. 227–31

Maharashtra State Gazetteers. Kolhapur District, Bombay 1962 (rev. edn.)

Maharashtra State Gazetteers. Ratnagairi District, Bombay 1962 (rev. edn.)

Maharashtra State Gazetteers. Satara District, Bombay 1962 (rev. edn.)

Mate, M.S., 'Daulatabad: Road to Islamic Archaeology in India', *World Archaeology*, 14/3 (1893), pp. 335–41

Michell, G., *Islamic Heritage of the Deccan*, Bombay 1986

Mysore State. Gazetteer of India. Bijapur District, Bangalore 1966

Mysore State. Gazetteer of India. Gulbarga District, Bangalore 1966

Mysore State. Gazetteer of India. Raichur District, Bangalore 1970

Racco, S., *Golconda and the Qutb Shahi*, Lahore 1920

Schotten Merklinger, E., 'Seven Tombs at Holkonda: a Preliminary Survey', *Kunst des Orients*, 10/1, 2 (1975), pp. 187–97

Schotten Merklinger, E., 'The Madrasa of Mahmud Gawan in Bidar', *Kunst des Orients*, 11/1–2 (1976), pp. 156–67

Schotten Merklinger, E., 'The Mosques of Raichur, Preliminary Classification', *Kunst des Orients*, 12/1, 2 (1978), pp. 79-94

Schotten Merklinger, E., 'Possible Seljuq Influence on the Dome of the Gol Gumbad in Bijapur', *East and West*, (n. s.) 28 (1978), pp. 257-61

Schotten Merklinger, E., 'Possible Seljuq Influence on the Dome of the Gol Gumbad', *Fifth International Congress of Turkish Art*, Budapest 1979, pp. 613-27

Schotten Merklinger, E., *Indian Islamic Architecture: the Deccan 1347-1686*, Warminster 1981

Sherwani, H.K., 'Tajud-Din Firuz and the Synthesis of the Bahmani Culture', *New Indian Antiquary*, 6/4 (1943-4), pp. 75-89

Sherwani, H.K., *The Bahmanis of the Deccan*, Hyderabad 1953

Shokoohy, M. and Shokoohy, N., *Hisar-i Firuza*, London 1988

Taylor, M., *Sketches of the Deccan*, London 1838

Taylor, M., *Architecture at Beejapore*, London 1866

Yazdani, G., 'The Antiquities of Bidar', *Archaeological Survey of India, Annual Report, 1914-1915*, Calcutta 1920

Yazdani, G., *Bidar: its History and Monuments*, Oxford 1947

Yusuf, S., *Antiquarian Remains in Hyderabad States*, Hyderabad 1953

Zebrowski, M., *Deccani Painting*, London 1983

KASHMIR

Fergusson, J., *Kashmir: an Historical Introduction*, London 1961, ch. 4, pp. 117-31

Kaul, M., *Kashmir: Hindu, Buddhist and Muslim Architecture*, New Delhi 1971

Nichols, J.R., 'Muhammadan Architecture (of Kashmir)', *Marg*, 8/2 (1955), pp. 76-92

Rai Mangat, M., 'Wooden Mosques of Kashmir', *Oriental Art*, 13/4 (1967), pp. 263-70

Sharma, Y.D., *Mosques of Kashmir*, New Delhi 1954

THE MUGHALS

Anand, M.R, 'Delhi under the Mughals', *Marg*, 20/4 (1967), pp. 31-67

Ashaf, H.M., *An Historical Guide to the Agra Fort*, New Delhi 1937

Asher, C.B., 'The Mausoleum of Sher Shah Suri', *Artibus Asiae*, 34/3-4 (1977), pp. 273-98

Asher, C.B., 'The Qal'a-i Kuhna Mosque: a Visual Symbol of Royal Aspiration', in A. Krishna (ed.), *Chhavi*, 2, Benares 1981

Asher, C.B., 'Legacy and Legitimacy: Sher Shah's Patronage of Imperial Mausolea', in K.P. Ensing (ed.), *Shari'at and Ambiguity in South Asian Islam*, 2, Berkeley 1988

Asher, C.B., *The New Cambridge History of India: Architecture of Mughal India*, 1/4, Cambridge 1992

Bakhsh, N., 'The Agra Fort and its Buildings', *Archaeological Survey of India, Annual Reports* (1903-4), pp. 164-93

Banerjee, S.K., 'Buland Darwaza of Fatehpur Sikri', *Indian Historical Quarterly*, 13 (1937), pp. 705-13

Banerjee, S.K., 'A Historical Outline of Akbar's Dar-ul-Khilafat, Fatehpur Sikri', *Journal of Indian History*, 21 (1942), pp. 198-215

Banerjee, S.K., 'Akbar's Khwabgah at Fatehpur Sikri', *Indian Culture*, 10 (1943), pp. 129-37

Banerjee, S.K., 'The Monuments of Aurangzib's Reign', *Journal of United Provinces Historical Society*, 16 (1943), pp. 138-47

Banerjee, S.K., 'The Administration Buildings of Akbar's Fatehpur Sikri', *Journal of Indian History*, 23 (1944), pp. 1-18

Banerjee, S.K., 'Marajam-ki-kothi or Sunahra Makam of Fatehpur Sikri', *Journal of the United Provinces Historical Society*, 17 (1944), pp. 103-10

Banerjee, S.K., 'Shaikh Salim Chishti, the Shaik ul-Islam of Fatehpur Sikri', *Bharata Kaumudi*, 1 (1945), pp. 69-76

Banerjee, S.K., 'The Historical Remains of the Early Years of Akbar's Reign', *Journal of the United Provinces Historical Society*, 1952

Bari, M.A., 'Mughal Mosques of Dhaka: a Typological Study', *Oriental Art*, 38/2 (1992), pp. 93-102

Begley, W.E., 'Amanat Khan and the Calligraphy on the Taj Mahal', *Kunst des Orients*, 12 (1978-9), pp. 5-60

Begley, W.E., 'The Myth of the Taj Mahal and a New Theory of its Symbolic Meaning', *Art Bulletin*, 61 (1979), pp. 7-37

Begley, W.E., 'Four Mughal Caravanserais built during the Reigns of Jahangir and Shah Jahan', *Muqarnas*, 1 (1983), pp. 167-79

Behr, H.G., *Die Mogulen*, Vienna and Düsseldorf 1979

Bhatia, H., *Fatehpur Sikri is a Hindu City*, New Delhi 1969

Brand, M. and Lowry, G., *Akbar's India: Art from the Mughal City of Victory*, New York 1985

Brand, M. and Lowry, G., *Fatehpur Sikri: a Sourcebook*, Cambridge 1985

Brown, P., 'Monuments of the Mughul Period', in *Cambridge History of India*, vol. 4, Cambridge 1937

Bukhari, Y.K., 'The Mosque Architecture of the Moghuls', *Indo-Iranica*, 9/2 (1956) pp. 67-75

Burton-Page, J., 'Fatehpur Sikri', in M. Wheeler (ed.), *Splendours of the East*, London 1965, pp. 142-153

Burton-Page, J., 'Lahore Fort', in M. Wheeler (ed.), *Splendours of the East*, London 1965, pp. 82–93

Burton-Page, J., 'The Red Fort', in M. Wheeler (ed.), *Splendours of the East*, London 1965, pp. 130–141

Burton-Page, J., 'Wazir Khan's Mosque', in M. Wheeler (ed.), *Splendours of the East*, London 1965, pp. 94–101

Chaghatai, M.A., 'The so-called Gardens and Tomb of Zeb-un-Niza at Lahore', *Islamic Culture*, 9 (1935), pp. 610–20

Chaghatai, M.A., 'Ustad Isa, the so-called Architect of the Taj', *Procedings of the 2nd Indian History Congress*, 1938, pp. 366–7

Chaghatai, M.A., 'Is there a European Element in the Construction of the Taj Mahall, Agra?', *Islamic Culture*, 14 (1940), pp. 196–206

Chaghatai, M.A., 'The Oldest Extant Muslim Architecture Relic in Lahore', *Journal of Pakistan History Society*, 12 (1964), pp. 60–81

Chaghatai, M.A., *The Badshahi Masjid (built by Aurangzeb in 1084/1674): History and Architecture*, Lahore 1972

Chaghatai, M.A., *The Wazir Khan Mosque, Lahore*, Lahore 1975

Chatterji, N., 'The Lotus-pillared Diwan-i-Khas of Fatehpur Sikri', *Indo-Asian Culture*, 4 (1956), pp. 450–54

Cole, H.H., *Illustrations of Buildings near Muttra and Agra*, London 1879

Davar, S., 'Fatehpur Sikri: the Origins and Growth of a Mughal City', *Architectural Association Quarterly*, 3 (1978), pp. 44–59

Dayal, M., *Rediscovering Delhi: the Story of Shahjahanabad*, New Delhi 1972

Faruqi, M., *Aurangzeb and his Times*, Bombay 1935

Frykenberg, R.E., *Delhi through the Ages*, Delhi 1986

Goetz, H., 'Moghul, scuola', in *Enciclopedia universale dell'arte*, Venice and Rome 1963, vol. 9, cols. 543–62

Goswami, A., *Glimpses of Mughal Architecture*, Calcutta 1953

Goulding, H.R., *Old Lahore*, Lahore 1924

Hambly, C. and Swaan, W., *The Cities of Moghul India*, London 1968

Hambly, G., *Cities of Moghul India: Delhi, Agra and Fatehpur Sikri*, with photographs by W. Swaan, New Delhi 1977

Haras, H., 'The Palace of Akbar at Fatehpur Sikri', *Journal of Indian History*, 4/1 (1925), pp. 53–68

Harve, L., 'Rédecouverte d'une capitale indienne abandonnée', *Connaisance des arts*, (1963) pp. 120–131

Havell, E.B., *A Handbook to Agra and the Taj, Sikandra, Fatehpur Sikri and the Neighbourhood*, 1924 (reprint New Delhi 1970)

Hoag, J., 'The Tomb of Ulugh Beg and Abdu Razzaq at Ghazni, a Model for the Taj Mahall', *Journal of the Society of Architectural Historians*, 27/4 (1968), pp. 234–48

Hosten, H., 'Who planned the Taj?', *Journal and Proceedings of the Asiatic Society of Bengal*, new series, 6 (1910), pp. 281–8

Husain, A.B., 'The Date of the Stone-Cutters Masjid at Fatehpur Sikri', *Journal of Asiatic Society of Pakistan*, 15 (1970), pp. 185–90

Husain, M.A., *A Guide to Fatehpur Sikri*, New Delhi 1937

Husain, M.A., *An Historical Guide to the Agra Fort*, New Delhi 1937

Irvine, W., 'Austin de Bordeaux', *Journal of the Royal Asiatic Society* (1910), pp. 1343–5

Jain, K., 'Fatehpur Sikri: Saving an Endangered Heritage', *Design* (1983), pp. 24–33

Jain, K., 'Fatehpur Sikri: some Unanswered Questions', *Design* (1983), pp. 37–46

Jairazbhoy, R.A., 'The Taj and its Critics', *East and West*, n. s. 6 (1956), pp. 349–52

Jairazbhoy, R.A., 'The Taj Mahall in the Context of East and West: a Study in the Comparative Method', *Journal of the Warburg and Courtauld Institutes*, 24 (1961), pp. 59–88

Jones, D. (ed.), *Lo specchio del principe, mecenatismi paralleli: Medici e Moghul*, Rome 1991

Kanwar, H.J., 'The Taj Mahall and the so-called Ustad Isa', *Indica*, 6 (1969), pp. 15–28

Keene's Handbook for Visitors to Agra, Calcutta 1909

Khalil, M., 'The Mausoleum of Emperor Jahangir', *Arts of Asia*, 13,/1 (1983), pp. 57–66

Khan, M.K., 'The Walled City of Lahore: Directions for Rehabilitation', *Conservation as Cultural Survival* (1978), pp. 43–5

Khan, M., 'Lahore Fort', *Journal of Pakistan Historical Society*, 10/2 (1973), pp. 45–60

Khan Wali, U.M., *Lahore and its Important Monuments*, Karachi 1959

Klingelhofer, W.G., 'The Jahangiri Mahal of the Agra Fort: Expression and Experience in Early Mughal Architecture', *Muqarnas*, 5 (1988), pp. 153–69

Koch, E., 'The Baluster Column: a European Motiv in Mughal Architecture and its Meaning', *Journal of the Warburg and Courtauld Institutes*, 45 (1982), pp. 251–62

Koch, E., 'The Lost Colonnade of Shah Jahan's Bath in the Red Fort of Agra', *The Burlington Magazine*, 124/951 (1982), pp. 331–9

Koch, E., *Mughal Architecture: an Outline of its History and Development (1526–1858)*, Munich 1991

Lall, J., *Taj Mahal and the Glory of Mughal Agra*, New Delhi 1982

Latif, S.M., *Agra, Historical and Descriptive with an Account of Akbar and his Court and of the Modern City of Agra*, Calcutta 1896

List of Muhammadan and Hindu Monuments, Delhi Province, 4 vols., Calcutta 1916-22

Lowry, G.D., 'Delhi in the 16th Century', *Environmental Design*, 1 (1983), pp. 7-17

Lowry, G., 'Humayun's Tomb: Form, Function and Meaning in Early Mughal Architecture', *Muqarnas*, 4 (1987), pp. 133-48

Mazumdar, K.C., *Imperial Agra of the Moghuls*, Agra 1934

Bras, M., Khan Mumtaz, K. and Khan, M., 'Upgrading and Conserving the Walled City of Lahore', *Adaptive Reuse*, no 3 of *Designing in Islamic Culture*, Aga Khan Program for Islamic Architecture, Cambridge 1983

Muckerjee, S.C., 'The Architecture of the Taj and its Architects', *India Historical Quarterly*, 9 (1933), pp. 872-9

Nadvi, S.S., 'The Family of the Engineers who built the Taj Mahall and the Delhi Fort', *Journal of the Bihar and Orissa Research Society*, 34 (1948), pp. 75-110

Naqvi, H.K., *Urbanization and Urban Centres under the Great Mughals*, Simla 1972

Naqvi, S.A., *Humayun's Tomb and Adjacent Buildings*, New Delhi 1947

Nath, R., 'Plan of Akbar's Tomb at Sikandra (Agra) and a Proposed Dome over it', *Indica*, 4/2 (1967), pp. 99-106

Nath, R., 'The Genesis of the Diwan-i Khass at Fatehpur Sikri', *Indica*, 5 (1968), pp. 25-36

Nath, R., 'Taj, Dream in Marble', *Marg*, 22/3 (1969), pp. 34-55

Nath, R., 'Bagh-i-Gul-Afshan of Babur at Agra', *Indo-Iranica*, 23/3 (1970), pp. 14-21

Nath, R., 'Mysteries of Phansighar at Agra Fort', *Journal of Indian History*, 48 (1970), pp. 673-690

Nath, R., 'Mausoleum of Maryam Zamani at Sikandra (Agra)', *Quarterly Review of Historical Studies*, 10 (1970-71), pp. 73-9

Nath, R., 'The Moti Masjid of the Red Fort', *Indica*, 81 (1971), pp. 19-26

Nath, R., 'Depiction of Fabulous Animals (Gaj-Vyala) at the Delhi Gate of Agra Fort', *Medieval India*, 2 (1972), pp. 45-52

Nath, R., *The Immortal Taj Mahall: the Evolution of the Tomb in Mughal Architecture*, Bombay 1972

Nath, R., 'The Diwan-i Khass of Fatehpur Sikri: a Symbol of Akbar's Belief in Surya-Purusa', *The Quarterly Review of Historical Studies*, 12/4 (1972-3)

Nath, R., 'Chauburj: the Tomb of Babur at Agra', *Islamic Culture*, 48 (1974), pp. 149-158

Nath, R., 'Depiction of Animate Motifs at the Tomb of I'timaud-ud-Daulah at Agra', *Islamic Culture*, 47 (1974), pp. 289-300

Nath, R., 'Mughal Concept of Sovereignty in the Inscriptions of Fatehpur Sikri, Agra and Delhi (1570-1654)', *Indica*, 11 (1974), pp. 90-100

Nath, R., 'The "Stone-Cutters" Mosque at Fatehpur Sikri', *Lalit Kala*, 16 (1974), pp. 48-9

Nath, R., 'Description of some Buildings in the Environs of Agra with Notes on the History of the City before the Time of the Emperor Akbar', *Transactions of the Archaeological Society of Agra*, 1975, pp. iv-xv

Nath, R., *History of Decorative Art in Mughal Architecture*, New Delhi 1976

Nath, R., *Some Aspects of Mughal Architecture*, New Delhi 1976

Nath, R., *Agra and its Monumental Glory*, Bombay 1977

Nath, R., 'Scrutiny of the Persian Data related to the Builders of the Taj Mahal' *Indo-Iranica*, 32/1-2 (1979), pp. 1-18

Nath, R., *History of Mughal Architecture*, [vol. 1, *Babur to Humayun*, vol. 2, *Akbar (1556-1605)*], New Delhi 1982

Nath, R., *Antiquities of Chittorgarh: Art and Architecture of Rajastan*, Jaipur 1984

Nicholls, W.H., 'Fatehpur Sikri', *Architectural Survey of India, Annual Reports*, 1903-4

Nicholson, L., *The Red Fort, Delhi*, London 1989

Nilsson, S., *The New Capitals of India, Pakistan and Bagladesh*, London 1973

Oak, P.N., *The Taj Mahall is a Temple Palace*, New Delhi 1974

Pal, P., et al., *Romance of the Taj Mahal*, New Delhi 1989

Paret, R., 'Fatehpur Sikri', in *The Encyclopaedia of Islam*, new edition, Leiden 1964, vol. 2, p. 840

Parihar, S., *Mughal Monuments in the Punjab and Haryana*, New Delhi 1985

'Patrons of Art: the Mughals and the Medici', *Marg*, 29/1, Bombay n.d.

Petruccioli, A., 'Studi per un piano di recupero per Fatehpur Sikri', *Architettura nei paesi islamici, Seconda mostra internazionale di architettura, Venezia, la Biennale, Catalogo della mostra*, Venice 1982

Petruccioli, A., 'C'era una volta in India: note su una grande capitale', *Al Farabi* (1984), pp. 54-6

Petruccioli, A., *Fatehpur Sikri: Urban Forms and Mughal Life*, Wiesbaden 1985

Petruccioli, A., *Fatehpur Sikri città del sole e delle acque*, Roma 1988

Pictorial Agra: Illustrated by a Series of Photographs of its Principal Buildings, Ancient and Modern, Agra 1911

Reuther, O., *Indische Paläste und Wohnhäuser*, Berlin 1925

Rizvi, S.A., *Fatehpur Sikri*, New Delhi 1972

Rizvi, S.A. and Flynn, J.V., *Fatehpur Sikri*, Bombay 1975

Rizvi, S.A., 'Mughal Town Planning: Fatehpur Sikri', *Abr Nahrain*, 15 (1974-5), pp. 99-112

Sanderson, G., 'Conservation Works at Agra and Neighbourhood', *Archaeological Survey of India, Annual Report*, 1910-11, pp. 94-103

Sanderson, G., 'The Moghul Architecture of Agra', *The Builder*, 103 (1912), pp. 434-6

Sanwal, B.D., *Agra and its Monuments*, London 1968

Saraswati, S.K., *Glimpse of Mughal Architecture*, Calcutta 1953

Sarda, H.B., *Ajmer: Historical and Descriptive*, Ajmer 1911

Sharman, G.S., 'Wall Paintings from Salim Chishti's Tomb, Fatehpur Sikri near Agra', *Journal of Indian Art*, 8 (1898), pp. 41-44

Siddiqi, W.H., *Fatehpur Sikri*, New Delhi 1972

Siddiqi, W.H., review of 'Fatehpur Sikri' by Rizvi, S. A. and Flynn, V. J., *Journal of the Indian Society of Oriental Art*, 8 (1976-7), pp. 82-7

Smith, E.W., 'Wall Paintings recently found in the Khwabgah, Fatehpur Sikri near Agra', *Journal of Indian Art*, 61 (1894), pp. 65-8

Smith, E.W., 'The Moghul Architecture of Fatehpur Sikri', *Archaeological Survey of India*, new imperial series, vol. 17, parts 1-4, Allahabad 1895-8 (reprint New Delhi 1985)

Smith, E.W., *Moghul Colour Decoration of Agra*, Allahabad 1901

Smith, H., *Fatehpur Sikri*, 4 vols., New Delhi 1894-1905

Smith, V.A., 'The Site and Design of Akbar's Ibadat Khana of Worship', *Journal of the Royal Asiatic Society* (1917), pp. 715-22

Spear, P., 'Mughal Delhi and Agra', A,. Toynbee (ed.), *Cities of Destiny*, London 1967

Terry, J., 'Fatehpur Sikri', *Marg*, 2/3 (1947-8), pp. 16-32

Tillotson, G.H., *Mughal India: Architecture Guide for Travellers*, London 1990

Toy, S., 'Fatehpur Sikri', *Strongholds of India*, London 1957, pp. 101-7

Vogel, J.P., *The Tile-mosaics of the Lahore Fort*, Karachi 1920

THE LATE MUGHALS

Andrews, P.A., 'Lucknow', in *Encyclopédie de l'Islam*, new edition, Leiden and Paris 1985, vol. 5, pp. 640-41

Arshi, P.S., *Sikh Architecture in the Punjab*, New Delhi 1986

Arshi, P.S., *The Golden Temple*, New Delhi 1989

Chatterji, N., 'The "Nawabi" Architecture of Luknow', *Journal of the United Provinces Historical Society* (1936), pp. 39-44

Goetz, H., 'The Qudsia Bagh at Delhi: Key to Late Mughal Architecture', *Islamic Culture*, 26/1, (1952), pp. 132-51

Gupta, N., *Delhi between Two Empires, 1803-31: Society, Government and Urban Growth*, New Delhi 1981

Joshi, M.C., *Dig*, New Delhi 1971

Kaye, G.R., *The Astronomical Observatories of Jai Singh*, Archaeological Survey of India, new imperial series, 40, Calcutta 1918

Khan, M.W., *Sikh Shrines in West Pakistan*, Karachi 1962

Khokhar, M., 'The Tomb of Sharaf un-Nisa Begum known as Servwala Maqbara at Lahore', *Pakistan Journal of History and Culture*, 3 (1982)

Llewellyn Jones, R., *A Fatal Friendship: the Nawabs, the British and the City of Luknow*, New Delhi 1985

Maliq, Z., *The Reign of Muhammad Shah*, New York 1977

Metcalf, T.R., 'A Tradition Created: Indo-Saracenic Architecture under the Raj', *History Today*, 32/9 (1982), pp. 40-45

Nilsson, S., *European Architecture in India, 1750-1850*, London 1968

Sharar, A.H., *Luknow: the Last Phase of an Oriental Culture*, Boulder 1975

Skelton, R., Topfield, A., Strong, S. and Crill, R., *Facets of Indian Art*, London 1986

Tillotson, G.H., *The Tradition of Indian Architecture*, New Delhi 1989

Uttar Pradesh District Gazetteer: Faizabad, Allahabad 1960

INDEX

Figures in *italics* refer to captions.
n after a figure refers to footnote on that page.

A
Abbasids 15, 17, 45
Achabal (garden), Kashmir 232
Adalaj: *waw* 127
Adil Shahi of Bijapur 152, 156, 162*ff.*
    Ali I (1557–80) 164, 165
    Ali II (1656–72) 171
    Ibrahim I (1534–57) 163
    Ibrahim II (1580–1627) 163, 166, 171
    Ismail 163
    Muhammad (1627–57) 165, 166, 168, 169, 170, 172
    Sikandar (1672–86) 171
    Yusuf (1489–1510) 150, 163
Afzal Khan 263*n*32
Agra 183, 185, 194, 204, 265
    Chauburj 185
    Chini-ka Rauza (tomb of Afzal Khan) 256, *256*
    The Fort 74, 204–5, *205*, 265
        Delhi Gate 142, 221, 242
        Diwan-i Amm 242, *243*
        Jahanara Begum Mosque 245
        Jajangir Mahall *203*, 205, 213, 221
        Khass Mahall 244, *245*
        Macchi Bhavan 244
        Moti (Pearl) Mosque 242, *243*, 244
        Musamman Burj 244
        pillared hall 205
        Shish Mahall 244–5
    gardens 185, 230
    Imarat Tilism 188
    Itimad al-Daula mausoleum 10, 92, *227*, *231*, 232, 254, *255*, 260
    Kachpura Mosque 188
    Kalan Mosque 58
    Kanch Mahall 237
    Muhammad Khan Mosque 238
    Shahi Madrasa Mosque 263*n*37
    Taj Mahall 228, 230, 237, *241*, 251–6, *253*, 273*n*9
Ahmad Shah *see* Gujarat
Ahmad Shah Durrani I 276
Ahmad Shah Durrani II 276, 277
Ahmedabad 46, 105, 106, 109–10, 128, 213, 270
    Ahmad Shah Mosque *110*, 110–11
    Ahmad Shah *rauza* 113
    Azam-Muazzam mausoleum 48, 116
    Bai Hari *waw* 127
    Bai Harir Mosque 119–20
    Bibi Achyut Kuki Mosque 116, *117*, 118
    Darya Khan mausoleum 115–16
    Darwish Ali Mosque 121
    Dastur Khan Mosque 118
    Haibat Khan Mosque 110, 111
    Ibrahim Sayyid Mosque 121
    jami masjid 106, *106*, 110, 111–13, *112*, 114
    Kankariya tank 115, 126
    Maliq Sarang Mosque 121
    Miyan Khan Chishti Mosque 116, 118
    Muhammad Ghaus Gwaliyori Mosque 121–2
    Rajapur funerary complex 115, 116
    Rani-ka Hujra 113–14
    Rani Rupavati Mosque 119–20, *120*
    Rani Sipari Mosque 116, *120*, 120–1
    Sakar Khan's tomb 114
    Sardar Khan Mosque 270
    Sayyid Alam Mosque 110, 111, 112
    Sayyid Usman complex 118
    Shah Alam mausoleum 118, 121
    Shah Alam Mosque 220
    Shah Khub Sayyid Muhammad Chishti Mosque 118, 121
    Shaikh Hasan Muhammad Chishti Mosque 122
    Sidi Beshir Mosque 225*n*12
    Sidi Said Mosque 89, *105*, 122, *123*, 220
    Tin Darwaza 110, 114
    see also Isanpur; Paldi-Kochrab; Sarkhej; Vatva
Ahmadnagar 156, 157, 203
    Damari Mosque 158, *158*
    Faria Bagh 158
    tomb of Salabat Khan (Chand Bibi Mahall) 158
Aibak *see* Qutb al-Din Aibak
Ainapur: mausoleum of Jahan Begum 170
Ajmer 17, 19, 23, 105, 224, 262, 270, 272
    Akbari Mosque 224–5
    Arhai-din-ka Jhompra Mosque 23, *25*, 28
    Badshahi Mahall 205
    Chashma-i Nur (Fountain of Light) 230
    fort 207
    idgah 282
    Lake Ana Sagar pavilions 230, *255*, 256
    Lake Pushkar hunting pavilions 230
    Mir Saadat Allah Mosque 282
    Muin al-Din tomb 271
    Shaikh Ala al-Din mausoleum (Sola Khamba) 272
Akbar, Mughal emperor (1556–1605) 10, 11, *18*, 19, 57, 70, 72, 78*n*8, 91, 102, 103, 105, 132, 142, 143, 172, 175, 179, 184, 188, 194, 199, 203*ff.*, 227, 242
    mausoleum, Sikandra 228–30, *229*
Akbar II, Mughal emperor (1806–37) 22, 277
al-Biruni 31
al-Fazl, Abu *see* Fazl, Abul
al-Jayush, Muhammad Zahir al-Din 44, *45*
al-Muntasir, caliph 45, 48*n*8
al-Rahman Khan, Abd 237
al-Samad, Abd 209
Ala al-Din Khalji *see* Khaljis
Alam I Bahadur Shah, Mughal emperor (1707–12) 275
Alawal Khan 196
Allahabad:
    Khusrau mausoleum 230
    palace-fortress 205
    Rani-ki Mahall 205
    Shah Begum mausoleum 228, 230
    Sultan Nisar Begum mausoleum 230
Alor, Sind 15, 16
Alwar: Fateh Jang mausoleum 259
Amanat Khan (Abd al-Haqq Shirazi) 230, 254, 261, 263*nn*26, 32 *and* 37
Amanat Khan caravanserai, nr Amritsar 260–1
Ambar, Malik 158
Amber:
    Diwan-i Amm 286, 287
    Jagat Shiromani 224
    Jai Mandir (Shish Mahall) 287
    Rajput palace 285, 286, *286*
    Sukh Niwas 287
Amritsar 295
    Doraha Serai 234, 235
    Golden Temple 288, 290, *291*
    see also Amanat Khan caravanserai
Arcot 282
Asaf Khan 228, 231, 251, 262*n*3
    mausoleum, Lahore 246
Asaf Khan (governor of Kashmir) 231
Ashoka 48*n*6
pillars 42, 43, 44, 228
Ashtur mausoleums 155
    Ala al-Din Ahmad II *154*, 156
    Khalil Ala 156
    Mahmud 156
    Shihab al-Din Ahmad I 155
Asirgarh: *jami masjid* 172
Assassins 48*n*9
Ata Allah 272
Aurangabad 158–9, 272, 273
    Bibi-ka Maqbara 271–2
Aurangzeb, Mughal emperor (1658–1707) 10, 11, 70, 162, 165, 170, 172, 177, 210, 238*n*8, 241, 242, 265*ff.*
Ausa: Adil Shahi mosque 171
Ayodhya 185, 187
Azam Shah, Mughal emperor (1707) 271

B
Babur, Mughal emperor (1526–30) 9, 10, 58, 183, 185–7, 198, 205, 206, 255
Badan Singh, Maharaja 285, 288
Badhan 145
Bagerhat: Sath Gumbad Mosque 86–7
Bagha: mosque 87
Baghnagar 162
Baha al-Din Tughrul, Malik 23, 25
Bahadur II, Mughal emperor (1837–57) 277
Bahadur Shah *see* Gujarat
Bahawalpur: Daud Gardizi mausoleum 65
Bahlolpur: tombs 223
Bahmanids 11, 19, 40, 48, 145, 146–56
    Ahmad I Wali (1422–36) 146, 150
    Ahmad III (1518–21) 151
    Ala al-Din Hasan Bahman Shah (1347–58) 145, 146, 148, 156
    Mahmud (1482–1518) 152–3, 156
    Muhammad I (1358–75) 146, 147, 148
    Muhammad II (1378–97) 146, 148
    Muhammad III (1463–82) 151, 156
    Taj al-Din Firuz (1397–1422) 149, 150
    mausoleum 148–9, *149*
Bairam Khan 203, 210, 237
Balban, Sultan *see* Ghiyas al-Din Balban
Baluchistan 203, 276
Bamzu *ziyarat* 177–8
Banassar Qila:
    fort 34, *35*
    minaret 58, *58*

315

Banbhore (Bhambur) 15–16, *16*, *17*
   Madina Mosque 16, *16*
Bangalore: Lal Bagh 282
baoli 42, 126–7, *138*, 171, *171*, 222, 272
Barbak, Ibrahim Naib 96, *96*
Barhi, Maliq Ahmad 157
Bari: Lal Mahall 259
Barid Shahi of Bihar 151, 152
   Ali Barid (1542–80) 153, 156
      mausoleum 156–7, *157*
   Amir Barid I (1504–43):
      tomb 156
   Qasim Barid I (d. 1504):
      tomb 156
   Qasim Barid II (1587–91):
      tomb 157
Bayana 23
   idgah 28
   Jajri (Water) Pavilion 224, *225*
   Kale Khan Gumbad 224, *225*
   Ukha Mandir 25–6
   Ukha Minar 25, 58
   Ukha Mosque 25, *33*, 34
      see also Banassar Qila
Baz Bahadur, Sultan of Malwa 132, 138
Benares 267
   Alamgiri Mosque 268
   Arhai Kanjura Mosque 102
   Golden Temple 290
   jami masjid 267, 268
   Lal Khan tomb 281
   observatory 288
   Scindia Ghat 291
Bengal 18, 19, 81*ff.*, 203, 294
Berar 156, 203
Berhampur: Baba Lului Mosque 122
Bhadreshwar 106
   Choti Mosque 108
   Dargah Lal Shahbaz
      mausoleum 106–7
   Sola Khamba Mosque 107–8
Bhamaria: *waw* 127
Bhambur *see* Banbhore
Bharatpur: palace 285
Bhera 295
Bhopal 281–2
   Taj al-Masajid 219
Bibi Raji 98, 99
Bidar 19, 46, 145, 150, 156
   Barid mausoleums 156–7, *157*
   Chaubara tower 155
   The Fort 150
      Diwan-i Amm 152
      Gagan Mahall 152
      Rangin Mahall 152–3, *153*
      Sola Khamba Mosque *153*, 153–4
      Takht Mahall *150*, 150–1
      Tarkash Mahall 151–2
   jami masjid 18, 153, 154
   Mahmud Gawan Madrasa *154*, 154–5
   Takht-i Kirmani 155

Bihar 18, 81, 53, 92, 271, 281
Bihar Sharif: Nauratan complex 273
Bijapur 19, 116, 150, 152, 156, 162, 163, 241, 266
   Adil Shahid Pir Mosque 171
   Ali II's tomb 171, *171*
   Anand Mahall 166
   Anda (Egg) Mosque 166
   Asar Mahall 170, *171*
   Batulla Khan Mosque 167
   Chand Baori 165
   Chini Mahall 170
   Gagan Mahall 164
   Gol Gumbaz 156, 168–70, *169*, 171
   Ibrahim *rauza* 166, *167*
   Ikhlas Khan Mosque 164
   Jal Mandir 166, *167*
   jami masjid (ancient) 163–4
   jami masjid (1576) 164, 165, 166
   Jod Gumbad (mausoleum) 172
   Karim al-Din Mosque 163
   Khwaja Jahan Mosque 163
   Malika Jahan Begum Mosque 166
   Mecca Mosque 163, 167
   Mihtar Mahall 166–7, *169*
   Mustafa Khan Mosque 167–8
   palace of Mustafa Khan 165–6
   Sat Manzil 170
   Shah Karim's mausoleum 172
   Sharza Burj 171
   Taj Bandi *baoli* 171, *171*
Bikaner:
   ancient palace 285, *286*
   Anup and Rang Mahall 288
   Junagarh Fort *286*
Bir: Adil Shahi Mosque 171
Bodhan 40
   Deval Mosque 146
Brahmanabad 8, 16
   see also Mansura
Brindavan: Govinda Deva 224
Broach 206
   jami masjid 108–9
Budagh Khan, Shah 143
Budaun:
   Great Mosque 28
   jami masjid 28, *28*
   musalla 28
   Shamsi *idgah* 26, 27–8
Bukhara: tomb of Ismail 27, 9n8, 48, 66, 157
Bukhari, Shaikh Farid 237
Bundelkand 203, 291
Bundi: palace 285
Burdwan: tomb of Pir Bahran 91
Burhan Nizam Shah I 158
Burhanpur 172, 251
   Badshahi Qila (Lal Bagh) 172
   Bibi-ki mosque 173

   tomb of Adil Shah 172
   tomb of Nadir Shah 172
   tomb of Shah Nawaz Khan 173
   tomb of Shah Shuja 172, *172*–3
Buria: Rang Mahall 262

C
Cambay 40, 105, 206
   jami masjid 106, 109, *109*
   Khtyar al-Daula mausoleum 109
caravanserais 234–5, 260–2
Champanir 116, 118, 122–3, *123*
   fort 224
   jami masjid 106, *106*, 123–4, *124*, 220
   Kamani Mosque 126
   Nagina Mosque and tomb 124, 126, *126*
   Shaer-ki Mosque 126, *126*
   tombs 124, 126
Chanderi 46, 133
   Badal Mahall Darwaza *142*, 143
   Delhi Darwaza 142
   Faqir Darwaza 142
   jami masjid 141, *141*, 218
   Kushk Mahall 48, 140–1, *141*, 142
   madrasa 141
   Nil Khant 143
   Nizam al-Din funerary complex 141, *142*
   Pathani Muhalla 142
   Shazadi-ka *rauza* 141, *142*, *142*, 218
Chandragiri: palace 293
Chatta: caravanserai 237
Chaukhandi, necropolis of 73, *74*
Chitor, Rana of 136
Chitori 73
   Talpur funerary complex 77–8, *78*
Chota Pandua:
   Bari Mosque 82–3
   victory tower 83
coins 16, 17, 31, 204
Cranganore: first mosque 8
Ctesiphon: Taq-i Kisra 32

D
Dahir 15, 16
Daira Din Panah: Abdi al-Walid mausoleum 67
Dakhni caravanserai 260
Dakor 291
Dara Shikoh 242, 247, 256, 259, 266
Daryapur: Fateh Mosque 121
Das, Tulsi: *Ramcarit-manas* 204
Datia: palace 285, *292*, 292–3
Daulatabad 39, 40, 145, 158, 241
   Chand Minar *154*, 155
   Chini Mahall 158
   citadel 40, *41*

   Great Mosque 34, *35*, 40
   jami masjid 145–6
Debal 8, 15–16, *16*
Deccan 8, 11, 31, 40, 145*ff.*
Delhi (*see also* Firuzabad;
   Jahan-Panah; Mehrauli;
   Nizam al-Din;
   Shahapur Jat;
   Shahjahanabad;
   Tughluqabad) 8–9, 18, 19, 28, 31, 37, 40, 51, 57, 183, 204, 237, 265, 270, 276, 277
   Adham Khan 53, *53*
   Afsarwala Gumbad and mosque *199*, 200
   Alai Darwaza 31, *32*, *32*, 54
   Alai Minar 32
   Anarvali Mosque 270
   Baburi Mosque 187
   Bara Darwaza 190
   Bara Gumbad, Lodi Gardens *51*, 54–5, *55*
   Bara Khaumba 57
   Bhuli Bhatiyari-ka Mahall 48
   Bijay Mandal *39*, 39
   Chaunath Khamba 237, *238*
   Chishti Nizam al-Din *dargah* 237
   Din-Panah of Humayun 142, 189
   Fakhr al-Masajid Mosque 276
   Fatehpuri Mosque 248, *249*
   Gold Mosque of Raushan al-Daula 277
   Hamid Ali Khan Mosque 277–8
   Hazar Sutun 39
   Humayun Darwaza 190–1
   Humayun mausoleum *197*, 198–9, 221
   Iltutmish tomb *14*, 26, 27
   Isa Khan complex 53, *194*, 195
   Jamali Kamali Mosque and mausoleum 186–7, *187*
   jami masjid of Sikandar Lodi 51, *53*
   Jantar Mantar 288
   Kabir al-Din Auliya tomb 39, 40
   Kabuli Darwaza 194
   Khair al-Manzil Mosque 193, 200
   Khalil Mosque 270
   Khan Jahan Tilangani mausoleum 45–6, 52–3
   Khan-i Khanan mausoleum 237, *238*
   Khwaja Qutb Salub Bakhtyar Kaki tomb 271
   Lal Bangala 277
   Lal Darwaza *193*, 194
   Lal Gumbad (Red Tomb) *200*, 201
   Lodi mausoleums 52, 54–5
   Moth Mosque 57, *57*, 186
   Moti Mosque 275–7, *276*

Mubarak Begum Mosque
    277–8
Muhtasib Mosque 276
Nila Gumbad 200
Nizam al-Din mausoleum 278
Phatak Tiliyan Palace 277
Purana Qila *189*, 189–90
Qasim Khan Mosque 277–8
Qila-i Kuhna Mosque 57, 189,
    191, *191*, 193–4,
    193, 195
Qudsia Begum complex 277
Qutb Minar 19, 22,
    22–23, 25
Quwwat al-Islam Mosque *21*,
    21–2, 22, 25, 31
Sabz Burj 200–1
Safdar Jang mausoleum
    278, *279*
Sayyid mausoleums 52–4
Shaikh Kabir al-Din Auliya
    mausoleum (Lal
    Gumbad) 39, 40
Shams al-Din Atgah Khan
    mausoleum *199*, 200
Sharaf al-Daula Mosque 276
Sher Mandal 189, *190*, 191
Shish Gumbad, Lodi Gardens
    54
Sikandar Lodi *jami masjid*
    51, 53, 54, 55, 57
Sikandar Lodi mausoleum
    55, *55*, 57
Sultan Ghari *26*, 26–7
Sunahri Mosques (1) 276, (2)
    276, (3) 277
Tahawwur Khan Mosque 276
Talaqi Darwaza *189*, 190
Tripolia Bazaar 276
Tripolia Gate 277
Zinat al-Masajid Mosque 276
Dhaka 91
    Lalbagh Fort 92
    tomb of Bibi Pari 92
Dhar 131
    Kamal Maula Mosque 132
    Lat-ki Mosque 132, *133*, 141
Dholka 40
    Alif Khan Mosque 116
    Hilal Khan Qazi Mosque 109
    Taka (Tanka) Mosque 109
Dholpur 185
    Bagh-i Nilufar (Lotus Garden)
        185
    Sadik Khan's tomb 230
    see also Bari
Dig: palaces 285, 288, *289*
Dindar Khan, Nawab 74
domestic architecture 16, 293–5
Doraha Serai, Amritsar 234, 235
Drakhan: Tahim tombs 75
Dwarka 291

E
Etawa: mosque 95, 103

F
Faizabad 259, 278
Faizi 204, 207, 221
Farukh Siyar (1712–19) 273*n*10
Faruqi dynasty 172, *172*
Fatehabad 46
    garden 272
    idgah 46, *47*
Fatehpur Sikri 46, 194, 201, 204,
    205–8, 222
    Abdar Khana (Girls' School)
        207, 208, 211
    Abul Fazl's home 207, 221
    Ankh Michauli (Michoni)
        207, 213
    Anup Talao pavilion (House
        of the Turkish
        Sultaness) 207, 209,
        210–11, *211*
    bazaars 207, 217
    Birbal Palace 207, 216–17
    Buland Darwaza 207, *207*,
        220, 235
    Diwan-i Amm 207, 209, 210
    Diwan-i Khass 18, 207, 210,
        211–13, *212, 214*
    Elephant Gate (Hathi Pol)
        207, 208, 216, 22
    Faizi's home 207, 221
    Fateh Bagh (Garden of
        Victory) 185
    Great Mosque 74, 207, *207*
    Hiran Minar 92, 207, 216,
        221, 221–2
    Ibadat Khana 203–4, 213
    Islam Khan mausoleum 221
    jami masjid 193, 219–20, 221
    Jodh Bai Palace 207, 209,
        215–16
    Khwabgah 207, 209–10
    Kutub Khana 209–10
    Maryam House (Rangin
        Mahall) 207, 217–18
    Masjid Sangtarashan (Stone
        Masons' Mosque) 141,
        207, 218, 221
    Nau Mahall 222
    Naubat Khana 207, 208–9
    palaces 207
    Panch Mahall 207, 210, 215,
        216, 230
    Rang Mahall 207, 218
    Salim Chishti mausoleum
        141, 207, *219*, 220–1
    Shaikh Salim Chishti
        mausoleum 141, 207,
        219, 220–1
    The Stables 217
    Taksal (the mint) 209
    Tansen's *baradari* 208, 210
Fath Khan Mahmud
        see Mahmud Begarha
Fazl, Abul 204, 207, 221,
        222, 224
Firuz Jalal al-Din *see* Khaljis
Firuz Khan 262, 263*n*38
Firuz Shah Tughluq *see* Tughluqs

Firuzabad (Delhi):
    jami masjid 42, 42–3
    Kotla Firuz Shah 41–2, *42*
    Kushk-i Shikar 43
    palaces 42

G
Galta: palace 288
Garaunda 259
    caravanserai 261–2
gardens 22, 158, 185, 222, 230–2,
    248–9, 250, 256–8, 262,
    272–3, 282
Gardizi, Shah Yusuf: mausoleum
    (Multan) *65*, 65–6
Gaur 81–2
    Akhi Suraj al-Din mosque
        and tomb 84
    Bara Sona Mosque *81*, 87,
        88, *89*
    Chamkatti Mosque 87
    Chika Building 85
    Chota Sona Mosque 84, 87,
        89–90
    Dakhil Darwaza 85–6, *86*
    Daraz Bari Mosque 87,
        88–9, 122
    Firuz Minar 90–1, *92*
    Gunmant Mosque 87, 89, *90*
    Jhanjhaniya Mosque 90, 92
    Kotwali Darwaza 84
    Nattan (Lattan) Mosque
        87, 90
    Qadam Rasul Mosque 87,
        90, *90*
    Tantipara Mosque *86*, 87, *88*
Gawan, Mahmud 146, 154, 156
Ghaznavids 8, 17, 19*n*6, 63, 64,
    64, 79
Ghazni 17, 18, 19, 19*n*5, 64
    palace of Masud III 78*n*2
Ghiyas al-Din Balban, Mamluk
        sultan 29, 81
    mausoleum, Delhi *28*, 28–9
Ghiyas al-Din Ghuri *see* Ghurids
Ghiyas al-Din Iwaz Husain,
    Sultan of Bengal 82
Ghiyas al-Din Tughluq
        see Tughluq Shahi
Ghiyas, Mirak Mirza 198
Ghurids 8, 17–18, 19, 19*n*6, 22,
    28, 46, 64, 70, 131
    Ala al-Din Ghuri 17, 19*n*6
    Dilawar Khan Ghuri 131, 132
    Ghiyas al-Din Ghuri 19*n*6, 22
    Muizz al-Din Muhammad
        Ghuri 8, 17, 18, 23, 105
        see also Hushang Shah
Golconda 19, 145, 156, 159,
    241, 266
    The Fort *158*, 159–60
    Moti Mahall 282
    Qutb Shahi mausoleums
        160, *160*
Gomal Valley: Lal Mahra Sharif
    mausoleum *65*, 65
Gondwana 203

Gujarat/Gujarati art 18, 19, 31,
    32, 40, 78, 105*ff*., 183,
    203, 206, 210, 213, 216,
    220, 294
    sultans:
        Ahmad Shah (1411–42) 105,
            106, 110, 111, 113, 114
        Bahadur (1526–37) 116,
            120, 132
        Mahmud I Begarha
            (1459–1511) 105, 106,
            114, 116, 121, 122–3;
            tomb, Sarkhej 115, *115*
        Mahmud III (1537–54) 120
        Muhammad Karim (1442–51)
            113, 114
        Muzaffar I (1391–1411) 105
        Muzaffar II (1511–26) 116,
            120, 121
        Qutb al-Din (1451–8) 114, 115
Gulbarga 145, 150
    Afzal Khan Mosque 149
    Bahmanid tombs 48, 148
    Bala Hisar 146
    Chor Gumbaz 149, *149*
    fortress 146
    Gesu Daraz *dargah* 149, *149*,
        172, 271
    Haft Gumbaz 148
    jami masjid 145, *147*, 147–8
    Langar-ki Mosque 150
    Shah Bazaar Mosque 148
    Shah Kamal Mujarrad *dargah*
        149
    Shaikh Siraj al-Din Junaydi
        dargah 149–50
    Taj al-Din Firuz mausoleum
        148–9, *149*
Gurgaon: caravanserai 261, 262
Gwalior 8, 188
    fort 224
    Great Mosque 270–1
    Man Mandir 205, 213
    Man Sing Tomar palace
        213, 215
    Muhammad Ghaus
        mausoleum *200*, 201

H
Habash Khan 224
Haibat Khan 224
Haidar, Nawab Nasir al-Din 280
Haidar Ali, Sultan of Mysore 282
Hajipur: Makhsus Khan Mosque
    224
Halol 129
    tomb of Sikandar Shah 129
Hampi *see* Vijayanagar
Hansi 34
    idgah 28
Hari Parbat fort 233
Hazrat Data Ganj Bakhsh 70
Hirapur: Adil Shahi mosque 171
Hisar 46
    Abu Bakr Jalwani Mosque 58
    Ali Mir Tijara tomb 58
    Chahar Diwan 58

Gujara Mahall 46, 47
Hansi Rauza of Shah
 Nimatullah 58
Jahaz Kothi 46, 47
Lat-ki mosque 46, 46, 47
Talaqi gate 46, 47
Holkonda 156
 dargah of Shaikh Mashyakha
  156, *157*
 tomb of Dilawar Khan 156
Hulagu 45, 48n9
Humayun, Mughal emperor
 (1530-40; 1555-6) 10,
 64, 183, 184, 187-91,
 194, 203, 204, 209
 mausoleum, Delhi *197*,
  198-9, 221
Hushang Shah, Sultan of Malwa
 (1406-32) 131, 133, 135
 tomb, Mandu *134*, 134, 141
Hyderabad 73, 160-1, *162*,
 164, 282
 Ashur Khana 161-2
 Char Kaman 161
 Char Minar *160*, 161
 jami masjid 161-2
 Kalhora mausoleums 75-6,
  77, *78*
 Mecca Mosque 162, *162*
 Talpur mausoleums 76-7, *78*
 Toli Mosque 162
hydraulic engineering works
 40, 222

I
Ibn Battuta 27, 38, 39, 40, 48
idgah 27-8
Iltutmish, Shams al-Din,
 Mamluk Sultan
 (1211-36) 8, 22, 23, 25,
 26, 27, 66, 70
 mausoleum, Delhi *14*, *26*, 27, 66
 inscriptions 34; *see also* Koranic
  and Kufic inscriptions
Irich: *jami masjid* 48, *49*
Isanpur:
 Gumti Mosque 121
 Imad al-Mulk Maliq Isan
  rauza 121
Islam Shah *see* Suri Shahi
Ismail 29n8

J
Jahan Junan Shah, Khan 45
Jahan-Panah (Delhi) 39, 40
 Begampuri Mosque 44-5,
  45, 98
 Khirki mosque 45, *45*, 148
 Sath Pala bridge 40
Jahanara Begum 247, 248, 250,
 262
Jahangir (1605-27) 11, 63, 71,
 138, 205, 208, 215, 219,
 221, 222, 227ff., 257
 mausoleum, Shadera 245,
  245-6, *246*
Jai Singh, Maharaja 285

Jaipur 285, 288
 Hawa Mahall 288, *289*
 observatory 288, *291*
Jaisalmer 285, *285*, 286
Jalal al-Din, Khwarezmshah
 16, 19n3
Jalal al-Din Muhammad Shah,
 Sultan 84
jali (screens) 25, 41, 100, 128-9
Jalor:
 idgah 129
 mosque of the fort 128
 Topkhana Mosque *128*, 128-9
Jam: Ghurid minaret 22
Jan Baba: tomb 72
Jats 11, 229, 238n8, 266
Jaunpur 46, 48, 95-6, 103
 Akbar bridge *102*, 103, 103n3
 Atala Mosque 48, 96, *97*, 98
 Chehil Sutun palace 103
 Firuz Shah mausoleum 100,
  101, 102
 forts 96, *96*, 103
 hammam 103
 Ibrahim Naib Barbak Mosque
  96, *96*
 jami masjid 99-100, *101*
 Jhanjiri Mosque 98
 Kalich Khan mausoleum 102
 Khalis Mukhlis Mosque 98
 Lal Darwaza Mosque 98-9, *99*
 Shah Zaman Khan
  mausoleum 102
 Sharqi mosques 44
  see also Etawa; Kanauj;
  Sharqi sultans;
  Zaffirabad
Javid Khan 277
Jhajjar 223, 259
 Hasan Shahid tomb 233, *234*
Jodhpur, Rajasthan 127
 palaces 285, 286, 288
Jullemdur: Nur Mahall Serai
 234-5
Junagadh 108, 116

K
Kabirwala: Khalid Walid
 mausoleum *64*, 65
Kabul 203, 208, 276
Kalanaur: Akbar's Throne 222
Kalhoras, the 71, 74, 75
 fort 77
 mausoleums 75-6, 77, *78*
Kalpi: Chaurasi Gumbad 58, *59*
Kaman: Chaurasi Khamba 23,
 25, 25
Kanauj:
 Bala Pir tomb *258*, 259
 mosque 102
 Said Shaikh Makhdum
  Jahaniya tomb complex
  102, 102-3
 Shaikh Mahdi tomb *258*, 259
Kandahar 203, 208, 228, 241,
 250-1, 276
Kandesh 156, 172-3

Kashmir 19, 175-9, 203, 294
 gardens 232, 257
Katak 40
Kathiavar 294
Khalji, Muhammad ibn
 Bakhtiyar 18
Khaljis 8, 31ff., 64, 131
 Ala al-Din Shah (1296-1316)
  8, 31-2, 33, 34, 40, 43,
  105, 131, 189
 Firuz Jalal al-Din (1290-6)
  31, 131
 Ghiyas al-Din, Sultan of
  Malwa (1469-1500) 136
 Mahmud I, Sultan of Malwa
  (1436-69) 131, 134, 136
 Nizam al-Din, Sultan of
  Malwa (1500-11) 138
  mausoleum 141, *142*
 Qutb al-Din Mubarak Shah
  (1316-20) 33, 34
Khanan, Abdur Rahim Khan-i
 78n8
Khirki 158
 Kala Mosque 158
 tombs 158
Khizr Khan 51, 64
Khudabad 73
 Great Mosque 74-5
 jami masjid 74, *76*
 tomb of Yar Muhammad 75
Khukaz, the 70
Khuldabad: Aurangzeb's tomb
 271
Khusrau (Jahangir's son) 227, 228
 mausoleum, Allahabad 230
Khusrau, Amir 31, 33
Khwaja Siah Posh: minaret 22
Koranic inscriptions 23, 27, 28,
 55, 66, 72, 193, 200
Kot Diji: fort 77
Kotah: palace 285
Kuban, Qutb-al-Din Kukaltash
 221
Kufa: mosque 16
Kufic inscriptions 16, 21, 27,
 29n3, 65
Kumatgi: palace 170

L
Lahore 17, 63, 64, 70, 204,
 239n15, 295
 Anarkali mausoleum 232
 Asaf Khan mausoleum 246
 Badshahi Mosque 268,
  269, *269*
 Chauburji gate 250, *251*
 Dai Anga mausoleum
  273, *273*
 Dai Anga Mosque 251, *253*
 The Fort 205, 232, 245, *233*,
  235, 239n14
  Alamgir Gate 269, *271*
  Diwan-i Amm 245
  Diwan-i Khass 245
  Kala Burj 232
  Moti (Pearl) Mosque 245

 Shish Mahall 245, 288
 Gulabi Bagh 250, 262
 Haveli of Nau Nihal Singh
  288
 Hazrat Dats Ganj Bakhsh
  mausoleum 70
 Hazrat Yakub Sadar Diwan
  Zinjani mausoleum 70
 Hazuri Bagh *baradari*
  pavilion 290
 Mardan Khan tomb 250-1
 Maryam al-Zamani Mosque
  232, 237
 Musamman Burj 239n14
 Niwi Mosque 70
 Nur Jahan mausoleum 246
 Ranjit Singh mausoleum
  288, 290
 Sikh buildings 278
 Sunahri Mosque 278, *279*
 Wazir Khan Mosque 249-50,
  251, 260
 see also Shadera
Lakshmeshwar: Kali Mosque 166
Lalitpur, Jhansi district: mosque
 58
Langahs, the 64
Larkana 73
 tomb of Shah Baharo 75
Larvand, Afghanistan: Masjid-i
 Sanji 19
Lashkar Khan Serai 272
Lodis, the 9, 48, 52, 54-5, 57-8,
 70, 183
 Bahlol (1451-89) 52, 54
 Ibrahim II (1517-26) 183
Lucknow 278, 279
 Asafi Mosque 279-80, *280*
 Chattar Manzil 280
 Great Imambara complex
  279-80
 Husainabad Imambara
  complex 280, *282*
 jami masjid 275, 280, 280-1
 late Mughal palace 282
 Martinière 280, *280*
 Roshanwali Kothi 280
 Shah Najaf Mausoleum
  frontispiece

M
madrasa 43, 82
Madurai: Tirumala Nayak Palace
 293
Mahal: hunting lodge 259
Maham 185
Maharaja palaces 285-6
Mahipalpur: Mahipalpur Mahall
 48
Mahmud of Ghazni (995-1050)
 8, 17, 19n5, 63, 70, 71,
 105, 108
Mahmud I Begarha *see* Gujarat
Mahmud I Khalji *see* Khaljis
Mahmud Shah of Jaunpur
 (1440-57) 98, 99

318

Mahmudabad 116, 118
    see also Bhamaria
Makli Hills: cemetery 72,
    72–3, 73
Makramat Khan 263nn5 and 26
Malda 81
    jami masjid 91, 92
    Nim Serai Minar 92
Malipura, Sind 15
Maliq Ikhtyar al-Din 74
Maliq Parviz 40
Malwa 31, 131ff., 183, 184, 203
Mamluks 8, 18, 22, 48n9, 186
    see Ghiyas al-Din
        Balban; Iltutmish;
        Qutb al-Din Aibak
Mamur Khan 239n14, 262n3
Man Singh, Raja 224, 228, 286
Mandasor 133
Mandu 131–2, 183
    Ashrafi Mahall 136, 137
    Baz Bahadur palace 138, 138
    Champa well 138
    Delhi Gate 133
    Diwan Khan Mosque 132
    Fort 224
    Gada Shah 140
    Hawa Mahall 138
    Hindola Mahall 48, 131, 135
    Hushang mausoleum 134,
        134, 141
    Jahaz Mahall 136–8, 137, 138
    Jal Mahall 140
    jami masjid 133, 133–4, 134
    Maliq Mughlis Mosque 132
    Pavilion of Rupmati 138, 140
Mangrol, Gujarat 129
Mansur 228
Mansura 8, 15, 16–17
    Friday mosque 64
Manuhar 235
Maragha: tomb of Hulaga's
    daughter 45, 48n9
Marathas, the 11, 255, 266,
    290–1
Mardan Khan, Ali 256, 257
Masud Saad Salman 70
Masum, Mir 74
Mathura 267
    idgah 268, 269
    jami masjid 268
    observatory 288
Medini Rai 140
Mehrauli (Delhi) 57
    Sultan Balban's mausoleum
        28, 28–9
Merta: Hajji Muhammad
    Mosque 270
Mirza Aziz Kulkatash 237
Mirza Ghazi Beg 74
Mirza Sultan Beg 259
Mongols 31, 33, 64, 70
Moro: tomb of Nur Muhammad
    75
Mubarak Khalji see Khaljis
Mubarak Khan 72, 78n7
Mughals 7, 9–11, 19, 52, 57, 63,
    64, 70, 91, 92, 106, 132,
    143, 157, 172, 177, 183ff.
    emperors see Akbar; Alam I;
        Babur; Humayun;
        Jahangir; Muhammad,
        Nasir al-Din, Shah
        Jahan; Shuja, Shah
Muhammad, the Prophet 19n2,
    45
Muhammad Ali Shah, Nawab
    (1837–42) 280, 281
Muhammad bin Qasim 8, 15,
    16, 65
Muhammad Karim see Gujarat
Muhammad Khan 230
Muhammad Quli see Qutb Shahi
Muhammad, Muizz al-Din
    see Ghurids
Muhammad, Nasir al-Din,
    Mughal emperor
    (1719–48) 208, 276, 277
Muizz dynasty see Mamluks
Multan 8, 15, 16, 17, 41, 63,
    64–5, 295
    Rukn-i Alam mausoleum 45,
        67, 67–8
    Shadna Shahid mausoleum
        65, 66–7
    Shah Yusuf Gardizi
        mausoleum 65, 65–6
    Shaikh Baha al-Din Zakariya
        mausoleum 29, 65,
        66, 66
    Shams Sabzawadi (Shams-i
        Tabrizi) mausoleum 65,
        66, 67
    Sultan Ali Khan mausoleum
        67–8
Mumtaz Mahall (Arjumand
    Banu Begum) 242, 251
Mun'im Khan, Khan-i Khanan
    Muhammad 103
    bridge 102, 103, 103n3
muqarnas 29n5
Murshid Quli Khan 92–3
Murshidabad 91, 92, 281
    Katra Mosque 92–3, 281
    Khwaja Anwar-i Shahid
        mausoleum 93
    Muni Begum Mosque 93, 281
    Shahbaz Mosque 93
Murtaza Nizam Shah I 158
Muzaffar I and II see Gujarat

N
Nagarcain 224
Nagaur 17
    Atarkin-ka Darwaza 28
    Bare Pir Sahib Dargah 58
    Husain Quli Khan Mosque
        224
    Shams Mosque 128, 128
Nakodar 259
    Hajji Jamal (Shagird)
        mausoleum 233–4,
        259–60
    Ustad's tomb 233–4

Naldrug: fort 146, 147
Narnala: fort 146, 222
Narnaul:
    Chatta Rai Bal Mukand Das
        262
    Ibrahim Khan mausoleum
        10, 183, 194, 195
    Jal Mahall 222
    Shah Quli Khan mausoleum
        222–3, 222
    Shah Quli Khan pavilion 222,
        223
Nasir al-Din Qubacha 64
naskhi inscriptions 21, 21,
    22, 29n3
nastaliq 27, 29n7
Nauraspur 163
Nilkhanthesvar 133
Nirun, Sind 15
Nizam al-Din (Delhi) 277
    Jamaat Khana 33
    Kalan Mosque 45, 148
Nizam al-Din, Sultan see Khaljis
Nizam al-Din Auliya 31, 33, 200
Nizam Shahi, of Ahmadnagar
    156, 158, 241
Nizamabad see Bodhan
Nur Jahan 10, 11, 138, 221, 227,
    228, 230, 231, 232,
    238nn4 and 11
    mausoleum, Lahore 246
Nur Mahall, Serai 234–5, 238

O
observatories, astronomical 288
Oljeytu, Ilkhanid 48n9
    mausoleum, Sultaniya 45
Orchha:
    Jahangir Mandir 291–2, 292
    palace 285, 291
    Raj Mandir 291
    Ramji Mandir 291
Orissa 203, 194

P
Palam (Delhi) 185
Paldi-Kochrab: Bawa Ali Shah
    Mosque 121
Pampur: mosque 179
Pandharpur 291
Pandua 81–2
    Adina Mosque 82, 82–3,
        85, 100
    Eklakhi mausoleum 84–5, 85
    Qutb Shahi Mosque 88, 89, 91
Panipat:
    Baburi Mosque 184, 185, 186
Parendra: fort 146
Patan 108, 213
    Adina Mosque 108
    Shaikh Farid mausoleum 108
Patna 271
    Haibat Khan mausoleum 281
    Mir Ashraf Mosque 281
    Rauza Mosque 271
    Sher Shah Mosque 194
Peshawar 276

Pilakhna 185
Pinjore, garden of 272–3
Poona: Shanwar Wada
    (Saturday Palace) 290–1
Pratap Singh, Maharaja Sawai
    100
propylons 96, 98, 100, 121
Punjab 8, 17, 63ff., 294, 295

Q
Qadam-i Sharif sanctuary, nr
    Delhi 45
Qadizi, Abd-al Razzaq 172
Qalam, Mir Abd Allah Mushkin
    228
Qandahar: mosques 40
Qubba al-Sulaybiya 45
Qudsia Begum (Udham Bai)
    277, 281
Quli Khan, Shah: mausoleum,
    Narnaul 222–3
Qutb al-Din Aibak, Mamluk
    Sultan (1206–10) 8,
    17–18, 21, 22, 23, 25,
    42, 70, 105
Qutb Shahi of Golconda and
    Hyderabad 156, 160
    Muhammad Quli (1580–1612)
        159, 160, 161, 162
    Quli Qutb Shah (d. 1543)
        159, 160
Quwwat al-Islam see Delhi

R
Rafi bin Shams bin Mansur 147
Raichur fortress 146
Rajmahal 81, 91, 92
    Akbari Mosque 92
    jami masjid 91–2, 224
    Man Singh's Palace 224
    Sanji Dalan 92
Rajputs, the 8, 10, 11, 17, 71, 183,
    184, 203, 224, 266,
    282, 285ff.
Rakhna, Sultan Hafiz 222
Ranjit Singh 290
    mausoleum, Lahore 288, 290
Raushan al-Daula Zafar Khan
    276, 277
Reza, Aqa 228
Rohtas:
    Habash Khan Mosque 91, 224
    fort 195, 224
    Man Singh's Palace 224
Rohtasgarh:
    jami masjid 194–5
    Shish Mahall 92
Rumi, Jalal al-Din 78n5
Rupbas: hunting lodge 259
Rupmati 138
Ruqayya Sultan Begum 210–11

S
Salim Chishti, Shaikh 204,
    205, 218
    mausoleum, Fatehpur Sikri
        141, 207, 219, 220–1

319

Salima Sultan Begum 210, 211
Samarqand 51, 199
Sambhal 185
    Mir Hindu Beg Mosque 186
Sammanagar 71
Samod: palace 285
Sarkhej 114
    Mahmud Begarha
      mausoleum 115, *115*
    Shaikh Ahmad Khattu
      complex 114–15,
      115, 201
Sasaram 53, 195
    Alawal Khan mausoleum
      198
    Hasan Khan Sur mausoleum
      196
    Islam Shah mausoleum
      196, 198
    Sher Shah mausoleum
      196–7, *197*
Sayyids, the 9, 48, 51–2, 58, 70
    mausoleums 52–4
Sehwan 73
    Lal Shahbaz Kalandar
      complex 74
    tomb of Shaikh Usman
      Marwandi 74, *74*
Seringapatnam 282
Shadera: Jahangir mausoleum
    245, 245–6, *246*
Shah Jahan, Mughal emperor
    (1628–57) 11, 19, *63*,
    70, 71, 204, 208, 220,
    221, 222, 228, 230,
    238nn3 and 11, 241ff.
Shahapur Jat: Tohfewala
    Gumbad 33
Shahi, Nizam 40
Shahjahanabad (Delhi) 46
    gardens 248–9
    jami masjid 248, *249*
    Raushan Ara tomb 248–9
    Red Fort 246
      Delhi Gate 246
      Diwan-i Amm 247
      Diwan-i Khass 247
      Hammam 247
      Jahanara's garden 248
      Khwabgah (Khass Mahall)
        247
      Lahore Gate 246
      Moti Mahall 247
      Moti Mosque 265, 267
      Rang Mahall 247
      Zeb al-Nisa's tomb 272
      Zinat al-Nisa Mosque 269–70
      Zinat al-Nisa tomb 272
Shaikhupura: Hiran Minar
    235–6, *236*
Shalimar gardens 257–9, *258*
Shams al-Din, Shah (Mirza
    Swati) 175
Shams al-Din Ilias, Sultan 83
Shams-i Tabrizi 78n5
    mausoleum, Multan 65,
      66, 67

shardula 190
Sharquis, the 44, 95, 100
    sultans of Jaunpur:
      Husain Shah (1458–79) 99,
        101, 102
      Shams al-Din Ibrahim
        (1402–40) 95, 96, 102
Sher Shah Sur (1540–45)
    see Suri Shahi
Sherpur: Kherua Mosque 91
Shuja, Shah, Mughal emperor
    (1657–60) 91, 92, 266
    mausoleum, Burhanpur
      172, 172–3
Shuja al-Daula, Nawab
    (1753–75) 278
Sighpur 133
Sikandar Butshikan
    (1393–1416) 175,
      175, 177
Sikandar Lodi (1489–1517) 22,
    57, 58, 95
    mausoleum, Delhi 55, *55*, 57
Sikandar Shah I (1358–89)
    82, 83
Sikandra 201
    Akbar's mausoleum
      228–30, *229*
    Maryam al-Zamani
      mausoleum 236–7
Sikhs 11, 70, 288, 290
Sind 8, 15, 17, 63, 71ff., 203, 276
Sirhind 58, 259
    Amm Bagh 222, 257
    Daulat Khana-i Khass 222
    Khwabgah 222
    Shish Mahall 222
Siri 33, 39, 189
    Hazan Sutun 33
    Muhammadwali Mosque 59
Sitpur: Tahir Khan Nahar
    Mausoleum 67
Siyar, Farukh 276
Sojali: Sayyid Mubarak Bukhari
    mausoleum 118–19
Sonepat 185
Srinagar 178–9
    Akhund Mulla Shah Mosque
      256, *256*
    Bamzu *ziyarat* 177
    gardens 222, 230, 231–2
    Hari Parbat Fort 230
    jami masjid 175, 177, *178*
    mausoleum of Zain
      al-Abidin's mother
      178, *178*
    Pattar Mosque 232–3, *234*
    Peri Mahall (Palace of the
      Fairies) 256
    Shah Hamadan Mosque
      177, *177*
    see also Shalimar
      gardens
Sukkur 73, 74
    Aram Gah 74
    tomb of Shah Ilah Khair
      al-Din 75

tower 74, *76*
Sultaniya 48n9
    mausoleum of Ilkhanid
      Oljeytu 45
Suri Shahi 10, 184
    Islam Shah (1545–52) 184,
      196, 197, 198
    Sher Shah (1540–45) 10, 184,
      188–9, 191, 194–8,
      204, 224

T

tah khana 45, 138
Taj al-Din Firuz *see* Bahmanids
Taj Mahall *see* Agra
takht 82–3
Talpurs 71
    mausoleums 76–77, *77*, *78*
Tamerlane *see* Timur
Tanjore 291, 293
Tansen (musician) 204, 208
Tarkhanids 71
    Isa Khan Tarkhan the
      Younger 72
    mausoleum 72, *73*
    Mirza Jani Beg 74, 78n8
    mausoleum, Makli Hills 72
Tarweh-Nauraspur: Sangat
    Mahall 164
Thalner 173
    tomb of Miran Mubarak 173
Thanesar 259
    Chiniwali Mosque 223–4
    Shaikh Chillie mausoleum
      259, *261*
Thatta 15, 64, 71
    Dabjir Mosque 71
    Great Mosque *63*, *70*,
      71–2, 262
Tilangani, Khan-i Jahan 44
    tomb, Delhi 52–3
Timur (Tamerlane) 8–9, 39, 42,
    43, 48, 51, 59n1, 64,
    70, 96, 175
Timurids 19, 51
Tipu, Sultan of Mysore 282
Tribeni: mosque and tomb 82
Trimbak 291
Tughluqabad (Delhi) 37–8, 46
    Adilabad fort 38, 39–40
    Ghiyas al-Din mausoleum
      9, *38*, 38
    tomb of Zafar Khan 39, 40
Tughluqs 19, 37ff., 51, 64,
    81, 145
    Firuz Shah (1351–88) 22,
      26–7, 28, 37, 40–1, 42,
      43, 44, 46, 47, 48, 51,
      67, 71, 95, 96, 128, 247
    Ghiyas al-Din Shah (1320–5)
      8, 37, 67, 105
    mausoleum, Delhi 9,
      38, *38*
    Muhammad Shah (1325–51)
      8, 37, 38, 39, *39*, 40, 41,
      45, 71
    Nasir al-Din Mahmud

      (1393–5; 1399–1413) 51
Tughril, Beg: pavilion tomb
    72–3
Turks 7, 8, 19, 40
    see also Mahmud
      of Ghazni

U

Uchchh Sharif:
    Abu Hanifa mausoleum
      70, *70*
    Baba al-Halim mausoleum
      68–9, *69*
    Bibi Jawindi mausoleum
      68–9, *69*
    Jahaniyan Jahan Gasht
      mausoleum 70
    Jalal Din Surkh Bukhari
      mausoleum 70
    Rajan Qattal mausoleum 70
Udaipur 133
    palace 285, 286, *286*
Ujjain 133
    gardens 272
    observatory 288
Umayyads 15, 16
Ustad Ahmad 253, 262n5, 272
Ustad Hamid 135, 262n5
Ustad Isa 253

V

Vatva: Qutb Alam mausoleum
    118, *119*
Vernag garden, Kashmir 232
Veroneo, Geronimo 253
Vijayanagar: Lotus Mahall
    293, *294*

W

Warangal:
    fort 135
    Hall of Shitab Khan 48
Wasit: mosque 16
waw see baoli
wells *see baoli*

Z

Zadibal: Madin Sahib *ziyarat*
    177–8
Zaffirabad:
    Char Angli Mosque 96
    Shaikh Barha Mosque 96
Zahir al-Daula Ibrahim 70
Zain al-Abidin 175, *175*, 177,
    179
    mother's mausoleum
      178, *178*
Zinat al-Nisa 269
Zulfikhan Khan 70